THE PSYCHOLOGY OF GOALS

The
Psychology
of Goals

edited by
GORDON B. MOSKOWITZ
HEIDI GRANT

THE GUILFORD PRESS
New York   London

KH

©2009 The Guilford Press
A Division of Guilford Publications, Inc.
72 Spring Street, New York, NY 10012
www.guilford.com

Printed in the United States of America

This book is printed on acid-free paper.

Last digit is print number: 9 8 7 6 5 4 3 2 1

Library of Congress Cataloging-in-Publication Data

The psychology of goals / edited by Gordon B. Moskowitz and Heidi Grant.
— 1st ed.
  p. cm.
 ISBN 978-1-60623-029-9 (hardcover : alk. paper)
 1. Goal (Psychology) 2. Motivation (Psychology) I. Moskowitz, Gordon B.
II. Grant, Heidi.
 BF505.6P78 2009.
 153.8—dc22

                                          2008050377

9/3/09

About the Editors

Gordon B. Moskowitz, PhD, is a social psychologist and Associate Professor of Psychology at Lehigh University. His research examines the relationship between social cognition and goals, with particular emphasis on the implicit nature of each. Person perception, social judgment, stereotyping, and stereotype control are typically used as the content areas in which these issues are explored. Dr. Moskowitz has received funding from the German Science Foundation and the National Science Foundation to support this research, and has written articles for the *Journal of Personality and Social Psychology*, *Journal of Experimental Social Psychology*, *Social Cognition*, *Personality and Social Psychology Bulletin*, *Advances in Experimental Social Psychology*, and *European Review of Social Psychology*. In addition to *The Psychology of Goals*, his other published books include *Cognitive Social Psychology* and *Social Cognition*. Dr. Moskowitz is currently investigating the implicit nature of control and self-regulation, with a focus on creativity goals and egalitarian goals and the impact of each on controlling stereotyping. Prior to his position at Lehigh University, Dr. Moskowitz was a faculty member at Princeton University for seven years and the University of Konstanz for one year. Prior to these posts, Dr. Moskowitz was a postdoctoral scholar at the Max Planck Institute for Psychological Research for one year, following doctoral training in psychology at New York University.

Heidi Grant, PhD, is a social psychologist and Assistant Professor of Psychology at Lehigh University. Her primary interest lies in understanding individual responses to setbacks and challenges, and how these responses are shaped by the types of goals pursued. Dr. Grant's research, funded by the National Science Foundation, has explored how goal content impacts self-regulation, achievement, person perception, persuasion, and well-being. She has coauthored articles in the *Journal of Personality and Social Psychology*, *Journal of Experimental Social Psychology*, *Personality and Social Psychology Bulletin*, *European Journal of Social Psychology*, and *Judgment and Decision Making*. Dr. Grant is currently investigating the impact of goal difficulty and obstacles to the pursuit of achievement goals, and the development of a successful classroom learning goal intervention. Prior to her position at Lehigh University, she was a postdoctoral researcher at New York University.

Contributors

John A. Bargh, PhD, Department of Psychology, Yale University, New Haven, Connecticut

Elliot T. Berkman, MA, Department of Psychology, University of California at Los Angeles, Los Angeles, California

Tanya L. Chartrand, PhD, Fuqua School of Business, Duke University, Durham, North Carolina

Ruud Custers, PhD, Department of Social and Organizational Psychology, Utrecht University, Utrecht, The Netherlands

Reuven Dar, PhD, Department of Psychology, Tel Aviv University, Tel Aviv, Israel

Andrew J. Elliot, PhD, Department of Clinical and Social Sciences in Psychology, University of Rochester, Rochester, New York

Melissa J. Ferguson, PhD, Department of Psychology, Cornell University, Ithaca, New York

Jens Förster, PhD, Department of Psychology, University of Amsterdam, Amsterdam, The Netherlands

Laura Gelety, BS, Department of Psychology, Lehigh University, Bethlehem, Pennsylvania

Yuichu Gesundheit, BA, Department of Psychology, Lehigh University, Bethlehem, Pennsylvania

Peter M. Gollwitzer, PhD, Department of Psychology, New York University, New York, New York

Heidi Grant, PhD, Department of Psychology, Lehigh University, Bethlehem, Pennsylvania

Deborah Hall, BA, Department of Psychology and Neuroscience, Duke University, Durham, North Carolina

E. Tory Higgins, PhD, Department of Psychology, Columbia University, New York, New York

Julie Y. Huang, MA, Department of Psychology, Yale University, New Haven, Connecticut

Nils B. Jostmann, PhD, Department of Social Psychology, University of Amsterdam, Amsterdam, The Netherlands

Andrew M. Kaikati, MBA, Carlson School of Management, University of Minnesota, Minneapolis, Minnesota

Peter Kerkhof, PhD, Department of Communication Science, Vrije Universiteit Amsterdam, Amsterdam, The Netherlands

Sander L. Koole, PhD, Department of Social Psychology, Vrije Universiteit Amsterdam, Amsterdam, The Netherlands

Catalina Kopetz, PhD, Department of Psychology and Center for Addictions, Personality, and Emotion Research, University of Maryland at College Park, College Park, Maryland

Arie W. Kruglanski, PhD, Department of Psychology, University of Maryland at College Park, College Park, Maryland

N. Pontus Leander, MA, Department of Psychology and Neuroscience, Duke University, Durham, North Carolina

Nira Liberman, PhD, Department of Psychology, Tel Aviv University, Tel Aviv, Israel

Matthew D. Lieberman, PhD, Department of Psychology, University of California at Los Angeles, Los Angeles, California

Leonard L. Martin, PhD, Department of Psychology, University of Georgia, Athens, Georgia

Sarah G. Moore, BA, Fuqua School of Business, Duke University, Durham, North Carolina

Gordon B. Moskowitz, PhD, Department of Psychology, Lehigh University, Bethlehem, Pennsylvania

Daniela Niesta, PhD, Department of Clinical and Social Sciences in Psychology, University of Rochester, Rochester, New York

Gabriele Oettingen, PhD, Department of Psychology, New York University, New York, New York

Elizabeth J. Parks-Stamm, MA, Social Psychology Program, New York University, New York, New York

Shanette C. Porter, MA, Department of Psychology, Cornell University, Ithaca, New York

Brandon J. Schmeichel, PhD, Department of Psychology, Texas A&M University, College Station, Texas

James Y. Shah, PhD, Department of Psychology and Neuroscience, Duke University, Durham, North Carolina

Elizabeth J. Stephens, MA, Department of Education, Psychology, and Human Kinetics, University of Hamburg, Hamburg, Germany

Abraham Tesser, PhD, Institute for Behavioral Research, University of Georgia, Athens, Georgia

Kathleen D. Vohs, PhD, Department of Marketing, Carlson School of Management, University of Minnesota, Minneapolis, Minnesota

Lioba Werth, PhD, Department of Economic, Organizational and Social Psychology, Chemnitz University of Technology, Chemnitz, Germany

Contents

Introduction
FOUR THEMES IN THE STUDY OF GOALS

GORDON B. MOSKOWITZ
HEIDI GRANT

"Goal." The word rings out from sports stadiums across the globe. In some instances it reflects a ball or puck moving into a net. In others it represents a player carrying a ball over a *goal* line and into an *end* zone. In others it represents a ball being shot through a hoop or rim (the field goal). Its colloquial use in sports captures the sense of how the word is used in psychology. It is the desired end state the individual reaches for; it is the ultimate aim of one's adopted action, the very cause of the action; it is the purpose toward which one is striving; it is the reason for doing and thinking. When in groups at stadiums "goals" make us scream with delight. When achieving more personal goals they deliver to us positive affect, such as pride and satisfaction (and maybe make us scream with delight). The goal is the essence of all that we think of when we think of what it means to be human. It is to have purpose that directs how we think and act.

Human responding (thought and action) can be divided into four broad classes: (1) reflexive responses (seemingly void of intent), (2) unintended/ accidental responses, (3) responses intentionally performed to bring about or maintain a desired state, and (4) responses intentionally performed to control or prevent an undesired state (colloquially known as "willpower"). The latter two, because they are guided by motivation, are in the domain of *self-regulation* or *control* (e.g., Baumeister & Vohs, 2004; Wegner & Bargh, 1998). The vast majority of meaningful human behavior is purposeful or willed or controlled (though not necessarily consciously so)—it is employed toward some end. It is these ends, or *goals*, that direct, ener-

1

gize, and sustain purposeful behavior over time. Goals are the "guides" that direct all nonreflexive and nonaccidental human responding. The goal is the most basic element of control. From the minute processes such as the deflection of attention from one stimulus to another and the categorization of a person according to either gender, race, occupation, or age, to grand gestures such as acts of heroism and striving to achieve, human responding is under the control of human goals.

Alfred Adler (1933, p. 3) once wrote, "We cannot think, feel, will, or act without the perception of some goal. . . . All activity would persist in the stage of uncontrolled gropings; the economy visible in our psychic life unattained." One advantage of the goal construct is that it brings just such "economy" to the study of psychic life as well, allowing for the prediction and explanation of whole patterns of cognition, affect, and behavior. Chronically pursued goals give us insight into the stability of personality within an individual, and differences among individuals. Management of multiple goals and changes in their situational accessibility help us understand variation in an individual over time and across situations. Moreover, goals contribute significantly to the meaning of events and outcomes—creating frameworks through which social information is processed, understood, and acted upon. Through our goals, all of our everyday thoughts, beliefs, desires, and fears are translated into action. When you think about it, how can we hope to understand and predict anyone's behavior in the absence of some sense of what that person is striving for, and how such strivings operate? How can we know how to act?

There are many psychological constructs, cognitive and motivational, that have been used to successfully predict and explain human behavior. Although cognitive and motivational explanations were once seen in opposition, whole volumes have been devoted to a newer, unified approach of merging cold cognition and hot motivation for a "warmer" look (the "New Look in Motivation"; see Kruglanski & Kopetz, Chapter 1)—understanding how our thoughts and desires act upon one another and in concert to create and sustain action (see, for illustration, Sorrentino and Higgins's (1986) *Handbook of Motivation and Cognition*). And nothing seems to better capture the essence of the warm approach than the goal—a construct that is at once cognitive (a mental representation subject to the laws that govern knowledge accessibility and use) and motivational (translating our desires into strivings, providing the reference point for self-regulation). It just doesn't get any warmer than goals.

This volume was intended to fill what we perceived to be a rather startling gap in handbook coverage; we believe it to be the first exhaustive psychological text to address this central and incredibly useful construct. It is meant to give the reader brief but thorough introductions to the key topics in understanding goals, from goal selection, to goal management, to goal pursuit. The idea for the book came from a simple goal of our own: We wanted to finally have a single text we could assign in advanced undergraduate and graduate courses that could address one of the singular most important concepts in psychology. We imagined a dream book—the "Big Book of Goals"—that covered everything you'd ever want to know about goals (but generally had to look in too many different places to find). This is that book, due largely to the dream team of authors who agreed to contribute short, complementary chapters that could cohere together as a text. We begin the book by identifying four themes that cut throughout the study of goals, and this book:

1. Goals, as mental representations that are linked to cues in the environment, connect the person to the situation through specifying desirability (affect and value) and feasibility (efficacy and opportunity).
2. Goals provide the person with meaning and a sense of having control over his/her environment.
3. Goals connect the wants of the person to instrumental activity (cognitive and behavioral activity), directing his/her commerce with the world.
4. Goals have consequences that do not require consciousness of either the goal or the consequences—one need not experience a sense of being willful.

Goals Connect the Person to the Situation

Kurt Lewin is generally credited as being a "founding father" of the field of social psychology and is often identified with the field's approach of studying the interaction of the person and situation. This credit is not unfounded, and his influence on the field has developed largely from Lewin's discussion of *field theory*. Kurt Lewin worked in 1920s Berlin, the center of the Gestalt psychology movement. It was the time of two (unrelated) regimes' rise to power: the behaviorists in psychology, and the Nazis in German political life. Lewin reacted against each. The latter influenced him to ultimately flee to the United States. The former led him to reject the position that to discover the basic psychological constructs that guide behavior we need to reduce the elements being studied to neurophysiology. Lewin instead believed behavior could only be understood within a field of stimuli, as an interaction of a person within a situation, who together made up a unit known as the "life space."

Lewin (1951) likened goal pursuit to the manner in which need states are satisfied, even going so far as to call intentions "quasi-needs." Intentions were likened to needs because having goals that are not attained was believed to lead the individual to experience a tension state that energizes goal-directed responses (just as need states are described as a tension arising from tissue deficits that energize responses to reduce the deficit). Lewin believed the tension associated with an intention could be reduced by multiple goal-relevant objects and multiple routes toward goal attainment. Rather than an intention representing an association between one stimulus and one course of action, the quasi-need was said to specify a "valence" being established between the goal and the various stimuli in the environment relevant to the goal.

The notion of valence is central to the person × situation interaction within the life space. It was Lewin's way of describing how the desires of the individual engage in her/his commerce with the opportunities present in the environment that afford one the possibility to potentially pursue those desires. Valence represents the strength and direction of the association between an object in the environment and the goal: the ability of the object to address the tension that one is experiencing due to the goal having been selected. Many possible objects can provide for one a means to attaining a given goal, with some of those objects present in the environment when others are not. Which of the viable means to the goal, from among the several means that are detected in the environment, is selected will depend on the valence that links each detected object/means to the goal. Thus, the direction of goal pursuit is in part dependent on the feasibility for each of the opportunities to a goal to actually allow the person to reach the goal. As Heider (1958) stated in his analysis of the concept "can," the feasibility of attaining a goal is based on the person and the situation. Feasibility asks not only whether the person has the efficacy to do something, but also whether the situation affords one the opportunity to do something. Feasibility thus captures the essence of a person with certain aptitudes in a situation with certain opportunities and obstacles. Feasibility concerns are reflected in Lewin's writings by the concept of "subjective probability," which is the probability that a particular means/behavior is readily available and will result in the goal being achieved. The opportunity with the highest subjective probability will develop the strongest valence to the goal and thus be the one selected. And if the selected means is blocked, the presence of other means to attaining the goal in the context can be adopted as a substitute (see Martin & Tesser, Chapter 10, for a review).

This approach conceives of goals as something attractive that the individual develops a commitment toward attaining. This establishes a link between the goal and the wants/desires of the individual, with the goal then pulling the individual in the direction of goal attainment. Although the feasibility of the various means in the environment help to specify the direction of the goal pursuit, the desires, wants, and wishes of the individual also help to specify the strength of the valence, providing it with its energy. Thus, it is not merely the case that a given goal must weigh the various opportunities to determine what the most feasible/viable route to attaining the goal will be, it is also the case that a given goal must compete with other goals, from among the many wants and desires of the person, to determine which goal will be selected. It is not feasible to pursue all of our goals at once! Thus, feasibility issues are complemented by desirability issues in the individual's negotiation of which goal and which means to the goal to pursue at any given time. This "Lewinian" perspective is reflected in modern goal theories such as the models of action control (e.g., Kuhl & Beckmann, 1994) and action phases (e.g., Heckhausen & Gollwitzer, 1987). We briefly review one of these two theories here, because Jostmann and Koole review the other in Chapter 13.

In their model of action phases, Heckhausen and Gollwitzer (1987) assumed that a person's motives produce more wishes and desires than can be realized. Therefore, one must choose a goal to pursue by a process of deliberating over the feasibility and desirability of one's wishes and desires. Only feasible and attractive wishes are turned into goals and initiate goal-directed behaviors. However, initiation of action is based also on the perceived suitability of the present situational context. All of this is considered in relation to the desirability and feasibility of other competing goals that press to be realized in the given situation and to possible future situational contexts that may be more or less suitable than the one at hand. Gollwitzer (1990) argued that a general cognitive orientation, with distinct features and procedures, becomes activated (a deliberative mindset) when one is attempting to deliberate among one's goals. When people are asked to engage in intensive deliberation of whether to turn an important personal wish or desire into a goal, a cognitive orientation with the following features originates: people are more open-minded when processing information; heeded information is processed more effectively while peripheral information is also encoded; people process desirability-related information more effectively than implementation-related information; the pros and cons of making a decision are analyzed in an impartial manner (e.g., feasibility-related information is analyzed in a relatively objective, nonillusionary way).

In conclusion, a fundamental assumption on which most goal work is predicated is that goals are analyzed with a consideration to the desirability and the feasibility of attaining the goal (see Atkinson, 1964). This logic has been incorporated into most of the theories reviewed in this book, with perhaps expectancy-value theories being the first fully formed models of goal pursuit to incorporate Lewin's concerns with desirability and feasibility (e.g., Fishbein's, 1967, theory of reasoned action; Atkinson's, 1957, motivation theory). These considerations connect the individual to the environment.

Goals Provide Meaning

Early researchers examining human inference about other humans specified one guiding principle of interpersonal perception: We attempt to infer the goals of others. We do so perhaps without thinking about it, we do so without necessarily knowing the rules we follow that provide us with inferences about intent, and we do so all the time, whenever we encounter another person in whom we anticipate (or observe) an action, and with whom we may expect an interaction that calls for us to produce behavior of our own. Humans are creatures of *goal inference*. Why infer goals? Because goals provide for us meaning about why other people act the way they do. Goal inferences define for us what we have seen and allow us to predict what will likely happen next. Goal inferences suggest the world is controlled, and feelings of control and agency are as essential to us as feelings of meaning and knowing the world around us.

This chapter was written during the 50th anniversary (sadly unheralded) of Heider's (1958) treatise *The Psychology of Interpersonal Relations*. It is generally regarded as a book that launched attribution theory, but the heart of Heider's beliefs about interpersonal perception hinge on two beliefs about goals. The first is a belief that interpersonal perception is pervasive and important precisely because it is purposive; it is a response that arises from what Heider considered a drive—the need to have meaning and understanding (epistemic needs). Heider (1944, p. 359) stated that "some authors talk of a general tendency towards causal explanation, a 'causal drive.'" The need for meaning is resolved through the motivation to make sense of other people and their action. This motive expresses itself through goals to form inferences and make predictions (with some degree of perceived accuracy) about what others are like and likely to do.

The second belief about goals that is central to Heider's (1958) writings is that the way in which we pursue our goal of having meaning, predictability, and control is by assuming that other people have goals. Assuming other people have goals allows us to feel as if we understand the cause for that person's behavior, and thus by knowing someone's goals, we can make veridical predictions about that person, and with the ability to predict comes the meaning and control we, as perceivers, desire. Heider famously spoke of the explanations we use to describe people being based either in the situation or the person. However, less known is that what Heider referred to when he spoke of "person causes" is *intentionality*. With person causes the perceiver comes to see the behavior as intentionally chosen by the person, and the perceiver's attributional task is to determine the reasons for that choice: Why did he/she *intend* to act as such? (Heider called these reason explanations.) When Heider spoke of the situation as the cause for an act he meant that the act was unintended by the person, not goal directed.

These two beliefs about goals in Heider's work were central to the emerging field of attribution theory, as seen in the following two quotes from Jones and Davis' (1965) seminal work. "The person perceiver's fundamental task is to interpret or infer the causal antecedents of action. The perceiver seeks to find sufficient reason why the person acted. . . . the perceiver's explanation comes to a stop when an intention or motive is assigned that has the quality of being reason enough" (p. 220). "A perceiver observes an action and at least some of its effects. His basic problem as a perceiver is to decide which of these effects, if any, were intended" (p. 221). How do perceivers make inferences about whether an actor intended an effect? Jones and Davis (1965) stated that several pieces of information are said to be considered: (1) does the actor have knowledge of the consequences of the action, (2) does the actor desire to bring about those consequences ("As the perceiver considers the multiple effects of action, he will usually assume that some of the effects were more desirable to the actor, and therefore more diagnostic of his intentions than others," p. 226), and (3) does the actor have the capability to bring about the desired consequences. In essence, they infer intentionality, desirability, and feasibility.

Thus, the field started with Heider's assertion that we have the goal to infer goals and moved onward to Jones and Davis' (1965) sets of rules regarding how we go about inferring what other people's goals are (even when we do not know those rules ourselves to consciously describe them to someone else). From there we saw the field move to the idea that we become so skilled at pursuing such goals that we come to make goal inferences spontaneously, so that not only do we not know we are using certain rules/procedures in pursuing our goal, but also we do not even know we are pursuing a goal at all (Uleman, Newman, & Moskowitz, 1996). This is a trend we see throughout this book, and throughout the literature on goals more generally. Researchers begin typically with work on goal content (such as the epistemic goals examined by Heider, 1958). Goal content ultimately gives way to examinations of process—the operations people pursue when trying to attain a goal, even if they do not consciously know the processes being used (such as the rules of inference examined by Jones & Davis, 1965). Finally, consciousness deserts not only awareness of the process, but also the awareness of the goal's existence (such as in work on spontaneous inference by Uleman et al., 1996).

Goals Provide a Basis for Instrumental Activity

Action has purpose. A goal is conceived of as something instrumental, capable of safely carrying us from one experience to the next. Without goals we are ill prepared to act in our environment. This can be seen colloquially in language. Few people in the English speaking world today have a working knowledge of Greek. Thus, you may be surprised to learn the root of words such as "practical" and "pragmatism" is from the Greek word for "action" (*praktikos*). When we use the term "practical"—defined as likely to be feasible; suitable for a particular purpose—we are infusing the Greek word for "action" with an analysis of feasibility and a purpose to which the action is suited. The way psychologists think of goals is in this instrumental fashion. Action typically has purpose, and this purpose is specified by a goal that varies in how feasibly it may be attained by the action.

Social psychologists adopted James's (1890/1950) pragmatist declaration that "my thinking is first and always for my doing." Allport (1954) paraphrased this pragmatic view when he stated, "thinking is basically an endeavor to anticipate reality. By thinking we try to foresee consequences and plan actions that will avoid whatever threatens us and will bring our hopes and dreams to pass" (p. 167). When we deliberate on the desirability and feasibility of a goal, when we form plans, when we evaluate the goal-relevant means in our environment, we are using goals to anticipate and guide behavior. Our goals are instrumental in that they tell us feasible and suitable ways to act in our environment.

This theme has cut across the study of goals from before the time psychologists studied these constructs in humans straight through the cognitive revolution and beyond. Behaviorists described the rat as purposive, running a maze with a goal. From their start, social cognition theories, like that of Jones and Davis (1965, quoted above), stated that people see their basic task as a perceiver to be to infer intent in others. This is accomplished (in part) by analyzing what the perceiver believes the other person was thinking about regarding the desirability and feasibility of a chosen action prior to having chosen that action. Because we believe our own behavior is goal directed, if we want to understand others, our job as a perceiver is to discern the goals that directs those others.

The scientific study of the instrumental nature of goals has many forms. One approach is to study goal content and to discern exactly how the framing of a goal and the specificity of the goal affects behavior. For example, Locke and Latham (1990) famously described drastically different effects on behavior as a function of how specific the goal is. The instrumentality of the goal changes as it moves from the vague to the specific. A specific and difficult goal such as "I will run 5 miles every other day" is better at delivering the desired end of "improved health" than a vague goal, such as "I will eat healthier" or "I will exercise more." The resulting behavior is marked by greater persistence, mobilization of effort, and desired action. Similarly, Higgins (Chapter 19) argues there is value from "regulatory fit." There is increased instrumentality to an action when the action fits one's goal orientation, such as a focus on either promotion or prevention. As one example, Chen and Bargh (1999) performed an experiment in which participants were asked to move a lever when a word appeared. The words were either positive or negative in valence, though participants were not asked to attend to this aspect of the stimulus. The action of moving the lever was manipulated so that some people were asked to pull the lever toward them and others were asked to push the lever away from their body, though participants did not know that pushing or pulling was being manipulated or mattered in any way. What was found was increased instrumentality of action when there was regulatory fit—when asked to pull toward the self, participants were faster to respond when the words were positive than negative. When asked to push the lever away from the body participants were faster when words were negative. The valence in the words is compatible with the appropriate corresponding response of approach (pull) or avoidance (push), with the goal of approaching and avoiding facilitated by fit.

Another approach to studying the instrumental nature of goals is to examine the processes through which goals get transcribed or transferred into action. If goals are instrumental they should determine action, yet people do not always act in ways that their goals suggest. We started this introduction by referring to two classes of goals that are unintended and accidental. This is not what we mean here. Instead, we refer to a class of theories that examine why and when intentions yield the desired act, and why and when goals, when they are activated, are prevented from taking life in the action of the individual (obstacles to goal-directed action). One example is the work of Gollwitzer (1990) on action phases that argued that for issues of goal choice, the classic motivational variables of desirability and feasibility may suffice. But when it comes to implementing a goal, the initiation of action, further variables need to be taken into account. For example, a different mind-set (i.e., general cognitive orientations with distinct features) should emerge when a person addresses the distinct tasks associated with implementing a goal (generating action) as opposed to deliberating about which goal to pursue. Action initiation, as opposed to goal deliberation, represents a shift to an implemental mind-set where one becomes focused and less distracted by irrelevant information. One also becomes effective in processing implementation-related issues (e.g., the sequencing of actions; Gollwitzer, Heckhausen, & Steller, 1990). Feasibility-related information is analyzed in a manner that favors illusionary optimism. Another example is the work of Gollwitzer and colleagues on planning. This work illustrates how the nature of action initiation changes as a function of the types of plans that accompany the goal (this work is reviewed in detail by Parks-Stamm & Gollwitzer in Chapter 14).

A final approach to studying the instrumental nature of goals is by examining how the goal system deals with and reacts to obstacles to goal pursuit. For example, Kuhl (1984) stated that for an ordered action sequence to occur, a current guiding goal has to be shielded from competing goal intentions (because at any given point many different action tendencies coexist). He called this process "action control," modeling it on Atkinson and Birch's (1970) theorizing on the dynamics of action. This model is reviewed by Jostmann and Koole in Chapter 13 of this book. Similar ideas regarding the shielding of goals in helping to promote action are described in Chapter 9 by Shah, Hall, and Leander. As a final example, the theory of planned behavior (Fishbein & Ajzen, 1975) examines why people, despite having an intention to behave a particular way, do not always act the way they intend. The intention is a function of many factors that can potentially disrupt action, such as subjective norms (including the beliefs about others regarding the behavior and one's desire to comply with those others) and perceived behavioral control (including one's assessment of one's efficacy in the behavioral domain and one's motivation to engage in the behavior).

Thus, goals are the liaison between the wants and needs of the person and the action that is taken to help the person satisfy those wants and needs. Goals do not always produce behavior, but behavior, when produced, is typically goal directed. Goals are instruments of action.

Goals and Consciousness

One of us spent an entire graduate school career illustrating that people engage in inference processes spontaneously (implicitly). When we see behavior in others, we infer traits about the people performing that behavior without knowing we do so or explicitly aiming to do so. Despite this being implicit cognition, unintended by the perceiver, it is still controllable by goals (Uleman & Moskowitz, 1994). Thus, this work makes the point that our explicit goals lead to implicit cognition. Of course, the nonconscious nature of the cognitive responses initiated when explicitly adopting a goal was not something Uleman and Moskowitz had discovered!

Much of cognitive psychology is about the implicit cognition that occurs after one adopts a goal. Although certainly true of any work explicitly about the study of executive function, it is also true of the study of language (where people are asked to adopt the goal of generating sounds), attention (where people are asked to focus on a specific set of stimuli and perhaps ignore others), memory (where people are asked to perform some set of functions, even if studying incidental memory, to a set of instructions), decision making (where people have the goal to explicitly choose between options or to indicate a preference), categorization (where people are asked to respond to stimulus items by either sorting them or merely identifying them as words), and skill acquisition (where a goal to respond a particular way on a task is practiced). As Kunda (1987) beautifully summarized, our cognition may be implicit but is the servant of our goals: "The cognitive apparatus is harnessed in the service of motivational ends. People use cognitive inferential mechanisms and processes to arrive at their desired conclusions, but motivational forces determine which processes will be used in a given instance and which evidence will be considered" (p. 637).

The reason this section starts with a discussion of spontaneous trait inference, therefore, is not because it is a unique example of people implicitly pursuing their intended goals. In fact, in some regard it is a bad example because the implicit inferences being formed in such research are unintended. The explicit goal of the perceiver in those experiments is to memorize the material, not to form impressions. In the fields of cognitive psychology mentioned above the implicit cognition is at least intended. For example, the person is trying to attend to a stimulus and is guided by implicit processes in how she/he successfully does so. The reason we started this section with a discussion of spontaneous inference is because it begs a larger question. If the explicit goal is not being serviced by the formation of spontaneous inferences, then what is being serviced? Why do people spontaneously form inferences all the time, without "trying"?

We suggest that this implicit cognition is servicing an *implicit goal*. People are trying to infer, they just don't know it. When Winter and Uleman (1984) first illustrated that people infer traits spontaneously, they provided one of the earliest empirical demonstrations of the wholly implicit nature of goal pursuit. That is, not only are the cognitive operations that follow the goal implicitly performed, but also the goal itself is implicit in its selection or adoption. This suggests that we are often not aware of either (1) our goals or (2) what we do to pursue those goals. What is the implicit goal being pursued when people form trait inferences? As reviewed above, people desire meaning and need to be able to predict what another person is likely to do. Attribution theories describe the rules we use to help us pursue such goals. One such rule is to determine how well behavior matches an underlying disposition. What the research on spontaneous trait inference reveals is that perceivers pursue this job so frequently and routinely that they ultimately come to do it efficiently and implicitly, inferring traits without knowing it (Moskowitz, 1993). The goal is to gain meaning, we pursue it constantly, and we become habitual in our execution.[1]

The preceding discussion illustrates that when one is chronically pursuing a goal, that goal can be removed from consciousness and function autonomous to the experience of the will. However, throughout this book we see, time and again, that chronic pursuit of a goal, though sufficient to render its selection "invisible," is not necessary. Bargh (1997) described the automaticity of everyday life and made a persuasive argument, augmented by several chapters in this book, that goals are implicitly triggered by the context even if the pursuit of the goal is not chronic. Bargh and Huang (Chapter 5) argue this is not only far more common than we expect, but also is far more natural than we expect. Indeed, Bargh and Huang argue that nonconscious goals are ingrained in our evolutionary past. Although perhaps less intuitively obvious than conscious goals, they argue that nonconscious goals are structurally more primary.

The nonconscious nature of goal pursuit raises several interesting issues aside from the issues relating to the possibility of its existence (such as "Are goals triggered without one knowing? or "Can people respond in goal-relevant ways without knowing they've responded?"). Two of these issues cast aspersions on consciousness itself: (1) the issue of whether the experience of will is an epiphenomenon and (2) the issue of whether consciousness merely introduces error to goal pursuit. A third issue poses the opposite question to the second. Instead of asking whether consciousness introduces error it asks whether implicit responses are errors that need to be corrected by consciousness. A final set of issues concerns the consequences of nonconscious goal pursuit, consequences arising from the inability to experience the will. Thus, the discussion of what it means to have free will, in philosophy and psychology, has been broadened by the concept of the implicit goal. Let us address each of the above issues.

We previously reviewed the idea that goals provide meaning for the individual and allow him/her to experience feelings of control. This presents the possibility that goals do not literally provide meaning and control but simply the feeling that one has meaning and control. Perhaps people use goals to help them feel agentic; perhaps they consciously assume behavior is willed so that the world is not seen as random and uncontrollable. This possibility implies that goals are epiphenomena. Indeed, there is a whole literature on people claiming willfulness for action initiated prior to consciousness, behavior that is clearly not willed. The "feeling of doing," as Ansfield and Wegner (1996) called it, is layered on top of the actual doing: "It seems to each of us that we have conscious will. It seems we have selves. It seems we have minds. It seems we are agents. It seems we cause what we do. Although it is sobering and ultimately accurate to call all this an illusion, it is a mistake to conclude that the illusion is trivial" (Wegner, 2002, p. 342).

One example is provided by Libet (1985). Libet measured electrical potential in the brain that occurs approximately a half-second before voluntary action. If brain activity causes a physical response, and if goals are what drive the response, it is only logical that the goal must be responsible for the change in electrical potential that precedes the action. But Libet found that consciousness of the goal to elicit a response occurs after the electrical potential has already increased. Action in the brain had already begun before people had the conscious experience of willing it to happen.

They felt as if they were causing an act, but the act was already occurring before they had the will to make it happen. The experience of willing exists, not actual willing. Wegner and Wheatley (1999) explained that the reason people experience conscious willing is because they make an inference about causality. They interpret their own thought, their goals, as the cause of their own actions (after all, they are paired together temporally).

The rejection of conscious willing as the cause for behavior leads naturally to the question: "Well what is the cause of action?" Wegner and Wheatley (1999) suggested it is unconscious mechanisms of mind—processes that we do not have conscious privy to. Because we lack awareness of what actually causes behavior, we generate a belief, and that belief is that we consciously will behavior. This has led some philosophers, bass players, and psychologists to refer to the will as a "ghost in the machine" (Ryle, 1949). The feeling of willing is like a spirit that haunts the efficient and implicit mechanisms of mind that actually produce the responses we mechanistically elicit. The unpleasantness of such a thought was captured well by William James (1890/1950), when he stated: "the whole sting and excitement of our voluntary life . . . depends on our sense that in it things are really being decided from one moment to another, and that it is not the dull rattling off of a chain" (p. 453). Yet some argue that much willed activity is rattled off in precisely this manner, taking advantage of the marvelous machine that is the mind. In chapter 5, Bargh and Huang argue that not only is the conscious will not needed, but also is sometimes opposed in its wants: "Active goals are the unit of control over higher mental processes, not the self or individual person, and active goals single-mindedly pursue their agenda independently of whether doing so is in the overall good of the individual person" (p. 131).

Now, even if the reader accepts this proposition wholeheartedly, it does not rule out that some behavior is consciously willed. It merely argues that much behavior is not, and that the mechanisms responsible for willed behavior often remain oblivious to the person. But does all this mean that goals are epiphenomena? We would argue no. It may mean that far more than one is likely to concede, the conscious experience of willing may be false. But the notion of nonconscious goals saves the notion of free will from being an illusion. Although we may not be able to correctly point consciously to the causes of our action, this does not mean that the cause of our action is not goal directed. The cause simply may be implicitly triggered and operating goals, and their corresponding operations. Although an argument can be made for conscious willing as epiphenomena in many cases, nonconscious willing is very much a phenomenon.

Let us turn next to the "flip side" of the issue just discussed. Although people may often see the conscious will as relevant to action when it is not, they may also sometimes fail to see the will as relevant when it actually is. Wegner and Wheatley (1999) argued the same cause is at root for both of these issues: people make inferences about causality. Thus, when it is difficult for people to see their role as the cause of an action, especially an action they did not want to perform, or a thought they did not wish to have, these responses seem somehow magical, to have appeared from out of the blue or delivered by the hand of God. Wegner and Erskine (2003) stated that "the feeling that an action is 'happening' rather than that one is 'doing it' can occur under a variety of conditions. People can experience such involuntariness when they are performing complicated, lengthy, goal-directed actions, and even when they are fully able to report the conscious goal of the action. Experiences of involuntariness occur regularly in hypnosis" (p. 685). Many examples of this phenomenon are reviewed throughout the book, so we will not linger here save to mention a few of them briefly.

Ansfield and Wegner (1996) described people who believe that Ouija boards can magically spell information that is important to the person. Ansfield and Wegner described the reality of the phenomenon as an example of nonconscious goals. The movement of one's hand to the letters is under the direction of goals that remain invisible to the person. They pit a "ghost in the machine" explanation against a "ghost in the Ouija board" explanation. Pendulum divining, where the swing of a pendulum's movement is in seemingly uncontrolled directions, Ansfield and Wegner similarly described as a case of control that is just not detected by the individual. If one cannot see oneself as cause, one may conclude that the movement must be mystical. Leander, Moore, and Chartrand (Chapter 18) describe people's experiences of moods as mysterious, arising from seemingly nowhere. Once again, it is the detachment between the nonconscious goal pursuit and the experience of goal pursuit (or better, the lack of experience) that causes moods resulting from goal pursuit to seem mysterious and lacking a cause. Finally, Wegner (1994) described an ironic effect from trying to suppress a thought. The very thoughts we are intending not to think seem to pervade consciousness in a way that belies our willing. Asking people "do not think about White bears" leads to an inexplicable rise in thoughts of those animals. Just like trying not to stereotype makes people stereotype more. Or trying not to think of cake makes you yearn for it more. As in the other examples, this is ironic because the response does not jibe with one's conscious intent and in fact opposes it. But also, as in the other examples, the response fits perfectly with the chain of nonconscious responses that the individual cannot see. The mental mechanisms required for not thinking something are rattled off as the nonconscious goal dictates (for a review of processes in thought suppression, see Moskowitz, Chapter 12). The person just does not know it.

We have just reviewed two types of "errors" arising from nonconscious goal pursuit: The "I did it" effect and the "I didn't do it" effect. That discussion, coupled with the idea that the consequences of nonconscious goal may be unintended, such as experiencing mystery moods and forming trait inferences, may lead to the impression that nonconscious goals are errors. Alternatively, they may lead to the impression that nonconscious goals are efficiently running passive mechanisms, and it is instead consciousness that is an error, layering false conclusions and interpretations on a perfectly well-oiled machine. A case could be made for both of these interpretations, and of course, to some degree they are true and false. Consciousness can be faulty but is not always so. And nonconscious goal operations may yield unintended and undesired outcomes, but so too may they yield exactly what was intended and desired.

For example, Bargh and Huang (Chapter 5) state: "Goal programs are the 'local agents' in the present that carry out genetic instructions from the distant past." They are linked to our genes, utilizing structures and brain processes developed separate from consciousness and prior, in our evolutionary past, to consciousness. Although "conscious goal pursuit makes use of the same underlying structures and processes as in evolutionarily older unconscious goal pursuit mechanisms," there is no necessity that while using those structures they do not alter the outputs in a nonmaximal (what some might call error-prone) way. Thus, in some instances we see nonconscious mechanisms of goal pursuit producing "better" outcomes for the individual than conscious pursuit, because consciousness introduces bias to processes that would work fine without it. Moskowitz (Chapter 12) reviews two such examples: one in the decision-making domain, the other in the creativity domain. In their work on creativity, Sassenberg and Moskowitz (2005) suggested that implicitly pursuing the goal of being creative leads to more creative behavior (and cognitive operations) than when people explicitly try to be creative. The conscious pursuit leads one astray from the implicit processes, not truly knowing how to yield the creativity it seeks. Dijksterhuis, Bos, Nordgren, and van Baaren (2006) also showed that in complex decision making, nonconscious processes of evaluation and rumination lead to better choices (selecting objectively better products from among a set of products) than conscious evaluation and rumination. The conscious pursuit introduces biases and errors that the nonconscious mechanisms avoid.

Of course, consciousness is not always bad! In some cases the conscious goal pursuits work in precisely the same manner as the nonconscious goal pursuits, as demonstrated by Chartrand and Bargh (1996). The implicit mechanisms implicated in pursuing a goal (in their case, the goal to form impressions of a person) are precisely the same and yield the same consequences, regardless of whether one consciously adopted the goal or had it implicitly primed. And, of course, we have already reviewed examples of how sometimes it is the nonconscious pursuits that lead us astray, rather than being the superior method of goal pursuit. Our point here is not to claim superiority of one form of goal pursuit over another. It is merely to point out that nonconscious goal pursuit exists and in fact may be the more natural, or at least rely on a biologically older set of mechanisms in the brain. And to point out that just because examples exist of intentional behavior opposing the will (such as thinking thoughts one tries to suppress, or performing behavior one had intended to avoid), it does not mean that implicit goals are not wanted, or that implicit operations are not still intended. We end this section where we started: Though in some sense it is correct to call trait inferences "unintended," they are also intended. They are great examples of why goals become implicit. Rather than being accidents, they allow our purpose and our pursuit of it to be invisible and efficient. Let us drive this home with the eloquence of James (1890/1950) on a goal's nonconscious nature:

> It is a general principle in Psychology that consciousness deserts all processes when it can no longer be of use. The tendency of consciousness to a minimum of complication is in fact a dominating law. . . . Now if we analyze the nervous mechanism of voluntary action, we shall see that by virtue of this principle of parsimony in consciousness the motor discharge *ought* to be devoid of sentience. If we call the immediate psychic antecedent of a movement the latter's *mental cue,* all that is needed for invariability of sequence on the movement's part is a *fixed connection* between each several mental cue, and one particular movement. For a movement to be produced with perfect precision, it suffices that it obey instantly its own mental cue and nothing else, and that this mental cue be incapable of awakening any other movement. Now the *simplest* possible arrangement for producing voluntary movements would be that the memory-images of the movement's distinctive peripheral effects, whether resident or remote, themselves should constitute the mental cues, and that no other psychic facts should intervene. (pp. 496–497)

The Psychology of Goals, the Book

The Psychology of Goals is organized into four parts. Part I, What (and Where) Are Goals?, examines the cognitive nature of goals (Kruglanski & Kopetz), distinguishes goals from (and relates them to) other motivational constructs (Elliot & Niesta), and points out how goals differ importantly from one another (Grant & Gelety). Also included in this section are discussions of the neural (Berkman & Liberman) and evolutionary (Bargh & Huang) underpinnings of goal-pursuit processes.

Kruglanski and Kopetz (Chapter 1) characterize goals as knowledge structures (cognitive representations that can be activated or primed, evaluated, and constrained by attentional resources), unique in that they represent states that can be attained through action. They review research on goal activation, interference, and means instrumentality, as well as commitment, multigoal management, and means substitution, highlighting the interplay of motivation and cognition as two inextricably linked aspects of the human psyche.

Elliot and Niesta (Chapter 2) clarify the goal construct and distinguish it from its antecedents, motives, and temperaments. They describe a hierarchical model in which goals serve these higher-order motivational propensities, translating inclinations into actions. In this model, temperaments and motives provide behavior with its energy (its why), while goals provide its specific direction (its how).

Grant and Gelety (Chapter 3) ask whether or not all goals operate according to the same principles. They examine differences in goal content and their impact on behavior and review some of the major content distinctions in the goal literature. In particular they emphasize those instances where goal type moderates the influence of aspects of goal pursuit often studied independent of content, such as the impact of expectancies or depressed affect on motivation.

Berkman and Liberman (Chapter 4) address the question of where goals reside, linking cognitive-behavioral theories of goal pursuit to recent neuroscientific evidence identifying the neural networks involved in various components of the goal-pursuit process, identifying ways in which each level of analysis can inform the other.

Bargh and Huang (Chapter 5) distinguish the active goal from conscious intention and argue not only that goals need not be consciously pursued, but that ultimate control of behavior rests not with the conscious self but with the autonomous operation of the goal that has been activated. They draw parallels between the "selfish" operation of genes, whose concern is only their own propagation (not the welfare of the host organism), and the "selfish" operation of goals, whose only concern is goal attainment (independent of what is best for the individual). Goal pursuits, they argue, do not require human consciousness—goals serve "as the liaison between genetic influences from the deep past and adaptive behavior in the present," not only in humans but also in all living things.

The chapters in Part II, How Are Goals Selected?, address the question of how people go from the state of not having a particular goal to having that particular goal. Goals can be adopted through processes that are conscious and deliberative (Oettingen & Stephens), through the association of potential future states with positive affect (Custers), and through the nonconscious priming of goals through cues in the environment (Moskowitz & Gesundheit). Once a goal is adopted, through whatever means, goals must be managed in concert with the demands of other, sometimes opposing goals—in other words, goal adoption is no guarantee of immediate goal pursuit (Shah, Hall, & Leander).

Oettingen and Stephens (Chapter 6) describe the different conscious self-regulatory strategies through which fantasies can be turned into binding goals: mentally contrasting aspects of the desired future with the present reality, indulging in aspects of the desired future, or dwelling on aspects of the present reality. Only through mental contrasting, they argue, do individuals experience the necessity to act and commit to goals as a function of their expectations for success.

Custers (Chapter 7) looks at the goal representation itself to better understand how accessible cognitions turn into motivated behavior. He argues that a goal made accessible through nonconscious means is translated into action through the presence of a positive affect component that signals the goal is desired and worth pursuing.

Moskowitz and Gesundheit (Chapter 8) focus on goal accessibility and review evidence suggesting that there are (a minimum of) six ways in which a goal can be made accessible and pursued, varying in the extent to which they are wholly or partially nonconscious, to fully conscious. This review shows that triggering of a goal through nonconscious means does not necessarily imply fully nonconscious goal pursuit, nor does conscious goal adoption guarantee full awareness of the processes at work in attaining a goal.

Shah, Hall, and Leander (Chapter 9) argue that goal pursuit does not exist in a vacuum, but rather in a complex, dynamic system subject to constantly changing situational needs and affordances. The regulation of multiple goal pursuits involves quite a bit of juggling, and whether or not resources are allocated to a particular goal at a particular point in time depends on features of that particular motivational "moment." They discuss not only how the moment for pursing a goal is determined by factors such as commitment, regulatory strength, and situational demands, but also how moments vary in duration, frequency and predictability, which in turn influence whether or not the moment will be seized or slip away.

The chapters in Part III, How Are Goals Pursued?, furnish the "hot" approach to discussing the selection of goals with somewhat "colder" cognitive processing accounts of how goals are regulated and pursued. These chapters begin at the point where Chapter 9 ends—acknowledging that goals reside in a system that manages the many goals against one another. Part III starts with a given goal having been selected and examines the factors that determine how that goal is pursued. The first four chapters of the section essentially place a detailed focus on each of the key steps specified by control theories, such as those of Carver and Scheier (1981) and Bandura (1989). For example, Carver and Scheier likened control to a negative feedback loop. The model starts with a goal having been selected according to inputs that are detailed in Part II of this book. The selected goal is equated with a standard, or reference criterion. The goal is essentially the discrepancy between the standard and one's current standing. For example, one may set the goal of achieving at basketball by setting a standard of making 10 consecutive foul shots. The current state is that 10 consecutive shots have not been made. A goal thus exists due to this discrepancy. The discrepancy energizes or motivates behavior aimed at reducing the discrepancy. Why? Because the discrepancy has associated to it a tension that the person experiences as aversive and unpleasant, and that one is driven to eliminate. The responses made in the service of such tension elimination need to be monitored so that the individual knows whether progress is being made, whether the goal is attained, and whether the rate or manner of responding needs to be altered. When the discrepancy is reduced, the goal is disengaged. Of course, other obstacles to goal pursuit may lead to disengagement as well, allowing the system to rotate to one of its other goals.

Martin and Tesser (Chapter 10) begin Part III with a focus on the discrepancy and its tension state. They argue for the essential nature of the tension state associated with the discrepancy: It is at the heart of the goal. Indeed, they specify what they call markers of a goal, markers that illustrate tension states are what energize the goal (and deenergize responding when the tension has been satisfied). This work starts the "colder" processing accounts with the idea that the mechanisms "rattled off" in the service of a goal are initiated by the "hot" notions of valence and tension that Lewin (1951) described.

Liberman and Dar (Chapter 11) place a fine-grained focus on the monitoring aspect of the negative feedback loop—the part that provides the feedback. To regulate responding one needs to know how the responses already enacted have fared. If not yet delivering the desired standard, the monitor feeds this negative status of the goal pursuit back through the system so that appropriate operations can supplement what responses have already transpired. The motivational advantages of concrete goals depend on continuous feedback on progress toward the goal. Importantly, they also note the disadvantages that monitoring can yield by linking dysfunction of several stripes to the functioning of this monitoring system (such as anxiety and obsessive–compulsive disorder).

Moskowitz (Chapter 12) picks up the movement through the negative feedback loop where Liberman and Dar (Chapter 11) left off. Once a standard (reference criterion) is selected and has been tested or monitored against existing perceptual input that determines the standard has not been attained, a response must be made. Operations are performed in which the cognitive and behavioral system is tuned toward reducing the discrepancy. The individual initiates responses to compensate for the discrepancy. In this manner cognition and behavior are compensatory, as one seeks to adjust an existing state so it conforms to a reference value.

This chapter focuses exclusively on this compensatory nature of purposive responding.

Finally, Jostmann and Koole (Chapter 13) allow us to understand how we exit this loop. Although strong engagement with attainable goals is essential for an individual's well-being, so too is disengagement from unattainable goals. Clearly, when persistence is useless, one's energy and resources are better spent elsewhere. What factors determine when and how and why an individual disengages from a goal pursuit? Their analysis is rooted in the Kuhl (1984) model of action control, including the critical role played by working memory, and the motivational orientations that facilitate the successful resolution of the conflict between goal persistence and disengagement. As such, the chapter provides an important connection between the regulatory processes of Part III, and the notion of goals in a system of goals that requires managing.

Despite strong goal commitment, individuals often fail to achieve their goals. Parks-Stamm and Gollwitzer (Chapter 14) suggest that the strategy of forming implementation intentions, or if–then plans, enables people to overcome the obstacles associated with unsuccessful goal pursuit. Specifically, if–then plans make opportunities to act more salient and initiate appropriate goal-direct automatically when opportunities arise. The authors review ample evidence as to the benefits of if–then planning, as well as more recent evidence suggesting there may be potential costs.

Förster and Werth (Chapter 15) review two strategies individuals use to reduce goal discrepancies, as a function of the goal's *regulatory focus*. When the goal has a promotion focus (involving ideal discrepancies), individuals employ eagerness or approach strategies (going for "hits") and are sensitive to opportunities framed as potential "gains." When the goal has a prevention focus (involving ought discrepancies), individuals use vigilance or avoidance strategies (avoiding mistakes) and are sensitive to potential "losses." Although both strategies are effective means to goal attainment, they differ in their implications for accompanying cognition (decision making, sensitivity to information), affective experience, and behavior (action initiation and persistence).

The chapters in Part IV, Consequences of Goal Pursuit, address the question of how lack of awareness over our goal pursuits and the processes through which those goal pursuits are carried out (even if we know we have goals we are pursuing) has important consequences for the person, across a variety of domains. The first chapter focuses on the draining nature of the goal pursuit itself, illustrating that there are downstream consequences of goal pursuit on one's subsequent resource-dependent activity. The second and third chapters focus on affect and mood that arises from goal pursuit. Finally, the book ends on a positive note, with value added from fit. Higgins's important idea is that strategy matters tremendously, that the framing of one's goals is able to improve the goal pursuit, even though people may not be aware that "matching" their means of goal pursuit to their motivational state adds value. Together these chapters reveal there are affective consequences to trying to "close the gaps" that our discrepancies specify, even if the affective responses are, as Ferguson and Porter (chapter 17) reveal, automatic. Goals shape implicit attitudes toward goal-relevant stimuli in ways that facilitate goal pursuit, thus making implicit affect a tool through which goals are instrumental. Further, goals not merely specify ends but strategies toward those ends that produce different types of discrepancies or tensions that can be associated with the same goal. These chapters identify the specific problems that arise in trying to close different types of gaps.

Vohs, Kaikati, Kerkhof, and Schmeichel (Chapter 16) review research relating to the idea that the capacity to successfully self-regulate in pursuit of goals, or self-regulatory strength, is a limited resource. When individuals pursue goals, they use up or deplete their regulatory strength, resulting in a loss of self-control on subsequent tasks. The authors discuss the nature and development of this resource, as well as the strategies people use to conserve or replenish it. This idea is essential to theories of action control and goal management that require the regulatory system to pursue its various ends given the constraints placed on the process by the limited nature of the resources available for action and cognition.

Ferguson and Porter (Chapter 17) discuss the "iterative and dynamic" relationship between goals and implicit attitudes, linking these two often-isolated literatures. In particular, they emphasize the role goals play in influencing implicit attitudes toward goal-relevant objects, and how implicit attitudes can help determine not only the direction of goal pursuit, but also its ultimate success.

Leander, Moore, and Chartrand (Chapter 18) examine the role of mood in goal pursuit, with particular emphasis on *mystery moods*—those affective states whose origins are not understood by the individual experiencing them. Mystery moods are the result of nonconscious processes (such as the operation of nonconscious goals) and can themselves be experienced without conscious awareness. Importantly, these moods can have tangible effects on subsequent information processing and goal pursuit.

Higgins (Chapter 19) identifies a source of value in goal pursuit that comes not from goal attainment itself, but from the *fit* between an individual's motivational orientation and the means used in pursuit of the goal—specifically, when the manner in which a person pursues a goal sustains rather than disrupts their motivational orientation. This *regulatory fit* makes people "feel right" about and engage more strongly in what they are doing, leading to greater perceptions of goal value and more effective performance.

In summary, the goal is a unique psychological construct. It is cognitive and motivational, fused with affect and expectancies. It has conscious and nonconscious components that interact in determining the person's commerce with and experience of the world. It also is a construct with great utility for understanding behavior. It is at the perfect level of abstraction for making predictions—not as broad in its conceptual nature and predictive value as the motive. Social cognition may describe the basic processes or operations that translate goals into action, that move us from states of wanting to states of having. But the operations of social cognition are the servants of the master, the goal.

Note

1. As an aside, it occurs to us now that another rule specified by attribution theories is that, as reviewed above, we want to infer the intent of others, their goals. Thus, it becomes wholly possible that the entire literature on spontaneous trait inference is not at all about inferring traits, but about inferring goals. The theory of correspondent inference makes an equally strong claim to assume these were in fact goal inferences that were being detailed in the research on spontaneous trait inference. Indeed, such spontaneous goal inferences were proposed and illustrated by Aarts, Gollwitzer, and Hassin (2004). Perhaps dozens of other experiments have already been run to bolster that case. Uleman, Moskowitz, Roman, and Rhee (1993) questioned whether spontaneous inferences refer to persons as opposed to representing mere summaries of the action being observed. But referring to persons does not require they refer to a person's traits. They could be inferences that refer to a person's goals.

References

Aarts, H., Gollwitzer, P. M., & Hassin, R. R. (2004). Goal contagion: Perceiving is for pursuing. *Journal of Personality and Social Psychology, 87,* 23–37.

Adler, A. (1933). *Individual psychology.* London: Kegan Paul.

Allport, G. W. (1954). *The nature of prejudice.* Reading, MA: Addison-Wesley.

Ansfield, M. E., & Wegner, D. M. (1996). The feeling of doing. In P. M. Gollwitzer & J. A. Bargh (Eds.), *The psychology of action: Linking cognition and motivation to behavior* (pp. 482–506). New York: Guilford Press.

Atkinson, J. W. (1964). *An introduction to motivation.* Princeton, NJ: Van Nostrand.

Atkinson, J. W. (1957). Motivational determinants of risk-taking behavior. *Psychological Review, 64*(6), 359–372.

Atkinson, J. W., & Birch, D. (1970). *The dynamics of action.* New York: Wiley.

Bandura, A. (1989). Self-regulation of motivation and action through internal standards and goal systems. In L. A. Pervin (Ed.), *Goal concepts in personality and social psychology* (pp. 19–85). Hillsdale, NJ: Erlbaum.

Bargh, J. A. (1997). The automaticity of everyday life. In R. S. Wyer, Jr. (Ed.), *Advances in social cognition* (Vol. 10, pp. 1–62). Hillsdale, NJ: Erlbaum.

Baumeister, R. F., & Vohs, K. D. (2004). Understanding self-regulation: An introduction. In R. Baumeister & K. Vohs (Eds.), *Handbook of self-regulation: Research, theory and applications* (pp. 1–12). New York: Guilford Press.

Carver, C. S., & Scheier, M. F. (1981). *Attention and self-regulation: A control theory approach to human behavior.* New York: Springer.

Chartrand, T. L., & Bargh, J. A. (1996). Automatic activation of impression formation goals: Nonconscious goal priming reproduces effects of explicit task instructions. *Journal of Personality and Social Psychology, 71,* 464–478.

Chen, M., & Bargh, J. A. (1999). Consequences of automatic evaluation: Immediate behavioral predispositions to approach or avoid the stimulus. *Personality and Social Psychology Bulletin, 25,* 215–224.

Dijksterhuis, A., Bos, M., Nordgren, L., & Van Baaren, R. B. (2006). On making the right choice: The deliberation-without-attention effect. *Science, 311,* 1005–1007.

Fishbein, M. (1967). *Readings in attitude theory and measurement.* New York: Wiley.

Fishbein, M., & Ajzen, I. (1975). *Belief, attitude, intention, and behavior: An introduction to theory and research.* Reading, MA: Addison-Wesley.

Gollwitzer, P. M. (1990). Action phases and mind-sets. In E. T. Higgins & R. M. Sorrentino (Eds.), *Handbook of motivation and cognition* (Vol. 2, pp. 53–92). New York: Guilford Press.

Gollwitzer, P. M., Heckhausen, H., & Steller, B. (1990). Deliberative vs. implemental mind-sets: Cognitive tuning toward congruous thoughts and information. *Journal of Personality and Social Psychology, 59,* 1119–1127.

Heckhausen, H., & Gollwitzer, P. M. (1987). Thought contents and cognitive functioning in motivational versus volitional states of mind. *Motivation and Emotion, 11,* 101–120.

Heider, F. (1944). Social perception and phenomenal causality. *Psychological Review, 51,* 358–374.

Heider, F. (1958). *The psychology of interpersonal relations.* New York: Wiley.

James, W. (1950). *The principles of psychology* (Vol. I & II). New York: Dover. (Original work published 1890)

Jones, E. E., & Davis, K. E. (1965). From acts to dispositions: The attribution process in person perception. In L. Berkowitz (Ed.), *Advances in experimental social psychology* (Vol. 2, pp. 219–266). New York: Academic Press.

Kuhl, J. (1984). Volitional aspects of achievement motivation and learned helplessness: Toward a comprehensive theory of action control. In B. A. Maher & W. A. Maher (Eds.), *Progress in experimental personality research* (pp. 99–171). New York: Academic Press.

Kuhl, J., & Beckmann, J. (Eds.). (1994). *Volition and personality.* Göttingen, Germany: Hogrefe.

Kunda, Z. (1987). Motivated inference: Self-serving generation and evaluation of causal theories. *Journal of Personality and Social Psychology, 53*(4), 636–647.

Lewin, K. (1951). *Field theory in social science: Selected theoretical papers.* New York: Harper & Row.

Libet, B. (1985). Unconscious cerebral initiative and the role of conscious will in voluntary action. *Behavioral & Brain Sciences, 8*(4), 529–566.

Locke, E. A., & Latham, G. P. (1990). *A theory of goal setting and task performance.* Englewood Cliffs, NJ: Prentice Hall.

Moskowitz, G. B. (1993). Individual differences in social categorization: The effects of personal need for structure on spontaneous trait inferences. *Journal of Personality and Social Psychology, 65,* 132–142.

Ryle, G. (1949). *The concept of mind.* London: Hutchinson.

Sassenberg, K., & Moskowitz, G. B. (2005). Don't stereotype, think different! Overcoming automatic stereotype activation by mindset priming. *Journal of Experimental Social Psychology, 41,* 506–514.

Uleman, J. S., & Moskowitz, G. B. (1994). Unintended effects of goals on unintended inferences. *Journal of Personality and Social Psychology, 66,* 490–501.

Uleman, J. S., Moskowitz, G. B., Roman, R. J., & Rhee, E. (1993). How spontaneous trait inferences refer to persons rather than merely behaviors. *Social Cognition, 11,* 321–351.

Uleman, J. S., Newman, L. S., & Moskowitz, G. B. (1996). People as flexible interpreters: Evidence and issues from spontaneous trait inference. In M. Zanna (Ed.), *Advances in experimental social psychology* (Vol. 28, pp. 211–280). San Diego, CA: Academic Press.

Wegner, D. M. (1994). Ironic processes of mental control. *Psychological Review, 101,* 34–52.

Wegner, D. M. (2002). *The illusion of conscious will.* Cambridge, MA: MIT Press.

Wegner, D. M., & Bargh, J. A. (1998). Control and automaticity in social life. In D. T. Gilbert, S. T. Fiske, & G. Lindzey (Eds.), *The handbook of social psychology* (4th ed., Vol. 1, pp. 446–496). Boston: McGraw-Hill.

Wegner, D. M., & Erskine, J. (2003). Voluntary involuntariness: Thought suppression and the regulation of the experience of will. *Consciousness and Cognition, 12,* 684–694.

Wegner, D. M., & Wheatley, T. (1999). Apparent mental causation: Sources of the experience of will. *American Psychologist, 54*(7), 480–492.

Winter, L., & Uleman, J. S. (1984). When are social judgments made? Evidence for the spontaneousness of trait inferences. *Journal of Personality and Social Psychology, 47,* 237–252.

PART I

WHAT (AND WHERE) ARE GOALS?

CHAPTER 1

What Is So Special (and Nonspecial) about Goals?

A VIEW FROM THE COGNITIVE PERSPECTIVE

ARIE W. KRUGLANSKI

CATALINA KOPETZ

The concept of "motivation" has been traditionally treated as an explanatory tool for understanding behavioral dynamics (Atkinson & Birch, 1970). Motivation has been assumed to frame an answer to the question why about an observed action, and motivational constructs have been invoked to account for organisms' voluntary shifts from one state to another. In social relations, divining one's interaction partners' motivations, understanding why they said what they said, did what they did, or felt how they did constitutes a ubiquitous concern driving a large proportion of human responses to their interpersonal environments. Ironically, motivational accounts themselves tended to be static. They have often consisted of identifying some condition, for example, based on a need, drive, instinct, or desire whose presence was assumed to instigate action. For instance, in social psychology a state of cognitive inconsistency such as imbalance or dissonance (Abelson, 1968; Heider, 1958; Festinger, 1957) was assumed to prompt cognitive activity intended to restore consistency. Perceived threat to one's self-esteem was assumed to drive defensive attributions (Kelley, 1987) and/or esteem-protective behavioral choices (e.g., Dweck, 1999; Williams, Forgas, von Hippel, & Zadro, 2005), and so on.

The last 17 years or so have marked a significant departure from such *motivational statics* in an approach characterized by a fresh, cognitive, look on motivation (Bargh, 1990; Dijksterhuis & Bargh, 2001; Kruglanski, 1996; Kruglanski et al., 2002; Kruglanski & Kopetz, 2009). Whereas in the past motivation was treated as separate from cognition (e.g., in models by Kruglanski, 1989; Petty & Cacioppo, 1986; Chaiken, Liberman, & Eagly, 1989) and was often juxtaposed to cognition (Bem, 1972; Miller & Ross, 1975) the "New Look in Motivation" recognized that motivational constructs are cognitively represented. In a sense, the New Look in Motivation mirrored the New Look in Perception of the late 1940s and the 1950s. Whereas the New Look in Perception was about how cognition is colored by motivation (Bruner, 1951) the New Look in Motivation was about how motivation is colored by cognition, or, better yet, about motivation as (a kind of) cognition. Of greatest importance, the "New Look" highlights motivational *dynamism* and *flux* as persons move through their environments and react to them (Kruglanski & Kopetz, 2009).

Goals as Knowledge Structures

Central to the New Look approach is the concept of goals. These can be characterized on three separate levels of analysis (Kruglanski, 1996). The most general level is that of knowledge structures whereby goals are governed by the same principles that apply to alternative cognitive structures as well (i.e., to categories, concepts, judgments, or opinions). According to this notion, just like other cognitive constructs goals can be activated or primed by various stimuli (retrieval cues). Furthermore, just like cognitive constructs that are deemed valid and believable, goals too require appropriate evidence as to their "worthiness" for adoption as objectives. Just like other cognitive constructs, goals can activate other constructs with which they are semantically linked. Furthermore, just like other cognitive constructs, goals too are constrained by limited attentional resources, such that the activation of a given goal may pull resources away from another goal.

Beyond the commonality they share with other cognitive constructs goals constitute a special category, representing the second level of analysis. Their contents or mental representations are unique and determine a variety of processes pertinent to their function. Unlike alternative cognitive concepts like tables, doctors, or butterflies, goals have a unique meaning: They are thought to represent states of affairs attainable through action serving as means to goal attainment (Kruglanski, 1996; Kruglanski et al., 2002). There potentially exist several alternative means to the same goal that could substitute for each other (*equifinality*), and any one means could potentially advance progress toward several goals, or to be multipurpose (*multifinality*). Goal attainment is conceived of as a positive event warranting positive affect, and a failure to attain a goal as a negative event warranting negative affect. Finally, goal attainment divests of value the means that (uniquely) served it and renders unnecessary the investment of effort in their pursuit.

Finally, at the third level of analysis goals vary in their unique substance as "all goals are not created equal" (Ryan, Sheldon, Kasser, & Deci, 1996). Goals may vary in several ways; for instance, they may differ in their abstractness or generality, in their remoteness from basic human needs, in the domain of endeavor to which they pertain, whether they are intra- or interpersonal, and so on. As implied above, much prior research on motivation belonged with this third analytic level, and Fiske (2003) importantly classified the various human motives within her "bucet" framework referring to motives related to belonging, understanding, controlling, enhancing, and trusting. In contrast, the New Look in Motivation related to the first two analytic levels, namely those of goals as knowledge structures, and as a specific category of knowledge structures. We now turn to review research of the latter two types.

The Role of Inference in Goal Pursuit

Goal Adoption

We define "goals" as subjectively desirable[1] states of affairs that the individual intends to attain through action (Kruglanski, 1996). The notion that the individual intends to attain a goal implies that the goal is perceived as attainable, apart from it being perceived as desirable. In other words, adoption of a goal entails a process of proof (Kruglanski, Pierro, Mannetti, Erb, & Chun, 2007) in which the individual confronts subjectively relevant evidence as to a given state's desirability and attainability. What constitutes evidence may vary widely across individuals, groups, and cultures. It rests on a syllogistic belief structure involving a *major premise,* a *minor premise,* and a *conclusion.* For instance, one may adopt a goal of going on a diet, because of a major premise whereby "If one wished an attractive figure, diet would be helpful." In conjunction with the minor premise "I wish to have an attractive figure," this yields the conclusion that "dieting is desirable." Another person might derive the same conclusion from entirely different premises, based, for example, on a physician's perceived expertise, that is, on the belief that "If something was recommended by my doctor it is beneficial to health, and hence desirable" (major premise), coupled with the belief that "my doctor indeed recommended dieting" (minor premise).

Recent research on goals in social cognition has paid relatively little attention to the process of goal adoption. Nonetheless, Liberman and

Förster (2000) discussed the inferential nature of goal adoption in their work on thought suppression (Wegner, 1994). Specifically, they argued that for reasons of conversational relevance (Grice, 1975) the experimental instruction to suppress a given thought, is taken as *evidence* for having the goal of thought expression, and so is persistence in suppression attempts despite the inherent difficulties of this endeavor.

An intriguing experiment that can be interpreted in goal-adoption terms was recently reported by Custer and Aarts (2005, Study 3). Using a subliminal priming technique, participants underwent an evaluative conditioning procedure in which course some activities (e.g., writing, walking) were associated with (prior) positively valenced conditioned stimulus (CS) words (e.g., "love," "happy"). Consequently, the former activities acquired a positive valence themselves; they were liked more than the same activities when paired with neutral stimuli. In present terms, the positive affect participants may have felt after exposure to the positive CS words may have been misattributed to the associated activities and produced the inference that they are desirable. Such an inference may have derived from a major premise of the sort "if something makes me feel good, it means I find it desirable [I like it]." That coupled with a (misattributed) minor premise "thinking of this activity makes me feel good," warrants the conclusion "this activity is desirable." In turn, the conditioned sense of desirability might have lent such activities goal-like properties. Indeed, Custer and Aarts (2005) found that in the case of positive evaluative conditioning participants reported stronger wanting to perform the activities than did their counterparts in the neutral condition.

Of interest, the interpretation above isn't the one adopted by Custer and Aarts (2005) who favor an explanation based on the distinction between "liking" and "wanting." To demonstrate the difference between the two they included a negative evaluative condition in which the activities are paired with prior negatively valenced CS words (e.g., death, pain). They found that even though the conditioning procedure was effective and the paired activities in this condition were "liked" less than those in the neutral condition (Study 4), there were no differences in "wanting" between the negative and the neutral conditions.

Admittedly, there could exist a substantial difference between "liking" and "wanting," in that not everything that one also likes or finds desirable (e.g., the *Mona Lisa* painting in the Louvre, a '59 bottle of Château Lafite Rothschild) one also wants or adopts as a goal. But it is also true that everything that one wants (i.e., a state that one wants to attain) one finds desirable as well, that is superior to one's present state (defining an approach goal) or a future state if threatened by an impending threat (defining an avoidance goal). In the present context, if participants were conditioned to find a given activity (e.g., studying, writing) undesirable they should have wanted less to perform it than participants in the neutral condition.

Why then didn't they? This isn't entirely clear at the moment. One possibility potentially worth exploring is that the negative affect might have reduced the activities' perceived sense of attainability that might have reduced the tendency to want to perform them. Thus, whereas in the case of positive conditioning, the procedure might have strengthened participants' sense that the activity is desirable and attainable, in the case of negative conditioning, the procedure established the activities' lower desirability, but also lowered their sense of attainability—these two tendencies canceling each other out. Further research is needed to investigate this issue.

Means Adoption

Webster's Dictionary (1986, p. 736) defines a "means" as "something useful or helpful to a desired end." To determine that an activity indeed constitutes a means and is believably "useful or helpful" one needs evidence of it being so. Such evidence may derive from a variety of sources, one's own experience with a given means (e.g., taking a given road may have been experienced as reliably leading to one's desired destination), a trusted "epistemic authority" (Kruglanski et al., 2005) (e.g., one may infer that a given road leads to a given destination based on an epistemic authority of a map, or a Global Positioning System [GPS] guidance). In all such cases, the conclusion that an activity is "useful or helpful" hence that it constitutes a means is syllogistically inferred from the appropriate premises, for instance "if something was helpful or useful in my past experience, it is likely to be so presently as well", or "whatever a trusted authority (e.g. a map, or GPS) pronounces as valid is in fact valid," and so on.

The process of means adoption may be involved in the intriguing "chameleon effect" (Chartrand & Bargh, 1999) and the broader phenomenon of mimicry that it may illustrate. We are referring here to findings that under some conditions people may unwittingly (and unconsciously!) adopt a way of doing things activated by an unrelated concept or event. Thus, in research by Bargh, Chen, and Burrows (1996) participants primed with words related to rudeness ("rude," "impolite," "obnoxious") were more likely to interrupt a conversation than those primed with neutral words, whereas participants primed with politeness words showed the least tendency to interrupt the conversation. Similarly, participants primed with words related to the elderly stereotype walked more slowly when provided the opportunity to walk.

In related work, people behaved with greater hostility after being primed with the African American stereotype versus the Caucasian stereotype (Chen & Bargh, 1997), and performed significantly better on a

Trivial Pursuit task when primed with the "professor" versus the "hooligan" stereotype (Dijksterhuis & van Knippenberg, 1998), and so on.

The present notion that mimicry may constitute a case of *means adoption,* that is adoption of a suggested activity perceived as helpful or useful to a given purpose, is implicit in the analysis by Chartrand, Maddux, and Lakin (2005) who viewed mimicry as a "strategy in the repertoire of behaviors that help people get along with others." In this vein, Chartrand and Bargh (1999, Study 2) showed that when a confederate mimicked the posture and mannerism of the participant during an interaction, participants liked the confederate better and perceived the interaction as unfolding more smoothly than when the confederate did not mimic the participant.

Behavioral mimicry has been shown to have other benefits as well. Van Baaren, Holland, Steenaert, and van Knippenberg (2003) showed that waitresses who mimicked their customers either verbally or physically received larger tips that waitresses who did not use mimicry. Moreover, participants mimicked by the experimenter in an alleged marketing study were more likely to engage in a prosocial behavior (picking up pens that were accidentally dropped by the experimenter) than participants who had not been so mimicked (van Baaren, Holland, Kawakami, & van Knippenberg, 2004).

These results speak to the instrumentality of unconscious imitation, suggesting that mimicry constitutes a general means to a better social fit. There is also the suggestion, however, that the general tendency toward mimicry may be qualified by situational appropriateness, and that it will not occur if inferred to be unhelpful or useless. Consistent with this line of reasoning, Dijksterhuis and van Knippenberg (1998) argued that the prime must trigger behaviors beneficial to performance on the subsequent task (more effort, smarter solving strategies). When the suggested behavior is incompatible with current behavioral goals hence being unhelpful to their pursuit, mimicry is significantly reduced. For instance, Macrae and Johnston (1998) showed that priming participants with "helpfulness" increased their tendency to help a confederate who dropped a number of objects. But when they were told that they were running late and had to hurry to the next experimental session, the goal of "hurry" overruled the priming effect. In this instance, primed helpfulness was apparently inferred to be non-instrumental, and in fact to impede the overriding goal of "hurry," hence it was not adopted.

In summary, extant data seem consistent with the notion that mimicry may be generally governed by a hard-wired (and unconscious) premise whereby it elicits sympathy and liking from one's interaction partners and hence is helpful and useful (i.e., it constitutes an instrumental means) to the ubiquitous social goal of acceptance and belonging (Fiske, 2003). Nonetheless, the means of mimicry may fail to be adopted if a particular suggested behavior was inferred to be useless, or unhelpful to one's currently predominant objective.

Inference of Goal Progress

The inference process may be involved in judging whether one had made sufficient progress toward a goal, and this may determine one's tendency to persist in an activity versus switching to other pressing tasks. These effects were recently examined in a series of studies by Fishbach and Dhar (2005). In one of the studies, progress toward the goal of a svelte figure was manipulated by asking dieters how far off they were from their ideal weight on a scale with either 5 pounds, or 25 pounds as the end points. The latter scale was assumed to lead dieters to believe that they had made sufficient progress because the same discrepancy from an ideal weight (e.g., of 4 pounds) would appear smaller with the wider, 25-pound scale than with the narrower, 5-pound, scale.

Participants' reasoning in this situation may have been something like the following: " If a large discrepancy from an ideal weight is defined by 25 pounds, then my own discrepancy (say, of 4 pounds) is small indeed; hence I have made considerable progress toward my goal, and can afford to attend to my other concerns." Fishbach and Dhar (2005, Study 1) assessed participants' tendency to pursue the dieting goal versus the food enjoyment by having them choose a chocolate bar versus an apple as a parting gift. Consistent with the inferred progress hypothesis, 85% of participants in the wide-scale condition chose a chocolate bar over an apple, whereas only 58% did so in the narrow-scale condition.

In their second study, Fishbach and Dhar (2005, Study 2) asked university students how much time they spent on their course work during the past day. Participants completed their answers on a survey form that was alleged to have been previously completed by another (fictitious) participant whose responses though erased were still quite visible. This fictitious respondent listed either 30 minutes of study evincing a low standard, suggesting that the amount of time participants invested (e.g., 2 hours) represented considerable progress, or 5 hours, representing a high standard and affording the inference that participants' time investment didn't represent acceptable progress. Accordingly, participants in the low-standard condition reported greater interest in non-academic activities (i.e., alternative goals) than those in the high-standard condition. This difference was mediated by perceived academic progress that was greater in the low versus the high-standard condition. On the whole then, results of various studies indicate that goal progress may be inferred from various types of evidence and that the inference of goal progress affects the tendency to persist in a given goal pursuit versus moving on to alternative objectives.

An Unintended Consequence of Promises

A false inference of goal progress may underlie the familiar "promises of the moment" phenomenon. A friend promises one to do something yet fails to deliver on that promise. One explanation of such a failure is that the act of promises may prompt the inference that progress toward the goal has already been achieved. Obviously, this could not be so universally. Some promises, after all, increase one's commitment to the promised activity. Thus the challenge is to identify the moderators of the "promises of the moment." In this vein, Orehek (2006) showed that making a promise (vs. no promise) to complete a self-set interpersonal goal resulted in decreased goal activation when other competing goals were also present and independently participants were led to experience positive affect after promising. However, when no other goals were activated and when the positive affect was absent, promising to fulfill one's goal had the opposite effect, of increasing goal activation. These results seem to suggest that "the promise of the moment" may serve as a substitution for action when people are motivated to infer goal progress because of alternative goals "waiting in the wings" and when there is additional evidence for goal progress such as positive affect experienced after promising. In such cases, inferring goal progress would allow one to move to the next goal while "feeling" good about the progress toward the current goal. In a related research, Fitzsimons (2006) showed that inferred goal progress led to more implicit approach and less implicit avoidance of their next important goal suggesting that participants were moving to another important goal system. Moreover, this effect was larger for individuals high (vs. low) on the locomotion dimension and low (vs. high) on the assessment dimension (Higgins, Kruglanski, & Pierro, 2003; Kruglanski et al., 2000).

Goal Activation

A prominent principle of mental representations is the accessibility principle according to which those cognitive constructs that come most readily to mind (are most accessible) are especially important determinants of social judgment and behavior (Taylor & Fiske, 1978; Higgins, Rholes, & Jones, 1977; Higgins, King, & Mavin, 1982; Devine, 1989). As knowledge structures, goals too fluctuate in accessibility. Hence, the likelihood of a certain goal being activated and of affecting one's course of action may vary across time and situations according to its momentary accessibility.

Much recent research on goals has tested the implications of this phenomenon focusing on the causes and effects of goal activation.

Sources of Activation

What kinds of stimuli can activate a goal? The literature on goal activation has uncovered a wide diversity of activation sources.

SEMANTIC ASSOCIATES

Semantic associates may activate a goal in the same manner that, say, a stereotype is activated by its semantic associates. In a now-classic study, Chartrand and Bargh (1996) primed participants with either an impression-formation goal (through words such as "opinion," "personality," "evaluate," and "impression"), or a memory goal (through words such as "absorb," "retain," "remember," and "memory"). In an allegedly unrelated second experiment participants were presented a series of predicates describing behaviors suggestive of different personality traits (social, athletic, intelligent, and religious). Participants were then given a surprise recall test. Those primed with the impression-formation goal clustered their recall more than did participants primed with the memory goal, just as did participants in the Hamilton, Katz, and Leirer (1980) study whose corresponding goals were induced via *explicit instructions*.

SOCIAL SOURCES OF ACTIVATION

A special case of the semantic activation of goals concerns the case wherein a node in a semantic network is represented by another person who in a perceiver's mind is associated with specific goals. For instance, other people (mother, father, friend) who have a given goal for an individual may activate it (Shah, 2003a, 2003b; Fitzsimons & Bargh, 2003). Priming by specific persons who have a given goal for themselves may activate it in others, producing *goal contagion* (Aarts, Gollwitzer, & Hassin, 2004). Furthermore, one's chronic goals or concerns may be activated in the presence of others. For instance, the presence of an ethnic minority member may activate one's long-term egalitarian goals (Moskowitz, Gollwitzer, & Wasel, 1999).

PRIMING BY MEANS AND OPPORTUNITIES

Often, an associative network including a goal may incorporate its means of attainment as well. In such a case, a means may activate the corresponding goal in a bottom-up fashion (Berkowitz & LePage, 1967; Shah

& Kruglanski, 2003). An opportunity to pursue a goal may also activate it if its mental representation was associated with the goal in an individual's mind. Accordingly, Shah and Kruglanski (2003) found that priming an opportunity to show one's capacity for "functional thinking" substantially interfered with participants' pursuit of a current task of anagram solution.

Idiosyncrasy of Associations

As the foregoing discussion suggests, any construct linked in an individual's mind to a goal may activate it. Many such linkages are common to members of the same culture and are based on general notions concerning norms of goal attainment (e.g., many Americans would associate the attainment of food with shopping at a grocery store). To some extent, however, the history of prior linkages may differ across individuals (Chen, Lee-Chai, & Bargh, 2001). Thus, very different stimuli can activate the same goal for different persons, and the same stimulus can activate different goals for different persons. In principle, any concept could activate a goal for some of the people under some of the circumstances. Whereas the word "table" may sound neutral enough, it could activate an achievement goal for an aspiring carpenter hoping to make outstanding tables, or for a gambler hoping to make a fortune at a baccarat table.

Spreading of Activation and of Other Properties

The concept of priming or knowledge activation is intimately connected to the notion of spreading activation among semantically associated constructs (Anderson, 1983). Many important self-regulation phenomena have been seen to result from the spreading of activation through goal systems. Evidence reviewed earlier suggests that once they have been automatically activated, goals are automatically pursued. This was presumed possible because goals are cognitively associated with their corresponding means of attainment, hence the activation of goals is spread intrasystemically to their corresponding behavioral plans (Bargh, 1990; Aarts & Dijksterhuis, 2000; Kruglanski et al., 2002) stirring individuals to action. Research by Shah and Kruglanski (2003) showed that the spreading of activation within a goal system is bidirectional: It flows not only from goals to means but also in the opposite direction from means to goals. Thus, goal activation increases in the presence of means perceived as instrumental to those particular goals, attesting to a "bottom-up" manner of goal activation.

In the context of goals research, the spreading activation process has been studied in reference to the transfer of various motivational properties from goals to means. For instance, a current goal may plausibly command greater affective investment than a goal not currently in place or a goal that had been already attained. Consistent with this notion, Fergusson and Bargh (2004) showed that an object is evaluated more positively when it is perceived as instrumental to a current (vs. already attained, or not currently pursued) goal.

Fishbach, Shah, and Kruglanski (2004) explored whether the strength of an association between goals and means moderates the transfer from goals to means of various motivational properties, such as degree of commitment, and the magnitude and quality of affect. In support of this idea, Fishbach et al. (2004, Study 1) found that the correlation between the magnitude of positive affect associated with participants' goals (e.g., a goal of "becoming educated") and the magnitude of affect associated with a corresponding means (e.g., a means of "studying") depended on strength of the goal–means association as assessed by the degree to which the goal primed the means. Moreover, the very same activity or means was experienced differently depending on the goal with which it happened to be associated. Participants in one study (Fishbach et al., 2004, Study 2) were primed either with the goal of "weight watching" or of "food enjoyment," or with no goal at all (control condition). They then rated the extent to which they experienced positive and negative emotions when they ate (1) vegetables, (2) fruits, (3) chocolate, (4) cakes, (5) fries, and (6) hamburgers. The low-calorie food was experienced equally positively in the weight watching, control, and food enjoyment conditions. But the high-calorie food was associated with less positive emotions in the weight watching compared to the control condition and with the most positive emotions in the food enjoyment condition.

Fishbach et al. (2004, Study 3) investigated whether the specific quality of positive affect, apart from its magnitude, may also be transferred from goals to means. In this experiment, participants listed either an "ought" goal or an "ideal" goal. Higgins' research (e.g., 1987, 1997) suggests that attainment of "ought" goals gives rise to such emotions as relief, calm, and relaxation. By contrast, attainment of "ideal" goals gives rise to the emotions of happiness, pride, or enjoyment. Participants then listed three acquaintances believed instrumental to attainment of either an ideal or an ought goal (i.e., to constitute "social means" to the goal in question). Following Higgins et al. (1982), we assumed that the order in which the acquaintances are listed reflects the strength of their association to the goal. Participants then rated their expected emotions following goal-attainment using three items related to ideal-type affect (happy, proud, enjoy) and three items related to ought-type affect (relieved, calm, relaxed). It was found that the affective qualities associated with ideal or ought goals were transferred to individuals related to these goals' attainment, and that the degree of transfer was proportionate to the order in which these persons were listed. Thus, for an ideal-type goal, ideal-type affect and not an ought-type affect felt with respect to the first person listed was more pronounced than ideal-type affect felt with regard to the second person listed, which in turn was more pronounced than the ideal-type affect felt with respect to the third person listed. Similarly, for the ought-type goal, the corresponding (ought-type) affect, and not the ideal-type affect, was stronger with respect to the first two persons listed than with respect to the third person listed.

Unconscious Goal Activation

A research trend in cognitive psychology that began in the late 1960s and the 1970s (Neisser, 1967; Posner & Snyder, 1975; Shiffrin & Schneider, 1977) has systematically demonstrated that psychological processes can occur without conscious guidance and intention that once were assumed to constitute the necessary ingredients of such processes. In line with this trend, much recent research in social psychology has revealed that goals too can be activated nonconsciously and can operate without awareness and cognizant guidance. People can behave, interact, and pursue their goals without knowing precisely why they are doing so, or what process has put various objectives in their mind (Nisbett & Wilson, 1977; Chartrand & Bargh, 1996; Bargh et al., 1996; Bargh, Gollwitzer, Lee-Chai, Barndollar, & Trotschel, 2001). Moreover, unconscious goal pursuit seems to produce the same outcomes as does conscious, explicit, goal pursuit (see Chartrand & Bargh, 2002, for a review). Indeed, a variety of research converges on the conclusion that unconscious goal activation leads to goal pursuit and to appropriate emotional reactions if the pursuit went well or poorly (e.g., Shah & Kruglanski, 2002, 2003; Shah, Friedman, & Kruglanski, 2002; Fishbach et al., 2004).

Research on unconscious goal activation and pursuit does not merely "echo" psychologists' old fascination with acting without knowing (traceable to Freud's notion of the unconscious). Instead it addresses a fundamental problem of goal-directed action, that of limited mental resources; accordingly, research on unconscious goal activation addresses the functional and adaptive nature of automatic goal pursuit when individuals' conscious abilities are limited. If constant attention was required for every goal-directed action, systems responsible for goal pursuit would be severely limited and persons would be incapable of pursuing more than one goal at any given time (say walking and talking) (Baumeister, Muraven, & Tice, 2000; Schmeichel, Vohs, & Baumeister, 2003). Research on automatic goal pursuit suggests the adaptive benefit of being able to pursue one's goals in a relatively automatic fashion, without the necessity of conscious deliberation at every turn.

To conclude, the accessibility principle of knowledge activation (Carlston & Smith, 1996; Higgins, 1996) has been shown to apply to goals. A considerable amount of research has demonstrated how goals, as knowledge structures, can become accessible through priming and how they subsequently guide one's actiivities. Study after study has revealed that a particular goal can be activated (or made accessible) through its semantic associates, its means of attainment, other people, and basically any concept cognitively associated with that goal. Moreover, goals can be activated and can operate in a nonconscious manner as well and efficiently as when they do so consciously. As Bargh and Chartrand (1999, p. 476) noted, "*the representation* does not care about the source of activation. . . ." Whether the goals are activated consciously or unconsciously, the mechanisms that underlie goal-directed behavior are the same. These findings constitute an important step forward from traditional motivation research in which one's consciousness and intentionality were necessary ingredients of goal-directed action, depicting individuals as permanently imprisoned by constraints of their own attentional resources. Although it violates the common sense idea of "freewill," automatic goal-directed behavior is highly adaptive, as it frees us from the burdens of goal operation and allows us to self-regulate with just "one third less effort than regular thinking" (Gilbert & Osborn, 1989).

Interconnectedness

Implicit in the notion of knowledge activation is the concept of "interconnectedness": Constructs are linked with each other; these linkages afford the activation of the constructs by one another. Carlston and Smith (1996) defined "linkages" as learned or inferred relationships among objects and concepts. In social cognition, different conceptual scheme for interconnections among concepts have been proposed including those of associative networks (Anderson, 1983; Carlston, 1992; Wyer & Srull, 1989) or of parallel distributed models (Gillund & Shiffrin, 1984; Hintzman, 1986). Similar to other cognitive webs of interconnected constructs, goals too may be linked with their corresponding means of attainment and with alternative goals, forming specific configurations or goal systems (Kruglanski et al., 2002). Goal systems are assumed to include facilitative as well as inhibitory links that vary in their form and strength. For instance, goals and means may be facilitatively connected, whereas the connections between competing goals may be inhibitory (Shah et al., 2002).

Goals as a Unique Category of Knowledge Structures

Much of the new research on goals (for discussion, see Kruglanski & Kopetz, 2009) explored the properties of goals by demonstrating that various cognitive processes (knowledge activation, spreading activation, unconscious activity) apply also to goal-related phenomena. Typically, the explicit focus in that work was on implementing a given cognitive manipulation such as supraliminal or subliminal priming and looking at its effect on various goal-related outcomes, such as action, performance, positive or negative affect engendered by goal progress, or lack of progress and so on. In that line of work, the goal-related outcomes were often based on plausible intuitive assumptions rather than on systematic analysis. For instance, in research where a goal was primed and an activity was observed (e.g., Aarts & Dijksterhuis, 2000; Bargh et al., 2001; Chartrand & Bargh, 1996) the intuitive assumption was that goals automatically lead to associated activities. In research on emotional transfer (Fishbach et al., 2004) the assumption was that goals are invested with positive affect that may be transmitted to the means, and that is diffused and released once the goal in question is attained (Fergusson & Bargh, 2004). In the following section, we focus on unique goal-related phenomena and consider them on their own, special, level of analysis.

Goal Schemas

The cognitive approach to the goal category regards it as a generic mental representation, or goal schema, characterized by a specific meaning and admitting a unique set of possibilities. As already noted, goals are understood and experienced as desirable[2] future states that one intends to pursue through action adjudged as helpful or useful (hence constituting means) to goal attainment. Goals may vary in their desirability or magnitude. The more desirable a goal, keeping attainability constant, the greater its power to incite goal-directed strivings. As possible future states, goals may also vary in their relation to current states. *Approach goals* represent future states that are more desirable than the current states, hence warranting actions designed to bring them about. In contrast, *avoidance goals* refer to impending future states that are less desirable than the current states, hence warranting actions designed to forestall them. [3]

The mental representation of the goal category allows the existence of several mutually substitutable or equifinal means to goal attainment and a means may be perceived as multifinal, that is, as capable of serving several different goals. Once a goal is perceived to be attained, or adequate goal progress is inferred to have occurred, it is implied that no further commitment of resources to that goal is necessary. In Kurt Lewin's (1935, p. 242) terms, a goal sets up a tension system. "This tension system drives toward discharge and causes activities which serve the execution of the purpose," such that "the tension system is discharged by the attainment of the goal" (p. 242).

The generic goal schema allows the possibility of a concurrent activation of several independent goals. Such goals may conflict and pull resources away from each other. Subjectively, the individual may strive to maximize desirability (or subjective utility) by allocating resources to goals of higher magnitude, and inhibiting, or pulling resources away, from lower magnitude goals. The relative experienced magnitudes of different goals may fluctuate considerably from one psychological context to the next. Thus, the degree of activation, effected by recent or frequent priming, or by situational salience (Higgins, 1996) might be taken as evidence for goal desirability and may create conditions under which a goal of normally lower desirability (e.g., a tasty yet caloric food item) may be experienced as of superior magnitude to a goal of normally higher desirability (e.g., a slim figure), in which case one may speak of "succumbing to temptation" (Fishbach, Friedman, & Kruglanski, 2003). The necessity to choose between goals and to resolve goal conflict through the withdrawal of resources from one of the concurrent objectives may be avoided if a means could be found that was multifinal, affording the concomittant attainment of both (or more) objectives.

We assume that the generic goal schema constitutes a fundamental cognitive structure, and that it probably represents a hard-wired feature of the human psyche. We are also assuming that the goal schema is capable of functioning unconsciously as well as consciously and that it can be instantiated by numerous specific goal contents, some representing basic social needs (Fiske, 2003), others representing their sociocultural derivatives that identify what states of affairs are worth striving for (approach goals) and worth avoiding (avoidance goals). The recent cognitive approach has inspired numerous experimental studies bearing on various aspects of the goal schema. These are reviewed in what follows.

Goal Magnitudes

Shah et al. (2002) found that activation of a given focal goal results in an inhibition of alternative goals reflected in the slowing down of lexical decision times to such goals. For instance, when a goal (vs. a control word) served as a prime this increased the lexical decision times to the alternative goals (vs. control words) attesting to their inhibition, the magnitude of such inhibition being positively related to participants' perceived magnitude, or importance, of the focal goal they were currently pursuing.

Fishbach et al. (2003) have shown that committed (vs. less committed) self-regulators may have learned to place more positive evaluations on their high magnitude goals and more negative evaluations on the temptation goals. As noted earlier, however, the momentary salience of temptations may render them highly attractive, suggesting a high goal magnitude, at a given instant. Effective self-control may consist in the ability to adjust for a momentary attractiveness surge of ordinarily low-magnitude goals, and to act according to the long-term relative magnitude of different goals. In a study addressed at this phenomenon, Fishbach and Shah (2006) used a method developed by Solarz (1960) to show that self-control may involve implicit predispositions toward approaching goal-related cues and avoiding temptations-related cues even though the goals and the temptations are similarly attractive in the moment. Participants were asked to respond to goal- and temptation-related words by either pulling a joystick toward them or pushing the joystick away from them. The results showed that participants were faster in pulling goal-related words versus temptation-related words and control words. Also, they were faster in pushing away temptation-related words than goal-related words and control words. Moreover, these results were qualified by (1) participants' experience of self-control conflict (whether they held an overarching goal or not) and (2) perceived appeal of temptations. Finally, the activation of these response patterns had behavioral implications regarding participants' intention to engage in goal-related behavior (how much time participants planned to invest in their homework that day when the overarching goal was studying) and their actual behavior (choice of a healthy vs. unhealthy snack when the overarching goal was dieting).

Goal Systemic Configurations: Equifinality

The equifinality configuration exists when several interchangeable means are connected to the same goal. This affords the possibility of substituting one means for another in case of thwarting or failure. The possibility of substitution should increase people's tendency to commit to a given goal by increasing the expectancy of goal attainment (if not one way, then another). In other words, the larger the equifinality set size the more subjectively likely goal attainment should be, and hence the stronger should be the tendency to adopt the goal and commit to it. On the other hand, existence of several interchangeable means should reduce individuals' commitment to any one means.

Pierro (2005) carried out a series of studies designed to address this problem. In one of the studies, participants, investment consultants in a large financial company in Rome, Italy, were asked to list two work goals they would be trying to attain in the next 6 months (they listed goals such as the acquisition of new clients, increasing the value of one's portfolio), and either a single means (e.g., use a mailing list, teamwork), or three separate means for attaining these goals. Pierro (2005) found that in the three versus the one means condition, participants exhibited weaker commitment to the first means but a stronger commitment to the goal. As expected, this effect was mediated by a greater likelihood of goal attainment in the three versus the one means condition.

The possibility of substitution has other, heretofore unexplored, implications. For instance, it suggests that the tendency to perform a given activity would be determined by the degree to which the means it was assumed to serve was already accomplished by a different activity. For instance, if activity B was thwarted and goal G was in place, individuals may move to perform activity A seen as a substitutable means to G, rather than to activity C perceived as a means to a different goal, G1. Similarly, if activity B was successful, and goal B was attained, individuals may prefer activity C (a means to a different goal, G1) over activity A (already accomplished by B). These issues could be profitably pursued in subsequent research.

Features of Multifinality

A fundamental aspect of the *equifinality* configuration is the necessity to choose between the interchangeable means, insofar as they represent distinct activities and couldn't be pursued all at the same time. Often, such choice may be guided by the principle of utility maximization across the entire spectrum of currently active goals. In other words, among the *equifinal* means the one selected may be the most *multifinal* means, that is, a means that in addition to a given focal goal serves other active goals as well. Chun, Kruglanski, Sleeth-Keppler, and Friedman (2005) explored the foregoing possibility. Their empirical point of departure was Wilson and Nisbett's (1978) classic research wherein passersby at a department store chose among four different nightgowns of similar quality, or among four identical pairs of nylon stockings. This research obtained a strong *position effect* was found such that the two rightmost objects in the array were heavily overchosen. Of interest, participants seemed entirely unaware of their bias. Instead, they justified their preferences exclusively in terms of the quality of the choice objects (the nightgowns or the stockings). Chun et al. (2005) hypothesized that the choice of the rightmost object was multifinal satisfying not only the *focal goal* of choosing the best-quality items, which goal would have been gratified equally well by any object in the array, but also a background goal of reaching quick closure after inspecting the entire array from left to right.

To test their analysis, Chun et al. (2005) conceptually replicated Wilson and Nisbett's (1978) with one modification. Participants' "focal goal" was kept constant while manipulating the presumptive "background goal" of closure. Participants were given the (focal) goal of choosing among four pairs of (actually) identical athletic socks, the pair that was of the best quality. To manipulate the "background goal" of closure, participants in one condition were placed under time pressure (Kruglanski, 2004; Kruglanski & Webster, 1996; Webster & Kruglanski, 1998; Kruglanski, Pierro, Mannetti, & De Grada, 2006). In another condition, participants were not placed under pressure and were given accuracy instructions intended to reduce their need for closure (Kruglanski & Webster, 1996). If the multifinality analysis is correct, the rightward bias should replicate in the time-pressure condition and be reduced or eliminated in the accuracy condition. This is precisely what happened: 81% of participants in the time-pressure (need for closure) condition chose the two rightmost choices replicating Wilson and Nisbett (1978). By contrast, only 33% of participants in the accuracy condition made these rightmost choices.

In the Wilson and Nisbett (1978) and Chun et al.'s (2005), study the various means presented (the stocking, the socks) were equally instrumental to the focal goal, hence they were truly equifinal. In a following study by Chun et al. (2005), these authors showed that if the means differed in their instrumentality, the power of the "background" goals may be overridden. In other words, if one of the means choices was more instrumental to the focal goal than to the background goal, whereas another was more instrumental to the background than to the focal goal—a focal override would take place, and the means more instrumental to the focal goal will be selected, sacrificing the background goal.

The hypothesis that unconscious goal states may influence one's choices in accordance with the principle of multifinality was further explored in a study conducted by Sleeth-Keppler (2005). In the study designed to test these notions, Winthrop University students were asked to make a choice between two identical sheets of construction paper, one dyed in the primary school color (garnet) and one dyed in blue (control color). Prior to making the choice, participants were subliminally primed with either a goal of identifying with their school or a goal of disidentifying with it. Next, the goal of self-affirmation was manipulated following the procedure employed by Cohen, Aronson, and Steele (2000). Assuming that the act of identifying or disidentifying with a group subserves the higher-order goal of self-affirmation, one could argue that fulfilling that goal in a manner unrelated to group identification should decrease participants' need to identify/disidentify with their group via a goal-consistent product choice.

In line with the predictions, 80% of participants in the Winthrop identification condition chose the garnet-colored paper when no alternative means to affirm the self was provided to them (i.e., in the no-affirmation control condition). This pattern of results was perfectly reversed when the Winthrop disidentification goal was primed and no alternative self-affirmation opportunity was provided. Quite a different pattern of results emerged in the affirmation condition. Only 30.8% of the participants chose garnet-colored sheet in the identification condition, whereas in the disidentification condition, 41.7% of participants chose the garnet-colored sheet after affirming the self. Again, without exception, participants justified their choices in terms of the focal goal of choosing the highest quality paper, citing such reasons as "the red piece of paper felt sturdier and looked much less grainy than the blue one," "the paper looked smoother and of higher quality," and so on.

Multifinality and Need for Closure

Beyond the "bang for the buck" it affords, *multifinality* could be appealing also because it eliminates the unnerving ambiguity of having one's alternative goal pursuits suspended while pursuing a current focal goal. Persons who are high on the need for closure should be particularly unnerved by such an ambiguity. Hence, such individuals should exhibit a particularly pronounced preference for multifinal means. Chun and Kruglanski (2005) obtained consistent support for this hypothesis in a series of studies. Participants high (vs. low) on need for closure reported that they

1. expected to attain more goals through the use of computers,
2. exhibited a stronger preference for a multifinal over a unifinal camera even though the unifinal one was of a higher quality,
3. exhibited a stronger preference for a multifinal over a unifinal cell phone even though the multifinal one was much more expensive, and
4. reported greater use of a multifinal soap (for the face and the body) versus two separate soaps, one for the face, the other for the body.

These findings were echoed by the results of Sleeth-Keppler (2005) that

5. individuals with high versus low need for closure prefer multifinal friends (i.e., "friends for all seasons" that gratify multiple needs over unifinal friends relevant to one type of need only).

The Price of Multifinality

Adoption of a multifinal means may appear to constitute a particularly desirable choice in that it maximizes subjective utility, and minimizes ambiguity about progress on various current goals. But like anything else in life, multifinal means "come with a price tag" and can entail significant trade-offs in comparison with a unifinal means. These trade-offs were recently examined in a series of studies by Zhang, Fishbach, and Kruglanski (2007) on the *dilution effect*. Specifically, consistent with Anderson's (1974) "fan effect," whereby the association between a construct and a cue is inversely proportionate to the number of cues associated with the construct, we assumed that strength of the linkage between a means and a goal will be inversely proportionate to the number of goals associated with the means (or, vice versa; Fishbach et al., 2004). In turn, we hypothesized that the diluted association strength may be interpreted as low instrumentality hence reducing the tendency to pursue the multifinal means when only one of the goals served by that means was activated. This general proposition was supported in six experimental studies.

For instance, in one of the studies (Zhang et al., 2007, Study 1) participants read short essays discussing aerobic exercise, consumption of tomatoes, and withdrawal from caffeine. In the one-goal condition participants read that aerobic exercise protects one from heart disease, whereas in the two-goals condition they read that aerobic exercise protects one from heart disease and also helps to maintain healthy bones. Participants in both conditions then rated the extent to which aerobic exercise protects one from heart disease, that is, is instrumental to that particular prevention goal. Across different topics addressed in the different studies we found that participants viewed as more instrumental the (same) activity when it was portrayed to serve that goal only, as compared to the case where it was portrayed to serve also another goal.

Goal Attainment and Limits of Cognitive Mechanisms

In the preface to their 1986 volume of the *Handbook of Motivation and Cognition,* Sorrentino and Higgins likened the motivation–cognition interface to the Moebius strip stating that "although there appear to be two sides to the figure, there is no point at which one side ends and the other side begins. You simply return to the place you began without ever crossing over from one side to the other. There is no point at which motivation ends and cognition begins. The two are synergistic. This synergism is what we call the "Warm Look" (p. vii).

The new goals research contains evidence consistent with these early insights. Thus, whereas in prior sections of this chapter we showed how cognitive principles (of priming, inference, accessibility, or interconnectedness) apply to goal systemic constructs, intriguing recent work also suggests that goal systemic considerations constrain the operation of cognitive mechanisms. In this vein, Liberman and Förster (2000) found in five studies that allowing participants to express suppressed thoughts, hence fulfilling their perceived need to do so (inferred from the suppression instructions), resulted in lower accessibility of the previously suppressed construct, than its accessibility following suppression (without the opportunity for expression), and its accessibility following expression without prior suppression (hence, without the inference of the motivation to express the construct).

What makes this finding particularly interesting is the fact that it runs counter to the cognitive principles according to which accessibility should increase as function of the frequency as well as the recency of activation. Specifically, allowing participants expression following suppression should increase the recency with which the pertinent constructs are expressed and add to the frequency of their activation. Yet the measured construct accessibility in this condition was lower than their accessibility in the suppression-only condition. It appears then that perceived goal attainment overrides the effect of the cognitive mechanisms.

Subsequent research adduced further evidence for this proposition. Thus, Förster, Liberman, and Higgins (2005) asked participants to search for a picture of a pair of glasses on a computer screen and found that during the search, but before participants found the target, the accessibility of words related to glasses was greater compared with the accessibility for those who were not searching for the target. However, once participants found the target, the accessibility declined below the level for control participants.

Cesario, Plaks, and Higgins (2006) hypothesized that priming a social category (e.g., the category "elderly") activates a goal to interact with members of the primed category. According to the postfulfillment inhibition hypothesis, that would imply that providing participants with an opportunity to interact (even symbolically) with a primed target should lead to a decrease in the accessibility of the category and related concepts. Consistent with this analysis, Cesario et al. (2006) showed that following social category activation and subsequent symbolic satisfaction of the interaction goal through writing an essay describing an interaction with an old man, the accessibility of the primed category (elderly) decreased compared with participants for whom the category was not activated.

Finally, in a study referred to earlier, Orehek (2006) has showed that making (vs. not making) a promise to complete a self-set interpersonal goal resulted in a decreased goal activation when (1) alternative competing goals were also present and (2) participants were led to experience positive affect after promising, allowing the inference of goal progress.

These various findings raise an intriguing possibility that cognitive mechanisms, such as the category activation via priming, generally operate within motivational constraints, and in the service of goal pursuit of one type or another. For instance, it is possible that frequency and recency of activation signal to the individual that the relevant constructs are goal relevant (representing important goals, or effective means to those goals) and that this inference of motivational relevance is critical to the increased construct accessibility as a consequence of frequent or recent priming. This suggests that if the inferred motivational relevance of the primed constructs could be controlled for, or negated, priming effects on construct accessibility might be attenuated if not completely removed.[4] These notions could be profitably probed in future research.

Summary and Conclusion

In this chapter we carried out a systematic (if a selective) review of recent cognitively oriented research on goal pursuit. Departing from the tri-partite distinction between the levels of analysis on which goal pursuit may be approached (Kruglanski, 1996) we proposed that the new goal research represents a conjunction of the knowledge structure level of analysis that treats goal constructs as subject to the same cognitive principle as other constructs, to the unique properties of goals as a category. The third level of analysis, that of specific goals or motives, though of considerable interest in the area of motivated social cognition (Fiske, 2003) has been deemphasized in the new goals research that focused, instead, on the general dynamic principles operating on all goals.

Typically, the new goal research has explicitly addressed cognitive level mechanisms (on knowledge structure level of analysis) stressing the possibility of goal *activation* via priming, and of doing so outside the actor's awareness. Research also addressed the cognitive process of *inference* as it may be involved in goal adoption (Custer & Aarts, 2005; Liberman & Förster, 2000), the perception of goal progress (Fishbach & Dhar, 2005) and that of means instrumentality (Zhang et al., 2007). Finally, research addressed the notion of *interconnectedness* and the spreading of activation and of other motivational properties as function of the degree of interconnectedness of goal systemic elements (e.g., Fishbach et al., 2004).

The new goals research also addressed (often intuitively and implicitly) the unique implications of the goal schema including the notions that

1. goals differ in their perceived magnitude or perceived importance affecting the degree of commitment they command,
2. goals may be activated simultaneously with other goals creating a problem of resource allocation,
3. such problem may be resolved by (a) inhibiting the less currently important objective (Shah et al., 2002) or (b) activating the more important objective that the pursuit of a less important objective threatens to undermine (Fishbach et al., 2003),
4. goal systemic configurations include the *equifinality* structure in

which several interchangeable means are seen to serve the same goal, posing the problem of choice among those means, as well as affording the possibility of substituting one means for another in case of failure or thwarting of goal pursuit via the use of a former means,

5. goal systemic configurations include also the *multifinality* structure in which the same means is attached to several different goals,

6. in the *equifinality* and *multifinality* configurations the presence of multiple connections dilutes their strength with appropriate consequences for the spreading of psychological qualities from goal to means (Fishbach et al., 2003) and for the inference of means instrumentality to goal attainment (Zhang et al., 2007).

Finally, we considered findings suggesting that motivational considerations may constrain the operation of basic cognitive mechanisms. Thus, the cognitive mechanisms of frequent and recent priming assumed to drive the phenomenon of construct accessibility may be overridden by motivational considerations suggesting that the goal represented by such constructs has been attained and is no longer in play (Liberman & Förster, 2000; Förster et al., 2005; Cesario et al., 2006). Such findings highlight the potentially recursive relations between motivation and cognition (of the Moebius strip variety) in which each of these two aspects of the human psyche is a handmaiden of the other.

Notes

1. The term "desirable" is meant here in a relative sense, that is, in comparison with some alternative state. Thus, action could be driven by *approach* goals (getting a PhD, spending more time with one's children) defining conditions valued as more desirable than the current state, but also by *avoidance* goals (protecting one's home against burglary, escaping an avalanche), defining conditions less desirable than the current state and which likelihood of occurrence one wishes to minimize.

2. In Kurt Lewin's (1951, p. 39) field theoretic terms, a "goal . . . [is] a positive valence."

3. In this sense, avoidance goals desirable future states of non-loss in light of the potential occurrence of desirability loss, in case no preventive action was taken.

4. Consistent with this notion are the findings of Zhang, Fishbach, and Kruglanski (2007) mentioned earlier that dilution of the association between the means and a given goal, leading to reduced accessibility of the goal when the means is activated, implied to participants a lower instrumentality of the means. If so, the opposite might also be true, namely that increased accessibility may imply increased instrumentality of the means.

References

Aarts, H., & Dijksterhuis, A. (2000). Habits as knowledge structures: Automaticity in goal-directed behavior. *Journal of Personality and Social Psychology, 78*(1), 53–63.

Aarts, H., Gollwitzer, P. M., & Hassin, R. R. (2004). Goal contagion: Perceiving is for pursuing. *Journal of Personality and Social Psychology, 87*(1), 23–37.

Abelson, R. P. (1968). Psychological implication. In R. P. Abelson, E. Aronson, W. J. McGuire, T. M. Newcomb, M. J. Rosenberg, & P. H. Tannenbaum (Eds.), *Theory of cognitive consistency: A sourcebook* (pp. 112–139). Chicago: McNally.

Anderson, J. R. (1974). Retrieval of propositional information from long-term memory. *Cognitive Psychology, 6*(4), 451–474.

Atkinson, J. W., & Birch, D. (1970). *The dynamics of action.* New York: Wiley.

Bargh, J. A. (1990). Auto-motives: Preconscious determinants of social interaction. In E. T. Higgins & R. M. Sorrentino (Eds.), *Handbook of motivation and cognition: Foundations of social behavior* (Vol. 2, pp. 93–130). New York: Guilford Press.

Bargh, J. A., & Chartrand, T. L. (1999). The unbearable automaticity of being. *American Psychologist, 54*(7), 462–479.

Bargh, J. A., Chen, M., & Burrows, L (1996). Automaticity of social behavior: Direct effects of trait construct and stereotype activation on action. *Journal of Personality and Social Psychology, 71*(2), 230–244.

Bargh, J. A., Gollwitzer, P. M., Lee-Chai, A., Barndollar, K., & Trotschel, R. (2001). The automated will: Nonconscious activation and pursuit of behavioral goals. *Journal of Personality and Social Psychology, 81*(6), 1014–1027.

Baumeister, R. F., Muraven, M., & Tice, D. M. (2000). Ego-depletion: A resource model of volition, self-regulation, and controlled processing. *Social Cognition, 18,* 130–150.

Bem, D. J. (1972). Self-perception theory. In L. Berkowitz (Ed.), *Advances in experimental social psychology* (Vol. 1, pp. 1–62). New York: Academic Press.

Berkowitz, L., & LePage, A. (1967). Weapons as aggression-eliciting stimuli. *Journal of Personality and Social Psychology, 7,* 202–207.

Bruner, J. S. (1951). Personality dynamics and the process of perceiving. In R. R. Blake & G. V. Ramsey (Eds.), *Perception: an approach to personality* (pp. 121–147). Oxford, UK: Ronald.

Carlston, D. E. (1992). Impression formation and the modular mind: The associated systems theory. In L. L. Martin & A. Tesser (Eds.), *The construction of social judgments* (pp. 301–341). Hillsdale, NJ: Erlbaum.

Carlston, D. E., & Smith, E. R. (1996). Principles of mental representations. In E. T. Higgins & A. W. Kruglanski (Eds.), *Social psychology: Handbook of basic principles* (pp. 184–210). New York: Guilford Press.

Cesario, J., Plaks, J. E., Higgins, E. T. (2006). Automatic social behavior as motivated preparation to interact. *Journal of Personality and Social Psychology, 69*(2), 318–328.

Chaiken, S., Liberman, A., & Eagly, A. H. (1989). Heuristic and systematic information processing within and beyond the persuasion context. In J. S. Uleman & J. A. Bargh (Eds.), *Unintended thought: Limits of awareness, intention, and control* (pp. 212–252). New York: Guilford Press.

Chartrand, T. L., & Bargh, J. A. (1996). Automatic activation of impression formation and memorization goals: Nonconscious goal priming reproduces effects of explicit task instructions. *Journal of Personality and Social Psychology, 71*(3), 464–478.

Chartrand, T. L., & Bargh, J. A. (1999). The chameleon effect: The perception-behavior link and social interaction. *Journal of Personality and Social Psychology, 76*(6), 893–910.

Chartrand, T. L., & Bargh, J. A. (2002). Nonconscious motivations: Their activation, operation, and consequences. In A. Tesser, D. A. Stapel, & J. V. Wood (Eds.), *Self and motivation: Emerging psychological perspectives* (pp. 13–41). Washington, D.C.: American Psychological Association.

Chen, M., & Bargh, J. A. (1997). Nonconscious behavioral confirmation processes: The self-fulfilling consequences of automatic stereotype activation. *Journal of Experimental Social Psychology, 33*(5), 541–560.

Chen, S., Lee-Chai, A. Y., & Bargh, J. A. (2001). Relationship orientation as a moderator of the effects of social power. *Journal of Personality and Social Psychology, 80*(2), 173–187.

Chun, W., Kruglanski, A. W., Sleeth-Keppler, D., & Friedman, R. (2005). *On the psychology of quasi-rational decisions: The multifinality principle in choice without awareness.* Manuscript submitted for publication.

Chun, W. Y., & Kruglanski, A. W. (2005). Consumption as a multiple goal pursuit without awareness. In F. R. Kardes, P. M. Herr, & J. Nantel (Eds.), *Applying social cognition to consumer-focused strategy* (pp. 25–43). Mahwah, NJ: Erlbaum.

Cohen, G. L., Aronson, J., & Steele, C. M. (2000). When beliefs yield to evidence: Reducing biased evaluation by affirming the self. *Personality and Social Psychology Bulletin, 26*(9), 1151–1164.

Custer, R., & Aarts, H. (2005). Positive affect as implicit motivator: On the nonconscious operation of behavioral goals. *Journal of Personality and Social Psychology, 89*(2), 129–142.

Devine, P. G. (1989). Stereotypes and prejudice: Their automatic and controlled components. *Journal of Personality and Social Psychology, 56*(1), 5–18.

Dijksterhuis, A., & Bargh, J. A. (2001). The perception-behavior expressway: Automatic effects of social perception on social behavior. In M. P. Zanna (Ed.), *Advances in experimental social psychology* (Vol. 33, pp. 1–40). San Diego: Academic Press.

Dijksterhuis, A., & van Knippenberg, A. (1998). The relation between perception and behavior, or how to win a game of Trivial Pursuit. *Journal of Personality and Social Psychology, 74*(4), 865–877.

Dweck, C. S. (1999). *Self-theories: Their role in motivation, personality, and development.* New York: Psychology Press.

Fergusson, M. J., & Bargh, A. J. (2004). Liking is for doing: The effects of goal pursuit on automatic evaluations. *Journal of Personality and Social Psychology, 87*(5), 557–572.

Festinger, L (1957). *A theory of cognitive dissonance.* Oxford, UK: Row, Peterson.

Fishbach, A., & Dhar, R. (2005). Goals as excuses or guides: The liberating effect of perceived goal progress on choice. *Journal of Consumer Research, 32*(3), 370–377.

Fishbach, A., Friedman, R., & Kruglanski, A. W. (2003). Leading us not into temptation: Momentary allurements elicit overriding goal activation. *Journal of Personality and Social Psychology, 84*(2), 296–309.

Fishbach, A., & Shah, J. (2006). Self-control in action: Implicit dispositions towards goals and away from temptations. *Journal of Personality and Social Psychology, 90*(5), 820–832.

Fishbach, A., Shah, J. Y., & Kruglanski, A. W. (2004) Emotional transfer in goal systems. *Journal of Experimental Social Psychology, 40*(6), 723–738.

Fiske, S. T. (2003). Five core social motives, plus or minus five. In S. J. Spencer, F. Steven, M. P. Zanna, & J. M. Olson (Eds.), *Motivated social perception: The Ontario Symposium* (Vol. 9, pp. 233–246). Mahwah, NJ: Erlbaum.

Fitzsimons, G. M. (2007). *Shifting goal systems maximizes success.* Symposium Presentation, Society for Personality and Social Psychology, Memphis, TN.

Fitzsimons, G. M., & Bargh, J. A. (2003). Thinking of you: Nonconscious pursuit of interpersonal goals associated with relationship partners. *Journal of Personality and Social Psychology, 84*(1), 148–163.

Förster, J., Liberman, N., & Higgins, E. T. (2005). Accessibility from active and fulfilled goals. *Journal of Experimental Social Psychology, 41*, 220–239.

Gilbert, D. T., & Osborne, R. E. (1989). Thinking backward: Some curable and incurable consequences of cognitive busyness. *Journal of Personality and Social Psychology, 57*(6), 940–949.

Gillund, G., & Shiffrin, R. M. (1984). A retrieval model for both recognition and recall. *Psychological Review, 91*, 1–67.

Grice, H. P. (1975) Logic and conversation. In P. Cole & J. Morgan (Eds.), *Syntax and semantics 3: Speech acts* (pp. 41–58). New York: Academic Press.

Hamilton, D. L., Katz, L. B., & Leirer, V. O. (1980). Cognitive representations of personality impressions: Organizational processes in first impression formation. *Journal of Personality and Social Psychology, 39*, 1050–1063.

Heider, F. (1958). *The psychology of interpersonal relations.* Hoboken, NJ: Wiley.

Higgins, E. T. (1987). Self-discrepancy: A theory relating self and affect. *Psychological Review, 94*(3), 319–340.

Higgins, E. T. (1996). Knowledge activation: Accessibility, applicability, and salience. In E. T. Higgins & A. W. Kruglanski (Eds.), *Social psychology: Handbook of basic principles* (pp. 133–168). New York: Guilford Press.

Higgins, E. T. (1997) Beyond pleasure and pain. *American Psychologist, 52*(2), 1280–1300.

Higgins, E. T., King, G. A., & Mavin, G. H. (1982). Individual construct accessibility and subjective impressions and recall. *Journal of Personality and Social Psychology, 43*(1), 35–47.

Higgins, E. T., Kruglanski, A. W., & Pierro, A. (2003). Regulatory mode: Locomotion and assessment as distinct orientations. In M. P. Zanna (Ed.), *Advances in experimental psychology* (Vol. 35, pp. 293–344). San Diego: Elsevier Academic Press.

Higgins, E. T., Rholes, W. S., & Jones, C. R. (1977). Category accessibility and impression formation. *Journal of Personality and Social Psychology, 13*(2), 141–154.

Hintzman, D. L. (1986). "Schemata abstraction" in a multiple-trace memory model. *Psychological Review, 93,* 411–428.

Kelley, H. H. (1972). Causal schemata and attribution process. In E. E. Jones, D. E. Knouse, H. H. Kelley, R. E. Nisbett, & S. Valins (Eds.), *Attribution: Perceiving the causes of behavior* (pp. 151–174). Hillsdale, NJ: LEA.

Kruglanski, A. W. (1989). *Lay epistemics and human knowledge: Cognitive and motivational bases.* New York: Plenum.

Kruglanski, A. W. (1996). Goals as knowledge structures. In P. M. Gollwitzer & J. A. Bargh (Eds.), *The psychology of action* (pp. 599–618). New York: Guilford Press.

Kruglanski, A. W. (2004). *The psychology of closed mindedness.* New York: Psychology Press.

Kruglanski, W., & Kopetz, C. (2009). The role of goal-systems in self-regulation. In J. Bargh, P. Gollwitzer, & E. Morsella (Eds.), *The psychology of action: Vol 2: The mechanisms of human action* (pp. 350–361). New York: Oxford University Press.

Kruglanski, A. W., Pierro, A., Mannetti, L., & DeGrada, E. (2006). Groups as epistemic providers: Need for closure and the unfolding of group centrism. *Psychological Review, 113*(1), 84–100.

Kruglanski, A. W., Pierro, A., Mannetti, L., Erb, H.-P., & Chun, W. Y. (2007). On the parameters of social judgment . In M. P. Zanna (Ed.), *Advances in experimental social psychology* (Vol. 39, pp. 255–303). San Diego: Elsevier Academic Press.

Kruglanski, A. W., Raviv, A., Bar-Tal, D., Raviv, A., Sharvit, K., Ellis, S., et al. (2005). Says who?: Epistemic authority effects in social judgment. In M. P. Zanna (Ed.), *Advances in experimental social psychology* (Vol. 37, pp. 346–392). San Diego: Academic Press.

Kruglanski, A. W., Shah, Y. J., Fishbach, A., Friedman, R., Chun, W. Y., Sleeth-Keppler, D. (2002). A theory of goal-systems. In M. P. Zanna (Ed.), *Advances in experimental social psychology* (pp. 331–376). San Diego: Academic Press.

Kruglanski, A. W., Thompson, E. P., Higgins, E. T., Atash, M. N., Pierro, A., Shah, J., & Spiegel, S. (2000). To 'do the right thing' or to 'just do it': Locomotion and assessment as distinct self-regulatory imperatives. *Journal of Personality and Social Psychology, 79*(5), 793–815.

Kruglanski, A. W., & Webster, D. M. (1996). Motivated closing of the mind: "Seizing" and "freezing." *Psychological Review, 103*(2), 263–283.

Lewin, K. (1935). *A dynamic theory of personality.* New York: McGraw-Hill.

Lewin, K. (1951). *Field theory in social science.* New York: Harper & Bros.

Liberman, N., & Förster, J. (2000). Expression after suppression: A motivational explanation of postsuppressional rebound. *Journal of Personality and Social Psychology, 79*(2), 190–203.

Macrae, C. N., & Johnston, L. (1998). Help, I need somebody: Automatic action and inaction. *Social Cognition, 16*(4), 400–417.

Miller, D. T., & Ross, M. (1975). Self-serving biases in the attribution of causality: fact or fiction? *Psychological Bulletin, 82,* 231–259.

Moskowitz, G. B., Gollwitzer, P. M., & Wasel, W. (1999). Preconscious control of stereotype activation through chronic egalitarian goals. *Journal of Personality and Social Psychology, 77*(1), 167–184.

Neisser, U. (1967). *Cognitive psychology.* New York: Appleton-Century-Crofts.

Nisbett, R. E., & Wilson, T. D. (1977). Telling more than we can know: Verbal reports on mental processes. *Psychological Review, 87,* 231–259.

Orehek, E. (2006). *"Easier said than done": Promises as false proxies in goal pursuit.* Unpublished master's thesis, University of Maryland.

Petty, R. E., & Cacioppo, J. T. (1986). *Communication and persuasion: Central and peripheral routes to attitude change.* New York: Springer Verlag.

Pierro, A. (2005). The possibility for means substitution increases people's commitment to a given goal. Unpublished raw data.

Posner, M. I., & Snyder, C. R. R. (1975). Facilitation and inhibition in the processing of signals. In P. M. A. Rabbit & S. Dornic (Eds.), *Attention and performance* (pp. 669–682). New York: Academic Press.

Ryan, R. M., Sheldon, K. M., Kasser, T., & Deci, E. L. (1996). All goals are not created equal: An organismic perspective on the nature of goals and their regulation. In P. M. Gollwitzer & J. A. Bargh (Eds.), *The psychology of action: Linking cognition and motivation to behavior* (pp. 7–26). New York: Guilford Press.

Schmeichel, B. J., Vohs, K. D., & Baumeister, R. F. (2003). Intellectual performance and ego-depletion: Role of the self in logical reasoning and other information processing. *Journal of Personality and Social psychology, 85,* 33–46.

Shah, J. (2003a). Automatic for the people: How representations of significant others implicitly affect goal pursuit. *Journal of Personality and Social Psychology, 84*(4), 661–681.

Shah, J. (2003b). The motivational looking glass: How significant others implicitly affect goal appraisals. *Journal of Personality and Social Psychology, 85*(3), 424–439.

Shah, J. Y., & Kruglanski, A. W. (2002). Priming against your will: How accessible alternatives affect goal pursuit. *Journal of Experimental Social Psychology, 38,* 368–383.

Shah, J. Y., & Kruglanski, A. W. (2003) When opportunity knocks: Bottom-up priming of goals by means and its effects on self-regulation. *Journal of Personality and Social Psychology, 84*(6), 1109–1122.

Shah, J. Y., Friedman, R., & Kruglanski, A. W. (2002). Forgetting all else: On the Antecedence and consequences of goal shielding. *Journal of Personality and Social Psychology, 83,* 1261–1280.

Shiffrin, R. M., & Schneider, W. (1977). Controlled and automatic human information processing: II. Perceptual learning, automatic attending, and a general theory. *Psychological Review, 82*(2), 127–190.

Sleeth-Keppler, D. P. (2005). *The multifinality principle in choice without aware-ness*. Unpublished manuscript, Winthrop University.

Solarz, A. K. (1960). Latency of instrumental responses as a function of compat-ibility with the meaning of eliciting verbal signs. *Journal of Experimental Psychology, 59,* 239–245.

Sorrentino, R. M., & Higgins, E. T. (1986). Motivation and cognition: Warming up to synergism. In R. M. Sorrentino & E. T. Higgins (Eds.), *Handbook of motivation and cognition: Foundation of social behavior* (Vol. 1, pp. 3–20). New York: Guilford Press.

Taylor, S. E., & Fiske, S. T. (1978). Salience, attention and attribution: Top of the head phenomena. In L. Berkowitz (Ed.), *Advances in experimental social psychology* (Vol. 11, pp 249–288). New York: Academic Press.

van Baaren, R. B., Holland, R. W., Kawakami, K., & van Knippenberg, A. (2004). Mimicry and prosocial behavior. *Psychological Science, 15*(1), 71–74.

van Baaren, R. B., Holland, R. W., & Steenaert, B. (2003). Mimicry for money: Behavioral consequences of imitation. *Journal of Experimental Social Psy-chology, 39*(4), 393–398.

Webster, D. M., & Kruglanski, A. W. (1998). Cognitive and social consequences of the motivation for closure. *European Review of Psychology, 8,* 133–173.

Wegner, D. M. (1994). Ironic processes of mental control. *Psychological Review, 101,* 34–52.

Williams, K. D., Forgas, J. P., von Hippel, W., & Zadro, L. (2005). The social outcast: An overview. In K. D. Williams, J. P. Forgas, & W. von Hippel (Eds.), *The social outcast: Ostracism, social exclusion, rejection, and bully-ing* (pp. 1–18). New York: Psychology Press.

Wilson, T. D., & Nisbett, R. E. (1978). The accuracy of verbal reports about the effects of stimuli on evaluations and behavior. *Social Psychology, 41*(2), 118–131.

Wyer, R. S., & Srull, T. K. (1989). *Memory and cognition in its social context.* Hillsdale, NJ: Erlbaum.

Zhang, Y., Fishbach, A., & Kruglanski, A. W. (2007). The dilution model: How additional goals undermine the perceived instrumentality of a shared path. *Journal of Personality and Social Psychology, 92*(3), 389–401.

CHAPTER 2

Goals in the Context of the Hierarchical Model of Approach–Avoidance Motivation

ANDREW J. ELLIOT
DANIELA NIESTA

Goals are of central importance to the study of motivation. Goals represent the hub of self-regulation and serve an integral role in explaining how dispositional proclivities, as well as situation-specific opportunities and threats, are translated into action. However, contemporary analyses of goals tend to define and conceptualize goals in a rather loose manner, making distinctions between constructs such as temperaments and motives, on one hand, and goals, on the other hand, difficult to discern. Without clear definitional and conceptual separation between constructs, motivational analyses of behavior lack clarity, precision, and ultimately, generativity, and utility.

In this chapter we define and conceptualize the goal construct in the interest of clearly differentiating it from other motivational constructs such as temperaments and motives. In addition, we delineate the different functions served by the goal, motive, and temperament constructs, and we describe the integrated functioning of these distinct constructs in the context of our hierarchical model of approach–avoidance motivation.

The Need for a Clear Definition and Conceptualization of the Goal Construct

Good science begins with good construct definition and conceptualization. This truism is perhaps particularly prone to violation in the social sciences in which the focal variables being studied are often unobservable abstractions, as opposed to readily observable, concrete entities. "Goal" is one such abstraction, and, simply put, this construct has neither been well defined nor well conceptualized in the motivational literature (Heckhausen & Kuhl, 1985).

A definition of "goal" is often not provided in contemporary theoretical and empirical work, even as the goal construct is used extensively and in integral fashion. The definitions that are provided by scholars exhibit considerable variation. Some definitions include reference to an internal representation (e.g., Caprara & Cervone, 2000), whereas others do not (e.g., Reeve, 1992). Some definitions include reference to a focus on the future (e.g., Kruglanski, 1996), whereas others do not (e.g., Austin & Vancouver, 1996). Some definitions include reference to a desired possibility (e.g., Locke & Latham, 1990), whereas others do not (e.g., Winter, 1996). Some definitions include reference to movement as well as an object that is the focal point of the movement (e.g., Ferguson, 2000), whereas others do not (e.g., Bandura, 1986). Some definitions include reference to commitment (e.g., Deckers, 2001), whereas others do not (e.g., Geen, 1995). Some definitions include reference to affect (e.g., Lewis, 1990), whereas others do not (e.g., Ford, 1992). More generally, some definitions are highly specific in nature (e.g., Pervin, 1983), whereas others are quite general (e.g., Maehr, 1989).

Variation is present not only in how goals are defined, but also in how they are conceptualized. Some equate goals with standards for behavior (e.g., Bandura, 1986), whereas others do not (e.g., Boldero & Francis, 2002). Some equate goals with essentially any form of desire (e.g., Ford, 1992), whereas others do not (e.g., Gollwitzer, 1990). Some collapse goals together with needs, motives, or temperaments (e.g., Pervin, 1983), whereas others do not (e.g., Brunstein, Schultheiss, & Graessman, 1998). Some posit that goals energize as well as direct behavior (e.g., Pintrich & Schunk, 1996), whereas others do not (e.g., Kuhl, 2000). Some use the term "goal" in reference to biological set points (e.g., Austin & Vancouver, 1996) and vegetative acts (such as a heartbeat or a flower turning toward the sun; e.g., Binswanger, 1986), whereas others do not. Some view virtually all behavior as goal directed (e.g., Beach, 1985), whereas others do not (e.g., Ferguson, 2000).

Clearly, there is considerable disagreement in the literature regarding how the term "goal" should be defined and conceptualized. We think that this lack of definitional and conceptual clarity poses several problems; we highlight two such problems herein (see Elliot & Fryer, 2008, for a more extensive analysis of this issue).

First, this lack of clarity makes it difficult to establish the boundaries of the goal construct. That is, without a clear delineation of what a goal is, how can one determine what should be included and what should be excluded from the goal construct? Potential problems loom in both directions. If goals are defined and conceptualized in an overly narrow fashion, their theoretical value and predictive utility may not be fully realized, and parsimony may be sacrificed as more constructs are used than are necessary to account for the phenomena under consideration. However, if goals are defined and conceptualized in an overly broad fashion, the term "goal" may become so overextended that it loses any precise meaning, and it is essentially utilized as a "wastebasket" or "kitchen sink" category.

Second, this lack of clarity makes it difficult to determine the functional properties of the goal construct. That is, without a clear delineation of what a goal is, how can one determine the role this construct serves in explaining motivated behavior, what additional constructs are needed to fully account for motivated behavior, and what relationship this construct has to these other constructs? One of two negative things tends to happen as a result. One is that the goal construct becomes meshed together with other motivational constructs such as motive, thereby losing its distinct identity. Another is that the goal construct becomes isolated from other constructs, thereby yielding a fragmented and incomplete account of motivation.

The Goal Construct: Defined and Conceptualized

Given the absence of a clear definition and conceptualization of "goal" in the contemporary psychological literature, and the importance of such clarity, we now offer a definition and conceptualization of the goal construct (see Elliot & Fryer, 2008, for additional details). The definition of "goal" provided herein in based on a linguistic analysis of the word, as well as an extensive historical analysis of the way that the term has been used by scholars over the centuries. Our definition is as follows: A goal is a cognitive representation of a future object that an organism is committed to approach or avoid. There are five basic features of the goal construct contained within this definition: (1) It is a cognitive representation, (2) it is focused on the future, (3) it is focused on an object, (4) it is a commitment, and (5) it entails approach or avoidance. Each of these basic features may be considered separately to articulate the conceptual nature of the goal construct in more detail (see also Elliot, 1997; Elliot & Fryer, 2008).

Cognitive Representation

As a mental representation, a goal shares many of the same features and operates according to many of the same principles as knowledge structures in general (Bargh, 1990; Shah & Kruglanski, 2003). However, a goal representation is also quite distinct from other forms of cognitive representation, in that it is inherently valenced (Custers & Aarts, 2005) and contains a commitment component. Much remains to be discovered about the precise ways in which goal representations differ, in structure and operation, from non-goal representations (for nascent speculation, see Herbart, 1850; Wyer & Srull, 1986), but what is clear is that our conception of the goal construct is restricted to animate organisms with representational capacities. As such, this conception excludes the standards, reference values, and set points in mechanical devices that are sometimes encompassed within the goal construct (see cybernetic models and some control theories; see also Austin & Vancouver, 1996).

Future

A goal focuses on a possibility that can be realized in the future, and goal pursuit entails using this future image as a guide to present behavior (Boldero & Francis, 2002). This future image may be something currently present that one is committed to keep or get rid of, or something currently absent that one is committed to get or keep away (Elliot, 2006). As a future possibility that guides present behavior, a goal is presumed to be the cause of observable action, and goal-directed behavior is viewed as proactive, not reactive.

Object

The object of a goal is the focal point of regulation. "Object" is used broadly to refer to an entity, event, experience, or characteristic that is the hub of the goal. Objects may be concrete or abstract, physical or psychological, observable or unobservable, and may be focused on an essentially limitless variety of contents (i.e., goals are idiographic in nature; Emmons, 1996; Little, 1999). The object of a goal is not the goal itself; rather a goal represents an object and some form of appetitive or aversive relation with regard to that object. The term "goal object" is best used to refer to the regulatory centerpiece of the goal per se.

Committed to

A goal is not just any cognitively represented future object that the organism would like to approach or avoid. Some such future possibilities simply represent wishes (Gollwitzer, 1990), wants (Heckhausen & Kuhl, 1985), or fantasies (Oettingen & Hagenah, 2005) and are best viewed as goal candidates (Elliot & Friedman, 2006). The goal label is only deemed applicable when an organism has made a commitment with respect to a future possibility. Furthermore, to be a goal, this commitment initially must be made consciously. That is, we think it is best to restrict the term "goal" to commitments that have their origin in conscious acts of volition ("conscious" is used here in a broad, inclusive sense; see Penrose, 1996). Once in place, a goal may be activated and may operate in a nonconscious, automatic fashion (Bargh & Ferguson, 2000).

Approach or Avoid

All objects that are the centerpiece of the goal are valenced, and goals delineate some sort of appetitive or aversive relation to the valenced object. Approach goals represent seeking to move toward or maintain a positively valenced object, whereas avoidance goals represent seeking to move away or stay away from a negatively valenced object (Lewin, 1926). Approach and avoidance "movement" with regard to objects may involve concrete physical movement or may involve abstract psychological movement. Much as the object of a goal may be of essentially infinite variety, the precise approach or avoidance movements with regard to the object may take on myriad forms.

What is the function of the goal construct in explaining motivation? Goals serve a directional role in motivation in that they guide or channel behavior toward or away from a specific possibility. Goals are used to regulate behavior, and such regulation may take place at a variety of different levels of abstraction. Goals may range from long-term personal projects (Little, 1983) or strivings (Emmons, 1986) to midrange aims or objectives (Elliot & Thrash, 2001) to task-specific aspirations (Lewin, Dembo, Festinger, & Sears, 1944) or targets (Locke & Latham, 1990) to action-specific intentions (Frese & Zapf, 1994). Multiple goals may be adopted within a given level of abstraction (Barron & Harackiewicz, 2000), and goals across levels may be used together in instrumental fashion in the regulation process (we have more to say on this issue in a later section of the chapter).

Motivation Underlying Goals: Temperaments and Motives

The definition and conceptualization of the goal construct offered herein is narrower and more constrained than that offered by many others in the literature. Our belief is that a more precise, restricted role for the goal construct is important because it affords clarity regarding not only the nature and function of goals, but also how goals fit within an overall analysis of motivation.

In our hierarchical model of approach–avoidance motivation (Elliot, 2006; Elliot & Church, 1997; Elliot & Thrash, 2001), goals are not viewed as sufficient to account for motivation. Instead, goals are considered in tandem with other constructs that underlie goals to more fully explain motivation. These other sources of goals are multifarious, but for the present purposes we focus on two important, fundamentally motivational constructs: temperaments and motives.

A temperament is a general neurobiological sensitivity to positive (approach temperament) or negative (avoidance temperament) stimuli (Elliot & Thrash, 2002). Temperaments naturally emerge from a broad network of interacting but partially independent sets of neuoanatomical structures and neurochemical/neuroendocrinological processes that are operative across the neuraxis (for specifics on such structures and processes, see Berridge, 2000; Cacioppo, Gardner, & Berntson, 1999; Davidson & Irwin, 1999; Elliot, in press; Panksepp, 1998). The joint operation of these structures and processes produces a net neurobiological sensitivity to valenced stimuli.

Approach and avoidance temperaments are conceptualized as core structural components of personality. They are at the root of and explain the shared variance among other personality dispositions such as trait adjectives, affective dispositions, and motivational systems. That is, approach temperament underlies extraversion, positive emotionality, and behavioral approach system sensitivity, and avoidance temperament underlies neuroticism, negative emotionality, and behavioral inhibition system sensitivity (Elliot & Thrash, 2002). These temperaments are presumed to be heritable, present in early childhood, consistent across situations, and quite stable across the life span.

Functionally, temperaments produce a perceptual vigilance for, an affective reactivity to, and a behavioral predisposition toward or away from valenced stimuli. Temperaments are responsible for immediate responses and inclinations to encountered or imagined stimuli and at any given moment describe the style or quality of expression of affect, cognition, and behavior (Allport, 1931; Winter, John, Stewart, Klohnen, & Duncan, 1998). These basic dispositions operate in a rather rigid manner, energizing individuals in a uniform manner across domains and types of valenced stimuli.

A motive is a dispositional tendency to desire or be fearful of a specific type of positive or negative experience in a particular life domain (McClelland, 1985). Two prominent domains of daily life are the achievement domain and the social domain, and appetitive and aversive motives are posited in each domain: the need for achievement and fear of failure in the achievement domain, and the need for affiliation and fear of rejection in the social domain (Atkinson, 1964). Motives emerge from socialization and experience involving natural incentives. For example, success is presumed to be rewarding for all individuals, but for some this experience becomes closely linked to joy and pride in many achievement situations over time, whereas for others it does not become linked to joy and pride across achievement situations in this manner. A strong need for achievement develops in the former, whereas a weak need for achievement develops in the latter (see McClelland, 1985; Schultheiss & Brunstein, 2005; Thrash & Elliot, 2001).

Motives develop early in life through preverbal felt experience and initially operate unconsciously. Over time, motives become more cognitively elaborated and differentiated (Elliot, McGregor, & Thrash, 2002), and individuals may acquire at least some degree of conscious access to the operation of their motives (Thrash & Elliot, 2002; Thrash, Elliot, & Schultheiss, 2007). Although some theorists posit separate constructs for the unconscious and conscious aspects of motives (i.e., implicit and self-attributed motives, respectively; McClelland, 1985), we think it best to conceptualize these two aspects as components or facets of a single, multidimensional motive construct (see Thrash & Elliot, 2002). Motives are presumed to be consistent within domain, and rather stable, but certainly not immutable, across the life span.

Functionally, motives produce an anticipatory orienting of individuals to particular types of affectively charged positive or negative experiences (Elliot, 1997; Heckhausen, 1991). Whereas temperaments energize the individual with respect to valenced stimuli in general, motives account for why some positive or negative experiences are more valued and evocative than others, in general and for some individuals in particular. Motives energize individuals with regard to, and orient them toward or away from, domain-specific types of experience such as social connection (in the case of need for affiliation) or failure (in the case of fear of failure).

Temperaments and motives are different in many ways. Temperaments are unlearned, domain-general predispositions that are part of our biological heritage, whereas motives are learned, domain-specific dispositions that are grounded in our socialization history. Although quite distinct conceptually, temperaments and motives are similar in that they represent broad forms of motivation that function as energizers of approach and avoidance behavioral tendencies, and that orient individuals to domain-general (temperaments) or domain-specific (motives) positive or negative possibilities. However, these temperaments and motives do not provide precise guidance for how the broad behavioral inclinations and desires/fears that have been evoked may be effectively addressed or regulated.

Differentiation of Constructs and the Need for an Integrative Model

As can be seen from the preceding definitional and conceptual considerations, goals are very different from temperaments and motives. Temperaments and motives represent dispositions that are stable over time and situations/domains and are difficult to change; goals represent situation-specific aims that can be highly malleable over time and situations/domains and can be easily and immediately changed (although some characterize goals in terms of dispositional tendencies to adopt particular types of aims, this designation is descriptive rather than explanatory and seems of questionable value; see Elliot, 2006). Temperaments and motives have a general, nomothetic focus on any valenced stimulus or any domain-specific experiential state; goals can vary in focus from general, nomothetic aims to highly concrete, idiographic aims. Temperaments and motives are fundamentally rooted in biological processes; goals are fundamentally cognitive in nature. Temperaments and motives operate automatically and without conscious intention; goals can operate automatically (Bargh, 1990), but initial goal adoption requires a conscious, intentional commitment. Temperaments and motives serve an energizing and orienting function in the motivational process; goals serve a directional function in the motivational process. This last, functional difference is of critical importance and is a central focus of the next section of the chapter.

Motivation encompasses the energization and the direction of behavior (Elliot, 1997). "Energization" refers to the instigation, activation, or "spring to action" (James, 1890/1950, p. 555) that orients the organism in a general manner. Energization, as used in this definition of "motivation," does not assume that the organism is passive until instigated to action. Instead, the organism is viewed as perpetually active, with instigation functionally representing a shift from one form of orienting to another (see Atkinson & Birch, 1970; Heider, 1958). Direction in this definition of "motivation" refers to the guiding or channeling of behavior in a precise way. A full account of motivation must attend to both of the energization and direction components of motivation, that is, to the questions of why and how individuals behave as they do. Accordingly, a full account of motivation must consider not only the goals that individuals pursue, but also the underlying temperaments and motives that give rise to goal pursuit in the first place.

One theoretical conceptualization that attends to the energization and direction components of motivation by utilizing temperament/motive and goal constructs is the aforementioned hierarchical model of approach–avoidance motivation. It is to this model that we now explicitly turn to illustrate and more clearly articulate the interrelation of goals, motives, and temperaments. Our discussion of the hierarchical model is brief and selective; further details on the model may be found in Elliot (1997), Elliot and Church (1997), Elliot, Gable, and Mapes (2006), and Elliot and Thrash (2001, 2002).

The Hierarchical Model of Approach–Avoidance Motivation

At the core of the hierarchical model is the premise that the distinction between approach and avoidance motivation is of such fundamental import that it may be used as a conceptual lens through which to view the structure and function of motivation. There is a considerable amount of empirical evidence in support of the fundamental nature of approach–avoidance motivation, and this evidence may be organized around four points.

First, approach–avoidance processes are present across phyla. Such processes are evident in amoebae, crustaceans, fish, octopuses, snakes, mice, birds, dogs, cats, wolves, cows, monkeys, and, of course, human beings (see Elliot & Covington, 2001, for a review). Second, approach–avoidance evaluative judgments are immediate (perhaps even primary) and ubiquitous in human functioning. Humans automatically evaluate most, if not all, encountered stimuli on a positive/negative dimension (Bargh, 1997; Osgood, Suci, & Tannenbaum, 1957), and these evaluations instantaneously evoke approach and avoidance behavioral predispositions (Corwin, 1921; Lewin, 1935). Third, approach and avoidance evaluative processes are essential for successful adaption to the environment. Basic approach–avoidance behavioral decisions are the most critical adaptive judgments that organisms have had to make in the evolutionary past (Davidson, 1992; Tooby & Cosmides, 1990), and it is likely that this adaptive function is the reason that approach–avoidance process are evident across animate forms of life (Schneirla, 1959). Fourth, approach–avoidance motivation is represented in many different and partially independent ways throughout the human body (Cacioppo & Berntson, 1994; Stellar & Stellar, 1985). Our evolutionary history appears to have produced multiple levels of valence-based evaluative mechanisms, ranging from rudimentary spinal cord reflexes to subcortical affective computions to high-level cortical processes. These multiple approach–avoidance processes operate in tandem and in sequence to produce the urges, affects, motor responses, and commitments that are the ingredients of motivated experience.

Clearly, approach–avoidance motivation is not only fundamental, but also is highly complex and multiply determined. As such, a theoretical model of approach–avoidance motivation must select a conceptual centerpiece with which to organize and structure the explanatory framework. In the hierarchical model, the goal construct has been selected as this conceptual centerpiece. There are two basic reasons that goals are granted a central place in the hierarchical model. First, throughout most of the history of scientific psychology, goal directedness has been considered a cardinal characteristic of human behavior (McDougal, 1908; Tolman, 1932; see Elliot & Fryer, 2008, for a review), and it is hard to imagine an intellectually satisfying account of human motivation that excludes the goal construct. Second, goals represent an intermediary construct that seem well positioned to hold together diverse aspects of the motivational process, ranging from general positive or negative evaluations to concrete approach or avoidance behavioral actions.

In the hierarchical model, goals are viewed as the carriers or servants of higher-order motivational propensities and dispositions such as temperaments and motives. Temperaments and motives are presumed to represent behavioral inclinations and desires/fears that orient the individual with regard to valenced possibilities. The rudimentary sense of direction provided by this orienting is usually insufficiently precise to regulate behavior effectively in that no specific standard or guideline for behavior is provided. Accordingly, goals are often selected and adopted to focus the individual on specific end-states that can address the higher-order inclination or desire/fear that has been activated. Temperaments and motives can and sometimes do lead directly to behavior, but such regulation often appears either rigid or unfocused (Elliot et al., 2002). Goals provide precise direction that can lead to more effective and efficient regulation.

Thus, temperaments/motives and goals commonly operate in concert in the motivational process, with temperaments/motives energizing and orienting the individual, and goals channeling this energization toward specific aims. In this way, temperaments and motives may be considered distal, indirect predictors of overt behavior, and goals may be considered more proximal, direct predictors of action. These constructs serve complementary and indispensable roles in explaining motivated behavior; temperaments and motives explain the why of behavior, whereas goals explain the how of behavior.

Before proceeding further, we would like to explicitly highlight two points that have already been noted in implicit form. First, temperaments and motives are not the only higher-order constructs that prompt goal adoption, many other higher-order intrapsychic constructs are also involved in the goal-adoption process (e.g, self-conceptions, perceptions of competence, implicit theories, attachment schemas, internalized values and norms, etc.). We selected temperaments and motives for illustrative purposes herein because these constructs are most directly and centrally involved in the energization function of motivation, and are thus perhaps most important to incorporate into a motivational analysis of behavior. Other intrapsychic constructs may indirectly implicate energization (e.g., attachment schemas are likely embedded, in part, in the motives need for affiliation and fear of rejection) or may influence goal adoption independently of energization processes (e.g., perceptions of competence may exert an entirely cognitive influence by providing information on what the individual expects to be able to accomplish given his or her skills and abilities).

Furthermore, goals may be induced by situational affordances, imped-ances, and prompts (e.g., the direct assignment of a goal by a supervisor), although the influence of external factors in such instances is likely medi-ated by the evocation of temperamental inclinations, motive-based desires/fears, and other intrapsychic processes in most instances.

Second, when we portray goals as direct, proximal predictors of behavior, it is important to bear in mind that this characterization is rela-tive, not absolute. Goals are direct, proximal predictors of behavior rela-tive to upper-level constructs such as temperaments and motives. We do not mean to communicate that goals operate alone to exert an unmediated influence on behavior. On the contrary, we think it is commonly the case that once a goal is adopted, individuals recruit a variety of other levels and types of goals to assist them in effective regulation. Lower-level goals that are instrumental to higher-order goals may be construed as subgoals that provide additional precision as to the ways through which the upper-level goals will be pursued (see Carver & Scheier, 1981; Elliot & Thrash, 2001; Harackiewicz & Elliot, 1998). "Subgoal" is an entirely functional designation; any goal may be a subgoal to another goal if it represents a more precise aim that is meant to help accomplish a broader aim. Such subgoals may be characterized as strategies (Cantor & Kihlstrom, 1989), plans (Miller, Galanter, & Pribram, 1960), means (Lewin, 1926), imple-mentation intentions (Gollwitzer, 1999), tactics (Baron, 1982), and so on (see Austin & Vancouver, 1996). Detailed explication of the various ways in which goals and subgoals lead to behavior is beyond the scope of this chapter, which is focused primarily on distinguishing goals from their higher-order motivational sources.

A central assumption of the hierarchical model is that goals and their underlying sources or "reasons" (Elliot & Thrash, 2001, p. 141) such as temperaments and motives must be defined and conceptualized as sepa-rate entities. However, goals and their underlying reasons are posited to operate together during the actual process of goal regulation. The under-lying impetus for goal pursuit is not simply left behind once a goal has been adopted, but instead this impetus remains connected to the goal and continues to influence affect, cognition, and behavior throughout the pro-cess of goal pursuit (see Lewin's 1926, 1935, discussion of the need–goal relation for a similar analysis). This dynamic intertwining of goal and its underlying source is construed as a third construct in and of itself in the hierarchical model, and is termed "goal complex" (Elliot & Thrash, 2001; Thrash & Elliot, 2001; see Murray's 1938, p. 110, "need integrate" con-struct for an example of a similar, compound construct).

A goal complex is a context-specific regulatory construct that is formed when a goal is adopted and is represented in memory until the goal is achieved or the reason for adopting the goal is abandoned, altered, or successfully addressed through another route. This mental representation is presumed to include information regarding the goal and the underlying reason that the goal is being pursued. In many instances, the reason underlying goal adoption is not consciously accessible and, therefore, cannot be articulated by the individual. When the reason underlying goal adoption *is* accessible, the goal complex may be characterized in the propositional form: "(goal) IN ORDER TO (underlying reason)." For example, if an individual with a strong fear of failure adopts a performance-avoidance goal in a classroom setting, the goal complex may taken on the form "Avoid doing poorly relative to others in this class IN ORDER TO not to feel the deeply painful shame of failure." It is the unique compendium of goal and underlying reason within a goal complex that is posited to be the actual predictor of affect, cognition, and behavior in a given situation. That is, the effect of pursuing any given goal can vary considerably as a function of the reason that the goal was adopted.

Implications of the Hierarchical Model

The definitional and conceptual separation of goals from their underlying sources such as temperaments and motives necessitates a narrowing and restricting of the goal construct. At first glance, it may seem as though this constraining of the goal construct would limit its applicability or minimize its explanatory power in analyses of motivation. On the contrary, we contend that greater precision regarding the goal construct actually enhances its importance and utility and affords a more thorough and complete account of motivation. Perhaps the most important benefit of our restricted conception of goals is that it clearly points to the need to integrate the goal construct with other motivational constructs. If, indeed, goals are limited to accounting for the directionality of behavior, it becomes clear that additional variables are needed to explain why individuals adopt and pursue goals in the first place. When goals are linked to their underlying sources, the result is a hierarchical model of motivation that, we submit, yields important insights into the motivational process.

The hierarchical model highlights the complexity of motivation. A goal is not a goal is not a goal; rather, the same goal has different effects on affect, cognition, and behavior depending on the reason underlying goal pursuit. For example, a person with the goal of forging deeper friendships may do so out of a dispositional desire to connect to others (i.e., a strong need for affiliation) or may do so out of a dispositional fear of social exclusion (i.e., a strong fear of rejection). The former goal complex is presumed to prompt more appetitive, open, and flexible responding in social situations than the latter. Likewise, upper-level constructs such as temperaments and motives have different effects on affect, cognition, and behavior depending on the goals through which these temperamental inclinations and motive dispositions are channeled. For example, a strong fear of rejection may prompt the adoption of an avoidance goal focused on negative relational possibilities or the adoption of an approach goal focused on positive relational possibilities. The latter goal complex is presumed to promote more positive processes and outcomes than the former.

The complexity of motivation comes into even bolder relief when one is reminded that the aforementioned examples represent isolated, simplified illustrations. A single goal can emerge from multiple sources. A single source such as a temperament or motive can prompt the adoption of multiple goals to serve it. Furthermore, once a goal is adopted, it is commonly pursued using a variety of different levels and types of subgoals (e.g., strategies, plans, implementation intentions). Clearly, from a hierarchical standpoint, motivation is an intricate and involved process. Nomothetic analyses can be informative with regard to understanding basic and relatively isolated motivational principles, but it is important to bear in mind that such work does not fully capture the idiographic reality of daily striving (Allport, 1937; Murray, 1938).

The hierarchical model highlights not only the complexity of motivation, but also the flexibility of regulation in human connation. Although the behavior of lower animals is directly and rigidly governed by biological mechanisms (see Schneirla, 1959), human behavior is more flexible, in that aspects of motivation beyond deeply engrained dispositional tendencies may be involved in producing action (Elliot & Thrash, 2002; Lang, 1995). One prominent role of the self is the executive function, which involves the monitoring and regulating of basic response predispositions (Baumeister, 2003). Through self-regulation, human motivation may involve either the support and extrapolation of initial approach or avoidance inclinations and desires/fears, or the overriding and rechanneling of such basic tendencies. Of course, one prominent form of this self-regulation is goal adoption and pursuit.

It is undoubtedly most common for goals to match the valence of their source. For example, individuals high in approach temperament, need for achievement, and need for affiliation typically adopt approach goals, whereas those high in avoidance temperament, fear of failure, and fear of rejection typically adopt avoidance goals (Elliot et al., 2006; Elliot & Sheldon, 1997; Elliot & Thrash, 2002; Gable, 2006). However, approach and avoidance are considered independent within (Cacioppo et al., 1999) and across hierarchical levels. Thus, for example, approach and avoidance motives may be activated and may operate simultaneously in a given situation, and an individual may adopt an approach goal in the service of an avoidance motive (e.g., a person high in fear of failure may strive to do well relative to others—in order to avoid failure).

Accordingly, neither biology nor socialization is destiny in human functioning; self-regulation allows hierarchical combinations of approach and avoidance that help the individual not only adapt, but also to mature and grow in optimal fashion. An individual with a strong avoidance temperament need not incessantly focus on negative possibilities across situations but can, via self-regulation, learn to override avoidance-based propensities and proactively seek positive outcomes. Although this overriding of basic tendencies would initially be difficult and would entail a large expenditure of attentional and ego-based resources (Elliot, Sheldon, & Church, 1997), over time and repetition such regulation may become more natural, efficient, and perhaps even automatic (Logan, 1988).

Avoidance motivation has been shown to have negative implications for functioning across different levels and forms of motivation (see Elliot, in press). Thus, it seems reasonable to suggest that in most instances in which self-regulation produces a valence mismatch, the pattern will be for upper-level avoidance to be overridden by lower-level approach. However, this will not always be the case. For example, if an individual with a strong need for achievement is faced with a task that requires careful monitoring and the avoidance of errors or negative events (e.g., accounting, air traffic controlling, goal tending), the adoption of an avoidance goal would likely be effective in serving this upper-level desire. Approach and avoidance are independent at the level of subgoals, as well as the level of goals and their upper-level sources, and mismatches induced by self-regulation may take place across the goal-subgoal levels, as well as across levels of subgoals. Indeed, mismatches may become more commonplace as one moves down the regulatory ladder, and avoidance motivation, although typically considered less optimal than approach motivation, may be less inimical at the subgoal than the goal (or above) level (Elliot, 2006).

In emphasis, if not fact, our hierarchical model of approach and avoidance motivation embraces a somewhat different position than motivational models that emphasize the benefits of matching. Some theorists seem to downplay the inimical nature of avoidance motivation, opting instead to point to any match between dispositions and states, traits and goals, or goals and subgoals as optimal in the regulatory process. For example, Tamir (2005) posited that a valence-based match between motivational traits and motivational states (e.g., affects) or goals increases task engagement, leading to optimal functioning. Thus, individuals high in neuroticism are viewed as accruing performance, enjoyment, and well-being benefits to the extent that they experience negative affects such as worry or use negative regulatory tools such as avoidance goals (Tamir & Diener, 2008). Likewise, Higgins (2000) proposed that a fit between promotion/prevention orientations and the promotion/prevention means used to pursue these orientations increases the intensity of motivation, leading to optimal functioning. Thus, promotion-oriented individuals who focus on gains and prevention-oriented individuals who focus on losses are thought to perform better, enjoy activities more, and value experiences and outcomes to a greater degree (Higgins, 2005).

It is a small step from pointing out the benefits of such matches to advocating interventions designed to alter situations and contexts to fit individuals' preexisting orientations. Keller and Bless (2006) proffered one such match-based intervention for educational contexts. These researchers have proposed that teachers should try to figure out their students' motivational dispositions and then frame educational environments to match these dispositional tendencies. Thus, they suggest that teachers should seek to put prevention-oriented students in contexts in which the avoidance of mistakes and failures is made salient. Unfortunately, this type of intervention runs contrary to a large body of research on test anxiety and fear of failure that clearly indicates that the worst possible context for a person with an aversive motivational orientation is one that makes salient the possibility of negative outcomes (Heckhausen, 1991; Zeidner, 1998). In short, a strong emphasis on the benefits of matching per se would seem to imply that existing dispositional orientations should be embraced, regardless of their inherent qualities. This position seems questionable in and of itself and leads to applications that seem quite untenable.

We agree with the proposition that matches across hierarchical levels are often beneficial and, as stated earlier, believe that these matches are the norm in the motivational process. However, we also think that some matches, especially those involving avoidance motivation, can be problematic and should be altered rather than embraced. For example, in general, we do not think that it is best for persons high in neuroticism to be encouraged to adopt avoidance goals or to select themselves into avoidance-based situations and contexts. Rather, we think it best for such individuals to seek to regulate their avoidance predispositions by rechanneling them using approach goals, and to expose themselves to approach-based contexts wherever possible. Likewise, we think that persons with a strong fear of failure would best adopt and pursue performance-approach or mastery-approach goals in achievement settings and would benefit most from achievement contexts in which failure was accepted as part of the learning process, rather than construed as an outcome to vigilantly avoid at all costs. We believe that this "approach in order to avoid" form of motivational regulation is not only optimal in the short run, but also might even affect some degree of positive change toward approach motivation in the long run. Temperaments and motives are quite stable over time, but some variation, especially in motives, is also exhibited (Elliot et al., 2002; Roberts, Caspi, & Moffitt, 2001), and such variation may very well be a function of efforts to regulate, rather than succumb to, problematic dispositional inclinations.

Approach and avoidance motivation are part of our evolutionary heritage, and we cannot survive, either physically or psychologically, without the operation of both. Certain tasks, situations, and contexts that we encounter in everyday life require focusing on and regulating according to negative possibilities and avoidance motivation is undoubtedly adaptive in such instances. Nevertheless, it is important to bear in mind two things regarding avoidance motivation. First, avoidance motivation is, by its very nature, aversive (Elliot, 2006), meaning that even when it is adaptive in a given instance, it may be characterized as necessary rather than optimal. All told, approach–approach matches are to be preferred over avoidance–avoidance matches. Second, avoidance motivation tends to be greatly overutilized, relative to what is necessary in everyday life. Avoidance motivation is designed to facilitate surviving and approach motivation is designed to facilitate thriving; individuals often utilize survival mode even when danger is not imminent, thereby missing positive opportunities for development and growth. It is for these reasons that the negative implications of avoidance motivation are highlighted in the hierarchical model. The necessity of avoidance motivation in some instances and the benefits of some forms of avoidance–avoidance matches are acknowledged, but only in the context of a broader perspective in which approach motivation, in general, is viewed as optimal relative to avoidance motivation.

Closing Statement

In this chapter we argued that either a loose definition of "goal" or an overextended conceptualization of "goal" is counterproductive for the goal construct, and motivational research and theory more generally. By precisely delineating the boundaries of the goal construct, and placing it in integrative context within the hierarchical model of approach–avoidance motivation, we feel that we have put goals in their proper place. This place just happens to be at the centerpiece of the motivational process. Goals are integral and indispensable in motivational analyses of behavior as they account for the focused and flexible way in which motivational energy becomes manifest in observable behavior.

References

Allport, F. H. (1937). Teleonomic description in the study of personality. *Character and Personality, 5,* 202–214.

Allport, G. W. (1931). What is a trait of personality? *Journal of Abnormal and Social Psychology, 25,* 368–372.

Atkinson, J. W. (1964). *An introduction to motivation.* Princeton, NJ: Van Nostrand.

Atkinson, J. W., & Birch, D. (1970). *The dynamics of action.* New York: Wiley.

Austin, J., & Vancouver, J. (1996). Goal constructs in psychology: Structure, process, and content. *Psychological Bulletin, 120,* 338–375.

Bandura, A. (1986). *Social foundations of thought and action.* Englewood Cliffs, NJ: Prentice Hall.

Bargh, J. A. (1990). Auto-motives: Preconscious determinants of social interaction. In E. T. Higgins & R. M. Sorrentino (Eds.), *Handbook of motivation and cognition: Foundations of social behavior* (Vol. 2, pp. 93–130). New York: Guilford Press.

Bargh, J. A. (1997). The automaticity of everyday life. In R. S. Wyer, Jr. (Ed.), *Advances in social cognition* (Vol. 10, pp. 1–61). Mahwah, NJ: Erlbaum.

Bargh, J. A., & Ferguson, M. J. (2000). Beyond behaviorism: On the automaticity of higher mental processes. *Psychological Bulletin, 126,* 925–945.

Baron, J. (1982). Personality and intelligence. In R. Sternberg (Ed.), *Handbook of human intelligence.* Cambridge, UK: Cambridge University Press.

Barron, K., & Harackiewicz, J. M. (2000). Achievement goals and optimal motivation: A multiple goals approach. In C. Sansone & J. Harackiewicz (Eds.), *Intrinsic and extrinsic motivation: The search for optimal motivation and performance* (pp. 229–254). San Diego: Academic Press.

Baumeister, R. F. (2003). Ego depletion and self-regulation failure: A resource model of self-control. *Alcoholism: Clinical and Experimental Research, 27*(2), 1–4.

Beach, L. R. (1985). Action: Decision-implementation strategies and tactics. In M. Frese & J. Sabini (Eds.), *Goal directed behavior: The concept of action in psychology* (pp. 123–131). Hillsdale, NJ: Erlbaum.

Berridge, K. C. (2000). Irrational pursuit: Hyper-incentives from a visceral brain. In I. Brocas & J. Carrillo (Eds.), *Psychology and economics* (pp. 1–15). Oxford, UK: Oxford University Press.

Binswanger, H. (1986). The goal-directedness of living action. *The Objectivist Forum, 7,* 1–10.

Boldero, J., & Francis, J. (2002). Goals, standards, and the self: Reference values serving different functions. *Personality and Social Psychology Review, 6,* 232–241.

Brunstein, J. C., Schultheiss, O. C., & Graessman, R. (1998). Personal goals and emotional well-being: The moderating role of motive dispositions. *Journal of Personality & Social Psychology, 75,* 494–508.

Cacioppo, J., & Bernston, G. (1994). Relationship between attitudes and evaluative space: A critical review, with emphasis on the separability of positive and negative substrates. *Psychological Bulletin, 115,* 401–422.

Cacioppo, J., Gardner, W., & Berntson, G. (1999). The affect system has parallel and integrative processing components: Form follows function. *Journal of Personality and Social Psychology, 76,* 839–855.

Cantor, N., & Kihlstrom, J. F. (1989). Social intelligence and cognitive assessments of personality. In R. Wyer & T. Srull (Eds.), *Social intelligence and cognitive assessments of personality* (pp. 1–59). Hillsdale, NJ: Erlbaum.

Caprara, G. V., & Cervone, D. (2000). *Personality: Determinants, dynamics, and potentials.* New York: Cambridge University Press.

Carver, C., & Scheier, M. (1981). *Attention and self-regulation: A control-theory approach to human behavior.* New York: Springer-Verlag.

Corwin, G. (1921). Minor studies from the psychological laboratory of Cornell University. *American Journal of Psychology, 32,* 563–570.

Custers, R., & Aarts, H. (2005). Positive affect as implicit motivator: On the nonconscious operation of behavioral goals. *Journal of Personality and Social Psychology, 89,* 129–142.

Davidson, R. J. (1992). Prolegomenon to the structure of emotion: Gleanings from neuropsychology. *Cognition and Emotion, 6,* 245–268.

Davidson, R. J., & Irwin, W. (1999). The functional neuroanatomy of emotion and affective style. *Trends in Cognitive Sciences, 3,* 11–21.

Elliot, A. J. (1997). Integrating "classic" and "contemporary" approaches to achievement motivation: A hierarchical model of approach and avoidance achievement motivation. In P. Pintrich & M. Maehr (Eds.), *Advances in motivation and achievement* (Vol. 10, pp. 143–179). Stanford, CT: JAI Press.

Elliot, A. J. (2006). The hierarchical model of approach–avoidance motivation. *Motivation and Emotion, 30,* 111–116.

Elliot, A. J. (in press). Goals. In N. Salkind (Ed.), *Encyclopedia of educational psychology.* Thousand Oaks, CA: Sage.

Elliot, A. J., & Church, M. A. (1997). A hierarchical model of approach and avoidance achievement motivation. *Journal of Personality and Social Psychology, 72,* 218–232.

Elliot, A. J., & Covington, M. V. (2001). Approach and avoidance motivation. *Educational Psychology Review, 12,* 73–92.

Elliot, A. J., & Friedman, R. (2006). Approach and avoidance personal goals. In B. Little, K. Salmela-Aro, & S. Phillips (Eds.), *Personal project pursuit: Goals, action, and human flourishing* (pp. 97–116). Hillsdale, NJ: Erlbaum.

Elliot, A. J., & Fryer, J. (2008). The goal construct in psychology. In J. Shah & W. Gardner (Eds.), *Handbook of motivational science* (pp. 235–250). New York: Guilford Press.

Elliot, A. J., Gable, S. L., & Mapes, R. R. (2006). Approach and avoidance motivation in the social domain. *Personality and Social Psychology Bulletin, 32,* 378–391.

Elliot, A. J., McGregor, H. A., & Thrash, T. M. (2002). The need for competence. In E. Deci & R. Ryan (Eds.), *Handbook of self-determination research* (pp. 361–387). New York: University of Rochester Press.

Elliot, A. J., & Sheldon, K. M. (1997). Avoidance achievement motivation: A personal goals analysis. *Journal of Personality and Social Psychology, 73,* 171–185.

Elliot, A., Sheldon, K., & Church, M. (1997). Avoidance personal goals and subjective well-being. *Personality and Social Psychology Bulletin, 23,* 915–927.

Elliot, A. J., & Thrash, T. M. (2001). Achievement goals and the hierarchical model of achievement motivation. *Educational Psychology Review, 12,* 139–156.

Elliot, A. J., & Thrash, T. M. (2002). Approach–avoidance motivation in personality: Approach and avoidance temperaments and goals. *Journal of Personality and Social Psychology, 82,* 804–818.

Emmons, R. A. (1986). Personal strivings: An approach to personality and sub- jective well- being. *Journal of Personality and Social Psychology, 51,* 1058– 1068.

Ferguson, E. D. (2000). Motivation: *A biosocial and cognitive integration of motivation and emotion.* New York: Oxford University Press.

Ford, M. (1992). *Motivating humans: Goals, emotions, and personal agency beliefs.* Thousand Oaks, CA: Sage.

Frese, M., & Zapf, D. (1994). Action as the core of work psychology: A Ger- man approach. In H. Triandis, M. Dunnette, & L. Hough (Eds.), *Handbook of industrial and organizational psychology* (2nd ed., Vol. 4, pp. 271–340). Palo Alto, CA: Consulting Psychologists Press.

Gable, S. (2006). Approach and avoidance social motives and goals. *Journal of Personality, 74,* 175–222.

Geen, R. G. (1995). *Human motivation.* Belmont, CA: Brooks & Cole.

Gollwitzer, P. M. (1990). Action phases and mind-sets. In E. T. Higgins & R. Sorrentino (Eds.), *Handbook of motivation and cognition: Foundations of social behavior* (Vol. 2, pp. 53–92). New York: Guilford Press.

Gollwitzer, P. M. (1999). Implementation intentions: Strong effects of simple plans. *American Psychologist, 54,* 493–503.

Harackiewicz, J. M., & Elliot, A. J. (1998). The joint effects of target and purpose goals on intrinsic motivation: A mediational analysis. *Personality and Social Psychology Bulletin, 24,* 675–689.

Heckhausen, H. (1991). *Motivation and action* (P. Leppman, Trans.). New York: Springer-Verlag.

Heckhausen, H., & Kuhl, J. (1985). From wishes to action: The dead ends and short cuts on the long way to action. In M. Frese & J. Sabini (Eds.), *Goal directed behavior: The concept of action in psychology* (pp. 134–159). Hills- dale, NJ: Erlbaum.

Heider, F. (1958). *The psychology of interpersonal relations.* New York: Wiley.

Herbart, J. F. (1850). Psychologie als Wissenschaft. In G. Hartenstein (Ed.), *Säm- mtliche Werke* (Vol. 5, pp. 191–514). Leipzig, Germany: Voss.

Higgins, E. T. (2000). Making a good decision: Value from fit. *America Psycholo- gist, 55,* 1217–1230.

Higgins, E. T. (2005). Value from regulatory fit. *Current Directions in Psycho- logical Science, 14,* 209–213.

James, W. (1950). *The principles of psychology.* New York: Holt. (Original work published 1850)

Keller, J., & Bless, H. (2006). Regulatory fit and cognitive performance: The inter- active effect of chronic and situationally induced self-regulatory mechanisms on test performance. *European Journal of Social Psychology, 36,* 393–405.

Kruglanski, A. W. (1996). Goals as knowledge structures. In P. Gollwitzer & J. Bargh (Eds.), *The psychology of action: Linking cognition and motivation to behavior* (pp. 599–618). New York: Guilford Press.

Kuhl, J. (2000). A functional-design approach to motivation and self-regulation: The dynamics of personality systems and interactions. In M. Boekaerts &

P. Pintrich (Eds.), *Handbook of self-regulation* (pp. 111–169). San Diego: Academic Press.

Lang, P. J. (1995). The emotion probe: Studies of motivation and attention. "American Psychologist, 50," 372–385.

Lewin, K. (1926). Vorsatz, Wille und Bedürfnis [Intention, will, and need]. *Psychologische Forschung, 7,* 330–385.

Lewin, K. (1935). *A dynamic theory of personality.* New York: McGraw-Hill.

Lewin, K., Dembo, T., Festinger, L., & Sears, P. S. (1944). Level of aspiration. In J. McV. Hunt (Ed.), *Personality and the behavior disorders* (Vol. 1, pp. 333–378). New York: Ronald Press.

Lewis, M. (1990). The development of intentionality and the role of consciousness. *Psychological Inquiry, 1,* 231–247.

Little, B. (1983). Personal projects: A rationale and method for investigation. *Environment and Behavior, 15,* 272–309.

Little, B. (1999). Personality and motivation: Personal action and the conative evolution. In L. Pervin O. John (Eds.), *Handbook of personality: Theory and research* (pp. 501–524). New York: Guilford Press.

Locke, E., & Latham, G. (1990). *A theory of goal setting and task performance.* Englewood Cliffs, NJ: Prentice Hall.

Logan, G. (1988). Toward and instance theory of automatization. *Psychological Review, 95*(4), 492–527.

Maehr, M. L. (1989). Thoughts about motivation. In C. Ames & R. Ames (Eds.), *Research on motivation in education: Goals and cognitions* (Vol. 3, pp. 299–315). San Diego: Academic Press.

McClelland, D. C. (1951). *Personality.* Oxford, UK: William Sloane.

McClelland, D. C. (1985). How motives, skills, and values determine what people do. *American Psychologist, 40,* 812–825.

McDougall, W. (1908). *An introduction to social psychology.* Boston: John W. Luce & Co.

Miller, G. A., Galanter, E., & Pribram, K. H. (1960). *Plans and the structure of behavior.* New York: Holt.

Murray, H. A. (1938). *Explorations in personality.* New York: Oxford University Press.

Oettingen, G., & Hagenah, M. (2005). Fantasies and the self-regulation of competence. In A. Elliot & C. Dweck (Eds.), *Handbook of competence and motivation* (pp. 647–665). New York: Guilford Press.

Osgood, C., Suci, G., & Tannenbaum, P. (1957). *The measurement of meaning.* Urbana: University of Illinois Press.

Panksepp, J. (1998). *Affective neuroscience: The foundations of human and animal emotions.* New York: Oxford University Press.

Penrose, R. (1996). *Shadows of the mind: A search for the missing science of consciousness.* Oxford, UK: Oxford University Press.

Pervin, L. A. (1983). The stasis and flow of behavior: Toward a theory of goals. In *Nebraska Symposium on Motivation* (Vol. 38, 1–53). Lincoln: University of Nebraska Press.

Pintrich, P., & Schunk, D. (1996). *Motivation in education: Theory, research, and applications.* Englewood Cliffs, NJ: Prentice Hall.

Reeve, J. (1992). *Understanding motivation and emotion*. Orlando, FL: Harcourt Brace Jovanovich College.

Roberts, B. W., Caspi, A., & Moffitt, T. E. (2001). The kids are alright: Growth and stability in personality development from adolescence to adulthood. *Journal of Personality and Social Psychology, 81,* 670–683.

Schneirla, T. (1959). An evolutionary and developmental theory of biphasic processes underlying approach and withdrawal. In *Nebraska Symposium on Motivation* (Vol. 7, pp. 1–42). Lincoln: University of Nebraska Press.

Schultheiss, O. C., & Brunstein, J. C. (2005). An implicit motive perspective on competence. In A. Elliot & C. Dweck (Eds.), *Handbook of competence and motivation* (pp. 31–51). New York: Guilford Press.

Shah, J. Y., & Kruglanski, A. W. (2003). When opportunity knocks: Bottom-up priming of goals by means and its effects on self-regulation. *Journal of Personality and Social Psychology, 84,* 1109–1122.

Stellar, J. R., & Stellar, E. (1985). *The neurobiology of motivation and reward.* New York: Springer-Verlag.

Tamir, M. (2005). Neuroticism, trait-consistent affect regulation, and performance. *Journal of Personality and Social Psychology, 89,* 449–461.

Tamir, M., & Diener, E. (2008). Approach–avoidance goals and well-being: One size does not fit all. In A. J. Elliot (Ed.), *Handbook of approach and avoidance motivation* (pp. 415–430). Hillsdale, NJ: Erlbaum.

Thrash, T. M., & Elliot, A. J. (2001). Delimiting and integrating the goal and motive constructs in achievement motivation. In A. Efklides, J. Kuhl, & R. Sorrentino (Eds.), *Trends and prospects in motivation research* (pp. 3–21). Amsterdam: Kluwer Academic Publishers.

Thrash, T. M., & Elliot, A. J. (2002). Implicit and self-attributed achievement motives: Concordance and predictive validity. *Journal of Personality, 70,* 729–755.

Thrash, T. M., Elliot, A. J., & Schultheiss, O. C. (2007). Methodological and dispositional predictors of congruence between implicit and explicit need for achievement. *Personality and Social Psychology Bulletin, 33,* 961–974.

Tolman, E. (1932). *Purposive behavior in animals and men.* New York: The Century.

Tooby, J., & Cosmides, L. (1990). The past explains the present: Emotional adaptions and the structure of ancestral environments. *Ethology and Sociobiology, 11,* 375–424.

Winter, D. G. (1996). *Personality: Analysis and interpretation of lives.* New York: McGraw-Hill.

Winter, D. G., John, O. P., Stewart, A. J., Klohnen, E. C., & Duncan, L. E. (1998). Traits and motives: Toward an integration of two traditions in personality research. *Psychological Review, 105,* 230–250.

Wyer, R. S., & Srull, T. K. (1986). Human cognition in its social context. *Psychological Review, 93,* 322–359.

Zeidner, M. (1998). *Test anxiety: State of the art.* New York: Plenum Press.

CHAPTER 3

Goal Content Theories
WHY DIFFERENCES IN <u>WHAT</u> WE ARE STRIVING FOR MATTER

HEIDI GRANT
LAURA GELETY

A quick glance at the chapter titles in this volume tells you something important about the way in which the study of goal setting and goal pursuit has been approached by the majority of researchers in the field, and with good reason. In pursuit of universal principles that cut across all goals or all self-regulatory processes, we have often emptied goal pursuit of its content—in other words, we don't care which particular goal you're pursuing, we just want to know what happens when people pursue goals in general. And the advantages of this approach are clear: It has generated principles that apply widely and can shed light on behavior across domains. Clearly, principles of goal setting, goal implementation, and goal conflict can be informative independent of particular goal content. One need look no further than this very book to see ample evidence of this.

The goal content approach—identifying particular types of goals and studying them in detail—has been useful, too. It has yielded deep insights into important phenomena, such as aggression, depression, achievement, and well-being. At its best, this approach can specify the processes involved in a way that illuminates the character of a phenomenon, and that allows one to chart its causes, follow its consequences, and design effective interventions. The potential limitation of this approach is that what one learns may be limited to that phenomenon or domain alone. Indeed, content distinctions have too often been conceptualized in a way that renders them less useful and largely unappealing to goal theorists who are seeking general laws or principles.

Ultimately, the most compelling argument that can be made to make goal theorists stand up and take notice of goal content is that, in fact, goal pursuit takes on a different character in pursuit of different goals—that though there may be some universal principles true of all goal pursuit, there are also those that do not apply, or apply differently, to the pursuit of particular types of goals. This is exactly the argument we are going to try to make, by reviewing the most influential goal content research (specifically, research on life goals, achievement goals, and regulatory focus) and pointing out along the way those instances where different types of goals are, for example, pursued by different means, affected differently by expectancies, are associated with different affective experiences, or contribute differently to well-being.

Life Goals

Our most meaningful and significant thoughts, feelings, and behaviors in our everyday lives occur in relation to the things we value and strive for, and much of our action is in the service of the attainment of valued goals. Often it has been assumed that as long as two goals hold the same value and performance expectancies, they will lead to the same quality of performance and emotional experience (Deci & Ryan, 2000). However, a large body of evidence now exists suggesting that this is not the case—specifically, that the kind of goal an individual tends to pursue in her everyday life can significantly affect her well-being, independent of the goal's value or likelihood of success.

Cantor and her colleagues (see Cantor et al., 1991) have used the term "life task" to describe the important goals that people pursue in daily life, often specific to a particular stage or time and context in the life span. Emmons' (1989) emphasis, not unlike Cantor et al.'s, is on personal strivings, or the typical kinds of goals a person is likely to have in different situations. Personal strivings are coherent patterns of goal pursuit, which are grouped by their content into thematically relevant categories. Examples of personal strivings include "Get to know new people," "Make a good impression," and "Avoid arguments when possible." Strivings can also be characterized along several more structural dimensions, including value, commitment, and expectancy for success. These approaches, along with those of Klinger (current concerns; 1977) and Little (personal projects; 1989), are highly individualized, in that each focuses on people's self-articulated, content-laden goals, which vary across domains and levels of abstraction.

However, by focusing on the differences in goals that people actually pursue on a regular basis, they have been able to utilize differences in goal content to tell us something unique about quality of life and well-being. For example, Emmons (1989) found that the experience of positive affect over time is predicted by the content as well as the value, importance, and past fulfillment of personal strivings. Salmela-Aro and Nurmi (1997) used Little's (1989) Personal Project Analysis (assessing family-related, self-related, and achievement-related goals) to predict well-being in a longitudinal study of first-year university students. They found that students who were focused on self-related goals at the beginning of the study experienced fewer positive life events. By contrast, students who had family and achievement-related goals at the beginning of the study experienced fewer negative life events, and those who pursued family-related goals also had higher self-esteem and lower levels of depression throughout the study. Finally, students' endorsement of these goals remained relatively stable over time. The results of this study provide just one example of the important role that goal content plays in affecting one's life experience and self-concept.

Self-Determination Theory

Perhaps the most influential approach to the study of differences in individuals' life goals has been Deci and Ryan's self-determination theory (SDT) (Deci & Ryan, 2000). Deci, Ryan, and their colleagues' (for a review, see Deci & Ryan, 2000) approach has been to focus on both the process of goal pursuit and the content of the goals being pursued. Specifically, SDT posits that people pursue goals to fulfill three basic psychological needs: competence, relatedness, and autonomy. These needs give goals their meaning and determine the regulatory processes selected to direct goal pursuit. SDT distinguishes between two classes of goals—intrinsic and extrinsic goals—and two self-regulatory processes involved in goal pursuit—autonomous and controlled processes. According to SDT, it is necessary to consider *both* the goal content and self-regulatory processes involved in goal pursuit to fully understand consequent behavior and well-being.

The self-regulatory process involved (whether autonomous or controlled) is important in determining effectiveness and well-being because these processes involve different amounts of need satisfaction. In general, autonomous processes predict better outcomes and well-being because they imply greater self-determination in goal pursuit. That is, people who pursue goals for autonomous reasons have greater intrinsic motivation for attainment and are not pressured by outside forces (e.g., peers, laws, etc.). On the other hand, because of their extrinsically based motivation, controlled processes tend to predict poorer outcomes and well-being. Support for these relationships have been found in studies involving a wide variety of domains (e.g., achievement, religious, and physical health).

For example, Vansteenkiste, Simons, Lens, Sheldon, and Deci (2004) conducted three field studies that tested the effects of intrinsic goals combined with autonomy-supportive climates on learning (specifically, deeper processing), performance, and persistence. In all three studies, the experimental tasks were framed in terms of either an intrinsic or extrinsic goal, and the learning climate was framed as autonomy supportive or controlled. Results supported SDT on a variety of measures, including self-reported superficial processing, self-report and behavioral measures of deep processing, graded performance, and free-choice persistence on activities.

In addition to considering the self-regulatory processes underlying goal pursuit, SDT maintains that the content of one's goals is also an important factor to consider, insofar as certain life goals are better suited to meeting basic psychological needs than others. Greater need satisfaction, in turn, leads to greater well-being. Intrinsic goals involve goals of affiliation, personal growth, and community contribution. These goals directly satisfy the three basic psychological needs of relatedness, competence, and autonomy. Extrinsic goals, on the other hand, involve goals of wealth, fame, and image attainment. These goals emphasize a focus on obtaining external contingent approval and signs of worth. As a result, extrinsic goals are not likely to yield need satisfaction and, thus, predict poorer subsequent well-being (that is, if one primarily pursues extrinsic life goals).

In general, SDT assumes that goal content and self-regulatory processes each uniquely and independently contribute to goal attainment and well-being. These two factors also interact with each other in goal pursuit (where intrinsic goals combined with autonomous motivation lead to the most optimal outcomes and well-being) (Sheldon, Ryan, Deci, & Kasser, 2004). For example, Sheldon and colleagues (2004) found that individuals report the highest levels of anticipated happiness in pursuit of future goals that are intrinsic and autonomously pursued. Further, those who had pursued such goals in the past reported the highest levels of current well-being.

Deci and Ryan (2000) suggest that by examining both sides of the goal-pursuit coin (the "what," or content of the goal, and the "why," or extent to which it is autonomously pursued), researchers gain a fuller understanding of the consequences of goal pursuit.

Cross-Cultural Differences in Life Goals

If, as a field, we are seeking universal principles that govern behavior, then we must ask to what extent the life-goal distinctions obtained in these studies exist in very different populations cross-culturally. Grouzet et al. (2005) attempted to determine the dimensions that organize the content of personal goals across 15 cultures. Although acknowledging the large body of work supporting the intrinsic/extrinsic distinction, they argued that there might be important differences between specific goals within each of these categories. Moreover, not all goals are explicitly intrinsic or extrinsic in nature, and thus other dimensions along which goal content distinctions fall must exist. Specifically, they proposed a second dimension that involves goals that range from being exclusively physical (i.e., hedonistic goals) to exclusively self-transcendent (i.e., spiritual goals). They hypothesized that goals could be organized into a circumplex model that includes both of these dimensions. Generally, the results of their cross-cultural study supported the circumplex model. That is, people from differing cultures (including those that differ greatly in terms of affluence) place value on similar goals that fall along extrinsic/intrinsic and self-transcendent/physical dimensions.

Achievement Goals

Considerable evidence (in fact, so considerable we can only skim the surface in our review) now exists to suggest that much of achievement motivation (e.g., persistence, strategy use, and intrinsic interest) can be understood in terms of the different goals individuals bring to the achievement context (Elliot & Harackiewicz, 1996; Elliott & Dweck, 1988; Grant & Dweck, 2003; see also Ames, 1992; Kaplan & Maehr, 2007; Nicholls, 1984; Pintrich, 2000; Urdan, 1997). Two classes of goals have been identified: *performance goals,* where the purpose is to perform well on a particular task (i.e., to display and validate one's competence), and *learning goals,* where the aim is to acquire new knowledge or skills (i.e., to increase one's competence).

Performance goals emphasize outcomes as measures of competence or opportunities to outperform others and have been shown to produce a vulnerability to helplessness and debilitation after a setback or negative feedback. In contrast, learning goals emphasize the acquisition of competence and consequently have been shown to facilitate persistence and mastery-oriented behaviors, including the increase of effort and maintenance of intrinsic motivation. (Butler, 1993; Elliott & Dweck, 1988; Grant & Dweck, 2003; Jagacinski & Nicholls, 1987; see Dweck & Elliott, 1983; Dweck & Leggett, 1988; Urdan, 1997, for reviews). Performance and learning goals have also been shown to predict real-world performance, including exam grades, course grades, and achievement test scores, controlling for past performance (Dweck & Sorich, 1999; Grant & Dweck,

2003; Elliot & Church, 1997; Elliot, McGregor, & Gable, 1999). These effects are obtained across a variety of ages from preschool children to adults (Dweck & Leggett, 1988; Elliot & Church, 1997; Smiley & Dweck, 1994) and in other achievement realms, such as sports (Duda & Nicholls, 1992) and business (Vandewalle, 1997).

The different patterns of behavior associated with performance and learning goals occur when they are experimentally manipulated (Butler, 1993; Elliott & Dweck, 1988; Gelety & Grant, 2008; Harackiewicz & Elliot, 1993), and when chronic goal orientations are measured (Dweck & Leggett, 1988; Elliot & Church, 1997; Grant & Dweck, 2003; Midgley, Anderman, & Hicks, 1995; Miller, Behrens, Greene, & Newman, 1993, Pintrich & DeGroot, 1990; Pintrich & Garcia, 1991). The fact that induced goals have been found to have strong impact is important for two reasons. First, it means that goals have a causal role in producing achievement patterns. Second, and practically speaking, it means that learning environments can be constructed in ways that enhance achievement.

Attributions and Expectancies

Individuals pursuing performance and learning goals have been shown to explain their achievement outcomes, particularly their failures, in importantly different ways. Decades of research have demonstrated that the different attributions individuals generate for their own outcomes lead to unique patterns of affect and motivation (see Weiner, 1985, for a review). Generally speaking, low-ability attributions (associated with performance-goal pursuit) after failure tend to produce a pattern of helplessness, negative self-evaluation, and negative affect, whereas effort attributions (associated with learning-goal pursuit) tend not to involve issues of the self to the same degree (Ames & Archer, 1988; Dweck & Leggett, 1988; Grant & Dweck, 2003). In fact, those individuals who make effort attributions report a sense of challenge and enthusiasm, and a belief that if they work harder and find new strategies they can master the task.

According to Weiner (1985), ability is generally considered stable and uncontrollable, and therefore attributing a failure to ability leads to low efficacy beliefs, whereas effort is considered unstable and controllable, and therefore these attributions lead to high efficacy beliefs. At the outset of goal pursuit, both learning and performance goal-oriented individuals tend to have high and equal expectancies for goal attainment (Elliot & Church, 1997). Not surprisingly, performance goals have been associated with larger drops in expectancies in the face of difficulty than learning goals (Gelety & Grant, 2008; Grant & Dweck, 2003). Moreover, decreases in expectancies for success seem to have a negative impact on motivation in pursuit of performance goals but do not appear to impair learning-goal pursuit (Elliott & Dweck, 1988; Gelety & Grant, 2008).

Intrinsic Motivation

Another mechanism through which goals might affect performance is their capacity to increase or decrease intrinsic motivation. Individuals who enjoy a task or subject and pursue it in their spare time are likely to do better on it in the future than those who do not (Butler, 1987; Deci & Ryan, 1985; Lepper, 1981). Performance and learning goals have been shown to affect intrinsic motivation, in terms of task enjoyment and free-choice persistence (Butler, 1987; Heyman & Dweck, 1992). Chronic learning goals predict increased intrinsic motivation (Elliot & McGregor, 2001; Grant & Dweck, 2003) whereas chronic performance-avoidance goals are associated with decreased intrinsic motivation (Elliot & McGregor, 2001; Cury, Elliot, Sarrazin, Da Fonseca, & Rufo, 2002).

Affect and Its Consequences

In the face of negative feedback, performance and learning goal–oriented individuals experience negative affect. More specifically, feelings of anxiety, frustration, and sadness are commonly reported when individuals encounter hardship. For instance, Dykman (1998) assessed college students' goal orientations, negative life events, and level of depression. The pursuit of performance (self-validation) and learning (self-growth) goals predicted increased depression after experiencing a negative life event. However, performance goal–oriented students experienced depression to a greater degree (see also Elliott & Dweck, 1988). Similarly, Grant, Baer, and Dweck (2008) found that while both chronically performance and learning goal–oriented participants reported experiencing depressed affect in response to daily stressors, the degree of depression was significantly greater in pursuit of performance (this may be particularly true for individuals pursuing performance-avoidance goals, see Pekrun, Elliot, & Maier, 2006). Perhaps more interesting, individuals pursuing learning goals utilized this negative affect in a more adaptive way. They seemed to take the experience of depression as a sign that their effort needed to be increased or that they should engage in more adaptive coping strategies, and consequently greater depressed affect was associated with more problem-focused coping, whereas the opposite pattern emerged in pursuit of performance goals (i.e., greater depression was associated with disengagement and helplessness). These findings have recently been replicated in the laboratory. Grant, Baer, Gelety, and Dweck (2008) manipulated goals and found that after experiencing difficulty depressed affect predicted better subsequent achievement for individuals assigned to a learning goal, and impaired achievement for those assigned to a performance goal.

Strategy Use and Information Seeking

Performance goals have been linked to less effective study strategies, including rote memorization and other forms of surface processing while learning goals predict the use of deeper processing strategies such as "elaboration" and "networking" (Elliot et al., 1999; Kaplan & Midgely, 1997; Pintrich & DeGroot, 1990). That is, wanting to document one's ability via test performance appears to lead to more superficial study strategies than does wanting to understand and master the material. Moreover, learning goals predict adaptive help seeking when one does not understand the material (Pintrich, 2000), whereas performance goals predict self-handicapping in the face of uncertain outcomes (Midgley et al., 1995). Students with performance goals would (ironically) often prefer to risk their achievement to preserve their perceptions of their ability. There is some evidence to suggest that learning goals also predict adaptive motivational strategy use. Wolters (1998), for example, found that among college students learning goals were related to attempts to regulate efficacy, interest, and value. Learning goals have also been shown to predict time regulation (Pintrich, 2000) and more cooperative information exchange with task partners (Poortvliet, Janssen, Van Yperen, & Van de Vliert, 2007), as well as the seeking of instructive information, rather than normative evaluation information, after disagreement with a task partner (Darnon, Muller, Schrager, Pannuzzo, & Butera, 2006).

Butler (2000) suggested that learning goals prompt individuals to find new and better ways to solve problems, whereas performance goals lead individuals to rely on familiar knowledge and strategies. Thus, each goal may lead to superior performance depending on the demands of the task—graded performance on tests of knowledge may be facilitated by performance goals, whereas the acquisition of complex skills may be facilitated by learning goal (see also Butler, 2006).

Task and Context

Performance and learning goals are also associated with different sensitivities to aspects of the task, context, and situation. Gelety and Grant (2008) found that performance goals led to more motivated and successful goal pursuit on easy tasks, but that this advantage disappeared with the introduction of obstacles or increases in perceived task difficulty. Elliot, Shell, Henry, and Maier (2005) found that students pursuing performance goals were motivated (and performed better) when future opportunities to obtain reward were contingent on their current performance relative to a contingency-free condition, whereas those pursuing learning goals were insensitive to the presence or absence of contingencies.

Distinguishing among Performance Goals

Although there is consensus regarding the predictive power of these two classes of goals, data regarding the nature of the impact of performance goals in particular have been somewhat inconsistent. Specifically, some studies have shown that performance goals relatively less adaptive strategies of goal pursuit, whereas others have shown performance goals to result in superior goal attainment. Consequently, several achievement goal theorists (e.g., Elliot & Harackiewicz, 1996; Grant & Dweck, 2003) have argued that important distinctions can and should be made among different types of performance goals.

Approach versus Avoidance Performance Goals

The distinction between approach and avoidance is an important distinction made throughout the motivational literature (see Carver & Scheier, 1982; Elliot & Niesta, Chapter 4, this volume; Förster & Werth, Chapter 15, this volume; Higgins, 1997). Elliot and his colleagues have distinguished between *approach* and *avoidance* forms of performance goals, where approach forms involve a focus on success and outperforming others, and avoidance forms involve a focus on avoiding failure or performing poorly relative to others. They maintain that debilitation occurs primarily when performance goals are avoidant in nature, and that approach forms can be highly beneficial for achievement (Elliot & Church, 1997; Maehr & Midgley, 1991). For example, Elliot et al. (1999) found that avoidance-performance goals predict maladaptive study strategies, decreased intrinsic motivation, and poorer performance in a college classroom, whereas approach–performance goals did not. More recently, Elliot and colleagues have argued that the approach–avoidance distinction should be applied to mastery goals as well, with data suggesting that only mastery-approach goals are associated with positive achievement outcomes (Elliot & McGregor, 2001).

Ability versus Normative Performance Goals

Grant and Dweck (2003) pointed out that studies of (approach) performance goal effects had operationalized these goals in critically different ways. For some researchers, the essence of a performance goal is seeking to do well and validate one's competence (operationalized by suggesting to the participant that his/her performance on a task measures the extent to which he/she possess a valued ability). Debilitation occurs when outcomes indicate a lack of competence, but performance enhancement can occur when success is expected (Ames, 1992; Dweck & Leggett, 1988; Nicholls, 1984). For others, the essence of a performance goal is a normative comparison (i.e., wanting to perform better than others), and a goal that is not normative (e.g., using an absolute standard such as a perfect score, or tying absolute performance to self-worth) is not considered a performance goal (Elliot & Church, 1997; Maehr & Midgley, 1991). Here, performance goals are often operationalized by simply informing the participants that their performance on a task will be evaluated normatively, or by measuring their agreement with statements such as "It is important to me to do well compared to others in this class" (Elliot & Church, 1997). According to this view, debilitation occurs only when one fails to outperform one's peers on a task.

Thus, it is important to distinguish between what Grant and Dweck (2003) termed "ability" performance goals, focused on validating a valued ability, and "normative" performance goals, focused on outperforming others. When pursuing ability goals, students interpret difficulty or a setback as evidence of low ability. In their studies, ability goals were associated with loss of self-worth, rumination, and loss of intrinsic motivation. In a difficult college course, after multiple setbacks, ability goals predicted lower grades. In contrast, normative goals were associated with a kind of competitive zeal that seemed to buffer students from the experience of setbacks or difficulty. Students with these goals reported higher levels of perceived ability, while engaging in less in-depth learning of course material. These findings helped to demonstrate the importance of emphasizing the psychological processes that accompany different types of goals, and of matching operationalizations to these conceptions. When thought of in this way, it becomes clearer when and why different goals—even ones that have typically been classified under the same name—will have different effects.

Performance and Learning in Other Domains

What kinds of goals do individuals pursue in their interactions with others? Ryan and Shim (2006) argued that social competence (social skills and abilities) is not unlike academic competence, in that individuals can seek either to develop and improve their social abilities, or demonstrate their already-existing abilities. Specifically, they found that people can pursue social-development goals (focused on improvement and growth), social demonstration–approach goals (focused on obtaining positive judgments from others) and social demonstration–avoidance goals (focused on avoiding displaying a lack of social competence). To the extent that participants endorsed social-development goals, they reported having more positive relationships with others, greater self-acceptance, and more personal growth, whereas social demonstration–avoidance goals predicted the absence of each of the same indices of adjustment.

A study by Erdley, Cain, Loomis, Dumas-Hines, and Dweck (1997) observed the effects of performance and learning goals in social interaction by manipulating children's social goals and observing their responses to a social setback. Erdley and colleagues informed a group of fourth- and fifth-grade children that they would be participating in a "pen-pal tryout." They were asked to write a letter to a potential pen pal and believed that this letter was transmitted to a peer rater, who would decide if the child could join the pen-pal club. After transmitting the letter, each child was told that the rater was "not sure whether to have you in the club" and would like the child to write another letter. After the second letter, all children were told that they had been accepted.

Before writing the first letter, however, each child was told either that "we'd like to see how good you are at making friends," setting up a performance goal, or that "this is a chance to practice and improve how you make friends," establishing a learning goal. The postrejection second letter was coded by independent raters, who found that letters written by children with performance goals, when compared to those written by children with learning goals, showed decreased effort and withdrawal from the task. This was evidenced among children with performance goals by a decrease in the number of strategies used by the writer, a decrease in overall message length, and a decrease in the amount of information about the writer contained in the letter. The performance-goal group was also more likely than the learning-goal group to attribute the initial social setback to uncontrollable factors.

These results illustrate how goals can influence the way in which a social setback is interpreted by an individual, and how goals are linked to coherent, meaningful patterns of responding in a social interaction. They also support the claim that there are goal content distinctions that cut across domains and predict analogous patterns of behavior.

Additionally, several researchers have found behavior patterns produced by what we would classify as performance and learning goals in the domains of social interaction (Goetz & Dweck, 1980), aggression (Erdley & Asher, 1996; La Greca, Dandes, Wick, Shaw, & Stone, 1988; Taylor & Asher, 1989), and intimate relationships (Brundage, Derlega, & Cash, 1977; Kamins, Morris, & Dweck, 1997), analogous to those found in the achievement domain. Taken together, this evidence suggests that having a performance goal during social interaction produces a seeking out of interaction partners who will validate the self and increase prestige, as well as a vulnerability to negative affect, negative evaluation of self or others, and withdrawal or aggression after a perceived rejection. In contrast, having a learning goal produces a seeking out of interaction partners that will help to develop and improve the self (even through criticism), and persistence, and new strategy generation after a perceived rejection (Erdley et al., 1997; Kamins et al., 1997).

Regulatory Focus

Research by Higgins and his colleagues on self-discrepancy theory (Higgins, 1987) and regulatory focus theory (see Förster & Werth, Chapter 15, this volume, for an extensive review) illustrates another way in which goal content determines the nature of goal pursuit. Self-discrepancy theory distinguishes between two different styles of self-regulatory socialization children can receive, that in turn influence the self-conceptualizations that guide their behavior. When the caretaker's message to the child is, "This is what I would *ideally* like you to do," the child develops a strong ideal self-guide. Ideal self-guides involve the individual's hopes, wishes, and aspirations and exist to satisfy the basic need for nurturance. When the caretaker's message to the child is, "This is what I think you *ought* to do," the child develops a strong ought self-guide. Ought self-guides involve the individual's duties, obligations, and responsibilities and exist to satisfy the basic need for security. Importantly, ideal and ought self-guides determine the nature of the *goals* one pursues.

Specifically, strong ideal self-guides result in an overall *promotion focus,* creating goals that concern aspirations, advancement, and accomplishments (or, more generally, the presence or absence of positive outcomes). Strong ought self-guides, in contrast, result in an overall *prevention focus,* creating goals that concern responsibilities, safety, and security (or, more generally, the presence or absence of negative outcomes). Situations can also temporarily induce either a promotion focus or a prevention focus, through task instructions or messages that are represented in terms of the presence or absence of positive outcomes (i.e., gain/nongain) or the presence or absence of negative outcomes (i.e., loss/nonloss) (Shah & Higgins, 1997; Shah, Higgins, & Friedman, 1998).

Motivation and Strategy Use

When a person has a promotion focus, his or her motivation is best characterized as *eagerness,* and in pursuing a particular goal, eagerness is increased by actual or anticipated gain and decreased by actual or anticipated nongain (Idson, Liberman, & Higgins, 2000). In contrast, when a person has a prevention focus, his/her motivation is best characterized as *vigilance,* and in pursuing a particular goal he/she is sensitive to the presence or absence of negative outcomes (loss/nonloss). Vigilance is increased by actual or anticipated loss and decreased by actual or anticipated nonloss (Idson et al., 2000). Several studies have found that the promotion focus concern with advancement and accomplishment involves the strategic inclination to *approach matches* to desired end-states, whereas the prevention focus concern with protection and safety involves the strategic inclination to *avoid mismatches* to desired end-states (see Higgins, Roney, Crowe, & Hymes, 1994; Shah et al., 1998).

A set of studies examined individuals' inclination to generate few or many means to attain each of their goals (Liberman, Molden, Idson, & Higgins, 2001). The process of generating alternative means to reach a goal involves a trade-off—each alternative produced represents a chance to offer a correct solution (i.e., to attain a "hit" and avoid a "miss"), but it also represents a chance to offer an incorrect solution (i.e., to commit an error of commission). Promotion-focused individuals, with their inclination to ensure "hits" and ensure against "misses," tend to generate more alternatives in the course of problem-solving than prevention-focused individuals, who are inclined to ensure "correct rejections" and to ensure against errors of commission.

Affect and Expectancies

Failure to successfully reach one's goal should lead to the experience of negative affect, but exactly what kind of negative affect? Because failure to attain a promotion-focused goal represents the absence of positive outcomes, individuals pursuing this type of goal are likely to experience dejection-related emotions such as feeling sad, disappointed, or discouraged. In contrast, failure to attain a prevention-focused goal represents the presence of negative outcomes, individuals pursuing prevention goals are likely to experience agitation-related emotions such as feeling, tense, nervous, or worried (Higgins, Grant, & Shah, 1999).

Do individuals pursuing promotion and prevention goals respond differently not only to failure but also to success? Förster, Grant, Idson, and Higgins (2001) looked at how success and failure feedback influence expectancies in an ongoing task for participants with either a promotion or prevention focus. Participants pursuing promotion goals reported very high expectancies for future performance when given success feedback, and moderate expectancies when given failure feedback. In contrast, those pursuing prevention goals reported only moderate expectancies when given success feedback, and low expectancies when given failure feedback.

Förster and colleagues (2001) argued that this asymmetry was the result of participants using expectancies strategically to maintain or increase motivation. Prevention-focused participants did not generate high expectancies, even after success feedback, because high expectancies would lead to less vigilance motivation, and subsequently poorer performance. Notably, they still had higher expectancies after success than after failure, but they had lower expectancies after the same success than did promotion-focused participants. Further, Grant and Higgins (2003) found that individuals with a history of successful promotion-goal attainment reported greater optimism, whereas those who had successfully attained prevention goals dampened their optimism to maximize future motivation.

In addition, the interactive effect of expectancy and value on motivation and decision making has been found to vary as a function of the strength of an individual's current promotion or prevention focus. A basic assumption of expectancy-value models is that in addition to there being main effects of expectancy and value on goal commitment, there is also an effect from their multiplicative combination (for a review, see Feather, 1982). The multiplicative assumption is that as either expectancy or value increases, the impact of the other variable on commitment increases. This assumption reflects the notion that the goal commitment involves a motivation to maximize the product of value and expectancy. Shah and Higgins (1997) suggested that the pursuit of promotion-focused goals is more likely to involve the motivation to maximize the product of value and expectancy. Goal pursuit with eagerness strategies would involve pursuing highly valued goals with the highest expected utility, which maximizes value expectancy. In contrast, goal pursuit with vigilance strategies would involve avoiding all unnecessary risks by striving to meet only responsibilities that are either clearly necessary (i.e., high value-prevention goals) or safely attainable (i.e., high expectancy of attainment). When goal pursuit becomes a necessity, such as ensuring the safety of one's child, one must do whatever one can to succeed regardless of the ease or likelihood of goal attainment. That is, although expectancy information would always be relevant, it would become relatively less relevant as goal pursuit becomes more like a necessity. Thus, Shah and Higgins (1997) predicted and found that as strength of prevention focus increased the interactive effect of value and expectancy becomes negative.

Taken together, it becomes clear not only that goal content tells us something important about the relationship between goal attainment and well-being, but also that the pursuit of different goals (performance vs. learning, promotion vs. prevention) lead to differences in strategy use, motivation, affective experience, task choice, and implications for changes in expectancies—aspects of goal pursuit that are often studied independent of goal content.

What Kinds of Content Distinctions Are Most Useful?

Returning to the achievement goal theories, which link the helpless and mastery-oriented patterns to differences in goal content, we can examine the goals of the students in the achievement situation at three salient levels of analysis (see Grant & Dweck, 1999a, 1999b). At the highest level of abstraction, there is the general need or value that one seeks to fulfill or attain (see Carver & Scheier, 1982; Gollwitzer & Moskowitz, 1996). In this example, both groups of students could be described as striving towards the same value—*competence* ("I want to possess competence"). This is a goal at a level of abstraction of such goals as *self-esteem* or *relatedness*. This level may be too abstract to predict specific behaviors, and it does not differentiate between the helpless and mastery patterns—though it may tell us something about an individual's overall well-being (see Deci & Ryan, 2000).

At a lower level of abstraction, individuals in an achievement situation generally want to solve as many problems as possible or complete the task assigned to them. Again, this level of abstraction will not provide us with predictions about specific patterns of responding because it is too concrete rather than too abstract.

Between these two levels lies the level of goal abstraction at which the superordinate goal takes a more specific form, and individuals' goals can be seen to diverge. At this level, the superordinate goal of possessing *competence* takes on a particular nature and determines the particular way in which the individual will self-regulate to achieve the competence goal. In the Elliott and Dweck (1988) achievement study, one group's goal was to demonstrate competence (performance goal), whereas the other's was to gain competence (learning goal). Once the method of fulfilling the superordinate need is delineated, corresponding behavioral responses to failure can be expected. Elliott and Dweck found that seeking to demonstrate competence resulted in a vulnerability to helplessness in the face of failure, whereas seeking to gain competence resulted in a tendency to display a mastery orientation. We propose that this is the level of goal abstraction that is conceptually the most useful in predicting the specific character of goal pursuit. It is the goal that is both the purpose of the lower, "nominal" level goal (solving the problems correctly), and the means through which the higher level goal (competence) is achieved.

This analysis of levels of goal abstraction is analogous to Powers' (1973) model of the hierarchical organization of control systems (see also Carver & Scheier, 1982). Most germane to our ideas are the highest levels of the nine-level hierarchy. The system concept level is the highest level of abstraction, corresponding to goals such as self-esteem, relatedness, and identity. The directly subordinate level is the principle control level, which specifies the way in which the system concept goal or need can be satisfied. In the case of the system concept "self-esteem," for example, the principle control level goal could be a promotion-focused goal ("look good in front of my friends") or a prevention focused-goal ("avoid being unpopular and socially isolated").

In other words, the principle level specifies how people self-regulate with respect to the system level. Often goal contents have been grouped together according to the need they satisfy (e.g., affiliation goals, moral goals, power goals). We are suggesting that goal content distinctions at the principle level of abstraction may generally be the most useful in predicting differences in the affective, cognitive, and motivational qualities of goal pursuit (see Grant & Dweck, 1999a, for a lengthier discussion).

Concluding Comments

We are far from the first to draw the distinction between content and structural or process models of goal-driven behavior (see Austin & Vancouver, 1996; Gollwitzer & Moskowitz, 1996; Kruglanski & Shah, 1997). However, is it really possible (or wise) to assume that a structural or process model can be content free, or are some content distinctions necessary to have a complete model of goal pursuit? We have argued that models of goal structure must take into account important content distinctions to more fully identify and understand the workings of particular structural or process dimensions of goal striving. However, we acknowledge that not all content distinctions have proven themselves particularly useful, and that much more attention must be paid to determining which kinds of goal distinctions predict real differences in cognition, affect, and behavior. This more integrative approach will give us a much richer and more complete picture of goal pursuit and self-regulation, and consequently it is our hope that future researchers will work in the spirit of a reunion of content and process.

References

Ames, C. (1992). Classrooms: Goals, structures, and student motivation. *Journal of Educational Psychology, 84*, 261–271.

Ames, C., & Archer, J. (1988). Achievement goals in the classroom: Students' learning strategies and motivation processes. *Journal of Educational Psychology, 80*, 260–267.

Austin, J., & Vancouver, J. (1996). Goal constructs in psychology: Structure, process, and content. *Psychological Bulletin, 120*, 338–375.

Brundage, L. G., Derlega, V. J., & Cash, T. F. (1977). The effects of physical attractiveness and need for approval on self-disclosure. *Personality and Social Psychology Bulletin, 3,* 63–66.

Butler, R. (1987). Task-involving and ego-involving properties of evaluation: Effects of different feedback conditions on motivational perceptions, interest and performance. *Journal of Educational Psychology, 79,* 474–482.

Butler, R. (1993). Effects of task- and ego-achievement goals on information seeking during task engagement. *Journal of Personality and Social Psychology, 65,* 18–31.

Butler, R. (2000). What learners want to know: The role of achievement goals in shaping information-seeking, performance, and interest. In C. Sansone & J. Harackiewicz (Eds.), *Intrinsic and extrinsic motivation: The search for optimal motivation and performance* (pp. 161–194). San Diego: Academic Press.

Butler, R. (2006). Are mastery and ability goals both adaptive? Evaluation, initial goal construction and the quality of task engagement. *British Journal of Educational Psychology, 76,* 595–611.

Cantor, N., Norem, J. K., Langston, C. A., Zirkel, S., Fleeson, W., & Cook-Flanagan, C. (1991). Life tasks and daily life experience. *Journal of Personality, 59,* 425–451.

Carver, C. S., & Scheier, M. F. (1982). Control theory: A useful conceptual framework in personality-social, clinical, and health psychology. *Psychological Bulletin, 92,* 111–135.

Cury, F., Elliot, A. J., Sarrazin, P., Da Fonesca, D., & Rufo, M. (2002). The trichotomous achievement goal model and intrinsic motivation: A sequential meditational analysis. *Journal of Experimental Social Psychology, 38,* 473–481.

Darnon, C., Muller, D., Schrager, S. M., Pannuzzo, N., & Butera, F. (2006). Mastery and performance goals predict epistemic and relational conflict regulation. *Journal of Educational Psychology, 98,* 766–776.

Deci, E. L., & Ryan, R. M. (1985). *Intrinsic motivation and self-determination in human behavior.* New York: Plenum Press.

Deci, E. L., & Ryan, R. M. (2000). The "what" and "why" of goal pursuits: Human needs and the self-determination of behavior. *Psychological Inquiry, 11,* 227–268.

Duda, J. L., & Nicholls, J. G. (1992). Dimensions of achievement motivation in school work and sport. *Journal of Educational Psychology, 84,* 290–299.

Dweck, C. S., & Elliott, E. S. (1983). Achievement motivation. In P. Mussen & E. M. Hetherington (Eds.), *Handbook of child psychology* (pp. 643–691). New York: Wiley.

Dweck, C. S., & Leggett, E. L. (1988). A social-cognitive approach to motivation and personality. *Psychological Review, 95,* 256–273.

Dweck, C. S., & Sorich, L. (1999). Mastery-oriented thinking. In C. R. Snyder (Ed.), *Coping* (pp. 232–251). New York: Oxford University Press.

Dykman, B. M. (1998). Integrating cognitive and motivational factors in depression: Initial tests of a goal-orientation approach. *Journal of Personality and Social Psychology, 74,* 139–158.

Elliot, A. J., & Church, M. A. (1997). A hierarchical model of approach and avoidance achievement motivation. *Journal of Personality and Social Psychology, 72,* 218–232.

Elliot, A. J., & Harackiewicz, J. M. (1996). Approach and avoidance achievement goals and intrinsic motivation: A mediational analysis. *Journal of Personality and Social Psychology, 70,* 461–475.

Elliot, A. J., & McGregor, H. A. (2001). A 2 × 2 achievement goal framework. *Journal of Personality and Social Psychology, 80,* 501–519.

Elliot, A. J., McGregor, H. A., & Gable, S. (1999). Achievement goals, study strategies, and exam performance: A mediational analysis. *Journal of Education Psychology, 91,* 549–563.

Elliott, E. S., & Dweck, C. S. (1988). Goals: An approach to motivation and achievement. *Journal of Personality and Social Psychology, 54,* 5–12.

Elliot, A. J., Shell, M. M., Henry, K. B., & Maier, M. A. (2005). Achievement goals, performance contingencies, and performance attainment: An experimental test. *Journal of Educational Psychology, 97,* 630–640.

Emmons, R. A. (1989). The personal striving approach to personality. In L. A. Pervin (Ed.), *Goal concepts in personality and social psychology* (pp. 87–126). Hillsdale, NJ: Erlbaum.

Erdley, C. A., & Asher, S. R. (1996). Children's social goals and self-efficacy perceptions as predictors of their responses to ambiguous provocation. *Child Development, 67,* 1329–1344.

Erdley, C. A., Cain, K. M., Loomis, C. C., Dumas-Hines, F., & Dweck, C. S. (1997). The relations among children's social goals, implicit personality theories, and responses to social failure. *Developmental Psychology, 33,* 263–272.

Feather, N. T. (1982). Expectancy-value approaches: Present status and future directions. In N. T. Feather (Ed.), *Expectations and actions: Expectancy-value models in psychology* (pp. 395–420). Hillsdale, NJ: Erlbaum.

Förster, J., Grant, H., Idson, L. & Higgins, E. T. (2001). When does the "goal loom larger"? Approach and avoidance strength as a function of regulatory focus and success versus failure feedback. *Journal of Experimental Social Psychology, 37,* 253–260.

Gelety, L. S., & Grant, H. (2008). *The impact of achievement goals and difficulty on mood, motivation, and performance.* Manuscript submitted for publication.

Goetz, T. S., & Dweck, C. S. (1980). Learned helplessness in social situations. *Journal of Personality and Social Psychology, 39,* 246–255.

Gollwizter, P. M., & Moskowitz, G. B. (1996). Goal effects on action and cognition. In E. T. Higgins & A. W. Kruglanski (Eds.), *Social psychology: Handbook of basic principles* (pp. 361–399). New York: Guilford Press.

Grant, H., Baer, A. R., & Dweck, C. S. (2008). *Personal goals predict the level and impact of dysphoria.* Manuscript submitted for publication.

Grant, H., Baer, A. R., Gelety, L. S., & Dweck, C. S. (2008). *Is depressed affect good or bad for performance? The moderating role of achievement goals.* Manuscript submitted for publication.

Grant, H., & Dweck, C. S. (1999a). Content vs. structure in motivation and self-regulation. In R. Wyer (Ed.), *Advances in Social Cognition* (Vol. 12, pp. 161–174). Mahwah, NJ: Erlbaum.

Grant, H., & Dweck, C. S. (1999b). A goal analysis of personality and personality coherence. In D. Cervone & Y. Shoda (Eds.), *The coherence of personality* (pp. 345–371). New York: Guilford Press.

Grant, H., & Dweck, C. S. (2003). Clarifying achievement goals and their impact. *Journal of Personality and Social Psychology, 85,* 541–553.

Grant, H., & Higgins, E. T. (2003). Optimism, promotion pride, and prevention pride as predictors of well-being. *Personality and Social Psychology Bulletin, 29*(12), 1521–1532.

Grouzet, F. M. E., Kasser, T., Ahuvia, A., Dols, J. M. F., Kim, Y., Lau, S., et al. (2005). The structure of goal contents across 15 cultures. *Journal of Personality and Social Psychology, 89,* 800–816.

Harackiewicz, J. M., & Elliot, A. J. (1993). Achievement goals and intrinsic motivation. *Journal of Personality and Social Psychology, 65,* 904–915.

Heyman, G. D., & Dweck, C. S. (1992). Achievement goals and intrinsic motivation: Their relation and their role in adaptive motivation. *Motivation and Emotion, 16*(3), 231–247.

Higgins, E. T. (1987). Self-discrepancy: A theory relating self and affect. *Psychological Review, 94,* 319–340.

Higgins, E. T. (1997). Beyond pleasure and pain. *American Psychologist, 52,* 1280–1300.

Higgins, E. T., Grant, H., & Shah, J. (1999). Self-regulation and quality of life: Emotional and non-emotional life experiences. In D. Kahneman, E. Diener, & N. Schwarz (Eds.), *Well-being: The foundations of hedonic psychology* (pp. 244–266). New York: Russell Sage.

Higgins, E. T., Roney, C., Crowe, E., & Hymes, C. (1994). Ideal versus ought predilections for approach and avoidance: Distinct self-regulatory systems. *Journal of Personality and Social Psychology, 66,* 276–286.

Idson, L. C., Liberman, N., & Higgins, E. T. (2000). Distinguishing gains from non-losses and losses from non-gains: A regulatory focus perspective on hedonic intensity. *Journal of Experimental Social Psychology, 36*(3), 252–274.

Jagacinski, C. M., & Nicholls, J. G. (1987). Competence and affect in task involvement and ego involvement: The impact of social comparison information. *Journal of Educational Psychology, 79,* 107–114.

Kamins, M. L., Morris, S. M., & Dweck, C. S. (1997). *Implicit theories as predictors of goals in dating relationships.* Poster presented at the Annual Meeting of the Eastern Psychological Association, Washington, D.C.

Kaplan, A., & Maehr, M. L. (2007). The contributions and prospects of goal orientation theory. *Educational Psychology Review, 19,* 141–184.

Kaplan, A., & Midgley, C. (1997). The effect of achievement goals: Does level of perceived academic competence make a difference? *Contemporary Educational Psychology, 22,* 415–435.

Klinger, E. (1977). *Meaning and void: Inner experience and the incentives in people's lives.* Minneapolis: University of Minnesota Press.

Kruglanski, A. W., & Shah, J. Y. (1997, October 23–26). *Intrinsic and extrinsic motivation: A little structure, a little substance.* Paper presented at the Meeting of the Society for Experimental Social Psychology, Toronto, Canada.

La Greca, A. M., Dandes, S. K., Wick, P., Shaw, K., & Stone, W. (1988). Development of social anxiety scale for children: Reliability and concurrent validity. *Journal of Consulting Clinical Psychology, 17,* 84–91.

Lepper, M. R. (1981). Intrinsic and extrinsic motivation in children: Detrimental effects of superfluous social controls. In W. A. Collins (Ed.), *Aspects of the development of competence: The Minnesota Symposium on Child Psychology* (Vol. 14, pp. 155–214). Hillsdale, NJ: Erlbaum.

Liberman, N., Molden, D. C., Idson, L. C., & Higgins, E. T. (2001). Promotion and prevention focus on alternative hypotheses: Implications for attributional functions. *Journal of Personality and Social Psychology, 80,* 5–18.

Little, B. R. (1989). Personal projects analysis: Trivial pursuits, magnificent obsessions, and the search for coherence. In D. M. Buss & N. Cantor (Eds.), *Personality psychology: Recent trends and emerging directions.* New York: Springer-Verlag.

Maehr, M. L., & Midgley, C. (1991). Enhancing student motivation: A schoolwide approach. *Educational Psychologist, 26,* 399–427.

Midgley, C., Anderman, E., & Hicks, L. (1995). Differences between elementary and middle school teachers: A goal theory approach. *Journal of Early Adolescence, 15,* 90–113.

Miller, R. B., Behrens, J. T., Greene, B. A., & Newman, D. (1993). Goals and perceived ability: Impact on student valuing, self-regulation, and persistence. *Contemporary Educational Psychology, 18,* 2–14.

Nichols, J. G. (1984). Achievement motivation: Conceptions of ability, subjective experience, task choice, and performance. *Psychological Review, 91,* 328–346.

Pekrun, R., Elliot, A. J., & Maier, M. A. (2006). Achievement goals and discrete achievement emotions: A theoretical model and prospective test. *Journal of Educational Psychology, 98,* 583–597.

Pintrich, P. R. (2000). An achievement goal theory perspective on issues in motivation terminology, theory, and research. *Contemporary Educational Psychology, 25,* 92–104.

Pintrich, P. R., & DeGroot, E. V. (1990). Motivational and self-regulated learning components of classroom academic performance. *Journal of Educational Psychology, 82,* 33–40.

Pintrich, P. R., & Garcia, T. (1991). Student goal orientation and self-regulation in the college classroom. In M. L. Maehr & P. R. Pintrich (Eds.), *Advances in motivation and achievement* (Vol. 7, pp. 371–402). Greenwich, CT: JAI Press.

Poortvliet, P. M., Jannsen, O.,Van Yperen, N. W., & Van de Vliert, E. (2007). Achievement goals and interpersonal behavior: How mastery and performance goals shape information exchange. *Personality and Social Psychology Bulletin, 33,* 1435–1447.

Powers, W. T. (1973). *Behavior: The control of perception.* Chicago: Aldine.

Ryan, A. R., & Shim, S. S. (2006). Social achievement goals: The nature and consequences of different orientations toward social competence. *Personality and Social Psychology Bulletin, 32,* 1246–1263.

Salmela-Aro, K., and Nurmi, J. (1997). Goal contents, well-being, and life context during transition to university: A longitudinal study. *International Journal of Behavioral Development, 20,* 471–491.

Shah, J., & Higgins, E. T. (1997). Expectancy X value effects: Regulatory focus as a determinant of magnitude and direction. *Journal of Personality and Social Psychology, 73,* 447–458.

Shah, J., Higgins, E. T., & Friedman, R. (1998). Performance incentives and means: How regulatory focus influences goal attainment. *Journal of Personality and Social Psychology, 74(2),* 285–293.

Sheldon, K. M., Ryan, R. M., Deci, E. L., & Kasser, T. (2004). The independent effects of goal contents and motives on well-being: It's both what you pursue and why you pursue it. *Personality and Social Psychology Bulletin, 30,* 475–486.

Smiley, P. A., & Dweck, C. S. (1994). Individual differences in achievement goals among young children. *Child Development, 65,* 1723–1743.

Taylor, A. R., & Asher, S. R. (1989). *Children's goals in game playing situations.* Paper presented at the Annual Meeting of the American Psychological Association, New York.

Urdan, T. (1997). Examining the relations among early adolescent students' goals and friends' orientation toward effort and achievement in school. *Contemporary Educational Psychology, 22,* 165–191.

Vandewalle, D. (1997). Development and validation of a work domain goal orientation instrument. *Educational and Psychological Measurement, 57,* 995–1015.

Vansteenkiste, M., Simons, J., Lens, W., Sheldon, K. M., & Deci, E. L. (2004). Motivating learning, performance, and persistence: The synergistic effects of intrinsic goal contents and autonomy-supportive contexts. *Journal of Personality and Social Psychology, 87,* 246–260.

Weiner, B. (1985). An attributional theory of achievement motivation and emotion. *Psychological Review, 92,* 548–573.

Wolters, C. A. (1998). Self-regulated learning and college students' regulation of motivation. *Journal of Educational Psychology, 90(2),* 224–235.

CHAPTER 4

The Neuroscience of Goal Pursuit
BRIDGING GAPS BETWEEN THEORY AND DATA

ELLIOT T. BERKMAN
MATTHEW D. LIEBERMAN

Goal pursuit is a multifaced enterprise that requires coordination among several psychological processes. For example, the goal of finding a job requires a plan to apply and interview, a mechanism to initiate the plan, a set of criteria for offer acceptance, and a way of monitoring progress along the way. An attempt to get a job with only some but not all of these parts would almost surely result in failure, as each element is necessary. Researchers in neuroscience have examined many of these processes, but often in isolation without considering the broader context of a goal-pursuit framework. This chapter links process-level neuroscience evidence to the cognitive-behavioral level of goal-pursuit theories. Utilizing psychological theory to organize neuroscience evidence offers advantages to both sides of the equation. New theoretical insights can be forged through patterns of association and dissociation among the neural networks involved in various goal-pursuit processes. Additionally, gaps in the current neuroscience literature on goal processes are conspicuous once the existing evidence is organized within a theoretical framework, providing avenues for new research. This chapter reviews a common model for goal pursuit in light of recent neuroscience findings, with the hope that it will prove useful to psychologists studying goal pursuit and social neuroscientists.

Overview

We take as our starting point several goal-pursuit models put forth by social and cognitive psychologists, such as the test–operate–test–exit (TOTE) cybernetic model (Carver & Scheier, 1998; Miller, Galanter, & Pribram, 1960), various discrepancy-reduction models (Higgins, Roney, Crowe, & Hymes, 1994; Wicklund & Gollwitzer, 1981), and action planning models (Gollwitzer, 1990; Kuhl, 1984). Rather than focus on any one model to adopt as a framework, we have selected three components common to most models of goal pursuit. We see each of the following steps as places where psychological theory and neuroscience data complement each other and help generate insights for both fields.

The first step in goal pursuit involves simply having a goal to pursue and holding it in memory. "Goal representation" refers to the mental process of maintaining a goal or desired end-state at least during a period of goal pursuit (e.g., be friendly during a brief interview for a job), and possibly much longer (e.g., being a nice person over the course of one's life). The second step in goal pursuit is the intention to pursue the goal (cf. Bargh and Chartrand, 1999, on automatic activation of goal pursuit). Intention typically serves as the motivating force that comes between holding a goal in memory and initiating goal-pursuit behavior. As such, intention seems to have a cognitive, planning aspect (e.g. "When X happens, I will do Y") and a motivational aspect (e.g., wanting to pursue the goal, expecting positive outcomes from pursuit). To act upon an intention is to engage in *goal action,* which is characterized in terms of four subcomponents: attention, motor control, response inhibition, and progress monitoring.

Few neuroscience studies explicitly address goal pursuit, but many address components (or subcomponents) of goal pursuit mentioned above. Our review focuses on findings regarding the goal-pursuit components, and particularly on those that seem to be integral to goal pursuit overall. In some cases, the available neuroscience evidence is tangential to the study of goal pursuit in general. For these cases, we identify which aspects of the research might be relevant to goal pursuit and try to point the way toward more pertinent studies. We review each component in turn, first giving a brief discussion of the social psychological research in the area then reviewing the relevant neuroscience findings. In addition, we point out connections to other components of goal pursuit and to related processes that have received attention in neuroscience. Comparing the psychology and neuroscience findings allows us to highlight the gaps in the extant neuroscience research for each component, and also divergences between the social psychology and neuroscience findings.

We conclude with a discussion of several caveats, complications, and further directions in the neuroscience of goal pursuit. First, one broad difference between the social psychological and neuroscience findings is the distinction between short- and long-term goal pursuits. In general, psychologists are concerned with long-term goal pursuit, lasting weeks, months, or years (such as weight loss, career success, etc.). In contrast, insofar as neuroscientists study goals, they tend to study short-term goals, lasting seconds or minutes (such as success on a laboratory task or on the next trial of a task). We attempt to answer some of the questions that this distinction raises and to capitalize on the commonalities across the literatures. Second, researchers in social psychology (Schneirla, 1959; Miller, 1959; Gray, 1970; Carver & Scheier, 1982; Higgins, 1997; Elliot & Thrash, 2002) and neuroscience (Cunningham, Raye, & Johnson, 2005; Canli et al., 2001) have investigated *approach and avoidance motivation* and its relation to goal pursuit. We believe that this is a crucial construct for goal pursuit and highlight findings that demonstrate the role of this individual difference during goal pursuit. Finally, recent research has begun to examine the possibility of goal pursuit outside of conscious awareness (e.g., Bargh & Chartrand, 1999; Mauss, Evers, Wilhelm, & Gross, 2006). For each component, we highlight what is known about the automatic and controlled parts and point to areas where further understanding is needed.

The Neuroscience of the Goal Pursuit

Goal Representation

From where do we get our goals? Two possible places are from internal sources—from the mental image of who we'd like to be, or our immediate desires such as finding something sweet to eat—and from external sources—the things other people would like us to do, or nonsocial cues from the environment (e.g., being in a library may help motivate studying). Previous empirical and theoretical work by social psychologists has investigated the analogous distinction between intrinsic and extrinsic goals (Sheldon, Ryan, Deci, & Kasser, 2004; Deci & Ryan, 2000). Findings from this area have emphasized the importance of three intrinsic goals or needs—competence, relatedness, and autonomy—for achieving and maintaining well-being. From this perspective, extrinsic goals are evaluated in terms of how well they become internalized to align with intrinsic goals. For example, an employee may be given a task by her boss (an extrinsic goal) but might think about the task differently so that it also fulfills her intrinsic goal of being a competent worker. In this theory, goal representation is an active process that frequently involves re-representing extrinsic goals as intrinsic in a process called "assimilation."

Research in neuroscience has also uncovered distinctions between internal and external mental representations, although only representation of extrinsic goals has been considered explicitly. However, findings from extensive neuroscience studies on introspection might apply to representation of intrinsic goals. Extrinsic goals are typically provided for us from the outside. A perhaps trivial (yet relevant) example is that of experimental participants, who accept the instructions from the experimenter as their own goal for the duration of the experiment. Internalization is not typically measured and may not occur in any meaningful way. At least for a few minutes, undergraduates are able to pursue a goal that was given to them from without. A vast body of literature suggests that the orbital and lateral parts of the prefrontal cortex (PFC) are essential for maintaining these *if–then*, rule-based performance goals (see Table 4.1; Miller, 1999; Cohen & Servan-Schreiber, 1992; Wise, Murray, & Gerfen, 1996). The conceptual distinction made by social psychologists between internally and externally generated goals is paralleled by a neural distinction of medial and lateral PFC networks, respectively (Lieberman, 2007).

The paradigmatic externally derived goal in psychology experiments is to succeed on a task such as the color-word Stroop task (Stroop, 1935; Macleod & Mathews, 1991). In this task, participants are presented with color words printed in an incongruent ink color (e.g., "red" written in blue ink). Although the automatic response is to read the word, the externally provided goal is to say the color of the ink. This task requires maintenance of an if–then rule in memory and also, on some trials, the top-down inhibition of a prepotent response, making it a popular laboratory approximation of the demands of "real-world" goal pursuit. This type of task typically activates the dorsolateral prefrontal and anterior cingulate cortices. However, it has only recently become clear how these regions each contribute to task performance. An experiment by MacDonald, Cohen, Stenger, and Carter (2000) dissociated the brain regions involved in the two parts of the task (rule maintenance, conflict detection) by inserting a delay between the instructions and the word presentation. In the first phase, participants were instructed to pronounce either the word ("word" trials) or the color ("color" trials) of the upcoming stimulus. After a pause of a few seconds, the stimulus was presented in the second phase. The first part of the task required only the maintenance of the trial-specific goal, and the second part of the task required top-down regulation (in the color trials). Consistent with other evidence regarding rule-based processing (Baker, Frith, Frackowiak, & Dolan, 1996; Fletcher, Shallice, & Dolan, 1998), the dorsolateral PFC was active only during the first portion of the task. Another region, the anterior cingulate cortex (ACC) was active only during the second portion, and within that portion, only active during trials that required inhibition of prepotent responses (e.g., during the color trials). We return to the ACC and its role in goal pursuit in subsequent sections. Critically, the authors conclude that the dorsolateral PFC

TABLE 4.1. Summary of Social-Psychological Findings, Neuroscience Findings, and Unanswered Questions for Goal Pursuit

	Pursuit					
	Representation	Intention	Attention	Motor control	Response inhibition	Progress monitoring
Psychological findings	Intrinsic versus extrinsic goals	Connect a behavior to a situation Translate abstract goals to concrete behavior Affected by approach–avoidance	Attention to goal in context Attention to goal-relevant cues Automatic activation of attention Modulated by approach–avoidance	Stimulus evaluations impact and are impacted by lever push–pull Motivation impacts push–pull	Self-control and self-regulation Situational and personality moderators	Discrepancy detection and discrepancy reduction Distinct effects of discrepancy from approach and avoidance goals
Brain regions involved	Intrinsic: medial PFC, medial parietal Extrinsic: lateral PFC, lateral parietal	Readiness potential: SMA, premotor cortex Prepatory set: dorsolateral PFC, SFG	Exogenous: ACC, SMA, FEF, TPJ, superior parietal cortex Endogenous: exogenous and anterior PFC	Primary motor cortex, SMA, premotor cortex Cerebellum and basal ganglia	Dorsolateral and ventral PFC, ACC	Detection: ACC Reduction: PFC
Unanswered questions	Representation of time duration? Representation of abstractness?	Neural correlates of approach–avoidance framing of intention?	For automatic goal pursuit, is attention impacted by awareness?	Separable neural systems for approaching/avoiding?	Further specificity within PFC? Different types of inhibition?	Is conflict detected in the planning or execution of action? Implications for long-term goals?

Note. ACC, anterior cingulate cortex; FEF, frontal eye fields (superior frontal gyrus); PFC, prefrontal cortex; SFG, superior frontal gyrus; SMA, supplementary motor area; TPJ, temporal parietal junction.

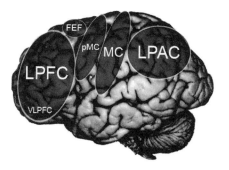 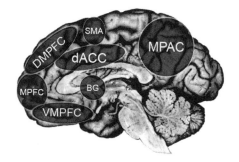

FIGURE 4.1. Key brain regions implicated in the pursuit of goals. BG, basal ganglia; dACC, dorsal anterior cingulate cortex; DMPFC, dorsomedial prefrontal cortex; FEF, frontal eye fields (superior frontal gyrus); LPAC, lateral parietal cortex; LPFC, lateral prefrontal cortext; MC, primary motor cortex; MPAC, medial parietal cortex; MPFC, medial prefrontal cortex; pMC, premotor cortex; SMA, supplementary motor area; VLPFC, ventrolateral prefrontal cortex; VMPFC, ventromedial prefrontal cortex. Note: The basal ganglia is a subcortical structure presented here on the medial surface for ease of presentation.

is integral in maintaining rules and planning rule-based action as in goal pursuit.

Other recent findings have sharpened these conclusions by separating the brain activations related to maintenance of the task goal from those related to processing the visual stimuli of the task. By employing several versions of the Stroop task across multiple stimulus types (e.g., pictures, words presented visually, words presented aurally), Banich and colleagues (Banich et al., 2000; Herd, Banich, & O'Reilly, 2006) found that regions in dorsolateral PFC and inferior parietal cortex are involved in the Stroop task independent of stimulus modality. Another study reported increased activity in lateral parietal regions during maintenance of rules during a visual response contingency task (Bunge, Kahn, Wallis, Miller, & Wagner, 2003). These studies converge on the finding that the dorsolateral PFC and parietal cortex are involved in representing the rules involved in maintaining extrinsic goals.

Although there have yet to be studies directly investigating the neural correlates of intrinsic goals, there is a growing number of conceptually related studies on introspection of internal states (Kihlstrom & Klein, 1997). Studies that compare internal appraisals about current states (e.g., "Do I like this painting?") or traits (e.g., "Do I possess this trait?") to matched non-self-judgments (e.g., "Is the picture of an indoor or outdoor scene?," "Is this a good or bad trait?") consistently find increased activation in medial PFC and medial parietal cortex (Ochsner et al., 2005; Lieberman, Jarcho, & Satpute, 2004; Gusnard, Akbudak, Shulman, &

Raichle, 2001; Ochsner et al., 2004). Finally, one study reported greater medial prefrontal cortical activation while reflecting upon personal hopes and aspirations than distraction (Johnson et al., 2006). In light of these findings it seems reasonable to speculate that the representation of intrinsic goals might make use of these self-reflective processes and the network of associated neural regions.

Evidence presented in this section leads us toward two observations regarding goal representation. First, the PFC broadly is involved in the generation and maintenance of goal representation. Second, there may be subdivisions within the PFC that make different contributions to goal representation. Insofar as goals are derived from sources internal to the actor such as traits, motives, and desires, those goals might be represented medially. Likewise, insofar as goals are derived from situational cues and maintained by if–then rules that are not internal to an actor, they seem to be represented laterally.

In addition to the distinction between intrinsic and extrinsic goals, psychologists have also discussed two other important dimensions of goal representation: abstractness and temporal duration. For example, on one hand brushing one's teeth and flossing are concrete goals that last only a few moments. On the other, maintaining oral hygiene is a more abstract goal that can endure over years and decades. Psychologists have noted that goals can often be represented hierarchically, with more abstract, longer-term goals at the top, and more concrete, shorter-term goals (sometimes called "plans") at the bottom (Elliot & Church, 1997; Carver & Scheier, 1998; Vallacher & Wegner, 1987). The hierarchy construct is useful because it allows clusters of related goals to be represented simultaneously and within the same framework, with abstract long-term goals (*oral hygiene*) being instantiated behaviorally by concrete short-term goals (*flossing, brushing*). Given that long- and short-term goals can be intrinsic and extrinsic (e.g., wanting to be a good person vs. being told to be a good American by the president; wanting a piece of candy vs. participating in an experiment), temporal duration and goal locus seem to be separate dimensions.

Neuroscientists have yet to examine long-term goals. Although methodological constraints limit our ability to examine the representation of long-term goals in a magnetic resonance imaging (MRI) scanner (e.g., imaging participants while they engage in the task of being a good American), an initial step would be to extend our existing knowledge of short-term goals to slightly broader ones, termed here "medium-term" goals. Medium-term goals would be brief in duration yet still conceptually connected to an individual's abstract, long-term goals, making them ideal for the present purposes. Although it would be difficult to investigate the long-term, abstract goal of physical well-being in a functional MRI (fMRI) scanner, it would be possible to characterize the representation of that goal by examining successful and unsuccessful episodes of constituent behavioral goals. For example, participants might be led to succeed at one task that requires selectively responding to healthy activities, but be led to fail at another task that requires inhibiting responses to unhealthy foods (or vice versa). Evaluations of goal progress will then differ depending on whether participants are focused on the immediate task or on the abstract goal. This design could clarify several questions regarding the duration of goal pursuit, such as whether a longer-term inhibitory goal recruits similar or different regions than a shorter-tem goal, whether the same inhibitory strategies are used for both types of goals, and which brain regions (if any) predict success at the long-term goal. This type of study would begin to build a more sophisticated model of if and how our brains use hierarchies to organize goals and connect long-term abstract objectives with concrete behaviors.

Goal Intention

Regardless of whether the source of a goal is internal or external, once an individual has a goal in mind it must be linked to behavior. Social psychologists have termed the critical link between goal representation and goal pursuit behavior intention, and examined it in the context of specific *implementation intentions*, or self-statements in the form of "in situation *x*, I will engage in behavior *y*" (Gollwitzer, 1996; Gollwitzer & Brandstatter, 1997). Implementation intentions serve a dual purpose in the goal-pursuit process. First, they connect a specific behavior to a specific situation, thereby creating a contextual association in memory. Once an implementation intention is formed, the situation itself becomes a cue that, when encountered, increases the likelihood of the action. For instance, Gollwitzer and Brandstatter (1997) found that participants who formed an implementation intention to counterargue a persuasive message at a certain point during the message did so more frequently and closer to the intended time than participants with no implementation intention. Second, implementation intentions provide a bridge from more abstract to more concrete aspects of the goal (Vallacher & Wegner, 1987). Whereas a highly abstract goal may have no obvious behavioral expression ("to be a good person"), creating an implementation intention demands a specific realization of that goal which can actually be implemented ("to help elderly people when I see them having trouble getting on the bus"). This translation from more abstract to less abstract also provides a means of transforming a long-term goal into a more specific and actionable short-term goal (Trope & Liberman, 2003).

A related thread regarding the leap from goal representation to goal-related behavior comes from the motivation literature, which suggests that intention can arise from personality-level approach and avoidance tendencies (Elliot & Church, 1997; Elliot & Thrash, 2002). In these conceptualizations, goal representations serve as the pathway from broad and abstract approach–avoidance tendencies to specific behavior. As such, internally generated goals reflect an individual's underlying motivations to approach incentives, avoid punishments, or some combination thereof, providing the why behind the goal intent's how. This theory has at least two implications for the current discussion. First, the goal representation itself might be modulated by approach–avoidance motivation. In an experimental context, a goal might be represented as "to do well on the task," or as "to avoid doing poorly on the task," in approach or avoidance orientations, respectively. Second, how an individual intends to pursue a goal might also be modulated by approach–avoidance motivation. Given the same goal, a relatively approach-oriented person might adopt a strategy designed to maximize rewards whereas a relatively avoidance-oriented person might adopt one that minimizes punishments. Furthermore, these differential strategies can lead to effects on performance (Elliot & Church, 1997; Higgins et al., 1994).

In contrast to the rich theoretical attention goal intention has received in social psychology, relatively few studies have explored the neural mechanisms underlying intention. The studies that have can be divided into two categories. The first category addresses the relation between conscious intention and the neural sources of that intention. Using electroencephalography (EEG) to measure neural activity, Libet and colleagues identified a neural event associated with voluntary movement—the readiness potential (RP)—that occurs 500–1000 milliseconds prior to movement, and even prior to the conscious experience of intending movement (Libet, Gleason, Wright, & Pearl, 1983; Libet, 1985). The RP has subsequently been localized to the supplementary motor area and precentral gyrus (Cheyne, Bakhatazad, & Gaetz, 2006). Converging evidence for this localization comes from a neural stimulation study, which found that stimulation of the supplementary motor area produced an urge to move a particular body part, or the subjective feeling of impending motion (Fried et al., 1991). Although there continues to be debate concerning exactly what the RP represents and its precise role in signaling intent (see Libet, 1999, for discussion), it is at least clear that supplementary motor areas in the frontal cortex precede behavior and are also associated with the experience of intention. Although these experiments did not involve goals per se, the processes involved in transforming action to behavior in general may be similar to those involved in goal pursuit.

The second category of studies that links mental representation of goals to future action examines neural control of visual saccades. Studies in this area have operationalized intent as *preparatory set*, or the set of neural events that immediately precedes voluntary action (Connolly, Goodale, Menon, & Munoz, 2002; Everling & Munoz, 2000; Funahashi, Chafee, & Goldman-Rakic, 1993; Schlag-Rey, Amador, Sanchez, & Schlag, 1997). In these experiments, participants in the scanner are first shown a central cue (e.g., a colored circle) that indicates later eye movement either toward a target (green) or away from the target (red). Next, after a brief pause, the target appears in the periphery, and the participant is instructed to saccade toward (prosaccade) or away (antisaccade) from the target according to the earlier cue. Although the prepotent orienting response is a prosaccade, participants are given enough onset latency that they can easily antisaccade with only a slightly longer response time. The crucial distinction is that pro- and antisaccade conditions contain rule-based planning for action, but only the antisaccade condition is necessarily "intentional" because it requires something other than the prepotent response. More precisely, the gap period after cue onset but before target onset is thought to reflect an intention to act in the antisaccade condition. By comparing the gap periods of the prosaccade and antisaccade conditions, these studies have isolated the preparatory set for intentional eye movements. Imaging results have shown greater relative activation during intention periods in the frontal eye fields (superior frontal gyrus), dorsolateral PFC, and dorsal premotor activity. Although the frontal eye fields (which are involved in control of eye movement) may be specific to intentional eye movement, the activity in prefrontal and premotor regions might be a reflection of intentional action across goal domains.

Although suggestive, the neuroscience studies thus far only capture the first layer of complexity in intentional goal pursuit. The antisaccade paradigm seems to map onto the structure of implementation intentions (e.g., "when I see a red cue, I will move my eyes away from the target") but does not capture either the underlying needs or motives within the individual that implementation intentions serve or broader, less context-dependent intentions (e.g., "I intend to study hard for the upcoming exam") that are unlikely to recruit motor processes. An examination of trait motivation in the context of intention can address these issues and provide a further avenue for neuroscience research. For example, it might well be possible that implementation intentions are flavored by dispositional approach and avoidance motivation, and that individual differences interact with the relative approach or avoidance framing of the goal. These differences have already been shown to affect performance (Elliot & Church, 1997); differences in the framing of the intention (e.g., whether to avoid failure or approach success) seem to be reasonable place to begin the search for pathways to performance. Employing neuroscience techniques, such as by examining neural pathways for reward and punishment, could further illuminate the approach- and avoidance-related changes in goal intention.

Goal Action

Following intention the next phase in most goal models is goal-oriented action itself: the actual goal-relevant behavior. For the present purposes, we have divided the goal-pursuit operation into four parts that occur in concert: attention to goal-relevant cues, direct motor control in service of goals, inhibition of distractions internal (e.g., emotions, irrelevant cognitions) and external (e.g., incorrect or task-irrelevant cues), and progress monitoring. Attentional processes must be recruited to direct attention to goal-relevant cues. This includes conscious attentional control (e.g., seeking out broccoli instead of French fries), and also possibly nonconscious attentional biasing toward goal-relevant or away from goal-irrelevant cues. Motor control is necessary to direct behavior toward the goal. Response inhibition is necessary to control goal-violating prepotent responses (e.g., avoiding tempting but unhealthy food for someone with the goal of eating less). Finally, an ongoing progress monitoring mechanism is necessary to continuously monitor behavior vis-à-vis the goal, draw attention to discrepancies when they are detected, and adjust behavior to advance progress toward the goal.

Attention

At least two forms of attention seem to be required for successful goal pursuit. For longer-term goals, which might not always be in the mental foreground (e.g., dieting), a process to identify goal-relevant contexts and to draw attention to the goal in these contexts is essential. For short-term goals, or once a long-term goal context is identified, attentional processes might be recruited to identify goal-relevant cues within the present context (Posner & Petersen, 1990). For instance, during dieting an individual first must recognize that the present meal is an opportunity to pursue the dieting goal. Next, it would be useful to attend to cues that are relevant to dieting, such as healthy items on the menu (goal-consistent) and unhealthy desserts to avoid (goal-inconsistent). Psychologists have investigated both processes. In terms of attending to long-term goals within a goal-relevant situation, implementation intentions seem to serve the purpose of drawing attention to goals by linking situational cues to those goals. Also, Bargh and colleagues (Bargh, 1990; Bargh, Gollwitzer, Lee-Chai, Barndollar, & Troetschel, 2001) have provided support for the possibility of nonconscious activation of goals simply by being exposed to a relevant context. At least for long-terms goals that are relatively practiced and familiar (e.g., achievement, cooperation), goal-context cues in and of themselves seem to be enough to launch behavioral goal pursuit, seemingly bypassing conscious attention to the goal.

Psychologists have also offered evidence of automatic attention to goal-relevant cues in short-term goal pursuit. Derryberry and Reed (1994) demonstrated that the approach- and avoidance-related personality dimensions of extraversion and neuroticism relate to differential attention to positive and negative cues. Specifically, under voluntary and involuntary orienting conditions, people high in approach but low in avoidance were slower to draw attention away from positive cues, and people low in approach but high in avoidance were slower to draw attention away from negative cues. Other psychologists have studied "goal shielding" (Shah, Friedman, & Kruglanski, 2002) demonstrating that as various factors such as goal commitment and fit between goal type and trait approach–avoidance motivation increase, attention to the primary goal increases and distraction from secondary goals decreases.

Decades of neuroscience studies have investigated voluntary control of visual attention, which consistently corresponds to increased activation in the anterior cingulate, supplementary motor area, the frontal eye fields, and the temporal-parietal junction (TPJ; Posner & Petersen, 1990; Ro, Henik, Machado, & Rafal, 1997; Posner, Walker, Friedrich, & Rafal, 1984). Studies that have attempted to separate neural systems involved in willful (i.e., endogenous) versus cued (i.e., exogenous) shifts in attention have been generally unfruitful, with two notable exceptions (Nobre et al., 1997; Rosen et al., 1999). Both of these studies found similar patterns of activation across endogenous and exogenous attention, except areas in the medial (Nobre et al., 1997) and dorsolateral PFC (Rosen et al., 1999), which were selectively active during endogenous control trials. The authors noted this difference in the PFC and concluded that both types of attention are mediated by a single system involving the frontal eye fields, supplementary motor area, superior parietal cortex, TPJ, and ACC. The tentative conclusion is that although visual attention in general recruits a network of premotor, motor control and visual areas, only willful control of attention recruits anterior parts of the PFC.

Research on attention-deficit/hyperactivity disorder (ADHD) presents another pathway to investigating attentional processes involved in goal pursuit. ADHD is characterized by persistent inattention, impulsivity, and hyperactivity (Barkley, 1997), indicating a lack of components essential to successful goal pursuit. Research has implicated several brain regions in the inattention component of ADHD. Regions that are relatively inactive in adults with ADHD may contribute to attention to goals in normal adults. One positron emission tomography (PET) study found reduced glucose metabolism in premotor and superior prefrontal cortex in adults with ADHD compared to unimpaired adults (Zametkin et al., 1990), and several fMRI studies have documented the role of the ACC in the attentional deficit component of ADHD (Bush et al., 1999; Carter et al., 1998; Bar-

kley, Grodzinsky, & DuPaul, 1992). Patients with ADHD in these studies demonstrate selective ACC hypoactivity during tasks with competition
among attentional resources, suggesting the ACC to be involved in modulating attention selection.

In light of social psychological studies on attention to goal cues, the
possibility of automatic and nonconscious attention is one notable gap in
the existing neuroscience data. Participants in several social psychological studies (e.g., Derryberry & Reed, 1994; Bargh et al., 2001) have been
shown to orient toward goal cues and engage in goal pursuit while being
completely unaware of both actions. The attentional processes engaged by
these participants seems qualitatively different than that in neuroscience
studies of exogenous attention shifts because the lack of awareness in the
former. It remains an open question as to whether unaware attention is
distinct from aware attention (voluntary or involuntary), and whether the
two processes recruit distinct or overlapping neural networks. A first step to
answering these questions would be to use fMRI to scan participants who
were involuntarily attending to different cues, but who are either aware or
unaware of their attention. The experiment could be done in an achievement context by flashing the same "achievement" cues for either 500 milliseconds (aware) or 50 milliseconds (unaware) centrally before participants
complete a task that measures attention such as the dot-probe task (Tamir
& Robinson, 2004). In both cases attention to the achievement-related
cues in the dot-probe would be involuntary, but participants in the shorter
cue condition would be unaware of the achievement prime. Results could
show that some of the same regions that had previously been associated
only with voluntary and aware attentional control were also associated
with involuntary and unaware attention.

Direct Motor Control

Although a complete review of psychological studies of motor control
would be well beyond the scope of this chapter, it is worth noting an interesting set of studies regarding approach–avoidance motivation and motor
control. Using a lever push–pull paradigm (Duckworth, Bargh, Garcia, &
Chaiken, 2002), several studies have demonstrated that positive stimulus
evaluations facilitate level pulling, and negative stimulus evaluations facilitate level pushing (Solarz, 1960; Chen & Bargh, 1999). Several other studies have demonstrated this effect on a trait motivation level, where dispositional approach facilitates pulling and dispositional avoidance facilitates
pushing (Neumann & Strack, 2000; Epley & Gilovich, 2001). One study
(Fishbach & Shah, 2006) even demonstrated that a brief training to "pull"
in response to healthy foods and "push" in response to unhealthy foods
increased subsequent interest in healthy foods.

Neuroanatomically, the main regions for motor control relative to goal pursuit are the primary motor cortex (BA4), the supplementary motor area and premotor cortex (BA6), the presupplementary motor area (BA8), and the cerebellum and basal ganglia (Kandel, Schwartz, & Jessell, 1995; Schmahmann & Pandya, 1997). Although there are no direct connections from the PFC to the primary motor cortex, the dorsolateral PFC (BA 46) is connected directly to the supplementary, presupplementary, and premotor areas, as well as to the cerebellum and basal ganglia (Bates & Goldman-Rakic, 1993). Furthermore, the basal ganglia seem to serve as a motor control hub, integrating information from several frontal motor regions and outputting them back to prefrontal, premotor, and motor regions. Their position in the motor network makes them essential to modulating motor control during goal pursuit (Graybiel, Aosaki, Flaherty, & Kimura, 1994).

Response Inhibition

People pursuing goals are faced with an assortment of hurdles along the way such as intrusive thoughts or emotions, attractive yet task-irrelevant behaviors, and prepotent or automatic behavioral responses that run counter to one's goal. For example, given the long-term goal of being healthy, a person might experience a feeling of dread in anticipation of exercise, might want to watch television instead of exercising, or might desire junk food rather than vegetables. A mechanism for response inhibition is crucial to maintaining goal pursuit by inhibiting goal-irrelevant responses—internal thoughts and emotions and external temptations and distractions. A vast body of social psychological research on self-control and self-regulation addresses this problem (Bandura, 1977; Metcalfe & Mischel, 1999; Muraven & Baumeister, 2000; Trope & Fishbach, 2000). Mediators of self-control can take the form of contextual variables such as available resources (Baumeister, Heatherton, & Tice, 1993; Ward & Mann, 2000) and individual difference variables such as self-efficacy (Bandura, 1982), motivation (Carver & Scheier, 1998; Higgins, Shah, & Friedman, 1997), and emotion regulation (Gross, 2002).

Models from neuroscience tend to be broad frameworks of control rather than specific theories like those in social psychology. Several models suggest that the PFC plays a role in response inhibition by biasing attention and behavior toward goals. These models conceptualize response inhibition as a battle between automatic, "bottom-up" behavior on one hand, and controlled, "top-down" goal behavior on the other. Many forces pull us away from or against our goals, and a major role of the PFC is to guide our attention and behavior through this gauntlet in a "top-down" or executive manner, in a process that is known as top-down excitatory biasing (TEB; Desimone & Duncan, 1995; Miller & Cohen, 2001; Cohen, Dunbar, & McClelland, 1990; Herd et al., 2006). Within a goal pursuit context, TEB can be thought of as a form of attentional control that serves to focus our cognitive resources on a goal or goal-relevant behavior to the exclusion of other temptations or distractions. The PFC is involved in top-down regulation of motor (Horn, Dolan, Elliott, Deakin, & Woodruff, 2003) and nonmotor responses such as cognitions and emotions (Lieberman, in press; Ochsner, Bunge, Gross, & Gabrieli, 2002).

Top-down control encompasses more than just response inhibition. Processes such as goal representation, conflict detection, and progress monitoring are all acting in concert, but they might recruit separable divisions within the PFC (Aron, Robbins, & Poldrack, 2004). Using converging evidence across several inhibitory tasks (e.g., task switching, go/no-go, stop signal), Aron and colleagues have suggested that, although dorsolateral PFC, ventral PFC, and ACC are each activated in tasks that involve inhibition, only the right ventral PFC (inferior frontal gyrus) is necessary for inhibition (Aron et al., 2004). This observation is supported by studies showing patients with lesions to right ventral PFC to have selective deficits in inhibition (Aron, Fletcher, Bullmore, Sahakian, & Robbins, 2003; Aron, Monsell, Sahakian, & Robbins, 2004).

Other evidence in support of this view comes from research on impulsiveness. Individual differences in impulsivity (or in the related construct of novelty seeking) have been linked to the ventral regions of the PFC as well as related subcortical regions in the ventral striatum (Horn et al., 2003). In one recent study, self-reported impulsivity was positively correlated with activity in the caudate and anterior cingulate cortex, and negatively correlated with bilateral ventral PFC during an inhibitory go/no-go task (Brown, Manuck, Flory, & Hariri, 2006). Main effects during the go/no-go task show that participants generally activate the ventral PFC, the ACC, and caudate in no-go relative to go trials. One interpretation of these data is that individuals who are impulsive have stronger impulses to regulate and also less regulatory ability. This interpretation is consistent with the "alarm" theory of the ACC (because participants who are impulsive show greater ACC during no-go relative to go trials), and also with TEB models of ventral PFC involvement in response inhibition (because ventral PFC is recruited more during no-go trials in general but less by individuals who are impulsive). Assuming this interpretation is correct, the construct of impulsivity serves as a wedge to illustrate distinctions within PFC during goal pursuit, with conflict detection being associated with ACC activity and conflict resolution being associated with ventral PFC activity.

In light of the converging evidence for the role of the PFC in TEB broadly and ventral PFC in response inhibition, one path for future research could be to investigate further divergences within that region. As noted above, psychologists have made distinctions between situational and personality moderators of inhibition, and between inhibition of motor and non-motor. Just as we observed differential roles for the medial and lateral parts of the PFC for goal representation, there might there be a comparable split for regulation of internal distractions (e.g., emotions) from external ones (e.g., alternative options), or of situational from personality moderators of response inhibition. Another intriguing question for future research is what neural machinery allows personality moderators such as approach–avoidance motivation to modulate response inhibition during goal pursuit. Clarifying the processes involved in successful response inhibition due to personality factors can further our understanding of those individual differences, and also generate new theories of response inhibition across domains.

Progress Monitoring

To adapt to changing contingencies across time and situations there must be a mechanism to monitor whether or not progress toward the goal is being made. If progress is not being made and is noticed, the relevant adjustment can be made. Progress monitoring is particularly useful for goal pursuit in novel or unexpected situations where previously formed intentions cannot be mapped to all of the contingencies involved in goal pursuit. For example, a smoker who intends to quit might have decided to throw away any cigarettes he might encounter in his desk drawer but still be caught off guard when an acquaintance offers him a cigarette. Ideally, a progress-monitoring mechanism would be active on some level of awareness to spotlight the fact that smoking is not in line with his quitting goal and guide behavior to overcome the habit. Clearly, progress monitoring shares some features of attention (discussed previously), so this review focuses on conceptual distinctions between the two.

Several goal-pursuit theories have incorporated a self-regulatory component in the form of reciprocal *discrepancy detection* and *discrepancy reduction* mechanisms. These mechanisms act in a loop that serves as an alarm when the current state is discrepant from the goal state and also as a guide to point the way toward discrepancy reduction. For example, the hallmark of Carver and Scheier's (1982, 1998) self-regulation model is the "test" phase, which, in a loop with the "operate" phase, guides behavior to reduce discrepancy. In this model, when discrepancies at a higher level of abstractness are detected, attention is drawn toward lower-order goals in the hierarchy. For example, after the holidays someone with the higher-order goal of "being healthy" might notice that his current state is discrepant from this goal and be moved to engage in a lower-order behavior such as exercise. A related theory by Higgins (1997) considers the affective consequences of goal discrepancies. In this theory, discrepancy from approach-oriented goals (called ideal goals) results in low-arousal negative affect such as sadness and dejection, whereas discrepancy from avoidance-oriented goals (called ought goals) results in high-arousal negative affect such as anxiety and tension. Both models feature a discrepancy gradient where the urgency or affect resulting from discrepancy increases with distance from the goal.

Much of the existing neuroscience research on discrepancies has focused on disentangling the process of discrepancy detection from the process of discrepancy reduction—in TOTE terminology, pulling apart the neural machinery of the "test" from the "operate" steps (Botvinick, Braver, Barch, Carter, & Cohen, 2001; MacDonald et al., 2000). This body of work adopts a view of the brain as a massive parallel-distributed network that engages in many task-relevant processes simultaneously. Engaging any behavioral goal launches several representational processes, some of which might conflict, and only one of which can be expressed behaviorally at any time. In this massive network, the role of the ACC is to sound a neural "alarm" whenever some of these processes produce conflicting responses. The ACC can do this in two ways. First, the ACC might be involved in action initiation by signaling discrepancy between the current state and the desired end-state. Second, the ACC might be involved in coordinating and directing ongoing action by signaling discrepancy among possible response options.

Botvinick and colleagues (2001) used three sources of evidence to support these conclusions. The first piece of evidence is that the ACC is active during tasks that require inhibition of prepotent responses that conflict with the correct response, such as the Stroop task (Bush et al., 1999; Carter, Mintun, & Cohen, 1995). The authors suggested that the ACC is associated with the discrepancy detection component of the Stroop task rather than the behavioral inhibition per se. In further support of this position, MacDonald et al. (2000) dissociated the discrepancy detection phase of the task from the response correction phase and showed that the ACC is uniquely related to the discrepancy detection phase. These results are consistent with the "alarm" theory of the ACC, which seems to respond to the simultaneous representation of the prepotent (but incorrect) and learned (and correct) response options. However, it is unclear whether the ACC activity during the detection phase reflects the detection of possible upcoming conflict or detection of conflict between the selected course of action and the correct response.

Second, underdetermined tasks (i.e., those with multiple correct responses) elicit activity in the ACC relative to those with only one correct response. For example, in the "F-A-S" fluency task participants are asked to generate lists of words beginning with the letters "F," "A," and "S," and this task produces increased ACC activity relative to simply echoing the cue (Friston, Frith, Liddle, & Frackowiak, 1993) or performing a lexical decision task (Frith, Frison, Liddle, & Frackowiak, 1991). The control tasks present only one correct response option, whereas the experience of completing the FAS task is a barrage of options becoming available after the cue. Again, the view of the ACC as an "alarm" that indicates the need to resolve the problem of conflicting response pathways is consistent with these findings. Other research demonstrating ACC activation even during silent word generation again suggests that the role of the ACC is in the initial conflict detection rather than during subsequent conflict reduction (Warburton et al., 1996; Wise et al., 1991).

Third, researchers using EEG have noted an event-related potential specific to commission of errors on speeded decision tasks (Gehring, Coles, Meyer, & Donchin, 1995; Falkenstein, Hohnsbein, & Hoorman, 1995; Amodio et al., 2004), which has since been localized to the ACC (Carter et al., 1998). These types of tasks often present participants with two response options (e.g., right/left), and in those cases participants will often re-respond with the correct answer shortly after the incorrect answer: They realize they have made an error and attempt to correct it. Gehring and Fencsik (2001) used electromyogram (EMG) to measure muscle movement in both hands during responding, and showed that activity in the ACC (assessed with EEG) corresponded to periods of response overlap between correct and incorrect button presses. This is perhaps the most direct evidence of the ACC's role in conflict between multiple response pathways. However, the ACC was active during behavior, making it unclear whether this activity reflects conflict detection (between the correct and incorrect representations), or conflict reduction (between the correct and incorrect responses).

Taken together, the studies reviewed here suggest that one role of the ACC is to reflect conflict among multiple representations of response options or among actual response behaviors (Botvinick et al., 2001; Carter et al., 2000). However, most of the studies discussed in this context conflate the intention or planning that occurs immediately before behavior (which involves parallel representation of the current state and the end-state, along with many possible plans) and the actual behavior (which involves parallel representation of different possible behaviors), so it is unclear whether the ACC is involved in only one or both.

One reason for this ambiguity is that laboratory tasks rarely differentiate between the planning and maintenance phases of goal pursuit. Tasks such as the Stroop or FAS occur relatively quickly, on a single-trial basis, and with little opportunity to dynamically adjust behavior across time to match task demands. Even during the time-delayed Stroop employed by MacDonald and colleagues (2000), it is unclear whether the ACC during the response inhibition trials reflects conflicting responses in planning (immediately before responding) or during execution (during responding). New paradigms involving longer-term goals that require planning and maintenance of behavior over the span of at least several minutes are necessary to untangle these possibilities. Although it seems plausible that the ACC is integral to both phases, more research in goal-pursuit paradigms is necessary to clarify its precise role.

Conclusion

Several conceptual threads ran through this review. First, there is a tension between the level of abstractness and temporal duration of the goals studied by social psychologists and neuroscientists, with psychologists generally concerned with more abstract, longer-term goals and neuroscientists investigating concrete, shorter-term goals. Second, dispositional and state approach–avoidance motivation has been found to be a key construct across multiple components of goal pursuit. Third, whether goal pursuit occurs within or outside of awareness, and whether this dimension significantly affects performance, remains an open question for several goal pursuit components.

Abstract/Concrete or Long-Term/Short-Term?

One recurrent theme in our discussion is the importance of temporal duration and scale in examinations of goal pursuit: Is there a process-level distinction to be made between brief goal-directed behavior (such as that examined on a trial-by-trial basis in the Stroop task) and longer-term goal pursuit (such as that involved in forming and pursuing a New Year's resolution)? Understanding the distinctions and commonalities between the two is an essential step toward translating what is already known about the neuroscience of short-term goals to the relatively unknown neuroscience of long-term goal pursuit that is of equal or greater importance outside the laboratory. Our review presents two related directions for future research that might provide insight into this question.

First, the literature on action identification (Vallacher & Wegner, 1987) bears on the distinction between concrete and abstract representations of goals. In the same way that individuals are capable of viewing the same action with varying levels of abstraction such as "moving my hand up and down," "brushing my teeth," and "maintaining good oral hygiene," so too might they distinguish between different levels of the same goal, as in "pushing the button as fast as possible," "doing well on the task," and "being a good experimental participant." Indeed, a key tenant of action identification theory is that any given action (such as engaging in goal pursuit) may be represented at multiple levels of abstraction, and that the level of representation has important implications for how the action is attended to, pursued, and monitored. Neuroscientists have also observed distinctions between levels of mental abstraction, such that more abstract representations activate more anterior regions and more concrete representations activate more posterior regions (Amodio & Frith, 2006). A natural extension of these findings would be to import action-identification paradigms into the scanner and attempt to find convergences between these two literatures. For example, one study observed that people who are alcoholics tend to represent drinking at more abstract levels than people who are not alcoholics, and thus have difficulty altering behavior (Wegner, Vallacher, & Dizadji, 1989). It might be the case that people who are alcoholics recruit more anterior regions when thinking about drinking, and that engaging more posterior regions would be associated with behavior change through transformations of abstract into concrete goals. Researchers can capitalize on the convergence between social psychological and neuroscience findings to forge new theories and even interventions for health behavior change.

Second, the construct of temporal construal, which grew out of the action-identification literature (e.g., Trope & Liberman, 2003; Nussbaum, Trope, & Liberman, 2003), could yield valuable insights about the dynamic processes in the relationship between short- and long-term goals. For example, construal level theory (CLT) explicitly connects the level of abstractness and the temporal duration of a goal. As noted above, our brains recruit different regions to represent and attend to goals as they move from being more abstract to more concrete. Taken together, these observations suggest that there might be a parallel gradient of prefrontal cortical representation of temporal duration moving from posterior (shorter-term) to anterior (longer-term). Furthermore, CLT research has made inroads into experimentally modulating the focus between more and less abstract features of goals (e.g., Liberman & Trope, 1998). Importing neuroscience methods into this field is an important next step toward understanding the regulatory mechanisms involved in shifting construals.

Approach–Avoidance Motivation in Goal Pursuit

Social psychologists have made distinctions at each step of the goal-pursuit process between approaching rewards and avoiding punishments. Whether a stimulus is appetitive or aversive has implications for how it is represented (Elliot & Church, 1997) and attended to (Derryberry & Reed, 1994), how it is acted upon (Fishbach & Shah, 2006), the impact of discrepancies (Higgins et al., 1997), and for progress monitoring (Carver & Scheier, 1998). Neuroscientists are only beginning to make these distinctions.

Although existing studies of neural activity have considered reward (e.g., Knutson, Adams, Fong, & Hommer, 2001) and punishment (e.g., Buchel, Morris, Dolan, & Friston, 1998) separately, we know from social psychological research that it is important to consider both processes in tandem. To date, relatively few neural investigations have done so (but see Seymour et al., 2005), even though there are two important reasons to consider both processes together. First, long-term goal pursuit often involves systems that engage appetitive and aversive stimuli. Dieting, for example, might involve avoiding wanted but goal-inconsistent junk food and also approaching unwanted but goal-consistent vegetables. As neuroscience studies of goal pursuit move forward they will begin to more closely examine long-term goal pursuit and will necessarily involve a mixture of approaching incentives and avoiding punishments.

Second, social psychological theories dating back to the beginning of the study of approach and avoidance motivation have included both systems simultaneously (e.g., Schneirla, 1959; Gray, 1970). Empirical findings have also highlighted the importance of examining individual differences in approach and avoidance motivation within the same experimental context. A recent series of studies from our lab involving a novel goal-pursuit task found that the approach system was related to success across trial types, and that the avoidance system was related to success only on trials where inhibition of prepotent responses was necessary. Furthermore, there was an interaction between the two systems such that individuals high on both systems were the most successful group on the task in general (Berkman, Lieberman, & Gable, 2006). Subsequent fMRI analyses revealed that these systems were related to differential activation in regions sensitive to reward, such as the caudate and nucleus accumbens, and conflict detection and reduction, such as the ACC and dorsolateral PFC (Berkman, Burklund, Gable, & Lieberman, 2007). We view these types of studies to be essential in understanding how individual differences in motivation affect goal pursuit, and what are their unique and additive effects.

Levels of Awareness

We noted in several places in this chapter how goal-pursuit processes might operate at some times in a conscious, controlled way, and at others in a nonconscious, automatic way. An example of the dual nature of goal-pursuit processes are implementation intentions, which are formed by a conscious, deliberative process, yet later become active in a goal-relevant context because of an automatic association between goal context and intent (Gollwitzer, 1996). We reviewed other associative models where goal attention, discrepancy, and even pursuit is activated by situational cues, all entirely outside of awareness (Bargh et al., 2001; Mauss et al., 2006).

One important question faced by researchers in this area is how goal pursuit at these different levels is conceptually similar or different. Intuitively, goal pursuit seems like something that might involve deliberative, rule-based, and conscious processes. Indeed, several of the main components reviewed above have been shown to involve prefrontal regions that are traditionally associated with this type of processing (Miller & Cohen, 2001; Lieberman et al., 2004). However, studies on automatic goal pursuit have demonstrated that people can engage in seemingly "controlled" operations such as enduring in the face obstacles without awareness (Bargh et al., 2001). Although it is possible that conscious awareness is not a prerequisite to prefrontal activity and that automatic goal pursuit recruits the same regions as controlled goal pursuit, it is also possible that automatic goal pursuit recruits entirely different brain systems to engage in the same behavior (Lieberman, 2007). Neuroscience techniques can be used to differentiate these possibilities.

Beyond adding to our understanding of how automatic and controlled goal pursuit works inside the brain, neuroscience can enhance our knowledge of automatic and controlled goal pursuit inside the person. Given what we know about the complex and multiple processes involved in long-term goal pursuit, it is likely that controlled and automatic processes are employed at some point. Each type of processing has advantages at different stages in goal pursuit; automatic processes are necessary to continuously monitor for goal-relevant cues without exhausting our limited cognitive resources, and controlled processes are useful during active goal pursuit for rule-based operations and inhibiting goal-counter responses. Drawing on existing neuroscience models such as "alarm" and top-down excitatory biasing theories, it is now possible to generate a coherent model of long-term goal pursuit combining social psychological insight and neuroscience data.

References

Amodio, D. M., & Frith, C. D. (2006). Meeting of minds: The medial frontal cortex and social cognition. *Nature Reviews Neuroscience, 7*(4), 268–277.

Amodio, D. M., Harmon-Jones, E., Devine, P. G., Curtin, J. J., Hartley, S. L., & Covert, A. E. (2004). Neural signals for the detection of unintentional race bias. *Psychological Science, 15*(2), 88–93.

Aron, A. R., Fletcher, P. C., Bullmore, E. T., Sahakian, B. J., & Robbins, T. W. (2003). Stop-signal inhibition disrupted by damage to right inferior frontal gyrus in humans. *Nature Neuroscience, 6*(2), 115–116.

Aron, A. R., Monsell, S., Sahakian, B. J., & Robbins, T. W. (2004). A componential analysis of task-switching deficits associated with lesions of left and right frontal cortex. *Brain, 127*(7), 1561–1573.

Aron, A. R., Robbins, T. W., & Poldrack, R. A. (2004). Inhibition and the right inferior frontal cortex. *Trends in Cognitive Science, 8*(4), 170–177.

Baker, S. C., Frith, C. D., Frackowiak, R. S., & Dolan, R. J. (1996). Active representation of shape and spatial location in man. *Cerebral Cortex, 6*(4), 612–619.

Bandura, A. (1977). Self-efficacy: toward a unifying theory of behavioral change. *Psychological Review, 84*(2), 191–215.

Bandura, A. (1982). Self-efficacy mechanism in human agency. *American Psychologist, 37*(2), 122–147.

Banich, M. T., Milham, M. P., Atchley, R., Cohen, N. J., Webb, A., Wszalek, T., et al. (2000). fMRI studies of Stroop tasks reveal unique roles of anterior and posterior brain systems in attentional selection. *Journal of Cognitive Neuroscience, 12*(6), 988–1000.

Bargh, J. A. (1990). Auto-motives: Preconscious determinants of social interaction. In E. T. Higgins (Ed.), *Handbook of motivation and cognition: Foundations of social behavior* (Vol. 2, pp. 93–130). New York: Guilford Press.

Bargh, J. A., & Chartrand, T. L. (1999). The unbearable automaticity of being. *American Psychologist, 54*(7), 462–479.

Bargh, J. A., Gollwitzer, P. M., Lee-Chai, A., Barndollar, K., & Troetschel, R. (2001). The automated will: Nonconscious activation and pursuit of behavioral goals. *Journal of Personality & Social Psychology, 81*(6), 1014–1027.

Barkley, R. A. (1997). Behavioral inhibition, sustained attention, and executive functions: Constructing a unifying theory of ADHD. *Psychological Bulletin, 121*(1), 65–94.

Barkley, R. A., Grodzinsky, G., & DuPaul, G. J. (1992). Frontal lobe functions in attention deficit disorder with and without hyperactivity: a review and research report. *Journal of Abnormal Child Psychology, 20*(2), 163–188.

Bates, J. F., & Goldman-Rakic, P. S. (1993). Prefrontal connections of medial motor areas in the rhesus monkey. *Journal of Comparative Neurology, 336*(2), 211–228.

Baumeister, R. F., Heatherton, T. F., & Tice, D. M. (1993). When ego threats lead to self-regulation failure: negative consequences of high self-esteem. *Journal of Personality and Social Psychology, 64*(1), 141–156.

Berkman, E. T., Burklund, L., Gable, S. L., & Lieberman, M. D. (2007, January). *Motivation in action: Neural correlates of approach–avoidance motivation during goal pursuit.* Paper presented at the Society for Personality and Social Psychology, Memphis, TN.

Berkman, E. T., Lieberman, M. D., & Gable, S. L. (2006, May). *Goal pursuit moderated by a behavioral activation / inhibition system (BAS/BIS) interaction.* Paper presented at the Association for Psychological Science, New York, NY.

Botvinick, M. M., Braver, T. S., Barch, D. M., Carter, C. S., & Cohen, J. D. (2001). Conflict monitoring and cognitive control. *Psychological Review, 108*(3), 624–652.

Brown, S. M., Manuck, S. B., Flory, J. D., & Hariri, A. R. (2006). Neural basis of individual differences in impulsivity: contributions of corticolimbic circuits for behavioral arousal and control. *Emotion, 6*(2), 239–245.

Buchel, C., Morris, J., Dolan, R. J., & Friston, K. J. (1998). Brain systems mediating aversive conditioning: an event-related fMRI study. *Neuron, 20*(5), 947–957.

Bunge, S. A., Kahn, I., Wallis, J. D., Miller, E. K., & Wagner, A. D. (2003). Neural circuits subserving the retrieval and maintenance of abstract rules. *Journal of Neurophysiology, 90*(5), 3419–3428.

Bush, G., Frazier, J. A., Rauch, S. L., Seidman, L. J., Whalen, P. J., Jenike, M. A., et al. (1999). Anterior cingulate cortex dysfunction in attention-deficit/hyperactivity disorder revealed by fMRI and the Counting Stroop. *Biological Psychiatry, 45*(12), 1542–1552.

Canli, T., Zhao, Z., Desmond, J. E., Kang, E., Gross, J., & Gabrieli, J. D. (2001). An fMRI study of personality influences on brain reactivity to emotional stimuli. *Behavioral Neuroscience, 115*(1), 33–42.

Carter, C. S., Braver, T. S., Barch, D. M., Botvinick, M. M., Noll, D., & Cohen, J. D. (1998). Anterior cingulate cortex, error detection, and the online monitoring of performance. *Science, 280*(5364), 747–749.

Carter, C. S., Macdonald, A. M., Botvinick, M., Ross, L. L., Stenger, V. A., Noll, D., et al. (2000). Parsing executive processes: strategic vs. evaluative functions of the anterior cingulate cortex. *Proceedings of the National Academy of Sciences USA, 97*(4), 1944–1948.

Carter, C. S., Mintun, M., & Cohen, J. D. (1995). Interference and facilitation effects during selective attention: an H2150 PET study of Stroop task performance. *NeuroImage, 2*(4), 264–272.

Carver, C. S., & Scheier, M. F. (1982). Control theory: A useful conceptual framework for personality—social, clinical, and health psychology. *Psychological Bulletin, 92*(1), 111–135.

Carver, C. S., & Scheier, M. F. (1998). *On the self-regulation of behavior.* New York: Cambridge University Press.

Chen, M., & Bargh, J. A. (1999). Consequences of automatic evaluation: Immediate behavioral predispositions to approach or avoid the stimulus. *Personality and Social Psychology Bulletin, 25*(2), 215–224.

Cheyne, D., Bakhtazad, L., & Gaetz, W. (2006). Spatiotemporal mapping of cortical activity accompanying voluntary movements using an event-related beamforming approach. *Human Brain Mapping, 27*(3), 213–229.

Cohen, J. D., Dunbar, K., & McClelland, J. L. (1990). On the control of automatic processes: a parallel distributed processing account of the Stroop effect. *Psychological Review, 97*(3), 332–361.

Cohen, J. D., & Servan-Schreiber, D. (1992). Context, cortex, and dopamine: a connectionist approach to behavior and biology in schizophrenia. *Psychological Review, 99*(1), 45–77.

Connolly, J. D., Goodale, M. A., Menon, R. S., & Munoz, D. P. (2002). Human fMRI evidence for the neural correlates of preparatory set. *Nature Neuroscience, 5*(12), 1345–1352.

Cunningham, W. A., Raye, C. L., & Johnson, M. K. (2005). Neural correlates of evaluation associated with promotion and prevention regulatory focus. *Cognitive, Affective & Behavioral Neuroscience, 5*(2), 202–211.

Deci, E. L., & Ryan, R. M. (2000). The "what" and "why" of goal pursuits:

Human needs and the self-determination of behavior. *Psychological Inquiry,*
11(4), 227–268.

Derryberry, D., & Reed, M. A. (1994). Temperament and attention: Orienting toward and away from positive and negative signals. *Journal of Personality and Social Psychology, 66*(6), 1128–1139.

Desimone, R., & Duncan, J. (1995). Neural mechanisms of selective visual attention. *Annual Review of Neuroscience, 18,* 193–222.

Duckworth, K. L., Bargh, J. A., Garcia, M., & Chaiken, S. (2002). The automatic evaluation of novel stimuli. *Psychological Science, 13*(6), 513–519.

Elliot, A. J., & Church, M. A. (1997). A hierarchical model of approach and avoidance achievement motivation. *Journal of Personality and Social Psychology, 72*(1), 218–232.

Elliot, A. J., & Thrash, T. M. (2002). Approach–avoidance motivation in personality: Approach and avoidance temperaments and goals. *Journal of Personality & Social Psychology, 82*(5), 804–818.

Epley, N., & Gilovich, T. (2001). Putting adjustment back in the anchoring and adjustment heuristic: differential processing of self-generated and experimenter-provided anchors. *Psychological Science, 12*(5), 391–396.

Everling, S., & Munoz, D. P. (2000). Neuronal correlates for preparatory set associated with pro-saccades and anti-saccades in the primate frontal eye field. *Journal of Neuroscience, 20*(1), 387–400.

Falkenstein, M., Hohnsbein, J., & Hoormann, J. (1995). Event-related potential correlates of errors in reaction tasks. *Electroencephalography and Clinical Neurophysiology Supplement, 44,* 287–296.

Fishbach, A., & Shah, J. Y. (2006). Self-control in action: implicit dispositions toward goals and away from temptations. *Journal of Personality & Social Psychology, 90*(5), 820–832.

Fletcher, P. C., Shallice, T., & Dolan, R. J. (1998). The functional roles of prefrontal cortex in episodic memory. I. Encoding. *Brain, 121*(Pt 7), 1239–1248.

Fried, I., Katz, A., McCarthy, G., Sass, K. J., Williamson, P., Spencer, S. S., et al. (1991). Functional organization of human supplementary motor cortex studied by electrical stimulation. *Journal of Neuroscience, 11*(11), 3656–3666.

Friston, K. J., Frith, C. D., Liddle, P. F., & Frackowiak, R. S. (1993). Functional connectivity: the principal-component analysis of large (PET) data sets. *Journal of Cerebral Blood Flow and Metabolism, 13*(1), 5–14.

Frith, C. D., Friston, K. J., Liddle, P. F., & Frackowiak, R. S. (1991). A PET study of word finding. *Neuropsychologia, 29*(12), 1137–1148.

Funahashi, S., Chafee, M. V., & Goldman-Rakic, P. S. (1993). Prefrontal neuronal activity in rhesus monkeys performing a delayed anti-saccade task. *Nature, 365*(6448), 753–756.

Gehring, W. J., Coles, M. G., Meyer, D. E., & Donchin, E. (1995). A brain potential manifestation of error-related processing. *Electroencephalography and Clinical Neurophysiology Supplement, 44,* 261–272.

Gehring, W. J., & Fencsik, D. E. (2001). Functions of the medial frontal cortex in the processing of conflict and errors. *Journal of Neuroscience, 21*(23), 9430–9437.

Gollwitzer, P. M. (1990). Action phases and mind-sets. In E. T. Higgins (Ed.),

Handbook of motivation and cognition: Foundations of social behavior (Vol. 2, pp. 53–92). New York: Guilford Press.

Gollwitzer, P. M. (1996). The volitional benefits of planning. In P. M. Gollwitzer (Ed.), *The psychology of action: Linking cognition and motivation to behavior* (pp. 287–312). New York: Guilford Press.

Gollwitzer, P. M., & Brandstatter, V. (1997). Implementation intentions and effective goal pursuit. *Journal of Personality and Social Psychology, 73*(1), 186–199.

Gray, J. A. (1970). The psychophysiological basis of introversion–extraversion. *Behaviour Research & Therapy, 8*(3), 249–266.

Graybiel, A. M., Aosaki, T., Flaherty, A. W., & Kimura, M. (1994). The basal ganglia and adaptive motor control. *Science, 265*(5180), 1826–1831.

Gross, J. J. (2002). Emotion regulation: Affective, cognitive, and social consequences. *Psychophysiology, 39*(3), 281–291.

Gusnard, D. A., Akbudak, E., Shulman, G. L., & Raichle, M. E. (2001). Medial prefrontal cortex and self-referential mental activity: relation to a default mode of brain function. *Proceedings of the National Academy of Sciences USA, 98*(7), 4259–4264.

Herd, S. A., Banich, M. T., & O'Reilly, R. C. (2006). Neural mechanisms of cognitive control: an integrative model of stroop task performance and FMRI data. *Journal of Cognitive Neuroscience, 18*(1), 22–32.

Higgins, E. T. (1997). Beyond pleasure and pain. *American Psychologist, 52*(12), 1280–1300.

Higgins, E. T., Roney, C. J., Crowe, E., & Hymes, C. (1994). Ideal versus ought predilections for approach and avoidance: distinct self-regulatory systems. *Journal of Personality & Social Psychology, 66*(2), 276–286.

Higgins, E. T., Shah, J., & Friedman, R. (1997). Emotional responses to goal attainment: strength of regulatory focus as moderator. *Journal of Personality & Social Psychology, 72*(3), 515–525.

Horn, N. R., Dolan, M., Elliott, R., Deakin, J. F., & Woodruff, P. W. (2003). Response inhibition and impulsivity: An fMRI study. *Neuropsychologia, 41*(14), 1959–1966.

Johnson, M. K., Raye, C. L., Mitchell, K. J., Touryan, S. R., Greene, E. J., & Nolen-Hoeksema, S. (2006). Dissociating medial frontal and posterior cingulate activity during self-reflection. *Social Cognitive and Affect Neuroscience, 1*(1), 56–64.

Kandel, E. R., Schwartz, J. H., & Jessell, T. M. (1995). *Essentials of neural science and behavior.* Stamford, CT: Appleton & Lange.

Kihlstrom, J. F., & Klein, S. B. (1997). Self-knowledge and self-awareness. *Annals of New York Academy of Science, 818*, 4–17.

Knutson, B., Adams, C. M., Fong, G. W., & Hommer, D. (2001). Anticipation of increasing monetary reward selectively recruits nucleus accumbens. *Journal of Neuroscience, 21*(16), RC159.

Kuhl, J. (1984). Volitional aspects of achievement motivation and learned helplessness: toward a comprehensive theory of action control. *Progress in Experimental Personality Research, 13*, 99–171.

Liberman, N., & Trope, Y. (1998). The role of feasibilty and desirability considerations in near and distant future decisions: A test of temporal construal theory. *Journal of Personality and Social Psychology, 75*(1), 5–18.

Libet, B. (1985). Mediation of slow-inhibitory postsynaptic potentials. *Nature, 313*(5998), 161–162.

Libet, B. (1999). How does conscious experience arise? The neural time factor. *Brain Research Bulletin, 50*(5/6), 339–340.

Libet, B., Gleason, C. A., Wright, E. W., & Pearl, D. K. (1983). Time of conscious intention to act in relation to onset of cerebral activity (readiness-potential). The unconscious initiation of a freely voluntary act. *Brain, 106*(3), 623–642.

Lieberman, M. D. (2007). Social cognitive neuroscience: A review of core processes. *Annual Review of Psychology, 58,* 259–289.

Lieberman, M. D. (in press). Why symbolic processing of affect can disrupt negative affect: Social cognitive and affective neuroscience investigations. In A. Todorov, S. T. Fiske, & D. Prentice (Eds.), *Social neuroscience: Toward understanding the underpinnings of the social mind.* New York: Oxford University Press.

Lieberman, M. D., Jarcho, J. M., & Satpute, A. B. (2004). Evidence-based and intuition-based self-knowledge: an FMRI study. *Journal of Personality and Social Psychology, 87*(4), 421–435.

MacDonald, A. W., 3rd, Cohen, J. D., Stenger, V. A., & Carter, C. S. (2000). Dissociating the role of the dorsolateral prefrontal and anterior cingulate cortex in cognitive control. *Science, 288*(5472), 1835–1838.

MacLeod, C., & Mathews, A. M. (1991). Cognitive-experimental approaches to the emotional disorders. In P. R. Martin (Ed.), *Handbook of behavior therapy and psychological science: An integrative approach* (Vol. 164, pp. 116–150). Elmsford, NY: Pergamon Press.

Mauss, I. B., Evers, C., Wilhelm, F. H., & Gross, J. J. (2006). How to bite your tongue without blowing your top: Implicit evaluation of emotion regulation predicts affective responding to anger provocation. *Personality and Social Psychology Bulletin, 32*(5), 589–602.

Metcalfe, J., & Mischel, W. (1999). A hot/cool-system analysis of delay of gratification: Dynamics of willpower. *Psychological Review, 106*(1), 3–19.

Miller, E. K. (1999). The prefrontal cortex: Complex neural properties for complex behavior. *Neuron, 22*(1), 15–17.

Miller, E. K., & Cohen, J. D. (2001). An integrative theory of prefrontal cortex function. *Annual Review of Neuroscience, 24,* 167–202.

Miller, G. A., Galanter, E., & Pribram, K. H. (1960). *Plans and the structure of behavior.* New York: Holt.

Miller, N. E. (1959). Liberalization of the basic S-R concepts: Extensions to conflict behavior, motivation, and social learning. In S. Koch (Ed.), *Psychology: A study of a science* (Vol. 2, pp. 196–292). New York: McGraw-Hill.

Muraven, M., & Baumeister, R. F. (2000). Self-regulation and depletion of limited resources: does self-control resemble a muscle? *Psychological Bulletin, 126*(2), 247–259.

Neumann, R., & Strack, F. (2000). Approach and avoidance: The influence of proprioceptive and exteroceptive cues on encoding of affective information. *Journal of Personality & Social Psychology, 79*(1), 39–48.

Nobre, A. C., Sebestyen, G. N., Gitelman, D. R., Mesulam, M. M., Frackow-iak, R. S., & Frith, C. D. (1997). Functional localization of the system for visuospatial attention using positron emission tomography. *Brain, 120*(3), 515–533.

Nussbaum, S., Trope, Y., & Liberman, N. (2003). Creeping dispositionism: The temporal dynamics of behavior prediction. *Journal of Personality & Social Psychology, 84*(3), 485–497.

Ochsner, K. N., Beer, J. S., Robertson, E. R., Cooper, J. C., Gabrieli, J. D., Kihsl-trom, J. F., et al. (2005). The neural correlates of direct and reflected self-knowledge. *NeuroImage, 28*(4), 797–814.

Ochsner, K. N., Bunge, S. A., Gross, J. J., & Gabrieli, J. D. (2002). Rethinking feelings: an FMRI study of the cognitive regulation of emotion. *Journal of Cognitive Neuroscience, 14*(8), 1215–1229.

Ochsner, K. N., Knierim, K., Ludlow, D. H., Hanelin, J., Ramachandran, T., Glover, G., et al. (2004). Reflecting upon feelings: an fMRI study of neural systems supporting the attribution of emotion to self and other. *Journal of Cognitive Neuroscience, 16*(10), 1746–1772.

Posner, M. I., & Petersen, S. E. (1990). The attention system of the human brain. *Annual Review of Neuroscience, 13*, 25–42.

Posner, M. I., Walker, J. A., Friedrich, F. J., & Rafal, R. D. (1984). Effects of parietal injury on covert orienting of attention. *Journal of Neuroscience, 4*(7), 1863–1874.

Ro, T., Henik, A., Machado, L., & Rafal, R. D. (1997). Transcranial magnetic resonance stimulation of the prefrontal cortex delays contralateral endog-enous saccades. *Journal of Cognitive Neuroscience, 9*, 433–440.

Rosen, A. C., Rao, S. M., Caffarra, P., Scaglioni, A., Bobholz, J. A., Woodley, S. J., et al. (1999). Neural basis of endogenous and exogenous spatial ori-enting. A functional MRI study. *Journal of Cognitive Neuroscience, 11*(2), 135–152.

Schlag-Rey, M., Amador, N., Sanchez, H., & Schlag, J. (1997). Antisaccade performance predicted by neuronal activity in the supplementary eye field. *Nature, 390*(6658), 398–401.

Schmahmann, J. D., & Pandya, D. N. (1997). The cerebrocerebellar system. *International Review of Neurobiology, 41*, 31–60.

Schneirla, T. C. (1959). An evolutionary and developmental theory of bipha-sic processes underlying approach and withdrawal. In M. R. Jones (Ed.), *Nebraska Symposium on Motivation* (pp. 1–42). Lincoln, NE: University of Nebraska Press.

Seymour, B., O'Doherty, J. P., Koltzenburg, M., Wiech, K., Frackowiak, R., Fris-ton, K., et al. (2005). Opponent appetitive-aversive neural processes underlie predictive learning of pain relief. *Nature Neuroscience, 8*(9), 1234–1240.

Shah, J. Y., Friedman, R., & Kruglanski, A. W. (2002). Forgetting all else: on the antecedents and consequences of goal shielding. *Journal of Personality & Social Psychology, 83*(6), 1261–1280.

Sheldon, K. M., Ryan, R. M., Deci, E. L., & Kasser, T. (2004). The independent effects of goal contents and motives on well-being: it's both what you pursue and why you pursue it. *Personality and Social Psychology Bulletin, 30*(4), 475–486.

Solarz, A. K. (1960). Latency of instrumental responses as a function of compatibility with the meaning of eliciting verbal signs. *Journal of Experimental Psychology, 59,* 239–245.

Stroop, J. R. (1935). Studies of interference in serial verbal reactions. *Journal of Experimental Psychology, 18,* 643–661.

Tamir, M., & Robinson, M. D. (2004). Knowing good from bad: the paradox of neuroticism, negative affect, and evaluative processing. *Journal of Personality & Social Psychology, 87*(6), 913–925.

Trope, Y., & Fishbach, A. (2000). Counteractive self-control in overcoming temptation. *Journal of Personality and Social Psychology, 79*(4), 493–506.

Trope, Y., & Liberman, N. (2003). Temporal construal. *Psychological Review, 110*(3), 403–421.

Vallacher, R. R., & Wegner, D. M. (1987). What do people think they're doing? Action identification and human behavior. *Psychological Review, 94*(1), 3–15.

Warburton, E., Wise, R. J., Price, C. J., Weiller, C., Hadar, U., Ramsay, S., et al. (1996). Noun and verb retrieval by normal subjects. Studies with PET. *Brain, 119*(1), 159–179.

Ward, A., & Mann, T. (2000). Don't mind if I do: disinhibited eating under cognitive load. *Journal of Personality & Social Psychology, 78*(4), 753–763.

Wegner, D. M., Vallacher, R. R., & Dizadji, D. (1989). Do alcoholics know what they're doing? Identifications of the act of drinking. *Basic and Applied Social Psychology, 10*(3), 197–210.

Wicklund, R. A., & Gollwitzer, P. M. (1981). Symbolic self-completion, attempted influence, and self-deprecation. *Basic and Applied Social Psychology, 2*(2), 89–114.

Wise, R., Chollet, F., Hadar, U., Friston, K., Hoffner, E., & Frackowiak, R. (1991). Distribution of cortical neural networks involved in word comprehension and word retrieval. *Brain, 114*(4), 1803–1817.

Wise, S. P., Murray, E. A., & Gerfen, C. R. (1996). The frontal cortex-basal ganglia system in primates. *Critical Reviews of Neurobiology, 10*(3/4), 317–356.

Zametkin, A. J., Nordahl, T. E., Gross, M., King, A. C., Semple, W. E., Rumsey, J., et al. (1990). Cerebral glucose metabolism in adults with hyperactivity of childhood onset. *New England Journal of Medicine, 323*(20), 1361–1366.

The Selfish Goal

JOHN A. BARGH
JULIE Y. HUANG

There has been a sea change in the past 20 years in our understanding of the role of consciousness in the selection and guidance of social behavior. Dominant theories of the 1970s and 1980s emphasized the central role of conscious choice and intention in the production of human behavior, as in the theory of reasoned action (Ajzen & Fishbein, 1980), self-efficacy theory (Bandura, 1977, 1986), and other motivational models (Locke & Latham, 1990; Mischel, 1973). Conscious choice of behaviors or goals to pursue was a bottleneck in these models: Nothing happened without the exercise of conscious will. Even today, proponents of these models hold that "human behavior is affected by conscious purposes, plans, intentions, tasks and the like . . . [which are] the immediate motivational causes of most human action" (Locke & Latham, 2002, p. 705).

However, two concurrent movements within social psychology have operated over the years to cast doubt on assumption that conscious processes are usually, if not always, in control. First and most important was the growing realization of the power of external situational variables in determining behavior, sometimes shown to be more powerful than internal causes such as personality or values (e.g., Darley & Latane, 1968; Milgram, 1963; Mischel, 1973; Ross & Nisbett, 1991). Second was the introduction of "dual-process" models (e.g., Posner & Snyder, 1975; Shiffrin & Schneider, 1977) that complemented conscious mental processes with "automatic," implicit, or nonconscious ones. Research within this dual-process framework amassed a good deal of evidence that there was another route to the selection and guidance of higher mental processes such as are involved in social judgment and behavior, a route that was triggered by relevant environmental stimuli and that bypassed the consciousness bottleneck (see reviews in Bargh, 2007; Chaiken & Trope, 1999).

Research on social-construct *priming* combines the situational and the nonconscious emphases of the past several decades. "Priming" refers to the passive, subtle, and unobtrusive activation of relevant mental representations by external, environmental stimuli, such that people are not and do not become aware of the influence exerted by those stimuli. In harmony with the situationist tradition, this priming research has shown that the mere, passive perception of environmental events directly triggers higher mental processes in the absence of any involvement by conscious, intentional processes (see reviews in Bargh & Ferguson, 2000; Dijksterhuis, Aarts, & Chartrand, 2007; Higgins, 1996). Following the initial success of priming research in the domain of impression formation (Higgins, Rholes, & Jones, 1977; Srull & Wyer, 1979), researchers extended it to other higher mental processes, such as evaluation (e.g., Fazio, 1986, 1990), stereotyping and prejudice (Devine, 1989), social behavior (e.g., Bargh, Chen, & Burrows, 1996; Dijksterhuis & van Knippenberg, 1998), and motivated goal pursuit (e.g., Bargh & Gollwitzer, 1994; Chartrand & Bargh, 1996).

For example, priming the concept of a library causes participants to speak more softly (Aarts & Dijksterhuis, 2003), the faint odor of cleaning fluid makes them more likely to tidy up after themselves when eating a crumbly cookie (Holland, Hendriks, & Aarts, 2005), and the mere presence of a briefcase versus backpack by the door of the experimental room causes them to be relatively competitive versus cooperative in a Prisoner's Dilemma game (Kay, Wheeler, Bargh, & Ross, 2004)—in each case, without any awareness of the role played by these external stimuli in the production of their behavior. The ease and ubiquity with which priming effects have been obtained have revealed the openness of the human mind to environmental influences. At the same time, it has by logical necessity reduced the presumed causal role of intentional, conscious processes in higher mental processes such as social behavior and goal pursuit (Bargh & Ferguson, 2000).

Up until quite recently, mainstream accounts of executive control or working memory within cognitive science held that all of the contents of working memory were accessible to conscious awareness; indeed, "working memory" and "conscious awareness" were considered synonymous terms (e.g., Smith & Jonides, 1998). Under this assumption it was difficult to understand how higher mental processes could make use of those executive control structures without the person being aware of it (see Bargh, 2005). This was especially a problem in the case of nonconscious goal pursuit, in which a primed goal operates on incoming informational input that is accessible to conscious awareness, while the goal-driven attentional selection and transformation of that information, and on-line guidance of behavior toward the goal, is occurring outside of conscious awareness.

That executive control structures could be operating without the person's awareness of their operation would seem to require the existence of dissociable component processes within executive control or working memory structures. Although these were not part of standard models of working memory at the time of the initial behavioral demonstrations of nonconscious goal pursuit (e.g., Bargh & Gollwitzer, 1994; Chartrand & Bargh, 1996), evidence of such dissociations had been reported in patients with "environmental dependency syndrome" (Lhermitte, 1986) that left them entirely at the mercy of externally suggested actions. Recently, supporting the existence of nonconscious forms of goal pursuit, cognitive neuroscience research has confirmed that distinct anatomical structures support the operating goal program, on the one hand, and the knowledge of its operation (i.e., consciously held intentions) on the other. Conscious intentions appear to be represented in the prefrontal and premotor cortex, but it is the parietal cortex that houses the representation used to guide action (Frith, Blakemore, & Wolpert, 2000).

That a goal can operate independently of conscious awareness of its operation would seem to imply the existence of a dissociation between the executive control structures in the brain responsible for "running" that goal's "program" and those that enable conscious awareness of the goal pursuit. Recent cognitive neuroscience research has confirmed this implication, with the finding that the operation of a goal program and one's awareness of its operation are located in separate anatomical structures within the frontal lobes (Frith et al., 2000). Further dissociation evidence comes from investigations of prefrontal lobe syndromes (Bogen, 1995; Lhermitte, 1986), the psychophysiology of dream consciousness, which involves prefrontal deactivations (Muzur, Pace-Schott, & Hobson, 2002), and demonstrations that control-structures in the brain (e.g., the frontal cortices) are not essential for the generation of consciousness (Koch & Tsuchiya, 2007). In light of this gathering evidence, it seems reasonable that goals can become active and operate to guide behavior independently of conscious intention and awareness (Bargh, 1990).

If a goal is capable of operating independently of any conscious intention or awareness of its operation, then active goals and conscious intentions cannot be the same things (Bargh, 1990). Self-theorists have distinguished between the "belief" (self-concept, self-esteem, self-efficacy) and the "agentic" (ego, volition) functions of the self: "Many crucial functions of the self involve volition: making choices and decisions, taking responsibility, initiating and inhibiting behavior, and making plans of action and carrying out those plans. The self exerts control over itself and over the external world" (Baumeister, Bratslavsky, Muraven, & Tice, 1998, p. 1252). Yet the self comprises many different, often-conflicting motives and goals, such as self-interest versus empathic concern for others, short-term pleasure versus long-term health and happiness, competition versus cooperation with others, and so on (Elster, 1990; Sen, 1978; see Mansbridge, 1990). Goal systems theory (e.g., Kruglanski et al., 2002) and supramodular interaction theory (Morsella, 2005), in fact, are specifically concerned with the structural relations between competing goal tendencies and how these conflicts are resolved within the self or individual.

Thus it is possible to make a useful distinction between the self and the currently active goal. In the case of nonconscious goal operation, it is clearly the goal that is in charge (of selective attention, evaluation, and behavior), not the "active" or conscious self. Modern self-theorists do acknowledge that "a great deal of human behavior is influenced by automatic or nonconscious processes," but contend that "undoubtedly some portion involves deliberate, conscious, controlled responses by the self . . . acting autonomously on its own behalf" (Baumeister et al., 1998, p. 1252). Our main point in this chapter is that ultimate control rests not with the self, but with the currently active goal, which will pursue its agenda autonomously even when doing so is not in the overall best interests of the individual (self)—and that this selfish goal principle holds for consciously pursued goals just as much as for automatic or nonconscious goal pursuits.

The relation between goals and the individuals holding them is strikingly similar to that between genes and their host organisms. In his classic work *The Selfish Gene*, Dawkins (1976) described how our genes have designed us (through the blind process of natural selection) to be their "survival machines" on which they depend for their propagation into future generations. The core of Dawkins's argument was that genes, not individual organisms, are the basic unit of natural selection. Moreover, genes were said to be essentially "selfish" in that their own propagation is their only concern, not the welfare of the host organism (except as it might affect propagation): "Each gene is seen as pursuing its own self-interested agenda against the background of the other genes in the gene pool" (p. ix).

That goals are to the self as genes are to the organism is more than just a metaphor. Evolutionary biologists and psychologists, as well as philosophers of science, view motivations as the crucial link between genetic influences and adaptive behavior (Campbell, 1974; Mayr, 1976; Neuberg, Kenrick, Maner, & Schaller, 2004; Pinker & Bloom, 1990, p. 468; Popper, 1972, pp. 256–280; Symons, 1992, p. 138; Tetlock, 2002; Tomasello, Carpenter, Call, Behne, & Moll, 2005; Tooby & Cosmides, 1992, p. 99). Because of constantly changing and shifting environmental conditions, coupled with the very slow rate of genetic change, direct genetic controls over behavior tend to be inflexible and unable to adapt fast enough to changes in the environment. Accordingly, genes provide us with general and specific motivations, which are translated into our nervous systems as "goal programs," and it is these goal programs that guide our behavior in the local environment (Mayr, 1976).

The close correspondence between genes and goals is further attested to by the prevalence of goal-directed behavior in the organic world, which largely lacks the strategic, conscious information-processing capabilities of humans. As the evolutionary theorist Ernst Mayr (1976, p. 389) stressed, "the occurrence of goal-directed processes is perhaps the most character-istic feature of the world of living organisms." For example, a predator stalking its prey or the prey fleeing from the pursuing predator, a bird starting on its migration, an insect selecting its host plant, a male display-ing to a female are acting purposefully yet unconsciously.

One reason why goal-directed and purposive behavior is common-place among living organisms (Mayr, 1976) is because goal programs are the "local agents" in the present that carry out genetic instructions from the distant past. Why do genes require the proxy of goals and motives? Because the rate of genetic change is very slow, too slow for direct genetic controls over behavior to adapt quickly enough to the constantly chang-ing and shifting environmental conditions over long stretches of time. The inflexibility of direct genetic control is the main reason why 99% of the species that ever existed are now extinct. Therefore, behavior is never directly controlled by the genotype but by a behavior program in the ner-vous system that results from the translation of the original genetic pro-gram. As Dawkins (1976) summarized the situation, "genes exert ultimate power over behavior. But the moment-to-moment decisions about what to do next are taken by the nervous system. Genes are the primary policy-makers, brains are the executives" (p. 19). And goal pursuits, we would add, are the executive processes of the brain.

Dawkins's (1976) main point was that genes, not their host organisms, are the unit of natural selection; further, that genes are essentially "selfish" in that their own propagation is their only concern, not the welfare of the host organism, except where it affects propagation. In an analogous fash-ion, we argue, active goals are the unit of control over higher mental pro-cesses, not the self or individual person, and active goals single-mindedly pursue their agenda independently of whether doing so is in the overall good of the individual person.

In advancing this argument, we first review evidence as to whether active goals operate in an autonomous fashion (autonomous with regard to the self and its conscious intentions and purposes). The evidence on this point comes mainly from experimental demonstrations of *nonconscious* goal pursuit. This leads us to the pivotal question of whether *conscious* goal pursuit is also characterized by autonomous goal functioning. We make a theoretical and an empirical case that it is: theoretically, because of the likelihood that conscious goal pursuit makes use of the same underlying structures and processes as in evolutionarily older unconscious goal pursuit mechanisms; empirically, because of the many other similarities between nonconscious and conscious goal pursuit that have already been demonstrated. We then report the findings of several experiments specifically designed to test whether conscious goals operate autonomously from conscious intentions—in other words, whether intended goal pursuit produces unintended (and, presumably, unwanted) consequences for the individual.

Do Goals Operate Autonomously?: Evidence from Goal-Priming Studies

The autonomy of active goals is clearly apparent in the case of nonconscious goal pursuit. The goal-priming literature has shown that goals can be activated without the individual knowing about or intending it—either through subliminal presentation of goal relevant stimuli, or through subtle and unobtrusive supraliminal presentation. A wide variety of environmental triggers have been demonstrated: not only verbal stimuli semantically related to the goal (as in many studies), but also material objects such as backpacks and briefcases (Kay et al., 2004), scents such as cleaning fluids (Holland et al., 2005), power-related features of a situation such as a professor's desk chair (Chen, Lee-Chai, & Bargh, 2001), and the names of one's significant others (Fitzsimons & Bargh, 2003; Shah, 2003).

These same studies have shown that once activated outside the person's knowledge, these goals operate autonomously, without any conscious guidance, to guide cognition and behavior toward the desired end-state (see reviews in Bargh, 2005; Bargh & Ferguson, 2000; Chartrand & Bargh, 2002; Dijksterhuis et al., 2007; Ferguson, Hassin, & Bargh, 2008; Fitzsimons & Bargh, 2004). Importantly, the same behavioral and judgmental outcomes are obtained in these studies as when the same goal is pursued consciously (see next section). Nonconscious goal pursuit has now been demonstrated across a range of goal types: information-processing goals such as judgment and memorization, achievement goals such as high performance on a task, and interpersonal goals such as to compete or cooperate.

How do nonconscious goals operate outside of awareness and intention when the stimuli and events they are operating on are in full view of conscious awareness? In one study, for example, the nonconscious (primed) goal to cooperate with one's game opponent produced equivalent increases in cooperative behavior to the experimental condition in which some participants were explicitly instructed to cooperate (Bargh, Gollwitzer, Lee-Chai, Barndollar, & Troetschel, 2001, Study 2). Yet only in the latter case were participants aware of having the goal to cooperate, as shown by postexperimental retrospective reports of how cooperative they had just been on the task. These participants thus gave every appearance of pursuing the cooperation goal without knowing they were doing so, while they were consciously aware of the task stimuli and of their own behavioral responses to them. Somehow the primed goal operated on stimuli and events relevant to it to produce the goal-appropriate outcomes, but without any foreknowledge of exactly what goal-relevant stimuli and events might occur during the experimental session. The active goal, therefore, had to be ready for whatever goal-relevant environmental input might occur, and then operate on it when it did occur.

The readiness of nonconsciously activated goals to operate on whatever goal-relevant input occurs in the environment illustrates the open-ended nature of human goal pursuit. Mayr (1976, p. 23) identified two types of inherited behavior programs in the organic world: open and closed. Closed programs are those containing a nearly complete set of ready-made responses to particular stimuli in the environment; these characterize organisms with short life spans or highly stable and unchanging environments, in which there is little time or need to benefit from experience or adapt to local variations. Because humans, on the other hand, enjoy longer life spans and also a long childhood under the supervision and protection of caregivers, most genetic behavior programs (goals) in humans are open. This is a great advantage to successful adaptation because it allows the general tendencies furnished genetically to be fine-tuned to the specific local conditions into which the infant happens to be born. A well-known example of an open-ended program in humans is the young child's ability to quickly learn the local language and absorb the local culture; any infant can be taken to any location on earth and over time will learn that language and that culture as well as if he/she had been born there (Pinker, 1994).

The open-ended nature of human goal pursuit also enables flexibility of behavior instead of fixed, rigid responses to specific stimuli. Many researchers have taken this flexibility as evidence of the autonomous nature of conscious self-control (e.g., Baumeister et al., 1998), but as the evolutionary psychologist Symons (1992) pointed out, this confuses the open-ended nature of means selection with a choice among goals themselves (i.e., desired end-states):

> One source of confusion is that we are used to thinking of human behavior as being uniquely flexible and responsive to environmental variation. Human behavior is flexible, of course, but this flexibility is of means, not ends, and

the basic experiential goals that motivate human behavior are both inflexible and specific. (p. 138; see also Tooby & Cosmides, 1992, p. 101)

To give one example, we have many ways of consuming sugar, but the goal of eating sugar remains the same: to experience the sensation of sweetness.

Moreover, flexibility of means cannot be the exclusive province of conscious goal pursuit and self-regulation because the empirical demonstrations of nonconscious goal pursuit could not have occurred if it did not have this same flexible quality. In fact, the most compelling demonstration of the open-ended nature of human goal pursuit is in the case of nonconscious goal pursuit. Given the largely unpredictable nature of future events (e.g., Dawes, 1993), participants cannot know in advance in these studies what goal-relevant stimuli might occur (they are not even aware of which stimuli are goal relevant and which are not). Nevertheless, the nonconscious goal is shown to operate on any and all such relevant information: driving selective attention toward such information when it is present (Chartrand & Bargh, 1996, Study 2; Neuberg et al., 2004), causing the differential evaluation of that information in terms of whether it facilitates or interferes with the goal (Ferguson & Bargh, 2004), transforming and manipulating the information in the service of the goal (McCulloch, Ferguson, Kawada, & Bargh, 2008), and guiding behavior toward the goal (e.g., Bargh et al., 2001).

Thus, the recent research on nonconscious goal pursuit has established the autonomy with which goals can be activated, operate, and guide cognition and behavior to successful completion of the goal, all independently of conscious intentions and guidance. Once again, the situation is closely analogous to how genes operate to guide our present-day behavior through open-ended motivational mechanisms. The nonconsciously active goal operates on whatever goal-relevant information happens to occur next in the experimental situation, which could not be known to the participant beforehand—just as genetic influences from the distant past programmed us through open-ended motivations to be capable of adapting to local conditions far into a future that could not have been anticipated in any detail (Dawkins, 1976).

Similarity of Nonconscious and Conscious Goal Pursuit

Do conscious goals also operate autonomously, once activated? The many similarities that recent research has revealed between conscious and nonconscious goal pursuit suggests that they might also share the feature of autonomous operation. First, as noted above, nonconsciously operating goals produce the same outcomes as when those same goals are pursued consciously, and as the recent study by McCulloch et al. (2008) showed in the case of the impression-formation goal, do so following the same processing stages as well. Second, nonconscious goal pursuit possesses the same phenomenal qualities previously demonstrated and ascribed to conscious, deliberate goal pursuit (Bandura, 1977, 1986; Gollwitzer & Moskowitz, 1996; Heckhausen, 1991; Lewin, 1926). These include persistence in the face of obstacles, resumption of interrupted goal pursuits in the face of intrinsically more attractive activities, and evaluative and motivational consequences of the goal pursuit attempt (see reviews in Chartrand & Bargh, 2002; Ferguson et al., 2008). Kawada, Oettingen, Gollwitzer, and Bargh (2004) demonstrated yet another similarity: Conscious and nonconscious goals, when active, are "projected onto" (i.e., attributed to) other people in the course of impression formation.

Cognitive neuroscience studies of the brain regions involved in motivated behavior also support the hypothesis that the same underlying mechanisms and processes are involved in conscious and nonconscious goal pursuit. Pessiglione et al. (2007) found that the same region of the basal forebrain moderates task-effort level in response to a consciously perceived and a subliminally presented reward signal, leading the authors to conclude that "the motivational processes involved in boosting behavior are qualitatively similar, whether subjects are conscious or not of the reward at stake" (p. 906).

What accounts for these close similarities in process and outcome between conscious and nonconscious forms of goal pursuit? As noted above, purposive behavior and goal pursuits are widespread in the world of living things, serving as the liaison between genetic influences from the deep past and adaptive behavior in the present (e.g., Mayr, 1976). Thus, goal pursuit is not something requiring human consciousness or its equivalent; for most organisms goal-directed behavior is driven entirely through unconscious means (Dawkins, 1976). Given that consciousness and strategic, intentional mental processes were relatively late arrivals in human evolutionary history (e.g., Dennett, 1991; Donald, 1991), human goal pursuit was largely unconscious in nature for most of evolutionary time. Thus, upon the arrival of conscious forms of information processing, it is probable that conscious methods of goal pursuit made use of the existing (unconscious) goal pursuit structures in the brain. In evolution, the formation of new structures (such as organs) involves complex, often competitive interactions with extant ones because intelligent design in nature builds on available existing structures in a gradual, incremental fashion, instead of creating entirely new ones each time from scratch (Allman, 2000; Dawkins, 1976).

For these reasons, then, we hypothesized that conscious and nonconscious goal pursuit would share another important feature, that of autonomous operation once active. Note that up to this point, potential similarities between the two modes of goal pursuit were assessed by testing whether nonconscious goal pursuit possesses qualities already established for conscious goal pursuit (Chartrand & Bargh, 2002; Fitzsimons & Bargh, 2004). Here we do the reverse: asserting that conscious goal pursuit shares a quality previously demonstrated only for nonconscious goal pursuit—that is, operating on any relevant (i.e., applicable; see Higgins, 1996) information in the environment regardless of whether the individual intends or is aware of it. In the case of conscious goals, the person is aware of pursuing them with regard to a specific target or set of targets; but just as nonconscious goals operate on any and all perceived information to which they are applicable, conscious goals will too—even information that was not the intended focus of the goal. If even consciously pursued goals operate in this independent manner, one can speak of the "selfish goal" pursuing its own agenda just as the "selfish gene" is ultimately concerned with its own propagation.

An Empirical Test of Conscious Goal Autonomy

We suggest that the "selfish goal" principle holds for all goal pursuits, conscious and unconscious alike. Previous research shows that primed, nonconscious goals to form an impression of a target person operate without the participant's knowledge and compute the evaluation in the same way as if the person consciously and intentionally had the goal to form an impression (Chartrand & Bargh, 1996). In that study, participants were unaware of having the goal of forming an impression and so also were not intending to form an impression of the particular target person. Thus, the experiment included an unintended goal and an unintended target of that goal; but because of the open-ended nature of the active impression goal, and the presence of relevant target information in the environment, impressions of that target were nonetheless formed and stored (see also McCulloch et al., 2008).

For consciously intended goal pursuits, on the other hand, the goal is of course intended and resident in conscious awareness, and so the autonomy of goal operation from conscious intentions and awareness would be manifested by its application to relevant targets that were not the intended focus of the goal. Thus, it is the open-ended nature of human goal pursuit that is expected to produce the unintended effects, with the active goal ready to operate on any goal-relevant information in the environment, even if it is not the intended focus of the goal.

We (Bargh, Green, & Fitzsimons, 2008) tested this hypothesis in two experiments by having participants watch a videotape of an ostensible job interview (in the control condition, participants were told it was of two people getting acquainted). They were told that the job in question was either a crime reporter for the New York *Daily News,* or a restaurant waiter position. The two jobs were pretested so that the desired personality characteristics were opposite of each other: the ideal crime reporter is tough and aggressive, whereas the ideal waiter is deferential and polite.

During the taped interview, the two principals were interrupted several times by secretaries and coworkers, as in an actual busy office situation. The behavior of one of these interrupters ("Mike") varied across the two experimental conditions. In one tape, Mike was very polite and deferential after interrupting; in the other, he was rude and aggressive. After the tape had been presented, participants were given a surprise impression task in which we did not ask about the job candidate at all (on which they had been consciously focused), but simply how much they liked Mike.

Under the hypothesis that the active conscious goal of evaluating a specific type of job candidate would also be applied to other people encountered at the same time, we expected that participants in the control and waiter-goal conditions would like "polite Mike" more than "rude Mike," but that those in the reporter-goal condition would actually like "rude Mike" better. Results confirmed this prediction. Because Mike's behavior matched the qualities that the active goal was looking for, and which would be evaluated positively by the active goal (see Ferguson & Bargh, 2004), participants in the reporter-goal condition showed a significant reversal of preferences compared to the other two conditions: They liked rude Mike more than polite Mike.

These findings support the hypothesis that conscious as well as nonconscious goals, once activated, operate autonomously in an open-ended fashion on any and all relevant information in the environment, even that which was not the original intended focus of the goal pursuit (in the case of conscious goals). Intended goal pursuits thus can have unintended consequences. As shown by the results of the control condition, we do not normally find rude, aggressive people likable, and it is doubtful we'd like "rude Mike" under normal circumstances—but we do tend to like him if we are concurrently evaluating others for some purpose in which rudeness and aggressiveness happen to be valued traits.

In a third study, some participants were instructed to help another participant (actually a confederate) with an experimental task, while others were not assigned this "helper" role. Consistent with the selfish-goal hypothesis, participants who were concurrently helping someone (compared to those who were not) showed a greater willingness to donate money to a charity, and also to commit their time to helping a stranger who stopped by the experimental room, asking if the participant would fill out a lengthy questionnaire for her. Note that these are costs that one would not choose to incur were it not for this unintended influence of the active goal (as shown by the control and deactivated-goal conditions of that study), just as one would normally like a polite person more than a rude one.

This last experiment also included a condition in which the conscious helping goal was completed and no longer active at the time of the further requests for help. Consistent with predictions as well as past theory and evidence on goal effects (Atkinson & Birch, 1970; Förster, Liberman, & Higgins, 2005; Kawada et al., 2004; Lewin, 1926), turning off the goal in this way also eliminated the selfish-goal effect of causing the participant to help anyone who asked for it, not only the person the participant consciously intended to help. It is the currently active goal that is in charge of attention, judgment, evaluation, and behavior, and turning off the goal turns off its property of operating on any and all relevant information in the environment.

Operation of the Selfish Goal

The preceding analysis suggests that it may be beneficial to depart from the traditional homuncular view of social (and much of cognitive: see Bargh & Morsella, 2008) psychology, with its agentic, autonomous self said to be in control of executive processes and goal pursuits, and instead conceptualize the human motivational system as a collection of self-interested entities. Increasingly, research is concluding that an organism can be optimally designed (i.e., the fittest organism by natural selection terms) of conflicting selfish agents (Dawkins, 1976; Kurzban & Aptikis, 2007; Livnat & Pippenger, 2006). As Livnat and Pippenger (2006) pointed out, "Unbeknownst to an agent, its actions may promote the goal of the collective, given the actions of the other agents and the computational limitations. Yet it does not necessarily follow that the agent's goal aligns with that of the collective or of any other agent by extension." Instead, the human goal system appears to have evolved as a collection of "selfish" agents, operating to attain their own end-states at whatever costs to other agents or even its host organism.

Therefore, instead of viewing our goals as always operating in direct service of our conscious agenda, in this section we ask an alternative question: How do our goals control us? In our view, the open-ended design and autonomous operation of the selfish goal is the key to how it pursues its own attainment. To document the variety of mechanisms through which active goals control our minds and behavior without our being aware of it, we review evidence bearing on how conscious and nonconscious goals operate as open-ended systems, following them from activation, through strategic operation, conflict with other selfish goals, and finally to completion (see also Gollwitzer & Moskowitz, 1996).

Selfish Goals Drive Attention, Perception, and Evaluation

Once active, the goal directs one's attention toward some (i.e., goal-relevant) stimuli and away from others; the world is filtered through the goal's "eyes." The active goal's effect on selective attention has long been known in the case of consciously pursued goals (Anderson & Pichert, 1978; Bruner, 1957; Hastie & Park, 1986), but more recent research shows this effect occurs in nonconscious goal pursuit as well (Chartrand & Bargh, 1996, Study 2; Maner et al., 2003; McCulloch et al., 2008; Neuberg et al., 2004). For example, a nonconscious impression formation goal causes greater selective attention to behavioral information inconsistent with the target's general pattern of behavior (Chartrand & Bargh, 1996, Study 2; McCulloch et al., 2008), and a nonconscious mating goal drives greater selective attention to the potential romantic partners shown on a video-screen (Maner et al., 2003; Neuberg et al., 2004).

The power of the effect of active goals on attention and memory is such that very salient, unusual events can be missed entirely, as in the "attentional blindness" research (Mack, 2003; Simons & Chabris, 1999). In one such study, participants given the explicit, conscious task of counting the number of ball tosses between actors on a computer display failed to notice a gorilla walking right through the ball-tossing game while they were busy counting tosses.

These effects on attention, encoding, and memory occur because the active goal is only interested in facilitating its own attainment—to the exclusion of other concerns, such as whether all available visual information has been relayed to its host. The power of selfish-goal effects on attention and encoding is further indicated by the power of the currently active goal to override otherwise automatic, chronic encoding tendencies. For example, there is much evidence of the automatic manner in which other people are encoded or categorized in terms of their race, age, and gender (e.g., Bargh, 1999; Brewer, 1988). However, if doing so hinders the successful completion of the currently active goal, this does not happen. Kurzban, Tooby, and Cosmides (2001, Study 2) gave participants the explicit goal of impression formation and subsequently presented them with a situation wherein allied targets were visibly linked by shirt color. The experimenters found that participants encoded targets using the most useful information current to that context, which in this case, was target shirt color, to a greater extent than race (which did not designate targets' group affiliations).

Moskowitz, Gollwitzer, Wasel, and Schaal (1999) provided a particularly powerful demonstration of the selfish goal dominating potentially antagonistic automatic processes. In their studies, those participants with a strongly held goal to treat others in an egalitarian fashion showed evidence of inhibiting automatically activated stereotypes toward minority groups. The active egalitarian goal, once again, overrode the otherwise automatic tendency to categorize people in terms of the group stereotype, because doing so would run counter to the active goal's aim of treating people the same regardless of race, gender, or ethnicity.

Treating other people fairly is a positive social goal of course, but in line with the notion that the self comprises of many, often-conflicting goals, people also have strong goals to protect their self-esteem. If this self-protective goal is active, for example following a threat to one's self-esteem (e.g., failure at a task), it can instead cause the stereotyping of minority group members, even under conditions known to normally prevent such stereotyping. In a series of experiments by Spencer, Fein, Wolfe, Fong, and Dunn (1998), automatic stereotyping effects were shown to be blocked by an attentional load (secondary task) manipulation, replicating earlier work by Gilbert and Hixon (1991). The secondary task thus created conditions under which it was difficult for automatic stereotyping of minority group members to occur.

Next, Spencer et al. (1998) threatened the self-esteem of some participants through bogus failure feedback, thus presumably triggering a goal to restore positive self-regard. This active self-protective goal was able to overcome the load conditions as automatic stereotyping effects were found to reemerge for this group: the goal of maintaining self-esteem using the means of denigration of others, strong enough to overcome the obstacle (attentional load) in its way.

The currently active goal also has the power to override chronic, automatic attitudes. Ferguson and Bargh (2004) showed that though a goal is active, stimuli that facilitate attainment of that goal are automatically (nonconsciously and immediately) evaluated positively, even if those stimuli are otherwise viewed negatively. When the goal was completed, evaluations were found to revert immediately back to their default state. These findings are reminiscent of the successful intervention by Sherif, Harvey, White, Hood, and Sherif (1961) in the famous Robbers' Cave summer camp study: Giving the two warring bands of campers a common goal, for which they needed the cooperation of the other group to succeed, made friends out of summer-long "enemies."

And in another demonstration of an active (nonconscious) goal overriding automatic, habitual responding, Sassenberg and Moskowitz (2005) primed a "think-different" goal of generating creative solutions to a problem. Participants in the think-different condition indeed generated more unusual uses for a given object and more uncommon answers in a free-association task, instead of the usual, more easily generated ones.

Successful Goals Are Self-Perpetuating

Once a goal pursuit attempt is completed, the goal deactivates (e.g., Atkinson & Birch, 1970; Lewin, 1926) and then inhibits the mental representations used to attain the goal (Förster et al., 2005). In the case of nonconscious goal pursuit, it is clear that the deactivation of the goal must occur independently of conscious intention and awareness (because the individual was not even aware the goal was active in the first place). Thus, several studies have found that once a nonconscious goal is satisfied, its influence on cognition and behavior disappears (e.g., Kawada et al., 2004). The same goal turn-off effect occurs for conscious goals as well, of course, even for positively valued, prosocial goals such as helping another person (Bargh et al., 2007, Study 3). Our point is that the goal turn-off is part of the autonomous operation of the (selfish) goal, and not under the individual's (or self's) awareness and control; this can be seen most clearly in studies where an unequivocally positive goal deactivates after fulfillment, actually inhibiting the individual from continuing to behave in this positive fashion! A dramatic example of this phenomenon is found in recent research on "moral credentials" (e.g., Monin & Miller, 2001).

Monin and Miller (2001) found that participants who were given the opportunity to disagree with blatantly sexist comments (thus fulfilling their goal to be egalitarian and nonsexist) were later more willing (compared to a control condition) to recommend a man for a stereotypically male job. According to the authors, after participants had been allowed to establish their moral credentials in the first part of the experiment, they stopped pursuing this goal in a subsequent part. Thus, after the egalitarian goal was fulfilled, it shut off, leaving its "host" individual vulnerable to behaving in a manner contrary to his or her egalitarian values.

The recently discovered "Macbeth effect" (Zhong & Liljenquist, 2006) provides another illustration of the goal-completion effect running against the individual's presumed values and behavioral intentions. In this study, participants were induced to consider performing some unethical behaviors and were then given a choice among several small gifts for taking part in the study. Compared to a control condition, these participants were more likely to choose an antiseptic tissue-wipe than other gifts. Most important, those who were given an opportunity to wash their hands after contemplating the unethical behavior subsequently were less likely to help a stranger. Considering an unethical act thus triggered the participants' goal to cleanse themselves in any way possible (i.e., morally or physically), and satisfying that goal by washing of the hands (physical cleansing) turned off the goal and made it less likely they would engage in ethical behavior (moral cleansing).

When participants who were morally threatened washed their hands, the selfish goal was fulfilled—and therefore no longer on the lookout for opportunities to restore its host's moral self. Consequently, participants who were morally restored were more likely to decline helping a person in need. Once again, as with the moral-credentialing effect, the effect of completion of the cleansing goal runs counter to the presumed conscious intentions of the individual. As one of the Macbeth-effect study's authors asked rhetorically in an on-line interview, "Do you really want your past sins to be easily washed away, which discourages you from engaging in ethical behaviors to help others?" (Hirshon, 2006).

The autonomy of selfish-goal operation even extends to its own perpetuation (another similarity between goals and genes). The consequences of conscious goal attempts for affective experience (mood) and the future strength of that goal have long been established (e.g., Bandura, 1977; Carver & Scheier, 1981; Heckhausen, 1991). Success at the attempt produces positive mood and increased tendencies to pursue that goal in the future; failure produces the opposite consequences. Research on nonconscious goal pursuit has shown that the same consequences accrue for goal attempts the individual is not even aware of making (Chartrand & Bargh, 2002). Participants were given an anagram task that was very easy or impossible to solve; the importance of this task was downplayed by the experimenter as a "filler task" in the larger study. However, for participants previously primed with the achievement (high-performance) goal, but not for control group participants, working on the easy anagram task (success condition) resulted in elevated mood and increased motivation to work on a subsequent verbal task, and working on the difficult anagram task produced depressed mood and lower effort on the subsequent task.

Thus, successful goals become stronger (more likely to be pursued again by the individual) and unsuccessful goals become weaker, all without the individual's knowledge or consent. Presumably this change in future goal strength is driven by the positive versus negative affect associated with the goal; that is, its "incentive value." As noted earlier, Pessiglione et al. (2007) showed this incentive value can be manipulated outside of conscious awareness, having the same effect on the individual's effort and performance as when manipulated explicitly and consciously. Similarly, recent experimental work by Custers and Aarts (2005, 2007) showed that conditioning a positive affective response to the name of a particular goal increases the chances the individual will pursue that goal over other possible alternatives, without the participants being aware of this influence on their choice of action. Thus, successful goals are self-perpetuating; more to the present point, their increase in strength and thus probability of being pursued in the future by the individual is determined autonomously, through mechanisms independent of the individual's conscious awareness and intent.

Conclusions

Just as genes are the unit of natural selection, not the individual organism or species (Dawkins, 1976), so too are active goals the unit of behavioral selection and control, not the individual pursuing them. We have reviewed evidence in support of the selfish-goal hypothesis that currently active goals operate independently of conscious awareness and purposes and can thus be shown to yield consequences that run counter to the individual's conscious intentions and values.

The theoretical parents of the selfish-goal hypothesis are "selfish-gene" theory (Dawkins, 1976) combined with the widely held view in evolutionary biology (and by some in evolutionary psychology) that motivations are the present-day agents of genetic influences from the distant past. Genes as the unit of natural selection pursue their own agenda (propagation) whether or not this is in the best interest of their host organism; similarly, goals (when active) as the proxies of genetic influences guide human cognition and behavior toward the goals' desired end-states, independently of conscious awareness and guidance by the individual. Goals, conscious and unconscious alike, are the local agents of genes, their instantiation in present time. Therefore, just as the selfish gene operates to further its own agenda independently of the interests of its host organism (for the gene, not the organism, is the unit of natural selection; see Dawkins, 1976; Dennett, 1995), the selfish goal has only its attainment "in mind" and not the overall interests of the goal holder. Accordingly, we have reviewed evidence from many domains that consistently show conscious and unconscious goal pursuit produce judgmental and behavioral outcomes that the person does not consciously intend and might well seek to avoid if aware of them.

We emphasize in closing that the fact of the "selfish goal" does not at all imply selfishness at the level of the individual person, mainly because the individual or "self" comprises many goals—self-interested ones to be sure, but also prosocial and morally principled ones as well (e.g., Mansbridge, 1990; Sen, 1978). Prosocial goals such as cooperation, helping, and putting the welfare of others over one's own have been shown to operate entirely automatically and nonconsciously, testifying to their innate or well-practiced nature (see Bargh et al., 2001, Study 2; Chen et al., 2001).

As selfishness means putting one's own welfare and needs above those of other people (Elster, 1990; Jencks, 1990), perhaps the best demonstration of a "selfless" (at the level of the individual) selfish goal comes from the Chen et al. (2001) study in which participants nonconsciously primed with the concept of power were given a choice of experimental tasks to complete, with full knowledge that an ostensibly late other participant would have to do the remaining tasks. For those participants with a communal relationship orientation (who tend to care more about the welfare of those they have power over; see Clark & Mills, 1993), the nonconscious effect of power was to activate their communal or altruistic goals, causing them to take more of the task burden on themselves, leaving less for the other person to do. And in another experiment (Bargh et al., 2001, Study 2), subliminal priming of the goal of cooperation caused participants playing the role of a fishing company to voluntarily put more fish back into a lake to replenish the fish population, thereby reducing their own profits in the game. These experimental findings were not driven by any self-presentational or "demand" effects given their nonconscious nature (the participants were not aware of the cause of their prosocial behavior), and thus demonstrate that goals that are selfish in terms of their own agenda, completion, and perpetuation are not selfish in terms of only pursuing the individual's own self-interest.

That goals can be selfish without making their "owners" selfish is a nice idea on which to end this chapter. It shows yet again that it is the active goal that is the unit of autonomous behavior control, not the individual human being (or "self")—just as Dawkins and others had shown earlier that the gene is the unit of natural selection, not the individual organism. The selfish goal pursues its agenda regardless of whether this fits the agenda of its individual host, just as selfish genes pursue their own propagation whether or not this is good for their host organisms. Conscious intentions and active goals are not the same thing, not at the level of brain physiology, nor at the level of the outcomes they produce. Little wonder then that to "know thyself," the task assigned to visitors by the ancient oracle of Delphi, is such a difficult one.

Acknowledgments

This research was supported by Grant No. MH R01 MH60767 from the U.S. Public Health Service. We thank Ezequiel Morsella for input and feedback.

References

Aarts, H., & Dijksterhuis, A. (2003). The silence of the library: Environmental control over social behavior. *Journal of Personality and Social Psychology, 84,* 18–28.

Ajzen, I., & Fishbein, M. (1980). *Understanding attitudes and predicting social behavior.* Englewood Cliffs, NJ: Prentice Hall.

Allman, J. M. (2000). *Evolving brains.* New York: Scientific American Library.

Anderson, R. C., & Pichert, J. W. (1978). Recall of previously unrecallable information following a shift in perspective. *Journal of Verbal Learning and Verbal Behavior, 17,* 1–12.

Atkinson, J. W., & Birch, D. (1970). *The dynamics of action*. New York: Wiley.

Bandura, A. (1977). Self-efficacy: Toward a unifying theory of behavioral change. *Psychological Review, 84*, 191–215.

Bandura, A. (1986). *Social foundations of thought and action: A social cognitive theory*. Englewood Cliffs, NJ: Prentice Hall.

Bargh, J. A. (1990). Goal Intention: Goal-directed thought and behavior are often unintentional. *Psychological Inquiry, 1*, 248–251.

Bargh, J. A. (1999). The cognitive monster: The case against controllability of automatic stereotype effects. In S. Chaiken & Y. Trope (Eds.), *Dual process theories in social psychology* (pp. 361–382). New York: Guilford Press.

Bargh, J. A. (2005). Bypassing the will: Towards demystifying behavioral priming effects. In R. Hassin, J. Uleman & J. Bargh (Eds.), *The new unconscious* (pp. 37–58). Oxford, UK: Oxford University Press.

Bargh, J. A. (Ed.). (2007). *Social psychology and the unconscious: The automaticity of higher mental processes*. Philadelphia: Psychology Press.

Bargh, J. A., Chen, M., & Burrows, L. (1996). Automaticity of social behavior: Direct effects of trait construct and stereotype priming on action. *Journal of Personality and Social Psychology, 71*, 230–244.

Bargh, J. A., & Ferguson, M. J. (2000). Beyond behaviorism: The automaticity of higher mental processes. *Psychological Bulletin, 126*, 925–945.

Bargh, J. A., & Gollwitzer, P. M. (1994). Environmental control over goal-directed action. *Nebraska Symposium on Motivation, 41*, 71–124.

Bargh, J. A., Gollwitzer, P. M., Lee-Chai, A., Barndollar, K., & Trotschel, R. (2001). The automated will: Unconscious activation and pursuit of behavioral goals. *Journal of Personality and Social Psychology, 81*, 1004–1027.

Bargh, J. A., Green, M. L., & Fitzsimons, G. M. (2008). The selfish goal: Unintended consequences of intended goal pursuit. *Social Cognition, 28*, 520–540.

Bargh, J. A., & Morsella, E. (2008). The unconscious mind. *Perspectives on Psychological Science, 3*, 73–79.

Baumeister, R. F., Bratslavsky, E., Muraven, M., & Tice, D. M. (1998). Ego depletion: Is the active self a limited resource? *Journal of Personality and Social Psychology, 74*, 1252–1265.

Bogen, J. E. (1995). On the neurophysiology of consciousness: II. Constraining the semantic problem. *Consciousness and Cognition, 4*, 137–158.

Brewer, M. B. (1988). A dual process model of impression formation. In T. K. Srull & R. S. Wyer, Jr. (Eds.), *Advances in social cognition* (Vol. 1, pp. 1–36). Hillsdale, NJ: Erlbaum.

Bruner, J. S. (1957). On perceptual readiness. *Psychological Review, 64*, 123–152.

Campbell, D. T. (1974). Evolutionary epistemology. In P. A. Schilpp (Ed.), *The philosophy of Karl Popper* (pp. 413–463). La Salle, IL: Open Court Publishing.

Carver, C. S., & Scheier, M. F. (1981). *Attention and self-regulation: A control-theory approach to human behavior*. New York: Springer-Verlag.

Chaiken, S., & Trope, Y. (1999). *Dual process theories in social psychology*. New York: Guilford Press.

Chartrand, T. L., & Bargh, J. A. (1996). Automatic activation of social information processing goals: Nonconscious priming reproduces effects of explicit conscious instructions. *Journal of Personality and Social Psychology, 71,* 464–478.

Chartrand, T. L., & Bargh, J. A. (2002). Nonconscious motivations: Their activation, operation, and consequences. In A. Tesser, D. Stapel, & J. Wood (Eds.), *Self and motivation: Emerging psychological perspectives* (pp. 13–41). Washington, DC: American Psychological Association Press.

Chen, S., Lee-Chai, A. Y., & Bargh, J. A. (2001). Relationship orientation as a moderator of the effects of social power. *Journal of Personality and Social Psychology, 80,* 173–187.

Clark, M. S., & Mills, J. (1993). The difference between communal and exchange relationships: What it is and is not. *Personality and Social Psychology Bulletin, 19,* 684–691.

Custers, R., & Aarts, H. (2005). Positive affect as implicit motivator: On the nonconscious operation of behavioral goals. *Journal of Personality and Social Psychology, 89,* 129–142.

Custers, R., & Aarts, H. (2007). In search of the nonconscious sources of goal pursuit: Accessibility and positive affective valence of the goal state. *Journal of Experimental and Social Psychology, 43,* 312–318.

Darley, J., & Latane, B. (1968). Bystander intervention in emergencies: Diffusion of responsibility. *Journal of Personality and Social Psychology, 8,* 377–383.

Dawes, R. M. (1993). Prediction of the future versus an understanding of the past: A basic asymmetry. *American Journal of Psychology, 106,* 1–24.

Dawkins, R. (1976). *The selfish gene.* New York: Oxford University Press.

Dennett, D. C. (1991). *Consciousness explained.* Boston: Little, Brown.

Dennett, D. C. (1995). *Darwin's dangerous idea: Evolution and the meanings of life.* New York: Simon & Schuster.

Devine, P. G. (1989). Stereotypes and prejudice: Their automatic and controlled components. *Journal of Personality and Social Psychology, 56,* 5–18.

Dijksterhuis, A., Aarts, H., & Chartrand, T. L. (2007). Automatic behavior. In J. A. Bargh (Ed.), *Social psychology and the unconscious: The automaticity of higher mental processes* (pp. 51–131). Philadelphia: Psychology Press.

Dijksterhuis, A., & van Knippenberg, A. (1998). The relation between perception and behavior or how to win a game of Trivial Pursuit. *Journal of Personality and Social Psychology, 74,* 865–877.

Donald, M. (1991). *Origins of the modern mind.* Cambridge, MA: Harvard University Press.

Elster, J. (1990). Selfishness and altruism. In J. J. Mansbridge (Ed.), *Beyond self-interest* (pp. 44–52). Chicago: University of Chicago Press.

Fazio, R. H. (1986). How do attitudes guide behavior? In R. M. Sorrentino & E. T. Higgins (Eds.), *Handbook of motivation and cognition* (Vol. 1, pp. 204–243). New York: Guilford Press.

Fazio, R. H. (1990). Multiple processes by which attitudes guide behavior: The MODE model as an integrative framework. In M. P. Zanna (Ed.), *Advances in experimental social psychology* (Vol. 23, pp. 75–109). New York: Academic Press.

Ferguson, M. J., & Bargh, J. A. (2004). Liking is for doing: The effects of goal pursuit on automatic evaluation. *Journal of Personality and Social Psychology, 87,* 557–572.

Ferguson, M. J., Hassin, R., & Bargh, J. A. (2008). Implicit motivation: Past, present, and future. In J. Shah & W. Gardner (Eds.), *Handbook of motivational science* (pp. 150–166). New York: Guilford Press.

Fitzsimons, G. M., & Bargh, J. A. (2003). Thinking of you: Nonconscious pursuit of interpersonal goals associated with relationship partners. *Journal of Personality and Social Psychology, 84,* 148–164.

Fitzsimons, G. M., & Bargh, J. A. (2004). Automatic self-regulation. In R. F. Baumeister & K. D. Vohs (Eds.), *Handbook of self-regulation: Research, theory, and applications* (pp. 151–170). New York: Guilford Press.

Förster, J., Liberman, N., & Higgins, E. T. (2005). Accessibility from active and fulfilled goals. *Journal of Experimental Social Psychology, 41,* 220–239.

Frith, C. D., Blakemore, S.-J., & Wolpert, D. M. (2000). Abnormalities in the awareness and control of action. *Philosophical Transactions of the Royal Society of London, 355,* 1771–1788.

Gilbert, D. T., & Hixon, J. G. (1991). The trouble of thinking: Activation and application of stereotypic beliefs. *Journal of Personality and Social Psychology, 60,* 509–517.

Gollwitzer, P. M., & Moskowitz, G. B. (1996). Goal effects on action and cognition. In E. T. Higgins & A. W. Kruglanski (Eds.), *Social psychology: Handbook of basic principles.* (pp. 361–399) New York: Guilford Press.

Hastie, R., & Park, B. (1986). The relationship between memory and judgment depends on whether the judgment task is memory-based or online. *Psychological Review, 93,* 258–268.

Heckhausen, H. (1991). *Motivation and action.* New York: Springer.

Higgins, E. T. (1996). Knowledge activation: Accessibility, applicability, and salience. In E. T. Higgins & A. W. Kruglanski (Eds.), *Social psychology: Handbook of basic principles* (pp. 133–168). New York: Guilford Press.

Higgins, E. T., Rholes, W. S., & Jones, C. R. (1977). Category accessibility and impression formation. *Journal of Experimental Social Psychology, 13,* 141–154.

Hirshon, B. (2006, October 5). Washing away your sins. *Science Update.* Available at *www.scienceupdate.com/show.php?date=20061005.*

Holland, R. W., Hendriks, M., & Aarts, H. (2005). Smells like clean spirit: Nonconscious effects of scent on cognition and behavior. *Psychological Science, 16,* 689–693.

Jencks, C. (1990). Varieties of altruism. In J. J. Mansbridge (Ed.), *Beyond self-interest* (pp. 53–67). Chicago: University of Chicago Press.

Kawada, C. L. K., Oettingen, G., Gollwitzer, P. M., & Bargh, J. A. (2004). The projection of implicit and explicit goals. *Journal of Personality and Social Psychology, 86,* 545–559.

Kay, A. C., Wheeler, S. C., Bargh, J. A., & Ross, L. (2004). Material priming: The influence of mundane physical objects on situational construal and competitive behavioral choice. *Organizational Behavior and Human Decision Processes, 95,* 83–96.

Koch, C., & Tsuchiya, N. (2007). Attention and consciousness: two distinct brain processes. *Trends in Cognitive Sciences, 11*, 16–22.

Kruglanski, A. W., Shah, J. Y., Fishbach, A., Friedman, R., Chun, W. Y., Sleeth-Keppler, D. (2002). A theory of goal systems. In M. P. Zanna (Ed.), *Advances in experimental social psychology* (pp. 331–378). San Diego: Academic Press.

Kurzban, R., & Aktipis, C. A. (2007). Modularity and the social mind: Are psychologists too self-ish? *Personality and Social Psychology Review, 11*, 131–149.

Kurzban, R., Tooby, J., & Cosmides, L. (2001). Can race be erased? Coalitional computation and social categorization. *Proceedings of the National Academy of Sciences USA, 98*, 15387–15392.

Lewin, K. (1926). Vorsatz, wille, und bedürfnis [Intention, will, and need]. *Psychologische Forschung, 7*, 330–385.

Lhermitte, F. (1986). Human anatomy and the frontal lobes: Part II: Patient behavior in complex and social situations: The "environmental dependency syndrome." *Annals of Neurology, 19*, 335–343.

Livnat, A., & Pippenger, N. (2006). An optimal brain can be composed of conflicting agents. *Proceedings of the National Academy of Sciences USA, 103*, 3198–3202.

Locke, E. A., & Latham, G. P. (1990). *A theory of goal setting and task performance.* Englewood Cliffs, NJ: Prentice Hall.

Locke, E. A., & Latham, G. P. (2002). Building a practically useful theory of goal setting and task performance: A 35-year odyssey. *American Psychologist, 57*, 705–717.

Mack, A. (2003). Inattentional blindness: Looking without seeing. *Current Directions in Psychological Science, 12*, 180–184.

Maner, J. K., Kenrick, D. T., Becker, D. V., Delton, A. W., Hofer, B., Wilbur, L. J., & Neuberg, S. L. (2003). Sexually selective cognition: Beauty captures the mind of the beholder. *Journal of Personality and Social Psychology, 85*, 1107–1120.

Mansbridge, J. J. (1990). The rise and fall of self-interest in the explanation of political life. In J. J. Mansbridge (Ed.), *Beyond self-interest* (pp. 3–22). Chicago: University of Chicago Press:

Mayr, E. (1976). *Evolution and the diversity of life.* Cambridge, MA: Harvard University Press.

McCulloch, K. D., Ferguson, M. J., Kawada, C., & Bargh, J. A. (2008). Taking a closer look: On the operation of nonconscious impression formation. *Journal of Experimental Social Psychology, 44*, 614–623.

Milgram, S. (1963). Behavioral study of obedience. *Journal of Abnormal and Social Psychology, 67*, 371–378.

Mischel, W. (1973) Toward a cognitive social learning reconceptualization of personality. *Psychological Review, 80*, 252–283.

Monin, B., & Miller, D. T. (2001). Moral credentials and the expression of prejudice. *Journal of Personality and Social Psychology, 81*, 33–43.

Morsella, E. (2005). The function of phenomenal states: Supramodular interaction theory. *Psychological Review, 112*, 1000–1021.

Moskowitz, G. B., Gollwitzer, P. M., Wasel, W., & Schaal, B. (1999). Preconscious control of stereotype activation through chronic egalitarian goals. *Journal of Personality and Social Psychology, 77,* 167–184.

Muzur, A., Pace-Schott, E. F., & Hobson, J. A. (2002). The prefrontal cortex in sleep. *Trends in Cognitive Sciences, 6,* 475–481.

Neuberg, S. L., Kenrick, D. T., Maner, J. K., & Schaller, M. (2004). From evolved motives to everyday mentation: Evolution, goals, and cognition. In J. Forgas & K. Williams (Eds.), *Social motivation: Conscious and unconscious processes* (pp. 133–152). New York: Cambridge University Press.

Pessiglione, M., Schmidt, L., Draganski, B., Kalisch, R., Lau, H., Dolan, R., et al. (2007, April 12). How the brain translates money into force: A neuroimaging study of subliminal motivation. *Science, 316,* 904–906.

Pinker, S. (1994). *The language instinct.* New York: William Morrow.

Pinker, S., & Bloom, P. (1990). Natural language and natural selection. *Behavioral and Brain Sciences, 13,* 707–784.

Popper, K. R. (1972). *Objective knowledge: An evolutionary approach.* Oxford, UK: Oxford University Press.

Posner, M. J., & Snyder, C. R. (1975). Attention and cognitive control. In R. L. Solso (Ed.), *Information processing in cognition: The Loyola Symposium* (pp. 55–85). Hillsdale, NJ: Erlbaum.

Ross, L., & Nisbett, R. E. (1991). *The person and the situation: Perspectives of social psychology.* New York: McGraw-Hill.

Sassenberg, K., & Moskowitz, G. B. (2005). Do not stereotype, think different! Overcoming automatic stereotype activation by mindset priming. *Journal of Experimental Social Psychology, 41,* 317–413.

Sen, A. K. (1978). Rational fools: A critique of the behavioral foundations of economic theory. In H. Harris (Ed.), *Scientific models and men* (pp. 317–344). New York: Oxford University Press.

Shah, J. Y. (2003). Automatic for the people: How representations of significant others implicit affects goal pursuit. *Journal of Personality and Social Psychology, 84,* 661–681.

Sherif, M., Harvey, O. J., White, B. J., Hood, W. R., & Sherif, C. (1961). *Intergroup conflict and cooperation: The Robbers Cave experiment.* Norman: University of Oklahoma.

Shiffrin, R. M., & Schneider, W. (1977). Controlled and automatic human information processing: II. Perceptual learning, automatic attending, and a general theory. *Psychological Review, 84,* 127–190.

Simons, D. J., & Chabris, C. F. (1999). Gorillas in our midst: Sustained inattentional blindness for dynamic events. *Perception, 28,* 1059–1074.

Smith, E. E., & Jonides, J. (1998). Storage and executive processes in the frontal lobes. *Science, 283,* 1657–1661.

Spencer, S. J., Fein, S., Wolfe, C., Fong, C., & Dunn, M. (1998). Stereotype activation under cognitive load: The moderating role of self-image threat. *Personality and Social Psychology Bulletin, 24,* 1139–1152.

Srull, T. K., & Wyer, R. S., Jr. (1979). The role of category accessibility in the interpretation of information about persons: Some determinants and implications. *Journal of Personality and Social Psychology, 37,* 1660–1672.

Symons, D. (1992). On the use and misuse of Darwinism in the study of human behavior. In J. H. Barkow, L. Cosmides, & J. Tooby (Eds.), *The adapted mind: Evolutionary psychology and the generation of culture* (pp. 137–159). New York: Oxford University Press.

Tetlock, P. E. (2002). Social functionalist frameworks for judgments and choice: Intuitive politicians, theologians, and prosecutors. *Psychological Review, 109*, 451–471.

Tomasello, M., Carpenter, M., Call, J., Behne, T., & Moll, H. (2005). Understanding and sharing intentions: The origins of cultural cognition. *Behavioral and Brain Sciences, 28*, 675–691.

Tooby, J., & Cosmides, L. (1992). The psychological foundations of culture. In J. H. Barkow, L. Cosmides, & J. Tooby (Eds.), *The adapted mind: Evolutionary psychology and the generation of culture* (pp. 19–136). New York: Oxford University Press.

Zhong, C.-B., & Liljenquist, K. (2006, Sept. 8). Washing away your sins: Threatened morality and physical cleansing. *Science, 313*, 1451–1452.

PART II

HOW ARE GOALS SELECTED?

CHAPTER 6

Fantasies and Motivationally Intelligent Goal Setting

GABRIELE OETTINGEN
ELIZABETH J. STEPHENS

The self-help industry would have us believe that to "think positive" is the single most effective means of getting what we want. And though empirical research does consistently find that optimistic beliefs foster motivation and successful performance (Bandura, 1997; Heckhausen, 1991; Seligman, 1991; Taylor & Brown, 1988), recent research reveals that alternate forms of positively thinking about the future (e.g., positive fantasies; Oettingen & Mayer, 2002; wishful thinking and other avoidant coping styles; Lengua & Sandler, 1996, Holahan & Moos, 1986) are less beneficial for effortful action, performance, and well-being. Although at first glance it seems contradictory that optimistic beliefs and positive thoughts should lead to such disparate motivational outcomes, whether one mentally indulges in a desired future (i.e., has positive fantasies about a desired future) or actually judges a desired future as within reach (i.e., has positive expectations about a desired future; Oettingen & Mayer, 2002) has very different implications for effortful action and successful performance.

Oettingen and Mayer (2002) distinguish between two ways of thinking about the future: expectations and fantasies. Expectations are judgments of how likely it is that certain events or behaviors will occur in the future (Bandura, 1977; Mischel, 1973; review by Olson, Roese, & Zanna, 1996). Based on experiences in the past, and thus on a person's performance history, expectations specify the probability of whether an event will actually happen or not. These expectancy judgments are conceptualized as self-efficacy expectations (i.e., whether one can perform a certain behavior in its relative context; Bandura, 1997), as outcome expectations (i.e., whether performing the behavior will produce the desired outcome; Bandura, 1997), as general expectations (i.e., whether a certain event will occur; Heckhausen, 1991; Oettingen & Wadden, 1991), or as generalized expectations (i.e., whether the future in general will be positive or negative; Scheier & Carver, 1992). Conversely, free fantasies are future events or behaviors that appear in the mind (Klinger, 1990; Singer, 1966), independent of whether it is likely or unlikely that they will occur. For example, despite perceiving the chances of competing in the Olympics to be low, a competitive swimmer can indulge in positive fantasies about receiving a gold medal at the next Olympic Games.

Moreover, the two ways of thinking about the future have different predictive values with regards to effortful action and performance. As expectations judge the likelihood of future outcomes by applying past facts to future events (Bandura, 1977, 1997; Mischel, 1973), these types of beliefs prove a valid base for strong behavioral investment and indeed are powerful predictors of future behavior (e.g., Bandura, 1978). In contrast, as positive fantasies embellish future events regardless of past performance and probability of future occurrences (Klinger, 1990; Singer, 1966), these types of thoughts fail to serve as a solid basis for acting. Furthermore, by seducing one to indulge in images of a desired and smoothly attained future these types of thoughts should yield little effort to achieve the desired future.

Several studies examining the predictive power of thinking about the future attest to the different motivating functions of expectations versus fantasies (Oettingen & Mayer, 2002). In one example, women who were obese enrolled in a weight reduction program with positive expectations about losing weight (e.g., "It is likely that I will lose weight") lost on average 26 pounds more than those with negative expectations (e.g., "It is unlikely that I will lose weight"). However, participants with positive fantasies (e.g., those who imagined easily resisting the temptation of a leftover box of doughnuts in the lunch room) lost on average 24 pounds fewer than participants with negative fantasies (e.g., those who imagined having a hard time resisting a leftover box of doughnuts in the lunch room; Oettingen & Wadden, 1991). In another example, participants with high expectations of success about finding a well-suited job after college graduation received more job offers and enjoyed higher salaries over the course of 2 years than those reporting more negative expectations of success. However, participants with positive fantasies about finding a well-suited job after college graduation were less successful in their job search over 2 years, sending out fewer applications, receiving fewer job offers, and ultimately earning less money than those with more negative fantasies (Oettingen & Mayer, 2002, Study 1). Other similar studies focusing on thoughts about entering a romantic relationship (e.g., starting a relationship with a secretly admired individual; Oettingen & Mayer, 2002, Study 2), achieving academic success (e.g., performing well on a midterm exam; Oettingen & Mayer, 2002, Study 3), and recovering from hip replacement surgery (e.g., increasing range of hip joint motion, walking on stairs, general recovery; Oettingen & Mayer, 2002, Study 4) provide further evidence that positive expectations predict high effort and performance, whereas positive fantasies predict low effort and performance.

If, as shown in the abovementioned studies, fantasies are problematic for effort and action, the question thus becomes what can be done with these thoughts to make them fruitful for effort and action? One possibility would be to question the unrestricted enjoyment of the desired outcome and its smooth attainment, for example, by considering present factors that potentially hinder attainment of the desired outcome (e.g., a wish about one day getting an A in Biochemistry is juxtaposed with a current lack of effective study skills). Because fantasizing alone about desired outcomes conceals the necessity to act, pairing these thoughts with thoughts about the present reality that stands in the way of fantasy realization could reveal an existing discrepancy between the present and desired future, that is, to achieve what one wants, one needs to make changes in the here and now. Moreover, grounding such thoughts in aspects of the present, impeding reality should facilitate the activation of judgments about whether or not one could actually reach the desired outcome. In other words, juxtaposing fantasies about a desired future with aspects of the present reality should prompt individuals to consider their expectations of reaching a desired outcome that in turn prove critical for effort and action.

As mentioned previously, expectations judge the likelihood of future outcomes by applying past facts to future events (Bandura, 1977, 1997; Mischel, 1973). Theories of motivation contend that beliefs guide action, that is, perceiving a future state or behavior as feasible (i.e., having high expectations) and desirable (i.e., high incentive) motivates individuals to act toward realizing that future (Bandura, 1997; summary by Heckhausen, 1991). However, although expectancy and incentive are the two main determinants of goal-directed behavior, these beliefs do not guarantee action. Certainly we have all had wishes (e.g., meeting a deadline) that were feasible (e.g., 6 months writing period for a 30-page chapter, experience writing successful chapters in the past) and desirable (e.g., happy editors, opportunity to highlight your recent work), yet we nevertheless failed to take the necessary action to realize those wishes. Therefore, for expectations to guide action they need to first become activated, yet how is this accomplished? To illustrate this notion we want to briefly consider some findings from animal psychology.

Edward C. Tolman (1925), a neo-behaviorist working with *Mus norvegicus albinus,* proposed that animals acquire expectations (i.e., "cognitive-like map"; Tolman, 1948) about the layout of a maze as a function of running through it. Tolman (1948) suggested that rats' expectations of the maze served to determine "what responses, if any, the animal will finally release" (p. 191). However, what he found was that only the rats with the motivation to search (i.e., they had to be hungry) were the ones who utilized their expectations (i.e., activated cognitive maps) to maneuver through the maze to find available food (i.e., incentive). That is, rats only then demonstrated that they had been building a cognitive map "once they were motivated to do so" (i.e., there was food at the end of the maze; Tolman, 1948, p. 193). What Tolman's findings therefore show is that unless expectations become activated, these seeds of behavior remain dormant, and that in rats, to activate expectations, and thus behavior, some type of incentive (e.g., food) is inherently necessary.

Yet are the factors, as described by Tolman, sufficient to activate human expectations and thus influence behavior? Desirability and feasibility, as mentioned before, play a role, but what more is necessary to activate our expectations (i.e., cognitive maps) and thus prompt us to act toward a coveted future? A recent model of fantasy realization (Oettingen, 2000; Oettingen, Pak, & Schnetter, 2001) proposes specific thought processes (e.g., self-regulatory strategy of mental contrasting; Oettingen, 2000) that serve to turn free fantasies about a desired future into binding goals. Specifically, the model assumes that mentally contrasting aspects of the future and reality activates expectations about attaining a desired future that in turn leads to persistent goal striving and effective goal attainment in the case of high expectations. This chapter focuses on this self-regulatory strategy (i.e., mental contrasting of future and reality) that people can use to help them commit to goals of realizing a desired future based on the perceived likelihood (i.e., based on expectations), in addition to two other self-regulatory strategies, indulging in aspects of the future and dwelling on aspects of the present reality, which make people form commitment to goals irrespective of expectations. This chapter begins by examining these strategies in detail, describing their effects and scope, then presents current research showing motivational and cognitive mechanisms of the three self-regulatory strategies. Finally, the last section of the chapter introduces translational research establishing how interventions that teach people how to use these strategies as a metacognitive tool can affect and improve their personal and professional lives.

Three Strategies of Fantasy Realization

Fantasy realization theory (Oettingen, 1999, 2000) elucidates three routes to goal setting that result from how people elaborate their fantasies about desired futures. One route leads to expectancy-based goal commitment, whereas the other two routes lead to goal commitment independent of expectations. This section describes these three self-regulatory strategies of fantasy realization, one in particular that helps people translate their expectations into appropriate goal-directed behavior.

Mental Contrasting

The expectancy-based route to goal commitment rests on mentally contrasting fantasies about a desired future with aspects of the present reality. When people use the self-regulatory strategy of mental contrasting (Oettingen, 1999), they first imagine a desired future (e.g., improving in academic or professional performance) and then reflect on the respective negative reality (e.g., having little time or being distracted). The conjoint elaboration of the positive future and the negative reality makes future and reality simultaneously accessible (Kawada, 2004) and activates the relational construct (Higgins & Chaires, 1980) of the negative reality standing in the way of realizing the desired future, thereby emphasizing a necessity to change the present reality to achieve the desired future. This necessity to act should activate relevant expectations of success, which then informs goal commitment. When perceived feasibility is high, people strongly commit to attaining the goal of changing the status quo and realizing the desired future; when perceived feasibility is low, people form weak goal commitment or none at all.

Indulging and Dwelling

The second route to goal commitment originates from solely fantasizing about a positive future. Such indulging in thoughts about the positive future seduces a person to mentally enjoy the future in the here and now because there are no reflections on the present reality that would point to the fact that the positive future is not yet realized. Thus, a necessity to act is not induced and expectations of success are not activated and used. Commitment toward fantasy realization solely reflects the individual's prior determination to attain the desired future. It should be independent of the perceived chances of success (i.e., expectations of success). As a consequence, people will try too hard when underlying expectations of success are low and not try hard enough when underlying expectations of success are high.

The third route to goal commitment is based on merely reflecting on the negative reality. Dwelling on the negative reality produces continual ruminations, as no fantasies about a positive future designate the direction to act. Hence, a necessity to act is not induced, and expectations are not activated and used. Commitment toward fantasy realization solely reflects the individual's prior determination to attain the desired future. Similar to indulging, commitment should be independent of the perceived chances of success (i.e., expectations of success).

Numerous studies show that mental contrasting turns free fantasies into binding goals by activating expectations, thus influencing subsequent goal commitment and goal-directed behavior (e.g., Oettingen, 2000; Oettingen et al., 2001). In one study (Oettingen et al., 2001, Study 4), freshmen in a vocational school for computer programming reported their expectations for excelling in math, a critical subject within their school, and then had to either engage in mental contrasting, indulging, or dwelling regarding math achievement. Teacher-rated study efforts and course grades, assessed 2 weeks after the experiment, showed that participants with high expectations in the mental contrasting group invested more effort and attained better grades than all other participants, whereas, in the indulging and dwelling groups, participants showed commitment independent of participants' perceived chances of success. The same pattern of results occurred in a study with 12-year-old middle school students where the desired future pertained to excelling in learning a foreign language (Oettingen, Hönig, & Gollwitzer, 2000, Study 1), in students wishing to solve an interpersonal problem (Oettingen et al., 2001, Studies 1 and 3), and in students being offered the opportunity to get to know an attractive stranger (Oettingen, 2000, Study 1).

Furthermore, two recent studies show that the range of mental contrasting effects extends from desired futures to which people readily commit (e.g., achievement-, interpersonal-, leisure/hobby-related desired futures), up to those that people are hesitant to commit to (e.g., offering and requesting help). After first establishing that people are indeed more hesitant to commit to goals that require help giving and help seeking, it was found that mental contrasting with high expectations helped pediatric nurses commit to goals of improving communication with patients' relatives, a critical help-giving job demand, as well as helped students commit to goals of asking comparatively unapproachable individuals for their assistance.

It is important to note that the outcomes of mental contrasting do not occur as a result of a change in expectations or incentive value, but rather as a result of the mode of self-regulatory thought, aligning commitment with expectations (Oettingen et al., 2001). Furthermore, it is important to mention here that the effects of mental contrasting are dependent upon the ensuing perception of the present standing in the way of the future. When engaging in mental contrasting, individuals first elaborate a desired future, establishing the positive future as their reference point and only thereafter elaborate aspects of the present reality, thereby perceiving the negative aspects as obstacles standing in the way of attaining the future.

Reversing this order (i.e., reverse mental contrasting), by first elaborating the negative reality followed by elaboration of the desired future, thwarts construal of the present standing in the way of the future and thus fails to elicit goal commitment congruent with expectations of success (Oettingen, et al., 2001, Study 3).

Summary

Thus far, evidence was presented that mental contrasting enables people to commit to their desired futures in line with their expectations of attaining the desired future, and that mental contrasting is effective in promoting commitment to goals that are initially hard to commit to. The cumulative results of these studies attest to the power of mental contrasting as a self-regulatory strategy to turn free fantasies into binding goals by facilitating the activation and transformation of high expectations into strong commitment and low expectations into weak or no commitment. Recent research extends these findings by uncovering the motivational and cognitive processes behind mental contrasting, essentially the mechanisms underlying how mental contrasting effectively translates beliefs into goal commitment and effective goal pursuit.

Mechanisms of Mental Contrasting

Previous research examining the thought processes of mental contrasting, indulging, and dwelling focused predominantly on the outcomes of the three self-regulatory strategies (i.e., expectation-dependent versus expectation-independent goal commitment; e.g., Oettingen et al., 2001). Still absent from the overall picture though was how mental contrasting influences expectation-congruent goal commitment and thus fosters effective goal pursuit. The next several studies present the underlying motivational and cognitive processes responsible for these effects and provide neural data substantiating and extending the theoretical principles.

Energization

Locke and Latham (2002) identified feelings of energization as paramount to promoting goal-directed behavior. They contended that commitment to realizing a desired future has an "energizing function" (i.e., activity incitement; Brunstein & Gollwitzer, 1996), for example, desired futures that prove more challenging to achieve (e.g., a seasoned marathon runner who sets her sights on beating a personal best time) give rise to greater effort than less challenging desired futures (e.g., a seasoned marathon runner who sets her sights on finishing an upcoming marathon; Locke & Latham). As previously discussed, mental contrasting, unlike indulging or dwelling, activates the perception of the present reality standing in the way of the desired future, which consequently prompts a need to act and catalyzes expectation activation. When the perceived chances of attaining the desired future appear high, feelings of energization should propel individuals forward on their quest toward goal attainment, ultimately resulting in strong goal commitment. Thus, whether energization serves as a mechanism responsible for the effects of mental contrasting on expectation-dependent goal pursuit is the focus of the next two studies (Oettingen, Mayer, Sevincer, et al., 2008).

Using an acute stress paradigm (i.e., videotaped public speaking; al'Absi et al., 1997), quantity and quality of goal striving were observed in the laboratory. Economics students participating in this study were informed that they were to deliver a speech in front of a video camera to help with the development of a measure of professional skills for a human resource department. Participants were randomly assigned to either a mental contrasting or an indulging condition. As dependent variables participants indicated their initial feelings of energization with a self-report measure (e.g., how energized do you feel when you think about giving your talk) and to gauge participants' evaluations of their own presentations they were asked to rate their actual performance. Persistence of goal striving was indicated by the length of each participant's presentation, and quality of goal striving was assessed via independent raters' evaluations of the quality of the videotape content (Oettingen, Mayer, Sevincer, et al., 2008, Study 2).

Consistent with previous mental contrasting studies, individuals in the mental contrasting group, in contrast to those in the indulging condition, evidenced a strong link between perceived expectations of success and goal pursuit as measured by subjective self-evaluations of performance and objective ratings of the videotaped presentations. Moreover, feelings of energization not only showed the same pattern of results as the goal pursuit variables (i.e., congruous with goal commitment and striving), but also predicted objective and subjective presentation quality. Additionally, in the mental contrasting condition feelings of energization significantly mediated the relationship between expectations of success and subjective and objective performance quality. Physiological data substantiate these findings by demonstrating the same pattern of results for mental contrasting as measured by cardiovascular responses (Oettingen, Mayer, Sevincer, et al., in press, Study 1). Cardiovascular responses, such as systolic blood pressure, are shown to be reliable indicators of physiological arousal states and effort mobilization (Gendolla & Wright, 2005; Wright & Kirby, 2001). Indeed in this study, objective measurement of energization via systolic blood pressure during the thought process of mental contrasting and indulging supported the familiar pattern of results and the notion that energization is a motivational mediator explaining the expectation–commitment link produced as a result of mental contrasting.

These two studies examining energization as a mediator of the effect of mental contrasting versus indulging not only highlight the role of energization in expectation-dependent goal commitment, but also point to one implication of feelings of energization, namely that energization resulting from mental contrasting in one domain could transfer to other potentially unrelated domains. This transfer effect could have implications, for example, when one engages in mental contrasting with regards to an interpersonal concern; energization resulting from this process could transfer to an unrelated task, like studying for an upcoming test, thus potentially influencing subsequent commitment and action toward an important, yet unrelated desired outcome.

Planning for Upcoming Hindrances

Failing to prepare and plan for upcoming hindrances on the way toward achieving a desired future compromises one's chances of success (Gollwitzer, 1999). Because mental contrasting influences individuals to view the negative aspects of the present reality as obstacles hindering the attainment of a desired future, mental contrasting individuals with high expectancies should prepare for potential impediments by planning out in advance strategies to help them tackle any future bumps in the road. Explicitly, mental contrasting individuals with high expectancies should spontaneously form if–then plans (i.e., implementation intentions: If situation X, then I will perform Y; see Gollwitzer 1999), shown to be highly effective facilitators of goal striving in a host of domains (meta-analysis by Gollwitzer & Sheeran, 2006). Moreover, because these plans are shown to materialize during the mental contrasting procedure (i.e., Oettingen et al., 2001, Study 1; Oettingen, Mayer, Thorpe, Janetzke, & Lorenz, 2005, Study 2), they should serve as a cognitive mechanism responsible for the effects of mental contrasting versus the other self-regulation strategies on goal commitment. Whether or not this tendency to form plans actually serves as a cognitive mechanism responsible for the different effects of the self-regulatory strategies on commitment serves as the basis for the next study.

For this recent study, participants first indicated an important interpersonal concern (e.g., solving a conflict with a friend, being friendlier to parents) and, thereafter, had to engage in either mental contrasting, indulging, dwelling, or reverse mental contrasting (i.e., participants started first with elaboration of the reality followed by elaboration of the future). Additionally, participants answered questions assessing their commitment to resolving their interpersonal concern (e.g., actively pursuing their desired outcome).

To assess the mediating variable for this study two independent raters content analyzed participants' elaborations of the negative aspects of the reality in either the mental contrasting, dwelling, or reverse contrasting conditions to assess the number of implementation intentions (e.g., "If I come home feeling overworked, then I will still spend at least half an hour with [my partner]") formed as a result of experimental condition. A significant benefit of this method is its ability to capture participants' plan formation during the process of mental contrasting versus noncontrasting thought (i.e., dwelling and reverse contrasting).

As presumed, plan formation emerged congruent with expectations in the mental contrasting condition and irrespective of expectations in the dwelling and reverse mental contrasting conditions (because negative aspects of the present reality fail to emerge in the indulging condition, determining plan formation in response to these negative aspects was not possible in this group). Specifically, the formation of if–then plans (i.e., implementation intentions; Gollwitzer, 1999) showed the same pattern of results as the goal-pursuit variables (i.e., congruous with goal commitment and striving) and also predicted participants' goal pursuit to resolve their concerns. Additionally, in the mental contrasting condition, forming implementation intentions fully mediated the relation between expectations of success and objective performance quality. Thus, when people are in the mental contrasting condition and have high expectations of success they begin to consider a course of action toward goal attainment and therefore make plans to overcome anticipated obstacles. Such planning in turn fosters goal attainment.

Thorough Obstacle Consideration

A person engaged in mental contrasting resembles a person challenged to problem solve: "He wants something and does not know immediately what series of actions he can perform to get it" (Newell & Simon, 1972, p. 72). According to Newell and Simon (1972) problem solving is effective inasmuch as an individual is capable of internalizing the objective task environment (e.g., the desired future and the negative reality standing in the way of attaining the desired future); mere awareness of one component (e.g., either the desired future or the negative reality) fails to provide a complete picture of the problem-solving task at hand. One result of the process of mental contrasting is promotion of effective problem solving through enabling conceptualization of "what series of actions he can perform [to attain a desired future]" (p. 72). Specifically, through the anticipation of obstacles that may impede fantasy realization one recognizes the course of action necessary to attain a desired future.

The essence of mental contrasting thus rests on calling to mind obstacles that impede the realization of a desired future. People who approach the problem of fantasy realization via mental contrasting should invest effort and time in generating obstacles. This hypothesis is in line with the finding that trying to arrive at a correct or comprehensive understanding of a given problem leads to expending more effort in retrieving and considering relevant information (Kruglanski & Freund, 1983; Chaiken, 1987; Sanbomatsu & Fazio, 1990; reviews by Kruglanski, 1996, and by Pittman, 1998). Thinking thoroughly about an issue involves retrieving less readily accessible but critical information from memory (Sanbomatsu & Fazio, 1990), as well as considering a greater number of pieces of information (Kruglanski, 1996). However, although individuals attend to obstacles during dwelling, this strategy should not lead to invested effort and time in generating obstacles because dwelling fails to provide a complete picture of the problem-solving task at hand. Thus after dwelling, the negative aspects of the present reality should not be scrutinized as critical pieces of information necessary for problem solving.

In this study college undergraduates first engaged in either mental contrasting, indulging, or dwelling pertaining to a leisure activity (e.g., finding more time for a hobby; Grant, Oettingen, Gollwitzer, & Schneider, 2008, Study 1). Thereafter, participants named their most important concerns in three other domains (e.g., achievement, interpersonal, and health) and listed obstacles related to those concerns. The dependent measure was the amount of time participants took to generate, in writing, the obstacles related to the other three concerns.

As predicted, individuals in the mental contrasting condition took more time than individuals in the indulging and dwelling conditions to generate obstacles standing in the way of the desired future. Moreover, thorough obstacle consideration held true across domains (e.g., academic, interpersonal, health), congruous with the transfer assumption of the Smith and Branscombe (1987) model of procedural strengthening and transfer (Gollwitzer, 1990), as participants who engaged in mental contrasting with respect to one domain (e.g., leisure activity) transferred the cognitive procedures to other subsequent domains (e.g., achievement, interpersonal and health). More specifically, those who engaged in mental contrasting focused on obstacles in one domain and thus carefully considered hindrances in another domain. Ostensibly, mental contrasting, as compared to indulging and dwelling, engages people in careful consideration of obstacles and additionally readies them to critically consider hindrances in regard to other concerns in their lives. That individuals in the dwelling condition did not expend more effort and time generating obstacles further illustrates that mental contrasting alone engrosses people in the aspects obstructing attainment of a desired future.

The research presented thus far concerning the mechanisms of mental contrasting used a combination of self-report measures, content analysis, and behavioral and physiological indicators to determine the resulting strength of commitment to strive toward a goal. However the following study elucidates the postulated cognitive components and processes of mental contrasting and indulging by looking at brain activity in relevant regions.

Neural Correlates

Mental contrasting, as opposed to indulging, presents itself as a cognitively demanding task, one requiring individuals to look into the future, past, and present, helping them to form goal commitment (i.e., intentions) in line with their expectations. As such, mental contrasting should be associated with greater activity in brain regions linked to *working memory processes* as mental-contrasting effects are based on mentally placing the present negative reality in the way of the desired future. However, mental contrasting should also lead to greater activity in brain areas associated with *episodic memory* because it demands the elaboration of obstacles. Such elaborations should recruit memories of relevant obstacles that were experienced in the past as well as relevant memories about past successes and failures in trying to overcome them. Mental contrasting should also be linked to heightened activity in brain regions that are related to vividly imagining events. As the mental-contrasting procedure demands switching back and forth from positive images about a desired future to images of impeding obstacles, images of the desired future and obstacles should become particularly vivid and crystallized. Finally, mental contrasting should lead to greater activity in brain regions that are related to *holding intentions* and *action preparation* because mental contrasting leads to the formation of strong goal commitment, given that relevant expectations of success are high.

Continuous magnetoencephalography (MEG), a brain-imaging technique measuring magnetic fields produced by electrical activity in the brain (Achtziger, Fehr, Oettingen, Gollwitzer, & Rockstroh, in press), was used to test the assumptions that mental contrasting and indulging appear as two different mental processes as illustrated by dissimilar patterns of brain activity in areas associated with working memory, episodic memory, intention maintenance, action preparation, and vivid visualization. Specifically, mental contrasting was predicted to show stronger activity in all regions of interest in comparison to indulging and resting.

First, university participants were pretested to identify those who could vividly and intensely represent the future and reality related to their concern, that is, those who were most able to self-induce both self-regulation strategies and who had high expectations for success of fully realizing their named concerns. Next, using a within-subject design, participants inside of the MEG machine relaxed during a 5-minute rest period, then *mentally* (as opposed to the standard written elaboration) engaged in either mental contrasting then indulging, or indulging then mental contrasting.

The dependent measures were the amount of activity in the brain regions of interest (i.e., pattern of dipoles per second) based on the mode of self-regulatory thought (i.e., mental contrasting vs. indulging versus resting). The results of the study verified the initial hypotheses. First, mental contrasting and indulging were identified as two distinct mental activities, and second, areas of greater brain activity in mental contrasting as compared to indulging and resting were observed, supportive of proposed cognitive components and processes ascribed to mental contrasting as per fantasy realization theory.

Specifically, mental contrasting heightened activity in brain regions responsible for working memory and intention formation suggesting that mental contrasting directs attention toward critical information, such as positioning the present, negative reality in the way of the desired future. Moreover, mental contrasting heightened activity in regions responsible for episodic memory and for vivid mental imagery suggesting that mental contrasting is rooted in the retrieval of past personal events, as well as the processing of complex stimuli, such as reexperiencing past incidents. Apparently, indulging relies less on episodic memory processes, that is, indulging in a positive future does not entail the mental exploration of past experiences, rather it should entail loose associations between the not-yet-experienced desired positive future (Oettingen, 2000; Oettingen et al., 2001). Furthermore, whereas mental contrasting forces a person to take a more critical look at the desired future and negative reality, thus evoking vivid images, indulging seemingly to a lesser extent evokes such images. This finding implies that mere daydreaming about a positive future is possible without having to closely attend to the images.

Mental contrasting appears to fulfill its task of turning high expectations into strong intentions by engaging working memory, episodic memory, and vivid imagery. Indulging, on the contrary, does not differ from resting, suggesting that indulging indeed involves no more than passively experiencing the desired future in the mind's eye. Going beyond prior research on the effects of mental contrasting on the attainment of personal goals, the present findings suggest that certain preliminaries have to be fulfilled such that mental contrasting can evidence its beneficial effects. For example, as mental contrasting taxes working memory, people should not be able to effectively perform mental contrasting whenever cognitive resources are blocked by dual task activities (e.g., being occupied by demanding cognitive tasks, coping with interpersonal stressors, extreme tiredness, or physical frailty and pain). Moreover, as mental contrasting is based on the effective retrieval of relevant obstacles experienced in the past, mental contrasting should be particularly effective for people who have carefully encoded past experiences with obstacles and thus can easily and accurately be retrieved from memory. Vividly depicted in this MEG study is the cognitive complexity of mental contrasting to promote expectation congruent goal commitment and goal pursuit.

Summary

As described, mental contrasting influences goal commitment via motivational (i.e., energization) and cognitive (i.e., thorough obstacle elaboration and planning) mechanisms and affects these processes in line with activity in corresponding brain regions. Although an understanding of the mechanisms underscoring the beneficial effects of mental contrasting is necessary and important for furthering goal theory, it is equally important to develop an understanding for if and how people can use these techniques on their own to enhance the quality of their everyday lives. Thus, the next section focuses on the metacognitive utility of mental contrasting as well as the combined strategy of mental contrasting and implementation intentions (i.e., MCII) as a first attempt to demonstrate the translation of years of laboratory research into practical applications to improve various aspects of people's lives.

Mental Contrasting: A Useful Strategy in Daily Life

The question of applicability of laboratory findings to everyday life is an increasing focus in the psychological community (National Advisory Mental Health Council, 2000). Translational research, as it is commonly called, is concerned with the translation of scientific discoveries into practical applications to benefit overall health and well-being. Regarding research looking at the outcomes and mechanisms of mental contrasting in areas of academic achievement, interpersonal concerns, professional development, and health, to name just a few, it is still largely unknown if and how people can apply the self-regulatory strategy in their everyday lives, essentially as a metacognitive tool. Therefore, whether or not these strategies can be used by individuals as metacognitive strategies to benefit their everyday lives, how these strategies affect job effectiveness and self-discipline, and if these strategies can influence critical health-related outcomes becomes the focus of the next section of the chapter.

Mental Contrasting on the Job

Ample evidence exists showing the positive outcomes related to achieving one's goals (e.g., positive emotional experience; Brunstein, 1993; life satisfaction; see Cantor & Blanton, 1996; Emmons, 1996, for review). However, many researchers also point out that striving for goals that cannot be brought to completion leads to a host of negative outcomes including negative affect (Higgins, 1987; Higgins, Roney, Crowe, & Hymes, 1994), anxiety (Pomerantz, Saxon, & Oishi, 2000), mental and physical problems (Emmons, 1996), and diminished well-being (Brunstein, 1993; Brunstein, Schultheiss, & Maier, 1999). In the same vein, researchers find that those who disengage from unattainable goals (e.g., bearing children after confirmed infertility) experience heightened well-being (Klinger, 1975, 1977; Wrosch, Scheier, Carver, & Schulz, 2003).

Given that mental contrasting allows individuals to commit to goal striving in accordance with perceived feasibility, it offers itself as a strategy to promote fruitful goal striving and also as a strategy to curtail futile goal striving. Thus, applying mental contrasting flexibly and independently in everyday life should help people discriminate between concerns that they are able to resolve and concerns that they should postpone or relinquish altogether. To the contrary, applying indulging in everyday life should make people invest in their everyday concerns irrespective of whether or not they will be able to resolve them. Such lack of discriminative competence should put them at risk for poor decision making and ineffective time management. Thus, the aims of a recent study were twofold: First, to examine if teaching people the self-regulatory strategies of mental contrasting or indulging enables them to apply these strategies in a metacognitive way toward their own problems, and second, how using the strategies affects job-related tasks.

For this intervention study, hospital personnel managers were trained in either mental contrasting or indulging regarding their own, everyday problems, and it was expected that those trained to use mental contrasting, in contrast to those trained to use indulging, should better discriminate between fruitful and futile concerns, resulting in better time management and more effective work-related behaviors. Hospital personnel managers were the target of this intervention because these individuals, whose daily obligations include managing employees, attending meetings, delegating responsibility, and presenting information, seemed particularly apt to benefit from a self-regulatory strategy effective at increasing fruitful and curtailing futile goal pursuit.

Indeed, in comparison to the managers assigned to the indulging condition, personnel managers in the mental contrasting condition reported better time management, less effortful decision making, increased project completion, and increased project relinquishment 2 weeks after receiving the initial training in one of the two strategies. The finding that mental contrasting can be used by individuals on a daily basis as a self-regulatory strategy to deal with a variety of personal and professional problems is all the more impressive because this strategy entails precise sequential execution of relatively complex cognitive processes. When chances of success were high, hospital managers in the mental contrasting condition should have actively pursued and completed ongoing projects, and when chances of success were low, hospital managers in the mental contrasting condition should have relinquished projects they perceived as less likely to have a good outcome (i.e., lower chance of success). Thus, in accordance with findings suggesting the beneficial effects of relinquishing infeasible goals (e.g., Wrosch et al., 2003; Klinger, 1975, 1977) these individuals should have forestalled psychological distress associated with the pursuit of unattainable goals, preserved their subjective well-being, and perhaps even benefited their health in doing so.

Mental Contrasting and Implementation Intentions: A Complementary Coupling

Mental contrasting helps people form strong goal commitments to desired futures they perceive are feasible to attain. However, even if people form strong goal commitment, they are not always successful at translating their strong goal commitment into effective goal-directed behavior. For instance, people may simply forget to act, they might be unaware of suitable situations for actions, or they may be distracted if and when a suitable situation presents itself. Implementation intentions (Gollwitzer, 1999), on the other hand, specify the when, where, and how of goal striving by guiding goal attainment (e.g., eating healthy) through the use of a cue ("If I have the urge to eat potato chips"), triggering an instrumental goal-directed behavior ("then I will eat a piece of fruit"). Therefore the coupling of these two self-regulatory strategies is indeed complementary: Mental contrasting when expectations of success are high fosters energization, individuals' readiness to plan, and the formation of strong goal commitments, whereas implementation intentions provide an effective strategy to turn plans and strong goal commitments into effective goal-directed behavior and goal attainment (Gollwitzer & Sheeran, 2006).

Effects on Self-Discipline

Self-discipline (i.e., self-control) has been defined as the ability to consciously and effortfully quell strong responses in the service of a higher goal (Duckworth & Seligman, 2006). Empirical evidence indicates that people high on trait measures of self-discipline have better outcomes in various aspects of life (e.g., academic performance, impulse control, psychological adjustment, interpersonal relationships; Tangney, Baumeister, & Boone, 2004). On the other hand, the bulk of social and personal problems (e.g., debt, violence, academic failure, addictions, procrastination, self-handicapping) seem to stem from deficiencies in self-discipline (Baumeister, Heatherton, & Tice, 1994). Thus, strategies, such as mental contrasting and implementation intentions, which help people develop a sense of self-discipline (Oettingen, 1999; Gollwitzer, 1999), seem all the more necessary as this skill has far-reaching implications for overall well-being.

To examine the influence of the Mental Contrasting Implementation Intention (MCII) intervention on self-discipline, undergraduate participants were either assigned to a MCII intervention group or to a control group (Oettingen, Barry, Guttenberg, & Gollwitzer, 2008). In the intervention group participants first learned how to use the mental contrasting strategy, then learned how to form implementation intentions by identifying the behavior necessary to overcome or circumvent the obstacle (e.g., noisy roommate as an obstacle to studying effectively for an upcoming test) generated during mental contrasting. To do so, participants imagined a desired outcome and a present obstacle in vivid detail, then created three "if–then" statements focusing on overcoming the obstacle (e.g., "If my roommate starts to get noisy again tonight, then I will talk to her about her behavior"), preventing the obstacle (e.g., "If the stereo is on when I come home at eight o'clock tonight, then I will immediately ask my roommate to turn the stereo off"), and planning to approach the desired outcome (e.g., "If I pass a drugstore on the way home, then I will buy myself a pair of ear plugs"). Students practiced using the MCII procedure so they could perform the strategy on their own for various everyday concerns over the course of one week.

As dependent measures, participants rated self-discipline at two time points: one week after the intervention in comparison to a respective baseline measure. The results showed that the MCII intervention directly enhanced MCII participants' reports of self-discipline, in comparison to control group participants' self-discipline, over a mere one-week period. These effects of the MCII intervention were not moderated by any other measured variables (e.g., sex, age, school year, depression, perceived stress, life satisfaction, troublesome events, college life satisfaction, self-efficacy). Presumably, MCII empowered individuals with self-regulatory skills, first by helping them sensibly commit to goals (i.e., to feasible but not to infeasible goals) and second by helping them to effectively achieve a goal. Thus, this powerful-yet-simple combination of strategies should have helped people recognize and realize their potential and feel a sense of self-discipline in the everyday lives.

Effects on Health Behavior

A common, yet troubling finding with regards to health behavior change is that though initial success is quite prevalent, long-term maintenance of the changed behavior is generally quite rare (Polivy & Herman, 2002). Extended behavior modification is however necessary if one is to reap the benefits of protective health behaviors (e.g., for regular exercise: Department of Health, 2004), yet roughly one-half of the individuals who begin a self-monitored exercise program abandon them within 6 months (Dishman, 1982, 1991). Therefore, it seems crucial to develop interventions to facilitate long-term behavior change.

One promising approach is to target goal commitment and goal implementation: People who fully commit to their goals for behavior change and plan goal implementation should be more successful, in the short and the long run. The next study we report was therefore conducted to determine whether participants who receive relevant information and learn the MCII technique would exercise more, immediately after the intervention and in the long run, than participants in an intervention-only control group (Stadler, Oettingen, & Gollwitzer, in press).

Middle-aged women were recruited to take part in this study focusing on healthy lifestyles. To begin, participants were randomly assigned to either an information control group or a MCII intervention group. In the information control group, women learned about the benefits of a healthy diet and exercise. In the MCII group, participants received the same information, additionally learning the MCII technique. First, participants learned the mental contrasting strategy and thereafter were instructed to form three implementation intentions regarding an obstacle standing in the way of exercising (e.g., feeling too tired in the evening to go for a run) in the form of "if–then" statements: one to overcome the obstacle generated by mental contrasting (e.g., "If I feel exhausted when I get home from work tonight, then I will put on my running shoes and go for a jog in the neighborhood"), one to prevent this obstacle (e.g., "If I hear the clock chime five o'clock, then I will pack my things and leave the office to go for a run"), and one identifying a good opportunity to act (e.g., "If the sun is shining, then I will go for a 30-minute jog in the park"). Participants learned the MCII technique with regards to short- and long-term health concerns.

As dependent measures participants maintained daily behavioral diaries to keep track of the amount of time they exercised every day. Specifically, participants recorded daily how much they had exercised in 15-minute intervals. Overall the MCII technique enhanced exercise more than the information intervention immediately after the intervention, and this effect remained stable for 4, 8, and 16 weeks after the intervention. The results for exercise behavior indicated that participants in the MCII group exercised nearly twice as much, that is, one hour more per week, than participants in the information control group. Thus, using the MCII technique was effective for initial success and long-term maintenance of improving exercise behavior. Moreover, as moderate amounts of physical exercise are shown to strengthen cardiovascular and respiratory systems, decrease risk for heart disease and Type 2 diabetes, help with weight control, improve stress and pain management, reduce risks of certain types of cancers, and improve quality of sleep (Mayo Foundation for Medical Education and Research, 2007), the MCII intervention should have far-reaching consequences for overall health.

Effects on Improving Mobility in Patients with Chronic Back Pain

A great challenge facing many physical therapists who work with patients with chronic back pain is motivating patients to exercise. One obstacle standing in the way of successful rehabilitation is that people who suffer pain anticipate pain in any activity-related situation and thus tend to avoid activity altogether. A second obstacle is patients' beliefs that "passive" treatments (e.g., surgery, massage) are the most effective or only avenue for pain control. Patients who hope that such "passive" treatments will eliminate their pain are less likely to learn how they themselves can effectively self-manage and overcome their pain, a difficult, yet necessary step for successful rehabilitation. Because long-term behavior change in the form of physical activity is necessary for these patients to recover and improve their quality of life, and as the maintenance of long-term behavior very often fails to persist over time (Marcus et al., 2000), strategies that translate fantasies about improved mobility into firm goal commitment with subsequent goal-directed action should be highly desirable for clinical applications as a means of increasing patients' physical activity and thus enhancing treatment and overall well-being.

In this study, the MCII intervention was adapted for a clinical sample of patients with chronic back pain (Schramm, Oettingen, Dahme, & Klinger, 2008). It was predicted that patients implementing the MCII technique in conjunction with the standard treatment offered to patients suffering from chronic back pain, in contrast to those only receiving the standard treatment, should evidence increased physical mobility. To test this assumption, participants with chronic back pain (i.e., existence of chronic pain of spine lasting longer than 6 months) were recruited from an outpatient rehabilitation center in Germany. Participants were randomly assigned to either a control group (i.e., standard outpatient back pain program) or an intervention group (i.e., standard outpatient back pain program and MCII intervention). The standard outpatient back pain program offered by the rehabilitation center entailed 3 to 4 weeks of treatment including individual informative seminars (e.g., relaxation techniques, handling stress), medical care and psychological consultation, physical therapy, and exercise. The experimental condition involved next to the standard back pain program, two one-half hour sessions: In the first session participants engaged in mental contrasting about realizing fantasies related to improved mobility (e.g., playing with a grandchild, becoming fit in everyday life), and during the second session participants identified behaviors in response to the obstacles generated in the first session to serve as the focus of an implementation intention (e.g., "If I see my baby granddaughter at our next family picnic, then I will carefully bend down to play with her"; "If I pass the door to the stairwell in my office building, then I will take the stairs up to my office").

The dependent variables for this study were physical strength, appropriate lifting behavior, and pain severity, once after 10 days and 3 months postintervention, and in comparison to respective preintervention baseline measures. To assess physical strength, participants completed one self-report measure to gauge their functional limitations in activities of daily living, and two objective measures, namely a lifting test (i.e., "handling load" of the Functional Capacity Evaluation, FCE; Gouttebarge, Wind, Kuijer, & Frings-Dresen, 2004) and a bicycle ergometer test. To assess severity of pain participants completed a self-report rating scale.

The findings of this test of a MCII-based intervention to change behavior in a clinical population as part of a therapy program indicate that this intervention, in conjunction with the standard treatment, improved physical mobility in patients with chronic back pain more so than the standard treatment only. The MCII intervention group increased physical mobility at about 2 weeks and 3 months as assessed by subjective and objective measures. These effects were independent of participants' experienced pain, which did not significantly differ between conditions during and after treatment. Furthermore the MCII intervention proved to be a time- and cost-effective behavior-change technique. Altogether, the intervention consisted of two sessions for a total of one hour. Other short-term psychological interventions take at least 4 to 6 hours (e.g., Linton & Nordin, 2006). Studies including problem-solving approaches contain multiple sessions (e.g., 19 half-day sessions over the course of 8 weeks in the study from van den Hout et al., 2003). The present findings suggest that MCII is a powerful, time- and cost-effective self-regulatory tool that in no more than an hour's time can help promote physical activity in a population known to have difficulties with rehabilitation.

Summary

Mental contrasting, also in conjunction with implementation intentions, can effectively be used as a metacognitive strategy to influence outcomes ranging from better time management, task effectiveness and reports of self-discipline, to improved health behavior and objective physical mobility in people suffering from back pain. Furthermore, as the results include samples from the United States and Germany, from young adults to middle-aged individuals, and include diverse domains ranging from professional and academic realms to improved health behavior, it seems evident that mental contrasting can be ubiquitously applied as a metacognitive strategy to help people manage and improve their everyday lives. These studies underscore the discriminative capabilities awarded to individuals who engage in mental contrasting (i.e., between fruitful and futile goals) as well as the beneficial personal outcomes associated with using mental contrasting as a metacognitive strategy. Using mental contrasting in their everyday lives should have helped participants in all of the studies either translate their potential and high expectations into strong commitment and action toward realizing a desired future, or to effectively disengage when chances of attaining the desired future appeared low.

Conclusion

As an old maxim advises, one needs serenity to accept the things one cannot change, courage to change the things one can, and the wisdom to know the difference. The self-regulatory strategy of mental contrasting, as shown throughout this chapter, bestows upon individuals just this, namely the capability to distinguish between the personally feasible and infeasible, the strength to change that which stands in the way of achieving the desirable, and the composure to let go of the things that are desirable, yet infeasible. Expressed in this proverb and garnered from the thought process of mental contrasting is the skill to simultaneously perceive one's strengths and weaknesses and to use this perception as a starting point for either translating desired (controllable) futures into binding goals or as an opportunity to creatively reengage in more promising prospects, a combination of skills which we newly refer to as *motivational intelligence*. Individuals who are motivationally intelligent are thus those individuals who engage in the self-regulatory strategies of fantasy realization in a motivationally adaptive manner. That is, those who engage in mental contrasting to create strong goal commitments when expectations of success are high, those who engage in mental contrasting to relinquish unachievable or unfavorable futures when expectations of success are low, those who engage in indulging to "stay in the game" when either goal relinquishment is not an option or when expectations are unclear, and finally those who cease indulging and engage in mental contrasting once expectations of success have been sufficiently strengthened. In essence this chapter underlines strategies that people can use to develop their wisdom to "know the difference," in other words, to develop their motivational intelligence.

The aims of this chapter were many. First, to show how mental contrasting as a self-regulatory thought process turns free fantasies about desired futures into binding goals by activating expectations, enabling people to commit to their desired futures in line with their perceived likelihood of attaining the desired future. Second, to reveal several motivational and cognitive mechanisms underlying the effects of mental contrasting, and to additionally illustrate the cognitive complexity of mental contrasting via neural correlates of this demanding self-regulatory thought process. Finally, to introduce translational research addressing the real-world benefits resulting from applying mental contrasting, also together with implementation intentions, showing how these strategies transcend the laboratory and positively affect the quality of everyday life. What this chapter reveals is that making fantasies come true is not merely the stuff of daydreams or fairy tales. To make our fantasies come true, a person needs the appropriate thought processes to activate expectations and commitment, in other words, making our dreams come true takes motivational intelligence.

References

Achtziger, A., Fehr, T., Oettingen, G., Gollwitzer, P. M., & Rockstroh, B. (in press). Strategies of intention formation are reflected in continuous MEG activity. *Social Neuroscience*.

al'Absi, M., Bongard, S., Buchanan, T., Pincomb, G. A., Licinio, J., & Lovallo, W. R. (1997). Cardiovascular and neuroendocrine adjustment to public speaking and mental arithmetic stressors. *Psychophysiology, 34*, 266–275.

Bandura, A. (1977). Self-efficacy: Toward a unifying theory of behavioral change. *Psychological Review, 84*, 191–215.

Bandura, A. (1978). The self system in reciprocal determinism. *American Psychologist, 33*, 344–358.

Bandura, A. (1997). *Self-efficacy. The exercise of control*. New York: Freeman.

Baumeister, R. F., Heatherton, T. F., & Tice, D. M. (1994). *Losing control: How and why people fail at self-regulation*. San Diego: Academic Press.

Brunstein, J. (1993). Personal goals and subjective well-being: A longitudinal study. *Journal of Personality and Social Psychology, 65*, 1061–1070.

Brunstein, J. C., & Gollwitzer, P. M. (1996). Effects of failure on subsequent performance: The importance of self-defining goals. *Journal of Personality and Social Psychology, 70*, 395–407.

Brunstein, J. C., Schultheiss, O. C., & Maier G. W. (1999). The pursuit of personal goals: A motivational approach to well-being and life adjustment. In J. Brandstädter & R. M. Lerner (Eds.), *Action & self-development: Theory and research through the life span* (pp. 169–196). Thousand Oaks, CA: Sage.

Cantor, N., & Blanton, H. (1996). Effortful pursuit of personal goals in daily life. In P. M. Gollwitzer & J. A. Bargh (Eds.), *The psychology of action: Linking cognition and motivation to behavior* (pp. 338–364). New York: Guilford Press.

Chaiken, S. (1987). The heuristic model of persuasion. In M. Zanna & J. Olson (Eds.), *Social influence: The Ontario Symposium* (Vol. 5, pp. 3–39). Hillsdale, NJ: Erlbaum.

Department of Health. (2004). *At least five a week: Evidence on the impact of physical activity and its relationship to health: A report from the Chief Medical Officer.* London: Author.

Dishman, R. K. (1982). Compliance/adherence in health related exercise. *Health Psychology, 1,* 237–267.

Dishman, R. K. (1991). Increasing and maintaining exercise and physical activity. *Behavior Therapy, 22,* 345–378.

Duckworth, A. L., & Seligman, M. E. P. (2006). Self-discipline gives girls the edge: Gender in self-discipline, grades, and achievement test scores. *Journal of Educational Psychology, 98,* 198–208.

Emmons, R. A. (1996). Striving and feeling: Personal goals and subjective well-being. In J. Bargh & P. M. Gollwitzer (Eds.), *The psychology of action: Linking motivation and cognition to behavior* (pp. 314–337). New York: Guilford Press.

Gendolla, G. H. E., & Wright, R. A. (2005). Motivation in social settings studies of effort-related cardiovascular arousal. In J. P. Forgas, K. D. Williams, & S. M. Laham (Eds.), *Social motivation: Conscious and unconscious processes* (pp. 71–90). New York: Cambridge University Press.

Gollwitzer, P. M. (1990). Action phases and mind-sets. In E. T. Higgins & R. M. Sorrentino (Eds.), *Handbook of motivation and cognition: Foundations of social behavior* (Vol. 2, pp. 53–92). New York: Guilford Press.

Gollwitzer, P. M. (1999). Implementation intentions: Strong effects of simple plans. *American Psychologist, 54,* 493–503.

Gollwitzer, P. M., & Sheeran, P. (2006). Implementation intentions and goal achievement: A meta-analysis of effects and processes. *Advances in Experimental Social Psychology, 38,* 69–119.

Gouttebarge, V., Wind, H., Kuijer, P. P. F. M., & Frings-Dresen, M. H. W. (2004). Reliability and validity of Functional Capacity Evaluation methods: A systematic review with reference to Blankenship system, Ergos work simulator, Ergo-Kit and Isernhagen work system. *International Archives of Occupational and Environmental Health, 77*(8), 527–537.

Grant, H., Oettingen, G., Gollwitzer, P. M., & Schneider, M. E. (2008). *Self-regulatory correlates and consequences of chronic mental contrasting.* Manuscript submitted for publication.

Heckhausen, H. (1991). *Motivation and action.* New York: Springer-Verlag.

Higgins, E. T. (1987). Self-discrepancy: A theory relating self and affect. *Psychological Review, 94,* 319–340.

Higgins, E. T., & Chaires, W. M. (1980). Accessibility of interrelational constructs: Implications for stimulus encoding and creativity. *Journal of Experimental Social Psychology, 16,* 348–361.

Higgins, E. T., Roney, C. J. R., Crowe, E., & Hymes, C. (1994). Ideal versus ought predilections for approach and avoidance distinct self-regulatory systems. *Journal of Personality and Social Psychology, 66*, 276–286.

Holahan, C. J., & Moos, R. H. (1986). Personality, coping, and family resources in stress resistance: A longitudinal analysis. *Journal of Personality and Social Psychology, 51*, 389–395.

Kawada, C. (2004). Self-regulatory thought in goal setting: Perceptual and cognitive processes. *Dissertation Abstracts International, 64*, 12B. (UMI No. 0419-4217)

Klinger, E. (1975). Consequences of commitment to and disengagment from incentives. *Psychological Review, 82*(1), 1–25.

Klinger, E. (1977). *Meaning and void: Inner experience and the incentives in people's lives.* Minneapolis: University of Minnesota Press.

Klinger, E. (1990). *Daydreaming: Using waking fantasy and imagery for self-knowledge and creativity.* Los Angeles: Tarcher.

Kruglanski, A. W. (1996). Goals as knowledge structures. In P. M. Gollwitzer & J. A. Bargh (Eds.), *The psychology of action: Linking cognition and motivation to behavior* (pp. 599–619). New York: Guilford Press.

Kruglanski, A. W., & Freund, T. (1983). The freezing and unfreezing of lay-inferences: Effects on impressional primacy, ethnic stereotyping, and numerical anchoring. *Journal of Experimental Social Psychology, 19*, 448–468.

Lengua, L., & Sandler, I. (1996). Self-regulation as a moderator of the relation between coping and symptomatology in children of divorce. *Journal of Abnormal Child Psychology, 24*, 681–701.

Linton, S. J., & Nordin, E. (2006). A 5-year follow-up evaluation of the health and economic consequences of an early cognitive behavioural intervention for back pain: A randomized, controlled trial. *Spine, 31*, 853–858.

Locke, E. A., & Latham, G. P. (2002). Building a practically useful theory of goal setting and task motivation: A 35-year odyssey. *American Psychologist, 57*, 705–717.

Marcus, B. H., Dubbert, P. M., Forsyth, L. H., McKenzie, T. L., Stone, E. J., Dunn, A. L. et al. (2000). Physical activity behavior change: Issues in adoption and maintenance. *Health Psychology, 19*, 32–41.

Mayo Foundation for Medical Education and Research. (2007). *Exercise: 7 benefits of regular activity.* Retrieved May 12, 2007, from *www.mayoclinic.com/health/exercise/HQ01676.*

Mischel, W. (1973). Toward a cognitive social learning reconceptualization of personality. *Psychological Review, 80*, 252–283.

National Advisory Mental Health Council. (2000). *Translating behavioral science into action: Report of the National Advisory Mental Health Council Behavioral Science Workgroup.* Bethesda, MD: National Institute of Mental Health.

Newell, A., & Simon, H. A. (1972). *Human problem solving.* Englewood Cliffs, NJ: Prentice Hall.

Oettingen, G. (1999). Free fantasies about the future and the emergence of developmental goals. In J. Brandstädter & R. M. Lerner (Eds.), *Action and self-*

development: Theory and research through the life span (pp. 315–342). Thousand Oaks, CA: Sage.

Oettingen, G. (2000). Expectancy effects on behavior depend on self-regulatory thought. *Social Cognition, 18,* 101–129.

Oettingen, G., Barry, H., Guttenberg, K., & Gollwitzer, P. M. (2008). *Improving self-discipline and self-esteem: A mental contrasting with implementation intentions intervention.* Manuscript submitted for publication.

Oettingen, G., Hönig, G., & Gollwitzer, P. M. (2000). Effective self-regulation of goal attainment. *International Journal of Educational Research, 33,* 705–732.

Oettingen, G., & Mayer, D. (2002). The motivating function of thinking about the future: Expectations versus fantasies *Journal of Personality and Social Psychology, 83,* 1198–1212.

Oettingen, G., Mayer, D., Sevincer, T., Stephens, E. J., Pak, H., & Hagenah, M. (in press). Mental contrasting and goal commitment: The role of energization. *Personality and Social Psychology Bulletin.*

Oettingen, G., Mayer, D., Thorpe, J. S., Janetzke, H., & Lorenz, S. (2005). Turning fantasies about positive and negative futures into self-improvement goals. *Motivation and Emotion, 29,* 237–267.

Oettingen, G., Pak, H., & Schnetter, K. (2001). Self-regulation of goal-setting: Turning free fantasies about the future into binding goals. *Journal of Personality and Social Psychology, 80,* 736–753.

Oettingen, G., & Wadden, T. A. (1991). Expectation, fantasy, and weight loss: Is the impact of positive thinking always positive? *Cognitive Therapy and Research, 15,* 167–175.

Olson, J. M., Roese, N. J., & Zanna, M. P. (1996). Expectancies. In E. T. Higgins & A. W. Kruglanski (Eds.), *Social psychology: Handbook of basic principles* (pp. 211–238). New York: Guilford Press.

Pittman, T. S. (1998). Motivation. In D. T. Gilbert, S. T. Fiske, & G. Lindsey (Eds.), *The handbook of social psychology* (Vol. 2, pp. 549–590). New York: McGraw-Hill.

Pomerantz, E. M., Saxon, J. L., & Oishi, S. (2000). The psychological trade-offs of goal investment. *Journal of Personality and Social Psychology, 79,* 617–630.

Polivy, J., & Herman, P. C. (2002). If at first you don't succeed: False hopes of self-chance. *American Psychologist, 57,* 677–689.

Sanbomatsu, D. M., & Fazio, R. H. (1990). The role of attitudes in memory-based decision making. *Journal of Personality and Social Psychology, 59,* 614–622.

Scheier, M. F., & Carver, C. S. (1992). Effects of optimism on psychological and physical well-being: Theoretical overview and empirical update. *Cognitive Therapy and Research, 16,* 201–228.

Schramm, S., Oettingen, G., Dahme, B., & Klinger, R. (2008). *Short term intervention consisting of mental contrasting and implementation intentions as a treatment for chronic back pain patients: A clinical intervention trial.* Manuscript submitted for publication.

Seligman, M. E. P. (1991). *Learned optimism.* New York: Knopf.

Singer, J. L. (1966). *Daydreaming.* New York: Random House.

Smith, E. R., & Branscombe, N. R. (1987). Procedurally mediated social inferences: The case of category accessibility effects. *Journal of Experimental Social Psychology, 23,* 361–382.

Stadler, G., Oettingen, G., & Gollwitzer, P. M. (in press). Long-term behavior change in exercise: A mental contrasting and implementation intention intervention. *American Journal of Preventive Medicine.*

Tangney, J. P., Baumeister, R. F., & Boone, A. L. (2004). High self-control predicts good adjustment, less pathology, better grades, and interpersonal success. *Journal of Personality, 72,* 271–322.

Taylor, S. E., & Brown, J. D. (1988). Illusion and well-being: A social psychological perspective on mental health. *Psychological Bulletin, 103,* 193–210.

Tolman, E. C. (1925). Purpose and cognition: The determinants of animal learning. *Psychological Review, 32,* 285–297.

Tolman, E. C. (1948). Cognitive maps in rats and men. *Psychological Review, 55,* 189–208.

U.S. Department of Health and Human Services. (2007). *Physical activity.* Retrieved April 5, 2007, from *www.healthierus.gov/exercise.html.*

Van den Hout, J. H. C., Vlaeyen, J. W. S., Heuts, P. H. T. G., Zijlema, J. H. L., & Wijnen, J. A. G. (2003). Secondary prevention of work-related disability in nonspecific low back pain: Does problem-solving therapy help? A randomized clinical trial. *Clinical Journal of Pain, 19,* 87–96.

Wright, R. A., & Kirby, L. D (2001). Effort determination of cardiovascular response: An integrative analysis with applications in social psychology. In M. P. Zanna (Ed.), *Advances in experimental social psychology* (Vol. 33, pp. 255–307). San Diego: Academic Press.

Wrosch, C., Scheier, M. F., Carver, C. S., & Schulz, R. (2003). The importance of goal disengagement in adaptive self-regulation: When giving up is beneficial. *Self and Identity, 2,* 1–20.

CHAPTER 7

How Does Our Unconscious Know What We Want?
THE ROLE OF AFFECT IN GOAL REPRESENTATIONS

RUUD CUSTERS

Human goal pursuit is often assumed to involve, and arise from, conscious process: We think before we act, put our mind to something, and then keep our eye on the prize. This intimate relationship between consciousness and goals resonates in most theories on goal pursuit: To attain a desired state, one needs to deliberate, form intentions, choose the proper means, and reflect on one's progress toward that state. According to this view, consciousness is what gets motivational, goal-directed behavior going and forms a prerequisite for successful attainment of a desired state.

But when asked for the reasons behind their intentions, strivings, and pursuits, people are notoriously bad in coming up with explanations (Wegner, 2002; Wilson, 2002). Why do we want to be successful scientists? What makes us decide to go for a drink this very moment? Most of the time, we can merely guess. This explanational void suggests that although people may—at least sometimes—be aware of setting and pursuing their goals, they do not always have conscious access to the actual source of their goal-directed behavior. This opens up the possibility that people's goal pursuits are in fact put in motion by external sources, without conscious intentions.

In line with this reasoning, Carpenter, followed by James more than a century ago, suggested that mere thoughts of behavior are enough to put them in motion (see Dijksterhuis & Bargh, 2001). Within social psychology, this idea of ideomotor action has developed in two distinct theoretical explanations. Based on findings in cognitive psychology suggesting that the cognitive representations that are activated upon the perception of specific actions are also the ones that are activated during the execution of the corresponding motor responses, it has been suggested that perceiving or activating the mental representation of an action can directly lead to its execution (see, for an overview, Dijksterhuis & Bargh, 2001). In addition to this behavior-priming explanation, it has been proposed that ideomotor effects stretch even further and that people's goals are mentally represented too, causing activation of these representations to be followed not by execution of simple motor responses, but by motivational, goal-directed behavior without conscious intentions (see Moskowitz, Li, & Kirk, 2004).

Over the last two decades, a growing number of studies have provided evidence in support of this hypothesis. Resorting to priming techniques to manipulate goal accessibility, these studies have reported goal-priming effects on cognitive and behavioral measures that are indicative of goal pursuit, such as the ability to overcome obstacles and sustained activation of the goal representation (see, for an overview, Moskowitz et al., 2004). Hence, the question of whether goal pursuit can be instigated by external primes seems to be settled. The challenge for researchers today is to figure out how it works. How do we get from accessible cognitions to motivational behavior?

In this chapter, I make an attempt to address the mechanisms by which priming of mental goal representations can instigate motivational, goal-directed behavior by taking a closer look at goal representations themselves. What do these mental representations look like? How do they develop? And most important, how can our brain recognize an accessible mental representation as a desired state that is worth pursuing and translate this information in motivational behavior? I argue throughout the chapter that goal priming can lead to goal-directed motivational behavior without conscious deliberations or intentions because a goal representation contains a positive affective component that signals that the primed goal is desired and worth pursuing, which is sufficient to put motivational behavior in motion. To better understand what functions should be fulfilled by mechanisms that make nonconscious goal pursuit possible, we first briefly turn to theories of goal pursuit and the role they assign to consciousness.

Consciousness and Theories on Goal Pursuit

"Goals" are widely defined as desired states one aims to attain, with "states" referring to outcomes or behaviors (see, e.g., Gollwitzer & Moskowitz, 1996). According to most contemporary theories on goal pursuit, these goals are the result of a deliberative process in which the desirability of the goal is determined and a conscious intention to realize the goal is formed (see, e.g., Baumeister & Vohs, 2004). Although people may readily retrieve previously stored knowledge about the potential goal state from memory to decide whether to pursue it or not, it is generally assumed that goal pursuit cannot arise without such a conscious fiat (see, e.g., Gollwitzer, 1990).

The most important criteria that serve as input for this decision to pursue a goal were formulated by Tolman (1932) as expectancy and value. The product of the value of a certain goal state and the expectancy of successfully attaining it (and/or the goal state yielding the anticipated affect) can be viewed as the main antecedent of motivational behavior. Whether one engages in the process of goal setting or considers to adopt a potential goal that is suggested or implied by others, one has to consider the expected value of the potential goal state, and—if this state is judged to be desirable—determine whether one has means of realizing it (Bandura, 1986; Fishbein & Ajzen, 1975; Gollwitzer, 1990; Locke & Latham, 2002).

Once a goal has been set or adopted, the goal has to be enacted. Goal enactment first requires a decision-making process that is similar to that of goal setting or adoption, in which people have to select the proper means to attain the goal. Second, progress toward the goal has to be monitored to secure attainment of the goal and potentially shift to different means or strategies (e.g., Carver & Scheier, 1998). Be it explicitly or implicitly, most theories of goal pursuit assume that all these aspects of goal pursuit (setting, adopting, and monitoring of goals) rely on conscious processes (see, for a more elaborate discussion, Custers & Aarts, 2005a).

But if one assumes that goal pursuit can be instigated and carried out outside conscious awareness, one is obliged to explain how goals can be set or adopted and finally enacted without conscious deliberations and intentions. In the remainder of this chapter, I present evidence supporting the idea that a goal representation contains not only directional information about the goal state (i.e., information about the state that is to be attained), but also information about the subjective or incentive value of the goal, which renders conscious deliberation in principle obsolete. I argue that affective information plays a role in instigating motivational processes that propel the execution of instrumental actions and maintain the accessibility of the goal representation in the service of the primed goal which makes persistent, flexible action possible. First, I scrutinize the existing evidence for nonconscious goal pursuit to see whether there is support for a moderating role of value in goal-priming effects on behavior.

Nonconscious Goal Pursuit

The Role of Accessibility

To demonstrate and investigate how the environment can influence people's behavior outside their awareness, researchers have mainly relied on priming techniques to simulate this process. With these techniques, it is possible to manipulate the accessibility of mental representations and investigate subsequent cognitive and behavioral effects without participants being aware of their true source. In one of the first studies that demonstrated priming effects on overt behavior, Bargh, Chen, and Burrows (1996) primed participants with words related to the stereotype of the elderly. They did so by hiding words as "bingo," "Florida," and "grey" in a word-search puzzle that participants had to solve. Upon completion of the experiment, the experimenters recorded the time it took participants to walk from the lab to the elevator. It was found that participants who were exposed to elderly related words walked more slowly than participants in the control condition, who completed a similar word-search puzzle that did not contain such words. Because the word "slow" was not among the words presented, this suggests that behavior was the result of the activation of the elderly stereotype (which includes the trait "slow"). Importantly, none of the participants was aware of the effect of the manipulation on their subsequent behavior. The construct "slow" that was activated through the stereotype, then, apparently influenced behavior outside people's conscious awareness.

This behavior, however, does not appear to be driven by any motivation or goal. First of all, there are no signs that are indicative of motivation (e.g., persistence, goal directedness) and second, the act of walking slowly does not seem very desirable in itself or instrumental in attaining a higher goal (but see Cesario, Plaks, & Higgins, 2006). Rather, these kinds of priming effects on behavior have been explained as the result of a direct link between perception and action. Because of an overlap in mental representations that are used to observe as well as execute actions, observing or activating the mental representation of an action can directly lead to its execution (see Dijksterhuis & Bargh, 2001). To demonstrate motivational effects of priming, it is necessary to test the resulting behavior for features that are characteristic of goal-directed, motivational behavior.

Such a demonstration was provided in a different line of studies by Bargh and colleagues (Bargh, Gollwitzer, Lee-Chai, Barndollar, & Trotschel, 2001). In several experiments, priming effects on cognition and behavior were tested for motivational qualities. In one experiment (Bargh et al., 2001, Experiment 4), the goal to achieve was rendered accessible by exposing participants to performance-related words in a word-finding task. During a second word-finding task, participants were after 2 minutes asked to stop working over an intercom. It was found that primed participants more often continued working on the task than nonprimed participants. This experiment demonstrates that people become more persistent as a result of merely activating the mental representation of achievement. Several other experiments revealed that behavior resulting from goal priming possessed other features that are characteristic of goal pursuit, such as the ability to overcome obstacles (see also Custers, Maas, Wildenbeest, & Aarts, 2008). Furthermore, it was shown that the accessibility of a primed goal representation does not decay after priming as would be expected for representations of other mental constructs.

These basic findings have been replicated and extended in a number of ways. It has been shown that primes as diverse as significant others, social category members, and other people's behavior can activate goals ranging from cooperation and achievement to making money and having casual sex (see, for an overview, Moskowitz et al., 2004). Thus, the question of whether goal priming works seems to be settled. To find out more about the underlying mechanisms, however, it may be worth looking at the boundary conditions of these effects.

People Do Not Pursue All That Is Primed

Some research suggests that people do not simply pursue anything that is primed, but that goal-priming effects are moderated by the subjective desirability of the goal. For example, in one of his studies, Shah (2003) primed participants with a significant other (i.e., their father) after which they participated in a task that was allegedly diagnostic for analytical reasoning. It was found that priming increased performance and persistence on the task, but only for participants who were close to a father who positively valued analytical reasoning. If one assumes that participants who were closer to their father were more likely to share his values, this research suggests that subjective desirability moderates goal-priming effects.

Similar findings come from research by Aarts and colleagues (Aarts, Gollwitzer, & Hassin, 2004). In their studies on goal contagion, they investigated whether people would adopt the goal to make money when it was rendered accessible through reading a description of another person's behavior. They found that when participants read a description that implied the goal to make money, they worked harder to earn an additional income, but that this effect was more pronounced when they were currently in need of money. These findings suggest that people only pursue a primed goal when the goal is desirable, in this case, as a result of their current needs.

Moreover, Aarts and colleagues (2004) found in another study that the intensity of priming effects on motivational behavior is decreased when existing goals are perceived in a negative light. Participants either read a short story describing the behavior of guy looking for a one-night stand with an old friend from high school, or a control story. For some of the participants who read the story implying the one-night stand the story was changed slightly in that the information was added that the guy was expecting a baby. It was found that compared to the control condition, the goal to seek casual sex proved to be contagious, in that the participants—all heterosexual males—spent more effort on helping the female experimenter. This effect, however, disappeared when the guy in the story was expecting to become a father. Under these conditions the accessible goal was rendered undesirable and was no longer pursued by the participants.

Together, these findings suggest that goal-priming effects are moderated by the subjective desirability of the goal or *goal strength*. This strength can be either increased by, for example, needs, or decreased if the goal is presented in a negative light. Apparently, there is no one-to-one relation between priming and goal pursuit. Somehow, the effect of accessibility on goal pursuit is gated by processes that take into account the desirability of the goal. But if we assume that these processes also operate outside of awareness, how can our unconscious "make decisions" about desirability that are by the majority of contemporary theories of goal pursuit assumed to require conscious deliberation?

How Does Our Unconscious Know What We Want?

One way to answer this question is to propose that the process of forming an intention to adopt and pursue a goal can take place outside awareness. This has resulted in the proposition of concepts such as nonconscious will (Bargh et al., 2001), implicit intention (Wood, Quinn, & Kashy, 2002), or implicit volition (Moskowitz et al., 2004). Although these terms certainly make excellent counterintuitive titles, they merely stretch the applicability of inherently conscious concepts featured in existing models to the unconscious level. This strategy has certainly helped to put the exciting notion of nonconscious goal pursuit on the scientific agenda, but it tells us little about how the unconscious can do what, until recently, was assumed to require conscious involvement.

Another approach is to make an inventory of what people can do unconsciously and construct a hypothesis in line with that knowledge. According to almost all models of goal pursuit, whether a goal is pursued or not depends on the expected value of the goal state. The best candidate for a mechanism that could determine the expected value of a primed goal outside conscious awareness would be one that relies on affective processes. It is known that affective processes play a fundamental role in motivating human action, are very fast, and can operate outside conscious awareness (see e.g., Berridge, 2001; LeDoux, 1996). Thus, if goal representations would contain an affective component that reflects the expected value of the goal, this information could be used to nonconsciously determine whether a primed goal is desired or not, which renders conscious deliberation redundant.

Positive Affect as Implicit Motivator

Incentive Theory

Support for the idea that positive affect associated with a goal state equips it with motivational properties comes from research on incentive theory. Incentive theory (see, e.g., Berridge, 2001) proposes that stimuli or states associated with positive affect form an incentive for which the organism will work. These theories grew out of several remarkable findings in different animal labs that shed new light on the role of reinforcement in learning processes following the S–R habit paradigm (Skinner, 1953; Watson, 1925). For instance, operant stereotypes or misbehaviors were discovered during operant conditioning experiments. One such behavior is auto-shaping (Brown & Jenkins, 1968). It has, for example, been observed that pigeons, for which free presentation of food was repeatedly paired with a light signal, started to vigorously pick at the light bulb although this behavior was not explicitly reinforced. This phenomenon, in which an animal shapes itself, occurs because the positive affect aroused by the food has now become linked to the light bulb, that therefore serves as an incentive for which the animal is motivated to work.

The idea that the positive affective valence of a behavior or activity motivates actions that are instrumental in realizing that behavior has been around for quite some time. That positive affect can be a powerful motivator was revealed by Olds and Milner (1954), who devised an apparatus by which rats could stimulate so-called pleasure centers in their own brain with small electric shocks by means of pressing a bar. The effect was astonishing. The rats were found to push the lever so vigorously that some literally collapsed after several thousands of presses. Moreover, hungry rats even neglected the opportunity to eat, and others crossed electrified shock grids to engage in pressing the bar. This demonstrates that if a particular neutral behavioral state (i.e., pressing the bar) becomes associated with positive affect, it becomes a desired state or goal for which the organism will exhibit enhanced motivation to accomplish it.

Dopamine and Motivation

Besides behavioral evidence, neuroscience provides more and more cues as to how affect may be involved in motivation. Recent studies show that the mesolimbic dopamine system, particularly the nucleus accumbens that was targeted in the self-stimulation studies of Olds and Milner (1954), is associated with motivated behavior (see, for an overview Berridge, 2007). The dopamine system responds very rapidly to delivery of rewards or engaging in behaviors that evoke positive affect, such as eating food and making money. This system is also activated instantly by cues referring to desired states, which shows that priming goal representations sets off neurological processes that are crucial for motivated behavior. Although the exact mechanism that produces goal-directed behavior is only partly understood, recent findings do suggest that dopamine is responsible for translating cues for incentive value in motivation.

Evidence for the Role of Positive Affect

Nonconscious Processing of Reward Signals

Recently, it has been demonstrated that reward information can be processed and subsequently increase motivational activity, even when it is presented below the threshold of conscious perception. Pessiglione et al. (2007) had participants engage in a task in which they could earn money by squeezing a hand grip. Before each trial, a picture of the maximal reward that could be earned—either that of a one pound or a one penny coin— was presented on the screen. It was found that even when this picture was presented subliminally, participants squeezed more forcefully than when they were exposed to a lower reward. This demonstrates that people are able to translate reward signals into motivation outside conscious awareness (see also Bijleveld, Custers, & Aarts, 2008).

Measuring the Affective Valence of Preexisting Goal Representations

In line with this finding, researchers have started to directly test the idea that the affective valence of goal representations is involved in translating primed goals in motivational, goal-directed behavior. Using implicit measures to determine the automatic affective responses that are triggered by words describing potential goals, they were able to test whether this affective valence moderates goal-priming effects on behavior.

In one of their experiments, Custers and Aarts (2007) subliminally primed participants with the concept of socializing and going out (presumably a goal for most of the students who participated) in an alleged letter-detection task and measured the effort they expended to realize that activity. They did so by telling participants after the letter-detection task that they would engage in a mouse-click task in which they would have to click with their mouse along several paths on the screen supposedly to study people's mouse movements. Crucially, participants were told that they might be participating in a second task in which they could win tickets for a popular students' party in the city center, if there would be enough time left. The reasoning behind this was that participants who were motivated to attain the goal would speed up their clicking behavior on the mouse-click task to be able to get a chance to win the tickets. Finally, after an extensive filler task, participants engaged in the Extrinsic Affective Simon Task (EAST; De Houwer, 2003), in which the affective valence of the potential goal of socializing and going out was assessed.

In the EAST, which is conceptually similar to the Implicit Association Task (IAT; Greenwald, McGhee, & Schwartz, 1998) participants have to respond to white and colored words that appear on a computer screen with a left or right key-press. Specifically, they are instructed to respond to white words based on their affective valence (e.g., press "left" for negative and "right" for positive words), but to base their responses to the other words on their color (e.g., press "left" for blue and "right" for green words). Hence, depending on the color of these words, people have to respond with a key that is also used for positive or negative responses to the white words. The idea behind the task is that responses to colored words should be faster if their valence is congruent, compared to incongruent with the response that is required based on color.

Words related to the goal of socializing and going out were presented as colored words. For each participant, an individual EAST score was computed. It was found that participants expended more effort to attain the goal state when the EAST score reflecting the valence of the goal was more positive, but only when the goal was primed. If one assumes that goals are mentally represented as (behavioral) states associated with positive affect, these results replicate the main finding in research on nonconscious goal pursuit that enhancing the accessibility of a goal representation motivates behavior aimed at realizing a desired state. Moreover, these effects cannot be explained in term of mere behavioral priming, as the findings demonstrate that this effect is conditional on a positive affective valence of the goal state. Only when a primed state preexists as a desired state associated with positive affect does goal priming induce motivational behavior. In other words, goal priming does not create goals. It merely causes preexisting goal representations to gain control over behavior.

Comparable findings have been reported by Ferguson (2007). She measured implicit attitudes towards the word "equal" using an affective priming task. Subsequently, participants were exposed to 60 words that they had to explicitly evaluate. Hidden among them for all participants was again the word "equal." Apart from implicitly measuring the affective valence of the concept "equal" and assessing its explicit evaluation, these two tasks ensured that the potential goal of being equal was rendered accessible. In a subsequent task it was tested how people reacted to inequality. It was found that the more positive people's evaluation of the concept "equal," the less they were inclined to support unequal government policies.

Creating Goal Representations by Linking Neutral Behaviors
to Positive Affect

Although the evidence presented above demonstrates a relation between the affective valence of goal representations and goal pursuit after priming, this evidence is only circumstantial when it comes to the causal role of positive affect in goal pursuit. That is, the correlations referred to above may be spurious in that another variable correlating with affect may produce the effect. To provide solid evidence for such a causal role of positive affect, one would have to simulate or manipulate the positive affective valence of potential goals.

One way to potentially do this would be to make use of operant conditioning: have people repeatedly engage in certain actions and after each time present them with a reward that elicits positive feelings. Such a method, though, would be accompanied with several problems. Although after various trials the mental representation of the activity would probably become associated with positive affect, participants would also develop conscious expectancies, predictions, and theories about the relation between the activity and the reward. With such a method, then, it would still be the question whether the positive affect itself does the trick.

These problems could, however, be circumvented by making use of evaluative conditioning techniques, which change the affective valence of mental representations in a more direct way. In evaluative conditioning research, pictures or descriptions of objects or behaviors are presented in temporal proximity with affective stimuli (e.g., affective words or photographs; for an overview, see De Houwer, Thomas, & Baeyens, 2001). As such, this type of conditioning relies more on coactivation of the mental representations of the stimulus that is being conditioned (CS), and the affective stimulus (US), than the actual experience of the affect. Coactivation is simply assumed to create a mental association between the two. Hence, evaluative conditioning techniques could be used to directly change goal representations, without having to have people actually pursue and attain those goals.

In a series of experiments, Custers and Aarts (2005b) manipulated the affective valence of potential goals through coactivation with positive affect. It has been demonstrated that changes in valence of the CS can be established even when the US and/or the CS are being presented subliminally (see De Houwer et al., 2001). Therefore, to rule out the possibility that participants were aware of what was being manipulated, the potential goal that was being conditioned (CS) was presented subliminally whereas affective stimuli were presented supraliminal and could hence be consciously perceived.

In a first experiment, effects of the affective valence of potential behavioral goals on participants' wanting to engage in those activities (Custers

& Aarts, 2005b; Study 1) was examined. Participants first completed an alleged dot-detection task, in which potential behavioral goals (e.g., doing puzzles, going for a walk, which could all be expressed in one word in Dutch) or nonwords were subliminally flashed on the screen, immediately followed by visible positive or neutral words. After this manipulation, participants' motivation to engage in the behaviors was assessed by having them respond to the potential behavioral goals that appeared on the screen, indicating quickly whether they wanted to engage in those behaviors or not. Results showed that participants' motivation to attain engage in the behaviors was higher when potential goals were subliminally flashed together with positive words, than when states were paired with neural words, or nonwords were presented with positive or neutral words. These findings demonstrate that priming of a neutral potential goal in itself does not increase motivation. It is the coactivation with positive affect that turns the neutral behavior into a desired state, which increases wanting.

To obtain more conclusive evidence for the primary and unique role of positive affect in motivational processes, in an additional study the effects of rendering neutral behavioral states more positively were compared to the effects of linking them to negative affect (Custers & Aarts, 2005b; Study 2a). Several theorists have argued that affect is not one single dimension that ranges from good to bad but actually consists of two separate dimensions—a positive and negative one—that independently contribute to motivation and behavior in opposite directions (see, e.g., Cacioppo & Berntson, 1999). Whereas positive affect is commonly associated with the preparation and instigation of motivated action, it has been proposed that negative affect attached to goal pursuits may reduce the motivation and operation of the given pursuits. However, when states are neutral, linking them to negative affect would not decrease people's motivation to attain those states, as they would not be motivated to pursue them to begin with. Hence, Custers and Aarts predicted that coactivating neutral states with negative affect would not decrease participants' motivation to attain them. This is exactly what was observed: Compared to a neutral control condition participants' reported motivation to attain the originally neutral states increased when these states were linked to positive affect but did not decrease when linked to negative affect.

To assess the motivational effects of positive affect on overt behavior, Custers and Aarts (2005b; Study 4) compared them to those of conscious goals. That is, they rendered the potential goal to do puzzles more positive making use of evaluative conditioning techniques, and compared this effect to a condition in which people only received the conscious goal to pursue this activity as well as to a third control condition. First, participants completed the manipulation in which words related to the neutral state of doing "number-sequence puzzles" were linked to positive affect or not. For people in the other two conditions the goal was left neutral. Subsequently, participants were informed that they would engage in the mouse-click task explained earlier and a number-sequence puzzle task, but that the latter task would only be given if there was sufficient time left. Additionally, participants in the conscious goal condition were told that the experimenter would appreciate it if they would get to the puzzle task (which explicitly attached desire to the goal state). It was expected that participants in both (conscious and nonconscious) goal conditions worked harder (i.e., faster) on the mouse-click task—which was in this setting a means to get to the puzzle task—because in both conditions the goals were rendered more accessible and desirable by respectively the explicit instructions, or the conditioning procedure. It turned out that this was indeed the case: participants were faster on the mouse-click task in both goal conditions compared to the control condition. Thus, unobtrusively manipulating the affective valence of a potential goal representation increases motivational behavior in the same way that a conscious goal or instruction does.

How Do Goal Representations Develop?

If, as the work discussed above suggests, positive affect forms a crucial part of goal representations, how do these representations develop in life outside the lab? There are several ways in which positive affect can become associated with a potential goal state. The most trivial one is perhaps conscious goal setting itself. As weighing pros and cons of a specific potential goal forms an essential part of the goal-setting process, a final positive impression is needed for the goal to be pursued (see Gollwitzer & Moskowitz, 1996). With increased practice, the contemplative decision process gradually changes into a more automatic one, aided by memory of past satisfactory experiences. That is, over time, the need for a conscious assessment ceases as the representation of the positive or desired goal is stored in memory, readily retrievable to motivate goal-directed behavior (see, e.g., Aarts, Verplanken, & van Knippenberg, 1998).

Additionally, mere attainment of a given goal is known to yield positive affect in itself (Bandura, 1986; Higgins, 1987). In a test of this hypothesis, Moors and De Houwer (2001) instructed participants to produce a specific result (i.e., to produce the color "blue" on the computer screen) by stopping rapidly alternating colors (blue and yellow) with a key press. Results revealed a classic affective priming effect: Immediate access to positive words was facilitated, and access to negative words was inhibited after the goal state (e.g., blue) was produced. This suggests that attainment of a given effect activates the representation of positive affect, which can then become associated with the result to form a goal, even though the result itself would not have yielded any positive affect at all were it not for the instructions.

In fact, goals can arise from any form of coactivation of the cognitive representation of a potential goal state and positive affect. Watching someone smile while eating blueberry muffins may, for instance, link that activity to positive affect, which creates a goal representation. Indeed, such observational or social learning is thought to be a basic way in which infants learn which behavioral states are desired and which ones are not.

But research on needs and deprivation suggests that the affective valence of objects and behaviors that are instrumental in lifting a state of deprivation is not static, but variable (see, e.g., Berridge, 2001). Through incentive learning, organisms aquire the knowledge that certain behaviors (e.g., drinking) are more rewarding (i.e., produce more positive affect) when they are deprived (e.g., of liquid) than when they are satiated. Hence, the representation of drinking should have a more positive affective valence for people who are deprived, but not for people who are not deprived and activating the mental representation of drinking should only induce the motivation to drink for people who are deprived.

In a recent study, Veltkamp, Aarts, and Custers (2008a) found just that. In two experiments, participants with high or low deprivation were either subliminally primed with words related to drinking or not before motivation to drink was assessed. In the first experiment, it was found that without priming, participants with low and high deprivation did not differ in reported motivation (wanting) to drink. Compared to this control condition, however, priming increased motivation for participants with high, but not low deprivation. In a second experiment, actual drinking behavior was measured in an alleged taste task. After the priming phase, participants were asked to sample and evaluate two drinks. The dependent variable was the amount of liquid that was consumed during tasting. Again, it was found that whereas participants with low and high deprivation consumed an equal amount of liquid in the control condition, priming increased the intake of liquid only for participants with high deprivation. These findings suggest that whereas deprivation alters the affective valence of deprivation reducing behaviors (i.e., makes them more positive), these representations still need to be activated, at least under conditions of mild deprivation, for motivation to arise.

In sum, goal representations can develop in various ways that involve coactivation of a mental representation of a state or behavior and positive affect, regardless of whether this affect is the result of a conscious assessment, experiences upon goal attainment, or mere observation.

Positive Affect and Goal Enactment

The research described above demonstrates that positive affect incorporated in goal representations promotes motivational goal-directed behavior. But how does positive affect guide actions on a concrete level? There is evidence to suggest that goals do not merely trigger instrumental actions through cognitive associations, but also facilitate goal pursuit through other processes that rely on the affective part of the representation.

Readiness for Goal Pursuit

An important way in which goals direct behavior is by biasing perceptual processes in favor of goal-related information. When one is, for example, motivated to drink, perceptual pronunciation of goal-related objects (e.g., a glass of water) in any way may be functional in the sense that it increases a person's chance of reaching the goal (Bruner, 1957). This accentuation would make lower-order actions involving the object (e.g., grabbing, drinking) more likely to occur.

Evidence for such a biasing effect on perceptual processes was obtained by Veltkamp, Aarts, and Custers (2008b). In line with research on functional perception, they hypothesized that objects related to goals that people are motivated to attain should be perceived as higher or bigger in size. In their classic study, Bruner and Goodman (1947), for example, established that children overestimated the size of coins as a function of their monetary value and that this effect was more pronounced for poor than rich children. Following this rationale, Veltkamp et al. asked participants to estimate the height of stimuli (e.g., a piece of a puzzle) that represented objects that were functional in attaining (initially neutral) potential behavioral goals (e.g., doing puzzles). These behavioral states were either linked to negative, neutral, or positive affective words in a within-participants design similar to that used in the evaluative conditioning procedure discussed above. It was found that compared to objects related to the neutral behavioral states, objects related to states linked to positive words were estimated to be higher, whereas no effect was found for objects related to behavioral states linked to negative words. Hence, positive affect incorporated in goal representations may lead to biased perceptual processes in favor of goal related objects.

Transfer of Affect from Goals to Goal-Related Objects

A second way in which positive affect may facilitate goal enactment is through transference of positive affect from goals to lower-order actions. As noted earlier, goal and means are associated in a hierarchical mental structure. It has been proposed that, not unlike activation, positive affect may "flow" from goals to means and related objects because of these associations (Kruglanski et al., 2002). In effect, positive affect associated with a goal representation would seep down to action representations lower in the hierarchy, furnishing them with motivational power, effectively creating subgoals.

Preliminary evidence for such a process was obtained in studies by Ferguson and Bargh (2004). In one experiment, they manipulated people's goal to drink. All participants were instructed to refrain from drinking in the 3 hours before the experiment. In the control group, participants were upon arrival in the lab submitted to an alleged taste test, in which they had to compare various drinks and should drink as much as possible. In the experimental group, participants had to taste different brands of pretzels, which should exacerbate their thirst. Subsequently, participants' implicit evaluations of goal-related objects and actions were measured. It was found that goal-related objects that could be used to quench their thirst evoked more positive affect in thirsty than in participants who were not thirsty.

Together, these findings suggest not only that goal priming facilitates goal enactment by rendering representations of instrumental actions more accessible, but also that positive affect associated with the primed goal biases perception toward goal-relevant objects by perceptually accentuating them. Moreover, the positive affect associated with the activated goal may "spill over" to lower goal-related actions and associated objects and thus facilitate (approach) reactions that are helpful in attaining the goal. As such, the selection of goal-directed actions may be driven not only by the cognitive part of the goal representation in that the representation of the desired state may render accessible representations of associated actions, but also by the affective part. This part biases perception toward goal-related objects and renders them more positive, which facilitates approach reactions.

Negative Affect and the Cessation of Nonconscious Goal Pursuit

The work discussed above demonstrates that the positive affective valence of goals determines whether a goal that is primed by the environment is pursued or not. Hence, nonconscious goal pursuit is based on learned relations between the goal state and positive affect. Although such a mechanism would be adaptive in that it allows people to pursue the goals that have proven to yield positive outcomes in the past, it could backfire if these goals are activated in a setting in which they are undesirable. Would the positive affect associated with the goal lead people astray in those situations and facilitate pursuit of the goal with unfavorable consequences?

This may not always be the case. In the studies of Aarts and colleagues (2004), for example, goal priming did not instigate motivational processes and even reduced desirability of the goal when the goal (having casual sex) was presented in a negative light (the guy pursuing the goal was going to be a father). One interpretation of these findings is that the negative contextual information may close down the motivational processes that would have been put in motion by the positive affect associated with the goal.

That is, affective processes may not only be involved in the production of motivation, they may also cease it.

This idea is supported by recent neurological findings suggesting that negative information modulates the activity of the dopamine system. Specifically, it appears that negative affect following the activation of a goal changes the effects of dopamine functioning in subcortical and cortical brain circuits involved in goal pursuit. Delgado, Nystrom, Fissell, Noll, and Fiez (2000), for example, gave participants the goal to guess whether the value of a card was lower or higher than the number "5." Each guess was immediately followed by a monetary reward or punishment. Neuroimaging data showed that, compared to a baseline condition, activation in the dopamine system was sustained following a goal reward but sharply decreased following goal punishment. These and other findings suggest that frequent priming of a goal in temporal proximity to the activation of negative affect may dampen activity in brain systems that control the motivation and resultant operation of the goal. If such a mechanism that takes into account changes in incentive value is hard wired in the brain, it may play an important role in modulating the effects of goal priming.

This hypothesis was specifically addressed by Aarts, Custers, and Holland (2007). Making use of the same conditioning paradigm discussed earlier, they repeatedly coactivated preexisting, positive goals in temporal proximity to negative affect. Effects were tested on a number of phenomena that are associated with the activation of goal representations. In a first empirical demonstration Aarts and colleagues (2007) subliminally primed undergraduates with the goal of partying (a goal they clearly perceived as a desired state) in temporal proximity of negatively valenced object words (e.g., war, trash) and tested effects of this affective goal treatment on the motivation to work to attain the goal in a goal-relevant task. They found that participants worked less hard to attain the goal when it was coactivated with negative affect, compared to conditions in which the goal was primed without negative affect. These findings fit those of Winkielman, Berridge, and Willbarger (2005), who found that thirsty participants having the active goal of drinking who were exposed to subliminal faces with negative emotions (anger) showed a decreased motivation to drink. Together, these findings suggest that coactivation of a goal with negative affect ceases the motivation to pursue this goal and this negative affect can be triggered by events that are not necessarily related to the goal, such as emotions or objects that are perceived in the environment.

Building on the idea that accessible preexisting goals are kept active over time, Aarts and colleagues (2007) also tested how the mental accessibility of a preexisting goal changes during a short time interval as a result of subliminally priming the goal in concert with negative affect. Specifically, they reasoned that the nonconscious activation of a desired goal triggers active maintenance (rehearsal) processes that can keep the goal alive in mind for several minutes. This in contrast to the activation of mere semantic knowledge, which shows a very rapid decay, usually returning to baseline within a couple of seconds. Thus, when a person becomes less motivated to pursue the goal (e.g., going out partying), its cognitive representation should, in principle, behave as any other semantic (nonmotivational) concept.

To test this hypothesis, Aarts and colleagues (2007) primed their participants either with the goal to party or not, and assessed the accessibility of the goal-related words (and goal-unrelated control words) in a lexical decision task 2.5 minutes later. Results showed that after that interval, the representation of the goal of partying was still more accessible in primed than in control participants, whereas no difference in the accessibility of the control words was observed. Importantly, for participants for whom the goal was primed and coactivated with negative affect, the activation level was not different from that of control participants. These findings suggest that when a preexisting goal is activated nonconsciously, the goal is mentally maintained or rehearsed to keep it at a heightened level of accessibility, and that this process disappears quickly when one becomes demotivated to pursue it as a result of negative signals accompanying the activation of the goal. Hence, people's goal pursuits may not only be guided by positive affect incorporated in the goal representation, but also be modulated by affective signals that co-occur with the stimuli that prime this representation.

Discussion

This chapter aimed to investigate how activation of mental goal representations can result in motivational, goal-directed behavior. Based on an analysis of the goal concept throughout psychology and its place in theories of goals, it was concluded that purely cognitive representations merely containing information about the state that is to be pursued cannot explain how goal-directed, motivational behavior emerges without conscious interventions. Given the evidence for the existence of such goal-priming effects, and based on the human capacity to process and use affective information efficiently and without conscious processes, it was hypothesized that affect incorporated in the goal representation reflects the (expected) value of the goal, rendering conscious assessments and deliberations obsolete.

The discussed research supporting this hypothesis suggests that positive affect can become associated to cognitive representations of the goal state through learning and as a consequence drive the instigation and enactment of goals. Furthermore, negative affect may be involved in modulating the motivational effects of preexisting goals. Together, these findings uncover the underlying mechanisms of nonconscious goal pursuit by showing how one of the most crucial parts in models of goal pursuit—assessment of the (expected) value of the goal—can occur without conscious involvement and is enough for primed goals to take control over behavior. In other words, because of the affective part of the goal representation, our unconscious "knows" what we want.

Distinguishing between Different Mechanisms by which the Environment Directs Behavior

The current analysis sheds new light on the currently fashionable topic of unconscious influences on human behavior. Most of all, it helps to further define and thereby distinguish nonconscious goal pursuit form other mechanisms, such as approach and avoidance reactions and behavior priming. Whereas behavior priming is an example of ideomotor action, relying on thoughts about or representations of behavior, approach and avoidance reactions can be categorized as sensorimotor actions: actions that are automatically put in motion by the sensory perception of a physical object in the immediate environment. As such, behavior priming is thought to rely on a purely cognitive mechanism, which involves the direct activation of motor programs that are associated with or incorporated in the representations of actions. Approach and avoidance reactions, on the other hand, rely on the affective signals emitted by perceived objects that trigger bodily reactions that either reduce or enlarge the physical distance between the object and the self. Whereas affect should not play a role in behavior priming, the content of the object representation should not matter much for approach and avoidance reactions.

Most of the time, however, the different mechanism are not easily told apart. Recent studies by Cesario and colleagues (2006) for instance, suggest that the finding by Bargh and colleagues (1996) that people walk more slowly when primed with words related to the elderly is not totally based on a direct perception–action link, but at least partly the result of motivational processes. First of all, they replicated the effect by demonstrating that priming people with "elderly" caused them to behave more slowly as compared to priming them with "youth." Second, they demonstrated that slowing down after elderly priming was more pronounced for people who implicitly evaluated the elderly as more positive (and less negative) and that speeding up after youth priming was more pronounced when youth was more positive (and less negative). Cesario and colleagues interpreted these effects as a motivated preparation to interact: People with more positive implicit attitudes toward the elderly would have a stronger goal to interact with members of this group and after priming behave in a way that would enable them to successfully attain that goal (i.e., behave more slowly). Hence, the effect that previously exemplified behavior priming appears to have at least partly been produced by motivational process. Thus, considering the affective valence associated with behaviors that are primed directly, or through concepts such as social stereotypes may help to determine whether motivational or nonmotivational mechanisms are operating.

In a recent study, Aarts, Custers, and Marien (2008) successfully differentiated between effects on preparation and motivation of behavior by manipulating the accessibility and affective valence of behavior representations related to exertion. Using the manipulation described earlier, all participants were exposed to supraliminally presented neutral and positive words. In the prime group, words related to exertion (exert, vigorous, strength) were subliminally primed prior to the neutral words, whereas in the prime + reward group these primes were presented prior to the positive words. In the control condition, no primes related to exertion were presented.

Subsequently, participants moved on to a task in which the effort they expended could be measured over time. Their task was to squeeze a handgrip for a time interval of 4 seconds when the word "squeeze" appeared on the computer screen. This task was repeated three times, and the force participants exerted was measured by the computer. It was found that compared to the control condition, participants were faster to respond to the squeeze instruction in the prime and the prime + reward condition, which indicates that in both conditions priming of the representation of exertion prepared the corresponding behavior. However, the total amount of effort expended in the task (mean force over the 4 seconds) was only increased in the priming + reward condition. This indicates that whereas activating a behavior representation leads to preparation of the corresponding action, motivation only results when the activation of a behavior representation is accompanied by positive reward signals.

The important role of affect in goal-priming effects should not lead people to confuse them with basic approach or avoidance reactions. It is by now well documented that positive objects facilitate approach reactions (e.g., extending one's hand), whereas negative objects elicit avoidance reactions (e.g., retreating one's hand). Although at a metaphorical level approaching a goal may seem similar to approaching a delicious piece of cake in front of you, there are important differences. Basic approach and avoidance reactions do, for instance, not rely on cognitions other than those that are required to categorize an object as good or bad, and knowledge of the location of the object. Affective categorization alone is enough to determine which of the two options apply: approach or avoid. Goal-directed behavior, on the other hand, does rely on cognitions. For one thing, goal-directed behavior is often triggered by mere thoughts of a certain goal state that is not present in the physical surrounding. As a consequence, cognitions about how to attain the goal are needed as extending or retreating a hand does not do the trick. Thus, although approach–avoidance reactions as well as goal-directed behavior may be propelled by affective processes, the use of cognitive representations makes the difference.

Consequences for Behavior Regulation and Behavioral Change

Recognizing the crucial role of affect in goal-directed behavior may have important consequences for behavior regulation and attempts to change behavior. Much work on behavior regulation already takes into account the unconscious influences of affect in this process. Fishbach and colleagues, for example, have been studying the interaction between goals and temptations across several lines of research (see, e.g., Fishbach, Friedman, & Kruglanski, 2003). In this research, affect is generally the source of unwanted approach reactions that are evoked by objects in the environment (temptations). Although the field of behavior regulations has contributed much to our understanding of the dynamics between motivation and environment, two implications of the current view on goal representations may be worth mentioning that may have important consequences for understanding behavior regulation and promoting behavioral change. First, the impact of the environment on our behavior may be far greater than assumed thus far. Objects in the environment may not only trigger approach reactions, but may also instigate goal-directed behavior that is potentially even more powerful. Thus, we may not only be tempted by a piece of pizza that is sitting right in front of us, but also may even walk an extra block to buy a slice if the thought about it is triggered in our mind. Although on the whole the ability to pursue goals without conscious thoughts may serve us well, it may also lead us to pursue the things we associate with positive affect, even when we have consciously and rationally decided not to.

Second, the power of nonconscious goal pursuit may also be used to our advantage if we can harness it. The work of Moskowitz and colleagues for example (2004) demonstrates that chronic or temporarily activated egalitarian goals help people to control their prejudiced responses that are often assumed to be out of the reach of conscious control. From the current analysis of the role of positive affect in goal representations it follows that such goals cannot only be activated through priming techniques, but that the strength of these goals can potentially also be altered by linking them to positive or negative affect. Such strategies that are to a certain extent already employed in cognitive therapy may prove effective in changing the strength of people's goals.

Although people often have the idea that their goal pursuits are the results of their conscious intentions, the work discussed in this chapter supports the idea that the processes underlying these intentions, specifically the assessment of the (expected) value of the goal, can also occur without deliberation and directly give rise to motivational, goal-directed behavior. The mechanism that makes this possible is one that relies on the cognitive as well as the affective information that is incorporated in the goal representation and takes into account affective signals that accompany goal priming. Thus, by processing and storing this affective representation along with other cognitive information about the goal, our unconscious keeps track of what we want so we do not have to deliberate on each potential goal, over and over again.

Acknowledgment

The writing of this chapter was supported by a grant from the Netherlands Organization for Scientific Research (NWO), VENI-grant 451-06-014.

References

Aarts, H., Custers, R., & Holland, R. W. (2007). The nonconscious cessation of goal pursuit: When goals and negative affect are coactivated. *Journal of Personality and Social Psychology, 92,* 165–178.

Aarts, H., Custers, R., & Marien, H. (2008). Preparing and motivating behavior outside of awareness. *Science, 319,* 1639.

Aarts, H., Gollwitzer, P. M., & Hassin, R. R. (2004). Goal contagion: Perceiving is for pursuing. *Journal of Personality and Social Psychology, 87,* 23–37.

Aarts, H., Verplanken, B., & van Knippenberg, A. (1998). Predicting behavior from actions in the past: Repeated decision making or a matter of habit? *Journal of Applied Social Psychology, 28,* 1355–1374.

Bandura, A. (1986). *Social foundations of thought and action: A social cognitive theory.* Englewood Cliffs, NJ: Prentice Hall.

Bargh, J. A., Chen, M., & Burrows, L. (1996). Automaticity of social behavior: Direct effects of trait construct and stereotype activation on action. *Journal of Personality and Social Psychology, 71,* 230–244.

Bargh, J. A., Gollwitzer, P. M., Lee-Chai, A., Barndollar, K., & Trotschel, R. (2001). The automated will: Nonconscious activation and pursuit of behavioral goals. *Journal of Personality and Social Psychology, 81,* 1014–1027.

Baumeister, R. F., & Vohs, K. D. (Eds.). (2004). *Handbook of self-regulation: Research, theory, and applications.* New York: Guilford Press.

Berridge, K. C. (2001). Reward learning: Reinforcement, incentives, and expectations. In D. L. Medin (Ed.), *The psychology of learning and motivation:*

Advances in research and theory (Vol. 40, pp. 223–278). San Diego: Academic Press.

Berridge, K. C. (2007). The debate over dopamine's role in reward: The case for incentive salience. *Psychopharmacology, 191,* 391–431.

Bijleveld, E., Custers, R., & Aarts, H. (2008). *Pupil size reveals strategic recruitment of resources in response to subliminal reward cues.* Manuscript under review.

Brown, P. L., & Jenkins, H. M. (1968). Auto-shaping of the pigeon's key-peck. *Journal of the Experimental Analysis of Behavior, 11,* 1–8.

Bruner, J. S. (1957). On percptual readiness. *Psychological Review, 64,* 123–152.

Bruner, J. S., & Goodman, C. C. (1947). Value and need as organizing factors in perception. *Journal of Abnormal Social Psychology, 42,* 33–44.

Cacioppo, J. T., & Berntson, G. G. (1999). The affect system: Architecture and operating characteristics. *Current Directions in Psychological Science, 8,* 133–137.

Carver, C. S., & Scheier, M. F. (1998). *On the self-regulation of behavior.* New York: Cambridge University Press.

Cesario, J., Plaks, J. E., & Higgins, E. T. (2006). Automatic social behavior as motivated preparation to interact. *Journal of Personality and Social Psychology, 90,* 893–910.

Custers, R., & Aarts, H. (2005a). Beyond priming effects: The role of positive affect and discrepancies in implicit processes of motivation and goal pursuit. In M. Hewstone & W. Stroebe (Eds.), *European review of social psychology* (Vol. 16, pp. 257–300). Hove, UK: Psychology Press/Taylor & Francis (UK).

Custers, R., & Aarts, H. (2005b). Positive affect as implicit motivator: On the nonconscious operation of behavioral goals. *Journal of Personality and Social Psychology, 89,* 129–142.

Custers, R., & Aarts, H. (2007). In search of the nonconscious sources of goal pursuit: Accessibility and positive affective valence of the goal state. *Journal of Experimental Social Psychology, 43,* 312–318.

Custers, R., Maas, M., Wildenbeest, M., & Aarts, H. (2008). Nonconscious goal pursuit and the surmounting of physical and social obstacles. *European Journal of Social Psychology, 38* 1013–1022.

De Houwer, J. (2003). The extrinsic affective simon task. *Experimental Psychology, 50,* 77–85.

De Houwer, J., Thomas, S., & Baeyens, F. (2001). Association learning of likes and dislikes: A review of 25 years of research on human evaluative conditioning. *Psychological Bulletin, 127,* 853–869.

Delgado, M. R., Nystrom, L. E., Fissell, C., Noll, D. C., & Fiez, J. A. (2000). Tracking the hemodynamic responses to reward and punishment in the striatum. *Journal of Neurophysiology, 84,* 3072–3077.

Dijksterhuis, A., & Bargh, J. A. (2001). The perception-behavior expressway: Automatic effects of social perception on social behavior. In M. P. Zanna (Ed.), *Advances in experimental social psychology* (Vol. 33, pp. 1–40). New York: Academic Press.

Ferguson, M. J. (2007). On the automatic evaluation of end-states. *Journal of Personality and Social Psychology, 92,* 596–611.

Ferguson, M. J., & Bargh, J. A. (2004). Liking is for doing: The effects of goal pursuit on automatic evaluation. *Journal of Personality and Social Psychology, 87,* 557–572.

Fishbach, A., Friedman, R. S., & Kruglanski, A. W. (2003). Leading us not into temptation: Momentary allurements elicit overriding goal activation. *Journal of Personality and Social Psychology, 84,* 296–309.

Fishbein, M., & Ajzen, I. (1975). *Belief, attitude, intention, and behavior: An introduction to theory and research.* Reading, MA: Addison-Wesley.

Gollwitzer, P. M. (1990). Action phases and mind-sets. In E. T. Higgins & R. M. Sorrentino (Eds.), *Handbook of motivation and cognition* (Vol. 2, pp. 53–92). New York: Guilford Press.

Gollwitzer, P. M., & Moskowitz, G. B. (1996). Goal effects on action and cognition. In E. T. Higgins & A. W. Kruglanski (Eds.), *Social psychology: Handbook of basic principles* (pp. 361–399). New York: Guilford Press.

Greenwald, A. G., McGhee, D. E., & Schwartz, J. L. K. (1998). Measuring individual differences in implicit cognition: The implicit association test. *Journal of Personality and Social Psychology, 74,* 1464–1480.

Higgins, E. T. (1987). Self-discrepancy: A theory relating self and affect. *Psychological Review, 94,* 319–340.

Kruglanski, A. W., Shah, J. Y., Fishbach, A., Friedman, R., Chun, W. Y., & Sleeth-Keppler, D. (2002). A theory of goal-systems. In M. P. Zanna (Ed.), *Advances in experimental social psychology* (Vol. 34, pp. 331–378). San Diego, CA: Academic Press.

LeDoux, J. (1996). *The emotional brain.* New York: Simon & Schuster.

Locke, E. A., & Latham, G. P. (2002). Building a practically useful theory of goal setting and task motivation: A 35-year odyssey. *American Psychologist, 57,* 705–717.

Moors, A., & De Houwer, J. (2001). Automatic appraisal of motivational valence: Motivational affective priming and simon effects. *Cognition and Emotion, 15,* 749–766.

Moskowitz, G. B., Li, P., & Kirk, E. R. (2004). The implicit volition model: On the preconscious regulation of temporarily adopted goals. In M. P. Zanna (Ed.), *Advances in experimental social psychology* (Vol. 36, pp. 317–404). New York: Academic Press.

Olds, J., & Milner, P. (1954). Positive reinforcement produced by electrical stimulation of septal area and other regions of rat brain. *Journal of Comparative and Physiological Psychology, 47,* 419–427.

Pessiglione, M., Schmidt, L., Draganski, B., Kalisch, R., Lau, H., Dolan, R. J., et al. (2007). How the brain translates money into force: A neuroimaging study of subliminal motivation. *Science, 316,* 904–906.

Shah, J. Y. (2003). Automatic for the people: How representations of significant others implicitly affect goal pursuit. *Journal of Personality and Social Psychology, 84,* 661–681.

Skinner, B. F. (1953). *Science and human behavior.* Oxford, UK: Macmillan.

Tolman, E. C. (1932). *Purposive behavior in animals and man*. New York: Appleton-Century-Crofts.

Veltkamp, M., Aarts, H., & Custers, R. (2008a). On the emergence of deprivation-reducing behaviors: Subliminal priming of behavior representations turns deprivation into motivation. *Journal of Experimental Social Psychology, 44,* 866–873.

Veltkamp, M., Aarts, H., & Custers, R. (2008b). Perception in the service of goal pursuit: Motivation to attain goals enhances the perceived size of goal-instrumental objects. *Social Cognition, 26,* 720–736.

Watson, J. B. (1925). *Behaviorism*. New York: Norton.

Wegner, D. M. (2002). *The illusion of conscious will*. Cambridge, MA: MIT Press.

Wilson, T. D. (2002). *Strangers to ourselves: Discovering the adaptive unconscious*. Cambridge, MA: Belknap Press of Harvard University Press.

Winkielman, P., Berridge, K. C., & Wilbarger, J. (2005). Unconscious affective reactions to masked happy versus angry faces influence consumption behavior and judgments of value. *Personality and Social Psychology Bulletin, 31,* 121–135.

Wood, W., Quinn, J. M., & Kashy, D. A. (2002). Habits in everyday life: Thought, emotion, and action. *Journal of Personality and Social Psychology, 83,* 1281–1297.

CHAPTER 8

Goal Priming

GORDON B. MOSKOWITZ
YUICHU GESUNDHEIT

Where do one's goals come from in a given moment? From among the multitude of goals an individual may wish to pursue in a given setting, what makes one goal jump ahead of the other goals one could possibly pursue? One may have the goal to listen to music, to study for an exam, to sleep in one's bed, use the phone, read a book, watch TV, and procrastinate by surfing the web all potentially ready to be pursued while in one's bedroom. One may have the goal to be helpful, selfish, egalitarian, oppressive, controlling, or merely the goal to identify and understand the behavior and words of another person (epistemic goals) potentially ready to be engaged when encountering a person. Often people consciously select a goal to pursue following a period of deliberation (for a review, see Oettingen & Stephens, Chapter 6, this volume) or following an instruction (e.g., Locke & Latham, 1990). Bargh (1990) pointed out that this is where research on motivation prior to 1990 begins: with people explicitly pursuing goals they consciously willed (or had willed for them). From work on the timing of goal pursuit (Bandura, 1989), to effort mobilization (Wright & Brehm, 1989), to deliberation regarding goal desirability and feasibility (Atkinson & Birch, 1970; Gollwitzer, 1990), to goal setting (Locke & Latham, 1990), to the role of expectancies in goal pursuit (Fishbein & Aizen, 1975), and to planning (Gollwitzer, 1993), people explicitly select (or are given) a goal and then perform behavior explicitly aimed at attaining the goal.

However, a watershed moment in the study of and understanding of goals occurred with the introduction of the notion of "auto-motives"

(Bargh, 1990). Bargh drew on existing illustrations of the effortless operation of the motivational system and the environment's ability to trigger
behavior (e.g., the "New Look" research reviewed by Bruner, 1957; Miller,
Galanter, & Pribam, 1960; Norman & Shallice, 1986; Zeigarnik, 1927) to
suggest that goals need not be consciously selected. Kruglanski and Kopetz
(Chapter 1, this volume), along with Bargh and Huang (Chapter 5, this
volume), bookend the previous section of this book with chapters on this
nonconscious nature of human goal pursuit.

Bargh (1990) described goals as cognitive structures, similar in many
respects to social constructs such as schemas and stereotypes. This development allowed for a novel answer to the question: "Where do one's goals
come from in a given moment?" Rather than being consciously selected by
a person, goals may also be triggered or primed by one's environment. This
idea freed goals from the grip of consciousness. And as Bargh and Huang
(Chapter 5, this volume) suggest (see also Wegner & Erskine, 2003), this
grip was perhaps, after all, an illusion: The need to consciously will behavior is something humans may desire to feel to experience a sense of personal agency and control, but may not be required for goal pursuit. Indeed,
conscious goal pursuit may be an evolutionary later development, one that
simply utilizes the nonconscious structures and processes developed in
our evolutionary past. From this view, nonconscious selection of goals is
not merely possible, but this relatively recent view is perhaps the one best
suited to capture the origin of one's goals in most everyday situations. As
Bargh (1990, p. 100) stated:

> Goals and intents are represented in the mind in the same fashion as are
> social constructs, stereotypes, and schemas. The probability that such social
> representations become activated directly by environmental information is
> a joint function of their applicability to the information and their accessi-
> bility in memory. . . . Just as other chronically accessible social representa-
> tions do, then, chronic goals and intents, and the procedures (Smith, 1984)
> and plans (Miller et al., 1960; Wilensky, 1983) associated with them, may
> become directly and automatically linked in memory with representations of
> environmental features to which they are frequently and consistently associ-
> ated. . . . The result of this automatic associative link is that the motive-goal-
> plan structure becomes activated whenever the relevant triggering situational
> features are present in the environment.

In summary, goals can be primed outside of awareness from the environment. This is especially likely to occur as part of social comprehension,
or the perceiver's attempt to make sense of the behavior of others by inferring intent and goals from the observed action (e.g., Brewer & Dupree,
1983; Trzebinski, 1989). And in some sense, this idea is not as novel as it
may seem. Bargh was not the first to discuss goals as mental representa-

tions. Tolman (1932) posited that cues in the environment become associated with need states of the organism when these external cues have, in the past, satisfied these need states. This association was said to be internally represented in the mind of the perceiving organism. The representation of the actions, outcomes, and objects associated with a need state was then described as ready in the mind and able to be brought to bear on a current context. When engaged in goal pursuit, the context one is in was said to be capable of triggering representations of similar goal pursuits in similar contexts, thus specifying what value stimuli encountered in the new context might have for the organism in terms of satisfying the goal.

Given that Tolman's (1932) organism of interest was a rat, and his school of thought was behaviorism, he was certain to clarify that "the reader will perhaps need constantly to remind himself that the use of the terms perception, mnemonization and memory implies nothing as to consciousness" (p. 134) or that the organism has sensations that we might label as intent or a feeling of purpose. Tolman's mental representation was merely a form of associative learning; an association exists between a need (such as hunger), a context (such as a certain type of maze), and incentives (food). The organism can then expect the incentive to exist when next entering the same context in the same need state. Lewin (1936) popularized the idea that humans differ from animals in the important respect that they have a far greater range of motives that operate like needs, calling them "quasi-needs." This allows the possibility to fuse notions of associative learning that links cues in the world to "need states" with notions of intent and a "feeling of purpose." Human goals, clearly borne of intent and purpose, can also be primed by contexts.

Goal Representations Have Implicit Accessibility

The idea that goals are mentally represented leads naturally to a related idea: These representations, just as with other types of representations, can vary in their accessibility. By "accessibility" it is meant that a representation stored in long-term memory, such as a goal (but including any representation from semantic knowledge to stereotypes to attitudes) is retrieved and placed in short-term (or working) memory. A concept may be retrieved even (often) without the person being aware this process has occurred. Once accessible, the goal (or any accessible construct) is now said to be "primed." Once priming has occurred that goal is ready to be used to help the person interpret and respond to the stimuli that greet him/her (e.g., Bruner, 1957).

What becomes accessible (primed) in your mind is partly determined by what you have been exposed to in your environment. A person need not consciously activate or awaken a goal from its temporary dormancy in memory. This responsibility is left partly to cues, or primes. Cues include information residing outside the mind (like features of a person encountered in the environment, or features of the environment itself) that have inherent or acquired associations with the goal to be activated. The presence of a cue in one's environment, once detected by the perceptual system (whether supraliminally or subliminally detected), will lead to attempts to categorize that cue, thus bringing associated representations (such as a goal) from long-term memory to its state of heightened accessibility in working memory. Of course, "environment" includes the internal mental life of the person as well, such that thoughts of a concept, or related concepts, will also operate as a cue to heighten the accessibility of a concept (which is why, as we soon see, thinking about one's mother can make goals relating to one's mother accessible). Finally, level of accessibility can be determined by personal factors (history of experience with the construct in question, as with chronic accessibility, e.g., Higgins, 1996).

It should be noted that this view does not conceive of humans as mere stimulus–response machines. Certainly the environment can push a particular goal to a heightened state of accessibility, but it is also the case that a given environment may contain many cues that are capable of pushing a wide array of goals to heightened accessibility. Which cues grab attention and push to accessibility one goal from among a variety of goals will also depend on how the opportunities for various goal pursuits in a given context relate to the value, strength, and commitment one has to each of his/her potentially activated goals (e.g., Lewin, 1936). The individual will be selective in evaluating which of the many potential goals to be activated are afforded the best opportunity to be successfully pursued in the environment.

Thus, accompanying the push of the environment is the pull of the motivational system that specifies what Lewin (1936) called a "valence," and what McArthur and Baron (1983) called an "affordance"—this is a relationship with both a strength and a direction between the opportunities presented in the environment and the goals one can potentially have made accessible. Rather than an environment representing an association between one cue and one goal, there is instead an interaction between the needs of the person, the strength of the goals associated with those needs, and the opportunities afforded the person to pursue those goals. Once again, there is no need to assume that such evaluations of what opportunities are best afforded a chance for success is something consciously performed.

Consider the relationship between the goal of writing a chapter and the affordances specified by the environment. Sitting in one's office might trigger activity relevant to this goal because cues such as one's computer and relevant readings on the desktop and bookshelves will be sufficient to trigger the goal. However, a different environment, such as riding a commuter train, might be less likely to trigger the goal of chapter writing despite the presence of the same, or similar, cues: one's laptop, a backpack full of relevant readings. Other cues in this setting, such as the bar-car, might be associated with a more strongly held goal, or to a goal that is perceived to be afforded a greater likelihood of success in this setting. And one might find oneself shoving the laptop under the seat and sidling up to the bar without having given any conscious thought to this decision at all.

The relationship between the environment and its relevant cues and the goals of the individual is, therefore, not a new idea. What is relatively new is the sense that the association between environment and goals can be implicitly triggered, without awareness of the motivational system being brought on-line reaching consciousness. The experimental evidence for the priming of goals is now overwhelming. The remainder of this chapter seeks merely to provide a sampling of the evidence for goal priming, focusing on six ways a goal can attain a heightened state of accessibility:

1. implicit priming of a goal without awareness of the mediating processes that give rise to the goal's accessibility;
2. implicit priming of a goal despite awareness of some component(s) of the processes that give rise to a goal's accessibility;
3. a conscious decision to pursue a goal followed by subsequent lack of awareness that the goal is accessible;
4. discrepancy detection—monitoring and/or feedback processes that indicate one is either failing at or doing poorly at goal pursuit, thus highlighting a discrepancy between a desired state and current state;
5. chronic accessibility; and
6. consciously selecting a goal and retaining conscious awareness the goal is accessible as one engages in behavior relevant to goal pursuit.

Implicit Priming: The Total Absence of Awareness of Goal-Relevant Processing

Bargh (1990, p. 100) stated that the environment can implicitly trigger goals when one has formed "direct and automatic mental links between representations of motives and goals in memory (and consequently the goals and plans associated with them) and the representations of the social situations in which those motives have been frequently pursued in the past." The strongest test of this assumption occurs when one is not only unaware of the fact a goal has been triggered, but also is not even consciously aware of the stimulus that is relevant to one's goals. That is, we said above that cues in the environment trigger goals without one knowing it; but does one have goals triggered by cues when one does not even know the cues exist? Such a possibility makes the strongest argument for the nonconscious nature of human volition.

Subliminal Priming

Chartrand and Bargh (1996) provided the first illustration of implicit goal priming by focusing on a known effect of conscious "impression" goals. When people have impression-formation goals there is a negative correlation between the impression they form on-line (as information is being presented) and recall for that information (Hastie & Kumar, 1979). Recall favors information incongruent with the impression formed. No such preference in recall for impression-incongruent information is found in people with memory goals. The logic is that memory goals, unlike impression goals, do not motivate us to attempt to make the information we learn about another person cohere together in some meaningful way. When we are trying to form an impression of a person, we are searching for coherence—some way to tie together the information we have learned about the person in a meaningful, unified way. What happens when some information does not fit the emerging impression? Such incongruent information is typically processed more deeply as one tries to reconcile how it fits with the overall impression. Incongruence creates difficulty of fit with what we think we know about the person, and this triggers deeper processing of such information, which ultimately makes it more memorable (because we have struggled more with how to make sense of it and make it fit). Chartrand and Bargh (1996) reasoned that implicit goals trigger these same set of complicated processes involved in making sense of a person, even though one is not aware of a processing strategy or having a goal.

Participants in this experiment were subliminally primed with words relating to either impression-formation goals or control words. These words were presented to participants on a computer screen too fast to be consciously detected. Despite the words not being "seen", did they trigger associated goals? Participants subliminally exposed to words not relating to impression-formation goals performed in a way that suggested they were not attempting to form impressions of the person in the material presented (at least in a way that attempted to make the material cohere together meaningfully). There was no relationship between the judgments they formed and the information they recalled. In contrast, the impressions of people subliminally primed with impression goals were correlated with memory for the information presented earlier. They were forming an impression on-line, and this led to information not easily integrated into the emerging impression to be processed more deeply, thus leading it to be better remembered. They concluded the goal to form impressions was implicitly triggered by the subliminal priming procedure, thus triggering processes of trying to integrate the information in a coherent way.

Another illustration is provided by Fitzsimons and Bargh (2003). Participants were subliminally primed with either the name of their best friend or another participant's best friend. After the priming stage, participants read a description of the behavior of a stranger and generated plausible causes for this person's behavior. A typical finding in social psychology is that people make internal attributions to others' behavior while generating external (situational) causes when thinking about the behavior of the self and close friends. In support of a goal having been implicitly primed by the name of their friend being subliminally presented, it was found that participants primed with a friend made fewer internal attributions for the target's behavior.

Shah and Kruglanski (2002) demonstrated that goals are activated by implicit perception of the means used for achieving those goals. In one experiment participants responded to words related to education and health goals (e.g., "educated" and "knowledgeable"; "strong" and "fit") by indicating as fast and accurately as possible whether a target word represented a characteristic or trait. Unknown to participants, subliminal priming of words representing the means for achieving each of these goals (e.g., "study," "read," "exercise," and "run") were presented on each trial just prior to the target word. They found that participants' responses to target words representing the education and fitness goals were faster following subliminal primes representing a means corresponding to a given goal than following a control word. Such faster reaction times are evidence of the goal's accessibility being heightened by subliminal exposure to the means.

The previous three experiments illustrate that we can prime goals, and it affects the complex set of thoughts we engage when thinking about a person. However, most people think about goals not in terms of their effects on how we think (though this is a common way researchers think about goals, as discussed by Moskowitz, Chapter 12, this volume), but in terms of how they affect how we act. Can subliminal goal priming change the way we behave as well as think? Shah (2003, Experiment 2) examined this issue by subliminally presenting participants with words relating to the concept "father." People who have close relationships with their father that involve specific goals should have those goals triggered despite never consciously seeing the word "father." If triggered, the goal should affect behavior relating to that goal.

Shah (2003) focused on people whose fathers either did or did not have goals relating to the domain of "analytical reasoning" for their child. Shah further assessed behavior in the domain of analytical reasoning by having participants solve anagram puzzles that were said to be an important measure of one's skill and ability at analytical reasoning. Participants worked on the puzzles after subliminal exposure to words relating to the concept "father" (and hence, for some people, subliminal goal priming). A first question is "was the goal accessible?" And the answer is "yes." For people who were close to their father and for whose father valued analytical reasoning, priming with father made the goal more accessible, despite participants not knowing they had been primed or that the goal was accessible. A second question, most pertinent to the current discussion, is "How did participants perform on the puzzles?" Their behavior depended on their goals and relationship with their father. People with a close relationship to a father who valued analytic reasoning performed better on the task if they had been subliminally exposed to the concept "father." Subliminal exposure to a cue relating to a goal (in this case, one's father) triggers the goal and guides behavior, all outside awareness of the individual (who simply feels as if he/she is working uninfluenced on puzzles).

Implicit Goal Priming from Implicit Inference

Increasing the accessibility of a goal (or any construct) does not require subliminal presentation. It is possible to implicitly activate constructs as an unintended consequence of some other activity in which one is consciously engaged. Moskowitz and Roman (1992) made the point that heightened accessibility is not a laboratory-bound phenomenon but occurs throughout the course of everyday life by the way in which we naturally think about the world. We do not need experimenters to subliminally flash words at us for those same concepts to become accessible to us! For example, one can consciously observe a person, or read about a person, yet implicitly engage in processes of spontaneous inference that remain outside of awareness. Inferring qualities about the people we see and read about is a consequence of the task that individuals not only do not intend, but also explicitly deny doing (e.g., Uleman & Moskowitz, 1994). And because people do not know they are doing it, those concepts are implicitly triggered/primed (Moskowitz & Roman, 1992).

This same logic holds for implicit goal priming: It can occur through spontaneous processes of inference formation, such as when we unknowingly infer the goals relating to the behavior of a person we have observed. Not only do we infer those goals in others without knowing it, we also adopt those goals, or catch those goals, ourselves (e.g., Hassin, Aarts, & Ferguson, 2005). Let us review an example of such implicit *goal conta-*

gion. Aarts, Gollwitzer, and Hassin (2004) had participants read about a person who worked on a farm. Half were told the person was doing volunteer work, the other half were told the person was receiving money to pay for a vacation. This made up the goal manipulation: half were to "catch" the goal of "volunteerism," the other to catch the goal of "getting paid." Did these goal inferences affect behavior? Participants next saw a message on the computer screen telling them another task would soon start, and following that task, if time permitted, they could perform yet a third task that would allow them to earn money. They predicted that the implicit goal of "making money" would be accessible for half the people, and this would motivate them to work extra fast on the middle task to get to that third task (so long as the participant also valued making money).

As predicted, Aarts et al. (2004) found that the speed with which people found their way to the final task (the cash-earning task) was moderated by not only the goals implied in the behavior of the person they read about, but also the financial status of the participant. People short on cash (who valued earning money more) were more susceptible to catching the goal. Participants who read about someone with the implied goal of making money were faster working their way through the "middle" experiment (relative to someone who read about a person volunteering on a farm), but only when they had a high need for or value of money. This reveals that goals are unknowingly triggered by observing those goals in others and then determine how we act. However, we need not fear mimicking the behavior of others who behave in non-normative and maladaptive ways. We only experience goal contagion if we already value the goal in question.

Liberman and Förster (2000; Förster & Liberman, 2001) illustrated yet another way a goal can be primed implicitly through the conscious initiation of a strategy that unintentionally (and without one's awareness) primes a goal. This is through attempts at thought suppression. They posit that people have difficulty suppressing thoughts and experience this difficulty as a mental sensation. Like most mental sensations, people attempt to link some meaning to the experience, employing a theory of why it occurs—a metacognitive belief about the meaning of the sensation. In this case, the difficulty experienced with trying to suppress a thought implies to the participant that he/she has the goal to think about that particular thought. The implicit triggering of the goal results from the metacognitive inference: "I must have really wanted to pursue this goal if attempting to not do it is so hard." Thus, goals get triggered when trying to not pursue them!

Liberman and Förster (2000) manipulated participants' goals through a suppression manipulation so that people either implicitly adopted the goal to use colors in describing a painting or had no goal relevant to the painting. The goal to use color words is implicit because participants are explicitly trying not to use colors. In the testing phase, all participants described their home. Of interest was the number of color words participants used when describing their homes. They found that participants who were trying to suppress the use of colors actually used colors more than control participants, indicting the accessibility of the goal (to support the idea this is a goal, this effect disappeared for some of the participants who were allowed to attain the goal of using colors just before describing their home, thus displaying one of the five markers of goals—*persistence-until*—that Martin & Tesser review in Chapter 10, this volume).

Implicit Priming: Awareness of the Stimuli but Not the Goal

Another way goals become accessible in everyday life, without an experimenter subliminally flashing something at us, is when we consciously see cues in the environment relating to our goals. This occurs even though we may not consciously/explicitly make the connection that those cues are relevant to our goals (and even if we do not recall paying any particular attention to those cues after we have seen them). The priming stimulus need not be subliminal for accessibility of the goal representation to be implicit. In such cases, an individual who has consciously detected a goal-relevant prime has the accessibility of that goal persist after the priming stimulus has been removed and the individual is no longer aware of its influence at the time of goal-relevant responding. Thus, being in a library (and obviously knowing one is in a library) triggers goals associated with a library even if one does not realize such goals have been adopted. Smelling cleaning fluid makes goals associated with cleaning accessible. This logic holds for people serving as cues, just as well as it does for environments and objects in those environments: Seeing one's mother, or thinking about one's mother, unknowingly triggers goals associated with her. Even reading words relating to a goal can unknowingly trigger the goals.

Goal Priming from Reading Goal-Relevant Words

Chartrand and Bargh (1996) focused again on impression-formation goals versus memory goals. People with impression goals engage in more elaboration and integration of material they are later asked to read, resulting in superior recall relative to people who have memorization goals. Chartrand and Bargh primed these goals by having research participants complete a paper-and-pencil "scrambled sentence test" in which a set of words presented in a jumbled order had to be arranged in a fashion that produced a coherent English sentence. For half of the participants the sentences contained words relating to the goal of forming an impression, for the other half of the participants the sentences contained words relating to the goal of memorization. Subsequently, participants completed an ostensibly unrelated task in which sentence predicates describing four trait categories were presented as part of a memory task. They found that participants primed with impression goals remembered more of the information than those primed with memory goals.

Many examples of this type of implicit accessibility (stemming from consciously reading goal-related words in a context irrelevant to those goals) can be seen. Bargh, Gollwitzer, Lee-Chai, Barndollar, and Trotschel (2001) made goals accessible by having participants solve word-search puzzles that contained words relevant to the goal of high performance (e.g., win, compete, succeed). The conscious triggering of the goal through the puzzle task nonetheless resulted in participants being unaware of this heightened accessibility during a later performance situation. Bargh et al. examined whether such goal priming influenced performance by measuring the number of solutions participants generated when solving subsequent word puzzles. These puzzles differed from the first set in that instead of activating a goal, each simply had a theme listed at the top of the page (e.g., foods, bugs, and colors), and participants were told to find as many members of the categories in the puzzle as they could. It was found that people exposed to the high-performance goal performed better on the subsequent word puzzles. Without people knowing why they performed better, the implicit goal nonetheless had them performing better.

In a second experiment, Bargh et al. (2001) once again manipulated accessibility of a goal using a "scrambled-sentence task." For half of the participants some of the sentences they constructed contained words related to the goal of cooperation. They next examined whether these people would cooperate more relative to a control group. To examine cooperative behavior they used a domain in which cooperation has important ramifications: a resource dilemma. In such dilemmas participants share a limited resource with another participant. Participants can choose to compete against the other player for their own maximum gain, but this will deplete the resource and ultimately render it useless. They can also choose to cooperate so that the shared resource thrives (at the cost of one not maximally benefitting). The dilemma they used involved creating a simulated experience of fishing from a lake with a limited number of fish. Participants performed against a bogus participant who was believed to be "fishing" from the same "lake." The task was set up such that if each participant caught the maximum amount of fish on each trial (competed rather than cooperated) they would quickly run out of fish (thus killing the lake for future fishing). As determined by the total number of fish returned to the lake, participants who had been exposed to the goal of cooperating cooperated significantly more.

Goal Priming from People We Consciously See or Think About

We have already seen that subliminal presentation of a person can trigger goals relating to that person (Shah, 2003). Similar effects emerge from consciously seeing or thinking about a person. Even strangers can trigger goals that are linked to the actions of those strangers. For example, Hafer (2000) proposed that people possess a goal to believe that the world is just, and this belief is triggered by cues in the environment that suggest injustice is prevalent. Such cues include the suffering of others, with certain types of victims posing a more potent threat to a sense of justice than others (e.g., victims who are innocent, victims whose attackers go unpunished). Ironically, seeing a suffering stranger leads to the triggering of goals relating to justice, but this makes us more likely to see the innocent victim as actually deserving of his/her lot (given that the world is just).

Of course not only strangers can cue goals, significant others have this power as well. Goals may often originate from external pressures put on us by significant others (such as parents and friends) until gradually we come to internalize the goals they have for us. Thus, representations of particular interpersonal relationships (mother, best friend, coworker) include the specific interpersonal goals relevant to that relationship (achievement, helping, understanding). The interpersonal goal may be made implicitly accessible by having consciously detected the person. Fitzsimons and Bargh (2003) illustrated the power of relationship partners to prime the specific goals linked with them: priming the relationship partner (in this case one's mother) activates the goal associated with that person (e.g., achievement).

They used the trait-priming paradigm from person perception research. In such research it has been found that participants primed by a particular trait concept are more likely to use the concept for interpreting a target person's behavior ambiguously related to the concept (e.g., Higgins, 1996). Thus if priming the participant's mother activates the relationship-relevant goal representation, that is, achievement, then the participant should view behavior ambiguously relevant to achievement as more achievement oriented than a participant who has been primed with a different relationship partner, for example, a friend. At the priming stage, the participants were asked to visualize the image of either their best friends or their mother and write about the appearance of these partners in a couple of lines. In the target-perception stage, the participants read a vignette about a college student whose behavior was ambiguously related to being successful at school and rated the extent that they believe the target person was motivated to be successful at school. Participants primed with their mothers saw the target person as more motivated to succeed than those primed with their best friend, indicating the goal linked to mother was accessible without one knowing it, despite one knowing they had previously been thinking about mom.

Environmental Cues Associated with Goals Trigger Goals

Being in an environment can increase the accessibility of goals associated with particular items in that environment. For example, Bargh and Williams (2007) examined the basic physical sensations associated with an object that were said to be triggering goals with which those sensations were metaphorically linked. Participants who were handed either a cup of hot coffee or iced coffee were asked to then evaluate a person. They were fully aware they were making evaluations of how warm versus cold the person is and fully aware of the coffee they were holding. What they were not aware of is that the coffee cup primes concepts of physical heat and coldness that trigger more basic, evolutionary-based goals relating to warmth and coldness. This implicit goal priming then affected the explicit judgment, leading people holding hot coffee to actually evaluate the target person as warmer, whereas those holding iced coffee saw the person as colder.

Kay, Wheeler, Bargh, and Ross (2004) focused not on the metaphorical associations to sensations associated with an object, but the goals linked to those objects. Participants were primed by having objects associated with the domain of business (e.g., boardroom tables and briefcases) present while participants knowingly engaged in activities that could be facilitated by the goals associated with the business environment, namely competition. The activities included tasks such as an "Ultimatum game" where investments were being made. Participants primed with objects relevant to business and competition versus control objects (e.g., briefcases vs. backpacks) were more competitive and stingier with their money in that they attempted to retain a greater amount for themselves. Simply detecting a briefcase made people adopt relevant goals.

Some objects aquire their association to a goal because of the origin of the object—where it comes from. For example, a nondescript computer may be associated with a goal such as checking mail or listening to music or doing work. However, advertisers and marketers have the job of associating products with specific goals that appeal to a particular demographic. Thus, "Apple computers" has, since their inception as a company, attempted to associate their brand with novelty, revolution, and being different. A nondescript computer may be linked to the goals specified above, but an "Apple" or even the company logo, can be associated with a wholly different set of goals that the company's advertisers have led the public to internalize. This is true of many products and companies—whether it be an Oakland Raiders football jersey or the "Trump" brand. Such objects come to be associated with specific goals to which they have been associated in the media, thus having those goals triggered when the product or company name is encountered. Fitzsimons, Chartrand, and Fitzsimons (2008) illustrated these very processes by priming participants with products from companies such as the Disney corporation and Apple computers. In one experiment they examined creative behavior and found that people who were primed with logos representing "Apple computers" displayed heightened creativity on the task when compared to people primed with the "IBM" brand and people in a control prime condition. A second experiment examined how honest people act following priming of cues representing either the "Disney corporation" or "E!" Disney leads people to act more honestly. Products and companies trigger goals (if the advertisers have done their jobs effectively).

Aarts and Dijksterhuis (2003) demonstrated how exposure to a pictorial image of an environment itself can increase accessibility of goals associated with particular items in that environment. Following a picture-viewing task in which participants studied images containing either a library or an exclusive restaurant, they were given a lexical decision task in which they had to indicate as fast and accurately as possible, over a series of trials, whether a string of letters formed a word (vs. a nonword). The stimuli varied so that the words were sometimes control words and other times were words related to the goals associated with the cues that had just been observed (e.g., library-related words). It was found that participants who had studied the library image as opposed to the other image responded faster to words associated with behavior appropriate for a library environment (e.g., silent, quiet, word, whisper) compared to control words. How do we know this reveals the priming of a goal as opposed to the semantic priming of concepts associated with the category "library"? These effects only occurred for those participants who were told that they would be visiting the library, suggesting that it is the actual goal of going to a library that increased the accessibility of the behavioral norms associated with being in a library, not simply the semantic content linked to the concept of a library.

Fishbach, Friedman, and Kruglanski (2003) argue that *temptations away from* a goal, things known to be *incompatible* with a goal, can also trigger that higher-order goal, setting in motion processes that override the temptation, or counteract the value of the temptation. A donut may seem attractive, but health goals incompatible with eating the donut, as opposed to the goal of embracing/eating the donut, should be triggered to counteract the value assigned to the donut. Donuts in this case would heighten the accessibility of a health goal to counteract the goal of comfort eating. Thus rather than increased donut consumption occurring when donuts are present, we should see heightened healthy eating. Such a counteractive effect would only be evidenced if the health goal was important, and if donuts were associated with the incompatible goal of being healthy. This is precisely what their research found.

Fishbach et al. (2003) found that a temptation (fattening foods) triggered the higher-order goal of being health conscious in one's eating behavior. Some participants were primed with a temptation by having them work in a room with magazines and photographs depicting fattening food. Others were primed, using a similar procedure, with the goal of dieting. The participants were asked to choose between a chocolate bar and an apple as a departure gift for having participated in the experiment. The participants who were food primed and diet primed were more likely than control participants to choose the apple rather than chocolate.

Even odors, or other sense-related stimuli in the environment, that one barely even consciously detects can trigger goals associated with those sensations. Holland, Hendriks, and Aarts (2005) placed some participants in a room that contained the faint odor of cleaning fluid, while others waited in a room without the odor. Participants were given a messy cookie to eat, one that crumbled to pieces on the table quite easily. Does the goal to be clean get triggered and guide behavior? Being in a room with a slight, hard-to-detect odor of cleaning fluid makes them more likely to tidy up after themselves when eating the cookie.

Consciously Selected Goals That Implicitly Retain Accessibility

The triggering of a goal by attending to a relevant stimulus, either implicitly or consciously, is not the only way in which individuals can have a goal in a heightened state of accessibility without the individual knowing it. A goal can be primed by consciously selecting to pursue that goal. However, a goal selected at one point in time, or in one context, can retain its accessibility later in time or in subsequent contexts where the individual is now unaware that the goal is accessible and guiding responding. One way this can be illustrated is with examples of one consciously selecting a goal yet subsequently either disengaging from that goal or entering a context where the goal is seemingly irrelevant. Despite conscious goal selection having been relinquished, goals retain accessibility. We review three examples to make the point.

Creativity

Creativity goals are characterized by one being productive of new things, or new, original, and atypical ideas. One is striving to be ingenious, innovative, and original. Sassenberg and Moskowitz (2005) posited that creativity is achieved by a mental system that inhibits typical associates to a category while simultaneously activating atypical or remote associates: thinking differently at the most basic level of what gets activated upon exposure to a stimulus. They further posited that giving people the goal to be creative would see the cognitive effects of that goal carryover to a new domain even though they were not asked to be creative on the next task, or knew they were pursuing the goal of creativity in the new context. Creativity was manipulated by having some participants describe a time in which they had strived to be creative, while others described instances of striving to be thoughtful. This task was described as a "pretest" for a future experiment, and participants were then asked to perform a new task seemingly irrelevant to creativity. Despite consciously disengaging from the consciously selected creativity goal, did the goal persist at an implicit level during the next task, affecting responses?

The new task was a lexical decision task, which on the face of it had no bearing to creativity. Strings of letters appeared on the screen and participants had to indicate, as fast as possible, whether the letters formed a word. They examined whether participants displayed a priming effect typical in the literature (e.g., Neely, 1977): a facilitated ability to respond to a target word (e.g., nurse) after a semantically relevant target had been presented as a prime (e.g., doctor). They found that this robust effect was controlled by people who previously had creativity goals triggered. These participants showed less facilitation (slower reaction times) for classifying the prime-relevant words than participants in the thoughtful condition. That is, responding to "nurse" is not facilitated following "doctor." The seeming irrelevance of the task to creativity, as well as the fast response times (see Bargh & Chartrand, 2000), suggest the creativity goal was implicitly accessible and guiding processes of categorization (in this case, inhibiting typical associates to a category). This was replicated with faces of members of a stereotyped group as the primes followed by stereotype-relevant or -irrelevant target words. The goal to be thoughtful did nothing to alter the typical finding: Seeing a face of a Black man facilitated responses to words relating to stereotypes of Black men (for a review, see Moskowitz, Chapter 12, this volume). However, creativity goals disrupted these typical associations such that stereotypes were not triggered following Black faces (people were not faster to stereotype-relevant words).

Rumination

This type of implicit goal accessibility following a conscious decision to pursue a goal can be seen in classic illustrations of goal pursuit. Zeigarnik (1927) illustrated that a goal that was at one point consciously selected, yet at another point consciously released, remained accessible at an implicit level, directing cognitive activity outside of conscious awareness and intent. People continue to ruminate on a task at an implicit level even after being asked to stop consciously deliberating/ruminating on the task. Participants were asked to work on a series of puzzles/problem sets until each set of tasks was completed. However, some of these activities were not completed but interrupted and removed from sight so participants could not continue to work on them. The participants then were given other tasks to complete to occupy consciousness and prevent them from thinking about the previous task. Had they stopped ruminating on the task, or did the goal stay implicitly accessible? Zeigarnik assessed this by unexpectedly asking participants to recall the tasks they had previously worked on. The unfinished tasks were recalled twice as much as the finished ones. This illustrated how the goal to ruminate on the task remained accessible despite participants consciously disengaging from it.

A more modern illustration of participants being guided by implicit rumination goals is provided by the "deliberation-without-attention" effect of Dijksterhuis, Bos, Nordgren, and Van Barren (2006). Research participants were given the goal of ruminating on the qualities of several products (from among four cars, for example) and then choosing the best option. Some participants were allowed to consciously ruminate on the qualities, engaging thus in explicit goal pursuit. However, others were prevented from thinking about the choices consciously. Rather than having time to consciously deliberate their attention was distracted, as was the case in the Zeigarnik (1927) research, with a task that consumed their conscious thought and prevented conscious rumination among the choices. Did being distracted from the goal lead to disengagement of the goal? No. In fact, better decisions were shown to have been made by the people prevented from consciously ruminating. Dijksterhuis et al. described this superior decision making following unconscious, versus conscious, deliberation as due to people ruminating over the choices nonconsciously. The goal to ruminate among the choices is accessible and directing cognition, allowing the individual to unconsciously deliberate among the products and yield a better choice. The conclusion is not that putting something out of consciousness is beneficial (in fact it is only beneficial when the decision to be made is complicated rather than simple). It is that for the desertion of consciousness to increase effectiveness, a goal must remain active in the unconscious (and the decision task complex) when the conscious goal is released.

Implementation Intentions

Rather than attempt to review the literally thousands of goals that could be released from consciousness and still affect responding, we end this section by discussing a style of approaching one's goals (no matter the goal) that can enable conscious goals to be triggered and pursued in the unconscious. Ach (1935) asserted that consciousness may be required to formulate a plan of action, but that there is no reason to assume it is required to trigger or implement the plan. Gollwitzer (1993) extended this logic, asserting that conscious planning can create an association between a goal, a behavior, and a cue such that the presence of the cue will trigger the goal and initiate the goal-relevant response without consciousness. Gollwitzer (1993) called such plans *implementation intentions* (for a review, see Chapter 14, this volume). We review two examples of consciously selected goals being linked to plans that thus allow cues specified in the plan to implicitly trigger the goal linked to the plan. The reader is directed to Chapter 14 (this volume) for a comprehensive review of implementation intentions.

Aarts, Dijksterhuis, and Midden (1999) reasoned that for a goal to be successfully pursued often requires the disruption of other, more routinized, behavior. Implementation intentions make the act of breaking such habits easier because they make goal-relevant cues in the environment more accessible, more likely to be detected, and opportunities to act more likely to be seized. Their experiment reveals increased rates of completion for intended acts following implementation intentions. Participants were all given the same goal: to get a coupon from the secretary's office. All participants were then given directions to the office (down the corridor, through the doors, near the red hose, etc.). Those participants given implementation intentions were asked to formulate a specific plan regarding how (what route they would take to the secretary's office) and when (what time of day) they would get the coupon. Next all participants were given a lexical decision task to perform as part of an ostensibly separate experiment. Among the words were a subset related to the environment (the path to the secretary's office) in which the intended behavior (getting a coupon) was to occur. These were words specifically mentioned in the directions to that location (words such as "red," "hose," and "corridor").

First, they found that participants with implementation intentions were more likely to perform the behavior specified by the goal. But they also found that this occurs because of the mental association made between the goal and the objects in the environment specified by the intention/plan. They found that reaction times to the critical words were reliably faster (almost 100 milliseconds faster) for people who had been asked to form implementation intentions than the control group. Additionally, after statistically controlling for the effects of the increased accessibility, the greater likelihood of getting the coupon for people with implementation intentions was no longer reliable. This suggests the increased accessibility of the implicit goal leads to goal-relevant cues being more easily detected, which in turn facilitates the execution of the intended behavior.

Bayer, Achtziger, Gollwitzer, and Moskowitz (in press) also examined whether a plan consciously formed at one point in time can be automatically triggered, leading to initiation of relevant action by a cue in the environment. This time the cue is implicit by being subliminally presented. The goal was to respond as quickly as possible by pressing a button on a response box whenever a specific geometrical figure (e.g., something round, something with angles) was present. Implementation intentions were introduced by asking participants to plan to respond to one specific type of figure especially fast, for example, a triangle. Following these instructions, participants performed the task by responding to rounded (e.g., oval, circle) and angular (e.g., square, triangle) geometrical figures as targets. This task was always preceded by a subliminal prime, which on some trials included a triangle and on other trials included other geometric shapes. Does subliminal presentation of a triangle facilitate one's goal to respond to angled objects? Yes, but only if one has an implementation intention that links triangles with the goal.

Although a square as a subliminal prime also facilitated responses (because it also has angles and facilitates responding that requires pushing a button for angled objects), subliminal presentations of triangles led to even faster responses to critical (e.g., a triangle) as compared to noncritical (e.g., a square, a circle) targets by implementation-intention participants.

Of course, because a square also has angles, being primed with triangle, which speeds up the pressing of the button marked "angled object" when one consciously sees a triangle, also speeds up responses when one consciously sees a square as opposed to a circle or oval (because the subliminally presented triangle primes the action of pushing the button for angled objects). A cue, even one not consciously seen, can trigger a goal and its associated action sequence, if one previously consciously selected the goal of responding to the cue with a specific action sequence.

Discrepancy Detection

The distinction between this category of goal priming and the former is subtle. Rather than a person deliberating and selecting a goal, the goal is consciously triggered by one detecting a discrepancy between a desired end-state and a current state (e.g., Carver & Scheier, 1981; Lewin, 1936; Powers, 1973). Such discrepancies can be caused by external agents, such as negative feedback being provided by a mentor, a lower-than-expected grade on an exam, and a significant other distancing himself/herself from you. Discrepancies can also be detected by the individual's own monitoring processes whereby one initiates processes of evaluation regarding one's progress toward the pursuit of a goal (for a review of monitoring, see Moskowitz, Chapter 12, this volume).

As reviewed by Martin and Tesser (Chapter 10, this volume) the detection of a discrepancy between one's current standing on a goal and one's desired standing triggers a psychological tension akin to a drive. This "drive" leads to goal pursuit (with markers and characteristics that identify it as goal pursuit that is tension driven) aimed at reducing the drive state (satisfying or releasing the tension). Once triggered, as with goals primed by consciously selecting the goal or consciously attending to goal-relevant cues, the goal may retain its accessibility when one is no longer aware one is pursuing it or in a goal-relevant context. This occurs in conditions where the discrepancy detection (goal priming) is temporally distanced from the response (so the goal is active but not salient) or by making the response one that is not linked to the goal in the mind of the individual.

Failure Feedback

Spencer, Fein, Wolfe, Fong, and Dunn (1998) had participants receive failure feedback on a test that was said to measure not merely intelligence, but also likelihood for future success. The person is thus detecting a discrepancy in relation to at least two goals: the goal of being intelligent and the goal of having high esteem (a person with good opportunities for future success and happiness). They then demonstrated that this discrepancy detection led to the automatic activation of stereotypes. Why? They posited that when a person receives a self-esteem threat, the goal to attain a positive sense of self is triggered. The goal is accompanied by a tension that the individual must reduce by responding in some way that will resolve or satisfy the tension. The individual has learned over the course of his/ her life that derogating others makes one feel good about the self. This is especially effective if the others are easy targets for derogation, such as members of disliked groups or minorities that are associated with clear negative stereotypes. Thus, the compensatory operations that follow discrepancy detection include implicit processes such as heightened stereotyping of members of stigmatized groups.

Spencer et al. (1998) found that stereotype activation was increased in participants whose self-esteem had been threatened. These effects were limited to stereotype-relevant words that were derogatory, suggesting that activation of the negative stereotype associated with a stigmatized group is employed as a means to compensate for the self-esteem threat. Fein and Spencer (1997) similarly illustrated heightened stereotyping following failure feedback. Participants received failure feedback on the same intelligence test. All participants next read a description of a target person who was either said to be gay or heterosexual. The measurement of interest was the explicit trait ratings made by the perceiver, particularly those related to stereotypes of gay men. They found that heightened stereotyping emerged, but only among participants who had been provided with goal-discrepant information (they rated the gay target as possessing more gay-stereotypic characteristics than the heterosexual target). In each case a goal is consciously triggered by the discrepancy detection, but participants do not know it is accessible and guiding responses when they are performing a new task in a new setting.

Koole, Smeets, van Knippenberg, and Dijksterhuis (1999) gave research participants a putative intelligence test consisting of unsolvable problems. This forced them to detect a discrepancy between their desired goal of being intelligent and their current state as indicated by the feedback on the test. The goal of being intelligent was then assessed across several experiments where participants did not know intelligence goals were accessible and being pursued (or assessed). In one experiment a lexical decision task was used to assess the implicit accessibility of the goal. Relative to control participants, those who had experienced the tension associated with discrepancy detection were faster to recognize words related to intelligence. Rumination about the test and the ability domain assessed by the test (intelligence) was found despite participants not knowing the goal was accessible when performing a new task.

Self-Reflection

Discrepancies can be consciously detected without an experimenter needing to tell one "you fail." They are often the result of people monitoring their own behavior and engaging in self-reflection. For example, Moskowitz (2002) had participants recall (and write about) a time in which they had failed to act in an egalitarian manner. This created a discrepancy relating to the goal to be egalitarian, which was evidenced in the experiment by participants implicitly redirecting their focus of attention. Items relating to egalitarianism in the environment were more easily detected than control items, even when people could not consciously perceive the items. This did not occur for people who had not reflected on a discrepancy in this domain. Consciously detecting a failure in a goal domain triggers that goal. This leads one to attend to items in the environment one cannot consciously recognize as being goal relevant, in a setting where one does not know the goal is accessible or relevant to the task.

Stone, Weigand, Cooper, and Aronson (1997) created a discrepancy in participants by having them publicly advocate for a position (using condoms). They then had people recall a time in which they acted in a way that opposed the position just advocated (not using condoms), with the hypocritical act now creating a tension state the individual is driven to reduce. The goal is clearly still explicit to participants when later in the experiment they are given the opportunity to purchase condoms at a discount. People with a discrepancy take advantage of the discount to a greater degree than people without a discrepancy. However, when the opportunity to purchase condoms is not present, the goal is still accessible even though participants are not focused on it. Participants given a chance to donate money to the homeless do so to a greater degree if they had a discrepancy triggered. Without knowing it, they are attempting to reduce the tension associated with being a hypocrite by stepping up their generosity and reaffirming their sense of self.

Priming Discrepancies

It is also possible that people can detect discrepancies somewhat implicitly. Custers and Aarts (2007) manipulated the existence of a discrepancy through priming. In one experiment, participants with the chronic goal to be "well groomed" were asked to perform a task where they read sentences and then indicated whether a word that followed the sentence had actually been in the sentence. Such a task has been shown to slow responses when the word presented is associated with the sentence in some way, but not actually present in the sentence (e.g., Uleman, Hon, Roman, & Moskowitz, 1996). On critical trials the sentences either presented a discrepancy with the goal of being well groomed ("your shoes are dirty") or control sentences ("your shoes have laces"). The following word was associated with reducing the discrepancy in that it was an instrumental act (polishing). Reactions to the target word were slowed only when the word was preceded by the discrepancy-inducing sentence.

Chronic Goals

Bargh (1990) asserted that the repeated pursuit of some goals (more consistently and habitually than other goals) leads to those goals acquiring a chronic state of heightened accessibility (for a review see Higgins, 1996). Such heightened goal accessibility persists across a variety of contexts. For example, it is not merely being proposed that some contexts trigger the goal of achievement. Rather, some people have the goal to achieve in a state of heightened accessibility across time and situations: It is accessible at work, when cooking dinner for a date, on the basketball court, when playing trivial pursuit with friends, and so on. These goals are associated with the individual's long-standing interests and most cherished values/motives. Chronic goals are thus always relatively ready to be used in construing the world. This has been demonstrated with illustrations of individual differences in how information is processed as a function of one's chronic goal pursuits in a wide variety of domains. These include locus of control, the depressive self-schema, attributional style, need for cognition, and uncertainty orientation. Other chronic goals do not generate an accompanying cognitive style but merely make the individual sensitive to goal-relevant cues across a variety of contexts, being able to detect opportunities to initiate goal pursuit efficiently. We direct the reader to Bargh (1990) for an excellent review of the research in support of the proposition that goals attain chronic accessibility.

We focus attention here on two illustrations of how chronically accessible goals affect thought and action. Moskowitz (1993) illustrated that chronic goals affect the formation of spontaneous trait inferences (STIs). STIs are social judgments made about the traits of other people, inferences that require neither conscious intent to form an inference nor the awareness of that any inferential activity has occurred. Inferences about the traits of others are a primary way we make sense of others and ascribe meaning to their action. Moskowitz posited that if trait inference serves this role of structuring the social environment, then the goal to have structure should facilitate trait inference formation. This should occur despite the fact that the goal is not being consciously activated and the trait inference is not being consciously formed.

Chronic goals to attain structure were assessed using the need for structure scale (Thompson, Naccarato, Moskowitz, & Parker, 2001). An individual possessing a high chronic need for structure has the goal to have organization, closure, structure, and clarity in most situations, with ambiguity proving troublesome and annoying. Moskowitz (1993) found that chronic need for structure led to heightened STI formation (using implicit memory as the means to detect if inferences had unknowingly occurred). Despite lacking awareness of having formed inferences and explicit denial that they used such a strategy as a mnemonic aid, participants were shown to be forming STIs when reading about people who were performing behavior that could be described by traits. This tendency to use STIs in making sense of the behavioral information was exacerbated in individuals with chronic goals to seek to structure. They also were more likely to link these inferences to the people being described in the sentences they were reading, indicating they were trying harder to understand those people and the cause for their actions.

Aarts and Dijksterhuis (2000) reasoned that some individuals have chronic tendencies associated with specific goals. One may habitualize the behavioral responses associated with a goal, and for these individuals the priming of the goal should trigger the behaviors/means chronically associated with that goal. Participants performed a task in which travel goals were implicitly primed, and the accessibility of the means to the goal (suitable and unsuitable locations for goal pursuit) was subsequently assessed in an ostensibly unrelated task. This was an association task in which different location words appeared on a monitor screen followed by a mode of transport. The task was to indicate whether the presented mode would constitute a realistic means of transport for the location. Finally, participants were asked to estimate their frequency of bicycle use in the recent past for different trips (to obtain information on whether they had formed habitual links between bicycle use and specific goal locales). They found that in a "no goal" condition, habitual participants' response latencies did not differ from those of nonhabitual participants. However, in the goal-priming condition, habitual participants responded faster to locations suitable for bicycle riding after being primed with travel goals related to bicycle riding. The goal primes the means to the goal to which it is habitually linked.

Consciously Selected Goals That Explicitly Retain Accessibility

This last category of goal priming is when one consciously selects a goal and maintains the conscious intent to pursue the goal as goal-relevant responses are made: wholly conscious goal pursuit. A primary example of this category of goal pursuit is work on achievement motivation, where people are explicitly given goals (such as performance goals vs. learning goals) and then explicitly asked to perform a task relevant to the goal (e.g., for a review see Grant & Gelety, Chapter 3, this volume). A second example is the bulk of the work on correction/control that evolved from dual process models in social psychology. For instance, research on the impact of accountability and accuracy goals typically has participants being explicitly asked to be accurate and then to explicitly form judgments regarding a target person (e.g., Fiske & Neuberg, 1990).

In some sense the history of cognitive psychology, which is not explicitly said to be about goals, follows this formula. In typical experiments participants are brought to the lab and provided with a goal and are then presented stimuli to which that goal is relevant. This occurs when participants are asked to perform a dichotic listening task (Cherry, 1953), name ink color (Logan, 1980), focus on the letter "g" as hundreds of such letters are used to construct a letter "x" (Navon, 1977), respond with one hand to an auditory stimulus and another to a visual stimulus (Pashler, 1991), switch tasks when responding to a stimulus that can be categorized in multiple ways (Arrington & Logan, 2004), make a lexical decision (e.g., Neely, 1977), or attend to a red triangle in a display of blue triangles (e.g., Treisman & Gormican, 1988).

As many of the above-cited experiments from cognitive psychology reveal, consciously activated goals that initiate explicit responses to stimuli that are quite explicitly relevant to the goal still affect implicit cognition. We have seen examples of this in experiments reviewed earlier. One described people with "impression-formation "goals who organize information they are consciously processing in a way that promotes coherence in the impression and deeper processing of incongruent items. Another involved people explicitly adopting a goal and then deciding if a string of letters encountered was a word. Responses on the task are facilitated by the goal. For example, Förster, Liberman, and Higgins (2005) asked participants to view schematic drawings, with some given the goal of identifying a drawing of eyeglasses followed by scissors. The hypothesis was that people with a goal related to eyeglasses would be vigilant to detect such objects, but people who had affirmed this goal (and thus no longer had it accessible, see the *persistence-until* notion, Martin & Tesser, Chapter 10, this volume) would not. Goal-relevant responding (vigilance) was assessed with a lexical decision task that had words associated with eyeglasses (e.g., read) and control words. The data revealed people to be faster at recognizing goal-relevant words, but only if the goal was accessible (it had not been previously attained).

Not all of the implicit effects of consciously selecting and pursuing a goal are intended by the person. Wholly conscious goal pursuit can result in unintended effects. Wegner and Erskine (2003) review many examples, such as when one consciously intends not to think a given thought (such as to suppress thoughts of white bears) only to experience the hyperaccessibility of those very thoughts (one has an increased prevalence of images of bears popping into one's mind). In our own lab, Uleman and Moskowitz (1994) examined how explicit goals shape whether or not implicit processes of trait inference occur. For example, some participants were asked to search stimulus sentences for instances of the letter "t," others to indicate whether a target word rhymed with any of the words in the sentences, whereas others had to decide how personally relevant the sentences were. The sentences were pretested to imply traits, and past research had shown that when simply asked to memorize the sentences, participants implicitly (spontaneously) infer the traits implied therein. Uleman and Moskowitz found an elimination of spontaneous inference in goal conditions incompatible with inference formation. The conclusion from these experiments was that the processing goals, though explicit, have associated with them implicit operations—sets of processing routines and plans required for the goal to be fulfilled—that direct processes in a manner the person may not have consciously intended or willed.

Conclusion

Goals are often consciously selected by an individual after a period of deliberation, weighing options, and calculating the opportunities that are presented and one's efficacy in regards to those opportunities. But this is not a complete accounting of why people adopt goals in a given moment. We reviewed many different ways goals are triggered in the mind of a person, some conscious to the person, others not. Nonconscious priming of goals by cues in the environment, even cues one does not consciously note ever having seen, initiate much of our everyday goal-directed thought and action. And we further described how even when a goal is consciously adopted it can still be pursued in ways that are outside of conscious aware-ness, in a fashion either intended or unintended by the conscious goal pur-suit.

However, it is important to note that priming by exposure to goal-relevant cues alone is insufficient for goal-relevant responding. An indi-vidual must value the goal and have positive affect associated with the outcomes specified by the goal for the priming to be considered more than mere semantic activation of the concept, and to instead be the activation of a goal. The triggering of the concept "achievement" is not the same as possessing the goal to achieve.

For example, in the experiments of Aarts et al. (2004) reviewed ear-lier, participants were observed to implicitly "catch" goals from others they had observed pursuing goals. However, if the person being observed was pursuing a goal that the observer did not value or desire, the goal was not contagious. Strahan, Spencer, and Zanna (2002) similarly illustrated that priming goal-relevant thoughts (semantic content) is insufficient for goal-relevant responding. There must simultaneously be a drive associated with the goal having not yet been attained. The participants were sub-liminally primed with goal-relevant words and then observed to see if they engaged in goal-relevant responding as a function of whether they had the *drive* to achieve the goal.

Strahan et al. (2002) asked participants to not eat or drink for 3 hours before the experiment. Upon arriving at the lab the participants performed a taste test. Half were then asked to cleanse their palate by drinking water and half did not have this opportunity. Participants had now been divided into two groups: thirsty and not thirsty. Next, they were asked to perform a lexical decision task, and in this task they were being subliminally primed with words relevant to thirst or control words. Finally, they performed a second taste test, this time with beverages. The measure of interest was beverage consumption. They found that when not thirsty, priming did not matter. However, people who were thirsty drank more when primed with "thirst"-related concepts as opposed to neutral concepts. The goal needed to be paired with the state of having not yet attained the goal for the prim-ing of the goal to affect behavior. Thus, one must value a goal and have a tension state associated with a goal for goal priming to be effective. Custers and Aarts (2007), reviewed earlier, similarly found that priming a discrepancy was able to create goal-relevant responding, whereas the absence of a tension state did not affect responding.

Custers (Chapter 7, this volume) describes converging evidence for this important caveat to goal priming by illustrating that when negative affect is associated with a goal it becomes "demotivated" or loses its power to guide responding. Similarly, implicitly associating positive affect with a concept can turn it into a goal, turning semantic accessibility into goal accessibility.

Thus, though goals are capable of being triggered without awareness, and even pursued without awareness, such a state of affairs does not mean the person is doomed to act or to initiate undesirable behavior. Nor does it mean free will is abandoned or surrendered to the environment. The association between goals and responses and contextual cues is one forged via conscious willing at some point in time. Additionally, if the individual does not value a goal, or does not experience a tension or striving when that goal state is contemplated/monitored, then it is not factual to discuss goals as relevant. In our view, the absence of consciousness does not diminish the role of the individual, volition, or free will. Instead we see it as making the will efficient and people more flexible. The assumption that volition, free will, and goals require consciousness is one that is an overly simplistic accounting of human motivation. Automaticity in goal pursuit is natural and should not be considered to somehow be counterintuitive or an oxymoron.

References

Aarts, H., & Dijksterhuis, A. (2000). Habits as knowledge structures: Automaticity in goal-directed behavior. *Journal of Personality and Social Psychology, 78,* 53–63.

Aarts, H., & Dijksterhuis, A. (2003). The silence of the library: Environment, situational norm, and social behavior. *Journal of Personality & Social Psychology, 84,* 18–28.

Aarts, H., Dijksterhuis, A. P., & Midden, C. (1999). To plan or not to plan? Goal achievement of interrupting the performance of mundane behaviors. *European Journal of Social Psychology, 29,* 971–979.

Aarts, H., Gollwitzer, P. M., & Hassin, R. R. (2004). Goal contagion: Perceiving is for pursuing. *Journal of Personality and Social Psychology, 87,* 23–37.

Ach, N. (1935). Analyse des Willens [The analysis of willing]. In E. Abderhalden (Ed.), *Handbuch der biologischen Arbeitsmethoden [Handbook of Biological Research Methods].* Berlin: Urban & Schwarzenberg.

Arrington, C. M., & Logan, G. D. (2004). The cost of a voluntary task switch. *Psychological Science, 15,* 610–615.

Atkinson, J. W., & Birch, D. (1970). *The dynamics of action.* New York: Wiley.

Bandura, A. (1989). Perceived self-efficacy in the exercise of personal agency. *The Psychologist: Bulletin of the British Psychological Society, 2,* 411–424.

Bargh, J. A. (1990). Auto-motives: Preconscious determinants of thought and behavior. Multiple affects from multiple stages. In E. T. Higgins & R. M. Sorrentino (Eds.), *Handbook of motivation and cognition: Foundations of social behavior* (Vol. 2, pp. 93–130). New York: Guilford Press.

Bargh, J. A., & Chartrand, T. L. (2000). The mind in the middle: A practical guide to priming and automaticity research. In H. T. Reis & C. M. Judd (Eds.), *Handbook of research methods in social and personality psychology* (pp. 253–285). New York: Cambridge University Press.

Bargh, J. A., Gollwitzer, P. M., Lee-Chai, A., Barndollar, K., & Trotschel, R. (2001). The automated will: Nonconscious activation and pursuit of behavioral goals. *Journal of Personality and Social Psychology, 81,* 1014–1027.

Bargh, J. A., & Williams, L. E. (2007). The nonconscious regulation of emotion. In J. J. Gross (Ed.), *Handbook of emotion regulation* (pp. 429–445). New York: Guilford Press.

Bayer, U., Achtziger, A., Gollwitzer, P., & Moskowitz, G. B. (in press). Responding to subliminal cues: Do if–then plans facilitate action preparation and initiation without conscious intent? *Social Cognition.*

Brewer, W. F., & Dupree, D. A. (1983). Use of plain schemata in the recall and recognition of goal-directed actions. *Journal of Experimental Psychology: Learning, Memory, and Cognition, 9,* 117–129.

Bruner, J. S. (1957). On perceptual readiness. *Psychological Review, 64,* 123–152.

Carver, C. S., & Scheier, M. F. (1981). *Attention and self-regulation: A control theory approach to human behavior.* New York: Springer.

Chartrand, T. L., & Bargh, J. A. (1996). Automatic activation of impression formation goals: Nonconscious goal priming reproduces effects of explicit task instructions. *Journal of Personality and Social Psychology, 71,* 464–478.

Cherry, E. C. (1953). Some experiments on the recognition of speech, with one and with two ears. *Journal of the Acoustical Society of America, 25,* 975–979.

Custers, R., & Aarts, H. (2007). Goal-discrepant situations prime goal-directed actions if goals are temporarily or chronically accessible. *Personality and Social Psychology Bulletin, 33,* 623–633.

Dijksterhuis, A., Bos, M., Nordgren, L., & Van Baaren, R. B. (2006). On making the right choice: The deliberation-without-attention effect. *Science, 311,* 1005–1007.

Fein, S., & Spencer, S. J. (1997). Prejudice as self-image maintenance: Affirming the self through negative evalutions of others. *Journal of Personality and Social Psychology, 73,* 31–44.

Fishbach, A., Friedman, R. S., & Kruglanski, A. W. (2003). Leading us not unto temptation: Momentary allurements elicit overriding goal activation. *Journal of Personality and Social Psychology, 84,* 296–309.

Fishbein, M. A., & Ajzen, I. (1975). *Belief, attitude, intention and behavior: An introduction to theory and research.* Reading, MA: Addison-Wesley.

Fiske, S. T., & Neuberg, S. L. (1990). A continuum of impression formation, from category-based to individuating processes: Influences of information and motivation on attention and interpretation. In M. P. Zanna (Ed.), *Advances in experimental social psychology* (Vol. 23, pp. 1–74). New York: Academic Press.

Fitzsimons, G. M., & Bargh, J. A. (2003). Thinking of you: Nonconscious pursuit of interpersonal goals associated with relationship partners. *Journal of Personality and Social Psychology, 84,* 148–164.

Fitzsimons, G. M., Chartrand, T. L., & Fitzsimons, G. J. (2008). Automatic effects of brand exposure on motivated behavior: How apple makes you "think different." *Journal of Consumer Research, 35*, 21–35.

Förster, J., & Liberman, N. (2001). The role of attribution of motivation in producing postsuppressional rebound. *Journal of Personality and Social Psychology, 81*, 377–390.

Förster, J., Liberman, N., & Higgins, E.T. (2005). Accessibility from active and fulfilled goals. *Journal of Experimental Social Psychology, 41*, 220–239.

Gollwitzer, P. M. (1990). Action phases and mind-sets. In E. T. Higgins & R. M. Sorrentino (Eds.), *Handbook of motivation and cognition* (Vol. 2, pp. 53–92). New York: Guilford Press.

Gollwitzer, P. M. (1993). Goal achievement: The role of intentions. In W. Stroebe & M. Hewstone (Eds.), *European review of social psychology* (Vol. 4, pp. 141–185). Chichester, UK: Wiley.

Hafer, C. L. (2000). Do innocent victims threaten the belief in a just world? Evidence from a modified stroop task. *Journal of Personality and Social Psychology, 79*, 165–173.

Hassin, R., Aarts, H., & Ferguson, M. J. (2005). Spontaneous goal inferences. *Journal of Experimental Social Psychology, 41*, 129–140.

Hastie, R., & Kumar, P. A. (1979). Person memory: Personality traits as organizing principles in memory for behavior. *Journal of Personality and Social Psychology, 37*, 25–38.

Higgins, E. T. (1996). Knowledge adtivation: Accessibility, applicability, and salience. In E. T. Higgins & A. W. Kruglanski (Eds.), *Social psychology: Handbook of basic principles* (pp. 133–168). New York: Guilford Press.

Holland, R. W., Hendriks, M., & Aarts, H. (2005). Smells like clean spirit: Nonconscious effects of scent on cognition and behavior. *Psychological Science, 16*, 689–693.

Kay, A. C., Wheeler, C. S., Bargh, J. A., & Ross, L. D. (2004). Material priming: The influence of mundane physical objects on situational construal and competitive behavioral choice. *Organizational Behavior and Human Decision Processes, 95*, 83–96.

Koole, S. L., Smeets, K., van Knippenberg, A., & Dijksterhuis, A. (1999). The cessation of rumination through self-affirmation. *Journal of Personality & Social Psychology, 77*, 111–125.

Lewin, K. (1936). *Principles of topological psychology*. New York: McGraw-Hill.

Liberman, N., & Förster, J. (2000). Expression after suppression: A motivational explanation of postsuppressional rebound. *Journal of Personality and Social Psychology, 79*, 190–203.

Locke, E. A., & Latham, G. P. (1990). *A theory of goal setting and task performance*. Englewood Cliffs, NJ: Prentice Hall.

Logan, G. D. (1980). Short-term memory demands of reaction-time tasks that differ in complexity. *Journal of Experimental Psychology: Human Perception and Performance, 6*, 375–389.

McArthur, L. Z., & Baron, R. (1983). Toward an ecological theory of social perception. *Psychological Review, 90*, 215–238.

Miller, G. A., Galanter, E., & Pribram, K. H. (1960). *Plans and the structure of behavior.* New York: Holt, Rinehart & Winston.

Moskowitz, G. B. (1993). Individual differences in social categorization: The effects of personal need for structure on spontaneous trait inferences. *Journal of Personality and Social Psychology, 65,* 132–142.

Moskowitz, G. B. (2002). Preconscious effects of temporary goals on attention. *Journal of Experimental Social Psychology, 38,* 397–404.

Moskowitz, G. B., & Roman, R. J. (1992). Spontaneous trait inferences as self generated primes: Implications for conscious social judgment. *Journal of Personality and Social Psychology, 62,* 728–738.

Navon, D. (1977). Forest before trees: The precedence of global features in visual perception. *Cognitive Psychology, 9,* 353–383.

Neely, J. H. (1977). Semantic priming and retrieval from lexical memory: Roles of inhibitionless spreading activation and limited-capacity attention. *Journal of Experimental Psychology, 106,* 226–254.

Norman, D. A., & Shallice, T. (1986). Attention to action: Willed and automatic control of behaviour. In R. J. Davidson, G. E. Schwartz, & D. Shapiro (Eds.). *Consciousness and self-regulation: Advances in research and theory* (pp. 1—18). New York: Plenum Press.

Pashler, H. (1991). Shifting visual attention and selecting motor responses: Distinct attentional mechanisms. *Journal of Experimental Psychology: Human Perception and Performance, 17,* 1023–1040.

Powers, W. T. (1973). Feedback: Beyond behaviorism. *Science, 179,* 351–356.

Sassenberg, K., & Moskowitz, G. B. (2005). Don't stereotype, think different! Overcoming automatic stereotype activation by mindset priming. *Journal of Experimental Social Psychology, 41,* 506–514.

Shah, J. Y. (2003). Automatic for the people: How representations of significant others implicitly affect goal pursuit. *Journal of Personality and Social Psychology, 84,* 661–681

Shah, J. Y., & Kruglanski, A. W. (2002). Priming against your will: How accessible alternatives affect goal pursuit. *Journal of Experimental Social Psychology, 38,* 368–383.

Spencer, S. J., Fein, S., Wolfe, C. T., Fong, C., & Dunn, M. A. (1998). Automatic activation of stereotypes: The role of self-image threat. *Personality and Social Psychology Bulletin, 24,* 1139–1152.

Stone, J., Wiegand, A. W., Cooper, J., & Aronson, E. (1997). When exemplification fails: Hypocrisy and the motive for self-integrity. *Journal of Personality and Social Psychology, 72*(1), 54–65.

Strahan, E. J., Spencer, S. J., & Zanna, M. P. (2002). Subliminal priming and persuasion: Striking while the iron is hot. *Journal of Experimental Social Psychology, 38,* 556–568.

Tolman, E. C. (1932). *Purposive behavior in animals and men.* New York: Appleton-Century-Crofts.

Thompson, M. M., Naccarato, M. E., Moskowitz, G. B., & Parker, K. J. (2001). The personal need for structure and personal fear of invalidity measures: Historical perspectives, current applications, and future directions. In G. B. Moskowitz (Ed.), *Cognitive social psychology: The Princeton Symposium on the Legacy and Future of Social Cognition* (pp. 19–40). Mahwah, NJ: Erlbaum.

Treisman, A., & Gormican, S. (1988). Feature analysis in early vision: Evidence from search asymmetries. *Psychological Review, 95*(1), 15–48.

Trzebinski, J. (1989). The role of goal categories in the representation of social knowledge. In L. A. Pervin (Ed.), *Goal concepts in personality and social psychology* (pp. 363–411). Hillsdale, NJ: Erlbaum.

Uleman, J. S., Hon, A., Roman, R. J., & Moskowitz, G. B. (1996). On-line evidence for spontaneous trait inferences at encoding. *Personality and Social Psychology Bulletin, 22*(4), 377–394.

Uleman, J. S., & Moskowitz, G. B. (1994). Unintended effects of goals on unintended inferences. *Journal of Personality and Social Psychology, 66,* 490–501.

Wegner, D. M., & Erskine, J. (2003). Voluntary involuntariness: Thought suppression and the regulation of the experience of will. *Consciousness and Cognition, 12,* 684–694.

Wright, R. A., & Brehm, J. W. (1989). Energization and goal attractiveness. In L. A. Pervin (Ed.), *Goal concepts in personality and social psychology* (pp. 169–210). Hillsdale, NJ: Erlbaum.

Zeigarnik, B. (1927). Das Behalten erledigter und unerledigter Handlungen [The retention of completed and uncompleted actions]. *Psychologische Forschung, 9,* 1–85.

CHAPTER 9

Moments of Motivation
MARGINS OF OPPORTUNITY IN MANAGING THE EFFICACY, NEED, AND TRANSITIONS OF STRIVING

JAMES Y. SHAH
DEBORAH HALL
N. PONTUS LEANDER

Research and theories on the nature of goals and their role in self-regulation have increasingly recognized that goals are adopted and pursued not in isolation from each other but rather in a dynamic situational context and as part of a structured motivational system. As mental representations, then, goals not only provide form, direction, and impetus to our needs and general motives, but additionally provide a broader "managerial" benefit in allowing us to more effectively oversee and prioritize these needs over time and in light of ever-changing environmental constraints and affordances (see Carver & Scheier, 1998; Emmons, 1986; Karoly, 1993; Pervin, 1989; Simon, 1967). Moreover, the challenge of such management only increases with the diversity and scope of our ambitions and with the well-documented limits in our self-regulatory capacities for addressing them (see Vohs, Kaikati, Kerkhof, & Schmeichel, Chapter 16, this volume). Everyday self-regulation, then, is commonly assumed to involve the skilled and simultaneous juggling of numerous and often-disparate goals, as any busy student or working parent already knows. Such juggling requires not only effective engagement with each goal individually, but also an efficient transition between them as our needs, resources, and circumstances change over time. The purpose of this analysis is to suggest how this juggling act may be fundamentally defined by the regulatory system of the pursuer and the situational constraints, affordances, and experiences that collectively define what is feasible and desirable in the present circumstances.

The Margins of Moments

This analysis begins by assuming that effective goal management requires consideration not only of how each goal should be pursued (e.g., the means or setting in which it should occur), but also when this pursuit should occur and given the diversity and dynamics of our various needs, the waxing and waning of our regulatory strength and social support and the growth in our regulatory experience and understanding (see also Gollwitzer, 1999; Higgins, 2006; Shah, 2005). We assume, then, that goals have their specific "moments" for pursuit. These moments represent the best possible conditions, for pursuing a goal as determined by the modulating motivation and regulatory strength of the pursuer as well as changes in the affordances, demands, and obstacles of the social environment (see Baumeister, Bratslavsky, & Muraven, 1998; Higgins, 2006; Shah, 2003: Shah & Kruglanski, 2003). We further assume that moments have margins: They vary in duration as well as in the frequency and predictability with which they return. Moments can change, then, as environmental and dispositional conditions change, and such changes are not always predictable or independent of other moments. The best conditions for one pursuit may emerge, perhaps unexpectedly, during a moment for another (providing another way to question if the best moments are indeed those that are shared).

Although perceiving and utilizing moments may often be difficult, especially when they overlap, we assume that moments can benefit goal pursuit and goal management not only by what it allows, but also by what it constrains. Not only do moments specify an easier, potentially more efficient, path to goal attainment, they also invaluably help confine pursuits to specific settings or occasions. Like Gollwitzer's (1999; see also Chapter 14, this volume) notion of implementation intentions, moments provide a cue to initiate goal pursuit (as a moment emerges) and the justification to put it aside (as the moment ends). But whereas implementation intentions specify goals by linking them directly to the particular conditions of their pursuit, moments specify dynamic environmental conditions by linking them to our own ends.

Constructing the Moment

Although moments of motivation are dynamic and occasionally surprising, they are hardly chaotic and unpredictable. Indeed, such moments are constrained by the regularity of individuals' needs and motives and by the priority and structure of the regulatory systems put in place to address these needs (see Carver & Scheier, 1998; Shah & Kruglanski, 2003). We assume then that to a large degree moments reflect individuals' current needs and goals and that change within and between motivational moments reflect the manner in which individuals have chronically organized their goals and means and the chronic style or tactics they employ in pursuing goals within these systems. Of course, goal systems also change over time as individuals' regulatory experience and understanding grows or because needs and resources change in predictable ways. And certainly moments may change with regular or gradual changes in the pursuer's social environment. Moments, then, can be seen as "structurally dynamic" in that their nature, and "fluctuation" is defined and constrained not only by predictable variation in need, but also by the manner in which they are mentally represented and associated with other mental representations and with each other. Although such representations reflect the needs and motives of the moment, they also reflect the cognitive qualities that goals share in common with other mental representations. Like other representations, for instance, goals have an accessibility that may vary dispositionally and situationally (see Shah & Kruglanski, 2003). They are also assumed to be organized hierarchically (see Bandura, 1997; Carver & Scheier, 1998; Shah & Kruglanski, 2000; Vallerand & Ratelle, 2002) with very general goals (e.g., achievement) giving rise to more concrete goals (e.g., success in school), which in turn give rise to more specific intentions (e.g., get an "A" in social psychology) and behaviors (e.g., study). Such an arrangement highlights that within a given system or more specific moment goals are (1) *end-states* for the more specific goals, intentions, or behaviors that they give rise to and (2) *means* for the more general or abstract goals they serve (see also Carver & Scheier, 1998; Emmons, 1992; Hyland, 1988; Powers, 1973).

Equally relevant to this analysis are the exhibitory and inhibitory "lateral connections" that may form between goals themselves, connections that may differ in their structural nature, complexity, and strength (see Read & Miller, 1998). In articulating his personal striving approach to personality, for instance, Emmons (1992) noted that one important way in which goals may vary is in the degree to which they are perceived to facilitate or conflict with each other—what Sheldon and Kasser (1995) later labeled "horizontal coherence." Such facilitation can be examined at the goal level or at the individual level. At the goal level, any one goal (e.g., doing well in school) may be viewed as facilitating or hindering one's other goals (e.g., to be social, to work out) or as unrelated to one's other pursuits. Such facilitation has been shown to have important implications for goal pursuit and psychological health. Emmons and King (1988) examined the influence of such facilitation and conflict on psychological and physical well-being and found that conflict among personal goals was associated with not only high levels of negative affect, depression, neuroticism, and psychosomatic complaints, but also with more frequent health center visits and illnesses over the course of an academic year. A separate study pointed to a possible cause as participants were more likely to ruminate on conflicting strivings, but less likely to act on them. Appraising a goal as potentially conflicting with other important pursuits can undermine commitment to this end-state, whereas perceiving a pursuit as potentially facilitating other goals provides yet another reason for pursuing it (see also Donahue, Robins, Roberts, & John, 1993).

Just as goals may be seen as facilitating other goals, so might they be seen as redundant (or substitutable) with these goals. Put another way, they may be perceived as fulfilling the same underlying need or motive. Although relatively little empirical work has examined goal substitutability directly, the significance of this goal quality has long been acknowledged in psychoanalytic theory (see Freud, 1923/1961). Similarly, Lewin (1935) noted that substitution of one goal for another was possible when both arose from the same tension system—that is, when both goals fulfilled the same underlying need or motive. More recently, the work of Steele and Liu (1983) and Tesser, Martin, and Cornell (1996) has illustrated how various psychological phenomena, including cognitive dissonance and self-affirmation, may represent substitutable goals for maintaining a positive self-view (see Tesser, Crepaz, Beach, Cornell, & Collins, 2000, as well as two chapters in this volume: Martin & Tesser, Chapter 10; Moskowitz, Chapter 12).

The conflict and redundancy of goal systems may affect the usefulness and dynamics of motivational moments. To the extent that conflict or redundancy between goals necessitates potentially paralyzing choices between goals, pursuers may readily seize on moments that make this a difficult choice for them. Conflict and redundancy among goals may also influence the transitions between moments, as success or failure in one moment may affect the utility of other goals in the next. Goal attainment in one moment, for instance, may encourage one to consider the next moment in terms of pursuits that benefited from this recent success and discourage consideration in terms of pursuits rendered unnecessary. Alternatively, a failure in the moment may encourage consideration of the next in terms of goals that could make up for this failure by addressing the same underlying (and still unfulfilled) need.

Terms of Engagement: Regulatory Rotation within and between Moments

Our use of the term "moment" also takes advantage of its typical scientific meaning: a tendency to produce rotation. We assume that motivational moments similarly produce rotation within and between goals. As illustrated in Figure 9.1, "volitional rotation" in the moment simply refers to the goal progress made in the moment through feedback loops (see Carver & Scheier, 1998). Regulatory rotation, however, also occurs among goals: The limits of motivational moments may encourage "horizontal" rotation among goals, as the moment for a particular pursuit begins, ends and begins again. Indeed, such horizontal rotation reflects a self-regulatory tendency to manage or juggle many "open" pursuits at once, rather than pursuing each exclusively until completion or abandonment. Regulating within and between motivational moments, then, requires that the priority, structure, and pacing of goal pursuits be continually updated. Such challenges can affect not only how goals are managed collectively, but also how each is defined, pursued, and maintained over time, as is discussed in turn.

Whether arising from significant others, (Fitzsimons & Bargh, 2003; Shah, 2003), role models (Lockewood & Kunda, 2000), or from the perceived pursuits in one's immediate environment (see Aarts, Gollwitzer, & Hassin, 2004), moment forces can certainly influence what we pursue, by either reinforcing an ongoing pursuit from the previous moment or introducing new possibilities that reflect the present or anticipate the future, at least within the boundaries of our general goal system. Indeed, recent work on regulatory fit by Higgins (2006; see also Chapter 19 in this volume) and his colleagues has extensively documented how the experience and perceived value of goals depend on the extent to which the defined moment "fits" individuals' general motivational orientation, such as their basic focus on promotion or prevention, though such fit is not always eas-

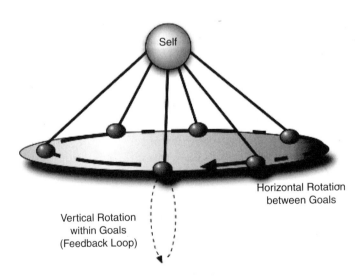

FIGURE 9.1. Regulatory rotation between and within goals.

ily attained (see Bauman & Kuhl, 2003; Deci & Ryan, 2000; Sheldon & Elliot, 2000).

The moment, however, may not simply reinforce or alter the value we place in goals but may also support or hinder their actual pursuit and attainment. As such, moments may be inspirational and instrumental: They may be perceived as crucial or rare opportunities to attain a goal more certainly or with less effort and time, even while having no impact on its perceived importance. Thus, when individuals anticipate many possible moments for pursuing a valuable goal, then they may readily put it aside to engage a less compelling goal if the present moment offers a relatively rare opportunity to attain this second goal more easily. Indeed, individuals' sensitivity to such opportunities may be so pervasive and basic to self-regulation that it may often be invoked automatically. Shah and Kruglanski (2003), for instance, found that goals may be automatically primed in a "bottom-up" fashion by the often idiosyncratic objects or settings that facilitate their attainment, even when such means have little general semantic relation to the goal concepts in question. Similarly, Gollwitzer and Brandstatter (1997) argued that goal pursuit can be significantly enhanced by linking it to specific settings (moments) and that even newly created implementation intentions can successfully prime goal pursuit in such moments (see Parks-Stamm & Gollwitzer, Chapter 14, this volume).

In short, then, this analysis assumes that regulatory moments change with modulations in our goal systems relating to predictable changes in our motivations, regulatory strength, and immediate environment. Such change is constrained by the nature and structure of our goal system as well as the regularity of dispositional and situational changes. Having provided a working definition of the motivational moment, we now focus on its potential self-regulatory impact for resource and goal management.

Rising to the Moment

The desirability and feasibility of goals may also lead us to redefine them, especially with regards to the markers for success and failure. When success feels more likely, for instance, one may naturally expect and strive for more. Some goals, of course, may be relatively resistant to redefinition, moment-to-moment, especially specific goals that are unique to particular moments (as when an athlete strives for a gold medal or a student strives for an "A"). Yet often the benchmarks of success and failure are not so easily recognized or universally defined. And this may be especially true of relatively abstract goals not tied to any particular moment, such as the abstract "be" goals that define who we are in a general sense (Carver & Scheier, 1998; Higgins, 1997; Lewin, Dembo, Festinger, & Sears, 1944; Markus & Ruvolo, 1989). Whether a exam grade of "B" is considered a success, for instance, may vary depending on the relevant circumstances of the moment (e.g., the class average that day).

Undoubtedly, such moment-to-moment differences may influence how one feels in that moment, and possibly beyond (e.g., Mento, Locke, & Klein, 1992). Moments in which the bar is set relatively high will undoubtedly produce fewer feelings of "success" than in less challenging moments, and these differences can have cumulative effects, especially for those particularly vulnerable to generalizing failure in the moment, such as those with fixed beliefs about their ability (see Dweck & Grant, 2007). Yet raising the requirements for success in the moment can also increase goal-related productivity, especially when the challenge is defined in a manner specific to the moment at hand. In their extensive work on goal-setting theory, Locke and Latham (1990, 2006) have consistently demonstrated that individuals induced to adopt challenging and specific goals in the moment show greater goal-related productivity than individuals adopting goals not uniquely tied to the moment at hand (e.g., "do your best" goals). In fact, the relationship between performance and goal challenge has been found to be quite robust, leveling off only at the limits of pursuers' ability and resources (Locke & Latham, 2006). At first glance, these findings appear to contradict those tenets of expectancy-value theory positing that higher levels of expectancy should lead to greater goal commitment, and presumably, greater goal-related performance (Feather, 1982). Locke, Motowidlo, and Bobko (1986), however, found that when goal level is constant (a general assumption of expectancy-value theories), higher expectancies lead to higher levels of performance. For a goal level set in the moment, then, higher expectancy has a positive impact on performance.

Individuals' willingness to "rise to the occasion" however, and take full advantage of a moment, may depend not only on how effectively it inspires or facilitates goal pursuit, but also on how frequently and consistently such moments occur and how easily they align with fluctuations in the regulatory strength of the pursuer, as is discussed in more detail below.

Moments of Strength and Weakness

That moments for goal pursuit are often fleeting may necessitate that goal pursuers are sensitive to the ongoing nature of this change. In particular, goal pursuit in the moment may require sensitivity to how the moment has just recently changed and how it will soon change again, as a function of situational changes as well as changes in the regulatory strength, or tolerance, of the pursuer and his/her system, defined here as the capacity for engaging in goal pursuit generally. Limits to this capacity can influence the degree to which individuals take advantage of moments and even whether they perceive moments at all. Indeed, a variety of self-regulatory theories and models have assumed that goal-related effort involves the momentary mobilization of potentially exhaustible self-regulatory resources that are generally applicable to goal pursuits (e.g., Kahneman, 1973; Kanfer, Ackerman, Murtha, Dugdale, & Nelson, 1994). Such resources include (but are not limited to) physical and mental energy (Zijlstra, 1996; Hockey, Battmann, & Dutke, 1996; Wright, Brehm, & Pervin, 1989) and various forms of executive functioning (e.g., impulse control and affect regulation see Schmeichel & Baumeister, 2004) and are generally understood to be limited and exhaustible. And unlike attentional load (see Baddeley, 2003; Norman & Shallice, 1986), the capacity for goal-related effort can only be restored gradually, and often not without expending additional effort (analogous to the time and fuel one may occasionally waste trying to find a gas station).

Undoubtedly, the effort put toward a current goal will depend on the goal's own motivationally relevant qualities. The energization model (Wright, Brehm, & Pervin, 1989), for instance, asserts that the effort put toward a goal is a function of its perceived value and difficulty. Whereas the difficulty of goal attainment establishes how much effort is necessary, the perceived value of goal attainment specifies the amount of effort individuals are actually willing to commit. Thus increases in goal difficulty lead to increases in effort until the effort required exceeds the effort one is willing to expend.

We assume, however, that engagement and exertion in the moment will be regulated not only with respect to what is presently required, but also what had been required in moments past and future. That is, our effort in the moment accounts for our most recent moments of exertion as well as upcoming moments of labor. Consistent with this argument, research by Wright, Martin, and Bland (2003) demonstrated that effort regulation in the present was moderated by the goal-related effort individuals exerted in the immediate past. The depletion of participants' capacity for effort through an initially difficult task goal was found to affect their subsequent effort regulation on a mental arithmetic task goal, such that the depleted participants exerted less effort on this second task when given a difficult performance standard in comparison to control participants who had not been initially depleted. An entirely different line of research by Muraven, Baumeister, and their colleagues on the phenomenon of "ego depletion" also suggests that goal-related effort regulation may depend on one's past exertions and present pursuits (see Vohs et al., Chapter 16, this volume). This work suggests that goal pursuits may deplete individuals' subsequent capacity for effort on unrelated goal pursuits and increase their tendency to regulate their effort, at least when such effort involves self-control (Muraven, Tice, & Baumeister, 1998; Muraven & Baumeister, 2000). Muraven and Baumeister (2000) found that the amount of self-control required to eat an unappetizing vegetable (a raw radish) decreased the subsequent effort put forth for completing an anagram task (as seen in participants' decreased performance). Similarly, Muraven et al. (1998) found that the regulation of thoughts or emotions decreased the subsequent physical effort that participants put forth in squeezing a handgrip. These depletion effects, however, also depend on the nature of one's present goal pursuit. Muraven and Slessareva (2003) found that individuals who were depleted who were led to believe that a current task (or their efforts) would benefit others did not demonstrate the detriments typically associated with ego depletion, suggesting that one's tendency to regulate effort after a previous exertion can be overridden by the general importance of a present pursuit. Finally, in addition to considering how much effort has recently been expended, exertion in the moment may additionally, and importantly, involve an anticipation of what is soon to be required from upcoming pursuits, especially those that will begin before capacity can be restored.

Thus, the limits of regulatory strength and to the duration of the moment require that individuals effectively regulate their energy and resources with respect not only to the goal they are pursuing in the moment, but also to former pursuits that may have drained their current resources as well as their anticipation of the resources required in upcoming moments. Such effort regulation may, of course, be rooted in our actual regulatory experiences of depletion, but they may additionally arise simply from general self-beliefs (accurate or not) about effort capacity (Mukhopadhayay & Johar, 2005) or from the realization that actual capacity is often difficult to gauge, even by the pursuer (leading coaches everywhere to play it safe and ask for 110%) . Moreover, this regulation can discourage and encourage exertion and engagement in the moment. Shah, Brazy, and Jungbluth (2007), for instance, found across five studies that anticipating an immediate upcoming moment of relative burden and difficulty, even implicitly, led participants to conserve resources on a task in the moment (and even replenish them when, e.g., they are given the option of drinking juice between trials). Alternatively, anticipating an immediate future moment of relative ease led participants to try harder on the task of the moment (and drink less juice).

The Urgency of the Moment

The perceived limits to the present moment may affect more than simply the effort exerted or withheld. Such limits may additionally affect how goals are pursued in the moment. Indeed, in preparation for upcoming moments, individuals may strive to be as efficient as possible in their present pursuits, relying on goal-related behaviors that are relatively easy, enjoyable, or automatic to employ (Aarts & Dijksterhuis, 2000; Sansone & Harackiewicz, 1996; Wood, Quinn, & Kashy, 2002). Although automatizing a current goal pursuit may come at some cost to flexibility (but see Gollwitzer, Parks-Stamm, Jaudas, & Sheeran, 2007), such choices would help individuals complete as much of the present pursuit as they can in the limited time remaining, while still retaining enough resources to take advantage of the new moments that lie ahead (see also Dijksterhuis & Bongers, 2005). Such an urgent reaction would be particularly useful when the present moment is not only fleeting but unlikely to return quickly or reliably.

Alternatively, moments for pursuing even important goals may often be squandered when the moment is understood to return regularly and often.

Enduring Moments

An understanding of motivational moments may also lend insight into how goals and behavioral means are maintained over time. The utility of moments for goal attainment, for instance, may encourage goal persistence simply by ensuring efficient progress. But if moments encourage persistence by instilling a sense of efficacy, their relatively confining nature may also offer important protection against the potential pull of competing alternatives. Indeed, evidence that goal pursuits may need to be defended or shielded from other goals has long been assumed in models of self-regulation. Ach (1935) suggested that the activation of an intention invokes a process of selective attention that magnifies one's focus on information pertaining to a current concern and diminishes the salience of information pertaining to alternative pursuits (see Kuhl, 1994). More recently, Shallice (1972) suggested that action systems (or general plans) may similarly struggle for conscious supremacy, causing each system, upon activation, to inhibit the others to maintain conscious dominance. The general significance of such everyday challenges is highlighted by classic motivational research demonstrating that the cognitive presence of alternative goals often creates an "approach–approach" conflict that hampers progress toward any of the involved objectives (Lewin, 1935, 1951; Miller, 1944; Zeigarnik, 1927/1938).

Shah, Friedman, and Kruglanski (2002) explored the role of goal inhibition in self-regulation by examining how the activation of goals may inhibit the salience of one's other important intentions. In five studies, they found consistent evidence of such "goal shielding," particularly when individuals were highly committed to an activated goal because of its perceived importance. For example, in one experiment participants first described a current goal to which they were either strongly or weakly committed. In the high-commitment condition they were instructed to list an attribute they had a strong rather than a slight desire to attain. In the low-commitment condition, they were instructed to list and attribute they had a slight rather than a strong interest in attaining. They then were asked to rate the importance of attaining the attribute, the difficulty of its attainment, the time they spent pursuing the attribute over the last month, and the progress they had made in that period of time. Participants were then asked to list other attributes that they were currently trying to possess and to rate its importance. Finally, they were asked to list the activities (means) they could perform to attain the attribute initially listed. The high-commitment group rated their initial goal as more important than those in the low-commitment group. The low-commitment group listed significantly more alternative goals than the high-commitment group. The listing of attainment yielded that opposite pattern, where the high-commitment group listed more means than the low-commitment group. A regression analysis of the listing of goal alternatives found that self-reported tenacity moderated the commitment effect, such that individuals who reported greater tenacity listed significantly fewer goals overall. This suggests that the inhibition of alternative goals was greater for those high in tenacity.

Another experiment examined whether implicit activation of a committed goal would automatically produce the inhibition of alternative goal constructs. Instead of having participants consciously generate goals, a focal goal construct was subliminally primed and implicit measures assessed the subsequent activation level of alternative goal constructs. Participants provided three one-word attributes it was their goal to possess (e.g., intelligent, happy). They also had to provide a positive attribute that they didn't want to currently possess as a goal (e.g., rugged). This served as a subsequent control word. Two other nonattribute words were also used as control words (house and planet). Goal commitment was assessed by having participants indicate how important it was to them to possess the three attributes they listed. Participants also rated their goal tenacity.

Participants then performed a task requiring them to determine whether a target stimulus represented a personal attribute or not. The target words were preceded by "prime words" that presented to participants either control words or personal attributes. There was an inhibitory effect for each of the participants' attribute goal primes: The participants were slower in recognizing goal attributes when first primed with another of their goals than when first primed with a control word. Responses to the non-goal attribute were not affected by the primes. Participants' commitment to each of their three goals was positively related to the degree to which each of these goals inhibited their other two goals. Goal-related tenacity and overall commitment to goals were positively related to the overall tendency to inhibit alternatives. Goal-related tenacity increased the degree to which commitment to these goals positively related to participants' overall tendency to inhibit alternatives.

Shah et al. (2002) also found evidence to suggest that goal shielding may depend on one's emotional state, in that the inhibition of alternative goals appears to be tied to participants' levels of anxiety and depression in different ways. Whereas depression seems to hinder intergoal inhibition, anxiety appears to strengthen it. The results of these studies also suggest that such inhibition does not occur equally for all alternatives. Rather, they found that goal activation more readily inhibits alternatives that fulfill the same regulatory need (i.e., goals that are substitutable with each other). Thus, for some individuals, the goal of playing tennis may readily inhibit the goal of jogging because both fulfill a higher-order need to get in shape. Alternatively, goal activation less readily inhibits alternatives the attainment of which is viewed as facilitating the salient focal goal. For other individuals, the goal of playing tennis may not inhibit the goal of jogging because the latter may help one attain the former. Finally, Shah and colleagues demonstrated that goal shielding may serve important self-regulatory functions because it has distinct consequences for how intensely goals are pursued and how likely they are to be attained. This was evidenced in participants' persistence and performance in pursuing specific task goals (Shah et al., 2002). In defining the specific terms of goal pursuit, then, moments may help compartmentalize pursuits in time and place, thereby sheltering them from each other.

Moments of Temptation

If goal persistence is encouraged when one is in the moment, it can also be discouraged by the perception of a new moment. Indeed, our attraction to moments may make us vulnerable to temptations, which are typically defined as relatively less important end-states that hinder a focal pursuit (see Trope & Fishbach, 2000; Trope & Liberman, 2003). Although we may recognize the relative unimportance of temptations and the threat they pose to a current pursuit, we may nevertheless be drawn to them when their moment for pursuit is relatively fleeting. Thus, although goals and temptations represent positive end-states, they may potentially be distinguished by the strength of their connection to long-term goals and to the immediate moment. Whereas a goal's benefit may be defined by the strength of its connection to higher-order goals and needs, the effectiveness of a temptation, and its link to the moment.

Moreover, if moments allow goals and temptations to be distinguished conceptually, they may also be primarily linked to different forms of goal defense. Whereas goal pursuits may be defended from alternative goals through shielding, the immediacy of temptations may make inhibition harder. Instead, effective self-regulators may react to the immediate threat of temptations by strengthening their focus on the goal at hand. Trope and Fishbach (2000), for instance, have suggested that when individuals perceive short-term temptations as a threat to their long-term (if more arduous) ambitions, they may counteract the threat of the temptation to discontinue goal pursuit by increasing the perceived importance of the goal. This may be especially likely if they are generally effective self-regulators. Individuals may also respond to the threat of temptations by simply increasing the salience of the goal that it would hinder. In support of this, Fishbach, Friedman, and Kruglanski (2003) found that among effective self-regulators and those committed to a goal, activation of a temptation-related construct (via priming) automatically activated constructs related to the goal that it would hinder. Moreover, consistent with the notion that this association is meant to prevent engagement in the temptation, this pattern of activation was unidirectional: Goal-related constructs showed a trend toward *inhibiting* temptation-related constructs.

When the Moment Passes

Finally, a consideration of moments and their margins may lend insight into the nature and consequences of goal disengagement. Indeed there has been an increasing recognition that such disengagement can often be useful, if not necessary, for self-regulation generally. In forgoing, or at least forestalling, the reward of goal attainment, disengaging from goals may nevertheless limit the costs, inefficiency, and ongoing stress of managing multiple goals by reducing our "regulatory load" (see Klinger, 1975). Heckhausen, Wrosch, and Fleeson (2001), for example, examined childbearing goals in a sample of women who were either approaching the point in adulthood after which the likelihood of giving birth to a healthy child significantly decreases (e.g., women between the ages of 27 and 33 years) or for whom this biological deadline had already passed (e.g., women between the ages of 40 and 46 years). For women who had passed the biological deadline, greater activation of the goal of childbearing was a significant predictor of negative affect. In other words, the inability of those women who had passed the ideal age for childbearing to disengage from the goal of having a child was predictive of lower psychological well-being, as measured by the presence of negative affect. In a second study, Heckhausen et al.

(2001) found that the inability to disengage from the goal of childbearing in a sample of older women was related to an increased presence of symptoms of depression. Similarly, Wrosch and Heckhausen (1999) investigated the goal of having a romantic partner in younger and older adults who had recently experienced a separation. Whereas pursuit of the goal of finding a romantic partner would indicate an adaptive response in the younger adults (ages 23–35), for whom a large pool of potential relationship partners still existed, the continued pursuit of this same goal would be a fairly maladaptive response for older adults (ages 49–59), for whom the likelihood of finding a new relationship partner would be considerably lower. Consistent with this hypothesis, younger adults who actively pursued relationship goals experienced greater improvement in emotional well-being over a 15-month period than younger adults who did not. In contrast, older adults who disengaged from the goal of having a romantic partner (and instead focused on other kinds of social goals) experienced greater improvement in emotional well-being over time than older adults who continued to pursue this goal. The findings of Wrosch, Carver, and their colleagues suggest another potential benefit of disengagement: It may free individuals to pursue even more desirable or socially supported pursuits. Indeed, even some of the typical self-regulatory drawbacks of disengagement can be mitigated when individuals find a ready alternative, or replacement, to their abandoned goal, an issue we return to later (see Wrosch & Heckhausen, 1999; Wrosch, Scheier, Miller, Schulz, & Carver, 2003; Wrosch, Shulz, & Heckhausen, 2002; Heckhausen et al., 2001).

Yet despite the potential desirability of disengagement, self-regulatory research has found that, for a variety of possible reasons, disengaging from goal pursuits often proves quite challenging. Lewin (1935) as well as Kuhl and Kazan (1999) noted the difficulty we have in mentally detaching from unfulfilled goals, even those experimentally generated goals with little personal significance (Kazan & Kuhl, 2005). Indeed, such difficulty can be seen in research suggesting how easily individuals can come to ruminate or even dream about unattained goals (see, for instance, Klinger, 1975; Kuhl & Kazan, 1999; Martin & Tesser, 1996). It is also evident in the persistence of goal accessibility over time. Indeed, the accessibility of goals, unlike other mental constructs, may persevere or even increase over time until the goal is finally attained or abandoned (Lewin, 1951; Forster, Liberman, & Higgins, 2005). Bargh, Gollwitzer, Lee-Chai, Barndollar, and Trotschel (2001), for example, demonstrated that the effects of achievement goal priming on behavior were even greater after a delay, in contrast to semantic (or nonmotivational) activation, which quickly decays over time (see Goschke & Kuhl, 1993; Higgins, Bargh, & Lombardi, 1985;

Srull & Wyer, 1979). Such persistence may only grow stronger as one approaches attainment when the goal "looms larger" psychologically (see Lewin, 1951; Miller, 1944).

This analysis of goal rotation suggests that disengagement may be difficult because of an inherent predisposition to return (rotate back) to the goal. It also suggests that goal disengagement may have a distinct dynamic complexity that is far from simply the absence of engagement. Rather than disengage "all at once," for instance, disengagement may often be in the gradual decrease in how often a goal reoccurs in rotation. It also suggests that, like goal engagement, disengagement my often unfold without deliberate awareness.

Moment to Moment

Finally, let us quickly note that in influencing rotation among goal pursuits moments may also influence the manner in which these pursuits come to relate to each other. That moments are limited in time, for instance, may encourage the economy and endurance of behavioral means. That means can often be applied to a variety of goals is a regulatory versatility that has been labeled "multifinality" as it pertains to a behaviors' "far-reaching" potential for addressing other relevant goals of the system (Kruglanski et al., 2002). Although the versatility of a means may lessen the strength of its association to any one goal (see Zhang, Fishbach, & Kruglanski, 2007), individuals may nevertheless come to value the versatility of general "regulatory tools" as their regular use across pursuits may increase how effectively they are employed while easing the often-abrupt turns in pursuit from one moment to the next.

Moments' End

In attempting to define how ongoing self-regulation may incorporate the constraints and challenges of the ever-changing motivational moment, this analysis seeks to integrate fundamental principles of goal pursuit and goal systems so compellingly demonstrated by social, cognitive, and motivational research into an approach that highlights the constrained changes of everyday goal pursuit and goal management. Although much remains to be to be specified, it is our hope that this analysis may provide at least an initial framework for understanding how optimal goal management requires a recognition of the magnitude and limits of opportunity.

References

Aarts, H., & Dijksterhuis, A. (2000). Habits as knowledge structures: Automaticity in goal-directed behavior. *Journal of Personality and Social Psychology, 78*(1), 53–63.

Aarts, H., Gollwitzer, P. M., & Hassin, R. R. (2004). Goal contagion: perceiving is for pursuing. *Journal of Personality and Social Psychology, 87*(1), 23–37.

Ach, N. (1935). Analyse des Willens. [Analysis of will.]. *Handbuch der Biologischen Arbeitsmethoden, Abt. 6, Teil E,* 460.

Baddley, A. (2003). Working memory: Looking back and looking forward. Nature reviews. *Neuroscience, 24,* 829–839.

Bandura, A. (1997). *Self-efficacy: The exercise of control.* New York: W. H. Freeman/Times Books/Henry Holt & Co.

Bargh, J. A., Gollwitzer, P. M., Lee-Chai, A., Barndollar, K., & Trotschel, R. (2001). The automated will: Nonconscious activation and pursuit of behavioral goals. *Journal of Personality and Social Psychology, 81,* 1014–1027.

Baumann, N., & Kuhl, J. (2003). Self-infiltration: confusing assigned tasks as self-selected in memory. *Personality and Social Psychology Bulletin, 29*(4), 487–497.

Baumeister, R., Bratslavsky, E., Muraven, M., & Tice, D. (1998). Ego depletion: Is the active self a limited resource? *Journal of Personality and Social Psychology, 74*(5), 1252–1265.

Carver, C. S., & Scheier, M. F. (1998). *On the self-regulation of behavior.* Cambridge, UK: Cambridge University Press.

Deci, E. L., & Ryan, R. M. (2000). The "what" and "why" of goal pursuits: Human needs and the self-determination of behavior. *Psychological Inquiry, 11*(4), 227–268.

Dijksterhuis, A., & Bongers, K. C. (in press). Conscious thought as a trouble shooting mechanism? The role of consciousness in goal pursuit. In E. Morsella, J. Bargh, & P. Gollwitzer (Eds.), *The psychology of action, Volume 2: Mechanisms of human action.* New York: Oxford University Press.

Donahue, E. M., Robins, R. W., Roberts, B. W., & John, O. P. (1993). The divided self: Concurrent and longitudinal effects of psychological adjustment and social roles on self-concept differentiation. *Journal of Personality and Social Psychology, 64,* 834–846.

Dweck, C., & Grant, H. (2008). Self-theories, goals, and meaning. In J. Y. Shah & W. L. Gardner (Eds.), *Handbook of motivation science* (pp. 405–416). New York: Guilford Press.

Emmons, R. A. (1986). Personal strivings: An approach to personality and subjective well-being. *Journal of Personality and Social Psychology, 51*(5), 1058–1068.

Emmons, R. A. (1992). Abstract versus concrete goals: Personal striving level, physical illness, and psychological well-being. *Journal of Personality and Social Psychology, 62*(2), 292–300.

Emmons, R. A., & King, L. A. (1988). Conflict among personal strivings: Immediate and long-term implications for psychological and physical well-being. *Journal of Personality and Social Psychology, 54*(6), 1040–1048.

Feather, N. T (1982). Actions in relation to expected consequences: An overview of a research program. In N. T. Feather (Ed.), *Expectations and actions: Expectancy-value models in psychology* (pp. 53–95). Hillsdale, NJ: Erlbaum.

Fishbach, A., Friedman, R. S., & Kruglanski, A. W. (2003). Leading us not into temptation: Momentary allurements elicit overriding goal activation. *Journal of Personality and Social Psychology, 84*, 296–309.

Forster, J., Liberman, N., & Higgins, E. T. (2005). Accessibility from active and fulfilled goals. *Journal of Experimental Social Psychology, 41*(3), 220–239.

Freud, S. (1961). The ego and the id. In J. Strachey (Ed. and Trans.), *The standard edition of the complete psychological works of Sigmund Freud* (Vol. 19, pp. 3–66). London: Hogarth Press. (Original work published 1923)

Gollwitzer, P. M. (1999). Implementation intentions: Strong effects of simple plans. *American Psychologist, 54*, 493–503.

Gollwitzer, P. M., & Brandstatter, V. (1997). Implementation intentions and effective goal pursuit. *Journal of Personality and Social Psychology, 73*(1), 186–199.

Gollwitzer, P. M., Parks-Stamm, E., Jaudas, A., & Sheeran, P. (2008). Flexible tenacity in goal pursuit. In J. Y. Shah & W. L. Gardner (Eds.), *Handbook of motivation science* (pp. 325–341). New York: Guilford Press.

Goschke, T., & Kuhl., J. (1993). Representation of intentions: persisting activation in memory. *Journal of Experimental Psychology: Learning, Memory, and Cognition, 19*(5), 1211–1226.

Heckhausen, J., Wrosch, C., & Fleeson, W. (2001). Developmental regulation before and after a developmental deadline: the sample case of "biological clock" for childbearing. *Psychology and Aging, 16*(3), 400–413.

Higgins, E. (1997). Beyond pleasure and pain. *American Psychologist, 52,* 1280–1300.

Higgins, E. (2006). Value from hedonic experience and engagement. *Psychological Review, 113*(3), 439–460.

Higgins, E. T., Bargh, J. A., & Lombardi, W. J. (1985). Nature of priming effects on categorization. *Journal of Experimental Psychology: Learning, Memory, & Cognition, 11*(1), 59–69.

Hockey, G. R. J. (1996). Energetical control processes in the regulation of human performance. In W. Battmann and S. Dutke (Eds.), *Processes of the Molar Regulation of Behavior* (pp. 271–287). Pabst: Berlin

Hyland, M. E. (1988). Motivational control theory: An integrative framework. *Journal of Personality and Social Psychology, 55*(4), 642–651.

Kahneman, D. (1973). *Attention and effort.* Englewood Cliffs, NJ: Prentice-Hall.

Kanfer, R., Ackerman, P., Murtha, T., Dugdale, B., & Nelson, L. (1994). Goal setting, conditions of practice, and task performance: A resource allocation perspective. *Journal of Applied Psychology, 79*(6), 826–835.

Karoly, P. (1993). Mechanisms of self-regulation: A systems view. *Annual Review of Psychology, 44*(1), 23–52.

Kazan, M., & Kuhl, J. (2005). Intention memory and achievement motivation: Volitional facilitation and inhibition as a function of affective contents of need-related stimuli. *Journal of Personality and Social Psychology, 89*(3), 426–448.

Klinger, E. (1975). Consequences of commitment to and disengagement from incentives. *Psychological Review, 82*(1), 1–25.

Kruglanski, A., Shah, J., Fishbach, A., Friedman, R., Chun, W., & Sleeth-Keppler, D., et al. (2002). A theory of goal systems. In M. P. Zanna (Ed.), *Advances in experimental social psychology* (Vol. 34, pp. 331–378). San Diego: Academic Press.

Kuhl, J. (1994). A theory of action and state orientations. In J. Kuhl & J. Beckmann (Eds.), *Volition and personality: Action versus state orientation* (p. 946). Seattle: Hogrefe & Huber.

Kuhl, J., & Kazen, M. (1999). Volitional facilitation of difficult intentions: Joint activation of intention memory and positive affect removes Stroop interference. *Journal of Experimental Psychology General, 128*(3), 382–399.

Lewin, K. (1935). *A dynamic theory of personality: Selected papers.* New York: McGraw-Hill.

Lewin, K. (1936). *Principles of topological psychology.* F. Heider & G. M. Heider (Trans.). New York: McGraw-Hill.

Lewin, K. (1951). *Field theory in social science: Selected theoretical papers.* 346. New York: McGraw-Hill.

Lewin, K., Dembo, T., Festinger, L., & Sears, P. S. (1944). Level of aspiration. In J. M. Hunt (Ed.), *Personality and the behavioral disorders* (pp. 333–371) New York: Roland Press.

Lewin, K., Heider, F., & Heider, G. M. (1966). Principles of topological psychology. *Mathematical representation and psychological theory* (pp. 76–83).

Locke, E. A., & Latham, G. P. (1990). *A theory of goal setting and task performance.* Englewood Cliffs, NJ: Prentice-Hall.

Locke, E. A., & Latham, G. P. (2006). New directions in goal-setting theory. *Current Directions in Psychological Science, 15,* 265–268.

Locke, E. A., Motowidlo, S. J., & Bobko, P. (1986). Using self-efficacy theory to resolve the conflict between goal-setting theory and expectancy theory in organizational behavior and industrial/organizational psychology. *Journal of Social and Clinical Psychology, 4,* 328–338.

Lockwood, P., & Kunda, Z. (2000). Outstanding role models: Do they inspire or demoralize us? In A. Tesser, R. B. Felson, & J. M. Suls (Eds.), *Psychological perspectives on self and identity* (pp. 147–171). Washington, DC: American Psychological Association.

Markus, H., & Ruvolo, A. (1989). Possible selves: Personalized representations of goals. In L. A. Pervin (Ed.), *Goal concepts in personality and social psychology* (pp. 211–241). Hillsdale, NJ: Erlbaum.

Martin, L. L., & Tesser, A. (1996). Striving and feeling: Interactions among goals, affect, and self-regulation, 408. Mahwah, NJ: Erlbaum.

Mento, A., Locke, E., & Klein, H. (1992). Relationship of goal level to valence and instrumentality. *Journal of Applied Psychology, 77*(4), 395–405.

Miller, N. E. (1944). Experimental studies of conflict. In M. V. Hunt (Ed.), *Per-*

sonality and the behavior disorders (Vol. 1, pp. 431–465). New York: Ronald Press.

Mukhopadhyay, A., & Johar, G. (2005). Where there is a will, is there a way? The effects of consumers' lay theories of self-control on setting and keeping resolutions. *Journal of Consumer Research, 31,* 779–786.

Muraven, M., & Baumeister, R. F. (2000). Self-regulation and depletion of limited resources: Does self-control resemble a muscle? *Psychological Bulletin, 126,* 247–259.

Muraven, M., & Slessareva, E. (2003). Mechanism of self-control failure: Motivation and limited resources. *Personality and Social Psychology Bulletin, 29,* 894–906.

Muraven, M., Tice, D., & Baumeister, R. (1998). Self-control as limited resource: regulatory depletion patterns. *Journal of Personality and Social Psychology,* 74(3), 774–789.

Norman, D. A., & Shallice, T. (1986). Attention to action: Willed and automatic control of behavior. In J. R. Davidson, G. E. Schwartz, & D. Shapiro (Eds.), *Consciousness and self regulation: Advances in research and theory* (Vol. 4, pp. 1–18). New York: Plenum Press.

Pervin, L. A. (Ed.). (1989). *Goal concepts in personality and social psychology.* Hillsdale, NJ: Erlbaum.

Powers, W. T. (1973). Feedback: Beyond behaviorism. *Science, 179,* 351–356.

Read, S. J., & Miller, L. C. (Eds.). (1998). *Connectionist models of social reasoning and social behavior.* Mahwah, NJ: Erlbaum.

Sansone, C., & Harackiewicz, J. M. (1996). "I don't feel like it": The function of interest in self-regulation. In L. L. Martin & A. Tesser (Eds.), *Striving and feeling: Interactions among goals, affect, and self-regulation* (pp. 203–228). Hillsdale, NJ: Erlbaum.

Schmeichel, B. J., & Baumeister, R. F. (2004). Self-regulatory strength. In R. F. Baumeister & K. D. Vohs (Eds.), *Handbook of self-regulation: Research, theory, and applications* (pp. 84–98). New York: Guilford Press.

Shah, J. Y. (2005). The automatic pursuit and management of goals. *Current Directions in Psychological Science, 14,* 10–13.

Shah, J. Y., Brazy, P. B., & Jungbluth, N. (2007). *Save it for later: Regulatory resource regulation in goal pursuit.* Manuscript under revision.

Shah, J., Friedman, R., & Kruglanski, A. (2002). Forgetting all else: on the antecedents and consequences of goal shielding. *Journal of Personality and Social Psychology,* 83(6), 1261–1280.

Shah, J. Y., & Kruglanski, A. W. (2000) The structure and substance of intrinsic motivation. In C. Sansone & J. M. Harackiewicz (Eds.), *Intrinsic and extrinsic motivation: The search for optimal motivation and performance* (pp. 105–127). San Diego: Academic Press.

Shah, J., & Kruglanski, A. (2003). When opportunity knocks: Bottom-up priming of goals by means and its effects on self-regulation. *Journal of Personality and Social Psychology,* 84(6), 1109–1122.

Shah, J., Kruglanski, A., & Friedman, R. (2003). Goal systems theory: Integrating the cognitive and motivational aspects of self-regulation. In S. J. Spencer,

S. Fein, J. M. Olson, & M. P. Zanna (Eds.), *Motivated social perception: The Ontario symposium* (Vol. 9, 247–276). Mahwah, NJ: Erlbaum.

Shah, J. Y., & Kruglanski, A. W. (2000). The structure and substance of intrinsic motivation. In C. Sansone & J. M. Harackiewicz (Ed.). *Intrinsic and extrinsic motivation: The search for optimal motivation and performance.* (pp. 259–298). Woodbine, NJ: Academic Press.

Shallice, T. (1972). Dual functions of consciousness. *Psychological Review, 79*(5), 383–393.

Sheldon, K. M., & Elliot, A. J. (2000). Personal goals in social roles: Divergences and convergences across roles and levels of analysis. *Journal of Personality, 68,* 51–84.

Sheldon, K. & Kasser, T. (1995). Coherence and congruence: two aspects of personality integration. *Journal of Personality and Social Psychology, 68*(3), 531–543.

Simon, H. (1967). Motivational and emotional controls of cognition. *Psychological Review, 74*(1), 29–39.

Srull, T. K., & Wyer, R. S. (1979). The role of category accessibility in the interpretation of information about persons: Some determinants and implications. *Journal of Personality and Social Psychology, 37,* 1660–1672.

Steele, C. M., & Liu, T. J. (1983). Dissonance processes as self-affirmation. *Journal of Personality and Social Psychology, 45,* 5–19.

Tesser, A., Crepaz, N., Beach, S. R. H., Cornell, D., & Collins, J. C. (2000). Confluence of self-esteem regulation mechanisms: On integrating the self-zoo. *Personality and Social Psychology Bulletin, 26,* 1476–1489.

Tesser, A., Martin, L. L., & Cornell, D. P. (1996). On the substitutability of self-protective mechanisms. In P. M. Gollwitzer & J. A. Bargh (Eds.), *The psychology of action: Linking cognition and motivation to behavior* (pp. 48–68). New York: Guilford Press.

Trope, Y., & Fishbach, A. (2000). Counteractive self-control in overcoming temptation. *Journal of Personality and Social Psychology, 79,* 493–506.

Trope, Y., & Liberman, N. (2000). Temporal construal and time-dependent changes in preference. *Journal of Personality and Social Psychology, 79*(6), 876–889.

Trope, Y., & Liberman, N. (2003). Temporal construal. *Psychological Review, 110*(3), 403–421.

Vallerand, R. J., & Ratelle, C. F. (2002). Intrinsic and extrinsic motivation: A hierarchical model. In E. L. Deci & R. M. Ryan (Eds.), *Handbook of self-determination research* (pp. 37–69). Rochester, NY: University of Rochester Press.

Wood, W., Quinn, J., & Kashy, D. (2002). Habits in everyday life: Thought, emotion, and action. *Journal of Personality and Social Psychology, 83*(6), 1281–1297.

Wright, R. A., & Brehm, J. W. (1989). Energization and goal attractiveness. In L. A. Pervin (Ed.), *Goal concepts in personality and social psychology* (pp. 169–210). Hillsdale, NJ: Erlbaum.

Wright, R. A., Martin, R. E., & Bland, J. L. (2003). Energy resource depletion, task difficulty, and cardiovascular response to a mental arithmetic challenge. *Psychophysiology, 40,* 98–105.

Wrosch, C., & Heckhausen, J. (1999). Control processes before and after passing a developmental deadline: Activation and deactivation of intimate relationship goals. *Journal of Personality and Social Psychology, 77*(2), 415–427.

Wrosch, C., Scheier, M., Miller, G., Schulz, R., & Carver, C. (2003). Adaptive self-regulation of unattainable goals: goal disengagement, goal reengagement, and subjective well-being. *Personality and Social Psychology Bulletin, 29*(12), 1494–1508.

Wrosch, C., Schulz, R., & Heckhausen, J. (2002). Health stresses and depressive symptomatology in the elderly: The importance of health engagement control strategies. *Health Psychology, 21,* 340–348.

Zeigarnik, B. (1938). On finished and unfinished tasks. In W. D. Ellis (Ed.), *A source book of Gestalt psychology* (pp. 300–314). New York: Harcourt, Brace & World. (Reprinted and condensed from *Psychologische Forschung, 1927, 9,* 1–85)

Zhang, Y., Fishbach, A., & Kruglanski, A. (2007). The dilution model: how additional goals undermine the perceived instrumentality of a shared path. *Journal of Personality and Social Psychology, 92*(3), 389–401.

Zijlstra, F. R. H. (1996). Effort as energy regulation. In W. Battmann & S. Dutke (Eds.), *Processes of the molar regulation of behavior* (pp. 219–235). Lengerich, Germany: Pabst Science Publishers.

PART III

HOW ARE GOALS PURSUED?

CHAPTER 10

Five Markers of Motivated Behavior

LEONARD L. MARTIN
ABRAHAM TESSER

Behavior can be goal directed in more than one way. Consider a healthy, exuberant, young man who is taking a walk with his frail grandmother. If the young man believes that his grandmother may have difficulty matching his brisk pace, then he may intentionally slow down to match his pace with that of his grandmother. If he finds that he has slowed down too much, then he may speed up to maintain his desired position alongside his grandmother. In other words, the man may modulate his behavior in relation to the outcome he hopes to attain (i.e., matching his pace with that of his grandmother).

Compare this man's behavior with that of a young man who has been subtly exposed to a series of words associated with the stereotype of the elderly (e.g., Florida, Bingo, shuffleboard). This man may also walk slowly, like an elderly person (Bargh, Chen, & Burrows, 1996), but his walking would not be directed toward the attainment of a desired end point (e.g., helping his grandmother) and would not be modulated relative to a reference point (e.g., the grandmother's pace). Because of these (and other) differences, we refer to the first man's behavior as motivated but refer to the second man's behavior as a simple by-product of passive knowledge activation.

In this chapter, we explore some features of behavior that mark behavior as motivated as opposed to passive. The distinction between motivated and passive behavior is relevant to a wide range of phenomena in social psychology. For example, there was a long running debate regarding the attitude change that can result when individuals engage in behavior inconsistent with their attitudes (e.g., Fazio, Zanna, & Cooper, 1977). The question was whether the attitude change was driven by a consistency motive (Festinger, 1957) or was the result of a passive inference process (Bem, 1967). There was also debate over the tendency of individuals to attribute their failures to external causes (e.g., the test was unfair). This tendency can be explained in motivational terms (Gollwitzer, Earle, & Stephan, 1982) or in terms of a passive, self-history inference process (Miller & Ross, 1975). More recently, questions have been raised about the extent to which stereotyping is motivated (Fein & Spencer, 1997) as opposed to automatic (Greenwald, Banaji, & Rudman, 2002). So being able to discriminate motivated behavior from behavior that is the result of more passive processes can help us understand a wide variety of social psychology phenomena.

Some of the features that distinguish motivated behavior from passive behavior have been known for years in the literature. Early in the last century, a number of researchers (e.g., Lewin, 1938; Tolman, 1932; Woodworth, 1921) explored motivational issues using animals in the context of a behaviorist philosophy. The animals, of course, could not say whether they were motivated, and the researchers were reluctant to infer a motivational state in the absence of observable behavioral evidence. To overcome these limitations, the researchers generated a list of observable features they could use to justify their inference that an animal's behavior was motivated. They suggested that it was reasonable to assume that a behavior was motivated if the behavior exhibited persistence-until, equifinality, and docility.

"Persistence-until" refers to the tendency of an organism to continue striving for a goal until it has attained the goal. If a person is searching for food, for example, obtains some food, eats it, and then stops searching, it is reasonable to assume that the person was motivated to eat. "Equifinality" refers to the ability of an organism to attain a goal through more than one means. A person motivated to reduce his hunger, for example, could eat a sandwich, snack on some cookies, or take a diet pill. Each of these means could reduce the person's hunger. "Docility" refers to the tendency of organisms to settle ultimately on the most efficient means of attaining a goal. A person may learn, for example, that eating a sandwich satisfies his hunger more than snacking on cookies or taking a diet pill. If so, then when the person is motivated to reduce his hunger, he is more likely to eat a sandwich. To summarize, a number of early researchers suggested that one could obtain observable, behavioral evidence that an organism's behavior is motivated when the organism attempted consistently to pursue the most efficient of various means to attain an outcome and no longer performed those means once the outcome had been obtained.

To these traditional features, we can add two more that have been shown in more recent research to be central to the definition of motivated behavior. These are affect and effort. In brief, progress toward a goal has been shown to be associated with positive affect, whereas movement away from a goal has been shown to be associated with negative affect. Also, when individuals are motivated to attain a goal, they may expend considerable effort especially if they experience difficulty progressing toward the goal. In the remainder of the chapter, we examine some evidence for persistence-until, equifinality, docility, affect, and effort as markers of motivated behavior. After that, we discuss ways in which these markers may allow us to distinguish behavior that is motivated from behavior that is the product of passive mechanisms.

Persistence-Until

Recall that "persistence-until" refers to the tendency of an organism to continue to pursue a goal until it has attained the goal. Perhaps the best known example of persistence-until is the Zeigarnik effect. In a classic experiment, Zeigarnik (1927/1938) asked participants to perform a series of tasks and allowed the participants to complete some of these tasks but not others. Later, she asked participants to recall the tasks they performed. Participants tended to recall more tasks they did not complete than tasks they did complete. Although subsequent research has revealed a number of qualifications on this recall effect (Butterfield, 1954), the more general principle demonstrated by Zeigarnik has held up well. Namely, information related to unattained goals tends to remain more accessible than information related to obtained goals.

For example, strong evidence for the persistence-until hypothesis was obtained by Goschke and Kuhl (1993). They presented participants with a short list of behaviors typifying two simple activities (e.g., setting a dinner table) and told participants which of these activities they would have to perform later in the experiment. Participants were also told that their memory for both sets of behaviors would be tested. Thus, participants were prepared to recall both sets of behaviors but had committed to performing only one. So if commitment to a goal leads to heightened accessibility of information related to that goal, then participants would have better memory of the behaviors they had committed to perform.

Goschke and Kuhl (1993) assessed memory in a speeded recognition test. Specifically, they flashed strings of letters on a computer screen and asked participants to indicate as quickly as they could whether the strings spelled out real words. Some of the real words reflected the behaviors making up each activity. Consistent with the persistence-until hypothesis, Goschke and Kuhl found that participants recognized words related to the activity they had committed to perform faster than words related to the activity they had not committed to perform.

This study constitutes a particularly strong test of the persistence-until hypothesis because the difference in recognition speed (i.e., accessibility) was observed even though participants knew they would have to recall the behaviors associated with each activity, and differences in imagery, selective encoding, and rehearsal of the two sets of behaviors were controlled. The results suggest, therefore, that it was the adoption of the goal and not passive activation of a goal-related script that caused the increase in accessibility.

As it turns out, this increase in accessibility can be a useful feature of motivated behavior. It can facilitate processing of stimuli related to the unattained goal. In fact, it may do so to such an extent that the goal-related stimuli may capture an individual's attention even if the individual is attempting to focus his/her attention elsewhere. Rothermund (2003), for example, had participants choose from a set of alternatives the closest synonym to a series of target words. On some trials, participants were led to believe that they had chosen correctly, whereas on other trials they were led to believe that they had chosen incorrectly. In goal-progress terms, when participants received the success feedback, they attained their goal of doing well on the task. When they received the failure feedback, they did not attain this goal. So, if goal nonattainment increases the accessibility of information related to the nonattained goal, then information related to the failure trials should be more accessible—hence more distracting—than information related to the success trials.

Rothermund (2003) assessed the amount of interference from the success and failure words by instructing participants to name a series of target words presented on a computer screen and to respond as quickly as they could when they heard a tone. On all trials, the target words were surrounded by two distractor words, some of which had been used in the earlier synonym task. Some of these words came from trials in which participants had received success feedback, whereas others came from trials in which participants had received failure feedback.

Consistent with the persistence-until hypothesis, the failure-related distractors, relative to the success-related distractors, increased the time it took participants to recognize the target words and respond to the tone. Thus, the heightened accessibility of information related to nonattainment goals (i.e., persistence-until) can facilitate the processing of goal-related stimuli and debilitate processing of goal-unrelated stimuli. This difference in the ability to process goal-related and goal-unrelated stimuli might help individuals attain their goals, especially when processing of the nonrelated stimuli could direct individuals away from their goal. A person who is dieting, for example, might be more successful at losing weight if he/she maintained thoughts of the goal (getting in better shape) while also minimizing thoughts of temptations (e.g., eating fattening foods). There is some evidence that this in fact is the case.

Fishbach, Friedman, and Kruglanski (2003) had participants generate a one-word description of a goal they were pursuing (e.g., study) and an activity they ought not to perform if they wanted to reach their goal (e.g., television). In this way, Fishbach et al. were able to obtain words related to a goal and temptation for each participant. Next, participants were asked to indicate as quickly as they could whether letter strings that appeared on a computer screen were real words or nonwords. On some trials, each participant's goal word was presented before the presentation of the goal word that preceded presentation of the temptation word, whereas on other trials, the converse was true.

Fishbach, Friedman, and Kruglanski (2003) found a difference in accessibility that would facilitate goal progress. Specifically, participants recognized their temptation-related word more slowly following presentation of their goal-related word but recognized their goal-related word more quickly following presentation of their temptation-related word. The results suggest that exposure to goal-related words led individuals to inhibit potentially counterproductive thoughts, whereas exposure to the temptation-related stimuli led participants to bring to mind the goal that was leading them to avoid the temptation in the first place. By keeping the overriding goal in mind (persistence-until) and reducing the activation of counterproductive thoughts, individuals may be more likely to obtain the outcomes they are motivated to pursue (Kuhl & Weiss, 1994).

In fact, Fishbach et al. (2003) obtained some evidence of the relation between accessibility and goal success in a follow-up study. They found that among women who were motivated to lose weight, those primed with diet-related stimuli (either the goal or the temptation) were more likely to choose an apple over a candy bar as a gift at the end of the experiment. In other words, the accessibility of information related to the unattained goal induced participants to engage in behavior that would help them attain their goal.

Of course, the heightened accessibility of information related to a goal would be beneficial only to the extent that individuals are still pursuing the goal. If individuals began pursuing other goals, then the accessibility of information related to the first goal might actually interfere. This is where the until aspect of persistence-until becomes important. One of the markers of motivated behavior is its tendency to decrease in probability after individuals have attained the goal that is motivating the behavior. If the accessibility of goal-related information is really the result of motivation (as opposed to passive priming), then it should be high before individuals attain the goal but low afterwards.

Evidence that accessibility does in fact vary as a function of goal attainment was obtained by Förster, Liberman, and Higgins (2005; see also Marsh, Hicks, & Bink, 1998). They asked participants to view a series of simple schematic drawings and to answer some questions about the drawings. Some participants were asked to notify the experimenter if they saw a drawing of eyeglasses followed immediately by a drawing of a pair of scissors. Others were not given this instruction. In this way, the former but not the latter were induced to adopt a goal related to eyeglasses. This means that the former should experience increased accessibility of information related to eyeglasses before they see the target drawings (eyeglasses followed by scissors), but decreased accessibility of this information after they see the target drawings.

The series of drawings was presented in four blocks, and the target drawings appeared in the third block. Thus, if the accessibility of goal-related information is motivated by goal nonattainment, then it should be high prior to Block 3 but low following Block 3. To measure accessibility, Förster et al. (2005) asked participants after each block to make word/non-word decisions about various strings of letters. In some cases, the strings spelled out words associated with eyeglasses (e.g., sun, read). Presumably, the more accessible the goal-related information, the faster participants will be at recognizing these words (i.e., goal related).

Consistent with the persistence-until nature of motivated behavior, Förster et al. (2005) found that when participants had not yet seen the target drawings, those instructed to notify the experimenter that they had seen the glasses–scissors pair recognized the eyeglass-related words more quickly than those not given this goal. After they had seen the target drawings, however, participants asked to notify the experimenter recognized these words more slowly than the non-goal participants. In other words, nonattainment of a goal increased accessibility of goal-related information, whereas attainment of the goal decreased it.

Förster et al. (2005) also found that these differences in accessibility were accentuated when participants were given an increased incentive to find the target drawings and/or believed that the drawings were highly likely to appear. In sum, it appears that motivation to attain a goal can increase accessibility of goal-related information and decrease accessibility of potentially interfering information, whereas attainment of the goal eliminates both of these effects, and both of these effects are enhanced by factors that enhance motivation. Moreover, none of these effects would be obtained if the accessibility of the goal-related information was the result of a passive, nonmotivational mechanism. The results suggest, therefore, that persistence-until is a defining characteristic of motivated behavior.

Equifinality

The second feature that distinguishes motivated behavior from passive behavior is equifinality. "Equifinality" refers to the tendency of motivated behavior to be directed more toward attainment of the desired outcome (i.e., the goal) than the means to obtain that outcome. This means that individuals can use a variety of means to attain their goal. A person looking to satisfy his hunger (goal), for example, may head out to a nearby burger restaurant (means). Finding that the restaurant is overly crowded, the person may opt to drive to the chicken restaurant (alternate means). Either restaurant will satisfy the person's goal—as long as that goal is defined abstractly such as "get something to eat." If it is defined more concretely, such as "get a burger from your favorite restaurant on the corner," then the chicken restaurant will not serve as a substitute means to attain the goal. Similarly, if the person's real goal for going to the burger restaurant is to flirt with the cute hostess, then going to the chicken restaurant would not reduce the motivation to go to the burger restaurant. As can be seen, the extent to which various means to a goal can reduce motivation to pursue that goal can tell us something about the nature of the goal. This is the logic of equifinality and it has proven itself useful in a variety of research programs.

Koole, Smeets, van Knippenberg, and Dijksterhuis (1999), for example, used the logic of equifinality to explore the motivation behind rumination (i.e., persistent intrusive thoughts). According to Martin and Tesser (1989, 1996, 2006), rumination is motivated by failure to make progress toward important higher-order goals. To the extent this is true, rumination should be turned off by attainment of the higher-order goal. It is unclear, though, what the higher-order goal might be in any given situation. If a student ruminates after failing a test, for example, is the rumination driven by a goal related specifically to the test or is it driven by a more general goal related to the class, to dropping out of school, to displeasing his parents, or to becoming a failure in life? We may be able to tell which goal is driving the rumination by seeing which kinds of attainment reduce the rumination.

Koole et al. (1999) hypothesized that the goal driving the rumination was a higher-order one involving self-evaluation (Martin & Tesser, 1989, 1996, 2006). If this hypothesis is correct, then having one's positive self-evaluation affirmed could reduce rumination even if the affirmation does not change the specific conditions that initiated the rumination (e.g., failure on a specific test). To test this hypothesis, Koole et al. had participants take what was ostensibly an intelligence test and gave all participants feedback that they had performed poorly on this test. In this way, participants were frustrated in their goal of demonstrating their intelligence. This means that the participants should ruminate about their poor performance—at least to the extent that they have not found some other means of attaining their goal (i.e., maintaining a positive self-evaluation).

Following the failure feedback, Koole et al. (1999) asked some participants to express their views on personally important issues but asked others to express their views on issues that were not important to them. In this way, the former attained the goal of having a positive self-evaluation (i.e., self-affirmation), whereas the latter did not. Koole et al. then used a lexical decision task to measure the accessibility of words related to the intelligence test. Specifically, they presented participants with strings of letters on a computer screen and asked participants to indicate as quickly as they could whether each string spelled out a real word or a nonword. Some of the real words were related to intelligence. So, the greater the rumination, the faster participants should be at recognizing the intelligence-related words.

If the rumination is motivated by factors specific to failure on the intelligence test, then attaining a positive self-evaluation by writing about one's important values should have no effect on the rumination. After all, writing about one's values does nothing to undo the failure on the intelligence test. If the rumination is motivated by the broader implications of the failure for one's self-evaluation, however, then participants who wrote about their important values should ruminate less than those who did not write about those values.

The results were consistent with the equifinality hypothesis. Participants ruminated more (faster recognition of intelligence-related words) when they had not affirmed their self than when they had. The results suggest, therefore, that the rumination was motivated by failure to maintain a positive self-evaluation. This is why the rumination could be turned off by either a positive performance on the intelligence test or by writing about their values (or, hypothetically, by any experience that allows the participants to attain the higher-order goal of maintaining a positive self-evaluation).

Equifinality is not a property of motivated behavior that can be observed only under controlled laboratory conditions. It can be easily observed in the real world. Consider the findings of Millar, Tesser, and Millar (1988) who noted that as individuals transition from high school to college, they often leave loved ones behind and have difficulty participating in activities they used to enjoy. The transition, however, can also open up the possibility of making new friends and engaging in new activities. If rumination is motivated by goal nonattainment, then students transitioning to college should ruminate about the individuals and activities they left behind, but only to the extent that they had not found substitutes for these persons and activities (i.e., alternate ways to attain the goal).

To test this hypothesis, Miller at al. (1988) had first-year college students identify the person with whom they were closest before coming to the university and to list activities in which they had regularly engaged with that person. The students were also asked to indicate the activities for which they had been able to find substitutes after coming to the university. Finally, the students were asked to rate the extent to which they were ruminating about the person they had left behind (e.g., "Memories of things we did together popped into my mind when I was trying to study, I spent time thinking about when we could see each other").

As expected, the more activities the students were no longer able to pursue, the more they reported ruminating. The more substitutes they found, they less they reported ruminating. The pattern is consistent with the equifinality feature of motivated behavior. It suggests that the students' rumination was motivated by a very broad goal (e.g., socialize) that could be satisfied in more than one way (e.g., spending time with old friend or spending time with new friends).

The logic of equifinalty has also helped researchers understand the motivation underlying behavior-induced attitude change. When individuals engage in behavior inconsistent with their attitudes, they often change their attitudes to be consistent with the implications of their behavior (Festinger, 1957). Steele and his colleagues (Steele, 1988; Steele & Liu, 1983) hypothesized that this attitude change was not the result of a specific motivation to maintain attitude-behavior consistency but by the more general goal of affirming the integrity of the self (i.e., perceiving the self as adaptive, competent, and able to control important outcomes).

Steele and Liu (1983) tested this self-affirmation hypothesis using the logic of equifinality. First, they induced participants to agree to write an essay in favor of raising tuition (a position the participants strongly opposed). Some participants were led to believe that they had high choice in writing the essay (high dissonance), whereas others were led to believe that they had little choice (low dissonance). Next, all participants filled out a questionnaire about economic values. For some of the participants, these values were important, whereas for others, they were not. As a result, the former attained the higher-order goal of maintaining their self-integrity, whereas the latter did not. Finally, Steele and Liu measured each participant's attitude regarding a tuition increase.

The classic cognitive dissonance effect occurs when individuals led to believe that they freely chose to write an essay inconsistent with their attitudes change their attitudes to make them consistent with the implications of their essay. In this case, participants would be more favorable to raising tuition. The question, though, is why the attitude change occurs. If it occurs because of a specific motivation to maintain consistency, then participants should display the attitude change regardless of whether they affirmed the self. The affirmation does not restore attitude-behavior consistency.

If the attitude change is in service of a more general motive to maintain self-integrity, however, then participants who wrote about their important values should not display the attitude change. Writing about their values is an alternate way to attain the higher-order goal that was threatened by engaging in attitude inconsistent behavior. The results supported the latter hypothesis. Affirming the self eliminated the participants' motivation to make their attitudes consistent with their prior attitude-inconsistent behavior.

There are at least two explanations for why self-affirmation can reduce the motivation aroused by cognitive dissonance. One possibility is that there is a hierarchical relation between cognitive dissonance and self-affirmation. Maintaining attitude-behavior consistency is a means for maintaining self-integrity. Another possibility is that self-integrity and attitude-behavior consistency are alternate means to an even higher-order goal, namely, maintaining a positive self-evaluation. This possibility was suggested by Tesser and his colleagues (e.g., Tesser, Crepaz, Collins, Cornell, & Beach, 2000; Tesser & Cornell, 1991; Tesser, Martin, & Cornell, 1996), and it becomes more intriguing when one considers the wide range of phenomena that have been linked to the self (e.g., rumination, self-affirmation, social comparison, self-evaluation maintenance, terror management, stereotyping; defensive processing, impression management). Do these phenomena stand in some hierarchical order relative to one another or is there a more general goal for each of these is an alternate means? Tesser and his colleagues used the logic of equifinality to find out.

Because the research programs addressing different self-related phenomena have generally proceeded independently of one another, it was difficult to determine whether the different phenomena reflected psychologically distinct goals or whether each reflected a different means to the same higher-order goal, namely, maintaining a positive self-evaluation (Tesser, 1988). If self-evaluation is a general higher-order goal, then different self-related phenomena should be substitutable for one another. For example, attaining a favorable social comparison should eliminate the motivation to restore attitude-behavior consistency, maintaining attitude-behavior consistency should reduce the need to engage in a favorable social comparison, attaining a favorable social comparison should reduce the need to affirm one's self-integrity, and so on.

If the different phenomena are motivated by independent systems, however, then the substitutability would not be possible. There is a simple strategy to assess the substitutability of the various self-related phenomena. One need only threaten or augment an individual's self-evaluation in one domain and measure the extent to which doing so affects the tendency of the individual to engage in self-augmenting behaviors in another domain.

Tesser and Cornell (1991), for example, gave some participants an opportunity to augment their self-evaluation by affirming themselves. Specifically, some participants filled out a questionnaire about a value important to the self, whereas others filled out a questionnaire about a less important value. Next, participants performed a task flowing from the social comparison literature (e.g., compare performance relative to others) and were asked to perform a version of this task that was either self-relevant or not. They also performed this task in the connection with a friend and a stranger. The main dependent measure was the extent to which participants helped or hindered the performance of the other participants.

Previous research and theory have suggested that being outperformed by a close other (i.e., a friend) on a self-relevant task is more threatening to the maintenance of a positive self-evaluation than being outperformed by a stranger. Thus, participants who had been outperformed by a close friend on a self-relevant task should be highly motivated to engage in behaviors aimed at restoring a positive self-evaluation. In the context of the experiment, these participants would offer less help to their friends (in an effort to lower their friend's performance) than to the strangers. When a task has little self-relevance, however, being outperformed is not very threatening to one's positive self-evaluation and may even result in a more positive self-evaluation because participants can bask in the reflected glory of their friend's good performance. So, when the task is low in relevance, participants who want to maintain a positive self-evaluation should help their friend more than the stranger.

Keep in mind, though, that the preceding predictions hold only to the extent that the participants are motivated to restore a positive self-evaluation. If self-affirmation and social comparison are in the service of the same general goal to maintain a positive self-evaluation, then affirming the self should reduce the motivation to bolster one's self-evaluation. Thus, participants who were not given the opportunity to affirm the self should help the stranger more than the friend when outperformed by the friend on a task of high self-relevance, but should help the friend more than the stranger when outperformed on a task of low self-relevance. Participants given the opportunity to affirm the self, on the other hand, should not display this pattern because the self-affirmation provided an alternate means to maintain a positive self-evaluation.

The results were consistent with these predictions. The results suggest, therefore, that self-affirmation and social comparison serve the same general self-evaluative goal. Subsequent research has shown that the substitutability among very different appearing mechanisms for maintaining self-evaluation is quite general (Tesser et al., 2000). Studies have shown that engaging in self-affirmation can reduce dissonance motivation as well as social comparison motivation, threats to self-evaluation via social comparison can increase dissonance motivation and the motivation to affirm the self, and threats to self-esteem via cognitive dissonance can increase the motivation to engage in social comparison strategies and self-affirmation strategies for maintaining a positive self-evaluation. The generality of substitutability among these disparate self-evaluation mechanisms suggest that they are not motivated by independent systems. Rather, each appears to be a means to attain a more general goal: the maintenance of a favorable self-evaluation. This general substitutability only makes sense in the context of a motivational model.

Docility

The third feature that identifies behavior as motivated is docility. This is the feature Tolman (1932) considered to be the most important marker of motivated behavior. He developed this belief in large part by watching animals attempt to escape from a puzzle box. He noticed that the animals would begin by emitting a wide range of responses but, over trials, drop the responses that did not lead to escape and perform more and more quickly the responses that proved to be successful. In other words, the animals selected among their many behaviors those that facilitated progress toward their goal. This selectivity makes no sense in the absence of a goal. Without a goal, one response is as good as another.

In humans, docility has been addressed in research on the development of skilled behavior (Spaeth, 1972) and expertise (Posner & Rothbart, 2007). In brief, the conclusions of this research closely parallel the observations of Tolman (1932). When first performing a task, individuals have difficulty distinguishing relevant from irrelevant responses. With practice, though, individuals begin to notice that some responses facilitate goal progress more than others. So, individuals maintain the former and eliminate the latter. They also organize their responses into higher-order units that require less and less attention to be performed.

When a person first begins to play the guitar, for example, he/she may not know how to hold the guitar, where to place his/her fingers, how to strum the strings, and so on. With practice, though, the person may begin to form chords, chord patterns, and then whole songs. Eventually, the person may become an expert, playing the chords cleanly, and progressing through complex chord patterns in skillful, melodic ways. This progression would not occur, of course, if at each stage, the individual had not dropped out the errors and maintained the behaviors that brought him/her closer to the desired goal of being a good guitar player. It is this dynamic relation between an individual's actions relative to the attainment of the goal that is the essence of docility. Passively guided behaviors do not display this kind of behavior–goal dynamism.

It is ironic, therefore, that behavior can become automatized precisely because individuals become especially skilled at them (Shiffrin & Schneider, 1977). Once individuals have developed a pattern of responding, they can emit this pattern with little attention to the details or the consequences. Doing so, however, reduces docility and yields a behavior that is no longer truly motivated. These well-practiced behaviors may reflect mindlessness (Langer & Imber, 1979) or misapplied competence (Reason, 1984).

In the absence of docility, individuals guide their behavior on the basis of well-established knowledge structures, such as scripts, and pay little attention to the details of their environment. For example, after purchasing an airline ticket, a traveler may automatically follow the "polite conversation" script. So when the travel agents says, "Have a good trip!" the traveler may reply, "You too," even though the agent is not taking a trip.

Truly motivated behavior requires a certain degree of updating and self-regulation. Individuals need to select the responses that help them attain their goal efficiently and reliably, but they also need to maintain an adaptive flexibility that allows them to adjust their behaviors should these behaviors no longer facilitate goal attainment. Passive or nonmotivated behavior does not display this dynamic flexibility.

Affect as a Marker of Motivated Behavior

Early motivational researchers speculated on the importance of persistence-until, equifinality, and docility. Research since then has not only supported the importance of these markers but has also highlighted two additional markers of motivated behavior: affect and effort. We discuss each in turn.

Given that a goal is a desired end point, it is not surprising to find that attainment of a goal is associated with positive affect, whereas nonattainment of a goal is associated with negative affect. Indeed, we can often see the state of a goal system by simply observing the affect in a person's face. Tesser, Millar, and Moore (1988), for example, invited participants to bring a friend with them to participate in a study. The participants and their friends were isolated from one another and asked to perform several trials of an esthetic judgment task and several trials of a logical thinking task. For some participants, logical thinking was relatively more relevant to their self-definition, whereas for others, esthetic judgments were more relevant to their self-definition. After each trial, a computer provided participants with feedback they had either outperformed their friend or been outperformed by their friend. Unknown to the participants, their facial expressions while receiving this performance feedback was videotaped.

According to the self-evaluation maintenance model (Tesser, 1988), individuals have a general higher-order goal to maintain a positive evaluation of the self. As noted earlier, individuals can attain a positive self-evaluation by outperforming a close other (e.g., a friend) on a self-relevant task or by being outperformed by a close other on a task that is not related to one's self-evaluation. This means that expressions of positive affect should be higher in these two conditions than in the other conditions (e.g., being outperformed by a stranger on a self-relevant task).

The videotapes were rated for the pleasantness of facial expression by coders who were blind to the experimental condition. The facial affect mapped nicely onto the pattern of goal attainment specified by the self-evaluation maintenance model. Participants displayed more positive facial expressions after outperforming a close other on a self-relevant task or after being outperformed by a close other on a non-self-relevant task. In other words, participants displayed more positive affect when they had attained their goal of a positive self-evaluation than when they had not.

It is important to keep in mind, though, that goal pursuit is not an either/or phenomenon. Individuals may be making progress toward their goals or retreating from them, and this movement may be either fast or slow. Thus, a full understanding of the relation between goals and affect will have to take into consideration not only the extent of discrepancy, but also the direction and rate of movement relative to the goal (Carver & Scheier, 1990). The relation between these three variables was captured succinctly by Hsee and Abelson (1991).

A second relation between outcome and satisfaction . . . is that satisfaction depends on the change in the outcome . . . the change relation can be interpreted in two forms: the displacement relation and the velocity relation. By displacement relation, we mean that satisfaction depends on the directional distance (i.e., displacement) between the original (reference) outcome position and the position after a change. The more (less) an outcome departs from its original position in a positive direction, the greater (less) the satisfaction. By velocity relation, on the other hand, we mean that satisfaction at a given time depends on the rate (i.e., velocity) at which the outcome is changing. The more (less) positive the velocity, the greater (less) the satisfaction. . . . Consider an example of how these two notions can lead to different predictions. Because velocity (when it is uniform) can be defined as the quotient of displacement over the time it takes, for the same amount of displacement there can be different values of velocity depending on the time. Suppose that two persons have the same displacement of +$200 in their savings. For one person, the time for the change is 40 days, and, hence, the velocity (suppose it is uniform) is +$5 per day; for the other person, the time is 10 days, and, hence, the velocity is +$20 per day. The displacement notion would predict the two persons to be equally satisfied because the final results of change are the same. On the other hand, the velocity notion would predict the second person to be happier because the velocity is more positive. (p. 341)

In a series of studies concerning imagined outcomes presented by questionnaire or computer graphics Hsee and Abelson (1991; see also Lawrence, Carver, & Scheier, 2002) found that all three proposed determinants of affect affected self-reported satisfaction. Goal attainment led to greater satisfaction than goal nonattainment, movement toward the goal led to greater satisfaction than movement away from the goal, and faster movement elicited stronger affective reactions. Obviously, these affect–performance relations make sense only in the context of motivated behavior. If behavior is not motivated toward a desired end point, then there can be no attainment, movement, or rate of movement.

Effort as a Marker of Motivated Behavior

A fifth marker of motivated behavior is effort. There is a general tendency for effort to increase with motivation, especially in the face of obstacles. The relations among effort, motivation, and obstacles to goal attainment have been investigated by Jack Brehm and colleagues (e.g., Wright & Brehm, 1989). They suggested that the effort expended on goal pursuit via a particular path is a function of the difficulty of the path, the likelihood that the path will pay off in goal satisfaction, and the value of the goal.

According to value expectancy theory (e.g., Atkinson & Burch, 1970), task effort is a function of the product of the value of the goal and the probability of reaching the goal. In contrast, Brehm and Wright suggested that the expected value is really the "potential" or maximum effort that an individual will invest in any instrumental response or particular path to a goal. Actual effort will be a function of task demands but only up to a point. Effort in a task will not exceed the expected value of the goal. If a task demands more than the value of the goal, then the individual will invest very little in the task regardless of task difficulty. If one's skills or ability is not up to the task, or task completion appears impossible, again, very little energy will be recruited for the task regardless of difficulty.

There is now a body of work consistent with Brehm's suggestions (Brehm & Self, 1989). In earlier research, effort had been indexed by in a variety of ways: running speed in animals, amplitude of instrumental responses, persistence on task, latent learning, and energization of irrelevant behaviors. In this research program, however, heart-related physiological measures of energization frequently have been used. Regardless of whether a task requires physical exertion or mental exertion, systolic blood pressure (SBP) and heart rate (HR) have been shown to be related to the amount of energy an individual subsequently invests in the task.

In a variety of elegant studies, Wright (1996) has shown that changes in SBP and HR behave as predicted by Brehm's theory. In one study (Wright & Gregorich, 1989), for example, participants were confronted with either a difficult or easy memorization task. Half the participants were led to believe that success on the task was very likely to lead to a prize, the remaining participants were led to believe that success at the task had only a small chance of leading to the prize. SBP was measured before working on the task. As predicted when success on the task was unlikely to lead to a prize there was little change in SBP regardless of task difficulty; however, when task success was highly likely to lead to a prize SBP covaried with difficulty,

In another study (Wright, Shaw, & Jones, 1990), incentive value was manipulated. Participants learned that they could avoid either a loud uncomfortable noise or a mild noise. Some participants learned that avoidance was contingent on successfully completing a difficult memorization task, others learned that avoidance was contingent on successfully completing an easy task. Brehm's theory suggests that task energization should covary with difficulty when the incentive is large but less so with a smaller incentive. Measure of SBP and HR were used as indicants of energy being recruited for the task. The results were consistent with the theory. When the incentive was high (loud noise) SBP and HR covaried with difficulty, greater task difficulty resulted in greater mobilization of energy. When the incentive was small, this relationship with task difficulty disappeared. These effects make sense only in the context of motivated behavior.

Distinguishing Passive from Motivated Behavior

There is accumulating evidence that passively priming individuals with stimuli that carry behavioral implications (e.g., a stereotype) can influence the behavior of the individuals. As noted earlier, exposing participants to words related to the elderly stereotype induces people to walk more slowly (Bargh et al., 1996). It is not clear, though, that this walking is motivated in the sense that we have used the term in this chapter. To be considered truly motivated, behavior must demonstrate persistence-until, equifinality, docility, and affective and effort-related consequences. Although we know of no evidence that addresses this issue directly, we suspect that behaviors that are the result of passive priming do not reveal these features.

Put yourself in the place of a participant in the Bargh et al. (1996) study. You are subtly exposed to a series of words associated with the stereotype of the elderly. Then, you exit the experiment and walk down the hall. As it turns out, you walk more slowly than participants not primed with words associated with the elderly. You clearly had no conscious goal to walk like an elderly person. The question, though, is whether you really had any goal at all? Were you motivated to walk like an elderly person? These questions can be answered by seeing the extent to which your behavior demonstrates the five markers of motivated behavior.

1. *Persistence-until.* When you were walking slowly, what was your goal (conscious or otherwise)? What would you use as evidence that you had attained that goal? If you had been prevented from walking slowly, would you have resumed slow walking as soon as you had the opportunity? Conversely, would you have stopped walking slowly and resumed your normal pace once you had successfully walked slowly? Had you not been motivated to exit the building, would you have experienced a desire to get up and walk?

2. *Equifinality.* Is there more than one means to attain your goal? If so, what behavior other than walking would have allowed you to attain that goal? Had you been unable to walk slowly, would you have tried to engage in some other behavior (e.g., forgetfulness, dwelling on the past) that would have allowed you to play out aspects of your stereotype of an elderly person? Would engaging in one of these behaviors reduce your tendency to walk slowly?

3. *Docility.* Would you alter your walking as a function of its success in allowing you to attain your goal? What reference value would you use to determine whether you needed to speed up or slow down?

4. *Affect.* Would your experience of positive affect increase or decrease as your own walking more or less approximated that of an elderly person? Would your affective experiences be influenced by the speed with which you were able to approximate the gait of an elderly person? What is the standard by which you would you measure your rate of progress toward the goal? How quickly should you be able to approximate the gait of an elderly person?

5. *Effort.* If you encountered difficulties in your attempt to walk like an elderly person, would you increase the amount of effort you devoted to walking slowly? Would the amount of effort you devoted to trying to walk slowly also vary as a result of chances of successfully matching the gait of an elderly person? If you met with continued frustration, would you eventually abandon your efforts to walk slowly?

Obviously, we have no way to provide definitive answers to these questions. The kind of data needed to provide such answers have not been collected. We suspect, though, that the answers to the questions would indicate that passively primed behavior does not manifest the features of true motivated behavior. We consider it more likely that such behavior reflects mindlessness (Langer & Imber, 1979) or misapplied competence (Reason, 1984).

In sum, the distinction between motivated and passive behavior is relevant to a large number of areas in psychology (e.g., dissonance, stereotyping, attribution). Researchers in these areas, however, have tended not to collect the kind of data needed to make a strong claim about whether a behavior is motivated or passive. We noted that the distinction has been important in the field for years, and markers of motivated behavior have been identified and empirically supported. Perhaps the best way to determine whether a behavior is motivated or passive is to assess the extent to which it manifests persistence-until, equifinality, docility, and affective and effort-related consequences.

References

Atkinson, J. W., & Birch, D. A. (1970). *A dynamic theory of action*. New York: Wiley.

Bargh, J., Chen, M., & Burrows, L. (1996). Automaticity of social behavior: Direct effects of trait construct and stereotype activation on action. *Journal of Personality and Social Psychology, 71*, 230–244.

Bem, D. J. (1967). Self-perception: An alternative interpretation of cognitive dissonance phenomena. *Psychological Review, 74*, 183–200.

Brehm, J. W., & Self, E. (1989). The intensity of motivation. *Annual Review of Psychology, 40*, 109–131.

Butterfield, E. C. (1954). The interruption of tasks: Methodological, factual, and theoretical issues. *Psychological Bulletin, 62*, 309–322.

Carver, C. S., & Scheier, M. F. (1990). Origins and functions of positive and negative affect: A control process view. *Psychological Review, 997*, 19–35.

Fazio, R. H., Zanna, M. P., & Cooper, J. (1977). Dissonance and self-perception: An integrative view of each theory's proper domain of application. *Journal of Experimental Social Psychology, 13*, 464–479.

Fein, S., & Spencer, S. J. (1997). Prejudice as self-image maintenance: Affirming the self through derogating others. *Journal of Personality and Social Psychology, 73*, 31–44.

Festinger, L. (1957). *A theory of cognitive dissonance*. Stanford, CA: Stanford University Press.

Fishbach, A., Friedman, R., & Kruglanski, A. (2003). Leading us not into temptation: Momentary allurements elicit overriding goal activation. *Journal of Personality and Social Psychology, 84*, 296–309.

Förster, J., Liberman, N., & Higgins, E. T. (2005). Accessibility from active and fulfilled goals. *Journal of Experimental Social Psychology, 41*, 220–239.

Gollwitzer, P. M., Earle, W. B., & Stephan, W. G. (1982). Affect as a determinant of egotism: Residual excitation and performance attributions. *Journal of Personality and Social Psychology, 43*, 702–709.

Goschke, T., & Kuhl, J. (1993). Representation of intentions: Persisting activation in memory. *Journal of Experimental Psychology: Learning, Memory, and Cognition, 19,* 1211–1226.

Greenwald, A. G., Banaji, M. R., & Rudman, L. A. (2002). A unified theory of implicit attitudes, stereotypes, self-esteem, and self-concept. *Psychological Review, 109,* 3–25.

Hsee, C. K., & Abelson, R. P. (1991). Velocity relation: Satisfaction as a function of the first derivative of outcome over time. *Journal of Personality and Social Psychology, 60*(3), 341–346.

Koole, S. L., Smeets, K., van Knippenberg, A., & Dijksterhuis, A. (1999). The cessation of rumination through self-affirmation. *Journal of Personality and Social Psychology, 77,* 111–125.

Kuhl, J., & Weiss, M. (1994). Performance deficits following uncontrollable failure: Impaired action control or global attributions and generalized expectancy deficits. In J. Kuhl & J. Beckmann (Eds.), *Volition and personality: Action versus state orientation* (pp. 317–328). Seattle: Hogrefe.

Langer, E. J., & Imber, L. G. (1979). When practice makes imperfect: Debilitating effects of overlearning. *Journal of Personality and Social Psychology, 37,* 2014–2024.

Lawrence, J. W., Carver, C. S., & Scheier, M. F. (2002). Velocity toward goal attainment in immediate experience as a determinant of affect. *Journal of Applied Social Psychology, 32,* 788–802.

Lewin, K. (1938). *The conceptual representation and measurement of psychological forces.* Durham, NC: Duke University Press.

Marsh, R. L., Hicks, J. L., & Bink, M. L. (1998). Activation of completed, uncompleted, and partially completed intentions. *Journal of Experimental Psychology: Learning, Memory, and Cognition, 24,* 350–361.

Martin, L. L., & Tesser, A. (1989). Toward a motivational and structural theory of ruminative thought. In J. S. Uleman & J. A. Bargh (Eds.), *Unintended thought* (pp. 306–326). New York: Guilford Press.

Martin, L. L., & Tesser, A. (1996). Some ruminative thoughts. In R. S. Wyer (Ed.), *Advances in social cognition* (Vol. 9, pp. 1–47). Mahwah, NJ: Erlbaum.

Martin, L. L., & Tesser, A. (2006). Extending the goal progress theory of rumination: Goal reevaluation and growth. In L. Sanna & E. Chang (Eds.), *Judgments over time: The interplay of thoughts, feelings, and behaviors* (pp. 145–162). New York: Oxford University Press.

Millar, K. U., Tesser, A., & Millar, M. G. (1988). The effects of a threatening life event on behavior sequences and intrusive thought: A self-disruption explanation. *Cognitive Therapy & Research, 12,* 441–457.

Miller, D. T., & Ross, M. (1975). Self-serving biases in the attribution of causality: Fact or fiction? *Psychological Bulletin, 82,* 213–225.

Posner, M. I., & Rothbart, M. K. (2007). Expertise. In M. I. Posner & M. K. Rothbart (Eds.), *Educating the human brain* (pp. 189–208). Washington, DC: American Psychological Association.

Reason, J. (1984, September/October). The psychopathology of everyday slips. *The Sciences,* 45–49.

Rothermund, K. (2003). Automatic vigilance for task-related information: Perseverance after failure and inhibition after success. *Memory & Cognition, 31,* 343–352.

Shiffrin, R. M., & Schneider, W. (1977). Controlled and automatic human information processing: II. Perceptual learning, automatic attending and a general theory. *Psychological Review, 84,* 127–190.

Spaeth, R. K. (1972). Maximizing goal attainment. *Research Quarterly, 43,* 337–361.

Steele, C. (1988). The psychology of self-affirmation: Sustaining the integrity of the self. In L. Berkowitz (Ed.), *Advances in experimental social psychology* (Vol. 21, pp. 261–302). New York: Academic Press.

Steele, C. M., & Liu, T. J. (1983). Dissonance processes as self-affirmation. *Journal of Personality and Social Psychology. 45,* 5–19.

Tesser, A. (1988). Toward a self-evaluation maintenance model of social behavior. In L. Berkowitz (Ed.), *Advances in experimental social psychology* (Vol. 21, pp. 181–227). San Diego: Academic Press.

Tesser, A., & Cornell, D. P. (1991). On the confluence of self processes. *Journal of Experimental Social Psychology, 27,* 501–526.

Tesser, A., Crepaz, N., Collins, J. C., Cornell, D., & Beach, S. R. H. (2000). Confluence of self defense mechanisms: On integrating the self zoo. *Personality and Social Psychology Bulletin, 26,* 1476–1489.

Tesser, A., Martin, L. L., & Cornell, D. (1996). On the substitutability of self-protective mechanisms. In P. M. Gollwitzer & J. A. Bargh (Eds.), *The psychology of action: Linking motivation and cognition to behavior* (pp. 48–68). New York: Guilford Press.

Tesser, A., Millar, M., & Moore, J. (1988). Some affective consequences of social comparison and reflection processes: The pain and pleasure of being close. *Journal of Personality and Social Psychology, 54,* 49–61.

Tolman, E. C. (1932). *Purposive behaviors in animals and men.* New York: Century/Random House UK.

Woodworth, R. S. (1921). *Psychology: A study of mental life.* New York: Columbia University Press.

Wright, R. A. (1996). Brehm's theory of motivation as a model of effort and cardiovascular response. In P. M. Gollwitzer & J. A. Bargh (Eds.), *The psychology of action: Linking cognition and motivatgion to behavior* (pp. 424–453). New York: Guilford Press.

Wright, R. A., & Brehm, J. W. (1989). Energization and goal attractiveness. In I. A. Irvin (Ed.). *Goal concepts in personality and social psychology* (pp. 169–210). Hillsdale, NJ: Erlbaum.

Wright, R. A., & Gregorich, S. (1989). Difficulty and instrumentality of imminent behavior as determinants of cardiovascular response and self reported energy. *Psychophysiology, 26,* 586–592.

Wright, R. A., Shaw, L. L., & Jones, C. R. (1990). Task demand and cardiovascular response magnitude: Further evidence of the mediating role of success importance. *Journal of Personality and Social Psychology, 59,* 1250–1260.

Zeigarnik, B. (1938). On finished and unfinished tasks. In W. D. Ellis (Ed.), *A source book of gestalt psychology* (pp. 300–314). New York: Harcourt, Brace, & World. (Reprinted and condensed from *Psychologishe Forschung, 1927, 9,* 1–85.)

CHAPTER 11

Normal and Pathological Consequences of Encountering Difficulties in Monitoring Progress toward Goals

NIRA LIBERMAN
REUVEN DAR

P eople pursue different goals. In an interview, we try to impress the interviewer. We study before an exam with the goal to understand and remember the study materials. We wash our hands to make them clean. But how do we know when to stop, and how do we know, in the process of goal pursuit, whether we need to exert more effort or may relax our effort? This chapter addresses these questions from the perspective of discrepancy-reduction models. We address difficulties in monitoring progress toward goals and discuss their antecedents and consequences. Finally, we propose to conceptualize obsessive–compulsive disorder as a pathology in monitoring goal progress and discuss its symptoms from that perspective.

We first review the basic components of the discrepancy-reduction process, and then discuss the motivational, emotional, and cognitive consequences of tight versus loose monitoring. We then turn to examine difficulties in monitoring: their antecedents (which goals are difficult to monitor) and consequences (possible strategies of coping with these difficulties).

Goal Pursuit via Discrepancy Reduction: An Overview

Lewin's Field Theory: Goals as Quasi-Needs

In Lewin's (1951) field theory, goals are viewed as quasi-needs. Like a need (e.g., hunger), a goal involves a discrepancy between an actual state and a desired state, a discrepancy that creates tension that a person tries to reduce by fulfilling the goal. This tension is motivation, a force directed toward goal fulfillment. According to Lewin (1951), goal-related tension is also reflected in the cognitive system as a preoccupation with (and better memory for) an unfulfilled goal. Modern cognitive theories showed that, indeed, an active goal enhances the accessibility of goal-related constructs whereas fulfillment of the goal inhibits the accessibility of goal-related constructs (Förster, Liberman, & Higgins, 2005; Liberman, Förster, & Higgins, 2007; for a review see Förster, Liberman, & Friedman, 2007). Unfulfilled and failed goals from which a person does not disengage create rumination—repeated and often-intrusive thoughts about the incomplete goal (Martin, Tesser, & Cornell, 1996). For example, research on current concerns has shown that they often emerge in dreams (Klinger, 1996). We refer to this state of being preoccupied with and focused on a goal and feeling motivated and energized in relation to the goal as "motivational tension" (to be distinguished from anxiety, e.g., due to anticipating a negative outcome).

Cybernetic Models of Goal Pursuit: The Feedback Loop and the Metamonitoring Loop

Lewin's field theory (1951) suggested that people work toward closing the discrepancy between the current state and a desired end-state, but it did not specify the process of discrepancy detection and reduction. This process was elucidated later in cybernetic models of goal-driven (i.e., teleological) systems. Miller, Galanter, and Pribram (1960) describe goal-directed actions in terms of a test–operate–test–exit (TOTE) system (also termed the "principle of feedback control"), in which the current state is compared to a goal state, exits the loop if no discrepancy is detected, and operates to reduce the discrepancy if a discrepancy is detected, after which the test phase is repeated.

Carver and Scheier (1999) added to the TOTE model a metamonitoring feedback loop, which takes as input the rate of discrepancy reduction, compares it to a reference value, and signals a need to speed up or an option to slow down, depending on the outcome of the comparison. In this model, the metamonitoring loop produces emotion. An acceptable rate of discrepancy reduction enhances positive emotion, whereas an unacceptably low rate of discrepancy reduction produces negative emotion (see also Hsee & Abelson, 1991; Hsee, Abelson, & Salovey, 1991). This means that people feel good not only when they attain a goal (i.e., eliminate the discrepancy), but also when they believe that they are making good progress toward goal attainment, irrespective of the discrepancy from goal attainment. For example, when only starting to work toward a goal, the discrepancy to the goal is relatively large, but rate of progress is high relative to the preengagement stage, and therefore the early stage of goal pursuit would be characterized by high spirits and positive affect. In contrast, attaining a goal (closing the discrepancy) is often characterized by slowing down, and thus produces negative emotion: the feeling of anticlimax. For example, upon completing a long and torturous graduate program and finally submitting a copy of the Ph.D. thesis, students often find themselves discouraged and sad instead of feeling the long-anticipated elation.

Rate of Approach and Avoidance

It is possible to look at rate of progress in moving away from the starting point, as well as at rate of progress toward the end point (Fishbach & Zhang, 2008). For example, a student who has to read 200 pages for an exam may consider the pages read so far or the pages that are still left. Advancing from page 20 to page 30 may be thought of as advancing by 50% of the material already covered (10/20), or as reducing by 6% the material that is still left to cover (10/170). Some goals allow monitoring progress from the starting point and the end point, and whether the former or the latter is chosen may depend on many situational, personal, and content factors. For example, it seems that initially the starting point is more salient, whereas close to goal completion, the end point is more salient. Correspondingly, early on, people would tend to monitor progress with respect to what has been done already, whereas later on, they would shift to regulating toward what still needs to be achieved. Regulatory focus (Higgins, 1997, 1998) may also moderate monitoring tendencies. A prevention focus, because of its concern with the presence and absence of negative outcomes, is likely to increase the tendency to monitor progress toward the end point. Conversely, a promotion focus, because of its concern with the presence or absence of positive outcomes, would increase the tendency to monitor progress from the starting point.

It should be emphasized, however, that for some goals the starting point and the end point are not equally clear. For example, in avoidance goals (e.g., in running away from a terrifying snake) the starting point is oftentimes specific but the end point is not, and one can only examine rate of progress from the starting point (Carver & Scheier, 1999; Brendl & Higgins, 1996).

Embedded Feedback Loops: Goal Hierarchies

Powers (1973) and Carver and Scheier (1990, 1999) introduced the notion of goal hierarchies, according to which each goal is subordinated to a higher-level goal, which answers the question of why the focal goal is being pursued, and is superordinate to a lower-level goal, which answers the question of how the focal goal is to be pursued (see also Vallacher & Wegner, 1987). For example, for the goal "call a friend" a superordinate goal, which answers the question why we call a friend, might be "express support," and a subordinate goal, which answers the question how we call a friend, may be "get the friend's phone number." In this hierarchy, "being goals" (e.g., to be successful, to be moral) are superordinate to "doing goals" (e.g., maintain social contact) and still lower are motor control goals (e.g., call a friend; Carver & Scheier, 1999). At the lowest level of the hierarchy are automatic physical actions that cannot be further reduced (e.g., take a pen, descend the stairs) in the sense that we cannot meaningfully specify how we do these actions. At the highest level of the hierarchy are basic needs that cannot be further reduced to (or derived from) other needs. Various theories identify the most fundamental human need as the pursuit of happiness (Gilbert, 2006), managing the terror of our imminent death (Solomon, Greenberg, & Pyszczynski, 1991, 2004), spreading one's genes (Dawkins, 2006), or seeking self-determination via autonomy, mastery and relatedness (Deci & Ryan, 2000).

In the hierarchical goal system, once a goal is fulfilled and the system exits the discrepancy-reduction loop of the goal in question, it immediately shifts to a superordinate goal, and, correspondingly, to regulate toward reducing discrepancies from the new goal. For example, once a person finds the friend's phone number, the goal of calling the friend is resumed, and further actions are taken toward fulfilling it. In this sense, achieving a goal is equivalent to making progress toward a superordinate goal.[1]

The Effect of Practice: Automatization

Some goals are pursued in an automatic, proceduralized manner. These goals do not require specification of subgoals. For example, most of us already know fairly well how to drive from our home to the office and do not require breaking this action down into subgoals (e.g., get into the car, get out of the parking lot, etc.).

Repeated goal-directed actions become easier, requiring less and less effort, and in that sense become automatic (Schneider & Shiffrin, 1977). With repetition, actions may also acquire other features of automaticity (Bargh, 1994): They may be more easily activated by a relevant cue and more difficult to stop once initiated. When a goal is performed in an automatic way, it requires only minimal monitoring, and the monitoring system may remain at a higher, superordinate level. For example, if driving to the office is automatic, a person can monitor the superordinate level ("today I need to prepare the week's teaching") instead of monitoring the subordinate goal of driving to the office.

Difficulties in Goal Pursuit: Lowering Level of Identification

When the monitoring system encounters difficulty in goal pursuit, the system shifts to a subordinate goal (Vallacher & Wegner, 1987). This process may be seen as the flip side of automatization, which fosters shifting to a superordinate goal as goal pursuit becomes easier. For example, when we want to call a friend and do not find her phone number, we may shift to a lower-level goal of finding the phone book. A difficulty in performing an automatic goal is likewise accompanied with adopting a lower-level goal, which, in this case, means deautomatization of performance. For example, if our usual way to the office is blocked, we will explicitly set getting to the office as a goal and will pursue it in a controlled way, instead of in the habitual, automatic mode.

The Effect of Monitoring

In the remainder of this chapter, we look more closely at the monitoring process. We examine some implications of monitoring (specifically of tight vs. loose monitoring) for motivation, emotion, self-evaluation, and cognition. We then turn to difficulties in monitoring and examine the conditions that give rise to such difficulties and the consequences of encountering difficulties in monitoring.

Motivation and Persistence

Suppose that you are working toward a goal but have not yet reached it: for example, you are trying to find a supermarket but have not found one yet. In that situation, it is easier to persist if you know that your efforts generate progress than if you do not have any feedback on progress. For example, you would be more likely to continue looking for a supermarket if you knew that you were getting closer to it, compared to a situation in which you did not have any indication of getting closer to your destination. Indeed, a vast literature has documented the advantages of extensive monitoring for motivation and persistence. For example, consider the classic finding in Locke and Latham's (1990, 2002) goal-setting theory that setting specific difficult goals (e.g., write 20 pages of the book every day) is more motivating (i.e., produce better performance, higher persistence, mobilization of more effort) than urging people to do their best. Importantly, these authors note that "Goal setting is . . . usually only effective when feedback allows performance to be tracked in relation to one's goals (Locke & Latham, 1990, p. 241; see Erez, 1977, for a similar point). It seems, then, that the motivational advantages of concrete goals depend on continuous feedback on progress toward the goal. In education, too, it is widely recognized that setting specific goals and providing feedback on progress increases persistence and improves performance (Kulik & Kulik, 1988; Bandura & Schunk, 1981), a principle that is widely advised in educational programs (Schunk, 2000).

Monitoring progress toward goal attainment creates a state of attention and concentration on goal-relevant activities. It keeps resources mobilized toward achieving the goal and minimizes distraction by non-goal-related activities (Locke & Latham, 2002; Schunk, 2000). For example, a tourist who looks up her map more frequently to assess her distance from a destination (e.g., the Eiffel Tower in Paris) would be more concentrated on reaching that destination, perhaps at the expense of not noticing other attractions on the way.

We mentioned earlier that goals enhance the accessibility of goal-related constructs, whereas goal fulfillment inhibits their accessibility (Förster et al., 2005). Although research is lacking on how monitoring is related to these effects, it is reasonable to predict that goal-related accessibility and postfulfillment inhibition would be more pronounced with more extensive monitoring. For example, we would predict that a tourist who closely monitors her progress to the Eiffel Tower in Paris would experience enhanced accessibility of related constructs compared to a less extensive monitor. Moreover, we predict that a person who closely monitors her progress would experience a stronger sense of completion after completing the visit, which would manifest itself in a stronger postfulfillment inhibition effect.

Emotion

Carver and Scheier (1999) proposed that during goal pursuit, emotions derive from registering sufficient or insufficient progress. An acceptable rate of discrepancy reduction is said to enhance expectancy and positive emotion, whereas an unacceptably low rate of discrepancy reduction is said to reduce expectancy and produce negative emotion. This analysis implies that more extensive monitoring would be accompanied with more intense emotions, positive and negative. For example, the tourist who more closely monitors her progress toward the Eiffel Tower, compared to a less intense monitor, would be happier upon noticing progress and more anxious upon noticing insufficient progress.

Difficulties in Monitoring Progress toward Discrepancy Reduction

Discrepancy-reduction models of goal pursuit provide a useful framework for thinking about human goal-directed behavior. These models originated with cybernetic models in engineering and were initially designed to describe fairly mechanistic goals, such as grasping an object, regulating the temperature in a room, or driving to a specific destination. Many of the goals that people pursue in everyday life, however, are of a different sort. Consider the goal of making a good impression on the interviewer, the goal of studying material for an exam or the goal of being open minded. How would one know if and when the goal is achieved? How would one know if enough progress is being made toward achieving the goal? Furthermore, when increasing efforts toward the goal, how would one know if the extra effort produced a corresponding decrease in the discrepancy between one's current state and the desired end-state?

More generally, how can discrepancy-reduction models apply to situations that are characterized by difficulties in monitoring goal attainment, rate of progress, and/or difficulties in evaluating the contingency between effort and rate of progress? We propose that when people encounter difficulty in monitoring, they do one of two things, which are quite similar to what people do when encountering any other difficulty: They either relax monitoring or increase monitoring attempts. In what follows, we first discuss the different types of difficulties in monitoring discrepancy reduction, then look at different types of goals that are likely to cause such difficulties. We then discuss the consequences of relaxing monitoring and of increasing monitoring attempts. Finally, we discuss factors that moderate the choice of relaxing versus increasing monitoring (see Figure 11.1 for a schematic representation of the main points).

Conditions that Give Rise to Difficulties in Monitoring

There are different reasons for why monitoring of discrepancy reduction may prove difficult. First, vague end-states may make it difficult to register goal attainment as well as to calculate the discrepancy from the current state. For example, the goals of "becoming famous" or "being a considerate person" provide only a vague idea of an end-state that would qualify as goal attainment. A second possible source of difficulty in monitoring is that it is often difficult to assess progress. For example, if one is being interviewed with the goal of being admitted to a graduate program, it might be difficult to get a clear sense of how well one is doing in closing the gap

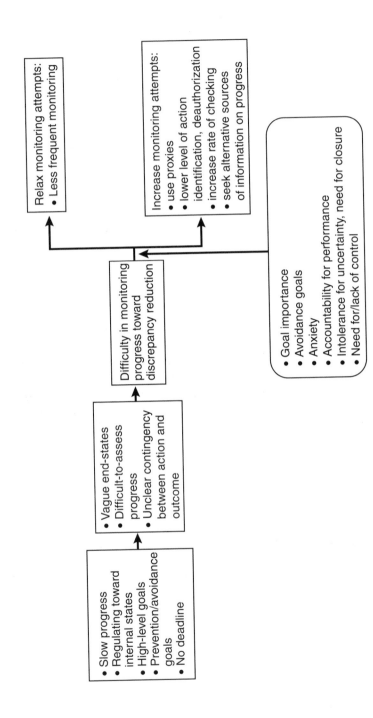

FIGURE 11.1. Causes and consequences of a difficult-to-monitor progress toward goal fulfillment.

to that (relatively clear) end-state. A third source of difficulty in monitoring is when the contingency between one's efforts and progress is unclear. For example, when competing for a job, a candidate may receive positive feedback on his chances along the way but feel uncertain as to what action on his part enhanced his or her prospects. Situations may include different combinations of these difficulties, as we see immediately. Regardless of the exact type of difficulty, it may have important implications for the monitoring process. We will now turn to examine several types of goal-pursuit situations that typically give rise to such difficulties.

Which Goal Pursuit Situations Are Difficult to Monitor?

Sometimes progress is slow and therefore is difficult to monitor. For example, on a diet, weight loss is slow and does not allow hour-to-hour (and even day-to-day) monitoring. Noticeable progress occurs over larger chunks of time, such as weeks or months. Similarly, children may find it difficult to monitor the effect of healthy food on their purported faster growing and increasing strength, which makes it rather difficult for them to pursue this goal.

Difficulty in monitoring may also arise when people regulate toward goals that are internal states and feelings, such as being in love or feeling interested in their job. Even understanding (e.g., understand the study material) is an internal state rather than an observable and easily identifiable end-state. Many times, such situations promote all three types of difficulty: difficulty in identifying the end-state (do I feel love?), difficulty in monitoring progress (am I getting more in love or less so?), and difficulty in understanding the effort–outcome contingency (does reading aloud make me understand the material better?)

To many people, regulating progress toward end-states that are feelings and emotions poses a considerable challenge. It is possible, however, that some people posses a clearer sense of their internal states as well as a better ability to control them (i.e., a clearer contingency between their efforts and emotional outcomes). Indeed, "emotional intelligence" (EI) is defined as the ability to identify and control emotional states (Mayer, Salovey, & Caruso, 2004). People high in EI would be more effective in regulating toward goals that are defined in terms of emotions and internal states. For example, consider a person who tries to feel less angry at the boss after being denied promotion. A person high in EI would be more likely to find strategies to do that and to monitor changes in her level of anger.

High-level goals tend to be vaguer than low-level goals, and "being" goals tend to be vaguer than "doing" goals. For example, "to be a friendly

person" is vaguer than "to go to the party." It is therefore oftentimes difficult to monitor discrepancy reduction toward higher-level goals than
toward lower-level goals. As we discuss later, lowering the level at which
a goal is identified may be used as a way to overcome the difficulty that
often accompanies regulating toward higher-level goals. Thus, instead of
pursuing the goal of "being knowledgeable," which is difficult to regulate
toward, a person may adopt the goal of "reading at least two newspapers
every day," which is more concrete and easier to monitor.

Self-determination theory (Deci & Ryan, 2000) distinguishes between
goals that subserve self-determination needs (the goals of competence,
relatedness, and autonomy), which people are intrinsically motivated to
pursue, and extrinsically motivated or introjected goals. For example, if
a student is doing homework because she finds the subject interesting and
wishes to master it, then she is intrinsically motivated. If, however, she is
doing homework to avoid punishment or in expectation of praise from her
mother, then her motivation is extrinsic. In the present context, it is interesting to note that it is difficult to monitor discrepancy reduction toward
self-determination needs. Competence, relatedness, and autonomy constitute inner feelings rather than a verifiable objective reality and do not have
a clear end-state (in fact, they do not have an end-state at all). We see that
some of the characteristics that are often ascribed to goals that subserve
self determination needs (e.g., intrinsic motivation, enjoyment of the means
rather than worrying about their instrumentality, open-mindedness, less
inhibition, and less disengagement after completion) may be conceptualized as the positive consequences of working toward goals that are difficult
to monitor.

Prevention and avoidance goals tend to have an end-state that is not
clearly specified. Some avoidance goals may allow feedback on progress if
progress is measured from the starting point, which is the state one tries to
avoid (Brendl & Higgins, 1996). For example, when running away from
a fire, one can monitor the distance from the fire and the rate at which it
increases. Sometimes, however, one may try to prevent a state that has not
yet occurred (e.g., a global epidemic), in which case feedback on progress
may become rather difficult to obtain, as neither the starting point nor the
end point is clear (e.g., it is not clear how far we are from an epidemic,
nor how close we are to the "safety zone"). It is interesting to note that
with such goals, feedback on progress may become easier to obtain once
the disaster happened (and one is working to overcome it) than before it
happened (and one is working to prevent it). For example, after the epidemic outbreak, the course of action is often clear, and the feedback on its
efficiency is obtainable; but prior to the epidemic breakout, it is often not
clear whether the various precautions indeed help or are taken in vain. It

is perhaps for this reason that hypochondriacs and pathological worriers often function much better when the feared disease or disaster actually strikes. A patient of the second author was chronically worried that some disaster would befall one of her parents, but when her mother was diagnosed with cancer, her anxiety immediately diminished and she took care of her mother rationally and effectively.

Goals that have no specified time point for implementation present a special case of difficulty to monitor progress, at least in comparison to similar goals that do have a deadline. For example, compare the goal of writing a novel to a goal of writing a novel by the end of the 8-week summer break. A failure to make any progress until the last week of the break signifies a potential failure in the latter case but has less clear implications for progress (or lack thereof) in the former case.

It is interesting to consider from this perspective "implementation intentions" (IIs), which are concrete plans as to when, how and where to pursue a goal (Gollwitzer, 1999). It has been demonstrated that forming IIs greatly increases the likelihood of goal fulfillment (for a review, see Gollwitzer, 1999). For example, if students think of how, when, and where they are going to write an assignment before leaving for a vacation, the likelihood that they will complete the goal of writing the assignment during the vacation greatly increases. It is likely that one of the advantages that IIs have is that by providing a clear deadline, they also enable better monitoring of progress.

Coping with Monitoring Difficulties

What do people do when they encounter difficulty in monitoring progress toward discrepancy reduction? We would like to suggest that they adopt one of two general strategies: they either relax or increase monitoring attempts. Below, we describe the consequences of using each of these strategies with different types of goals (summarized in Table 11.1). We then look at variables that may determine the choice of one strategy over the other.

Relaxing Monitoring Attempts in the Face of Monitoring Difficulty

An obvious possible reaction to encountering difficulty in monitoring is to relax one's monitoring attempts. For example, when writing this chapter, we were unable to monitor whether our efforts led us to making a significant contribution. We gave up on monitoring our progress toward this goal and instead adopted a more relaxed attitude that enabled us to enjoy the process (which probably explains the large delay in submitting the chapter). The expected consequences of more relaxed monitoring directly follow from the effects of monitoring: people would be less concentrated on their goal and would have more resources for non-goal-related stimuli. For example, a tourist who does not have a map and cannot closely monitor her progress toward her destination may feel more relaxed and may be freer to notice other things on the way than a person who closely monitors her progress. Of course, there are less positive consequences of reduced monitoring: A student who studies for an exam and loosens monitoring of her progress may find herself sidetracked by irrelevant activities and unable to prepare for the exam on time.

We propose that relaxing monitoring of progress toward goal attainment would also lead the individual to perceive her actions as being performed for their own sake, rather than as being a means toward the goal. In that sense, the experience of loose monitoring may resemble that of intrinsic motivation (see Kruglanski, 1975, for a definition of an intrinsically motivated action as being performed in end of itself rather than being a means toward another goal). For example, a tourist may enjoy the way to the Eiffel Tower rather than being concentrated on reaching the destination, or a student may enjoy reading the material rather than perceive studying only as a means to passing the exam. Closer, more intense monitoring, therefore, means more task orientation and less experience orientation, whereas loose monitoring facilitates experience orientation but not task orientation. The distinct advantages and drawbacks of task orientation and experience orientation are thus part and parcel of loosening versus tightening monitoring of progress toward a goal.

As noted earlier, it is possible that looser monitoring would reduce the extent not only of goal-related accessibility, but also of postfulfillment inhibition. For example, a tourist who less closely monitors her progress toward the Eiffel Tower would not only have the destination less accessible on her way, but would also inhibit it to a lesser extent after the visit. Similarly, a student who less closely monitors her progress toward preparing for the exam would forget less of the study materials after the exam is over. In a similar vein, intrinsically motivated actions, as compared to extrinsically motivated actions, seem to be characterized by less extensive postaction inhibition and disengagement. For example, more intrinsically motivated students are more likely to remain interested in the course study materials after the course is over (Deci & Ryan, 2000). This suggests once more a parallel between loosely monitored actions and intrinsically motivated actions.

When monitoring is relaxed and information on progress is vague, there is more room for subjective construal of the extent of progress.

Depending on personal tendencies and situational determinants, this may lead to self-enhancement or to self-deprecation. When trying to make a good impression on the interviewer, the lack of clear feedback can lead one person to think highly of her performance, whereas a less confident or optimistic interviewee may feel that she is doing terribly. In addition, relaxed monitoring may enhance the effect of irrelevant sources of input on perception of progress. For example, positive (or negative) mood may mislead one to think that she is making good (or poor) progress, thereby making her reduce (or increase) efforts with no actual need.

Increasing Monitoring Attempts in the Face of Monitoring Difficulty

Difficulty in monitoring progress may lead individuals to increase rather than to relax their monitoring attempts. Below, we examine strategies that people may use in their attempts to increase monitoring in the face of difficulty and the consequences of applying these strategies. Later, we discuss in more detail what makes people increase versus relax monitoring attempts.

Proxies for Progress

Instead of regulating toward goals that pose difficulties in monitoring, people may generate or try to find proxies that would be easier to regulate toward. For example, a person who tries to impress her interviewer and finds it difficult to rely on the vague feelings of internal satisfaction might resort to subgoals, such as sitting straight, smiling, and maintaining eye contact. A person who is trying to understand study materials and finds it difficult to rely on the vague sense of understanding may try to resort to counting pages or rehearsing sentences.

Although the proxies are easier to monitor than the original goals, using them often incurs a cost. One obvious problem with proxies is that they are not the real thing. Counting pages is not the same as understanding the material. If one concentrates on monitoring how many pages he has read instead of monitoring his understanding, this may result in a poorer understanding of the material. Likewise, if one is busy monitoring her posture and her rate of smiling, she may forget to monitor more relevant (albeit vague) aspects of the interview, such as how attentive and how friendly she appears. Darley (2004) referred to the problem of substituting goals with clearer proxies on the level of institutions. An organization that desires to reward performance that is fairly vaguely defined (e.g., academic excellence), in an attempt to provide a clearer, more objective criterion (e.g., number of published papers), might end up creating undesirable, counter-productive behaviors (e.g., publishing more worthless papers à la publish or perish) that make its workers and eventually the entire institution drift away from the original goal.

A special case of substituting difficult-to-monitor goals with easier-to-monitor goals is when feelings and internal states are substituted with external signals. For example, a person who wishes to feel loved and finds it difficult to tolerate the ambiguity inherent in monitoring this state might resort to monitoring the rate and price of the gifts her partner gives her, which may shift attention and efforts toward relatively less important aspects of the relationships.

Another problem is that at closer examination, proxies may lose their apparent clarity and engender further substitution. For example, on a date, a person may substitute the goal of impressing his partner, which is difficult to monitor, with a goal of sounding professional. The latter goal, however, may also prove to be difficult to monitor, leading to further substitution with the goal of using a great deal of professional lingo. As this example demonstrates, the process of goal substitution, if used repeatedly, may lead further and further away from the original goal.

Lower Level of Action Identification and Deautomatization

We mentioned earlier that in response to encountering a difficulty in goal pursuits people adopt a lower level of action identification. If the action in question is automatic, this would mean deautomatization (e.g., if encountering a difficulty in driving to the office). This strategy may also be adopted when encountering a difficulty in monitoring progress to the goal. For example, a person that cleans the house may find it difficult to monitor progress toward the overall goal of achieving cleanliness, and monitor, instead, progress toward the means of vacuuming each square inch of the floor, a goal that is much easier to monitor. Typically, lower-level goals are more concrete and thus allow for better monitoring than higher-level, abstract goals (Vallacher & Wegner, 1987).

Increased Frequency of Checking for Progress

When feeling uncertainty as to one's progress toward discrepancy reduction, one may simply attempt to monitor progress more closely. For example, a student may decide to check her understanding of the study material more frequently. A public health worker who wishes to prevent an epidemic may repeatedly check whether no disaster has yet occurred.

Increased frequency of monitoring attempts may incur various costs. In the case of avoidance goals, increased monitoring is likely to increase anxiety. For example, checking more frequently if one has cancer would increase anxiety, despite repeated negative findings, by increasing attention to and accessibility of this possibility. When progress is naturally slow, increased frequency of monitoring may engender frustration and disappointment. For example, a dieter who repeatedly weighs herself is likely to feel more frustrated than a dieter who checks her weight less frequently.

Close monitoring is especially counterproductive when the goals are feelings and internal states. When these feelings and states are desirable, attempts to increase monitoring are likely to make them disappear. For example, a person that wishes to feel in love and frequently checks the extent to which she has achieved this desired state may ironically reduce her chance of experiencing love. A person who repeatedly asks herself if she is happy diminishes the prospect of experiencing genuine happiness. Conversely, when the goal is to avoid negative feelings or states, such as distressing thoughts or unpleasant sensations, increased monitoring is likely to facilitate exactly the thoughts and feelings one is trying to avoid (Wegner, Schneider, Carter, & White, 1987; Wegner, 1994). We elaborate on these ironic processes when we discuss the relevance of this perspective to obsessive–compulsive disorder.

Alternative Sources of Information about Progress

When sufficient feedback on progress does not come from the feedback loop, one may attempt to receive it from other sources. One may seek the opinion of experts or friends or rely on social comparison and other sources of information. For example, a student who does not know if she is making sufficient progress in studying for the exam may ask other students or consult her teacher. Whether or not this strategy proves useful depends, of course, on the quality and relevance of the information obtained in that way. For example, the fellow students who are used for social comparison may or may not be a relevant comparison standard and may or may not provide correct information. In addition, when the goals are internal states and feelings, there may be very few, if any, alternative sources of information on progress other than one's own monitoring system.

In discussing many of the above strategies of increasing monitoring, we described how increased monitoring efforts may have unintended, negative effects. This is not always the case, of course. Increased monitoring can sometimes have the intended positive effect. Lowering level of action identification, more frequent checking, and social comparison may sometimes supply the desired feedback on progress. For example, counting the number of pages read in preparing for an exam may sometimes be an effective means of monitoring progress and could actually help the student remain task oriented and focused.

Relaxing versus Increasing Monitoring Attempts: Moderating Variables

When difficulty is encountered in monitoring progress toward discrepancy reduction, what makes either alternative, relaxing versus increasing monitoring, more likely than the other? In the following, we consider potential moderators of the reaction to difficulty in monitoring progress, including personality variables, situational variables, and goal characteristics. We then illustrate how these factors join to explain the development of repetition, rules, rituals and other symptoms of obsessive–compulsive disorder.

Importance of Goal

Obviously, it is more difficult to loosen monitoring of more important, relative to less important, goals. For example, it is more difficult to relax monitoring of how one is doing during an interview if the interview is to determine one's professional future than if it does not have crucial importance.

Prevention and Avoidance Goals

It is generally more difficult to relax monitoring of prevention and avoidance goals relative to promotion and approach ones. Research has shown, for example, that prevention goals call for more immediate action than do promotion goals (Freitas, Liberman, Salovey, & Higgins, 2002; Pennington & Roese, 2003). It is reasonable to assume that a need for more immediate action also means a need for tighter monitoring of progress because assigning positive value to immediacy implies the need to monitor whether progress is sufficiently fast. In addition to fostering more immediate action, prevention goals typically necessitate pursuit of all possible means (e.g., all the doors must be secured to ensure safety), whereas promotion goals typically have interchangeable means, any of which may suffice for goal achievement (e.g., any way of earning big money suffices to make you rich). The need to pursue all means is likely to necessitate closer monitoring as compared to a situation in which any means is sufficient.

Anxiety

Anxiety is closely associated with increased monitoring; in fact, the main evolutionary role of the anxiety mechanism may be to increase vigilance and monitoring. According to Gray (1982), for example, anxiety is a state of increased vigilance and extensive monitoring of the environment in response to potential anticipated danger (as opposed to fear, which is the response to actual perceived danger). In case of monitoring difficulty, anxiety should therefore be associated with increased rather than relaxed monitoring.

Accountability for Performance

Sometimes, people are accountable for their performance to another person, often a person of higher authority. Accountability and external monitoring would make relaxed monitoring less likely. A worker who is being closely supervised by her boss would be less likely to relax monitoring when she faces difficulty in monitoring compared to a worker who is not being closely supervised.

Authority may be internalized, in which case it would be difficult to relax monitoring even without the physical presence of another person who supervises one's actions. Sometimes the process of internalization remains incomplete, and although goals are pursued in the absence of the authority figure that originally introduced them, they are not fully integrated with one's self, and one feels coerced when working toward them (e.g., a child might tidy her room in the absence of her parents but still feel forced to do that). With such introjected goals (Deci & Ryan, 2000), as compared with internalized goals, it may be more difficult to relax monitoring. For example, imagine a child who is doing her homework and finds it difficult to monitor her progress (e.g., she does not know if she is fast enough in solving the math problems). We would predict that if she does homework to please her mother (an introjected motivation) she would be more eager to resume monitoring of her progress (e.g., by repeated checking of the number of pages completed) and would be less likely to relax monitoring compared to a child who does her homework because she thinks that studying is important (an internalized motivation). This prediction represents yet another way in which relaxed monitoring is related to intrinsic motivation.

Intolerance for Uncertainty and Need for Closure

People vary in their tolerance for ambiguity or uncertainty, and situations vary in the extent of tolerance for ambiguity that they foster. "Intolerance for uncertainty" is defined as the tendency to have negative emotional, cognitive, and behavioral reactions to uncertain situations and events (Dugas, Buhr, & Ladouceur, 2004). Related to intolerance for uncertainty is need for closure (NFC; Kruglanski & Webster, 1996), which is the tendency to seek definite answers and dislike for situations of indecision and uncertainty. People high in NFC, compared to people low in NFC, prefer to reach an early decision and stick to it longer in the face of disconfirming evidence. We would expect people who are intolerant for ambiguity and people who have high need for closure to be less tolerant for situations of ambiguous feedback on their progress. Thus, they will be less likely to relax monitoring in the face of monitoring difficulties.

Need for and Perception of Personal Control

Difficulties in monitoring progress toward discrepancy reduction may induce a sense of lack of control. Relaxing monitoring may be seen as accepting lack of control. Therefore, high need for personal control and low perceived personal control should be associated with attempting to increase monitoring (rather than relax it) when confronted with monitoring difficulties.

Interrelations between the Moderators

Our list of moderators of increasing versus relaxing monitoring of progress includes goal importance, anxiety, prevention versus avoidance goals, accountability, intolerance of ambiguity and need for closure, and need for and perception of control. It is easy to see that these various moderators are closely related to each other. As it is beyond the scope of this chapter to review all these interrelations, we would only note that all these variables were shown to be related to anxiety. For example, NFC was related to increased anxiety in a decision task that involved uncertainty. Moreover, this distress increased gradually as long as the situation remained ambiguous and a decision had not been reached. Research conducted in the framework of regulatory focus theory documented that failing a prevention goal, more than failing a promotion goal, produces anxiety. Low perceived control, which relates to one's perceived ability to affect the outcome of situations and events, has been associated with high levels of anxiety (Endler, Macrodimitris, & Kocovski, 2000). In the same vein, experimentally increasing individuals' perceptions of control leads to reduction in levels of anxiety (Sanderson, Rapee, & Barlow, 1989; Zvolensky, Eifert, Lejuez, & McNeill, 1999). It is easy to see also how accountability increases anxiety over one's performance (e.g., Mero, Guidice, & Anna, 2006). It appears, therefore, that many of the antecedents of increased monitoring involve the experience of anxiety.

Let us also emphasize the important role of need for control in increasing monitoring attempts in the face of monitoring difficulty. Monitoring is an essential part in control. For example, to control our food intake, we need to monitor it. In fact, it is possible that mere monitoring, with no actual control of outcomes, may sometimes satisfy the need for control. For example, if we closely monitor another person's actions, we may feel that we control them. It is possible that some of the moderators we mention, such as goal importance, accountability, and prevention goals, enhance monitoring efforts by increasing need for control.

To conclude this section on moderators of increased monitoring, we would like to note that some of these moderators, including anxiety, prevention focus, need for control, and intolerance of ambiguity, describe characteristics of situations and stable individual differences (i.e., personality traits). We think that both aspects of these variables are relevant to our framework. Obviously, the nature of the goal people pursue affects the importance they attach to monitoring progress—whether it produces anxiety, whether it fosters ambiguity, or whether it involves prevention. Stable individual differences may bias some people to perceive situations in personality congruent ways. For example, an anxious person or a prevention-focused person would be more likely to experience a situation as anxiety provoking or as involving prevention, respectively. It is for that reason that we anticipate both situational variance and stable individual differences in the tendency for increased monitoring of progress towards goals.

In the final section of this chapter, we illustrate how the analysis of difficulties in monitoring progress can be applied to the understanding of obsessive–compulsive disorder (OCD).

Obsessive-Compulsive Disorder

Obsessive–compulsive disorder (OCD) is defined by the presence of repetitive and distressing obsessions and compulsions, which tend to increase in severity during the natural course of the disorder (American Psychiatric Association [APA], 1994). One of the principal symptoms in OCD is persistent doubt, which can invade many domains of actions or feelings. It is well established that people with OCD distrust their memory (e.g., Brown, Kosslyn, Breitler, Baer, & Jenike, 1994; Dar, Rish, Hermesh, Fux, & Taub, 2000; Foa, Amir, Geshuny, Molnar, & Kozak, 1997; MacDonald, Antony, MacLeod, & Richter, 1997; McNally & Kohlbeck, 1993), a finding that has been associated with the common symptom of repeated checking. But theorists of OCD have observed that these patients also doubt their own perception, feelings, preferences, comprehension, and other internal states (e.g., Rapoport, 1989; Reed, 1985; Shapiro, 1965). For example, a patient with OCD may feel uncertain that she feels attracted to her partner or doubt that she fully understands the meaning of a simple word even if she cannot find any objective reason for these doubts. Such pervasive doubts may lead to a variety of pathological behaviors typical of OCD, including excessive self-monitoring, checking, mental reconstruction, incessant questions, and requests for external validation or reassurance.

According to the classic description of obsessive–compulsive (OC) style by David Shapiro (1965), people with OC tendencies have lost "the experience of conviction." These individuals have diminished ability to access their own feelings, wishes, and preferences directly and must resort to external indicators to infer these internal states. To use a metaphor by Shapiro, individuals with OC tendencies can be likened to pilots flying at night, who must rely on flight instruments instead of their vision. When asked whether they like someone, believe in something, or prefer one thing to another, most people usually feel that they simply "know" the answer. In contrast, individuals with OC tendencies, according to Shapiro, must deduce their answers from external indicators or base them on general rules or norms. A similar model was advanced by Reed (1985), who proposed that the clinical symptoms of OCD should be seen as manifestations of a functional impairment in the spontaneous organization and integration of experience. According to Shapiro and Reed, individuals with OCD are able to function well despite this deficit by using various compensation strategies, such as adopting rules and norms to guide their behavior. For example, a man with OC tendencies may conclude that he must be in love with his partner because she possesses all the "right" attributes (Shapiro).

The idea that OCD is related to a disturbance in the subjective experience of conviction has been adopted in a recent model of OCD (Szechtman & Woody, 2004). This model suggests that OCD is related to a disturbance in the "feeling of knowing," defined as "a subjective conviction functionally separate from knowledge of objective reality (p. 115)." In a recent study, Woody and colleagues demonstrated that hand washing in nonclinical participants was intensified by hypnotic suggestion that blocked the sense of satisfaction usually associated with washing (Woody et al., 2005). In a related vein, Joel and Avisar (2001) developed and tested an animal model of OCD that is based on the proposition that obsessions and compulsions result from a deficient response–feedback mechanism. In several studies, Joel and her colleagues demonstrated that attenuation of external feedback for operant behavior leads to excessive emission of this behavior in rats (see Joel, 2006, for a review). In the context of this chapter, we examine the symptoms of OCD from the perspective of feedback control systems. We suggest that OCD and its psychological correlates, including anxiety and compulsion, can be understood in terms of a difficulty in monitoring progress combined with a tendency to increase monitoring attempts in the face of this difficulty.

We begin by noting that the goals that individuals with OC tendencies typically pursue present difficulties in monitoring. The great majority of these goals are prevention or avoidance goals, such as not running over a pedestrian when driving or not contracting AIDS. As shown above, progress with this type of goal is difficult to monitor, as a minor error or a momentary lack of attention is sufficient for disastrous failure. This state of affairs necessitates monitoring of all possible ways of failing to achieve the goal, which are practically infinite. Other goals that people with OCD pursue may not be avoidance goals but still lack a clear end-state. A prime example is hand washing, the most common ritual in this disorder: Cleanliness is an ambiguous goal which lacks a clearcut end-state. Finally, in many of the goals that individuals with OC tendencies pursue, there is no feedback on the contingency between their acts (e.g., hand washing or repeated checking) and progress toward the desired goal (avoiding contamination or preventing harm to loved ones).

As discussed above, when individuals are faced with difficulties in monitoring progress, they can either relax or attempt to tighten monitoring (Figure 11.1). Individuals with OCD, however, do not have the option of relaxing monitoring. First, their goals are extremely important to them: No one can accept what feels like a high risk of a hit-and-run accident or of contracting a serious illness. Second, as our model suggests, a high need for control as well as high need for closure leads to increased rather than decreased monitoring attempts in the face of monitoring difficulties. As OC tendencies are associated with high need for control (Moulding & Kyrios, 2006; Reuven-Magril, Dar, & Liberman, 2008) and high NFC (Mancini, D'Olimpio, Del Genio, Didonna, & Prunetti, 2002), individuals with OC tendencies are unable to relax monitoring. Third, OCD is classified as an anxiety disorder and anxiety is believed to be the main motivation for the performance of rituals (APA, 1994). From the perspective of the present model (Figure 11.1), anxiety would be expected to increase vigilance and tighten monitoring, which in turn would enhance the accessibility of the avoidance goal. In the absence of clear progress, this would lead to a cycle of ever-increasing anxiety and monitoring. Finally, we suggested that accountability would also lead to enhanced, rather than to relaxed, monitoring. In OCD, accountability takes the form of exaggerated guilt and "inflated responsibility" concerning one's actions (e.g., Rachman, 1993; Rhéaume, Ladouceur, Freeston, & Letarte, 1995), which would also lead to increased monitoring attempts.

In our model, the symptoms of OCD can be conceptualized as the consequences of intensified monitoring attempts in the face of monitoring difficulty. As Figure 11.1 shows, these include increased checking, deautomatization, using proxies for progress, and seeking alternative sources of information on progress. Repeated checking, as mentioned above, is one of the most common symptoms in OCD. Patients may check again and again that doors are locked, that light switches and turned off, or that appliances are unplugged. In conducting these checking rituals, as well as other rituals like hand washing, patients with OCD monitor their actions very closely, attempting to be as focused and attentive as possible.

Tight monitoring, however, becomes a challenge when these actions are repeated many times, as normal learning mechanisms tend to make these actions habitual and automatic. Such automatization poses a threat for a person with OCD, who perceived it as a loss of control. Presumably as a response to this threat, OC rituals, including checking and washing, tend to become more and more elaborate, thus preventing automatization and enabling continued close monitoring (see Boyer & Liénard, 2006, for a similar point).

Similarly, an important function of rituals in OCD may be to serve as proxies for progress when monitoring is difficult. Counting the number of times each line or page is read, for example, may serve as a proxy for progress toward a higher-order goal of understanding the text. A washing ritual may serve as a proxy for avoiding contamination or preventing harm to others. Finally, patients with OCD often seek alternative sources for feedback on progress. Examples include relying on rules and norms or asking for reassurance or "objective" information from others. For example, a patient with OCD with a fear of driving may only be willing to drive with a close friend or a spouse who can serve as a reliable witness to reassure the patient she has not accidentally run over someone.

Checking may get especially tricky when the goal is a specific internal state, rather than an external goal. Patients with OCD may repeat an act many times until a specific subjective state (commonly a reduction in anxiety or a feeling of "just right") has been achieved (Dar & Katz, 2005). As people with OC tendencies appear to have a deficient sense of their own subjective states, as postulated by many models of OCD (see above), they encounter difficulties in monitoring these states. Coupled with the low tolerance for uncertainty associated with OCD (Tolin, Abramowitz, Brigidi, & Foa, 2003), these difficulties lead people with OC tendencies to increase monitoring of their own subjective experiences. As discussed above, such increased monitoring is likely to further undermine confidence in these already vague and fleeting internal states. Some of the rules and rituals common to OCD may serve as proxies aimed to compensate for the attenuation of direct experience. For example, a young patient with OCD of the second author began to worry that he did not fully understand the material he had learned in school. The more he questioned and attempted to monitor his own level of understanding, the more his uncertainty about his understanding grew. To compensate, he developed the rule that he should know the material by heart, which has become his proxy for understanding.

This model can also account for the subjective experience of people with OCD, including vigilance, anxiety, and a sense of compulsion. As noted above, vigilance and anxiety are endemic to tight monitoring. Compulsion, a defining feature of OC experience, can be conceptualized as an extreme form of extrinsic motivation and is also a consequence of tight monitoring (see Table 11.1). As in the case of introjected goals, this sense of compulsion, in turn, leads to even tighter monitoring and a further increase in the sense of compulsion. According to this analysis, then, anxiety and sense of compulsion can be antecedents as well as consequences of close monitoring.

Finally, we should note that the perspective suggested here may contribute to the understanding not only of OCD but of other psychopathological conditions. Most anxiety disorders involve avoidance goals without clear end point. As a result, people with these disorders often develop elaborate "safety behaviors" that may be seen as proxies for progress toward achieving the vague goal of safety. For example, a patient with agoraphobia may map out every emergency room on her route to work, and a patient who panics may respond to increased heart rate by sitting down and resting to avoid a heart attack. Rituals are found in many disorders other than OCD, perhaps for similar reasons. Examples are developmental disorders, including autism and Asperger's syndrome (e.g., Russell, Mataix-Cols, Anson, & Murphy, 2005). This analysis would suggest that in these disorders, rituals would also be associated with a deficient accessibility of internal experiences, higher need for control, and lower sense of control, intolerance of ambiguity, and anxiety.

Notes

1. Of course, oftentimes goals are not fulfilled but just become irrelevant, or forgotten, or are pushed away by other more urgent goals. Moreover, sometimes we fulfill a goal only to discover that the superordinate goal has changed. In our chapter, we address only the relatively simple case of stable goal hierarchies and do not examine more complicated cases of goal disengagement or dynamic hierarchies.

References

American Psychiatric Association. (1994). *Diagnostic and statistical manual of mental disorders* (4th ed.). Washington, DC: Author.

Bandura, J. A., & Schunk, D. H., (1981). Cultivating competence, self-efficacy, and intrinsic interest through proximal self-motivation. *Journal of Personality and Social Psychology, 41,* 586–598.

Bargh, J. A. (1994). The four horsemen of automaticity: Awareness, efficiency, intention, and control in social cognition. In R. S. Wyer, Jr., & T. K. Srull (Eds.), *Handbook of social cognition* (2nd ed., pp. 1–40). Hillsdale, NJ: Erlbaum.

Boyer, P., & Liénard, P. (2006). Why ritualized behavior? Precaution systems and action parsing in developmental, pathological and cultural rituals. *Behavioral and Brain Science, 29,* 595–613.

Brendl, M. C., & Higgins, E. T. (1996). Principles of judging valence: What makes events positive or negative? In M. Zanna (Ed.,) *Advances in experimental social psychology* (pp. 95–160). San Diego: Academic Press.

Brown, H. D., Kosslyn, S. M., Breitler, H. C., Baer, L., & Jenike, M. A. (1994). Can patients with obsessive–compulsive disorder discriminate between percepts and mental images? A signal detection analysis. *Journal of Abnormal Psychology, 103,* 445–454.

Carver, C. S., & Scheier, M. F. (1990). Principels of self regulation: Action and emotion. In E. T. Higgins & R. M. Sorrentino (Eds.), *Handbook of motivation and cognition: Foundations of social behavior* (Vol. 2, pp. 3–52). New York: Guilford Press.

Carver, C. S., & Scheier, M. F. (1999). Themes and issues in the self regulation of behavior. In R. S. Wyer (Ed.), *Perspectives on behavioral self regulation* (pp. 1–106). Mahwah, NJ: Erlbaum.

Dar, R., & Katz, H. (2005). Action Identification in obsessive–compulsive washers. *Cognitive Therapy and Research, 29,* 333–341.

Dar, R., Rish, S., Hermesh, H., Fux, M., & Taub, M. (2000). Realism of confidence in obsessive–compulsive checkers. *Journal of Abnormal Psychology, 109,* 673–678.

Darley, J. M. (2004). Commitment, trust and worker effort expenditure in organizations. In R. M. Roderick & K. S. Cook (Eds.), *Trust and distrust in organizations: Dilemmas and approaches* (pp. 127–151). New York: Russel Sage Foundation.

Dawkins, R. (2006). *The selfish gene* (30th anniversary edition). New York: Oxford University Press.

Deci, E. L., & Ryan, R. M. (2000). The "what" and "why" of goal pursuits: Human needs and the self determination of behavior. *Psychological Inquiry, 11,* 227–268.

Dugas, M. J., Buhr, K., & Ladouceur, R. (2004). The role of intolerance of uncertainty in etiology and maintenance. In R. G. Heimberg, C. L. Turk, & D. S. Mennin (Eds.), *Generalized anxiety disorder: Advances in research and practice* (pp. 143–163). New York: Guilford Press.

Endler, N. S., Macrodimitris, S. D., & Kocovski, N. L. (2000). Controllability in cognitive and interpersonal tasks: Is control good for you? *Personality and Individual Differences, 29,* 951–962.

Erez, M. (1977). Feedback: A necessary condition for the goal-performance relationship. *Journal of Applied Psychology, 62,* 624–627.

Fishbach, A., & Zhang, Y. (2008). Together or apart: When goals and temptations complement versus compete. *Journal of Personality and Social Psychology, 94,* 547–559.

Foa, E. B., Amir, N., Geshuny, B., & Molnar, C., & Kozak, M. (1997). Implicit and explicit memory in obsessive–compulsive disorder. *Journal of Anxiety Disorders, 11,* 119–129.

Förster, J., Liberman, N., & Friedman, R. S. (2007). Seven principles of goal activation: A systematic approach to distinguishing goal priming from priming of non-goal constructs. *Personality and Social Psychology Review, 11,* 211–233.

Förster, J., Liberman, N., & Higgins, E. T. (2005). Accessibility from active and fulfilled goals. *Journal of Experimental Social Psychology, 41,* 220–239.

Freitas, A. L., Liberman, N., Salovey, P., & Higgins, E. T. (2002). When to begin? Regulatory focus and initiating goal pursuit. *Personality and Social Psychology Bulletin, 28,* 121–130.

Gilbert, D. T. (2006). *Stumbling on happiness.* New York: Alfred A. Knopf.

Gollwitzer, P. M. (1999). Implementation intentions: Strong effects of simple plans. *American Psychologist, 54,* 493–503.

Gray, J. A. (1982). *The neuropsychology of anxiety: An enquiry into the functions of the septo-hypocampal system.* New York: Oxford University Press.

Higgins, E. T. (1997). Beyond pleasure and pain. *American Psychologist, 52,* 1280–1300.

Higgins, E. T. (1998). Promotion and prevention: regulatory focus as a motivational principle. In M. P. Zanna (Ed.), *Advances in experimental social psychology* (pp. 1–46). New York: Academic Press.

Hsee, C. K., & Abelson, R. P. (1991). Velocity relation: Satisfaction as a function of the first derivative of outcome over time. *Journal of Personality and Social Psychology, 60,* 341–347.

Hsee, C. K., Abelson, R. P., & Salovey, P. (1991). The relative weighting of position and velocity in satisfaction. *Psychological Science, 2,* 263–266.

Joel, D. (2006). The signal attenuation rat model of obsessive-compulsive disorder: A review. *Psychopharmacology, 186,* 487–503.

Joel, D., & Avisar, A. (2001). Excessive lever pressing following post-training signal attenuation in rats: A possible animal model of obsessive-compulsive disorder? *Behavioural Brain Research, 123,* 77–87.

Klinger, E. (1996). Emotional influences on cognitive processing, with implications for theories of both. In P. M. Gollwitzer & J. A. Bargh (Eds.), *The psychology of action: Linking cognition and motivation to behavior* (pp. 197–218). New York: Guilford Press.

Kruglanski, A. W. (1975). The endogenous–exogenous partition in attribution theory. *Psychology Review, 82,* 387–406.

Kruglanki, A. W., & Webster, D. M. (1996). Motivated closing of the mind: "Seizing" and "freezing." *Psychological Review, 103,* 263–283.

Kulik, J. A., & Kulik, C. C. (1988). Timing of feedback and verbal learning. *Review of Educational Research, 58,* 79–97.

Lewin, K. (1951). *Field theory in social science.* New York: Harper.

Liberman, N., Förster, J., & Higgins, E. T. (2007). Accessibility and completed vs. interrupted priming: The role of post-fulfillment inhibition. *Journal of Experimental Social Psychology, 43,* 258–264.

Locke, E. A., & Latham, G. P. (1990). *A theory of goal setting and task performance.* Englewood Cliffs, NJ: Prentice Hall.

Locke, E. A., & Latham, G. P. (2002). Building a practically useful theory of goal setting and task motivation. *American Psychologist, 57,* 705–717.

MacDonald, P. A., Antony, M. M., MacLeod, C. M., & Richter, M. A. (1997). Memory and confidence in memory judgments among individuals with obsessive compulsive disorder and non-clinical controls. *Behaviour Research and Therapy, 35,* 497–505.

Mancini, F., D'Olimpio, F., Del Genio, M., Didonna, F., & Prunetti, E. (2002). Obsessions and compulsions and intolerance for uncertainty in a non-clinical sample. *Journal of Anxiety Disorders, 16,* 401–411.

Martin, L. L., Tesser, A., & Cornell, D. P. (1996). On the substitutability of self-protective mechanisms. In P. M. Gollwitzer & J. A. Bargh (Eds.), *The psychology of action: Linking cognition and motivation to behavior* (pp. 48–68). New York: Guilford Press.

Mayer, J. D., Salovey, P., & Caruso, D. (2004). Emotional intellicgence: Theory, findings and implications. *Psychological Inquiry, 15,* 197–215.

McNally, R. J., & Kohlbeck, P. A. (1993). Reality monitoring in obsessive–compulsive disorder. *Behaviour Research and Therapy, 31,* 249–253.

Mero, N. P., Giodice, R. M., & Anna, A. L. (2006). The interacting effects of accountability and individual differences on rater response to a performance-rating task. *Journal of Applied Social Psychology, 36,* 795–819.

Miller, G. A., Galanter, E., & Pribram, K. H. (1960). *Plans and the structure of behavior.* New York: Holt, Rinehart & Winston.

Moulding, R., & Kyrios, M. (2006). Anxiety disorders and control related beliefs: The exemplar of obsessive–compulsive disorder (OCD). *Clinical Psychology Review, 26,* 573–583.

Pennington, G. L., & Roese, J. L. (2003). Regulatory focus and temporal distance. *Journal of Experimental Social Psychology, 39,* 563–576.

Powers, W. T. (1973). *Behavior: The control of perception.* Chicago: Aldine.

Rachman, S. (1993). Obsessions, responsibility and guilt. *Behaviour Research and Therapy, 31,* 149–154.

Rapoport, J. L. (1989). *The boy who couldn't stop washing: The experience and treatment of obsessive–compulsive disorder.* New York: Dutton.

Reed, G. F. (1985). *Obsessional experience and compulsive behaviour: A cognitive-structural approach.* Orlando, FL: Academic Press.

Reuven-Magril, O., Dar, R., & Liberman, N. (2008). Illusion of control and behavioral control attempts in obsessive–compulsive disorder. *Journal of Abnormal Psychology, 117,* 334–341.

Rhéaume, J., Ladouceur, R., Freeston, M. H., & Letarte, H. (1995). Inflated responsibility in OCD: Validation of an operational definition. *Behaviour Research and Therapy, 33,* 159–169.

Russell, A. J., Mataix-Cols, D., Anson, M., & Murphy, D. G. (2005). Obsessions and compulsions in Asperger syndrome and high-functioning autism. *British Journal of Psychiatry, 186,* 525–528.

Sanderson, W. C., Rapee, R. M., & Barlow, D. H. (1989). The influence of an illusion of control on panic attacks induced via inhalation of 5.5% carbon dioxide-enriched air. *Archives of General Psychiatry, 46,* 157–162.

Schunk, D. H. (2000). *Learning theories: An educational perspective* (3rd ed.). Columbus, OH: Merrill.

Schneider, W., & Shiffrin, R. M. (1977). Controlled and automatic human information processing: I. Detection, search, and attention. *Psychological Review, 84,* 1–66.

Shapiro, D. (1965). *Neurotic styles*. New York: Basic Books.

Solomon, S., Greenberg, J., & Pyszczynski, T. (1991). A terror management theory of social behavior: The psychological functions of self esteem and cultural worldviews. In M. P. Zanna (Ed.), *Advances in experimental social psychology* (pp. 91–159). San Diego: Academic Press.

Solomon, S., Greenberg, J., & Pyszczynski, T. (2004). The cultural animal: Twenty years of terror management theory and research. In J. Greenberg, S. L. Koole, & T. Pyszynski (Eds.), *Handbook of experimental existential psychology* (pp. 13–34). New York: Guilford Press.

Szechtman, H., & Woody, E. (2004). Obsessive–compulsive disorder as a disturbance of security motivation. *Psychological Review, 111*, 111–127.

Tolin, D. F., Abramowitz, J. S., Brigidi, B. D., & Foa, E. B. (2003). Intolerance of uncertainty in obsessive–compulsive disorder. *Journal of Anxiety Disorders, 17*, 233–242.

Vallacher, R. R., & Wegner, D. M. (1987). What do people think they're doing? Action identification and human behavior. *Psychological Review, 94*, 3–15.

Wegner, D. M. (1994). Ironic processes of mental control. *Psychological Review, 101*, 34–52.

Wegner, D. M., Schneider, D. J., Carter, S., & White, L. (1987). Paradoxical effects of thought suppression. *Journal of Personality and Social Psychology, 53*, 5–13.

Woody, E. Z., Lewis, V., Snider, L., Grant, H., Kamath, M., & Szechman, H. (2005). Induction of compulsive-like washing by blocking the feeling of knowing: An experimental test of the security-motivation hypothesis of obsessive–compulsive disorder. *Behavioral and Brain Functions, 1*, 11.

Zvolensky, M. J., Eifert, G. H., Lejuez, C. W., & McNeill, D. W. (1999). The effects of offset control over 20% carbon-dioxide-enriched air on anxious responding. *Journal of Abnormal Psychology, 108*, 624–632.

CHAPTER 12

The Compensatory Nature of Goal Pursuit
FROM EXPLICIT ACTION TO IMPLICIT COGNITION

GORDON B. MOSKOWITZ

I magine you are in a café, hungry, thirsty, and in need of caffeine. These are needs, specified by physiological states, and they produce motives that yield goals: to eat breakfast and to drink a caffeinated beverage. Imagine now you have finished your meal and feel satisfied yet are not satisfied. Though no longer hungry, thirsty, or in caffeine withdrawal, you now are in a café alone and in need of human companionship. You are lonely and feeling bored. These are not physiological needs but have many of the same qualities. These are psychological needs, what Lewin (1951) called "quasi-needs," that also ultimately yield goals: calling a friend (addressing the loneliness) whom you invite to go to the gym (addressing the boredom).

The two imagined scenarios described above share the requisite features of goal pursuit, features discussed in chapters of this book by Custers (Chapter 7), Liberman and Dar (Chapter 11), Martin and Tesser (Chapter 10), and Shah, Hall, and Leander (Chapter 9). Let us now succinctly review all these features, together. The first feature is an idea popularized by Lewin's (1936, 1951) field theory: that at the heart of understanding human motivation and goal pursuit is the *discrepancy*. The discrepancy in question is one between a desired state and one's current state, whether that discrepancy is physiological or psychological. For example, the body needs a certain level of sustenance, and the system may detect insufficient sustenance—a discrepancy between what is needed to operate well and what the system currently contains in terms of nutrients. As reviewed in Chapters 6 and 8, discrepancies may result from consciously deliberating among goals, or from goals being implicitly primed. This issue of the source of the discrepancy may be important in determining which from among one's many goals (the many discrepancies detected) is selected to be pursued at a given moment. But the first feature of goal pursuit is simply that, regardless of its source, a discrepancy is experienced (whether consciously experienced by the person or not).

The remaining features involve the way discrepancies motivate cognition and action. Features two through five involve processes that, on the surface, seem "cold" and mechanistic. The second feature is that when one experiences a discrepancy, a tension state arises. This can be a physiological state: For example, one may experience the pangs of hunger. The experienced tension may also be a psychological state: For example, one may experience longing associated with not having some desired object, or the uncomfortable sense of unease of receiving negative feedback that hints at failure. The third feature of goal pursuit is that the tension that arises from detecting a discrepancy is aversive and unpleasant. Like a drive, the aversive state aroused by the tension must be reduced: Responses must be taken to eliminate the tension. Goal striving arises to reduce the tension and eliminate the discrepancy. For example, when experiencing the pangs of hunger, one adopts the goal "to eat" and initiates appropriate responding. The fourth feature is that when the tension is satisfied, goal-relevant responding ends. If not satisfied, responding continues and may be adjusted. Thus, feedback regarding progress toward a goal, and rate of progress, inform the system's "decisions" regarding pace of responding and cessation of responding. The fifth feature is that to know when to cease (see Jostmann & Koole, Chapter 13, this volume) versus continue responding, the system is engaged in monitoring processes that allow you to know how you are doing (Liberman & Dar, Chapter 11, this volume). For example, combining features four and five, rather than eat ceaselessly, responding is eventually brought to a halt because one monitors (consciously or not) progress toward resolving the hunger, and ends responding when such monitoring provides appropriate feedback that the goal is reached, the tension is eliminated.

Miller, Galanter, and Pribram (1960) summarized this series of control steps in the test–operate–test–exit (TOTE) model of control (which grew out of Craik's [1947] engineering system analysis, and Wiener's [1948] cybernetic control theory). One tests for the degree of consistency between the desired state and the current state, operates a control action or response to attempt to reduce the discrepancy between them (if one exists), then tests again for the degree to which a discrepancy exists. If a discrepancy persists, the control action is continued. If the discrepancy is reduced, one exits this loop, terminating the goal pursuit. These actions of control constitute a *negative feedback loop,* or a closed-loop control system (Carver & Scheier, 1981). The term "negative feedback" loop refers to the fact that one's response is dependent on feedback regarding one's current state as it relates to a desired state. The response is performed as long as there is a negative state of goal attainment (a discrepancy) being fed back through the system.

Bandura (1989) provided a similar cognitive view that conceives of goals as specifying a performance standard. If the standard is attained then a positive self-evaluation prevails, whereas actions that fail to rise to the standard lead to negative self-evaluation. The individual is pushed by the negative self-evaluation associated with the discrepancy and pulled by the anticipated positive self-evaluation that is "intrinsically" linked to reducing the discrepancy. Thus, goals stimulate acting toward goal attainment only when people cognize a discrepancy between the standard and their current standing in goal pursuit. Bandura and Cervone (1983) also stated that people are expected to engage in efforts to reduce the discrepancy only when they feel self-efficacious with respect to the required actions. The most pronounced difference between the cybernetic models and that of Bandura is the role of affect. Bandura's explicitly describes tensions as associated with affective states that push and pull one's responses in a compensatory fashion. Cybernetic models require only that the comparator has discovered a discrepancy. Additionally, in this model goal pursuit does not necessarily end when the goal is reached. Goal attainment may raise feelings of self-efficacy, which can result in one setting more challenging goals, creating new discrepancies that stimulate new efforts at discrepancy reduction.

As stated above, both of these models describe processes of goal pursuit that make humans sound similar to machines, regulating thought and action the way a thermostat regulates release of heat. However, the final set of features fuse this cognitive perspective with the Lewinian motivational perspective. Goals are not simply "cold" cognitions specifying standards and discrepancies between "tested" current conditions and those standards. Goals are cognitively explicated and elaborated needs (Nuttin, 1980). Further features of goal pursuit make the point that affect, desire, commitment, and needs determine the selection and implementation of the goal, the inputs to the loop determining which discrepancy is being regulated, and why that discrepancy is the most relevant one to be pursued at a given moment. The selection and implementation of goals require the examination of the feasibility and desirability of various goals and the manner in which these goals relate to one's needs (the importance or strength of the goal, one's determination and commitment to the goal). The remaining set of features, thus, warm the model with the "hot" motivational perspective.

The sixth feature of goal pursuit is that many possible subgoals may be able to reduce the tension (several goals may satisfy the tension). Retaining the running example of the higher-order goal to eat, one may decide to eat eggs, croissants, bagels, or pancakes. Each subgoal can satisfy the goal to eat, and one may be a quite able to substitute for the other should an obstacle to one goal arise. But a given subgoal is selected from among the possibilities: for example, one adopts the goal to eat eggs. The seventh feature is that once a given goal is selected several possible means may be used to attain the goal. For example, the goal of consuming eggs can be attained by drinking them raw from a glass like Rocky Balboa, boiling them, getting them scrambled at a restaurant, and so on. Finally, the last feature is that a given goal does not exist in isolation but resides in a goal system, where one is balancing the pursuit of many goals and the resources needed to pursue those goals (with decisions about which goal to pursue made by analyzing forces such as the value of a goal, commitment to a goal, and opportunities in the environment to pursue it).

In summary, the control system involves the triggering of goals and the experience of discrepancies. This initiates required operations or responses that will eliminate the discrepancy, resolve its accompanying tension, and help one attain the goal. The operations are monitored through a feedback system so they can be adjusted and stopped when necessary. Finally, the specific goals one will select and the specific operations used in pursuing those goals are conceived of as linked to the wants/desires of the individual. Thus, goals are brimming with affect and commitment. However, the selection and implementation of a goal is dependent on an analysis of not merely the desirability of the goal, but the feasibility of attaining it given the means and opportunities present in the current context. This allows goal-relevant cues in the world to "speak to" goals, to establish what Lewin (1951) called valence: a force that connects, in terms of direction and strength, the tension of the individual and cues in the environment.

This chapter focuses on one feature of goal pursuit (and related issues), given that previous chapters have addressed the remaining features. The questions of interest addressed here concern the third feature of goal pursuit: Responding initiated to reduce a tension state one is experiencing and to eliminate to compensate for a discrepancy that defines a goal. The focus is on the "O" in the TOTE model: operations performed in the service of a goal. What determines which operations are performed? What is the nature of the operating system? What is the relationship between discrepancies and responses, or, how do goals shape compensatory thought and action?

Operation

Drawing from the features of goal pursuit reviewed above, a simple assertion is made: The responses or operations made in human goal pursuit are compensatory in nature. What does it mean to say responding is compensatory in nature? A goal specifies a desired state (which can include ending, or moving away from, a negative state). The desired state specified by the goal is not yet currently achieved. Responses that move the person toward that desired state (or away from an undesired state) are engaged to compensate for the discrepancy between the current state and the desired state. The operations initiated are compensatory in that they exist to address the fact the person is currently falling short of, or incomplete in movement toward, a desired end-state. Operation is, therefore, intimately tied to monitoring processes and to feedback. The nature of the monitoring process is reviewed in detail by Liberman and Dar (Chapter 11, this volume) and thus is not dealt with extensively here. But the relationship between monitoring and operations underscores the compensatory nature of the operations. Essentially, what is being monitored is whether a state exists (a discrepancy) for which one is thus required to compensate in his/her operations. If not, the operations are stopped. If so, specific operations that will address the detected discrepancy (compensate for it), revealed by the monitoring process, will be initiated.

Compensatory operations span the entire range of human responding, from minute responses of focusing attention on features of the stimulus environment and categorizing the objects/people detected, to overt action and conscious evaluation of objects and people. Thus, compensatory responses include not only the fairly intuitive notion of people taking goal-relevant action to help them achieve goals, but also the less intuitive notion of implicit cognition being in the service of one's goals. It is argued that the goal system implicitly directs where attention is focused, how a person is categorized, what concepts become activated or inhibited, and what goals (and means) will become accessible. Moskowitz (2001) labeled these less-than-intuitive compensatory responses "compensatory cognition."

The Empty Net (or the Invisible Man)

Compensatory responses can thus be conscious or nonconscious. Additionally, compensatory responses can occur to address goals one has consciously selected or to goals that are nonconsciously triggered (see Chapter 8, this volume). Moskowitz and Ignarri (in press) noted that a minimum of four classes of goal pursuit emerge from these distinctions: conscious responses to address conscious goals, conscious responses to address implicitly triggered goals, implicit responses that serve consciously triggered/selected goals, and implicit responses that are in the service of implicitly primed goals. The last two categories, in particular, suggest that as we tend to our goals, initiating our responses and monitoring our progress, the goaltender is not aware of the goaltending. Goals are being pursued, but it is like an "invisible man" is at the helm, not seen nor heard, but moving the individual along desired pathways.

Using a sports analogy from hockey, lacrosse, and soccer, it appears as if there is no goaltender, that there is an empty net. Yet the goal of keeping the ball/puck from the net is accomplished just the same, one simply cannot see the goaltending. This analogy of the empty net helps to illustrate the counterintuitive notion of implicit goal pursuit. Just as it is difficult for us to accept the idea that there is an invisible man playing goal and tending/guarding the net, it is difficult for us to accept the idea that we can engage in willed behavior and act in goal-driven ways without us being able to see the goals, let alone the responses/actions/operations. A large distinction between the sports analogy and the idea of implicit goal pursuit is that goalies cannot literally be invisible, but people can literally invisibly engage in control over thought and action. An empty net with an invisible man is a metaphor, but the invisible manner of goal pursuit is not.

How do operations become implicit? First, it is important to distinguish between implicit operations associated with a goal and those triggered by the environment, without the need of an intervening goal. James (1890/1950) asserted that behavior is mentally represented, and the representation can be triggered, leading to behavior in the absence of conscious thought or intent. He labeled this "ideo-motor action" (for a review, see Dijksterhuis & Bargh, 2001). Hull (1931) also stipulated that behavior is a mental representation and posited that unconsciously triggered action is not an error, but "that ideo-motor acts are in reality anticipatory goal reactions and, as such, are called into existence by ordinary physical stimulation . . . these anticipatory goal reactions are pure stimulus acts and, as such, guide and direct the more explicit and instrumental activities of the organism" (p. 502). Thus, in some instances responses precede a goal, in anticipation of a goal (a learned response that some stimuli are associated with behavior that has relevance to goals). Examples of this are offered by James (1890/1950), such as the person who lies in bed consciously dreading the cold awaiting outside the covers who nonetheless is soon dressed and making coffee without consciously having left the bed. Or the person who completes a big meal and is too stuffed to eat, only soon found to be stuffing candies into his/her mouth once seeing them on the table. In each case the goal is to not do something, but even without a goal the perception of cues (the clock, candy) linked to a behavior (get dressed, eat) triggers the response.

But the concern here is not responses that are not triggered by goals, but responses that are triggered by goals, just goals one does not see (and responses one may not know are being performed). Just as the "means" that are relevant to a goal can trigger a goal without one's awareness of the goal's accessibility (or even without one's awareness of the prime, see

Chapter 8, this volume), goals trigger goal-relevant responding. This can happen without conscious awareness in the same manner in which the implicit association between a goal and its means develop (see Chapter 9, this volume). Automatic processes develop through routinely performing tasks that we need and desire. Just like any skill acquisition, the responses associated with a goal develop an implicit link to that goal (capable of being triggered without consciousness) through practice and routine pursuit. James (1890/1950, p. 519) stated "often-repeated movements follow on their mental cue. An end consented to as soon as conceived innervates directly the centre of the first movement of the chain which leads to its accomplishment, and then the whole chain rattles off *quasi*-reflexly." The pairing of/association between the goal, the means to the goal, the contexts in which means are encountered, and the operations performed when encountering those means can be made automatic. This occurs through practice, frequent/routine pursuit, and specificity in association.

In summary, goal operations can be implicit and do not require one has an accompanying feeling of determination or a sense of willing. This does not make the response any less willed or driven by one's goals. Goal-tending can be an invisible process. Long ago, William James (1890/1950) wondered whether anything else is required in the mind to produce willed responses other than a "mental conception made up of memory-images of [passive movement] these sensations, defining which special act it is" (p. 492). James answered this by saying, "there need be nothing else, and that in perfectly simple voluntary acts there is nothing else in the mind but the kinaesthetic idea, thus defined, of what the act is to be" (pp. 492–493). A feeling of determination or of willing a response is not required for it to be volitional. Given that responses become implicit only after having made a conscious decision to enact and engage them when encountering a specific cue that is related to a specific goal, this position makes clear that consciousness is not an epiphenomenon. Consciousness is essential for the development of implicit operations but can be removed from being involved once those operations become implicitly associated with a goal.

Explicit Compensatory Responses

This chapter seeks to (1) illustrate the wide range of phenomena in which the compensatory nature of goal pursuit is evidenced (e.g., cognitive dissonance, achievement, thought suppression, prejudice, creativity, and decision making) and (2) illustrate the implicit, as well as explicit, nature of compensatory responding. Given the influence of Kurt Lewin over the field of social psychology, it is not surprising that almost any "classic" experiment in the field could be viewed as people exhibiting compensatory responding to a perceived discrepancy. When do bystanders intervene? Only when they note a discrepancy between what they should do (a desired end-state) and what they are doing. If they characterize the situation as one not in need of one's personal intervention (either through pluralistic ignorance or diffusion of responsibility) they do not experience a tension and thus do not act. Why do people shock a "learner" at an experimenter's insistence? Because they struggle between two goals (to obey and be kind), each not yet being met in their behavior. Ultimately one goal wins, and the discrepancy is reduced by a compensatory response to that goal: one either obeys and shocks, or exits. Why do people persuade and prostelytyze after a tragedy does not occur? Why do people label an experienced physiological state with an emotion identified by the cues in the environment? Why do people conform in naming line lengths? Because these are compensatory responses to tension states, states that arise from having detected a discrepancy. A sampling of the literature follows.

The Theory of Symbolic Self-Completion

We can conceive of people as striving to attain certain higher-order goals, called "self-defining goals." The desired end-state of such goals is specifying an identity (such as being a professional musician, or a research scientist, or an athlete, etc.). As there are many potential indicators that one possesses a given identity, a given identity can be serviced by many lower-order goals. Wicklund and Gollwitzer (1982) proposed that people are engaged in an ongoing process of pursuing goals that allow one to collect indicators or symbols of having attained the desired identity. For example, attaining the identity of "successful musician" may include pursuing and attaining goals that allow one to attain symbols of that success such as being invited (and paid) to play gigs, developing fans, and accruing sales of one's recorded music. But what happens if a given identity is challenged and an important sense of self is undermined?

Wicklund and Gollwitzer (1982) postulated that when shortcomings with respect to the pursuit of a goal are encountered, the individual experiences self-definitional incompleteness. The sense of incompleteness is equivalent to the tension state reviewed earlier. The discrepancy reviewed above is represented in their model by one's detected failure or shortcoming in a goal pursuit. They posited that one manner people act toward goal attainment, or to produce a sense of self-completion to replace the sense of incompleteness surrounding the challenged identity, is by acquiring symbols that suggest one possesses qualities associated with the goal. Thus, the name "the theory of symbolic self-completion." To summarize, upon detecting a discrepancy, a sense of self-definitional incompleteness in the goal domain drives the person to *compensatory efforts* aimed at pointing to the possession of alternative symbols representing the goal or to acquiring new symbols. The tension will be greatest when an individual is committed to a goal domain, when it is self-defining. We compensate for failures and shortcomings by attempting to display to ourselves and others that we actually are not failures in the domain in question but successes.

What type of symbols can the individual attempt to point to or acquire that will play this compensatory role and restore self-completion? The model is quite specific in asserting that these need to be symbols that are perceived to be relevant to the undermined identity. If one values being a musician, and has one's sense of being a good or successful musician challenged (e.g., one fails to get gigs in the local clubs), then one needs to acquire symbols that reassert success in this specific domain. Affirming the self in an irrelevant domain by acquiring symbols that point to one being a good cook will not compensate for the incompleteness. Nor will acquiring symbols that point to one's success in an important domain, such as being a good father, but not the domain that has been undermined. The compensatory behavior must restore completeness in the domain that has produced the tension/incompleteness. For example, if one's identity as a musician is challenged, symbols that one would attempt to collect as compensation include things such as purchasing equipment, getting gigs, and rehearsing. Collecting such symbols would indicate that one is moving in the correct direction, thus reducing the tension.

In one illustration of this model, Gollwitzer, Wicklund, and Hilton (1982) asked students to list six mistakes they had made in either a self-defining domain (musician) or an irrelevant domain (cooking). Listing mistakes in these domains created a discrepancy between the current state (incompleteness) and the desired state (success in the goal domain). Participants then were asked to write a biographical essay about their involvement in the domain for which they had listed failures. They were asked not to linger too long on this essay task and were additionally told that there was an alternative (more attractive) task they could turn to once finished. However, the biography afforded participants an opportunity to collect symbols of self-completion, to *compensate* for the failures previously listed by now listing successes.

The model predicts that though all people experienced failure, only failure in a relevant domain would trigger incompleteness and compensatory strivings. Failing at something we do not care about creates a discrepancy, but not one that triggers a tension associated with it. As predicted by the theory, compensatory behavior was exhibited only for people whose failures had accompanying states of incompleteness. Relative to the control group, participants undermined in a relevant dimension/identity wrote biographical essays for a longer period of time before turning to the alternate task. They used the task as an opportunity to reflect positively on their accomplishments in the domain in question. Although it is possible participants did not explicitly set out (deliberately) to dedicate more time to these essays, it is hard to argue that the essay was not explicitly seen as an opportunity to reaffirm their sense of self in the challenged domain.

Self-Discrepancy Theory

Higgins (1989) also focused on self-defining goals. Higgins posited there are different types of discrepancies that can be experienced. The nature of the discrepancy relates to the type of standard one uses for representing a self-defining goal. One's actual standing in relation to a goal pursuit can be compared against a standard that specifies what one ought to have attained (i.e., what one should accomplish) or against a standard that specifies what one can ideally attain (i.e., what one would hope to accomplish). Thus, the goal domain may stay the same, but the discrepancy that is experienced, and the type of tension associated with that discrepancy, can change dramatically dependent upon the standard being used to represent that domain. For example, a failure or shortcoming in the domain of being a musician will lead to the experience of one type of tension if the standard for being a musician is what one ought to accomplish as a musician, and it will lead to the experience of a wholly different tension if the standard of what one ideally hopes and dreams to accomplish as a musician is used. The current state is the same, but the standard changes from ought ("I ought to be sustaining myself financially, I ought to be playing gigs, I ought to be doing solid work") to ideal ("I hope to tour with a band in large clubs, I hope to be financially secure and saving for my future, I hope to be recording and selling music").

In some sense this is merely stating that different subgoals produce unique experiences for the individual. But in another sense it is saying far more: that the framing of the same general goal, in terms of wishes, hopes, and ideals versus what one ought to or should do, has systematic and predictable effects on the type of tension that is experienced, regardless of the goal domain that is being challenged. A discrepancy between one's actual state and the state one ought to have attained leads to the experience of agitation-related emotions (such as anxiety, fear, guilt, and restlessness). However, a discrepancy between one's actual state and an ideal state (what one hopes to attain) will lead to dejection-related emotions (such as sadness, depression, disappointment). Thus, the experience of a discrepancy from a standard has different consequences for the type of psychological tension experienced as a function of the type of standards one uses as a self-guide. But the type of tension experienced, assuming the standard being used is the same, cuts across different goal domains. Thus, one experiences agitation and guilt whether one experiences a discrepancy with how one ought to be pursuing the goal of being a musician or whether one experiences a discrepancy with how one ought to be pursuing the goal of being generous (assuming both goal domains are self-defining for the person).

The logical extension of this is that different types of compensatory behaviors are appropriate if the nature of the tension state changes. What is deemed relevant as a compensatory response will depend on what one is compensating for. For example, how one responds to the fact that one is not always egalitarian (goal failure) will be different dependent on whether the standard being used for evaluating that failure is the fact that one ought to be egalitarian or the fact that one ideally would like to be egalitarian. Each discrepancy triggers a different tension. Similarly, a discrepancy will only trigger a tension if it is self-defining. A person who experiences a discrepancy between the fact that he/she is not always egalitarian and the fact that he/she should be egalitarian will experience guilt and agitated tension states only if that goal is in fact important to him/her and self-defining. A person high in prejudice would detect the discrepancy, but not experience the tension state, because being egalitarian is not important to them.

The relationship between compensatory behavior and self-discrepancies has been examined in research on egalitarianism and prejudice. Devine (1989, Experiment 3) induced people high and low in prejudice to fail at the goal of being egalitarian. As part of an experiment ostensibly about how people informally talk about groups, participants were asked to list as many labels for the group "Blacks" as they could, even slang words and negative words. For participants low and high in prejudice this task represents a failure, pointing out the discrepancy that they have used words they know that they ought to not use. People high in prejudice and people low in prejudice should react to this discrepancy in drastically different ways: for one group there is a tension aroused from having violated a self-defining ought standard, the other group has violated nothing self-defining. The model predicts different compensatory responding to the exact same discrepancy because of differences in the experienced tension state. People low in prejudice should compensate in their subsequent behavior, people high in prejudice should not.

To test this prediction Devine (1989) next had participants list their personal thoughts about these labels and about Blacks as a group more generally. This "thought-listing" task can be conceived of as an opportunity to acquire symbols that represent compensatory actions. That is, to compensate for having discussed the "terrible" things that others may sometimes say about the group, and that the individual was now coerced into expressing, the person could now espouse personal beliefs that reveal how egalitarian one actually is. Indeed, participants low in prejudice used this task to express far more positive beliefs about Black Americans than participants high in prejudice, and to use far fewer negative and stereo-typic descriptions regarding the group.

Monteith (1993) extended the finding that compensatory acts, specific to the type of tension associated with an "ought" standard, arise from detecting a self-discrepancy. Monteith (Experiment 1) triggered a discrepancy by telling participants they were biased toward gay men. This was done by giving them what they believed were applications to law school to evaluate, with an applicant's sexual orientation—gay or straight—provided in the folder. People who read a gay student's application were given (false) feedback that their evaluation revealed an antigay bias. Measures were then taken to see if the tension associated with an ought discrepancy (psychological states such guilt and agitation) and compensatory acts were evidenced.

Similar to previous research (e.g., Devine, Monteith, Zuwerink, & Elliot, 1991) ratings of guilt were higher for participants experiencing a discrepancy. Additionally, a thought-listing task measured compensatory responses by assessing the extent to which participants ruminated on their discrepancy. Participants experiencing the tension state associated with the discrepancy compensated for this by focusing their explicit thoughts on their discrepant feelings/behavior. Finally, when given an essay to read about why discrepancies occur and what can be done to reduce them in the future, these participants dedicated more time to reading the essay and had better memory for the evidence the essay provided. Thus, attention was allocated to stimuli relevant to the discrepancy, and a search was initiated for indications of the discrepancy. These responses are compensatory in that they allow the individual to specify the conditions that produced the discrepancy and to establish coping strategies useful for fighting the discrepancy.

Monteith (1993, Experiment 2) provided another example of how tension states motivate people to consciously attempt to correct for, or compensate for, the undesired use of stereotypes. Participants were asked to evaluate jokes, some invoking the stereotype of gay men. Participants who were low in prejudice did not have a problem with these jokes, unless these participants had recently been made, by previous experimental procedures, to experience a discrepancy between how egalitarian and unbiased they should be and their actual behavior. Participants with a discrepancy compensated for the tension state in their unfavorable evaluation of the jokes.

Behavioral Inhibition Theory

Monteith and Voils (2001) provided a theory of how specific compensatory responses are triggered by a tension state that is associated with a specific type of discrepancy. Focusing on prejudice, they argued that a set of compensatory processes aimed at controlling bias are triggered by the experience of prejudice-related tension. Their model posits that an association develops between detection of a discrepancy in one's sense of self as unbiased (acting in a nonegalitarian fashion), an experienced tension state, the cues in the environment that trigger that discrepancy and tension (e.g., the presence of a Black or gay person), and appropriate compensatory responses. Initially this is all explicit to the person—one must first recognize a discrepancy with one's personal standards of prejudice, which initiates the associated tension state—in this case experienced as feelings of guilt and disappointment. Cues associated with the aversive state lead one to attempt to compensate for the undesired behavior (the discrepancy). The cues (people who may potentially be evaluated in a biased way) serve as a warning to the discrepancy between how one should respond and how one does respond, triggering the compensatory response.

Monteith and Voils (2001) argued that the compensatory response triggered is the operation of the behavioral inhibition system (BIS). What is the BIS? Monteith, Ashburn-Nardo, Voils, and Czopp (2002) described it as a motivational system associated with a specific brain structure that causes heightened arousal and a momentary pausing/interruption of one's current behavior. This brief stoppage of action allows one to increase attention to stimuli that are relevant to one's discrepancy and to determine what might have caused the discrepancy as well as to explore and search for indicators of the discrepant response. Monteith and Voils (p. 382) stated, "when [cues for control] are present in subsequent situations, the BIS should be activated again, causing heightened arousal and a slowing of ongoing behavior (i.e., behavioral inhibition). Consequently, the response-generation process should be slowed and executed more carefully." In sum, one explicitly compensates for a discrepancy when its associated cues are detected.

To illustrate the compensatory nature of the BIS-related responses, Monteith et al. (2002) undermined participants' goal of being nonprejudiced. Equipment said to measure physiological arousal provided computer-generated "feedback" indicating negative response to images. The feedback led some participants to believe they responded with negative arousal to pictures with racial content. Control participants were informed they had low negative arousal to the same stimuli (and high arousal to nonracial pictures). Participants were instructed to press the space bar after they received the feedback to advance to the next picture. The time between getting feedback and pressing the spacebar was the measure of behavioral inhibition. Participants with a discrepancy had slower responses to pressing the spacebar relative to the control group.

In another experiment feedback was provided to participants by having them take the Implicit Association Test (IAT). Being informed of their (actual) implicit bias served as the triggering of the discrepancy. Participants next completed two tasks. The first task involved viewing words on the monitor and pressing a button to indicate if the word was a living or nonliving thing. The items contained filler words as well as words from the IAT. The second task asked participants to indicate like or dislike to the same words presented in reverse order. The rationale was that the Black names from the IAT task would now serve as cues for control in the like–dislike task, but only among participants who experienced a discrepancy associated with their previous IAT performance. They found that following Black names, participants were less likely to generate racially biased responses and responded slower when presented with the Black name. But this only occurred for people who felt guilty about their IAT performance. Behavioral inhibition was triggered in people compensating for a discrepancy relating to a self-relevant goal.

The Theory of Cognitive Dissonance: The Case of Hypocrisy

Of course, the idea that a psychological tension compels people to strive to reduce the tension by compensatory responding is a central tenet of one of social psychologies oldest and most well-known theories: Festinger's (1957) theory of cognitive dissonance (not surprising, given the intellectual link between Lewin and Festinger). One way of instantiating the tension labeled as "dissonance" is by inducing in people a feeling of hypocrisy. That is, detecting a discrepancy between how you should act and how reality reveals you do act is, in another language, a case of detecting your own hypocrisy. Stone, Aronson, Crain, Winslow, and Fried (1994) found that hypocrisy is a powerful motivator of compensatory behavior.

Stone et al. (1994) illustrated this in one experiment by making people aware of their hypocrisy in the domain of sexual behavior: use of condoms. Participants recorded a message, that the experimenter said would be shown to others, about the importance of using condoms during sex to prevent the spread of AIDS. Hypocrisy was aroused in some participants by making them aware of how their own past behavior was discrepant with the position they just espoused and recorded. They have at times not used condoms. Does the discrepancy trigger compensatory behavior? Participants who experienced the discrepancy (hypocrisy) were more likely to engage in compensatory behavior that addressed the hypocrisy (purchasing condoms).

Is the compensatory response specific to the goal domain that had been threatened (condom use, in this case)? Or does it make people want to do anything self-affirming to stop feeling bad? To investigate this question, Stone, Weigand, Cooper, and Aronson (1997) followed the procedures of Stone et al. (1994) but offered more than one behavioral strategy for "feeling good" to participants, one irrelevant to their hypocrisy and one relevant to it. Some participants were provided the opportunity to purchase condoms at the end of the experiment and the opportunity to donate money to the homeless. Some only had the option of donating money. The results show that when only asked to donate money, 83% of participants aware of their hypocrisy donated to the homeless. However, when the opportunity to buy condoms was present along with the opportunity to donate to a homeless shelter, 78% chose to purchase condoms and only 13% chose to donate to the shelter. Thus, rather than just doing something affirming (giving money to the homeless), people are attempting to compensate quite specifically for a goal-relevant tension.

Self-Affirmation Theory

What the previous experiment illustrates is that when not given the opportunity to compensate in the specific domain, people still attempt to compensate for their goal-related tension state by responding in the most appropriate fashion to the opportunities that are present. This is consistent with self-affirmation theory (e.g., Steele, 1988). A discrepancy between a standard/reference point/desired goal and one's current state of goal pursuit is essentially providing the person with negative feedback. They are incomplete in an important identity-relevant domain. Steele (1988) proposed this represents not merely a specific type of discrepancy in a given domain, but also a threat to the integrity of one's entire self-belief system. Steele (1988) asserted that one can maintain a positive view of the self in the face of negative feedback by focusing not on the feedback, but by engaging in self-affirmation whereby one focuses on retrieving and contemplating positive aspects of one's self-concept that are not currently under threat. Thus, according to the theory, affirming self-esteem is a compensatory response to a more global discrepancy between higher-order goals of having positive esteem and one's current standing.

Many experiments illustrate the affirmation of the self-system in the face of such negative feedback, or a discrepancy to the positive sense of self. We focus on one example in which the route to compensation is the derogation of and prejudice toward members of low-status/stigmatized groups, who serve as targets of downward comparison. Fein and Spencer (1997) had participants receive either negative or positive feedback on a bogus intelligence test, thus either affirming or threatening their positive sense of self. All participants next reviewed a description of a woman as part of a job application. Her name either implied she was Jewish or non-Jewish. The experiment examined whether participants compensated for their discrepant self-esteem by assessing their ratings of the target's qualification for the job and personality. People who were given negative feedback (had an active discrepancy) rated the target more negatively on job qualification and traits if she was Jewish. This stereotyping effect did not emerge among participants who had received positive feedback.

Additionally, self-esteem was measured after participants received the bogus feedback on the intelligence test, and again after completing the evaluation of the target. The participants who received negative feedback had lower-state self-esteem than those given positive feedback. Further, the opportunity to derogate the Jewish woman seemed to repair self-esteem. Participants who received negative feedback and had the opportunity to derogate showed a larger increase in self-esteem after the rating task than other participants (although the statistical tests fell short of conventional levels of significance). The compensatory nature of stereotyping as a response to self-esteem threat was further illustrated in another experiment where participants once again received bogus feedback on an intelligence test. Rather than manipulating whether the feedback was good or bad, it was all bad, and they manipulated instead whether the feedback was perceived to be accurate or faulty. Among participants whose self-esteem had been undermined, a gay target was rated as possessing more gay-stereotypic characteristics than a heterosexual target. This stereotyping effect did not emerge for participants who were told the feedback was inaccurate and faulty (and thus spared from self-esteem threat and the discrepancy it causes). The goal to restore esteem appears to be regulated through compensatory processes of stereotyping.

Dual-Process Theories

At the risk of overkill, let it be noted that the entire body of work in social cognition covering the large part of the last three decades describes cognition as compensatory responses to explicit goals that either are delivered to the person by the experimenter, or perceived by the person through his/her own monitoring processes. In dual-process models, across all varieties of dual-process models, the heart of the switch from one process (heuristic or peripheral or stereotypic) to another (systematic or central or personalized) is a goal. In most models it is made quite explicit that this goal arises from a tension state that is caused by not meeting some desired end or standard/ threshold. Just to give one example, Chaiken, Liberman, and Eagly (1989) referred to one having the goal of forming a sufficiently good judgment in which one is confident. The end-state is marked by a sufficiency threshold, and the act of systematic processing compensates for a confidence gap—an experienced tension state arising when one's judgments do not meet the level specified by threshold (a discrepancy). One compensates with increased processing until the threshold is reached (the discrepancy is reduced and the tension is eliminated).

Most dual-process models share this logic, if not using the exact same terms, and differ typically in the domain they examine—from contrast effects in correction processes, to stereotyping and stereotype control, to persuasion, to impression formation, and priming effects. For example, correction models that explain contrast effects (e.g., Moskowitz & Roman, 1992; Strack & Hanover, 1996; Wegener & Petty, 1995; Wilson & Brekke, 1994) are essentially describing people as compensating for perceived bias. Wegener and Petty (1995) described contrast as emerging from a perceived a discrepancy between how one should respond and how one does respond. The tension state is described by their model as a metacognitive belief: thinking about the meaning of one's mental sensations associated with the discrepancy. These beliefs initiate a correction in the opposite direction to overcome and compensate for the perceived bias in one's judgment. Wilson and Brekke (1994) described people as attempting to remove what they experience as mental contamination. The contamination is the discrepancy, the feeling of having inadequate judgments is the tension state, and the removal/correction processes employed are the explicit attempt to reduce the discrepancy—what they refer to as "decontamination."

Rather than reviewing all the types of correction processes that can possibly be initiated by people who suspect bias in their responding, one example is discussed at length to illustrate the compensatory nature of the operations that are triggered in dual-process accounts. Research on accountability and accuracy goals (e.g., Fiske & Neuberg, 1990; Tetlock, 1985) has revealed that when people are given the goal of being accountable for their judgments and evaluations of other people (or forming accurate judgments), the way in which one attends to, evaluates, and acts toward that person changes. People do not use the easiest, most accessible interpretation for another person's behavior to explain why they act as they do (Thompson, Roman, Moskowitz, Chaiken, & Bargh, 1994) and instead consider a wider range of qualities in describing the person. Nor do they attribute the cause for the person's behavior to the person's disposition and the person's desire to bring about the particular consequences that were observed (Tetlock, 1985). They stereotype less and minimize the extent to which self-fulfilling prophecies emerge. These outcomes from accountability goals are all due to compensatory acts.

Neuberg (1989) examined how stereotypes affect cognition and behavior in the domain of job interviews but more importantly illustrated how an accuracy goal leads to attempts to compensate for one's perceived inaccuracy in those settings, thus reducing stereotyping. How were stereotypes assessed? A job interview is a forum for gathering information and testing hypotheses about a person, so if people are thinking and acting in ways guided by stereotypes, confirmatory processes should predominate. People would ask confirmatory questions that elicit answers affirming their stereotypes. Additionally, the stereotypes of the interviewer should work their way into the behavior of the person being interviewed—a self-fulfilling prophecy. The interviewer's behavior will restrict the interviewee's ability to respond and lead to expectancy-confirming responses. However, these stereotype-confirming processes should be attenuated when one has accuracy goals. Interviewers should compensate for their perceived discrepancy between their desired level of accuracy and their currently biased thinking. They can do this by altering how they think and act. They should attempt to gather more comprehensive and less biased information and treat the interviewee in a more complex and expectancy-inconsistent behavior (thus producing less stereotypic responses from those people).

Neuberg (1989) asked participants to interview and assesses two job applicants. They receive negative information about one of the applicants, and no information about the other. Half of the interviewers are given explicit goals to be accurate in their interview, half are given no goals. The interviews occur (and are taped), and ratings of the applicants are made. The behavior of the interviewers (the types of questions they ask, the number of speech errors they make while conducting the interview) and responses of the interviewee are then analyzed from the tape. The results revealed that people without accuracy goals form more negative impressions of the person for whom they had a negative, versus no, expectancy. People with accuracy goals did not show this bias. What sort of compensatory acts are indicative of their attempts to be nonbiased and accurate? They listen more to the person they had a negative expectancy toward than to people they had no expectancy toward. They are more encouraging in the questions they ask (being more affirming with interjections such as "mmm-hmmm"). Finally, they ask more open-ended, novel, and positively framed questions. These types of questions led interviewees to act in ways that were more favorably received by neutral observers.

Implicit Compensatory Responses

Although it is intuitively obvious that people explicitly act in ways to stop unpleasant sensations that they explicitly know exist, the precise manner in which they do so is perhaps not so obvious, as the preceding section hopefully illustrated. Additionally, it also illustrated that people explicitly compensate for tensions even when they may not realize that they are compensating. It is unlikely that Fein and Spencer's (1997) participants knew they were stereotyping more to restore self-esteem. The same is true of the behavioral inhibition responses observed by people in Monteith et al.'s (2002) experiments. This section takes this possibility to its logical extreme. It is suggested and illustrated that people often compensate without knowing they are engaging in any response and even compensate without knowing that any goal or discrepancy or tension state exists (they do not explicitly recognize these things). Is this less intuitive? Perhaps not. In two paragraphs I can illustrate how common implicit compensation is.

Please try to recall your early history lessons and the story of Archimedes running naked through the streets of Syracuse yelling "Eureka." Although running naked is hardly an implicit response, the epiphany that drew Archimedes to the streets was. Archimedes was consciously grappling with a dense and difficult problem: how to measure the purity of gold. He was stumped and frustrated. So he consciously decided to place his ruminations on this problem on hold so he could instead relax in the bath. Something we all do. As is the case with many of us, Archimedes had his best idea while distracted in the bath, supposedly relaxing. The displacement of the water by his body triggered the answer to the thought his mind had been grappling with. I contend that the use of the past tense in that description is inaccurate. It is not that his mind "had been" grappling with this problem. It is that his conscious mind had been doing so and currently was not. But this does not mean he was not still pursuing this goal at the nonconscious level. Archimedes was, as you and I often are, engaged in nonconscious cognition that was pursuing the goal (discrepancy) consciousness had vacated for other pastures. The shock of the solution appearing out of the blue, springing into consciousness as if delivered from God, led him to his famous shout of exuberance: "Eureka" (and to become perhaps the first streaker on record).

Just in case you do not know the story of Archimedes, simply think back to the last time you had difficulty retrieving some bit of trivia (or perhaps even something important) from memory. When trying to retrieve information from memory (e.g., what was the name of the man who shot and killed Robert Kennedy?), we sometimes experience a "tip-of-the-tongue effect" where the desired information feels as if it is knowledge you possess and is about to become accessible to you. But despite feeling like it will come to you, you cannot produce the response. Struggling with this for some time ultimately leads you to consciously disengage from the task. Interestingly, the desired information often comes rushing into consciousness at some later time (e.g., "it was Sirhan Sirhan!") when you were not trying to retrieve it. This is an example of nonconscious, yet compensatory, cognition. You had consciously disengaged from the goal yet preconsciously continued to pursue it without intending to or being aware the goal was active and being regulated. Just as in the Archimedes story, you solve a problem without trying; But you were actually trying, you simply were trying to pursue the goal preconsciously, and thus the solution to the task, the attainment of the goal, is delivered to your conscious mind seemingly magically—it pops into consciousness as if from nowhere (or as if by divine intervention).

Implicit Rumination as Compensatory Cognition

Anecdotes of Archimedes aside, there is empirical evidence to support this idea that implicit operations promote the attainment of one's goal. The Zeigarnik effect (see Chapter 8, this volume) is a seminal example. The soon-to-be seminal "deliberation-without-attention" effect of Dijksterhuis, Bos, Nordgren, and van Baaren (2006) is another. Participants were given the explicit goal of ruminating on the qualities of several products (from among four cars, for example) and then choosing the best option. Until the choice is made we can state that a discrepancy exists between the desired end (expressing a judgment built from weighing the options) and one's current state of uncertainty and being middeliberation. Some participants were allowed to consciously ruminate on the qualities, engaging thus in explicit operations that can compensate for this discrepancy. However, other participants had their attention distracted and thus were prevented from consciously thinking about and deliberating over the choices.

Did being prevented from consciously deliberating and ruminating over the choices mean that no operations of deliberation and rumination were being conducted? No. Participants continued to work on the problem at a nonconscious level, allowing them to weigh and consider the options without knowing they were doing so (unlike Archimedes, they kept their clothes on). How did Dijksterhuis et al. (2006) discern that nonconscious deliberation was being engaged as what I am referring to as a "compensatory response" to their goal having been unattained? They evaluated the quality of the decisions that participants produced. Better decisions were shown to have been made by the people prevented from consciously ruminating. The goal to ruminate among the choices is accessible and directing cognition, allowing the individual to unconsciously deliberate among the products and yield a better choice despite the conscious goal having been released.

Similar compensatory rumination, despite the implicit nature of the goal and the rumination processes, was illustrated by Koole, Smeets, van Knippenberg, and Dijksterhuis (1999). Their work couples two ideas: that ruminative thinking is goal directed, and it may be evidenced by implicit measures. The goal participants pursued is to enhance self-esteem, a goal triggered by discrepancy detection. Participants receive feedback that they have failed a test that assessed their intelligence. Rumination about the test and intelligence is then assessed across several experiments. In each experiment the participants have a goal triggered by a discrepancy being detected, and in each implicit cognition that steers the cognitive system toward goal-relevant stimuli is initiated. In support of the idea that these are indeed discrepancy-driven processes, in each case these implicit processes are brought to a halt when the tension is released by the person receiving goal-affirming feedback. For example, in one experiment a lexical decision task was used to assess implicit accessibility of the goal. Relative to control participants, those whose feedback was tantamount to discrepancy detection were faster to recognize words related to intelligence. Rumination about the test and about intelligence was found despite participants not knowing the goal was accessible when performing the lexical decision task.

Implicit Creativity

Sassenberg and Moskowitz (2005) similarly illustrated implicit operations in the service of a goal, focusing on creativity goals. It has been illustrated that conscious attempts at pursuing creativity are wrought with error. They posited that when the goal is pursued through implicit operations, the goal is facilitated and creativity more likely to emerge. What are these implicit operations (compensatory responses)? Creativity requires novelty and innovation: ingenuity. They hypothesized that this can be delivered by a cognitive system that triggers a specific set of implicit operations with the goal to be creative: the inhibition of typical associations to whatever concept one is attempting to think creatively about, and the increased accessibility of atypical associates to the same concept. These operations alter the types of thoughts that come to mind and thus the strategies people engage when performing behavior calling for creativity.

In one experiment, Sassenberg and Moskowitz (2005) examined whether participants displayed a typical priming effect: a facilitated ability to respond to a target word (e.g., nurse) after a relevant target is presented (e.g., doctor). They found that people with creativity goals had less facilitation (slower reaction times) for classifying the prime-relevant words than control participants. Responses to the word "nurse" were not faster when it followed the word "doctor." In a second experiment a similar finding emerged using faces of members of a stereotyped group as primes and following such faces with words that were either stereotype relevant or irrelevant. Participants in a control condition had facilitated responses to words relating to stereotypes of Black men after seeing a face of a Black man. However, those with creativity goals did not have this typical association triggered. There appears to be an implicit operation whereby when a discrepancy exists relating to the goal of being creative people compensate for this state by implicit inhibitory processes that prevent typical associates to a category from attaining heightened accessibility. The seeming irrelevance of the task to creativity, as well as the fast response times (see Bargh &

Chartrand, 2000), suggest the creativity goal was implicitly accessible and guiding responses.

Subsequent research illustrates that these implicit operations affect behavior. Sassenberg, Moskowitz, Kessler, and Mummendey (2009) showed that participants exhibit greater creative behavior when implicitly primed with creativity than when explicitly asked to be creative. The task was to generate names for a new pasta product as part of a purported marketing study. Some participants were explicitly asked to do so in a creative way, by not duplicating existing pasta names such as "spaghetti," "linguini," and "fettucini." They found participants with explicit goals were not creative but instead had responses anchored to existing product names (e.g., they suggest "fellini"). People implicitly primed with creativity show no such bias. Examining the product names generated, they are able to offer novel names that are not as heavily dependent on the examples that had been provided.

Implicit Processes in Thought Suppression

Many goal pursuits involve a mix of explicit and implicit operations, sometimes working in conjunction, and sometimes with the implicit process yielding unexpected and undesired effects that the explicit goal had not intended. Perhaps the most well known example of an unintended, unexpected, and even intention-opposing result of the implicit operations used in goal pursuit is the work that illustrates the difficulty people have in suppressing or avoiding unwanted thoughts. Thought suppression—whether it be dieters avoiding thoughts of food, managers and personnel officers avoiding thoughts of stereotypes, or jilted lovers trying to avoid thinking about their "ex"—is difficult to attain. We often end up thinking of the very thoughts we intend to avoid. Why do we experience this unwanted and unintended thought?

Wegner (1994) proposed a theory implicating two concurrent systems that are triggered when pursuing the goal of thought suppression (in the language of this chapter, when one is attempting to compensate for the fact that one has a discrepancy: thoughts one does not wish to have and desires to suppress). One system involves the conscious, intended operation of thinking about something else: replacement thoughts. This system occupies the mind with thoughts that are not the unwanted thought, even seeking items inconsistent with the unwanted thought to replace it in consciousness. But a second system is also implicated, an efficient one that runs implicitly: a monitoring process. Monitoring processes (described in detail by Liberman & Dar, Chapter 11, this volume) involve the checking, or testing, of one's standing in goal pursuit. In this case, it involves searching for failures of control, detecting for references to the unwanted thought. This requires holding in mind (at least below consciousness) the very thought that is not to enter consciousness. Wegner (1994) suggested that the operating system requires cognitive resources: one is consciously trying to occupy the mind with replacement thoughts. Monitoring can be implicit, however, and Wegner proposed that in this case it is. The monitor's task is simpler and is relatively free from capacity restrictions.

These concurrent processes, one implicit, one explicit, are what result in the unintended, what Wegner (1994) called ironic, consequences of thought suppression—the "rebound" of the unwanted thought. Because of its implicit operation, the monitoring process functions efficiently, whereas the operating process is disabled, when there are drains on cognitive resources, such as a "cognitive load." The disabling of the operating system, while the monitor continues to function, results in the unwanted thought being undeterred from reaching consciousness. Additionally, monitoring, by searching for unwanted thoughts to keep them from consciousness, results in the repetitive priming of those thoughts. Wegner and Erber (1992) referred to suppressed thoughts as being *hyperaccessible*. So long as the explicit goal to not think these thoughts is in place, this heightened accessibility does not influence one's responses. But a change in explicit goals should leave the consequences of the monitoring process—heightened accessibility of the unwanted thought—now in a state of increased likelihood to be used. In sum, either cognitive load or no longer trying to suppress can result in unwanted thoughts usurping consciousness.

An illustration of suppressed thoughts becoming highly accessible and more likely to affect thought and action is provided by research on the suppression of stereotypes. Macrae, Bodenhausen, Milne, and Jetten (1994) had participants write a story about a member of a stereotyped group shown in a picture. Half were told to suppress stereotype use in their story. Next, participants had to write a second story about a different person, with no instructions to suppress a stereotype. Although people, when asked, successfully suppressed the stereotype in their first story, their use of the stereotype was heightened in the second story. Suppressors actually stereotype more than people not trying to suppress. A subsequent experiment using an implicit measure of stereotype accessibility (response times on a lexical decision task) revealed a similar finding. People who suppressed a stereotype in one task later had increased accessibility of that stereotype. In both action (stories told) and thought (concepts coming to mind), compensatory responses meant to suppress a thought led to the unintended effect of that thought being more prevalent.

The Macrae et al. (1994) experiments just described, as well as a host of other experiments on thought suppression, focus on the ironic effect of suppression. The irony being the increased (hyper) accessibility of the stereotype, as well as its increased use. However, though suppression goals triggers implicit operations that increase stereotype accessibility, Galinsky and Moskowitz (2007) argued they also trigger implicit compensatory responses that facilitate goal pursuit. These are nonironic, intended, effects of stereotype suppression, such as the increased accessibility of counterstereotypic thoughts. Galinsky and Moskowitz gave participants the goal of suppressing stereotypic thoughts. They found that it is not merely the case that unwanted thoughts have heightened accessibility, but goal-relevant thoughts do as well. Stereotypes were accessible, but so were counterstereotypes, words that were the opposite of the stereotype. This simultaneous activation of the to-be-suppressed thoughts as well as goal-relevant thoughts clearly illustrates that thought suppression involves implicit operations that, though ironically giving rise to unwanted thoughts, also give rise to not-so-ironic, goal-relevant cognition.

When suppressing stereotypes, an individual can replace stereotypic items that spring to mind (e.g., hostile, criminal for African Americans) with the opposite construct or the antonym of the stereotypic item (e.g., kind, honest). The ability to not think a certain thought requires thinking something in its stead. Initially, people trying not to stereotype might need to focus conscious awareness on this process. As Wegner (1994) proposed, the operating process is an explicit and conscious one of replacing undesired thoughts with other thoughts. However, over time, the task of generating replacements may become an implicit part of the process. Suppressing stereotypes, if something one has practice at, will come to involve the implicit activation of counterstereotypes in addition to stereotypes.

The finding that a stereotype and counterstereotype are accessible is in contrast to what is typically found in the stereotyping and categorization literature. Social categorization is driven by an interplay of excitatory and inhibitory mechanisms (Andersen, Moskowitz, Blair, & Nosek, 2007; Macrae, Bodenhausen, & Milne, 1995). The active inhibition of competing, but relevant, constructs is what is usually seen. Priming a stereotype has previously been shown to inhibit stereotype-inconsistent traits (Dijksterhuis & van Knippenberg, 1996). Similarly, category-label primes increase the ability to retrieve typical category members, simultaneously limiting access to atypical members (Rothbart, Sriram, & Davis-Stitt, 1996). Galinsky and Moskowitz' (2007) findings highlight the compensatory nature of the implicit operations. A stereotype-suppression goal requires one to overcome the use of stereotypes. The compensatory processes serving this goal may involve the implicit monitoring for the stereotype's occurrence, but also implicit processes of replacing a stereotype.

Goal Shielding and Inhibition

Shah et al. (Chapter 9, this volume) review the idea that goals do not exist in isolation but reside within a system that is juggling many potential goal pursuits. Thus, as part of a given goal pursuit selected in a given moment, we often see operations triggered to "shield" or protect the goal from potential distractions to its pursuit, including shielding it from the pursuit of different goals in the system. Their review illustrates that implicit processes of inhibition are triggered when a goal is being pursued, with the inhibition being directed at goals that are in direct competition with the focal goal. Shah et al. defined temptations in this language as well, calling them goals that are attractive in the short run but compete with a potentially more attractive goal that one is pursuing over the long run. Thus, for the goal of dieting, a piece of cake is a temptation: the goal of eating it is attractive in the short run, but opposed to the long-term goal, which is more important than the momentary pleasure of tasting the cake. The temptation reminds us the goal is not yet reached, and we compensate for that state with implicit operations such as inhibiting the temptation.

Fishbach, Friedman, and Kruglanski (2003) highlighted the compensatory nature of these operations by labeling the process "counteractive control." The operations that are implicitly performed are taken to counteract the pull of the temptation. The desire associated with the temptation is discrepant with the ends and standards specified by the focal goal. This discrepancy needs to be counteracted, or compensated for. How is this done? Fishbach et al. showed that the very temptation (in our example, a piece of cake) that should be triggering an alternate goal (in our example, eating cake) is counteracted by a strengthening and heightened accessibility of the focal goal (in our example, dieting). Thus, dieters who are exposed to chocolate cake actually show heightened health consciousness in their subsequent food choices and have the goal of dieting more accessible. Although dieting goals inhibit goals associated with eating cake (goal shielding), thoughts of cake do not inhibit a dieting goal but make it more accessible. Implicit operations shield goals, even making temptations to a goal cues that make the goal stronger.

Inhibition of competing goals and distractions to goal pursuit are common in interpersonal goals as well. Earlier in this chapter, the research of Monteith (1993), Monteith et al. (2002), and Montieth and Voils (2001) illustrated compensatory processes explicitly aimed at helping people be nonbiased and egalitarian. Implicit operations are employed in pursuing this goal as well and include the type of goal-shielding processes discussed above. For example, when a woman or an African American is observed by a White man, such a person could be viewed as an opportunity to begin pursuing the goal of stereotyping, or as an opportunity to begin pursuing the goal of being egalitarian. People who are experiencing a discrepancy associated with their "sense of self as egalitarian," or simply people who are striving to be more egalitarian, should respond to these cues (people) in quite specific ways that reflect the compensatory operations that will move them toward their goal.

What operations implicitly address one's desired egalitarianism and compensate for one not yet reaching this state? Moskowitz and Ignarri (2008) asserted this includes the inhibition of one's stereotypes.

Moskowitz, Gollwitzer, Wasel, and Schaal (1999) reasoned that if compensatory processes of stereotype inhibition are triggered by egalitarian goals, such inhibition would be observed in people skilled at pursuing those goals: people with chronic goals to be egalitarian (see Chapter 8, this volume for a review of chronic goals). Their experiments recruited participants with chronic goals of being egalitarian to women and nonchronics. The task primed the participants with faces of women and then examined their reaction times to words relevant to the stereotype of women and control words in a task that participants did not know was about stereotyping. They found evidence of control over stereotyping across two experiments, with one experiment showing that participants inhibit stereotypes of women when they are exposed to faces of women, if and only if those participants are egalitarian. Because of the implicit nature of the task, these results complement the explicit compensatory responses shown by Monteith et al. (2002). Indeed, they extend such findings by showing an implicit operation, inhibition of unwanted stereotypes.

Moskowitz, Salomon, and Taylor (2000) used a similar procedure, except using African American faces as primes, words relevant to the stereotype of African Americans in the reaction time task, and chronic goals relating to African Americans in recruiting participants. They replicated the control of stereotype activation among chronics. Moskowitz et al. further reasoned that goal shielding is not merely about the inhibition of goals and responses that detract from a goal, but also facilitating responses that promote the goal. A person with egalitarian goals toward African Americans should be prepared to see such people as opportunities to move toward their goal. They have a heightened readiness to detect African Americans in the environment and should have forged an association between African Americans and one's egalitarian goals. A second experiment explored the implicit association between egalitarian goals and African Americans. Participants were shown faces of African American and White men as primes in one task and performed a separate task that they did not know had anything to do with stereotyping. Once again, their speed in responding to words was assessed, with some of the words being relevant to egalitarian goals. Participants with chronic goals showed facilitated response times when the words were preceded by faces of African American men, but only if the words were relating to egalitarianism. Facilitation did not occur for the nonchronic participants. People with egalitarian goals perform implicit operations that scan the environment for opportunities to pursue those goals, having the goal accessibility heightened when opportunities are detected.

Further support for these implicit operations in pursuing egalitarian goals is provided by Moskowitz and Ignarri (2008). The compensatory nature of these implicit operations is made evident by a switch from using people with chronic goals to recruiting nonchronics who have the goal made accessible by having them experience a discrepancy. Participants were asked to describe recent instances of having failed at the goal of being egalitarian to African Americans (control participants described either recent successes at egalitarianism or recent failures in a different domain). The egalitarian-failure conditions were hypothesized to create a discrepancy that can be compensated for by the implicit processes of goal shielding described above: inhibiting stereotypes and scanning the environment for opportunities to be egalitarian (selective attention). Once again, a task was used in which participants were primed with faces and then responded to words (where the faces and words are manipulated to be either relevant to the stereotype of African Americans or not). The question of interest is whether stereotypes are activated for people in the control condition, but actually implicitly inhibited for people in the "discrepancy" condition. Across a set of experiments this is indeed what is found, with people shown to be inhibiting stereotypes on a task that they do not recognize as being about stereotypes, and by controlling responses that are occurring too quickly to be governed by conscious control.

A subsequent set of experiments also illustrates the "scanning" element of the implicit operations by showing that people with "discrepancies" relating to the goal of being egalitarian implicitly scan their environment in search of African Americans. In one experiment faces of men were presented to participants four at a time, with the task of detecting the man with a bow tie (one of the four has a bow tie). The faces were presented so that in some instances an African American male was in the array at the same time as the focal stimulus (a White man in a bow tie). The issue at hand is whether the face of an African American man, as an opportunity to start pursuing one's egalitarian goals, disrupts focused attention. What is found is that when an egalitarian goal had previously been triggered, responses are slowed to the focal task only when the face of an African American is in the display. This slowdown does not occur for people not experiencing a discrepancy. Why? One of the operations to compensate for the discrepancy is the scanning of the environment, implicitly, for opportunities to pursue the goal. No discrepancy, no scanning.

How can we be sure such goal-directed attention is being carried out implicitly, without the person knowing he/she is doing it or trying to do it? One way to test this is to make it so that people cannot consciously detect the items they are directing attention toward. The previous experiment had people moving attention to a face they clearly could see. It was argued they did not know this face had anything to do with goal pursuit, or that they were pursuing goals in this task. The implicit nature of this compensatory process was illustrated more directly in an experiment by Moskowitz (2002). Once again, participants were asked to write about a time in which they failed to live up to the principles that would be exhibited by an egalitarian person. Participants next went to a different room for a "separate" experiment assessing perceptual ability. In this task two objects moved on the screen, one vertically, the other horizontally. The task was to report whether the direction of movement for the vertically moving object was up or down. Participants did not know it, but these objects were actually words moving too quickly for them to detect the content. But the content was essential. On some trials the words moving horizontally (to be ignored) were related to the goal of egalitarianism.

Moskowitz (2002) found that when goals had been triggered by the discrepancy being induced, attention was being preconsciously directed to goal-relevant items. This was evidenced by the fact that on the trials of the experiment where the goal words appeared, participants were slower at performing the task (naming the direction of the word moving vertically). If the word relevant to their goal appeared in the to-be-ignored spot (it moved horizontally), it distracted attention away from the task they were supposed to be focused on (detecting the direction of the word moving vertically) and slowed their performance on the task at hand. This occurred despite participants not knowing words relevant to their goals were presented (or that any words were being presented!) or that basic processes of attention were being assessed. They presumably did not even know they were trying to affirm their sense of being an egalitarian person (that this goal was triggered and relevant in the current context).

Conclusions

Humans have a natural tendency toward homeostasis, balance, and equilibrium. Imbalance, tension, and disequilibrium need to be reduced. As Asch (1952, p. 44) stated: "The organism is a biological unit whose internal activities tend toward a relation of equilibrium. To maintain these functions and their equilibrium the organism directs itself in the strongest way to the surroundings, engaging in a constant commerce with them." The discrepancy between the desired state and the current state, the disequilibrium, people find aversive. As such, people engage in compensatory responses in their environment, taking advantage of the opportunities it affords. This process is seen in the consistency theories emerging from Festinger (1957), the dual-process theories emerging from the 1980s, as well as in studies of emotion (Schachter & Singer, 1962), the development of intelligence (Piaget, 1972), and conformity (Asch, 1946).

Although conscious goals are known to lead to effortful attempts to explicitly compensate for our goal strivings, the pursuit of equilibrium can be implicit. Both the goals that represent the disequilibrium, as well as well as the operations or compensatory responses that can restore the equilibrium, may be implicit. It is common for people to discuss the implicit nature of goal pursuit as one associated with error, or associating implicit processes with unintended effects. Wegner and Erskine (2003) referred to "voluntary involuntariness" to describe unintended effects or involuntary activity implicitly arising from attempts at control. They discussed two types of "errors." The first is when people fail to accurately detect the role of their own will in producing their own behavior. They discussed a wide range of seemingly "magical" behavior in which people fail to see their goal system at work: Ouija board spelling, pendulum divining, automatic writing, and water dowsing. The second is when people consciously will one thing, but the act of will results in an opposite, involuntary act of will. This is evidenced by the work on thought suppression. The research and ideas reviewed in this chapter hopefully illustrate that implicit goals and their associated compensatory operations are both intentional and desired, not errors: that people do much of what they intend without knowing they are intending or doing.

Finally, there are studies in the literature, for example those reviewed in the section on implicit goal priming of Chapter 8, this volume, where the reader may ask, "Where's the tension?" In studies of goal priming, is it correct to call the responses compensatory? It seems as if a discrepancy is not being detected, a cue in the environment is merely triggering the goal. I would argue that the tension is part of the goal, and that priming the goal primes the tension, otherwise, it is not a goal being primed. Martin and Tesser touch on this in Chapter 10, this volume, by the marker of goal pursuit they call "persistence-until." I illustrate the point here using an example not reviewed in their chapter. Bargh, Gollwitzer, Lee-Chai, Barndollar, and Trotschel (2001) primed achievement goals in participants, who then achieved more. Is there a discrepancy? The answer is provided by their finding that attaining the goal, or shutting down the tension, eliminates goal striving. The implication is that in conditions in which there is no goal attainment, the individual continues to have a tension state associated with the triggered goal, and it is this tension that drives the goal-based responses of heightened achievement. Once that tension is satisfied, the response is eliminated. Thus, even goal priming involves the priming of a tension state, which is one of the components of the mental representation of the goal (see Moskowitz & Ignarri, in press). In goal priming too, responses are compensatory.

References

Andersen, S. A., Moskowitz, G. B., Blair, I. V., & Nosek, B. A. (2007). Automatic thought. In A. W. Kruglanski & E. T. Higgins (Eds.), *Social psychology: Handbook of basic principles* (2nd ed., pp. 138–175). New York: Guilford Press.

Asch, S. E. (1946). Forming impressions of personality. *Journal of Abnormal and Social Psychology, 41,* 258–290.

Asch, S. E. (1952). *Social psychology.* New York : Prentice Hall.

Bandura, A. (1989). Self-regulation of motivation and action through internal standards and goal systems. In L. A. Pervin (Ed.), *Goal concepts in personality and social psychology* (pp. 19–85). Hillsdale, NJ: Erlbaum.

Bandura, A., & Cervone, D. (1983). Self-evaluative and self-efficacy mechanisms governing the motivational effects of goal systems. *Journal of Personality and Social Psychology, 45,* 1017–1028.

Bargh, J. A., & Chartrand, T. L. (2000). The mind in the middle: A practical guide to priming and automaticity research. In H. T Reis & C. M. Judd (Eds.), *Handbook of research methods in social and personality psychology* (pp. 253–285). New York: Cambridge University Press.

Bargh, J. A., Gollwitzer, P. M., Lee-Chai, A., Barndollar, K., & Trotschel, R. (2001). The automated will: Nonconscious activation and pursuit of behavioral goals. *Journal of Personality and Social Psychology, 81,* 1014–1027.

Carver, C. S., & Scheier, M. F. (1981). *Attention and self-regulation: A control theory approach to human behavior.* New York: Springer.

Chaiken, S., Liberman, A., & Eagly, A. H. (1989). Heuristic and systematic information processing within and beyond the persuasion context. In J. S. Uleman & J. A. Bargh (Eds.), *Unintended thought* (pp. 212–252). New York: Guilford Press.

Craik, K. J. W. (1947). Theory of the human operator in control systems: I. The operator as an engineering system. *British Journal of Psychology, 38,* 56–61.

Devine, P. G. (1989). Stereotypes and prejudice: Their automatic and controlled components. *Journal of Personality and Social Psychology, 56,* 5–18.

Devine, P. G., Monteith, M. J., Zuwerink, J. R., & Elliot, A. J. (1991). Prejudice with and without compunction. *Journal of Personality and Social Psychology, 60,* 817–830.

Dijksterhuis, A., & Bargh, J. A. (2001). The perception-behavior expressway: Automatic effects of social perception on social behavior. In M. P. Zanna (Ed.), *Advances in experimental social psychology* (Vol. 33, pp. 1–40), San Diego: Academic Press.

Dijksterhuis, A., Bos, M., Nordgren, L., & Van Baaren, R. B. (2006). On making the right choice: The deliberation-without-attention effect. *Science, 311,* 1005–1007.

Dijksterhuis, A., & van Knippenberg, A. (1996). The knife that cuts both ways: Facilitated and inhibited access to traits as a result of stereotype activation. *Journal of Experimental Social Psychology, 32,* 271–288.

Fein, S., & Spencer, S. J. (1997). Prejudice as self-image maintenance: Affirming the self through negative evaluations of others. *Journal of Personality and Social Psychology, 73,* 31–44.

Festinger, L. (1957). *A theory of cognitive dissonance.* Stanford, CA: Stanford University Press.

Fishbach, A., Friedman, R. S., & Kruglanski, A. W. (2003). Leading us not unto temptation: momentary allurements elicit overriding goal activation. *Journal of Personality and Social Psychology, 84,* 296–309.

Fiske, S. T., & Neuberg, S. L. (1990). A continuum of impression formation, from category-based to individuating processes: Influences of information and motivation on attention and interpretation. In M. P. Zanna (Ed.), *Advances in experimental social psychology* (Vol. 23, pp. 1–74). New York: Academic Press.

Galinsky, A. D., & Moskowitz, G. B. (2007). Further ironies of suppression: Stereotype and counter-stereotype accessibility. *Journal of Experimental Social Psychology, 42,* 833–841.

Gollwitzer, P. M., Wicklund, R. A., & Hilton, J. L. (1982). Admission of failure and symbolic self-completion: Extending Lewinian theory. *Journal of Personality and Social Psychology, 43,* 358–371.

Higgins, E. T. (1989). Self-discrepancy theory: What patterns of self-beliefs cause people to suffer? In L. Berkowitz (Ed.), *Advances in experimental social psychology* (Vol. 22, pp. 93–136). New York: Academic Press.

Hull, C. L. (1931). Goal attraction and directing ideas conceived as habit phenomena. *Psychological Review, 38,* 487–506.

James, W. (1950). *The principles of psychology* (Vol. I & II). New York: Dover. (Original work published 1890)

Koole, S. L., Smeets, K., van Knippenberg, A., & Dijksterhuis, A. (1999). The cessation of rumination through self-affirmation. *Journal of Personality & Social Psychology, 77,* 111–125.

Lewin, K. (1936). *Principles of topological psychology.* New York: McGraw-Hill.

Lewin, K. (1951). *Field theory in social science: Selected theoretical papers.* New York: Harper & Row.

Macrae, C. N., Bodenhausen, G. V., & Milne, A. B. (1995). The dissection of selection in person perception: Inhibitory processes in social stereotyping. *Journal of Personality and Social Psychology, 69,* 397–407.

Macrae, C. N., Bodenhausen, G. V., Milne, A. B., & Jetten, J. (1994). Out of mind but back in sight: Stereotypes on the rebound. *Journal of Personality and Social Psychology, 67,* 808–817.

Miller, G. A., Galanter, E., & Pribram, K. H. (1960). *Plans and the structure of behavior.* New York: Holt, Rinehart & Winston.

Monteith, M. J. (1993). Self-regulation of prejudiced responses: Implications for progress in prejudice reduction efforts. *Journal of Personality and Social Psychology, 65,* 469–485.

Monteith, M. J., Ashburn-Nardo, L., Voils, C. I., & Czopp, A. M. (2002). Putting the brakes on prejudice: On the development and operation of cues for control. *Journal of Personality and Social Psychology, 83,* 1029–1050.

Monteith, M. J., & Voils, C. I. (2001). Exerting control over prejudice responses.

In G. B. Moskowitz (Ed.), *Cognitive social psychology: The Princeton Symposium on the legacy and future of social cognition* (pp. 375–388). Mahwah, NJ: Erlbaum.

Moskowitz, G. B. (2001). Preconscious control and compensatory cognition. In G. B. Moskowitz (Ed.), *Cognitive social psychology: The Princeton Symposium on the legacy and future of social cognition* (pp. 333–358). Mahwah, NJ: Erlbaum.

Moskowitz, G. B. (2002). Preconscious effects of temporary goals on attention. *Journal of Experimental Social Psychology, 38,* 397–404.

Moskowitz, G. B., Gollwitzer, P. M., Wasel, W., & Schaal, B. (1999). Preconscious control of stereotype activation through chronic egalitarian goals. *Journal of Personality and Social Psychology, 77,* 167–184.

Moskowitz, G. B., & Ignarri, C. (2008). Implicit goals and a proactive strategy of stereotype control. *Social and Personality Psychology Compass.*

Moskowitz, G. B., & Ignarri, C. (in press). Implicit volition and stereotype control. *European Review of Social Psychology.*

Moskowitz, G. B., & Roman, R. J. (1992). Spontaneous trait inferences as self generated primes: Implications for conscious social judgment. *Journal of Personality and Social Psychology, 62,* 728–738.

Moskowitz, G. B., Salomon, A. R., & Taylor, C. M. (2000). Implicit control of stereotype activation through the preconscious operation of egalitarian goals. *Social Cognition, 18,* 151–177.

Neuberg, S. L. (1989). The goal of forming accurate impressions during social interactions: Attenuating impact of negative expectancies. *Journal of Personality and Social Psychology, 56,* 374–386.

Nuttin, J. (1980). *Motivation, planning, and action.* Leuven, Belgium: Leuven University Press.

Piaget, J. (1972). Intellectual evolution from adolescence to adulthood. *Human Development, 15*(1), 1–12.

Rothbart, M., Sriram, N., & Davis-Stitt, C. (1996). The retrieval of typical and atypical category members. *Journal of Experimental Social Psychology, 32,* 1–29.

Sassenberg, K., & Moskowitz, G. B. (2005). Don't stereotype, think different! Overcoming automatic stereotype activation by mindset priming. *Journal of Experimental Social Psychology, 41,* 506–514.

Sassenberg, K., Moskowitz, G. B., Kessler, T., & Mummendey, A. (2009). *When automaticity outperforms intentions: Priming creativity as a strategy to initiate the generation of original ideas.* Manuscript under review.

Schachter, S., & Singer, J. E. (1962). Cognitive, social, and psychological determinants of emotional state. *Psychological Review, 69,* 379–399.

Steele, C. M. (1988). The psychology of self-affirmation: Sustaining the integrity of the self. In L. Berkowitz (Ed.), *Advances in experimental social psychology* (Vol. 21, pp. 261–302). New York: Academic Press.

Stone, J., Aronson, E., Crain, A. L., Winslow, M. P., & Fried, C. B. (1994). Inducing hypocrisy as a means of encouraging young adults to use condoms. *Personality and Social Psychology Bulletin, 20*(1), 116–128.

Stone, J., Wiegand, A. W., Cooper, J., & Aronson, E. (1997). When exemplification fails: Hypocrisy and the motive for self-integrity. *Journal of Personality and Social Psychology, 72*(1), 54–65.

Strack, F., & Hannover, B. (1996). Awareness of influence as a precondition for implementing correctional goals. In P. M. Gollwitzer & J. A. Bargh (Eds.), *The psychology of action: Linking cognition and motivation to behavior* (pp. 579–596). New York: Guilford Press.

Tetlock, P. E. (1985). Accountability: The neglected social context of judgment and choice. *Research in Organizational Behavior, 7,* 297–332.

Thompson, E. P., Roman, R. J., Moskowitz, G. B., Chaiken, S., & Bargh, J. A. (1994). Accuracy motivation attenuates covert priming effects: The systematic reprocessing of social information. *Journal of Personality and Social Psychology, 66,* 259–288.

Wegener, D. T., & Petty, R. E. (1995). Flexible correction processes in social judgment: The role of naive theories in corrections for perceived bias. *Journal of Personality and Social Psychology, 68,* 36–51.

Wegner, D. M. (1994). Ironic processes of mental control. *Psychological Review, 101,* 34–52.

Wegner, D. M., & Erber, R. (1992). The hyperaccessibility of suppressed thoughts. *Journal of Personality and Social Psychology, 63,* 903–912.

Wegner, D. M., & Erskine, J. (2003). Voluntary involuntariness: Thought suppression and the regulation of the experience of will. *Consciousness and Cognition, 12,* 684–694.

Wicklund, R. A., & Gollwitzer, P. M. (1982). *Symbolic self-completion.* Hillsdale, NJ: Erlbaum.

Wiener, N. (1948). *Cybernetics: or control and communication in the animal and the machine.* Cambridge, MA: MIT Press.

Wilson, T. D., & Brekke, N. (1994). Mental contamination and mental correction: Unwanted influences on judgments and evaluations. *Psychological Bulletin, 166,* 117–142.

CHAPTER 13

When Persistence Is Futile
A FUNCTIONAL ANALYSIS OF ACTION ORIENTATION AND GOAL DISENGAGEMENT

NILS B. JOSTMANN
SANDER L. KOOLE

As the ancient Greek hero Sisyphus knew, there may be no more dreadful fate than performing some futile activity without end. Sisyphus was condemned to incessantly rolling a rock to the top of a mountain, from where it would fall back from its own weight. Existentialist philosophers have regarded Sisyphus' condition as a metaphor for the futility of life itself (Camus, 1955). From a psychological perspective, however, one may wonder why Sisyphus never disengaged from his frustrating activity even though he knew it was pointless.

The problem of how to disengage from unattainable goals does not only concern classical heroes but also modern-day people. Contemporary Western culture has glorified "go-getters" who persist in the face of insurmountable obstacles and dismisses those who give up as "losers." However, a number of psychologists have suggested that disengagement can often be an adaptive response to situations in which further investment of time and resources is in undue proportion to the expected outcomes (Baumeister & Scher, 1988; Klinger, 1975; Wrosch, Scheier, Carver, & Schulz, 2003). Disengagement from unattainable goals can indeed have many benefits such as financial gains (Gilovich, 1983), improved decision making (Brockner, 1992), enhanced emotional well-being (Wrosch & Heckhausen, 1999), and better health (Wrosch, Miller, Scheier, & Brun de

Pontet, 2007). These findings suggest that disengagement may be an adaptive strategy when persistence is futile.

Previous research has offered a variety of explanations why and when people might disengage from unattainable goals. Classic explanations emphasized the importance of people's beliefs regarding the costs and benefits of further goal persistence or goal disengagement (e.g., Carver & Scheier, 2005; Klinger, 1975). In this chapter, however, we take a functional perspective, which is grounded in recent theories of human action control (Kuhl, 2000). In our view, goal disengagement involves the updating of working memory such that unattainable goals are erased and alternative goals can be processed. Updating of working memory is facilitated among individuals who are action oriented compared to state oriented, especially under demanding or threatening conditions. In the remainder of this chapter, we first present a theoretical analysis of goal disengagement and action orientation versus state orientation. Next we discuss existing evidence that supports our analysis. Finally, we present some ideas that might further advance the understanding of goal-disengagement processes.

Goal Dilemmas: Hanging on or Letting Go?

Reality imposes substantial constraints on the kind and number of goals that people can achieve simultaneously, or even in a lifetime. Therefore, most people will try to select goals that they expect to be attainable rather than unattainable. Unfortunately, however, expectations can be wrong and circumstances change, so that initially prioritized goals become more difficult than expected. Unforeseen difficulties confront people with a fundamental goal dilemma. On the one hand, people should not let go of their goals too easily but protect them against time delays, setbacks, and distracters. Indeed, failure to persist in the presence of obstacles may lead to incoherent and erratic behavior. On the other hand, however, people should not hang on to their goals at all costs. Indeed, never altering the course of one's strivings makes behavior inflexible and rigid. When goals become unexpectedly difficult, the dilemma thus lies in reconciling the opposing requirements of goal persistence and goal disengagement (Carver & Scheier, 2005; Goschke, 2003; Mayr & Keele, 2000).

Previous theorizing has identified two important factors that predict whether people hang on or let go during unexpected difficulties. One factor relates to the perceived value of the goal. If the goal is highly valuable, people are more inclined to hang on to it than when the goal is less valuable. The second factor relates to the expectancy that one is able to attain the goal. When people expect that they still have the capacity to attain the goal, they are more likely to persist compared to when they consider their capacities as insufficient. Expectancy and value have interactive effects on goal commitment. If value and expectancy are high, people are more likely to hang on than when only value or only expectancy is high (Brehm & Self, 1989; Carver & Scheier, 2005; Klinger, 1975; Shah & Higgins, 1997).

Expectancy and value can change during goal pursuit. In his classic analysis, for instance, Klinger (1975) suggested that frustration about unexpected difficulties makes people regard the frustrated goal as more valuable. As a consequence, people increase their efforts and strive for their goal more vigorously. When the goal remains frustrated despite increased efforts, however, a downswing into depression follows. During this stage, people experience depressive symptoms such as disappointment, apathy, and grief. A possible adaptive function of the depressive stage is devaluation of the goal. Devaluation of the goal leads to disengagement and finally, if new valuable goals emerge, to recovery from the depressive symptoms.

People thus invest more effort when the goal is rendered more difficult (Brehm & Self, 1989). When even high effort is futile, however, people change their expectations and consider the goal as no longer attainable. People may remain nevertheless committed to their unattainable goal. The resulting immobility can cause distress and feelings of helplessness (Wrosch et al., 2003). Dissolving one's commitment is especially difficult when no valuable alternatives are available (Aspinwall & Richter, 1999), or when past investments were high and people believe that they are drawing ever closer to the goal (Arkes & Blumer, 1985). Another problem is that people do not always take into account past experiences. Optimism, confidence, and other positive illusions may indeed turn "losses into near wins" (Gilovich, 1983), thereby leaving people more likely to persist. By contrast, pessimism and doubt leave people more likely to disengage from a failing goal (Carver & Scheier, 2005).

A Functional Perspective on Goal Disengagement

As we have seen, previous research on goal disengagement has traditionally emphasized the role of people's beliefs regarding the costs and benefits of further persistence versus disengagement. However, beliefs do not always predict actual behavior (Eagly & Chaiken, 1993). For instance, people may hold pessimistic beliefs about their unattainable goals but nevertheless fail to disengage from them. Likewise, people may fail to mobilize their efforts even though their expectancies of success are high. To explain these and other shortcomings of the expectancy-value approach, various theorists have sought to develop a functional perspective on goal disengagement (Gollwitzer, 1996; Jostmann & Koole, 2006; Kuhl, 1984, 2000).

A functional perspective examines how basic cognitive and affective processes shape goal-disengagement processes irrespective of the specific contents of people's beliefs (Kuhl, 2000). Notably, a functional perspective does not disregard the importance of belief systems. In line with the expectancy-value perspective, the functional perspective acknowledges that different beliefs can lead to different classes of behavior. However, a unique element of the functional perspective is the focus on the mental mechanisms that cause beliefs to have an impact on behavior. The two perspectives are thus partly based on similar assumptions, but there also exist important differences. The functional perspective should therefore be regarded as a complement to the classic expectancy-value perspective rather than as an attempt at its replacement. Indeed, contemporary theorizing on goal disengagement often includes elements from both perspectives (e.g., Brandtstädter & Rothermund, 2002; Carver & Scheier, 2005; Kuhl, 1981).

According to the present functional perspective, goals constitute symbolic mental representations of action plans that guide people toward the attainment of particular incentives or toward the avoidance of particular disincentives ("I will do behavior X in order to attain situation Y or to avoid situation Z"). After their formation, goals often remain represented in an implicit format that does not require conscious attention until enactment is initiated by appropriate situational cues, or after a predefined period of time has elapsed (Gollwitzer, 1996). However, goals can also be represented in an *explicit* format. Explicit goals are not consciously represented at all times. However, they remain in a state of heightened activation that makes them easily accessible for conscious awareness (Anderson, 1983; Goschke & Kuhl, 1993).

Explicit goal formats are especially appropriate when goal pursuit is rendered unexpectedly difficult because explicit formats facilitate deliberate planning and analytical thinking (Bongers & Dijksterhuis, 2009; Mayr, 2004; Norman & Shallice, 1986). Accordingly, the explicit format may be the most relevant format in the context of goal disengagement. The cognitive system that supports explicit goal formats is referred to as "working memory" (Baddeley, 1986; Engle, Tuholski, Laughlin, & Conway, 1999).[1] Working memory belongs to a greater network of executive functions that consists of short-term storage components and attentional control processes. Due to capacity constraints, working memory can only process a limited amount of explicit information simultaneously.

Unlike other mental representations, goals can remain activated for extended periods of time despite changes in the environment or one's motivational states. A likely purpose of such "self-sustained activation" (Anderson, 1983) is to ensure behavioral stability and coherence over time and during changing conditions. Self-sustained activation forms the basis of some of the key features of goal pursuit such as persistence in the presence of obstacles or the resumption of interrupted goals. It usually vanishes not until a goal has been successfully attained (cf. Mayr & Keele, 2000). A well-known instance of self-sustained activation is the so-called Zeigarnik effect, which reflects privileged cognitive availability in working memory of uncompleted relative to completed or nonintended activities (Zeigarnik, 1927; cf. Förster, Liberman, & Higgins, 2005; Goschke & Kuhl, 1993).

Sustained activation of goals in working memory is conducive to goal persistence during obstacles or delays. In the case of unattainable goals, however, sustained goal activation becomes problematic because it impedes goal disengagement. Sustained activation of unattainable goals can cause recurrent, uncontrollable thoughts and unwanted feelings (cf. Blascovich & Mendes, 2000; Martin & Tesser, 1996; Savitsky, Medvec, & Gilovich, 1997). One can distinguish between two types of conditions (Baumann, Kaschel, & Kuhl, 2005; Carver & Scheier, 2005; Higgins, 1987). First, people who ruminate about goals that they ideally would like to attain may experience reduced positive affect and feelings of weariness, dissatisfaction, or depression. In the present context, we term such a condition "demanding," whereas we term the absence of such a condition "nondemanding." Second, people who ruminate about goals that they ought to attain may experience increased negative affect and feelings of worry, agitation, or anxiety. We term such a condition "threatening," whereas we term the absence of such a condition "nonthreatening."

Demand and threat strain the limited capacity of working memory. As a consequence, attentional focus unduly prioritizes irrelevant information that is related to unattainable goals at the cost of relevant information that is related to new and potentially attainable goals (Cohen, Dixon, & Lindsay, 2005; Klein & Boals, 2001). Moreover, if goal activation continues for some time, it can reduce people's limited energy resources until insufficient resources remain available for the processing of new goals (Schmeichel, 2007). In view of these undesirable consequences, it is important that people are able to terminate the sustained activation of unattainable goals in working memory. From this functional perspective, terminating sustained goal activation can be regarded as one of the key indicators of successful goal disengagement.

Updating of Working Memory

How can people terminate the activation of unattainable goals in working memory? One possibility is that people deliberately direct their attention away from the goal. Recent research indeed suggests that people can clear their minds from negative experiences when they engage in new tasks that require working memory (Van Dillen & Koole, 2007). Unfortunately, people may lack the energy or opportunity to find such new tasks. Moreover, deliberate attempts to focus on something else may leave goals in a subconscious state of heightened activation, from where they can easily return into focal attention. Indeed, the deliberate suppression of unwanted thoughts or unpleasant feelings often causes rebound effects after some time (Wenzlaff & Wegner, 2000). Thus, people may not be able to terminate sustained goal activation effectively through deliberate strategies.

In this chapter, we suggest an alternative mechanism for refreshing the contents of working memory that does not rely on deliberate processing. Specifically, we suggest that sustained activation of unattainable goals terminates when working memory opens up to external information. Recall that, for the sake of behavioral stability and coherence, goals are usually protected against external information. When such protection is taken away, however, stored goals in working memory become aligned with perceptual information about the environment or with one's motivational preferences. As a consequence of such alignment, unattainable goals may be revised, replaced by alternative goals, or even completely relinquished. We refer to this process as the "updating" of working memory (cf. Braver & Cohen, 2000; Kuhl, 2000).

In functional terms, working memory updates its contents when the cognitive pathways between working memory on the one hand and perceptional and motivational systems on the other hand are facilitated. Based on recent theories of human action control (Kuhl, 2000), we suggest that two systems are particularly relevant for the updating of working memory (see Figure 13.1). The first system is referred to as the "intuitive behavior control" (IBC) system. The IBC regulates automatic behavior based on stored associative links between perceptual input and behavioral output. It operates largely on unconscious levels and can simultaneously process perceptual information from various modalities including information about the external world and internal states (e.g., hunger). Through a cognitive pathway, IBC can communicate with working memory. During such systems interactions, perceptual input can enter working memory and align its contents.

The second system is referred to as "extension memory" (Kuhl, 2000), an extended network of cognitive-emotional information that operates largely on unconscious levels and according to parallel-distribution principles. One important function of extension memory is to provide access to one's implicit motives, or unconscious motivational preferences (cf. McClelland, Koestner, & Weinberger, 1989; Schultheiss, 2008). Extension memory thus provides information about which incentives people find particularly valuable (e.g., to affiliate with others, to control others, or to achieve), and which types of actions are likely to lead to their attainment. Through a cognitive pathway, extension memory informs working memory what incentives are important to strive for under the current circum-

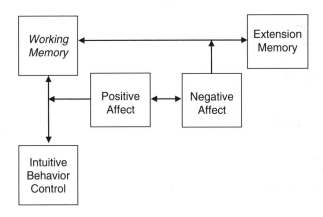

FIGURE 13.1. A model of working memory updating. Data from Kuhl's (2000) action control theory. Labels in *italics* deviate from original connotations.

stances and what action alternatives are potentially worthwhile to replace the failing goal that is currently processed in working memory.

According to recent theories of action control (Kuhl, 2000; cf. Braver & Cohen, 2000), the cognitive pathways between working memory, IBC, and extension memory are modulated by positive and negative affect. First, the pathway between working memory and IBC is modulated by positive affect. When positive affect is decreased, the pathway is blocked thereby inhibiting the communication between the two systems. By contrast, when positive affect is increased, the pathway blockage is released so that working memory and IBC can interact (cf. Dreisbach & Goschke, 2004; Kuhl & Kazén, 1999). Second, the pathway between working memory and extension memory is modulated by negative affect. When negative affect is increased, the pathway is blocked. Conversely, interactions between working memory and extension memory are facilitated when negative affect is decreased (cf. Baumann & Kuhl, 2002, 2003).

Frustrated goal pursuit can thus impair the flow of information between cognitive systems. When people experience threat because they fail at goals that they ought to attain, increased negative affect renders extension memory inaccessible. Consequently, threat renders the alignment of explicit goals in working memory with implicit motives in extension memory difficult. When people encounter demands because they fail at goals that they would like to attain, decreased positive affect reduces the influence of IBC on working memory. Under high demands, explicit goals thus cannot be sufficiently aligned with current information about the external world or internal states. Moreover, because decreases in positive affect can lead to increases of negative affect, low positive affect may also contribute indirectly to the inaccessibility of extension memory (Kuhl, 2007). In sum, aversive affective reactions during demanding or threatening situations render goal disengagement more difficult because they impair the updating of working memory.

The Moderating Role of Action versus State Orientation

At first glance, demanding and threatening conditions seem to have conflicting effects on goal pursuit. On the one hand, demand and threat impair the updating of working memory thereby rendering disengagement from unattainable goals difficult. On the other hand, however, demand and threat signal that working memory should update its contents and potentially disengage from the goal because unexpected difficulties have occurred. The paradox can be resolved if one considers that demand and threat represent an initial, evaluative response to unexpected difficulties. Adaptive goal pursuit likely requires a secondary, regulatory response to initiate appropriate corrective adjustments (cf. Botvinick, Braver, Barch, Carter, & Cohen, 2001; Carver & Scheier, 2005). We suggest that an important regulatory response to demand or threat is the updating of working memory.

People may not always be able to deal effectively with demands or threats. Accordingly, there might be moderators that determine whether people can successfully update their working memory under demands or threat. Based on action control theory (Kuhl, 1984, 2000), we suggest that one important moderator may be a person's *action orientation* versus *state orientation*. Action orientation is associated with high coping abilities during demand and threat, whereas state orientation is associated with low coping abilities. There are two major dimensions of action versus state orientation. First, action versus state orientation on the demand-related dimension (AOD) is characterized by initiative and decisiveness (action orientation) versus hesitation and indecisiveness (state orientation) during demands. Second, action versus state orientation on the threat-related dimension (AOT) determines whether people become challenged (action orientation) or remain threatened (state orientation) during situations that potentially jeopardize their well-being or self-image.[2] AOD and AOT are interrelated but independent regulatory dimensions. Accordingly, a person can be action oriented on one dimension but state oriented on the other dimension and vice versa.

Action orientation can be considered a skill that people acquire depending on their socialization experiences (Koole, Kuhl, Jostmann, & Finkenauer, 2006; Kuhl, 2000). Environments that encourage people to motivate themselves during hindrances are likely to promote action orientation in dealing with demands. By contrast, environments that discourage people from motivating themselves (i.e., overly controlling or neglecting environments) are likely to promote state orientation in dealing with demands. Moreover, environments that are comforting when people express their motivational preferences (which is functionally equivalent to the activation of extension memory) during stressful situations are likely to foster action orientation in dealing with threatening conditions. By contrast, a state orientation in dealing with threatening conditions develops when such comforting responses to expressions of one's motivational preferences are absent or inadequate.

Through repeated learning experiences, people may acquire a stable disposition toward action versus state orientation in dealing with demands or threats. Based on this assumption, Kuhl (1994) developed a self-report questionnaire to assess individual differences in action versus state orientation. Each item on the questionnaire presents an aversive situation and an action-oriented or state-oriented way to respond to the situation. The demand-related dimension (AOD) and the threat-related dimension (AOT) are measured on two different subscales. Illustrative items can be found in Table 13.1. Based on people's responses, they can be classified as either predominantly action oriented or predominantly state oriented in each of the two dimensions. During young adulthood, research populations in Germany, the Netherlands, and the United States have often been found to consist of equal numbers of individuals who are action oriented and state oriented (e.g., Diefendorff et al., 1998; Koole, 2003; Kuhl, 1994). During later life periods, however, increased experiences in coping with

TABLE 13.1. Example Items of the Demand-Related Subscale (AOD) and the Threat-Related Subscale (AOT) of the Action Control Scale (ACS-90) (Kuhl, 1994)

Items of the AOD subscale

When I know I must finish something soon:
  A. I have to push myself to get started*
  B. I find it easy to get it done and over with

When I have a lot of important things to do and they must all be done soon:
  A. I often don't know where to begin
  B. I find it easy to make a plan and stick with it*

Items of the AOT subscale

When I have lost something that is very valuable to me and I can't find it anywhere:
  A. I have a hard time concentrating on anything else
  B. I put it out of my mind after a little while*

When I am being told that my work is completely unsatisfactory:
  A. I don't let it bother me for too long*
  B. I feel paralyzed

Note. Action-oriented responses are marked with an asterisk (*).

aversive situations may render people more action oriented (Gröpel, Kuhl, & Kazén, 2004).

We suggest that better coping skills among individuals who are action compared to state oriented are due to their more effective updating of working memory under high demands or threat. Under high demands, the tendency toward initiative and decisiveness of individuals who are action oriented likely reflects the efficient use of working memory. By contrast, the tendency toward hesitation and indecisiveness of individuals who are state oriented under demands may indicate that they use their working memory inefficiently because information is processed extensively, even when quick decisions are appropriate. Likewise, the tendency to terminate excessive ruminations under threat of individuals who are action oriented may reflect efficient working memory use. By contrast, the tendency to remain preoccupied with threatening experiences of individuals who are state oriented indicates inefficient use of working memory. Taken together, individuals who are action oriented on either dimension of this personality construct may be better able to update their working memory compared to their counterparts who are state oriented.

Better updating of working memory among individuals who are action oriented compared to individuals who are state oriented likely facilitates goal disengagement. However, updating may not indiscriminately erase explicit goals from working memory. Rather, updating is likely to lead to disengagement from only those goals that are unattainable or disproportionally costly to pursue. When a goal is difficult but still attainable, however, updating may even lead to greater persistence. The latter case arises when IBC and extension memory inform working memory that, in spite of the current difficulties, the current goal remains the most viable option. Consequently, individuals who are action oriented under demand or threat presumably disengage from their goals when updating reveals valuable alternative options, but they persist when such options are absent.

Based on recent insights on human action control (Kuhl, 2000), we propose that goal disengagement is a function of successful exchange of information between cognitive systems. The quality of the disengagement process is reflected by the workings of the individual systems and also by the overall behavioral outcome of the interaction between systems. We therefore suggest that goal disengagement can be decomposed into *cognitive disengagement* or efficient clearance of intrusive thoughts from working memory, *affective disengagement* or effective downregulation of unwanted feelings, and *motivational disengagement* or rejection of explicit goals that are not in line with one's implicit motives. On the level of overall systems interactions, goal disengagement is reflected by *behavioral disengagement* or the ability to successfully switch to new activities. An overview of these various types of disengagement and their definitions is provided in Table 13.2.

TABLE 13.2. Functional Components of Goal Disengagement

Component	Definition	System	Illustrative findings
Cognitive disengagement	Clearance of intrusive thoughts from working memory	Working memory Affect systems	Jostmann & Koole (2006); Kuhl (1981); Stiensmeier-Pelster (1994)
Affective disengagement	Downregulation of unwanted feelings	(Working memory) Affect systems (Extension memory)	Koole & Jostmann (2004); Kuhl (1983); Rholes, Michas, & Shraff (1989)
Motivational disengagement	Rejection of explicit goals that are incompatible with implicit motives	Working memory Affect systems Extension memory	Baumann & Kuhl (2003); Baumann, Kaschel, & Kuhl (2005); Brunstein (2001)
Behavioral disengagement	Switching to new activities	Working memory Intuitive behavior control Affect systems (Extension memory)	Jostmann & Koole (2007); Kuhl (1981); Palfai, McNally, & Roy (2002)

Note. Systems in parentheses may not always be involved during disengagement.

Empirical Evidence on Action versus State Orientation

Empirical research over the past 25 years has revealed that action versus state orientation moderates goal pursuit across a broad range of different domains including education, health, work, and sports (for reviews, see Diefendorff, Hall, Lord, & Strean, 2000; Kuhl & Beckmann, 1994b). For instance, individuals who are action oriented compared to state oriented have been found to be more successful in pursuing their academic careers (Diefendorff et al., 1998), recover more quickly from medical surgery (Kuhl, 1983), perform better at the workplace (Diefendorff et al., 2000), and display greater athletic performance, especially when performance pressure is high (Heckhausen & Strang, 1988).

In this section, we consider evidence suggesting that action versus state orientation moderates the updating of working memory and, consequently, goal disengagement under demanding or threatening conditions. As noted above, we decompose goal disengagement into the more specific components of cognitive disengagement, affective disengagement, motivational disengagement, and behavioral disengagement. We first review research on goal disengagement among individuals who are action versus state oriented under high demands (AOD), followed by a review of research on goal disengagement among individuals who are action versus state oriented during threatening conditions (AOT).

Goal Disengagement under High Demands

High demands occur when individuals have to pursue their goals in the face of great difficulties. In the literature on action versus state orientation, these difficulties have been operationalized in various ways, for instance, as time pressure (Stiensmeier-Pelster, 1994), demanding relationship partners (Jostmann & Koole, 2006), performance pressure (Heckhausen & Strang, 1988), or prospective memory load (Jostmann & Koole, 2007). Throughout these various operationalizations, demand-related action orientation emerged consistently as a moderator of goal-disengagement processes. In this section, we review relevant research findings on the AOD facet of action orientation.

Cognitive Disengagement

"Cognitive disengagement" refers to the important task of clearing intrusive thoughts from working memory. Various strands of evidence suggest that individuals who are action oriented are more efficient at cognitive disengagement than their counterparts who are state oriented, particularly under high demands. Individuals who are action oriented report fewer everyday lapses of attention (Kuhl & Fuhrmann, 1998) and fewer intrusive thoughts (Kuhl & Goschke, 1994) than individuals who are state oriented. Moreover, individuals who are action oriented use more efficient and parsimonious decision-making strategies under time pressure than individuals who are state oriented (Stiensmeier-Pelster, 1994). Additional research suggests that cognitive disengagement among individuals who are action-oriented occurs under high demands but not under low demands (Jostmann & Koole, 2006). In this research, participants first either visualized interacting with a demanding person or with an accepting person. Subsequently, all participants performed an operation span task, which measures how efficiently individuals can utilize their working memory (cf. Turner & Engle, 1989). Participants who had visualized a demanding person had higher operation spans when they were action oriented than when they were state oriented. No similar effects were found among participants who had visualized an accepting person.

Affective Disengagement

"Affective disengagement" refers to the task of downregulating unwanted feelings. Are individuals who are action oriented indeed more efficient at affective disengagement than individuals who are state oriented? The available evidence suggests an affirmative answer to this question.

One relevant study revealed that college students who were action but not state oriented display increments in positive affect and energy over the course of a semester (Brunstein, 2001). Additional research suggests that individuals who are action oriented improve their affective states especially during aversive experiences. Specifically, individuals who are action compared to state oriented report higher personal well-being (Baumann et al., 2005) and less depression (Bossong, 1998) during stressful life periods. Recently, Koole and Jostmann (2004) showed that individuals who are action oriented regulate their affective states on an intuitive level that may not rely on conscious awareness. Specifically, individuals who are action oriented under high demands were faster to provide positive responses to negative target words in an affective Simon task (cf. De Houwer & Eelen, 1998). Moreover, individuals who are action compared to state oriented under high demands were faster to detect happy faces in crowds of angry faces in a face-discrimination task (cf. Öhman, Lundqvist, & Esteves, 2001).

In a further demonstration of affective disengagement (Jostmann, Koole, Van der Wulp, & Fockenberg, 2005), participants were first subliminally primed with angry, neutral, or happy faces, after which their affective responses were measured. Affective reactions of individuals who were state oriented were congruent with the affective valence of the subliminal prime. When individuals who were state oriented were primed with angry faces, they gave more negative affective reactions than when they were primed with neutral or happy faces. By contrast, affective reactions of individuals who were action oriented were not congruent with the subliminal prime. Importantly, among participants who were primed with angry faces, those with an action orientation displayed fewer negative affective responses than those with a state orientation. In sum, these findings reveal greater affective disengagement among individuals who were action compared to state oriented even when affect is triggered outside conscious awareness.

Motivational Disengagement

"Motivational disengagement" refers to the rejection of explicit goals that are not in line with one's implicit motives. According to our theoretical analysis, individuals who are action oriented should be more efficient at motivational disengagement than their counterparts who are state oriented, particularly under high demands. In one relevant study (Brunstein, 2001), individuals who were action compared to state oriented were more likely to commit themselves to explicit goals that were congruent with their implicit motives as measured by a projective technique similar to the Thematic Apperception Test (cf. Murray, 1943). In an experimental investigation, forming explicit self-control goals was associated with greater accessibility of motivational preferences in a subsequent free-choice task among individuals who were action compared to state oriented (Baumann

& Kuhl, 2005). In a different investigation, Baumann and colleagues (2005) measured individuals' explicit achievement goals and individuals' implicit achievement motives. Among individuals who reported that their current lives were very demanding, individuals who were action oriented displayed higher congruence between explicit achievement goals and implicit achievement motives than individuals who were state oriented. Such differences were absent among individuals who reported less demanding lives.

Behavioral Disengagement

"Behavioral disengagement" refers to the ability to switch to new activities at appropriate moments. Are individuals who are action oriented better at behavioral disengagement than individuals who are state oriented? In one relevant investigation, high demands led individuals who were action oriented to switch more easily from an unattractive to a more attractive activity (Kuhl & Beckmann, 1994a). In a different study, individuals who were action compared to state oriented under high demands were more likely to change directions in a motor movement task (Dibbelt, 1997). Moreover, individuals who were action oriented were found better able to let go of goals that are related to unhealthy or dangerous behavior (e.g., Palfai, McNally, & Roy, 2002).

In a further test of behavioral disengagement processes (Jostmann & Koole, 2007, Study 1), a group of individuals who were action versus state oriented first worked on an operation span task and then had to switch to a Stroop color-naming task. Performance on the operation span task is energy depleting and thus becomes increasingly demanding. Because demands were thus still low at the beginning of the task, participants who were action and state oriented displayed similar operation spans. However, when participants had to switch to the Stroop task during the second part of the investigation, performance differences emerged such that Stroop performance was better among participants who were action compared to state oriented. The performance decrements among participants who were state compared to action oriented can be explained by the difficulty of individuals who were state oriented after sustained task engagement to disengage from the operation span task and switch to the Stroop task.

In a follow-up study (Jostmann & Koole, 2007, Study 2), participants did not need to switch between tasks but performed one extended version of the Stroop task. Akin to the operation span task, performing the Stroop task depletes resources. Accordingly, demands are lower at the beginning of the task compared to later phases of the task. During early phases of the Stroop task, individuals who were state and action oriented performed similarly well. However, during later phases of the task, performance among individuals who were action oriented was much better than performance among individuals who were state oriented. Accordingly, under high demands, individuals who were action compared to state oriented were better able to persist on the task when it was not possible to switch to a different task. Taken together, the two studies (Jostmann & Koole, 2007) suggest that, under high demands, having an action orientation rather than a state orientation facilitates disengagement if people have to switch to a new task but also facilitates persistence if switching is not possible.

Goal Disengagement under Threat

High threat occurs when individuals have to pursue their goals in the face of setbacks, uncertainty, or negative affect. In the literature on action versus state orientation, threat has been operationalized in various ways, for instance, as repeated failure (Kuhl, 1981), negative mood (Baumann & Kuhl, 2003), or mortality salience (Koole & Van den Berg, 2005). Throughout these various operationalizations, threat-related action orientation (AOT) emerged consistently as a moderator of goal-disengagement processes. In this section, we review relevant research findings on the AOT facet of action orientation.

Cognitive Disengagement

Some of the earliest studies on AOT found evidence that individuals who were action compared to state oriented are less likely to report ruminative thinking about the causes of past failures or the potential aversive consequences of future failures (Kuhl, 1981). This findings has since then been replicated in several other experiments (e.g., Baumann & Kuhl, 2003; Brunstein & Olbrich, 1985). Using a response-time measure, Koole and Van den Berg (2005) found that individuals who were action oriented were better able to suppress death thoughts in a threatening environment than individuals who were state oriented. Taken together, it appears that individuals who were action oriented are more efficient at cognitive disengagement than individuals who were state oriented.

Affective Disengagement

Repeated experimentally induced failure experiences led individuals who were action oriented to report less negative affect and self-blame than individuals who were state oriented. Moreover, stressful life events were found to have more aversive effects on depression among individuals who were state compared to action oriented (Rholes, Michas, & Shroff, 1989).

Action compared to state orientation is further associated with lower incidence of psychosomatic symptoms during stressful life events (Baumann et al., 2005), and greater therapeutic success during the treatment of phobia (Schulte, Hartung, & Wilke, 1997). In addition, among patients who were hospitalized, those with an action orientation reported less subjective pain, lower use of pain killers, and reduced fear after surgery than patients with a state orientation (Kuhl, 1983). Finally, a recent investigation found that individuals who were action compared to state oriented recovered faster from a negative encounter with their relationship partner as indicated by better mood and higher self-reported satisfaction with their relationships (Karremans, Finkenauer, & Jostmann, 2008).

Motivational Disengagement

One investigation revealed that individuals who were state but not action oriented lose access to their emotional preferences during phases of negative affect (Guevara, 1994). Moreover, individuals who were state compared to action oriented are more likely to misperceive externally assigned goals as self-chosen. Notably, differences between individuals who were action and state oriented in false self-ascription of assigned goals were found especially after the induction of negative affect (Baumann & Kuhl, 2003). Finally, during threatening life events, individuals who were action compared to state oriented were found to display more coherence between explicit achievement goals and implicit achievement motives (Baumann et al., 2005).

Behavioral Disengagement

In an early investigation, Kuhl (1981) exposed participants who were action and state oriented to uncontrollable failure during a training task. Subsequently, participants were to switch to an unrelated activity. Individuals who were action compared to state oriented were better able to disengage from the training task as indicated by improved performance on the second task. In line with a functional perspective, better performance among individuals who were action compared to state oriented was not related to participants' expectancies regarding the attainability of the second task.

A more recent investigation examined disengagement from failure experiences on the level of single trials during a modified flanker task. When participants expected to be rewarded for correct responses, those with an action orientation were more accurate than those with a state orientation on trials that followed an incorrect response (De Lange & Van Knippenberg, 2008). Finally, a recent study demonstrated that among participants who missed an initial attractive action opportunity (e.g., getting a low-priced bargain), those with an action orientation were less likely than those with a state orientation to also miss a similar but somewhat less attractive action opportunity, as indicated by the inaction–inertia effect (Van Putten, Zeelenberg, & Van Dijk, 2008). Taken together, these studies reveal that action-oriented individuals are better able to disengage from a failing course of action and initiate new courses of action.

Summary, Discussion, and Implications

In this chapter, we suggested that unexpected difficulties during goal pursuit leave people with a fundamental goal dilemma whether they should hang on to their goal or let it go. From an expectancy-value perspective, the dilemma is solved on the basis of people's beliefs regarding the costs and benefits of further persistence versus disengagement. If people perceive the goal as less valuable than alternative goals, or if they expect that the goal has become unattainable, they are more likely to disengage from a failing goal compared to situations in which the goal's perceived value or people's success expectancies remain high. One limitation of the expectancy-value approach is, however, that it fails to explain why people's beliefs (e.g., the goal is unattainable) sometimes do not lead to corresponding behavior (e.g., disengagement). We have therefore advanced a functional perspective on the basic cognitive and affective processes that are involved during goal disengagement.

According to our functional perspective, unexpected difficulties during goal pursuit activate explicit goal representations in working memory. Because goals possess the property of self-sustained activation, they remain activated until their completion. In the case of unattainable goals, self-sustained activation leads to uncontrollable intrusions and unwanted feelings that strain the limited capacity of working memory and deplete energy resources. We have termed situations "demanding" when people face difficulties with goals that they ideally like to attain, and experience decreased positive affect. By contrast, we have termed situations "threatening" when people face difficulties with goals that they ought to attain, and experience increased negative affect (cf. Carver & Scheier, 2005; Higgins, 1987).

To disengage from unattainable goals during demand or threat, people have to update their working memory such that information related to the unattainable goal becomes erased and information to new and potentially attainable goals can be processed (cf. Braver & Cohen, 2000). During updating, information in working memory becomes aligned with current perceptual information about the external environment and internal states and with information regarding people's implicit motivational preferences. Based on recent insights on human action control (Kuhl, 1984, 2000), we have suggested that updating relates to the facilitation of the cognitive pathway between working memory on the one hand and perceptual systems (i.e., intuitive behavior control, IBC) and motivational systems (i.e., extension memory) on the other hand. Information flow between working memory and IBC is facilitated by increased positive affect, whereas information flow between working memory and extension memory is facilitated by decreased negative affect.

We have further suggested that the updating of working memory is facilitated by action orientation compared to state orientation. Following Kuhl (1984, 1994), we distinguish two dimensions of action versus state orientation. Individuals who are action oriented on the threat-related dimension (AOT) are likely better able to disengage from unattainable goals during threatening situations compared to their counterparts who are state oriented. Moreover, individuals who are action oriented on the demand-related dimension (AOD) are likely better able to disengage from unattainable goals during demanding situations compared to their counterparts who are state oriented.

Goal disengagement is reflected by the workings of the individual cognitive-affective systems but also by the interaction of the systems. Accordingly, the overall phenomenon of goal disengagement can be decomposed into cognitive disengagement, affective disengagement, motivational disengagement, and behavioral disengagement. A literature review revealed that individuals who are action compared to state oriented during high demands and threat display greater disengagement on the cognitive, affective, motivational, and the behavioral levels. Importantly, individuals who are action oriented do not invariably disengage from goals. Instead, individuals who are action oriented have been found to disengage only from goals that cannot longer be pursued, but to persist on goals if switching to new tasks is not possible (Jostmann & Koole, 2007). Taken together, empirical evidence confirms that action compared to state orientation is an important moderator of disengagement from unattainable goals during demand or threat.

Whereas classic analyses have emphasized the value of goals and people's confidence in their attainability, the functional perspective examines the affective-cognitive processes that facilitate the cessation of goal activation in working memory. Nevertheless, the functional perspective can be integrated with classic perspectives. For instance, the functional perspective can be related with the well-established finding that people respond to difficulties with increasing effort until their confidence in successful task completion falls below a critical level (Brehm & Self, 1989). However, if goal attainment is highly important people may continue investing even extreme levels of effort in spite of low confidence. Such extreme persistence can move people into a zone of "hysteresis" during which minor setbacks can lead to abrupt and potentially catastrophic switches from persistence to disengagement (Carver & Scheier, 2005).

Based on our functional perspective, we suggest that individuals who are who are action oriented enter hysteresis under different conditions than individuals who are state oriented. Individuals who are action oriented are more likely to display extreme persistence when the current goal is in line with their implicit motives. When high goal importance is due to pressure that comes from outside the self (e.g., social pressure, time pressure, etc.), individuals who are action oriented are more likely to devaluate the importance of their goals and, consequently, disengage earlier and therefore less abruptly from their goals compared to individuals who are state oriented. By contrast, when goal importance is strongly supported by people's implicit motives, alignment of current goals under threat or demand among individuals who are action oriented may reconfirm the high importance of a goal thereby making them even more likely candidates for hysteresis than individuals who are state oriented.

The present functional analysis can further inform life-span perspectives on goal disengagement (e.g., Schulz & Heckhausen, 1996). Past research has found that goal disengagement becomes more important during later life periods as indicated by an age-related shift from "assimilative" coping strategies (e.g., tenacious goal pursuit in the face of difficulties) towards "accommodative" strategies (e.g., flexible goal adjustment; Brandtstädter & Rothermund, 2002). We suggest that such a shift is facilitated by action compared to state orientation. In line with this assumption, people have been found to become more action oriented during later life phases (Gröpel et al., 2004). Future research may explore, whether such age-related increases in action orientation actually facilitate successful accommodation to aging.

Conclusion

Like Sisyphus, many people sometimes end up on a mission impossible. Fortunately, unlike this tragic hero, people have the possibility to disengage from their unattainable goals. Previous research has emphasized the importance of people's beliefs regarding the costs and benefits of further persistence versus disengagement. Our functional analysis extends this view by considering the role of sustained goal activation in working memory. Moreover, we have reviewed evidence that individuals who are action compared to state oriented are better able to update their working memory and hence terminate the activation of unattainable goals. As for Sisyphus, his tragedy might have been that he lacked action orientation, which led him to persevere even when his action was futile.

Notes

1. To simplify the present discussion, our definition of working memory subsumes characteristics of intention memory and object recognition systems (cf. Kuhl, 2000).
2. The labels "demand-related" and "threat-related" action versus state orientation were suggested by Koole and Jostmann (2004) to replace the original "decision-related" and "failure-related" action versus state orientation, respectively (Kuhl, 1994). The new labels fit better with relevant concepts in action control theory (cf. Baumann et al., 2005).

References

Anderson, J. R. (1983). *The architecture of cognition*. Cambridge, MA: Harvard University Press.

Arkes, K., & Blumer, C. (1985). The psychology of sunk costs. *Organizational Behavior and Human Decision Processes, 35*, 124–140.

Aspinwall, L. G., & Richter, L. (1999). Optimism and self-mastery predict more rapid disengagement from unsolvable tasks in the presence of alternatives. *Motivation and Emotion, 23*, 221–245.

Baddeley, A. (1986). *Working memory*. Oxford, UK: Oxford University Press.

Baumann, N., Kaschel, R., & Kuhl, J. (2005). Affect regulation and motive-incongruent achievement goals: Antecedents of subjective well-being and symptom formation. *Journal of Personality and Social Psychology, 89*, 781–799.

Baumann, N., & Kuhl, J. (2002). Intuition, affect, and personality: Unconscious coherence judgments and self-regulation of negative affect. *Journal of Personality and Social Psychology, 83*, 1213–1223.

Baumann, N., & Kuhl, J. (2003). Self-infiltration: Confusing assigned tasks as self-selected in memory. *Personality and Social Psychology Bulletin, 29*, 487–497.

Baumann, N., & Kuhl, J. (2005). How to resist temptation: The effects of external control versus autonomy support. *Journal of Personality, 73*, 443–470.

Baumeister, R. F., & Scher, S. J. (1988). Self-defeating behavior patterns among normal individuals: Review and analysis of common self-destructive strategies. *Psychological Bulletin, 104*, 3–22.

Blascovich, J., & Mendes, B. (2000). Challenge and threat appraisals: The role of affective cues. In J. P. Forgas (Ed.). *Feeling and thinking: The role of affect in social cognition* (pp. 59–82). New York: Cambridge University Press.

Bongers, K. C. A., & Dijksterhuis, A. (2009). Consciousness as a trouble-shooting device? The role of consciousness in goal-pursuit. In E. Morsella, J. A. Bargh, & P. M. Gollwitzer (Eds.), *The Oxford handbook of human action* (pp. 589–604). New York: Oxford University Press.

Bossong, B. (1998). *Stress und handlungskontrolle* [Stress and action control]. Göttingen, Germany: Hogrefe.

Botvinick, M. M., Braver, T. S., Barch, D. M., Carter, C. S., & Cohen, J. D. (2001). Conflict monitoring and cognitive control. *Psychological Review, 108,* 624–652.

Brandstädter, J., & Rothermund, K. (2002). The life-course dynamics of goal pursuits and goal adjustments: A two-process framework. *Developmental Review, 22,* 117–150.

Braver, T. S., & Cohen, J. D. (2000). On the control of control: The role of dopamine in regulating prefrontal function and working memory. In S. Monsell & J. Driver (Eds.), *Attention and performance XVIII: Control of cognitive processes* (pp. 713–737). Cambridge, MA: MIT Press.

Brehm, J. W., & Self, E. A. (1989). The intensity of motivation. *Annual Review of Psychology, 40,* 109–131.

Brockner, J. (1992). The escalation of commitment to a failing course of action: Toward theoretical progress. *Academy of Management Review, 17,* 39–61.

Brunstein, J. C. (2001). Persönliche Ziele und Handlungsorientierung: Wer bindet sich an realistische und bedürfniskongruente Ziele? [Personal goals and action orientation: Who commits to realistic and need-congruent goals?]. *Zeitschrift für Differentielle und Diagnostische Psychologie, 22,* 1–12.

Brunstein, J. C., & Olbrich, E. (1985). Personal helplessness and action control: Analysis of achievement-related cognitions, self-assessments, and performance. *Journal of Personality and Social Psychology, 48,* 1540–1551.

Camus, A. (1955). *The myth of Sisyphus.* New York: Random House.

Carver, C. S., & Scheier, M. F. (2005). Engagement, disengagement, coping, & catastrophe. In A. J. Elliot & C. S. Dweck (Eds.), *Handbook of competence and motivation* (pp. 527–547). New York: Guilford Press.

Cohen, A. L., Dixon, R. A., & Lindsay, D. S. (2005). The intention interference effect and aging: Similar magnitude effects for young and old adults. *Applied Cognitive Psychology, 19,* 1177–1197.

De Houwer, J., & Eelen, P. (1998). An affective variant of the Simon paradigm. *Cognition and Emotion, 12,* 45–85.

De Lange, M. A., & Van Knippenberg, A. (2008). *To err is human: How regulatory focus and action orientation predict performance following errors.* Manuscript submitted for publication.

Dibbelt, S. (1997). *Change and maintenance of goals as functional components of action control.* Unpublished doctoral dissertation, University of Osnabrück, Germany.

Diefendorff, J. M., Hall, R. J., Lord, R. G., & Strean, M. L. (2000). Action-state orientation: Construct validity of a revised measure and its relationship to work-related variables. *Journal of Applied Psychology, 85,* 250–263.

Diefendorff, J. M., Lord, R. G., Hepburn, E. T., Quickle, J. S., Hall, R. J., & Sanders, R. E. (1998). Perceived self-regulation and individual differences in selective attention. *Journal of Experimental Psychology: Applied, 4,* 228–247.

Dreisbach, G., & Goschke, T. (2004). How positive affect modulates cognitive control: Reduced perseveration at the cost of increased distractibility. *Journal of Experimental Psychology: Learning, Memory, & Cognition, 30,* 343–353.

Eagly, A. H., & Chaiken, S. (1993). *The psychology of attitudes.* Orlando, FL: Harcourt Brace Jovanovich.

Engle, R. W., Tuholski, S. W., Laughlin, J. E., & Conway, A. R. A. (1999). Working memory, short-term memory, and general fluid intelligence: A latent-variable approach. *Journal of Experimental Psychology: General, 128,* 309–331.

Förster, J., Liberman, N., & Higgins, E. T. (2005). Accessibility from active and fulfilled goals. *Journal of Experimental Social Psychology, 41,* 220–239.

Gilovich, T. (1983). Biased evaluation and persistence in gambling. *Journal of Personality and Social Psychology, 44,* 1110–1126.

Gollwitzer, P. M. (1996). The volitional benefits of planning. In P. M. Gollwitzer & J. A. Bargh (Eds.), *The psychology of action: Linking cognition and motivation to behavior* (pp. 287–312). New York: Guilford Press.

Goschke, T. (2003). Voluntary action and cognitive control from a cognitive neuroscience perspective. In S. Maasen, W. Prinz, & G. Roth (Eds.), *Voluntary action: brain, minds, and sociality* (pp. 49–85). Oxford, UK: Oxford University Press.

Goschke, T., & Kuhl, J. (1993). Representation of intentions: Persisting activation in memory. *Journal of Experimental Psychology: Learning, Memory, and Cognition, 19,* 1211–1226.

Gröpel, P., Kuhl, J., & Kazén, M. (2004, July 4–7). *Toward an integrated self: Age differences and the role of action orientation.* Paper presented at the Third International SELF Research Conference, "Self-concept, Motivation and Identify: Where to from Here?" Berlin, Germany.

Guevara, M. L. (1994). *Alienation und Selbstkontrolle: Das Ignorieren eigener Gefühle* [Alienation and self-control: Ignoring one's preferences]. Bern, Switzerland: Lang.

Heckhausen, H., & Strang, H. (1988). Efficiency under record performance demands: Exertion control—an individual difference variable? *Journal of Personality and Social Psychology, 55,* 489–498.

Higgins, E. T. (1987). Self-discrepancy: A theory relating self and affect. *Psychological Review, 94,* 319–340.

Jostmann, N. B., & Koole, S. L. (2006). On the waxing and waning of working memory: Action orientation moderates the impact of demanding relationship primes on working memory capacity. *Personality and Social Psychology Bulletin, 32,* 1716–1728.

Jostmann, N. B., & Koole, S. L. (2007). On the regulation of cognitive control: Action versus state orientation moderates the impact of high demands in Stroop interference tasks. *Journal of Experimental Psychology: General, 36,* 593–609.

Jostmann, N. B., Koole, S. L., Van der Wulp, N. Y., & Fockenberg, D. A. (2005). Subliminal affect regulation: The moderating role of action versus state orientation. *European Psychologist, 10,* 209–217.

Karremans, J., Finkenauer, C., & Jostmann, N. B. (2008). *Affect regulation in romantic relationships: Action orientation protects against relationship threat.* Unpublished manuscript, Radboud University Nijmegen, Nijmegen, The Netherlands.

Klein, K., & Boals, A. (2001). The relationship of life event stress and working memory capacity. *Applied Cognitive Psychology, 15*, 565–579.

Klinger, E. (1975). Consequences of commitment to and disengagement from incentives. *Psychological Review, 82*, 1–75.

Koole, S. L. (2003). Action versus state orientation among 1,457 Dutch college students. Unpublished raw data, VU University Amsterdam, Amsterdam, the Netherlands.

Koole, S. L., & Jostmann, N. B. (2004). Getting a grip on your feelings: Effects of action orientation and social demand on intuitive affect regulation. *Journal of Personality and Social Psychology, 87*, 974–990.

Koole, S. L., Kuhl. J., Jostmann, N. B., & Finkenauer, C. (2006). Self-regulation in interpersonal relationships: The case of action versus state orientation. In K. D. Vohs & E. J. Finkel (Eds.), *Self and relationships: Connecting intrapersonal and interpersonal processes* (pp. 360–383). New York: Guilford Press.

Koole, S. L., & Van den Berg, A. E. (2005). Lost in the wilderness:Terror management, action orientation, and nature evaluation. *Journal of Personality and Social Psychology, 88*, 1014–1028.

Kuhl, J. (1981). Motivational and functional helplessness: The moderating effect of state versus action orientation. *Journal of Personality and Social Psychology, 40*, 155–170.

Kuhl, J. (1983). Motivationstheoretische Aspekte der Depressionsgenese: Der Einfluss von ageorientierung auf Schmerzempfinden, medikamentenkonsum und Handlungskontrolle [Motivation-theoretical aspects of the development of depression: The influence of state orientation on the experience of pain, drug consumption and action control]. In M. Woltersdorf, R. Staub, & G. Hole (Eds.), *Der depressive Kranke in der psychiatrischen Klinik: Theorie und Praxis der Diagnostik und Therapie* (pp. 411–424). Weinheim, Germany: Beltz.

Kuhl, J. (1984). Volitional aspects of achievement motivation and learned helplessness: Toward a comprehensive theory of action control. In B. A. Maher (Ed.), *Progress in experimental personality research* (Vol. 13, pp. 99–171). New York: Academic Press.

Kuhl, J. (1994). Action versus state orientation: Psychometric properties of the Action Control Scale (ACS-90). In J. Kuhl & J. Beckmann (Eds.), *Volition and personality* (pp. 47–59). Göttingen, Germany: Hogrefe & Huber.

Kuhl, J. (2000). A functional-design approach to motivation and self-regulation: The dynamics of personality systems interactions. In M. Boekaerts, P. R. Pintrich, & M. Zeidner (Eds.), *Handbook of self-regulation* (pp. 111–169). San Diego: Academic Press.

Kuhl, J. (2007). *Individual differences in self-regulation.* Unpublished manuscript, University of Osnabrück, Osnabrück, Germany.

Kuhl, J., & Beckmann, J. (1994a). Alienation: Ignoring one's preferences. In J. Kuhl & J. Beckmann (Eds.), *Volition and personality: Action versus state orientation* (pp. 375–389). Göttingen: Germany: Hogrefe & Huber.

Kuhl, J., & Beckmann, J. (1994b). *Volition and personality: Action versus state Orientation.* Göttingen, Germany: Hogrefe & Huber.

Kuhl, J., & Fuhrmann, A. (1998). Decomposing self-regulation and self-control: The volitional components inventory. In J. Heckhausen & C. S. Dweck (Eds.), *Motivation and self-regulation across the life-span* (pp. 15–49). Cambridge, UK: Cambridge University Press.

Kuhl, J., & Goschke, T. (1994). State orientation and the activation and retrieval of intentions in memory. In J. Kuhl & J. Beckmann (Eds.), *Volition and personality* (pp. 127–154). Göttingen, Germany: Hogrefe & Huber.

Kuhl, J., & Kazén, M. (1999). Volitional facilitation of difficult intentions: Joint activation of intention memory and positive affect removes stroop interference. *Journal of Experimental Psychology: General, 128,* 382–399.

Martin, L. L., & Tesser, A. (1996). Some ruminative thoughts. In R. S. Wyer (Ed.), *Advances in social cognition* (Vol. 9, pp 1–47). Mahwah, NJ: Erlbaum.

Mayr, U. (2004). Conflict, consciousness, and control. *Trends in Cognitive Sciences, 8,* 145–148.

Mayr, U., & Keele, S. W. (2000). Changing internal constraints on action: The role of backward inhibition. *Journal of Experimental Psychology: General, 129,* 4–26.

McClelland, D. C., Koestner, R., & Weinberger, J. (1989). How do self-attributed and implicit motives differ? *Psychological Review, 96,* 690–702.

Murray, H. A. (1943). *Thematic Apperceptive Test manual.* Cambridge, MA: Harvard University Press.

Norman, D. A., & Shallice, T. (1986). Attention to action: Willed and automatic control of behavior. In R. J. Davidson, G. E. Schwartz, & D. Shapiro (Eds.), *Consciousness and self-regulation: Advances in research and theory* (Vol. 4, pp. 1–18). New York: Plenum Press.

Öhman, A., Lundqvist, D., & Esteves, F. (2001). The face in the crowd revisited: A threat advantage with schematic stimuli. *Journal of Personality and Social Psychology, 80,* 381–396.

Palfai, T. P., McNally, A. M., & Roy, M. (2002). Volition and alcohol-risk reduction: The role of action orientation in the reduction of alcohol-related harm among college student drinkers. *Addictive Behaviors, 27,* 309–317.

Rholes, W. S., Michas, L., & Shroff, J. (1989). Action control as a vulnerability factor in dysphoria. *Cognitive Therapy and Research, 13,* 263–274.

Savitsky, K., Medvec, V. H., & Gilovich, T. (1997). Remembering and regretting: The Zeigarnik effect and the cognitive availability of regrettable actions and inactions. *Personality and Social Psychology Bulletin, 23,* 248–257.

Schmeichel, B. J. (2007). Attention control, memory updating, and emotion regulation temporarily reduce the capacity for executive control. *Journal of Experimental Psychology: General, 36,* 241–255.

Schulte, D., Hartung, J., & Wilke, F. (1997). Handlungskontrolle der Angstbewältigung: Was macht Reizkonfrontationsverfahren so effektiv? [Action control in treatment of anxiety disorders: What makes exposure so effective?]. *Zeitschrift für Klinische Pyschologie, 26,* 118–128.

Schultheiss, O. C. (2008). Implicit motives. In O. P. John, R. W. Robins, & L. A. Pervin (Eds.), *Handbook of personality: Theory and research* (3rd ed., pp. 603–633). New York: Guilford Press.

Schulz, R., & Heckhausen, J. (1996). A life span model of successful aging. *American Psychologist, 51,* 702–714.

Shah, J. Y., & Higgins, E. T. (1997). Expectancy X value effects: Regulatory focus as determinant of magnitude and direction. *Journal of Personality and Social Psychology, 73,* 447–458.

Stiensmeier-Pelster, J. (1994). Choice of decision-making strategies and action versus state orientation. In J. Kuhl & J. Beckmann (Eds.), *Volition and personality* (pp. 167–176). Göttingen, Germany: Hogrefe & Huber.

Turner, M. L., & Engle, R. W. (1989). Is working memory capacity task dependent? *Journal of Memory and Language, 28,* 127–154.

Van Dillen, L. F., & Koole, S. L. (2007). Clearing the mind: A working memory model of distraction from negative mood. *Emotion, 7,* 715–723.

Van Putten, M., Zeelenberg, M., & Van Dijk, E. (2008). *Dealing with missed opportunities: Action versus state orientation moderates inaction inertia.* Unpublished manuscript, University of Tilburg, the Netherlands.

Wenzlaff, R. M., & Wegner, D. M. (2000). Thought suppression. *Annual Review of Psychology, 51,* 59–91.

Wrosch, C., & Heckhausen, J. (1999). Control processes before and after passing a developmental deadline: Activation and deactivation of intimate relationship goals. *Journal of Personality and Social Psychology, 77,* 415–427.

Wrosch, C., Miller, G. E., Scheier, M. F., & Brun de Pontet, S. (2007). Giving up on unattainable goals: Benefits for Health? *Personality and Social Psychology Bulletin, 33,* 251–265.

Wrosch, C., Scheier, M. F., Carver, C. S., & Schulz, R. (2003). The importance of goal disengagement in adaptive self-regulation: When giving up is beneficial. *Self and Identity, 2,* 1–20.

Zeigarnik, B. (1927). Über das Behalten von erledigten und unerledigten Handlungen [On remembering finished and unfinished activities]. *Psychologische Forschung, 9,* 1–85.

CHAPTER 14

Goal Implementation
THE BENEFITS AND COSTS OF IF–THEN PLANNING

ELIZABETH J. PARKS-STAMM
PETER M. GOLLWITZER

Although the relationship between goals and behavior is substantial (Webb & Sheeran, 2006), even very motivated individuals at times fail to act on their goals. In this chapter, we discuss the role of plans in linking goals with actual behavior. We focus specifically on a certain type of plan, an if–then plan known as an implementation intention, and review its place in the course of goal striving. We review the mechanisms underlying the effects of implementation intentions. Then, we address the benefits and costs associated with these mechanisms of implementation intentions, as well as if–then planning in general. Last, we discuss what personal and situational factors moderate the effectiveness of implementation intentions, as well as the formation of implementation intentions.

Implementation Intentions
and the Rubicon Model of Action Phases

The relationship between goals, planning, and behavior is outlined in the "Rubicon model of action phases" (Heckhausen & Gollwitzer, 1987; Gollwitzer, 1990). In this model, goal striving is temporally organized into four phases, which differ in both the tasks that are to be accomplished and the mind-sets associated with these tasks. The first predecisional phase involves considering the desirability and feasibility of various unattained wishes and desires. Its associated deliberative mind-set is associated with open-mindedness and even-handed consideration of alternatives, such as when deciding between various wishes to pursue or even the choice between action and inaction (Heckhausen & Gollwitzer, 1987; Beckmann & Gollwitzer, 1987). This predecisional stage culminates in a *goal intention*, a desired end-state the individual is committed to achieve: "I intend to perform Behavior *X*/to reach Outcome *X*" (e.g., to exercise regularly, to get an "A" in Introductory Psychology). This transformation from considering unattached wishes and desires to forming a goal intention is described as "crossing the Rubicon," because it is at this point that goal pursuit begins; from this point, one can either succeed or fail in achieving the goal intention. However, most goal-directed actions do not flow directly from this goal intention; often individuals fail to initiate any goal-directed behaviors after forming their goal intention. This may occur because individuals forget to act on their goal after it is formed, they miss good opportunities to act toward their goal, or they succumb to initial reluctance to act as is the case with goals that require overcoming unpleasant experiences at the start (e.g., starting to exercise; Gollwitzer & Sheeran, 2006). But even if people succeed with starting to act on their goals, there is always a risk that they will be derailed by difficulties, distractions, and disruptions (Gollwitzer, Bayer, & McCulloch, 2005). These problems associated with starting and continuing to act toward one's goals can be ameliorated by planning out how one's goals may be reached.

The time for planning comes in the preactional phase of goal pursuit, where the individual may arrange when, where, and how to act to realize the committed goal. Such planning is associated with an implemental (i.e., means-oriented) mind-set. This mind-set has been found to focus attention on information relevant to goal achievement (Beckmann & Gollwitzer, 1987) and away from the pros and cons of the selected or nonselected goals (Taylor & Gollwitzer, 1995; Gollwitzer, Heckhausen, & Steller, 1990). Ideally, this implementation-focused reasoning may result in one or more if–then plans, known as *implementation intentions* (Gollwitzer, 1993, 1999). This type of plan specifies an anticipated concrete situation that may signal an appropriate time to initiate goal-directed behaviors, and a response that could be used to work toward achieving the goal intention (i.e., an instrumental goal-directed response).

In the third stage of the model, the action phase, the goal-directed actions are actually initiated. This may involve enacting one planned behavior (e.g., getting the oil changed in the car as intended) or maintaining a number of goal-directed responses over a period of time. For example, to achieve an "A" in Introductory Psychology as intended, a student must carry out numerous studying behaviors, or enact one planned study behavior numerous times throughout the semester. Thus, the action phase may be short or long in duration.

Finally, in the postactional phase, the outcomes of the goal-directed actions are evaluated against what was desired when the goal intention was formed (e.g., the student compares the final grade with the desired "A"). If there is still a gap between the desired state and the current situation, the individual may start to engage in new planning on how to reach the goal, or even in new deliberation on whether the goal should be given up and other goals should be pursued instead.

Thus, it is in the preactional phase that implementation intentions are formed, but they are then carried by the individual into the action phase. From there, implementation intentions drive goal pursuit "in the moment" in a largely automatic fashion. The automaticity of the goal-directed behaviors carried out in the action phase resulting from a plan determined in the preactional phase make implementation intentions a resource-saving strategy when the opportunity to act has arrived.

Why is the temporal placement of goals and plans important? Implementation intentions are not merely a strategy that one appends to a desire to facilitate goal achievement, but a concrete plan for how to implement a selected goal pursuit. Indeed, research has demonstrated that implementation intentions facilitate goal achievement only when the related goal intention is activated. Sheeran and colleagues found that their participants benefited greatly from implementation intentions when they were linked to a strong goal intention, but not when the goal intention was weak (Sheeran, Webb, & Gollwitzer, 2005). So implementation intentions affect behavior only when they plan out the implementation of a valued goal intention. How do they accomplish this? Because of the if–then structure of implementation intentions, their underlying mechanisms may differ from some other types of plans (e.g., the "rational" planning and organization behaviors assessed by the Galotti-Simons Planning Survey; Simons & Galotti, 1992). We review the unique contributions of these underlying mechanisms next.

The Mechanisms Underlying the Effects of Implementation Intentions

To form an implementation intention, the individual identifies a future goal-relevant situational cue (i.e., the if-component) and a related planned response to that cue (i.e., the then-component). Whereas a goal intention specifies the desired event in the form of "I intend to perform Behavior X/ to reach Outcome X" (e.g., to exercise regularly/ to get an "A" in Introductory Psychology), an implementation intention specifies both an anticipated goal-relevant situation and a proper goal-directed response. Thus, an implementation intention that served the goal intention to "get an 'A' in Introductory Psychology" would follow the form "*If* Situation Y arises (e.g., when I'm going to bed on Sunday night), *then* I will perform Behavior Z (e.g., set my alarm early to read the textbook before lecture)." An implementation intention is subordinate to its related goal intention, as it exists only to aid goal achievement (Gollwitzer, 1993, 1999). The added benefit of an implementation intention is clear: A meta-analysis by Gollwitzer and Sheeran (2006) involving over 8,000 participants in 94 independent studies reported an effect size of $d = 0.65$. This medium-to-large effect size (Cohen, 1992) represents the additional facilitation of goal achievement by implementation intentions compared to goal intentions alone. As goal intentions by themselves already have a positive effect on behavior enactment (Webb & Sheeran, 2006), the size of this effect is quite astounding.

How do implementation intention effects come about? The theory of implementation intentions separates the effects of the if-component from those of the then-component, as the theory proposes two processes associated with these components through which implementation intentions facilitate goal attainment (Gollwitzer, 1993). First, specifying an anticipated goal-relevant situational cue in the if-component is proposed to increase the accessibility of the critical situation. Secondly, linking a specified goal-directed response to this cue in the then-component is proposed to automate the execution of this response upon contact with the specified cue. By forming implementation intentions, people can strategically switch from conscious and effortful action initiation (guided by goal intentions in the action phase) to having their goal-directed responses automatically elicited by the specified situational cues (through the implementation intention formed during the preactional phase). We review evidence for the heightened activation of the situational cue specified in the if-component (i.e., the if-process), and the automaticity of performing the response specified in the then-component (i.e., the then-process).

The If-Process

Specifying a goal-relevant situation in the if-component of an implementation intention is proposed to increase the activation of the mental representation of this situation, thereby making the situational cues more accessible (Gollwitzer, 1999). Research has directly tested this accessibility hypothesis by investigating whether the cues associated with the critical situation are more accessible in individuals who have formed implementation intentions relative to those with mere goal intentions.

Aarts, Dijksterhuis, and Midden (1999) found support for the idea that implementation intentions increase the accessibility of the situational cues

related to the goal by employing a lexical decision task. First, all participants were given the goal to redeem a coupon in the middle of a mundane
behavioral script (i.e., walking through the cafeteria to the building exit),
as well as information about expected situational cues that would signal
an opportunity to act on that goal. Half of the participants were asked to
organize this information into an if–then plan. Before participants were
given the opportuntity to act on their goal, they completed a lexical decision task. Aarts and colleagues found that individuals who had formed if–
then plans identified words related to the anticipated situational cue faster
than individuals who merely had the goal to redeem the coupon. In addition, the formation of the implementation intention significantly increased
participants' redemption of the coupon. Importantly, the faster lexical
decision latencies for these critical words (i.e., their heightened accessibility) mediated the relationship between planning and goal attainment. This
study provides support for the hypothesis that the if-process of implementation intentions increases the accessibility of the situational cues.

The Then-Process

Specifying a goal-directed response in the then-component of an implementation intention has been shown to automate the initiation of the planned
behavior upon contact with the situational cue, thereby allowing for goal
pursuit that exhibits features of automaticity (Bargh, 1994). The automaticity of the response specified in the then-component has been supported
in several studies demonstrating its immediacy (Gollwitzer & Brandstätter, 1997; Orbell & Sheeran, 2000), efficiency (Brandstätter, Lengfelder, &
Gollwitzer, 2001; Lengfelder & Gollwitzer, 2001), and initiation without
conscious intent (Bayer, Achtziger, Gollwitzer, & Moskowitz, in press).
We will review evidence for each of these features of automaticity in turn.

   The immediacy of the response specified in the implementation intention relative to responses guided by goal intentions alone has been supported by a laboratory experiment by Gollwitzer and Brandstätter (1997,
Study 3). All participants were given the goal to express counterarguments
to a proponent of discrimination against foreigners in Germany (presented
in a video clip), and some were asked to form implementation intentions to
specify a plan for how to do so. They found that participants with implementation intentions initiated the counterargument more quickly (without
a cost to the quality of the arguments presented) than the participants who
had merely formed the goal to counterargue. Orbell and Sheeran (2000)
also found support for the immediacy of action initiation through implementation intentions in a field study of patients who had undergone joint
replacement surgery. Patients who had formed implementation intentions
about their recovery behaviors engaged in activities sooner than those
who had not. The formation of implementation intentions mediated the

relationship between expectations of recovery and the speed of action initiation. These two studies provided evidence that the initiation of the response specified in the then-component of an implementation intention exhibits immediacy.

A second feature of automaticity has been supported by Brandtstätter and colleagues, who used a go/no-go task to test the efficiency of the initiation of the response specified in an implementation intention (Brandtstätter et al., 2001). Participants formed the goal intention to press a button as quickly as possible when a number appeared on the screen, but not to respond when a letter appeared. Participants in the implementation intention condition additionally formed a plan to press the response button particularly quickly if the number "3" was presented. This go/no-go task was then completed by participants merely as a secondary task in a dual-task paradigm. The efficiency of implementation intentions was supported by evidence that the response latencies to the number "3" were reduced in the implementation intention condition compared to the goal-only group, regardless of whether the simultaneous primary task was easy or difficult to perform. Brandtstätter et al. found that the speed-up of the response specified in the implementation intention was unaffected by the cognitive demand of the primary task to be performed at the same time (e.g., a memorization task in Study 3 and a tracking task in Study 4). These findings provide support for the hypothesis that performing the behavior specified in the then-component of implementation intentions in response to encountering the situational cue specified in the if-component does require minimal cognitive resources.

Last, two studies by Bayer et al. (in press) tested whether implementation intentions could allow an individual to respond in a goal-directed manner without conscious intent. This line of research investigated whether implementation intentions, formed consciously in the preactional phase of goal striving, can automatically guide behavior in the action phase without a second conscious act of will. In Study 1, all participants had the goal to confront a rude individual. When the face of the rude individual was presented subliminally in a sequential priming task (in which participants were asked to read target words as quickly as possible), the words to be used in complaining to her about her rude behavior (e.g., offensive, mean, and conceited) were read more quickly by implementation intention participants than goal-only participants. This suggests that the subliminally presented situational cue enabled participants to begin bolstering themselves to act toward their goal, preparing the response specified in the then-component, even without conscious awareness of the cue. Study 2 further examined whether implementation intentions could enable actual action initiation without conscious intent. In this experiment, participants were assigned the goal to classify various figures into two categories: round or angular. Those in the implementation intention condition formed a plan about one of these angular figures (e.g., "If I see a triangle, then I will press the right button particularly fast."). Bayer et al. found that participants in the implementation intention condition had faster response latencies for the angular figures (but not the rounded figures) when the specified situational cue (i.e., the triangle) was first presented subliminally than when it was not; no such effect was observed with goal intention participants. These subliminal priming effects suggest that the goal-directed behavior specified in an implementation intention is triggered by the anticipated situational cue without the need for a further conscious intention. Action initiation without conscious intent satisfies a central criterion for automatic action control.

The research reviewed above suggests that the two components of an implementation intention produce distinguishable effects during goal striving: The if-component heightens the activation of the specified situational cue, whereas the linked then-component automates the planned behavioral response upon contact with the cue. Often these two processes work together to enhance goal attainment. Webb and Sheeran (2007) simultaneously tested the impact of the cue accessibility associated with the if-component and the automatic response initiation associated with the then-component of the implementation intention on goal attainment. In their study, participants were either instructed to familiarize themselves with a target nonword (*avenda*) so they could respond quickly to that item (the goal-only condition), or to form a plan to respond quickly to this target nonword (the implementation intention condition). Participants were told that they would be searching for this nonword (along with others) in a word-search puzzle. Before they completed the word search, a sequential priming paradigm was used to measure the accessibility of this target nonword (i.e., the if-process) as well as the association between the target nonword and the planned response (i.e., the then-process). They found that the strength of each of these processes associated with implementation intentions independently mediated the effect of implementation intentions on goal attainment. In this experimental paradigm, both the if-process and the then-process facilitated goal attainment. However, depending on the goal being pursued and what behaviors are needed to act effectively toward that goal, these processes may help or hinder goal pursuit. The next section examines the potential benefits and costs of the if- and then-processes of implementation intentions.

The Benefits and Costs of Implementation Intentions

What are the implications of these two mechanisms of implementation intentions for goal pursuit? In terms of goal-related outcomes, there are benefits and costs of both the heightened activation of the specified cue afforded by the if-component (the if-process), and the automatization of the response afforded by the linked then-component (the then-process).

The Benefits and Costs Associated with the If-Process

Benefits

One outcome of the heightened accessibility of the specified situational cues is that these cues are more easily identified. In an early investigation of facilitated cue detection, participants searched for a figure in an embedded figures task (Steller, 1992). Participants exhibited superior detection of the figures specified in the if-part of an implementation intention. Webb and Sheeran (2004) investigated whether this improvement in cue identification was due to increased activation or response bias. They found that participants with implementation intentions responded faster to critical cues than did goal participants but were not more likely to respond to similar but inappropriate cues (Webb & Sheeran, 2004, Study 3), supporting the heightened accessibility explanation of the enhanced identification. Thus, the if-component of implementation intentions may help individuals to quickly recognize goal-relevant opportunities when they arise.

One self-regulatory problem that this enhanced cue identification may help solve is the failure to seize a goal-relevant opportunity when it is available (Gollwitzer & Sheeran, 2006). Missing potential opportunities to act is particularly a problem for behaviors that must be initiated during a certain window of opportunity (i.e., short-fuse behaviors; Dholakia & Bagozzi, 2003). In daily life, one must act during a limited frame of time to catch a plane, vote, attend a meeting, pick up dry cleaning, or attend an exercise class. It is clear, even from this short list of examples, that many common goals are served by short-fuse behaviors. Research has shown that implementation intentions do help individuals seize the opportunity to act when it is presented briefly; in their study of short-fuse behaviors, Dholakia and Bagozzi (2003) found 70% of participants who had formed implementation intentions took advantage of the opportunity during the allotted time compared to only 33% of participants with goals alone. In a meta-analysis of 20 tests of seizing opportunities (with over 2,000 participants), Gollwitzer and Sheeran (2006) found a medium-to-large effect size of implementation intentions relative to mere goals ($d = 0.61$).

Another benefit of the heightened accessibility of the situational cues specified in implementation intentions is the superior recall of the planned opportunities. In one study, research participants formed implementation intentions specifying when, where, and how they would perform an experimental task from numerous predesigned options. Immediately, or 48 hours later, participants were given a surprise task to recall all of the situational cues they had been provided. Those cues specified in implementation intentions were more successfully recalled than nonspecified cues, whether recall was tested immediately or at a later point in time (i.e., 2 days later; Achtziger, Bayer, & Gollwitzer, 2008).

Facilitated recall of specified opportunities may be especially beneficial for goal striving when opportunities to work toward the goal are rarely encountered. Sheeran and Orbell (1998) reported a strong negative correlation between the latency to act and goal achievement, illustrating that the longer the time interval between the goal intention and the opportunity to act, the less likely it is that intentions will be realized. In these cases, goal achievement may be prevented simply because individuals fail to recall how they wanted to act on their goal intention (Gollwitzer & Sheeran, 2006). For example, in an intervention designed to promote breast self-examination, 64% of women who had formed an implementation intention did perform a breast self-exam, whereas only 14% of those in the control group did. Of the participants in the control group who failed to perform a self-exam, 70% blamed their failure on forgetting to act on their goal (Orbell, Hodgkins, & Sheeran, 1997). Thus, people who have specified select opportunities in which to act on their goals will more easily recall when and where they wanted to act on them, and thus will be more likely to act in these situational contexts (e.g., a page to be marked in a booklet; Chasteen, Park, & Schwarz, 2001). According to Gollwitzer and Sheeran (2006), in their meta-analysis of 11 studies associated with remembering to act, the impact of implementation intentions was medium-to-large in size ($d = 0.54$).

Another benefit of the heightened accessibility of the situational cues in the if-component is that they may be observed even when one is busy with other things. The heightened accessibility means that the specified cues command attention, disrupting even attention that is focused elsewhere. Using a dichotic-listening paradigm, Gollwitzer et al. (2002) found that words related to a specified anticipated situation presented in the unattended channel were more disruptive to focused attention for implementation intention participants than goal intention participants. Individuals who had formed a plan specifying the anticipated goal-relevant situation showed a reduction in their performance in the primary task when they heard cue-related words. The disruption of focused ongoing activity demonstrates the heightened accessibility of these cues; even when endeavoring to ignore them, the cues specified in the if-component of an implementation intention readily capture attention. This disruption of otherwise-focused attention is clearly a benefit for goal pursuits that involve unexpected opportunities to act as goal-relevant cues may appear when one is engaged in another activity or thought.

In addition, situational cues may be especially easy to miss when one is engaged in a mundane behavioral script that requires little attention to the environment. In the Aarts et al. (1999) study described earlier, participants were presented with the opportunity to act while walking through a commonly used cafeteria to the building exit—a mundane behavioral script that required little attention to the external environment for the students. Aarts and colleagues argued that it is the increased accessibility of the situational cues that allowed participants to interrupt their mundane behavioral script and recognize the opportunity to act toward their goal. Thus, implementation intentions disrupt attention focused on goal-irrelevant topics, whether they are external or internal. These two examples represent very common situations that may impede recognition of the opportunity to act in real life. These studies provide examples of ways that the heightened accessibility of the situational cue afforded by the if-component of implementation intentions can provide benefits to goal pursuit.

Costs

The heightened activation of the situational cue specified in a plan can also result in costs for goal pursuit. When there are multiple possible situations or various appropriate opportunities in which to engage in a given goal pursuit, this heightened activation of one approach to the goal may become a liability for overall goal pursuit. Parks-Stamm, Gollwitzer, and Oettingen (2007, Study 1) found that the facilitated identification of the planned situation specified in the if-component of an implementation intention is associated with a reduced identification of alternative goal-relevant situations relative to goal-only participants. In this study, participants were given the goal to identify all the five-letter words in a story by typing in the first letter of the word. Thus, the if-process (i.e., counting letters in words to identify the goal-relevant situation) was difficult and required much cognitive capacity, but the then-process (i.e., typing in the first letter of the word to respond) was quite easy. Because implementation intentions only aid in difficult tasks, the effect of implementation intentions on the if-process would be seen in this task. Participants were then given information about two anticipated situational cues ("Laura" and "mouse"), which would account for only half of the presented opportunities to act toward the goal. Half of the participants formed implementation intentions with these situational cues (e.g., "And if I hear Laura, then I will press L," "And if I hear mouse, then I will press M"), and the goal participants merely familiarized themselves with these target words and the correct response. As one might expect, individuals who formed implementation intentions about these situational cues were better at identifying the situational cues specified in their implementation intentions. However, they were also worse than goal-only participants at identifying alternative, nonspecified cues that were equally valid means to achieve the desired goal.

Thus, when there are many routes to a goal, and one's implementation intention only specifies one or two of these opportunities, the heightened accessibility of the planned route may draw attention away from novel opportunities to act, harming overall goal pursuit. For example, if I have the goal intention to include more vegetables in my diet, and I make an implementation intention specifying broccoli as my situational cue (e.g., "if I see broccoli on the menu, then I will order that plate!"), this should increase my broccoli intake in restaurants. However, this may lead me to pass over the salads, carrots, and mixed vegetable plates. This plan may actually harm my ability to recognize other, possibly more valuable, goal-relevant situations in which to work toward my goal.

In addition to costs in identifying alternative goal-relevant opportunities to act in any given goal pursuit, planning one goal pursuit may also result in costs to other concurrent goal pursuits. The heightened accessibility of the cues specified in the if-component of implementation intentions may create costs because these cues automatically attract attention even when they are not relevant to one's current focal goal. As described above, Achtziger and colleagues (2008) showed in a dual-task paradigm that the heightened accessibility of the specified cues presented in an unattended channel disrupted performance on a primary task. The heightened accessibility of the situational cues specified for one goal pursuit thereby impeded a concurrent goal pursuit in this dual-task paradigm. This suggests that the heightened accessibility of the situational cues could result in a cost in pursuing alternative goals, as well.

Costs to alternative concurrent goal pursuits should be especially pronounced when there is an overlap between the planned situational cues and the cues currently encountered. Wieber and Sassenberg (2006) explored the effect of implementation intentions when a current (alternative) goal pursuit requires one to attend to different cues, but the specified situational cues were still present. Thus, the cues specified in the if-component of the implementation intentions for one task were actually distractors for the second task. In two studies, participants showed costs in their performance when pursuing a secondary goal because attention was drawn to the now-irrelevant cues from the prior implementation intention. Their results suggest that these costs are a result of implementation intentions drawing away limited attentional resources, rather than a derivative of the motor response system. These findings illustrate the costs planning may have for concurrently pursued goal pursuits. It also suggests that costs may be especially likely when the selected cues are commonly encountered in goal-irrelevant situations. If the cues are relevant to other goal pursuits, or are best left ignored to pursue other goals, the increased accessibility of these cues could be especially distracting.

However, even this cost has its limitations. The extent to which actual behavior is affected by an implementation intention appears to depend on the activation of the respective superordinate goal. There is evidence that implementation intentions do not compulsorily affect behavior any time the critical situation specified in the if-part of the implementation intention is encountered, but only when its respective superordinate goal is activated (Sheeran et al., 2005, Study 2). It appears then that the heightened accessibility of the situational cues specified in the if-component of an implementation intention may automatically capture attention away from a focal goal pursuit only if the nonfocal goal that had been furnished with an implementation intention is also activated.

The Benefits and Costs Associated with the Then-Process

Benefits

The automaticity afforded by the then-component of an implementation intention provides clear benefits for goal pursuit. Individuals are able to initiate the specified goal-directed behaviors immediately (Gollwitzer & Brandstätter, 1997; Orbell & Sheeran, 2000), efficiently (Brandstätter et al., 2001; Lengfelder & Gollwitzer, 2001), and without a second conscious act of will (Bayer et al., in press). Through implementation intentions, planned goal-directed behaviors essentially become habits that are initiated effortlessly (Aarts & Dijksterhuis, 2000). The possible benefits associated with each of these features of automaticity will be addressed individually below.

There are certain goal pursuits for which response immediacy is important and beneficial. For example, short-fuse behaviors (Dholakia & Bagozzi, 2003) must be performed in a given window of time. In these cases, responding quickly can be a benefit to goal pursuit. If people delay, considering their options and responses, the window of opportunity could pass without goal striving being initiated. Responding quickly is also particularly important for behaviors and responses that are always enacted immediately. Emergency room doctors and nurses often need to make split-second decisions in life-threatening cases, where deliberating about what response to enact could waste precious time. Providing these practitioners with implementation intentions that specify a response that can be initiated immediately when these dangerous situations are encountered could save lives when time is limited.

One benefit deriving from the efficiency of the then-response is that acting with an implementation intention allows an individual to work toward a goal without tiring as quickly as one acting on goal intentions alone. Muraven and Baumeister (2000) proposed that self-regulation failure often occurs because self-control is a limited resource, and the exertion of self-control leads to a reduction (or "depletion") of these resources. The result is a state known as *ego depletion*. In a typical demonstration of ego depletion, participants who were first asked to suppress certain thoughts (a difficult self-regulatory task) later gave up more quickly (i.e., were able to persevere for less time) on a subsequent anagram task (Muraven, Tice, & Baumeister, 1998, Study 2). What becomes of individuals who are self-regulating based on an implementation intention?

Because of the efficiency of the response specified in the then-component, implementation intentions provide a reduction in these ego-depletion effects, improving long-term self-regulation. Webb and Sheeran (2003) found that participants who acted based on implementation intentions on a first cognitive task (i.e., a Stroop task) showed greater persistence on a second cognitive task (i.e., an anagram task) than individuals who were only acting on goals in the first task. Bayer, Trötschel, Sumner, and Gollwitzer (2006) replicated this finding, showing that even when the first task did not challenge similar cognitive resources (i.e., participants had to control their emotions while watching a movie in the first task, and solve difficult anagrams as a second task), ego depletion was reduced as evidenced in a heightened anagram performance. In a second study, Webb and Sheeran (2003) found that implementation intentions helped participants perform better after being ego depleted. The automaticity that implementation intentions afford therefore not only preserves energy for other goal pursuits (or toward maintenance of the necessary goal-directed behaviors), but also allows individuals to work efficiently toward their goals even when tired from earlier self-regulatory exertions (i.e., when in a state of ego depletion). Accordingly, in their meta-analysis, Gollwitzer and Sheeran (2006) found a particularly large effect of implementation intentions when participants were ego depleted ($d = 1.28$). It does not come as a surprise then that patients with schizophrenia (who are burdened by uncontrollable thoughts) and persons in a state of withdrawal from a substance to which they are addicted (who are burdened by unwanted thoughts related to the drug urge) were found to benefit much in their action control by forming implementation intentions (Brandstätter et al., 2001, Studies 1 and 2).

A third benefit deriving from the automaticity afforded by the then-component of implementation intentions is that responses need not be considered at the time of behavior enactment. Because implementation intentions plan out a goal-directed response in advance, a second conscious act of will (or thinking up a possible response) is unnecessary. As was seen in the Bayer et al. (in press) studies, even subliminally presented critical cues were able to activate the responses specified in the then-component. Thus, even without conscious awareness of the cue, the response specified in the then-component of the implementation intention can be initiated. This automaticity would be very beneficial for individuals encountering dangerous situations in which complex thinking and decision making is not possible. For example, military personnel and police officers often must respond to dangerous and emotional situations. Rather than formulating a viable response in situ, these individuals may enact their planned responses through implementation intentions directly.

Like a habitual response formed through repeated pairing, the behavior specified in the then-component is directly triggered by the situational cue (Aarts & Dijksterhuis, 2000). The benefits of such "strategic automaticity" (Gollwitzer, 1999) created by forming implementation intentions are similar to the benefits of positive habits for daily self-regulation. Because habitual behaviors are enacted automatically, they take up little cognitive resources, so that even when a person is ego depleted they can be maintained (Neal, Wood, & Quinn, 2006). Research has also demonstrated that behaviors controlled by habits are enacted without necessitating the prefrontal regions associated with more reflective or effortful cognitive action control (Owen, 1997). The Lengfelder and Gollwitzer (2001) finding that frontal lobe patients benefit in their action control as much from forming implementation intentions as control patients or college students suggests that the prefrontal cortex is less involved in action control by implementation intentions as well.

Recently, Gilbert, Gollwitzer, Cohen, Oettingen, and Burgess (2008) tested this hypothesis more directly in an fMRI study. In two comparable prospective memory tasks (pressing the space bar whenever a critical stimulus configuration appeared in a classification task as part of a dual task) performed consecutively in the scanner, each participant formed an implementation intention for performing one prospective memory task and a goal intention for the other. Activation was then compared within participants across these counterbalanced tasks. The results indicated that in these two tasks, the behavioral data were in line with past research in that prospective memory performance was enhanced by implementation intentions, and that this enhanced performance did not compromise the performance on the ongoing dual task. Most important, in the goal-intention condition, successful prospective memory performance was found to be based on the activation of the frontal-parietal network that is known to be associated with working memory and high-level cognitive control. In contrast, in the implementation intention condition, successful prospective memory performance was based on the activation of the premotor cortex involved in low-level motor planning and located at more posterior parietal areas of the cerebral cortex.

How does automating one planned goal-directed response affect alternative possible goal-directed responses that might be equivalently instrumental to attaining the intended goal? Unlike the process associated with the if-component, the process associated with the then-component of implementation intentions does not reduce one's use of alternative routes to the desired goal (Parks-Stamm et al., 2007, Study 2). Because forming an implementation intention automates the initiation of the planned goal-directed response, enacting the behavior specified in the then-component of an implementation intention requires a reduced amount of time, cognitive capacity, and willpower. This efficient response allows the individual to initiate alternative goal-directed responses with the same ease as is possible for individuals without a plan. In this study, participants were given the goal to count the number of letters in every word that began with a "D." Thus, the if-process (i.e., identifying words starting with a "D" to identify the goal-relevant situation) was quite easy, but the then-process (i.e., typing in the number of letters of the word to respond) was difficult and required cognitive capacity. Because implementation intentions only aid in difficult tasks, the effect of implementation intentions on the then-process would be seen in this task. Participants were told that the two most common D-words they would encounter would be "Danny" and "dragon," which consist of five and six letters, respectively. Those in the goal condition merely memorized this information, whereas those in the implementation intention condition formed if-then plans involving this information (e.g., "If I hear 'Danny,' then I will press the 5," "If I hear 'dragon,' I will press the 6"). However, responding to these two target words represented only half of the available responses to achieve the overarching goal. In this study, participants with implementation intentions responded more frequently to the two target words than those with a goal intention, without exhibiting a cost in their response to alternative D-words. Thus, the then-component processes lead to increased initiation of the planned behavior without costs to alternatives; the automaticity associated with the then-component does not result in reductions in one's ability to enact nonspecified goal-directed behaviors.

Costs

The automaticity of the planned goal-directed behavior in response to the specified situational cue (i.e., the then-process) may lead to costs with respect to a different aspect of goal pursuit. When the implementation intention specifies a suboptimal approach to the goal, or the planned response is no longer applicable, it might be difficult for individuals to disengage from a plan that occurs immediately, efficiently, and without a second act of will. To explore this possibility, Jaudas, Achtziger, and Gollwitzer (2006) gave participants a faulty plan and examined participants' ability to disengage from the plan. All participants were given the goal to find the shortest possible way through various mazes. They were also told that a green arrow would appear at some junctions to indicate a shortcut. Participants in the implementation intention condition additionally formed an if–then plan involving the green arrow, "And if the green arrow appears, then I'll quickly press the button." This plan then turned out to be a poor plan for achieving their goal: The green arrow correctly indicated a shortcut only 30% of the time. As compared to participants with mere goal intentions, costs in terms of a reluctance to give up the faulty plan emerged among participants with implementation intentions when no explicit failure feedback was given (i.e, participants needed to evaluate the effectiveness of their plan by themselves). The automaticity of the response (in this case, not an instrumental response) thus appears to make it more difficult to disengage from a faulty plan, perhaps because the planned response is enacted quickly and without conscious thought, thus precluding a reevaluation of the plan. This interpretation of the participants' sluggishness to disengage from the faulty plan is supported by an additional observation in the present study. When the experimenter gave explicit failure feedback (to trigger evaluative thought) sluggish disengagement from the plan was no longer observed.

Another possible cost of the automatic then-processes includes the enactment of planned responses when the situation has changed, or when the goal is no longer present. Would response initiation occur automatically, even when the environment dictates this planned response is no longer appropriate? Further research is needed on this topic. However, because of the goal-dependent automaticity of implementation intentions, it seems possible that this type of rigidity would not be observed. Seehausen, Bayer, and Gollwitzer (1994) found that when participants were told that they no longer needed to reach an assigned goal, the effect of the former implementation intention disappeared, and Sheeran at al. (2005) reported that implementation intention effects require that the respective superordinate goal is still strong (i.e., people feel strongly committed) and in a state of high activation.

Recent work by Achtziger (2003) on prejudicial feelings toward soccer fans also indicates that implementation intentions can be applied flexibly, as their application depends upon the situation. In this study, a sequential priming paradigm was used in which pictures of soccer fans served as primes and relevant person attributes served as targets (e.g., rowdy, comradely) that had to be read as quickly as possible. Participants were given an implementation intention to block negative feelings toward soccer fans (e.g., "if I see a soccer fan, then I will not evaluate him negatively!"). Half of the pictures of soccer fans were accompanied by a tone, and participants were told that the implementation intention would only apply when the tone was heard. Implementation intention effects (i.e., relevant positive attributes were read faster than negative attributes) were observed only when the depiction of soccer fans was accompanied with a signal tone. This research suggests that implementation intentions may be applied flexibly, depending on the situation in which the situational cues are encountered. Still, the rigidity- related costs of the automaticity afforded by the then-component of implementation intentions demand further research.

Other Benefits and Costs of Implementation Intentions

In addition to the benefits and costs that come directly from each of the component processes that make up implementation intentions (i.e., the if-process and the then-process), forming an if-then plan itself may have benefits and costs for goal pursuit. The following section therefore lists some other benefits and costs of if–then plans that cannot be attributed to either the if- or the then-process triggered by having formed an implementation intention. Benefits of if–then planning include ameliorating dysfunctional thoughts and emotional responses as well as overcoming strong unwanted behavioral tendencies (such as bad habits), whereas costs include rigidity associated with the sense of obligation resulting from committing to a plan.

Ameliorating Dysfunctional Cognitive and Emotional Responses

One benefit of if-then planning is that it seems to reduce the planning fallacy. The planning fallacy describes the finding in which people believe they will accomplish their goals more quickly than they actually do (Kahneman & Tversky, 1979). Koole and Spijker (2000) found that individuals with implementation intentions completed their goals faster than those with a goal intention only, and that because of this performance enhancement the unrealistic optimism (actual minus the predicted rate of goal completion) was significantly less in the implementation intention condition. In fact, those with implementation intentions did not exhibit an optimistic bias at all as they fully achieved the predicted optimistic rate of goal completion.

Research by Kruger and Evans (2004) suggests another mechanism by which implementation intentions may reduce the planning fallacy, especially when more than one implementation intention is formed. They reported that breaking down a goal into subcomponents (as is necessary when concretely planning) resulted in longer predicted times for completion and thus less optimistically biased estimates. It was also found that the more complex the task, the greater the influence of considering each of its subcomponents on planning time.

Bayer and Gollwitzer (2007) combated dysfunctional beliefs in difficult academic tasks (e.g., taking the Raven intelligence test). Even when people begin a test with high self-efficacy beliefs, encountering a difficult test item may lead to weakened self-efficacy beliefs for subsequent test items. To counter such self-doubts, Bayer and Gollwitzer asked participants to form implementation intentions specifying a self-efficacy strengthening response: "And if I start a new test item, then I'll tell myself: I can solve it!" Participants in the implementation intention condition performed better than those with mere high-achievement goal intentions or those with a self-efficacy strengthening goal intention alone. This work suggests that in addition to the typical behavioral or cognitive responses normally specified in the then-component of implementation intentions, motivation-enhancing inner speech can also be specified and thus automated through if-then planning. Thus, another benefit of if-then plans is that they may be used to address dysfunctional motivational thought (in the present case, self-doubts in the form of reduced self-efficacy beliefs).

Recent research has also explored whether adding implementation intentions to emotion-regulation goals would make these goals more effective (Schweiger Gallo, Keil, McCulloch, Rockstroh, & Gollwitzer, in press). In one study, participants were exposed to a series of pictures used to elicit disgust. When participants formed a response-focused implementation intention ("if I see disgusting scenes, then I'll stay calm and relaxed"), they exhibited a reduction in arousal compared to a control group. As anticipated, participants who operated on mere goals to not get disgusted could not willfully reduce their arousal to the disgusting pictures. A second study analyzed the control of spider fear in people with spider phobias. Both participants with response-focused implementation intentions ("if a see a spider, then I will stay calm and relaxed") and antecedent-focused implementation intentions ("if I see a spider, then I'll ignore it") experienced less negative affect in the face of spider pictures than a no self-regulation control group; again, mere goal intentions to not get frightened failed to achieve this effect. Moreover, people with spider phobias using implementation intentions even managed to control their fear to the low level observed with a sample of participants who were preselected on the basis of having no fear of spiders at all. In a final study using dense-array electroencephalography, the effectiveness of ignore-implementation intentions for the control of spider fear in people with spider phobias was replicated, and the obtained electrocortical correlates revealed that those participants who furnished their goal intention with an ignore-implementation intention showed a significantly reduced early visual activity in response to spider slides, as reflected in a smaller P1. The ignore-implementation intention seemed to function in the first 120 milliseconds after the spider pictures were presented. As conscious efforts to inhibit the activation of the mental representation of a presented stimulus are commonly assumed to show their effects no earlier than 300 milliseconds after stimulus presentation (overview by Bargh & Chartrand, 2000), the smaller P1 produced by ignore-implementation intentions also supports the hypothesis that implementation intentions lead to strategic automation of the goal-directed responses spelled out in their then-part.

A final way that planning can ameliorate dysfunctional thought is by blocking its influence on action control. For example, in negotiations the framing of potential negotiation outcomes as losses commonly leads to both suboptimal negotiation outcomes (when both parties operate under a loss frame rather than a gain frame) and unfair negotiation outcomes (when one of the parties operates under a loss frame and the other under a gain frame). These negative consequences of loss frames are observed even when the negotiators are assigned prosocial goals (to cooperate, to be fair). However, when Trötschel and Gollwitzer (2007) assigned prosocial goals to negotiators and then asked them to supplement them with implementation intentions, the negative effects of loss frames on negotiation outcomes were blocked. Forming if-then plans allowed negotiators to recruit cognitively more complex negotiation strategies which in turn facilitated the discovery of integrative solutions which served the different interests of the negotiation parties equally well.

Breaking Unwanted Behavioral Orientations

Another benefit of planning is that plans are able to break old habits and create new ones (Holland, Aarts, & Langendam, 2006). In general, breaking bad habits is very difficult to do. Even when individuals have strong intentions to change habitual health behaviors, these interventions are usually unsuccessful (Aarts, Paulussen, & Schaalma, 1997). For example, Verplanken and Faes (1999) found that implementation intentions formed to serve the goal of eating in a healthy manner did increase healthy food intake but did not reduce the habitual intake of unhealthy food. However, when implementation intentions are formed that compete with habitual behaviors, the planned behavior is able to replace the habit. For example, Holland and colleagues (2006) found that implementation intentions designed to replace environmentally unfriendly disposal habits with recycling were effective in reducing unwanted habits. The new habits replaced these past habitual behaviors even 2 months after the implementation intention was formed.

But implementation intentions can be used to break unwanted behavioral tendencies not only when these responses are based on habits but also when they originate from task sets. After having performed one task for a while, individuals experience costs in terms of errors and reaction times when they attempt to switch to a new task (Rogers & Monsell, 1995). In such cases, successful performance of the new task is only possible when responding in terms of the old task is effectively inhibited. Commonly, such inhibition is insufficient and switch costs (reduced performance on the new task) arise even when individuals have a full second to prepare for responding to the new task (Allport, Styles, & Hsieh, 1994). Could implementation intentions also be applied here, to ease the difficulty individuals experience in switching to the different responses required for the new task? Cohen, Bayer, Jaudas, and Gollwitzer (2008, Study 1) found that implementation intentions do indeed reduce switch costs. Participants only had to specify the behavior demanded in the new task and link it to an anticipated critical cue (stimulus) to respond immediately to the new task.

Finally, implementation intentions have been shown to allow the execution of a new response even in situations that have always been responded to in a different manner. Cohen et al. (2008, Study 2) used the Simon task that takes advantage of such ingrained responses: stimuli presented on the left side of a person are commonly responded to by the left arm, whereas stimuli presented on the right side are responded to by the right arm. In the Simon task, tones are presented which simultaneously feature relevant (low or high pitch) and irrelevant (left or right location) attributes. For example, the participants must answer if a tone's pitch is low or high by pressing a key with their left or right hand, respectively. In this example, responses to low-pitch tones presented on the left side (and high-pitch tones presented on the right side) are typically faster compared to responses to high-pitch tones presented on the left side and low-pitch tones presented on the right side. This congruence effect on response times is termed the "Simon effect."

The Simon effect is a robust phenomenon that can be replicated for different stimuli and in different modalities (for an overview see Lu & Proctor, 1995); it is commonly explained by so-called two-route models. One of the most cited two-route models is the dimensional overlap model (Kornblum, Hasbroucq, & Osman, 1990). According to this model, the stimulus attributes (relevant and irrelevant) are processed along two different routes. The processing of the irrelevant attribute (spatial location) is automatic and thus immediately activates a respective response. The relevant stimulus attribute is processed by the slower, more controlled processes instigated by the task goal. If processing along both routes activates the same response, one finds shorter reaction times. On the other hand, when the responses activated by the two routes are different (or incongruent) then this results in a conflict that produces longer reaction times. This "race" between information processing along the automatic and task goal routes is supported by experiments investigating the temporal relationship between coding of the irrelevant stimulus attribute and coding of the relevant attribute (e.g., De Jong, Liang, & Lauber, 1994). Cohen et al. (2008) found that forming implementation intentions designed to focus the individual on the relevant stimulus attributes (i.e., pitch of the tone) reduced the effect of spatial location for the cue specified in the implementation intention. Thus, implementation intentions eliminated the Simon effect in terms of error rates and reaction times for the critical stimulus specified in the implementation intention.

Finally, implementation intentions can be used to break a behavioral tendency that has been described as "throwing good money after bad," or the escalation of commitment. Henderson, Gollwitzer, and Oettingen (2007) investigated the effectiveness of implementation intentions in overcoming the tendency to remain committed to a failing course of action. Participants who had chosen a certain strategy for a given goal either formed an implementation intention that specified a complex reflection response ("If I receive disappointing feedback, then I'll think about how things have been going with my strategy!") or a more simple action response ("If I receive disappointing feedback, then I'll switch my strategy!"), or merely the goal to always use the best strategy available. Henderson et al. (2007) observed that action-implementation intentions facilitated disengagement as a response to experienced failure no matter whether there were signs that things were picking up or that they would continue to stay bleak. Reflection-implementation intention participants, on the other hand, integrated information about recent improvement in forming their disengagement decision (i.e., they were less willing to disengage when things were picking up). In sum, these studies show that implementation intentions can be used to curb the escalation of behavioral commitment commonly observed when people experience failure with a chosen strategy of goal striving. Using reflection-implementation intentions (as compared to action-implementation intentions) even allows for flexible disengagement in the sense that recent turns to the better are respected in one's decision to switch (or not) to a different goal-striving strategy.

Rigidity from Social Obligation

Costs from forming implementation intentions may originate when people feel that by having formed this particular plan they are now socially obligated to act as planned, which may obstruct individuals from taking advantage of alternative opportunities to achieve their goals. Häfner (2000) explored this question by asking participants to fill out a questionnaire at the end of the experiment. Then, during the experiment, the computer "unexpectedly crashed." The experimenter then informed the participants that it would take about 5 minutes for the computer technician to come by to fix the problem, which was enough time to fill out the questionnaire lying on the table next to the computer monitor. Significantly more participants in the goal intention condition used this unexpected opportunity than in the implementation intention condition (57% vs. 34%), demonstrating that the implementation intention hampered participants in their goal striving by binding them to the specified opportunity. A posttest questionnaire revealed that although 98% of participants responded that they noticed that the computer breakdown offered a good opportunity to complete the questionnaire, 38% reported that they felt that the experimenter would not want them to complete it during that time. When these participants were excluded, there was no longer a difference between the goal intention condition and the implementation intention condition. Thus, assuming that one is obligated to act on one's goals as specified in one's implementation intention may very well create a burden to overall goal attainment as it prevents people from taking advantage of unexpected (unplanned) opportunities.

Moderators of Implementation Intention Effects

There are numerous moderators to this relationship between planning and goal attainment including features of the goal itself and character-istics of the individual. One characteristic of the goal that moderates the success of implementation intentions is the extent to which it reflects the individual's actual interests and values. Koestner et al. (2006) show that the positive effects of implementation intentions on goal attainment are partially dependent on whether they are formed in the service of intrinsic (high-autonomy) versus extrinsic (low-autonomy) goals. Implementation intentions that furnish intrinsic goals are more effective than those that furnish extrinsic goals. Another characteristic of the goal that moderates the effectiveness of implementation intentions is its difficulty. It is com-monly found that difficult rather than easy goals are benefited by imple-mentation intentions (Gollwitzer & Brandstätter, 1997).

As implementation intentions are subordinate to goal intentions, the strength of implementation intention effects should also be moderated by the activation of the related goal. Sheeran et al. (2005, Study 2) tested this assumption by implicitly priming half of their participants with speed-related words, thereby activating a speed goal in one condition. After the speed goal had been activated (or not), all participants formed an imple-mentation intention on how to be fast in solving puzzles. Sheeran and colleagues found that the if–then plan only increased the speed of solv-ing puzzles when the superordinate goal of being fast had been activated. Analogously, Seehausen et al. (1994) found that when participants were told that they no longer needed to reach an assigned goal, the effect of the related implementation intention disappeared. Once the goal was no longer activated, the common implementation intention effect of enhanced memory for the critical situation specified in the if-part of the implementa-tion intention could not be observed any more.

Another moderator of the effect of implementation intentions is the strength of the underlying goal intention. For instance, Orbell et al. (1997) found that forming implementation intentions that specified when and where participants wanted to perform a breast self-exam in the coming month resulted in an increased occurrence only in those participants who held a strong goal intention to perform a breast self-exam. Following up on this finding, Sheeran et al. (2005, Study 1) investigated the moderation of implementation intention effects depending on the strength of the goal intention to study. They found a significant interaction between goal-intention strength (i.e., number of intended study hours) and the effect of implementation intentions. When the goal intention to study was weakly held, the presence or absence of implementation intentions did not predict behavior; when it was moderate, implementation intentions increased their predictive validity; and when the goal intention was strong, the prediction of behavior by implementation intentions was at its highest.

In addition to features of the goal, characteristics of the individual can moderate the relationship between if–then planning and goal attainment. Implementation intentions have been found to be especially useful for individuals with poor self-regulatory abilities. People with schizophrenia, substance addicts in withdrawal (Brandstätter et al., 2001, Studies 1 & 2), and frontal lobe patients (Lengfelder & Gollwitzer, 2001) have been found to benefit as much (or even more) from forming implementation intentions than respective control groups. This is also true for children with attention-deficit/hyperactivity disorder (ADHD) who are known to have difficulties with tasks that require response inhibition (e.g., go/no-go tasks). First, it was observed that response inhibition performance of children with ADHD in the presence of stop signals can be improved by forming implementation intentions (Gawrilow & Gollwitzer, 2008). Second, this improved response inhibition is even reflected in the P300 component of electroencephalogram data (Paul et al., 2007). Typically, the P300 component invoked by no-go stimuli has greater amplitude than the P300 invoked by go stimuli. This difference is less pronounced in children with ADHD. Paul et al. (2007) found that if–then plans improved response inhibition and increased the P300 difference (go/no-go) in children with ADHD. These recent findings encourage the application of the self-regulation technique of making if–then plans in addition (or even as an alternative) to common medical therapy of ADHD.

There is one group of individuals in whom implementation intentions have been found to have a negative effect. Socially prescribed perfectionists characterized by self-critical tendencies, rejection of external control, and hypersensitivity to criticism actually experience reductions in goal attainment after having formed implementation intentions (Powers, Koestner, & Topciu, 2005). For these individuals, planning was associated with negative affect. However, the authors reported that in individuals whose perfectionism is driven by personal standards (as is the case with perfectionists who are self-oriented) implementation intentions do not obstruct but rather facilitate goal progress. In sum, both characteristics of the goal (e.g., difficulty, activation, strength) and characteristics of the individual (e.g., perfectionism) moderate the effectiveness of implementation intentions.

What, on the other hand, moderates the formation of implementation intentions? More research is needed to explore the circumstances under which people are most likely to form if–then plans. Because implementation intentions are formed during the preactional phase of goal pursuit, it is likely that the individual's anticipation of difficulties in striving for one's goal will influence whether he/she can and wants to make plans (i.e., whether implementation intentions are formed or not). In a recent intervention study geared at changing middle-aged women's eating and exercise behavior, these women were first taught to mentally contrast a desired future of healthy eating and regular exercise with impediments (obstacles) of present reality (for details of the mental contrasting technique see Oettingen, Pak, & Schnetter, 2001). Only then they were asked to form implementation intentions that linked these perceived obstacles (if-part) to relevant goal-directed behaviors (then-part). In comparison to control participants who received persuasive information that depicted a healthy diet and regular exercise as highly desirable and feasible, women in the intervention group (mental contrasting plus implementation intentions) showed an immediate increase in healthiness of diet and regular exercise that was still observed 4 months later (Stadler, Oettingen, & Gollwitzer, in press).

Because implementation intentions require focusing on the low-level features of the goal striving (i.e., the when, where, and how of the implementation), it is also likely that being in a concrete mind-set during the preactional phase of goal pursuit that focuses on how things are done will facilitate forming implementation intentions (Freitas, Gollwitzer, & Trope, 2004). An abstract mind-set that focuses on why things are done, on the other hand, would likely draw the individual away from forming if–then plans. In the latter case, people should be in a worse position to detect obstacles and think of instrumental behaviors that are then linked together by making concrete if–then plans.

The formation of implementation intentions may also be moderated by characteristics of the individual. Implementation intentions may be more likely to be formed by some individuals than others because they differ in their ability to create links between anticipated situations and planned behaviors. Grant, Gollwitzer, and Oettingen (2006) developed a behavior-based diagnostic test of individual differences in forming strong if–then links. In this test, individuals were asked to plan out how to achieve their goals in different domains (e.g., academic, personal), including situational cues (i.e., when and where) and planned responses (i.e., how). Participants were then presented with each situation they had listed as a cue and were asked to recall the planned behavior they had generated. The response latency for this response was taken as an indication of the individual's capability of forming strong implementation intentions. This approach was validated by a separate study, which demonstrated that those in an implemental mind-set (i.e., a mind-set focused on goal implementation) were faster in recalling the behavior portion of their implementation intentions when cued with the corresponding situation than those in the deliberative mind-set condition (i.e., a mind-set focused on estimating the feasibility and desirability of goals). This individual difference measure of the chronic tendency to form strong if–then links in implementation intentions showed discriminant, convergent, and predictive validity, and it was found to be stable over time.

Conclusion

Implementation intentions are a powerful tool that can facilitate goal striving, but they must be formed thoughtfully. It is clear that forming implementation intentions are associated with great benefits, but they also can result in costs for goal striving. Because the enhanced activation of opportunities to act toward the goal is associated with a reduced identification of alternative cues (Parks-Stamm et al., 2007), one must be careful to select cues that have a high frequency of appearance. If one selects an infrequently encountered cue in the if-component of an implementation intention, this may actually hinder taking advantage of the majority of opportunities to act toward the goal that are encountered. To maximize the benefits that are afforded by the if-process of implementation intentions, individuals planning a goal pursuit should consider how effective the planned situational cue is.

Second, because the if-process results in automatic attentional capture of the situational cues specified in the if-component of implementation intentions, these cues can be distracting to alternative goal pursuits (Wieber & Sassenberg, 2006). If an individual specifies a situational cue in the if-component of an implementation intention that is often encountered in non-goal-relevant situations, this cue will be distracting and therefore result in costs in alternative goal pursuits. This suggests that individuals planning their goal pursuit should be careful to select cues that arise in situational contexts that are conducive to initiating goal striving. For example, to serve the student's goal of achieving an "A" in his Introductory Psychology course, he might make the implementation intention, "If I see my book, then I will begin reading it!" However, it is not appropriate for students to read their Intro book every time it is perceived, and this cue will only serve as a distraction when it is encountered in a non-goal-relevant situation. During lecture, it is possible the book will distract him, resulting in costs for his current goal to pay attention to his professor. Thus, the student should specify a situational cue that is most likely to be encountered when a good opportunity to act has really arrived.

Third, because the response specified in the then-component is associated with automaticity, individuals with implementation intentions are sometimes more delayed in realizing when a plan is not effective. Two solutions to this problem have been offered above. First, participants may pay attention to feedback because feedback has been shown to eliminate this effect. Second, participants may form "reflection"-implementation intentions (Henderson et al., 2007). Implementation intentions that specify a more complex, reflective response in the then-component may allow individuals to consider the effectiveness of the current course of action. Third, considering the effectiveness of a chosen course of action (i.e., its instrumentality) before forming implementation intentions could eliminate this cost before it is encountered. Again, forming implementation intentions thoughtfully before goal striving begins could eliminate these costs and allow for the many benefits from implementation intentions to aid in goal achievement.

By returning to the Rubicon model, we can see that possible costs of if–then planning can be alleviated by taking much care in forming proper implementation intentions in the preactional stage of goal pursuit. By thoughtfully selecting situational cues and responses in the service of the desired goal, the individual can ensure that implementation intentions are optimally effective.

References

Aarts, H., & Dijksterhuis, A. (2000). Habits as knowledge structures: Automaticity in goal-directed behavior. *Journal of Personality and Social Psychology, 78*, 53–63.

Aarts, H., Dijksterhuis, A., & Midden, C. (1999). To plan or not to plan? Goal achievement or interrupting the performance of mundane behaviors. *European Journal of Social Psychology, 29*, 971–979.

Aarts, H., Paulussen, T., & Schaalma, H. (1997). Physical exercise habit: On the conceptualization and formation of habitual health behaviors. *Health Education Research: Theory & Practice, 12*, 363–374.

Achtziger, A. (2003). *A cognitive analysis of the willful inhibition of stereotypes.* Unpublished dissertation thesis, University of Konstanz, Konstanz, Germany.

Achtziger, A., Bayer, U. C., & Gollwitzer, P. M. (2008). *Committing to implementation intentions: Attention and memory effects for selected situational cues.* Manuscript submitted for publication.

Allport, D. A., Styles, E. A., & Hsieh, S. (1994). Shifting intentional set: Exploring the dynamic control of tasks. In C. Umilta & M. Moscovitch (Eds.),

Attention and performance XV: Conscious and nonconscious information processing (pp. 421–452). Hillsdale, NJ: Erlbaum.

Bargh, J. A. (1994). The four horsemen of automaticity: Awareness, intention, efficiency, and control. In R. S. Wyer, Jr., & T. K Srull (Eds.), *Handbook of social cognition* (Vol. 10, pp. 1–61). Mahwah, NJ: Erlbaum.

Bargh, J. A., & Chartrand, T. L. (2000). The mind in the middle: A practical guide to priming and automaticity research. In H. T. Reis & C. M. Judd (Eds.), *Handbook of Research Methods in Social and Personality Psychology* (pp. 253–285). New York: Cambridge University Press.

Bayer, U. C., Achtziger, A., Gollwitzer, P. M., & Moskowitz, G. B. (in press). Responding to subliminal cues: Do if–then plans facilitate action preparation and initiation without conscious intent? *Social Cognition.*

Bayer, U. C., & Gollwitzer, P. M. (2007). Boosting scholastic test scores by will-power: The role of implementation intentions. *Self and Identity, 6,* 1–19.

Bayer, U. C., Trötschel, R., Sumner, M., & Gollwitzer, P. M. (2006). *Self-regulation by implementation intentions is void of ego depletion and rebound.* Manuscript submitted for publication.

Beckmann, J., & Gollwitzer, P. M. (1987). Deliberative versus implemental states of mind: The issue of impartiality in pre- and postdecisional information processing. *Social Cognition, 5,* 259–279.

Brandstätter, V., Lengfelder, A., & Gollwitzer, P. M. (2001). Implementation intentions and efficient action initiation. *Journal of Personality and Social Psychology, 81,* 946–960.

Chasteen, A. L., Park, D. C., & Schwarz, N. (2001). Implementation intentions and facilitation of prospective memory. *Psychological Science, 12,* 457–461.

Cohen, A. L., Bayer, U. C., Jaudas, A., & Gollwitzer, P. M. (2008). Self-regulatory strategy and executive control: Implementation intentions modulate task switching and Simon task performance. *Psychological Research, 72,* 12–26.

Cohen, J. (1992). A power primer. *Psychological Bulletin, 112,* 155–159.

DeJong, R., Liang, C. C., & Lauber, E. (1994). Conditional and unconditional automaticity: A dual-process model of effects of spatial stimulus–response correspondence. *Journal of Experimental Psychology: Human Perception and Performance, 20,* 731–750.

Dholakia, U. M., & Bagozzi, R. P. (2003). As time goes by: How goal and implementation intentions influence enactment of short-fuse behaviors. *Journal of Applied Social Psychology, 33,* 889–922.

Freitas, A. L., Gollwitzer, P. M., & Trope, Y. (2004). The influence of abstract and concrete mindsets on anticipating and guiding others' self-regulatory efforts. *Journal of Experimental Social Psychology, 40,* 739–752.

Gawrilow, C., & Gollwitzer, P. M. (2008). Implementation intentions facilitate response inhibition in children with ADHD. *Cognitive Therapy and Research, 32,* 261–280.

Gilbert, S. J., Gollwitzer, P. M., Cohen, A.-L., Oettingen, G., & Burgess, P. W. (2008). *Separable brain systems supporting cued vs. self-initiated realization of delayed intentions.* Manuscript submitted for publication.

Gollwitzer, P. M. (1990). Action phases and mindsets. In E. T. Higgins & R. M. Sorrentino (Eds.), *Handbook of motivation and cognition: Foundation of social behavior* (Vol. 2, pp. 53–92). New York: Guilford Press.

Gollwitzer, P. M. (1993). Goal achievement: The role of intentions. *European Review of Social Psychology, 4,* 141–185.

Gollwitzer, P. M. (1999). Implementation intentions: Strong effects of simple plans. *American Psychologist, 54,* 493–503.

Gollwitzer, P. M., Bayer, U. C., & McCulloch, K. C. (2005). The control of the unwanted. In R. Hassin, J. Uleman, & J. A. Bargh (Eds.), *The new unconscious* (pp. 485–515). New York: Oxford University Press.

Gollwitzer, P. M., & Brandstätter, V. (1997). Implementation intentions and effective goal pursuit. *Journal of Personality and Social Psychology, 73,* 186–199.

Gollwitzer, P. M., Heckhausen, H., & Steller, B. (1990). Deliberative vs. implemental mind-sets: Cognitive tuning toward congruous thoughts and information. *Journal of Personality and Social Psychology, 59,* 1119–1127.

Gollwitzer, P. M., & Sheeran, P. (2006). Implementation intentions and goal achievement: A meta-analysis of effects and processes. *Advances in Experimental Social Psychology, 38,* 69–119.

Grant, H., Gollwitzer, P. M., & Oettingen, G. (2006). *Individual differences in the self-regulation of goal striving by forming implementation intentions.* Unpublished manuscript.

Häfner, S. (2000). *Machen Vorsätze rigide?: Eine experimentelle Studie zum Erkennen und Nutzen günstiger Handlungsgelegenheiten* [Do implementation intentions make a person rigid?: An experimental study on seizing good opportunities to act]. Unpublished master's thesis, University of Konstanz, Konstanz, Germany.

Heckhausen, H., & Gollwitzer, P. M. (1987). Thought contents and cognitive functioning in motivational vs. volitional states of mind. *Motivation and Emotion, 11,* 101–120.

Henderson, M. D., Gollwitzer, P. M., & Oettingen, G. (2007). Implementation intentions and disengagement form a failing course of action. *Journal of Behavioral Decision Making, 20,* 81–102.

Holland, R. W., Aarts, H., & Langendam, D. (2006). Breaking and creating habits on the working floor: A field-experiment on the power of implementation intentions. *Journal of Experimental Social Psychology, 42,* 776–783.

Jaudas, A., Achtziger, A., & Gollwitzer, P. M. (2006, March). *Bedingungen der effektiven Nutzung von Vorsätzen* [Determinants of the effective use of implementation intentions]. Paper presented at the 48th Meeting of Experimental Psychologists, Mainz, Germany.

Kahneman, D., & Tversky, A. (1979). Prospect theory: An analysis of decisions under risk. *Econometrica, 47,* 313–327.

Koestner, R., Horberg, E. J., Gaudreau, P., Powers, T., Di Dio, P., Bryan, C., et al. (2006). Bolstering implementation plans for the long haul: The benefits of simultaneously boosting self-concordance or self-efficacy. *Personality and Social Psychology Bulletin, 32,* 1547–1558.

Koestner, R., Lekes, N., Powers, T. A., & Chicoine, E. (2002). Attaining personal goals: Self-concordance plus implementation intentions equals success. *Journal of Personality and Social Psychology, 83*, 231–244.

Koole, S., & Van 't Spijker, M. (2000). Overcoming the planning fallacy through willpower: Effects of implementation intentions on actual and predicted task completion times. *European Journal of Social Psychology, 30*, 873–888.

Kornblum, S., Hasbroucq, T., & Osman, A. (1990). Dimensional overlap: Cognitive basis for stimulus-response compatibility—A model and taxonomy. *Psychological Review, 97*, 253–270.

Kruger, J., & Evans, M. (2004). If you don't want to be late, enumerate: Unpacking reduces the planning fallacy. *Journal of Experimental Social Psychology, 40*, 586–594.

Lengfelder, A., & Gollwitzer, P. M. (2001). Reflective and reflexive action control in patients with frontal brain lesions. *Neuropsychology, 15*, 80–100.

Lu, C.-H., & Proctor, R. W. (1995). The influence of irrelevant location information on performance: A review of the Simon and spatial Stroop effects. *Psychonomic Bulletin and Review, 2*, 174–207.

Muraven, M. R., & Baumeister, R. F. (2000). Self-regulation and depletion of limited resources: Does self-control resemble a muscle? *Psychological Bulletin, 126*, 247–259.

Muraven, M., Tice, D. M., & Baumeister, R. F. (1998). Self-control as limited resource: Regulating depletion patterns. *Journal of Personality and Social Psychology, 74*, 774–789.

Neal, D., Wood, W., & Quinn, J. M. (2006). Habits: A repeat performance. *Current Directions in Psychological Science, 15*, 198–202.

Oettingen, G., Pak, H., & Schnetter, K. (2001). Self-regulation of goal setting: Turning free fantasies about the future into binding goals. *Journal of Personality and Social Psychology, 80*, 736–753.

Orbell, S., Hodgkins, S., & Sheeran, P. (1997). Implementation intentions and the theory of planned behavior. *Personality and Social Psychology Bulletin, 23*, 945–954.

Orbell, S., & Sheeran, P. (2000). Motivational and volitional processes in action initiation: A field study of the role of implementation intentions. *Journal of Applied Social Psychology, 30*, 780–797.

Owen, A. M. (1997). Cognitive planning in humans: Neuropsychological, neuroanatomical, and neuropharmacalogical perspectives. *Progress in Neurobiology, 53*, 431–450.

Parks-Stamm, E. J., Gollwitzer, P. M., & Oettingen, G. (2007). Action control by implementation intentions: Effective cue detection and efficient response initiation. *Social Cognition, 25*, 247–264.

Paul, I., Gawrilow, C., Zech, F., Gollwitzer, P. M., Rockstroh, B., Odenthal, G., et al. (2007). If–then planning modulates the P300 in children with Attention Deficit Hyperactivity Disorder. *NeuroReport, 18*, 653–657.

Powers, T. A., Koestner, R., & Topciu, R. A. (2005). Implementation intentions, perfectionism, and goal progress: Perhaps the road to hell is paved with good intentions. *Personality and   Social Psychological Bulletin, 31*, 902–912.

Rogers, R. D., & Monsell, S. (1995). Costs of a predictable switch between simple cognitive tasks. *Journal of Experimental Psychology: General, 124,* 207–231.

Schweiger Gallo, I., Keil, A., McCulloch, K. C., Rockstroh, B., & Gollwitzer, P. M. (in press). Strategic automation of emotion control. *Journal of Personality and Social Psychology.*

Seehausen, R., Bayer, U., & Gollwitzer, P. M. (1994, September). *Experimentelle Arbeiten zur vorsätzlichen Handlungsregulation.* Paper presented at the biannual meeting of the German Psychological Association, Hamburg, Germany.

Sheeran, P., & Orbell, S. (1998). Do intentions predict condom use? Meta-analysis and examination of six moderator variables. *British Journal of Social Psychology, 37,* 231–250.

Sheeran, P., Webb, T. L., & Gollwitzer, P. M. (2005). The interplay between goal intentions and implementation intentions. *Personality and Social Psychology Bulletin, 31,* 87–98.

Simons, D. J., & Galotti, K. M. (1992). Everyday planning: An analysis of daily time management. *Bulletin of the Psychonomic Society, 30,* 61–64.

Stadler, G., Oettingen, G., & Gollwitzer, P. M. (in press). Effects of a self-regulation intervention on women's physical activity. *American Journal of Preventive Medicine.*

Steller, B. (1992). *Implementation intentions and the detection of good opportunities to act.* Munich, Germany: tuduv Verlagsgesellschaft.

Taylor, S. E., & Gollwitzer, P. M. (1995). Effects of mindset on positive illusions. *Journal of Personality and Social Psychology, 69,* 213–226.

Trötschel, R., & Gollwitzer, P. M. (2007). Implementation intentions and the willful pursuit of goals in negotiations. *Journal of Experimental Social Psychology, 43,* 579–598.

Verplanken, B., & Faes, S. (1999). Good intentions, bad habits, and effects of forming implementation intentions on healthy eating. *European Journal of Social Psychology, 29,* 591–604.

Webb, T. L., & Sheeran, P. (2003). Can implementation intentions help to overcome ego-depletion? *Journal of Experimental Social Psychology, 39,* 279–286.

Webb, T. L., & Sheeran, P. (2004). Identifying good opportunities to act: Implementation intentions and cue discrimination. *European Journal of Experimental Social Psychology, 34,* 407–419.

Webb, T. L., & Sheeran, P. (2007). How do implementation intentions promote goal attainment? A test of component processes. *Journal of Experimental Social Psychology, 43,* 295–302.

Webb, T. L., & Sheeran, P. (2006). Does changing behavioural intentions engender behavior change? A meta-anylsis of the experimental evidence. *Psychological Bulletin, 132,* 249–268.

Wieber, F., & Sassenberg, K. (2006). I can't take my eyes off it—Attention attraction effects of implementation intentions. *Social Cognition, 24,* 723–752.

CHAPTER 15

Regulatory Focus
CLASSIC FINDINGS AND NEW DIRECTIONS

JENS FÖRSTER
LIOBA WERTH

G oals and desired end-states can be connected to security or to growth. Whether a goal entails security or growth depends on structure, personality, and the situation. For example, an authoritarian or fundamentalist system that monitors all production and communication processes may constantly activate security-related goals in people, whereas a democratic system that aims for economic increase and personal self-development may activate goals of growth. Similarly, a person whose education focused on security concerns, on potential failures, and responsibilities may be more concerned with security-related issues than one who was raised to fulfill her ideals, had hopes, and learned to focus on wins and positive outcomes. As a consequence, for these people the very same event can be perceived in different ways. For example, a person with a focus on oughts may get married to be safe and protected, whereas a different person may rather want to grow with her partner, to experience new things, and to share her life with someone. Independent from a person's personality, social events and tasks can also be framed in terms of security or growth. If, for example, friends and family convey the message that a marriage provides shelter and security, one may eventually adopt this point of view, whereas if they encourage the perspective that marriage is the romantic start of a wonderful lifetime journey, people may embrace this idea instead. Similarly, a field trip to a museum for students can be framed in different ways: a teacher conveying to her students that learning about art is a duty for a well-educated person and announces punishments for those that misbehave during the trip may increase security concerns in all of her students, whereas a teacher that frames the same trip as a learning adventure thought to increase creativity and curiosity may raise awareness of ideals and growth.

When people pursue goals of security versus growth was examined in the field of regulatory focus theory (RFT; Higgins, 1997, 1998; for recent reviews see Higgins & Spiegel, 2004; Higgins & Molden, 2003; Molden, Lee, & Higgins, 2007). According to RFT people can fulfill their goals applying two different self-regulatory systems: if the need for self-realization and to maximize positive events takes control, then attention is focused on reaching ideals and wins. If, instead, the need for security and safety takes precedence, then minimizing of losses becomes of the essence. In the first case people find themselves in a *promotion focus,* whereas in the second case they are in a *prevention focus.* The foci can evolve from education as a personality trait (see Higgins & Silberman, 1998), they can be induced in the situation or could be superimposed by structure. Thus, RFT is a personality and a social psychology theory and, as the aforementioned examples indicate clearly, has the potential of becoming a sociological, economic, and political theory as well (see Welzel, 2007).

Psychologically, different strategies are the result of such foci (Higgins, 2000). People adopt *eager* strategies to fulfill their need for self-realization, therefore maximizing positive results while minimizing negative outcomes: They dedicate their full attention to a goal, to make sure of the occurrence of a positive outcome, and concentrate on those activities that are tied to wishes, ideals, and hopes (so-called ideal/maximal goals). When people approach promotion goals, they think about hits: Not getting this hit would therefore be the negative outcome. Strategic eagerness relates to means of advancement. To give an example, a person with a promotion focus looking to land an attractive job that promises more freedom to develop his plans will try to present his positive traits and to raise himself above the other candidates. He will possibly focus on the "big picture" during the interview and how he thinks he and the company can develop.

To realize their needs for protection and security, and to prevent uncomfortable situations (e.g., failures) from happening, people use *vigilant* strategies. They focus on activities that allow them to fulfill their responsibilities and duties and that are in service of their own safety (so-called oughts) (Shah & Higgins, 1997). When people pursue prevention goals, they think about losses: Not experiencing a loss would then be seen as the positive outcome. On their way of attaining a goal, they try to prevent mistakes and avoid possible dangers. Strategic vigilance relates to means of being careful. An unemployed person who fears not getting a job because she definitely needs it to feed her children will do anything to fulfill the requirements, to behave well, and to not give a bad impression of herself: A rather conventional way of self-representation would be the result, and she would avoid making too risky claims that could potentially be harmful.

Notably, vigilant and eager strategies are functional, effective, or "positive," depending on the situation or the task at hand. Similarly, security and growth needs or a promotion versus prevention focus are functional and are related to positive end-states. People like security and growth. Thus, RFT is no "bad guys—good guys" theory. It implies that most behaviors are functional, that is, they are goal directed and meaningful when the situation is appropriate. Of course, mistakes or inefficiencies can occur if the strategy does not fit the task (e.g., if a hiker who is inexperienced and promotion focused underestimates the danger of leaving the path in the mountain or if a too careful prevention focus prevents a person from talking to an interesting stranger), because it is possible that structure, a persons' personality, or the situation might erroneously activate inappropriate behavior.

Success or failure to goal attainment are experienced differently in the respective foci. Because ideals, hopes, and aspirations naturally involve a focus on *gains*, their achievement is experienced with joy, happiness, or so-called *cheerfulness-related* emotions (see Higgins, Grant, & Shah, 1999). Notably, being in a promotion focus does not prevent anticipating failure or negative outcome expectations; however, failure in a promotion focus is a mismatch to the goal or a *nongain,* rather than a loss. To illustrate, an Academy Award nominee that fails to win the award will usually not experience this as a loss, rather she will think of it as a lost opportunity (i.e., a nongain). According to RFT, she will likely experience *dejection-related emotions,* such as sadness or depression. Not attaining a prevention goal, such as not being punctual for an exam, is however experienced as a *loss,* leading to *agitation-related* emotions, such as anxiety or nervousness. Attaining this goal is a *nonloss,* and it will not make the person happy, rather it will lead to *quiescence- related* positive emotions, such as feeling relieved or calm. Again, these contingencies are independent from anticipation: A person in a prevention focus can very well be optimistic in meeting the date. Regulatory focus is thus independent from *regulatory anticipation* (Higgins, 1997) that drives behavior in its own right. Additionally, as can be seen, RFT entails a rather specific emotion theory, as well, that predicts different emotional experiences due to promotion versus prevention foci.

Vigilant and eager strategies have immense implications for information processing and motivation. We now summarize some of the results; however, because research on regulatory focus is exploding the summary can by no way be exhaustive.

Regulatory Focus and Its Effects

RFT has implications for decision making, affect and motivational direction, encoding and memory, and ways of thinking and processing. We start our overview with decision making, affect, motivational direction, and information processing. Notably, all these effects have been explained with a signal detection logic underlying RFT. We end this chapter by focusing on yet a different aspect of RFT, namely, that it can change perception at a very basic level, and outline some implications.

Decision Making

One can either adopt an eager (moving toward the desired end-state by approaching matches to it) or a vigilant strategy (moving toward the desired end-state by avoiding mismatches to it) in responding, and those strategies are correlated with conservative and risky tactics of goal pursuit in case of a neutral or a positive end-state. A lot of situations are ambiguous or uncertain: If your favorite dessert is chocolate tart, but the chef recommends his famous cheesecake—would you try it? To give another example: If we are only 50% sure that the French Revolution started around 1780, should we mark this answer in a quiz as correct or skip it because it is a freebie? Moreover, a lot of (if not most) tasks in modern life entail speed/accuracy conflicts. For example, when would we sloppily finish a paper, thereby risking a lot of mistakes, and when would we ask the editor for more time because we want to deliver an accurate product? Research on RFT demonstrates that strategic eagerness in a promotion focus leads to risky and fast behavior, whereas strategic vigilance in a prevention focus leads to careful and slow behavior if the end-state is positive or neutral (see Scholer & Higgins, 2008).

In recognition memory tasks, for example, individuals in a promotion focus want to ensure recognizing a true target (i.e., they want many "hits") and ensure against omitting a true target (i.e., they want few "misses" or errors of omission), thereby producing an overall yea-saying bias (Crowe & Higgins, 1997). Individuals in a prevention focus want to ensure rejecting a false distractor (i.e., want many "correct rejections") and ensure against failing to reject a false distractor (i.e., want few "false alarms" or errors of commission), thereby producing an overall nay-saying bias. In other words, if a person experiences a feeling of familiarity for an item in a recognition test, which could be due to the fact that it appeared in the study list but could also be the result of other factors (such as that the person thought about related concepts before the study), a person in a promotion focus would rather say, "Yes, I have probably studied it," because he wants to obtain a hit and would be afraid of not getting it, whereas a person in a prevention focus would rather say, "No, I have probably not studied it," to prevent for a mistake.

A study by Crowe and Higgins (1997) tested these predictions: Participants were told that they would first perform a recognition memory task and then would be assigned a second, final task. A liked and disliked activity had been selected earlier for each participant to serve as the final task. The participants were told that which of the alternative final tasks they would work on at the end of the session depended on their performance on the initial recognition task. The relation between the initial memory task and the final task was described as contingent for everyone, but the framing varied as a function of regulatory focus (promotion vs. prevention) and valence (self-regulation succeeding [pleasure] vs. self-regulation failing (pain). Valence was included to test whether regulatory focus influences decision making independent of participants' imagining pleasant versus painful outcomes (i.e., independent of regulatory anticipation; see Higgins, 1997). More specifically, the contingency framing was as follows: (1) Promotion succeeding: "If you do well on the word recognition memory task, you will get to do the (liked task) instead of the other task"; (2) Promotion failing: "If you don't do well on the recognition memory task, you won't get to do the (liked) task but will have to do another task instead"; (3) Prevention succeeding: "As long as you don't do poorly on the word recognition memory task, you won't have to do the (disliked task) but will have to do the other task instead"; and (4) Prevention failing: "If you do poorly on the word recognition memory task, you will have to do the (disliked task) instead of the other task."

The study found, as predicted, that participants in the promotion-focus condition had a risky yea-saying bias in the recognition memory task, whereas participants in the prevention-focus condition had a nay-saying bias. Moreover, these regulatory focus effects were independent of the valence of the framing (i.e., success vs. failure framing), which itself had no significant effects. Using the same paradigm, Crowe and Higgins (1997) found in a second study that when individuals work on a task where generating any number of alternatives is correct, those in a promotion focus generate more distinct alternatives (ensuring hits) whereas those in a prevention focus are more repetitive (ensuring against errors of commission).

Other research examined the influence of RFT on speed/accuracy tasks. Förster, Higgins, and Taylor Bianco (2003), for example, induced the foci with a framing similar to that of Crowe and Higgins (1997) described above and asked participants to connect numbered dots with a pen so that the result would be a cartoon figure. Participants were asked to mark the dots accurately and to be fast and were told that evaluation would be based on a combined score of accuracy and speed. Participants in a promotion focus were faster and less accurate than participants in a prevention focus who were accurate (i.e., did not miss the dots to such an extent) but slower. The study replicated the findings with a personality measure of RFT (Higgins, Shah, & Friedman, 1997) showing that when the task instructions were the same for everybody (and no valence or focus was manipulated), participants who were chronically promotion focused were fast and inaccurate whereas participants who were chronically prevention focused were slow and accurate.

Such findings were replicated when, instead of reward/punishment contingencies, negative versus positive stereotypes (Seibt & Förster, 2004) were activated and when more subtle manipulations were used (i.e., promotion vs. prevention focus priming; Friedman & Förster, 2001, see below).

These findings have implications beyond those basic laboratory tasks. For example, people differ in their RF-dependent sensitivity to risks and wins in their investment choices: People in a prevention focus invest more conservatively (e.g., in bonds), whereas people in promotion focus show a higher acceptance of risks (they might therefore invest in stocks) (Zhou & Tuan Pham, 2004). Moreover, the strategic orientations dependant on RF are also found to be significant in group activities: It was thus shown that induced RF in a small-group situation influenced whether the group opinion converged toward the risky or the conservative direction (see group polarization; Levine & Moreland, 1998; Levine, Higgins, & Choi, 2000). Finally, a recent study showed that employers in a promotion focus set themselves more challenging goals than employers who were prevention focused (Steidle & Werth, 2008).

Eagerness and vigilance also relate to openness to novelty. Liberman, Idson, Camacho, and Higgins (1999) for example, demonstrated that participants in a prevention focus preferred continuing an already-begun and interrupted task than start a new one, whereas the opposite was true for participants in promotion focus. Given that novel events are unknown and thus involve the risk of being worse than the conservative and well-known alternative (see Bornstein, 1989; Richards, 1997), these studies showed another important implication of eager versus vigilant strategies. This also expands to the social domain: Förster, Higgins, and Werth (2004) showed that people in a promotion focus are more likely than those in a prevention focus to be interested in meeting a person that contradicts gender stereotypes and thus bring the risk of experiencing conflicts with expectancies and preexistent schemas. Moreover, when people have or want to have friends they use different strategies: Participants with a chronic ideal promotion focus are more likely to select friendship tactics that involved eager strategies to approach matches to this goal (e.g., "Be supportive to your friends") than tactics that involved vigilant strategies to avoid mismatches (e.g., "Stay in touch. Don't lose contact with friends"), whereas for participants with a chronic ought prevention focus the reverse was true. The influence of RF was also found in the art of social discrimination between groups (Sassenberg, Kessler, & Mummendey, 2003; Shah, Brazy, & Higgins, 2004). People who are promotion oriented gain distinctiveness (or social identity; see Tajfel, 1978) by favoring their own group (ingroup) and allocating them more positive resources, but in people who are prevention oriented it is more the devaluation of other groups (outgroups) that is the typical strategy for distribution of negative resources (= the removal of positive resources). This differentiation in choice of strategy in turn coincides with the different direction of attention on positive or negative events, and therewith the preferred approach or avoidance strategies for promotion and prevention foci.

Due to their focusing on gains and nongains, negotiators in a promotion focus make more extreme bids (resulting in an anchor effect; Galinsky & Mussweiler, 2001), claim more resources for themselves at the bargaining table, and in the end achieved more advantageous distributive outcomes than negotiators in a prevention focus (Galinsky, Leonardelli, Okhuysen, & Mussweiler, 2005).

Whereas eagerness may help in negotiation situations, the focus on losses and nonlosses, however, and the resulting vigilance may help to resist temptations, because this is the strategy that fits the situation. After all, temptations are failures to goal pursuit, and avoiding them is necessary. Research by Freitas, Liberman, and Higgins (2002) shows that when in a prevention focus participants like tasks better that involve avoiding distracters and that outperform participants with a promotion focus (but do not do so in nondistracting control conditions).

Theoretically, these findings qualify—if not challenge—the principle of loss aversion, which assumes that people evaluate losses more extremely than gains of similar size (Kahneman & Tversky, 1979). This principle can explain why people are usually more afraid of what they can lose than what they can win and thus keep what they already have (e.g., money) rather than exchange it or invest in new projects (e.g., the endowment effect; see Kahneman, Knetsch, & Thaler, 1990, 2005). More generally, the principle of loss aversion either implies or explicitly predicts a general tendency for conservatism, a general reluctance against novelty, and on average more careful than eager behaviors in people. Research cited above shows that this general notion is correct for people in a prevention focus but incorrect for those in a promotion focus: They would rather want to exchange what they have for a new objects or tasks, eagerly approach hits, and prefer risky over careful behavior (Liberman et al., 1999; see also Higgins, 2002).

Importantly, however, differential risk propensity is a correlate but not a defining characteristic of RFT. Usually, achieving gains (promotion) increases risks, and avoiding losses decreases risks. In situations where capturing gains does not entail greater risk and avoiding losses does not entail lower risk, promotion is not expected to trigger risk seeking nor is prevention expected to trigger risk aversion (see Pham & Higgins, 2005; Zhou & Tuan Pham, 2004). More recently, Scholer, Stroessner, and Higgins (2008) challenged the general notion of eagerness = risky behavior and vigilance = careful behavior. They stated that most of the experiments in the domain of decision making and RFT entailed current or initial states of goal pursuit of neutral or positive valence and that for this state the notion is true, however, that for negativity a risky tactic can serve a vigilant strategy. The authors proposed that strategic concerns (e.g., eagerness, vigilance) and the tactical means (e.g., risky vs. conservative bias) are theoretically separable; Whereas strategies direct behavior generally but do not suggest the specific instantiation of behavior, tactics reflect the specific ways in which a strategy is enacted in a particular context. Thus, a given strategy (being vigilant) may be served by different tactics given different situations, and different tactics will be used for negative compared with positive input when individuals are in a prevention focus.

More specifically, a negative stimulus may suggest a challenge to the primary concern of an individual under prevention focus: maintaining safety and security. Consequently, individuals who are prevention focused might be especially motivated not to "miss" negative input. When negative input is involved, individuals in a prevention focus might modify their typical tactics (i.e., the conservative tactic of attaining correct rejections while minimizing false alarms) and show a willingness to incur false alarms to ensure that negative stimuli are detected (i.e., a risky tactic). In six studies using recognition measures with negative and positive targets, Scholer, Stroessner, and Higgins (2008) found support for their predictions: False alarm rate (and bias) for negative stimuli was higher for participants with a prevention focus. In line with this analysis is a recent study showing that drivers in a prevention focus judge a traffic situation as more dangerous and therefore brake earlier than people in a promotion focus (Werth & Förster, 2007). Thus, it is not the case that people in a prevention focus are always slower as suggested by findings by Förster et al. (2003), rather if speed serves the strategy of vigilance—and this is the case when end-states are negative–participants who are prevention focused become faster.

All the research listed above included some kind of decision (e.g., risky vs. vigilant, fast vs. accurate, hits vs. losses). In the following, we present research showing that success and failure are experienced differently when in a specific focus.

Experiences, Motivational Direction, Persistence, and Initiation

We all strive to get closer to those things we like and to distance ourselves from those things we do not like. We all like success and dislike failure, and we feel good after having accomplished our goals and feel bad when we missed a goal. This hedonic principle (see Freud, 1923; Gray, 1982; Pfaffman, 1960) has been at the base of many motivation theories, for example, in Atkinson (1964), Gray (1982), McClelland (1961, 1985), Miller (1944), Mowrer (1960), and Murray (1938), to name just a few.

However, as mentioned above, a person's regulatory focus has direct repercussions on the kind of affective experiences of people. Promotion-focus success should lead to cheerfulness-related emotions and promotion-focus failure to dejection-related emotions, whereas prevention-focus success should lead to quiescence-related emotions and prevention focus failure to agitation-related emotions. Importantly, a promotion focus is theoretically not more "positive" than a prevention focus: It can well be the case that a person with a chronic prevention focus experiences quiescence as truly rewarding, or that a person with a chronic promotion focus can suffer immensely from sadness or depression. Thus, RF operates beyond the hedonic principle or (positive vs. negative) valence of experiences and qualifies it. Moreover, RFT qualifies the hedonic principle with respect to motivational directions: It predicts that the motivation for people in a promotion focus is generally approach, whereas for people in a prevention focus it is generally avoidance. This is a challenge because, as has been said repeatedly, when in a promotion focus people can think of nongains (negative) and when in a prevention focus people can think of nonlosses (positive). We first summarize findings on affective experiences and then report findings on approach versus avoidance motivation.

Affective Experience

Research shows that discrepancies between the actual state and ideal versus ought goals in adulthood can have serious consequences: People who deviate strongly from their ideal goals (i.e., chronic promotion focus) are frequently found to suffer of depression, whereas people with high discrepancies regarding their obligations (i.e., chronic prevention focus) show high scores in fearfulness (Strauman, 1988, 1992; Strauman & Higgins, 1987, 1988).

Such emotions can be directly experienced when participants with actual-ideal discrepancies and actual-ought discrepancies are reminded of (or primed with) ideals or oughts tested in the lab. Higgins, Bond, Klein, and Strauman (1986), for example, asked participants with both kinds of discrepancies and those with neither to think about themselves as related to their ideals or their oughts. It was shown that in those who had both types of discrepancies, when reminded of ideals, they experienced more dejection-related affect whereas those reminded of oughts experienced more agitation-related affect. For participants who had neither discrep-

ancies no such changes occurred, presumably because for those participants these discrepancies could not be reactivated. Further studies showed
that independent from discrepancies between actual states and ideal or
oughts, mere concerns or accessibility of ideals versus oughts can predict
participants' feelings. A computer measure that inquired participants to
type in their ideals and oughts and their discrepancies, thus measuring
the reaction time of such answers, was used by Higgins et al. (1997). With
it they showed that independent from self-discrepancies, accessibility of
ideals versus oughts predicted dejection when promotion was not working, cheerfulness when it was working, agitation when prevention was not
working, and quiescence when it was working.

Roney, Higgins, and Shah (1995) asked participants to work on a
task and framed it in terms of promotion or prevention similarly to the
paradigm used by Crowe and Higgins (1997; see above). All participants
experienced success afterwards; but whereas after promotion framing
participants cheerfulness increased, after prevention framing quiescence
increased. Idson, Liberman, and Higgins (2000) further showed that this
is also true for anticipated emotions, and that losses are experienced as
agitation whereas nongains as dejection (see Shah & Higgins, 2001).

Studies by Roese, Hur, and Pennington (1999) also showed that emotions elicit a certain focus that further has repercussions. The authors reasoned that failure usually elicits counterfactual thinking ("If only I had . . .
") but that the type of counterfactuals differs as a function of RF. The
authors predicted and showed that people with induced promotion-focus
emotions of dejection tend to reflect upon earlier nonactions (e.g., "Had I
only sold the stock, then . . . "), whereas people with induced prevention-
focus emotions of agitation rather generate alternatives they could have
taken to their actions (e.g., "Had I only not sold the stock, then . . . ").
This phenomenon can probably be traced back to a signal-detection process, which entails that people in a promotion focus are concerned with
acquisition of a desired goal and are sensitive to omissions along the way
to the goal. If promotion fails, counterfactual specification of the addition
of some omitted action may therefore come to mind. In a prevention focus
that is more concerned with preservation of the status quo, people are
sensitive to commissions that threaten that goal. Thus, if prevention fails,
they are concerned with the subtraction of the action that brought about
the negative event.

Feedback Affecting Motivation

Eagerness and vigilance are also motivational experiences. In a promotion
focus, success (i.e., the appearance of a positive event) results in feelings of
satisfaction and enthusiasm, as well as a simultaneously increasing moti-

vational intensity. In case of a failure, disappointment and dejectedness set in, and the intensity decreases accordingly.

In a prevention focus, the occurrence of a positive event (i.e., nonappearance of a negative event) gives rise to feelings of relief and reassurance, and motivation decreases. Instead, when there is failure, tenseness and worry take hold and motivation increases (see Förster, Higgins, & Idson, 1998; Higgins et al., 1999; Higgins et al., 1986; Higgins, Grant, & Shah, 1999).

Thus, positive or negative feedback should also differentially affect people's feelings and their motivation. Notably, the fact that RFT is independent of the valence of goal states offers the opportunity to study such focus × valence interactions. From this perspective, positive and negative feedback play different roles for people in one or the other focus. People in a prevention focus mainly orient themselves toward the appearance and disappearance of negative events (punishment and its absence) and are therefore more sensitive to negative feedback. For people in a promotion focus, instead, the occurrence and nonoccurrence of positive events (reward and its absence) is of greater importance, so that positive feedback and successes increase the motivation to approach strategies.

This escalation of motivation, which follows success for people in a promotion focus and failure for people in a prevention focus, can be found for anticipated feedback (without actual task revision; Van Dijk & Kluger, 2004; Werth & Förster, 2007, Experiment 2), anticipated costs or benefits (Spiegel, Grant-Pillow, & Higgins, 2004). for process feedback (feedback during task revision; Roney et al., 1995), as well as for performance feedback (feedback after task revision; Förster, Grant, Idson, & Higgins, 2001; Idson, & Higgins, 2000; Spiegel & Higgins, 2001; Werth & Förster, 2007). To give one example from a recent study within the applied context of idea management in a business setting: employees who were promotion oriented were more motivated to hand in an improvement proposal after one of their earlier suggestions was accepted (success), whereas employees who were prevention oriented were more motivated to engage in a new attempt following a failure (their suggestion was not taken into consideration; Werth & Förster, 2007, Experiment. 2).

Direction of Motivation

Maybe the most counterintuitive prediction derived by a motivational theory is a relation between avoidance behavior and positive outcomes or approach behavior and negative outcomes: RFT makes such predictions, derived from the notion that when in a promotion focus, people are eager whereas when in a prevention focus they are vigilant. This is true even when people who are promotion focused work toward negative outcomes (which for them are nongains) and when people who are prevention focused work toward positive outcomes (which for them are nonlosses; Higgins, 1997, 1998).

On a strategic level, people with a promotion focus approach matches to their goals, whereas people with a prevention focus avoid mismatches to their goals. This may be illustrated by two runners, both working toward the goal of winning a medal. Let us assume that both anticipate success for good reasons: Both are successful runners and are well prepared. Thus, both are working toward a desired end-state and are optimistic (i.e., anticipate success). However on the strategic level one of them focuses on the goal and tries to exploit all the bodily and mental energy she has, whereas the other one is focusing on not turning her head around and not to waste energy by making unnecessary movements. The former strategically approaches the goal, and the latter strategically avoids obstacles to it. Evidence keeps being put forward to demonstrate the link between prevention focus and its preference for avoidance strategies and promotion focus and its preference for approach strategies even when both of them work toward positive end-states and are equally optimistic/pessimistic.

One property of approach versus avoidance motivation is that it increases the closer to the goals (the "goal looms larger" effect; Brown, 1948; Lewin, 1951; Miller, 1944, 1959), and thus it should be predicted that the closer the goal is (which implies increasing motivational intensity), the stronger the approach behavior in people in a promotion focus, and the stronger the avoidance behavior in people in a prevention focus. Förster et al. (1998) used a subtle online measurement of approach versus avoidance motivation to test these theses in an experiment where participants had to work on several anagrams that were framed with a promotion focus ("If you perform well, you will win an extra dollar [gain] or if you do not perform well, you will not win an extra dollar [nongain]") or with a prevention focus ("If you do not perform well, you will lose a dollar [loss] or if you perform well, you will not lose a dollar [nonloss]"). While working on the task participants were asked to press a copper plate with their palm either from above or below, thus inducing arm flexion, a motor action used to pull desired objects toward the body, or arm extension, a motor action used to push undesired objects away from the body (see Cacioppo, Priester, & Berntson, 1993). It was shown that approach arm-flexion pressure increased anagram by anagram the closer participants were to the goal—when they focused on gaining or not gaining the dollar—whereas there was no approach gradient in the prevention focus condition. However, avoidance arm extension increased as a function of the distance to the goal when focusing on losing or not losing a dollar, whereas there was no avoidance gradient in the promotion focus condition. The same effects could be replicated with RF as a chronic trait variable as measured by the aforementioned regulatory strength questionnaire (Higgins et al., 1997). In sum, these studies show that approach behavior increases in a promotion focus even when the task is framed as a nongain, whereas avoidance increases in a prevention focus even when the task is framed as a nonloss. Because "nongain" is defined as a negative event and "nonloss" as a positive event in most motivational theories on the hedonic principle, they would be unable to predict the specific interactional pattern observed in the studies. The relation between strategic approach and a promotion focus and strategic avoidance and a prevention focus is meanwhile supported by many studies (Förster et al., 2001; Higgins, Roney, Crowe, & Hymes, 1994; Higgins et al., 2001; Higgins et al., 1997; Leung & Lam, 2003).

This general relation can further enlighten more social phenomena. For example, a recent study showed that people with a promotion focus liked high-power groups better than people with a prevention focus, who actually preferred low-power groups (Sassenberg, Jonas, Shah, & Brazy, 2007). The model predicting such an outcome was based on former research showing that high-power groups use strategic approach means to attain their goals whereas low-power groups use avoidance means (see Keltner, Gruenfeld, & Anderson, 2003). Thus, a *regulatory fit* (Higgins, 2000) between group power and strategic means predicts the value of groups for people with different motivational orientations.

Gradients, that is constant increase of vigilance versus eagerness, can also expand to speed and accuracy. For example, people who are promotion oriented demonstrate an increase of speed and a decrease of accuracy in tasks that require both these elements the closer the goal is. People who are prevention oriented will show the opposite effect: a decrease in speed and an increase in accuracy (Förster et al., 2003).

We should caution that contrary to the classic notion of goal gradients, motivation does not necessarily increase closer to the goal (for a recent discussion and review of this topic, see Liberman & Förster, 2007). For example, our motivation to write a paper does not necessarily increase as we get closer to actually writing it. A careful analysis of how distance to the goal affects value and expectancy is necessary to predict whether motivation will increase or decrease closer to the goal. For example, Liberman and Förster (in press) argued that expectancy has been related to probability of outcome (e.g., Edwards, 1951), task difficulty (e.g., Atkinson, 1964), control and self efficacy (the extent to which one feels capable of bringing about the desired outcome; Bandura, 1982), and necessity (e.g., difficulty to compensate for not having started). Whereas probability of success may increase with the distance to the goal, subjective difficulty may remain similar, may decrease or may increase (e.g., the "cold-feet" phenomenon), self-efficacy may increase or decrease (depending on whether one thinks one can control the outcome), and necessity may increase when there is a deadline, whereas it may not do so when there is no deadline. Some predictions can be made for RF: Because individuals who are prevention oriented are driven by necessity and are generally more sensitive to necessity than individuals who are promotion oriented (see Shah & Higgins, 1997; Freitas, Liberman, Salovey, & Higgins, 2002; Liberman, Idson, Higgins, & Molden, 2000; Roese et al., 1999), individuals who are prevention focused, compared to individuals who are promotion focused, should show steeper gradients when expectancy changes with distance due to necessity but not when expectancy changes because of other components of motivation. For example, individuals who are prevention focused, more than individuals who are promotion focused, are expected to exhibit increased motivation closer to a deadline, but not in a similar situation that does not involve a deadline.

Persistence and Initiation

When in a promotion focus, goals may be construed as maximal goals, whereas when in a prevention focus they may be construed as minimal goals (Brendl & Higgins, 1996). This can have consequences for persistence in tasks, because achievement of maximal goals is, among others, less clearly defined than achievement of minimal goals. For example, it is harder to say when one has accomplished the goal of being a "good person" or a "smart guy" than to acknowledge that one has arrived on time or solved an assigned math task. An example for this was illustrated by an anagram task in which participants had to find as many usable solutions as possible: A person working on a maximal goal of appearing smart may think, "Maybe there's still something to be won" that may encourage persevering in the task (i.e., increase approach motivation), whereas working toward the minimal goal of, for example, "following experimenter's instructions" might cause one to break off a task as soon as this goal is reached: "Three solutions already show my compliance, I could only worsen the status quo by pursuing" (i.e., increased avoidance motivation). As a result, generally, persistence is higher in a promotion focus (cf. Roney et al., 1995).

Moreover, because minimal prevention goals are likely necessities whereas promotion goals are not, people in a prevention focus begin tackling a single task earlier than people in a promotion focus (Freitas et al., 2002, Experiments 1–3): they literally "need to be done." In a different experiment, Freitas et al. (2002, Experiment 4) asked participants to do different tasks that were either framed in a promotion- or a prevention-focused way. They were asked to do the tasks in whichever order they wanted to. In this case, consistent with the notion that prevention goals are necessities and thus have priority, participants started from the prevention-oriented task, independently of which focus they were in. These findings can be traced back to the fact that prevention-oriented goals concerned with responsibilities, duties, security, and providing shelter resemble basic needs that must be followed first: They cause a sort of inner pressure, and thus we strive to complete these tasks as soon as possible.

To sum up, RFT's emotion theory challenges current and classic theories in several ways. It shows that beyond valence different emotions result from RF and that approach and avoidance operate independent from valence of the outcome. Furthermore, RFT can predict when we start and how much energy we invest while working on a task. RFT also makes important predictions about sensitivity to information, which we summarize now.

Sensitivity to Information

Attention, Encoding, and Memory

People in a prevention focus care for different contents than do people in a promotion focus. Accessibility of promotion versus prevention concerns should facilitate encoding of compatible information (see Higgins, 1996; Förster & Liberman, 2007). Consistently, Higgins and Tykocinski (1992) showed that people in a prevention focus remembered the presence or absence of negative biographical events for a fictitious person (e.g., "Because I didn't want to say anything dumb, I preferred not to say anything at all in class") than people in a promotion focus, whereas this relationship was reversed for the presence or absence of positive events (e.g., "Since I wanted to buy something nice for my best friend, I went shopping and looked for a present"). Seibt and Förster (2004, Experiment 1) replicated these results with situationally inducing RF via stereotypic expectations ("members of your ingroup can do this task" vs. "people from your ingroup cannot do this task"). They proposed that negative self-stereotypes (which produce stereotype threat; Steele, 1997) induce a prevention focus, whereas positive self-stereotypes induce a promotion focus.

Beyond content, participants encode stereotype-inconsistent information better if they hold the stereotype relevant and are at the same time in a prevention focus (Förster, Higgins, & Strack, 2000; Förster et al., 2004). It was suggested that stereotypes serve the function of quasi-theories predicting outcomes in the social environment. For example, for a sexist, the belief that women do not like sports is an important theory about what the group of women are like. If the sexist is a prevention-focused person, a violation of such a theory that helps to control the social environment is a threat (i.e., failure to predict behavior), leading to vigilant behavior.

Vigilance should lead to a search for an explanation in the surroundings of the threat. Consistently, a series of studies found that people high in sexism and chronic prevention focus remember inconsistent information better and as a result of vigilant search also remember the source wherein it appeared better (i.e., the color of paper the information was printed on).

Beyond inconsistency and content, recent research showed differences in the foci in relation to global versus local processing styles (Förster & Higgins, 2005). According to this, a chronic promotion focus leads to a faster perception of the entirety of a stimulus, whereas a chronic prevention would lead to a faster processing of the local details of an object. One may argue that when in prevention focus (because of its struggle for safety), goals are constructed more concretely and that the locating of solid strategies to reach the goal is of the essence, whereas in promotion focus (because of its predominant aspect of self-realization) goals are constructed more abstractly, and the realization of the underlying structure and internal connections serves attainment of the goal. We come back to this issue below.

The Effect of Information

Focus-compatible information is not only better encoded but usually preferred over incompatible information and seems to be more convincing (Avnet & Higgins, 2003; Cesario, Grant, & Higgins, 2004; Higgins, Idson, Freitas, Spiegel, & Molden, 2003; Lee & Aaker, 2004; Pham & Avnet, 2004). People in a promotion focus are more strongly convinced by growth-related information (e.g., "increases energy" in a medicament); people in a prevention focus instead are convinced more by safety-related information (e.g., "lowers risk of getting cancer") (Aaker & Lee, 2001). Accordingly, products that show compatibility with the RF of the buyer receive better reviews (Chernev, 2004; Freitas et al., 2002; Werth & Förster, 2006; see also Florack, Scarabis, & Gosejohann, 2005). To give one example, buyers in a prevention focus pay more attention to the dependability of the product, whereas buyers in a promotion focus look more to its innovative value (Higgins, 2002; Safer, 1998; Werth & Förster, 2006). Thus, a prevention-relevant dimension is more important to people in a prevention focus when making decisions, whereas promotion-relevant information is more important to people in a promotion focus. People are then a lot faster in their assessment when the evaluation dimension coincides with their focus: This is because processing is facilitated by regulatory fit (Semin, Higgins, DeMontes, Estourget, & Valencia, 2005).

Finally, beyond the contents, information that is formulated in a form compatible to the focus (i.e., more abstract in promotion focus, more concrete in prevention focus) has the greatest influence on peoples' evaluations and decisions. Förster and Higgins (2005) showed that people assigned a higher value to a selected item when it could be located within a global or local processing style, according to which focus the person was in, and Semin et al. (2005) showed that using more abstract language convinces participants in a promotion focus more than concrete language, whereas for participants with a prevention focus the opposite is true.

More generally, research on regulatory fit (Higgins, 2000, 2002, and Chapter 19, this volume) shows repeatedly that people assign higher value when they process information in a focus-compatible situation. In one study, for example, Higgins, Idson, et al. (2003) measured participants' chronic promotion and prevention strength and asked them to choose between a mug and a pen. The instructions induced participants to make their choice either in an eager manner (i.e., asked them to think about what they could gain by choosing the mug or choosing the pen) or in a vigilant manner (i.e., asked them to think about what they would lose by not choosing the pen or not choosing the mug). The experiment was set up so that most of the participants chose the mug. When asked what they thought was the price of the chosen mug, the participants assigned it a much higher price when their chronic focus fit the instructions (promotion-eager, prevention-vigilant) than when their focus and the instructions did not fit (promotion-vigilant, prevention-eager).

Regulatory fit may also predict why people with a promotion focus are more motivated by positive role models, whereas those in a prevention focus are motivated by negative role models (Lockwood, Jordan, & Kunda, 2002; Lockwood, Sadler, Fyman & Tuck, 2004). Similarly, negative, health-related models gain importance with age due to the fact that prevention focus increases with the years (Lockwood, Chasteen, & Wong, 2005). Preferred models also vary according to culture area: people in collectivist (= prevention oriented) cultures prefer negative role models, whereas individualist (= promotion oriented) cultures favor positive role models (Lockwood, Marshall, & Sadler, 2005).[1]

Regulatory fit, which is summarized in more detail later, shows that from the notion of distinct RF, models can be derived that are remote from a signal detection logic. The mere fit between strategies and RF is experienced as positive affect (feeling right) and drives value (Higgins, 2000). In the following section we introduce RFT's effects on complex thinking and delineate yet a different relative of RFT on creative thinking.

Complex Thinking Styles

People in a promotion focus produce more creative and often more numerous ideas; people in a prevention focus instead, as a result of their slow, methodical approach, are superior in analytical tasks (Friedman & Förster,

2001, 2005, 2007; see also Förster, Friedman, Özelsel, & Denzler, 2006). For example, when people test hypotheses, those in a promotion focus compile a larger number and variety of hypotheses, whereas those in a prevention focus compile less diverse hypotheses (Liberman, Molden, Idson, & Higgins, 2001). Friedman and Förster (for a summary see 2007) showed on a multitude of measures reflecting creative generation, restructuring, and breaking fixed mental set (Schooler & Melcher, 1995) that promotion increases creative thinking whereas prevention impedes it. Several processes can underlie such effects. For example, Liberman et al. (2001) explained their results using signal detection logic: Usually, generating more ideas ensures against misses and increases likelihood of hits, whereas generating fewer ideas prevents for finding a wrong idea and increases likelihood of correct rejections. In support of such an explanation, they showed that people in a prevention focus were more likely to discount rejected hypotheses, whereas participants in a promotion focus showed less discounting (i.e., kept several possible alternatives in mind).

On the other hand, global versus local processing has been related to creativity and breadth of conceptual scope, and based on this correlation, Friedman and Förster (2007) proposed a creativity model integrating RFT, attentional tuning theory, and brain research that we now describe in detail. We hasten to add that this model is not the only recent relative of the general notion of regulatory foci. However, it exemplifies how inspiring RFT can be in building new models for special domains, in this case, creative thought.

Tucker and his colleagues' (Tucker & Williamson, 1984; see also, Derryberry & Reed, 1998; Derryberry & Tucker, 1994; Luu, Tucker, & Derryberry, 1998) neuropsychological model suggests that aversive arousal reduces the range of cues that an organism uses (Easterbrook, 1959) and constricts the scope of perceptual attention (i.e., the extent to which attention is trained upon local versus global details). Analogously aversive arousal is said to reduce the scope of what might be termed "conceptual attention," the attentional selection of stored mental representations in long-term memory as opposed to the selection of sensory-based percepts (cf. Anderson & Neely, 1996). Just as a narrower scope of perceptual attention entails focusing upon a smaller number of external percepts, a narrower scope of conceptual attention entails cognitive activation of fewer constructs in memory (typically those with the highest a priori level of accessibility in a particular context). Furthermore, Tucker and his colleagues suggested that appetitive arousal (arousal that is associated with approach motivational states; e.g., elation) will broaden, as opposed to narrow, perceptual and conceptual attentional scope. More specifically, elated arousal is predicted to bias attention to the gestalt of a stimulus set and to facilitate detection of peripheral cues on the perceptual level, whereas it is posited to promote activation of mental representations with lower a priori accessibility (e.g., subordinate semantic associates) on the conceptual level. Tucker and his group assumed that such effects are hard wired and originate in distinct brain systems (Derryberry & Tucker, 1994; Tucker & Williamson, 1984). The *phasic* system associated with appetitive arousal is conceived of as right lateralized. In the face of approach-worthy incentives it spontaneously elicits a *habituation bias,* expanding attentional scope and enabling access to perceptually peripheral or cognitively inaccessible information. In contrast, the tonic system associated with aversive arousal is proposed to reside in the left hemisphere. Upon exposure to threat cues, it spontaneously elicits a *redundancy bias,* constricting the scope of attention and "choking off" access to "remote" stimuli and constructs. Even though there is considerable evidence for the link between elated and aversive moods and global perceptual/conceptual processing, the link between moods and hemispheric activation is highly controversial, because some studies find positive mood in the right and some in the left hemispheres (for a summary, see Friedman & Förster, 2007; Schwarz & Clore, 2007).

In Friedman and Förster's (2007) model, these seeming inconsistencies are resolved by borrowing Heller's notion that tense arousal (i.e., anxiety) may be subdivided into a somatic component, reflecting the physiological excitation associated with avoidance motivational states (i.e., panic), as well as a cognitive component reflecting the anticipation of threats (i.e., worry). Moreover, she and her colleagues have put forth evidence suggesting that the cognitive component is associated with greater relative left-hemispheric activation than is the somatic component (see, e.g., Heller, Koven, & Miller, 2003; Heller & Nitschke, 1998; Heller, Nitschke, Etienne, & Miller, 1997; Nitschke, Heller, Palmieri, & Miller, 1999). Assuming that the cognitive component of anxiety to which Heller refers is akin to a prevention focus, a focus on the prospect of undesired outcomes (Higgins, 2000; Higgins et al., 1997), it is therefore possible that avoidance motivational states may indeed shunt activation toward the left hemisphere as proposed by attentional tuning theory (see Derryberry & Reed, 1998, for an analogous proposition). Following this reasoning, it is likewise possible that approach-related states, or more specifically the promotion foci associated with these states, engender diminished relative left-(increased relative right) hemispheric activation, consistent with Tucker's hypotheses. Similar to Heller's model, RFT's emotion theory decouples arousal from anticipation: One can, for example, vigilantly avoid mistakes without feeling anxious or worried (see Higgins, 1997, 2000, 2002, Chapter 19, this volume). Friedman and Förster (2007) suggested that while focusing on hits or positive outcomes, people who are promotion focused may activate the right hemisphere, whereas while focusing on negative outcomes, people who are prevention focused may activate the left hemisphere. However, when people experience negative affect, the right hemisphere would be activated, whereas when they experience positive affect, the left hemisphere is activated. In a recent study, the authors manipulated emotional arousal and regulatory focus separately and assessed relative hemispheric activation with a behavioral measurement (Friedman & Förster, 2005, Experiment 3). Specifically, to induce RF without eliciting affect, participants were asked to guide a cartoon mouse out of a maze. Procedurally and semantically priming security versus nurturance, in one maze participants approached a cheese whereas in the other they avoided an owl hovering around the mouse and had to find the entry hole of the mouse's nest. In this study, a variant of the maze tasks was also used to elicit affective arousal. In the appetitive arousal group, participants were asked write a vivid story to be titled "The Happiest Day in the Life of the Mouse" about the cheese maze in which the mouse gradually approaches the cheese and eventually eats it. Those in the aversive arousal group were asked to write a story to be titled "The Terrible Death of the Mouse" about the owl maze in which the mouse attempts to escape the owl but eventually gets caught, killed, and eaten. A manipulation check revealed a significant effect of this writing manipulation on their current mood, whereas in line with earlier studies there was no effect of the standard maze manipulation on self-reported affectivity (see Fazio, Eiser, & Shook, 2004; Friedman & Förster, 2001).

Following these manipulations, participants completed a behavioral task measuring relative hemisphere activation (Milner, Brechmann, & Pagliarini, 1992), showing that within the emotional arousal condition, those in whom appetitive arousal was induced demonstrated significantly greater relative left-hemispheric activation than those in the aversive arousal group (see Coan & Allen, 2003, for a review). In contrast, following predictions, within the regulatory-focus condition a prevention focus was associated with greater relative left-hemispheric activation than was a promotion focus. This suggests that the sheer cognitive orientation toward desired versus undesired end-states may indeed entail a pattern of hemispheric activation that is essentially the opposite of that associated with appetitive versus aversive emotional arousal (see also Friedman & Förster, 2005, Experiments 1–2; Förster & Friedman, 2008). The authors also showed that relative right-hemisphere activation predicted creativity in subsequent tasks, whereas relative left-hemisphere activation predicted analytic thinking independent of mood. In sum, these studies show that emotions and outcome orientations are in fact psychologically different and that regulatory focus rather than valence drives the effect of mood on creative thought. More generally, the mechanisms suggested operate beyond decision-making tasks and do not necessarily involve a signal detection logic. We think that both are correlates of RF and future research should further examine them independently as well as their interaction.

Conclusion

As was shown, people not only take different paths to get to the same goal, but also generate very different performances using the same procedure according to context. Thus, the fit of the regulatory focus between a person and a to-be executed task influences how motivated the person is in pursuing the goal, which emotions awaits him/her for the different choice alternatives, how he/she evaluates past decisions, what value he/she assigns to objects as well as how he/she behaves within social interactions. At the base of RFT we can therefore explain differences in emotion, thinking, and behavior. Additionally, we can expound on this by matching tasks and demands to the focus of a person. Furthermore, RFT is a fruitful starting point for new theorizing in psychology research that eventually can help us to better understand people's behavior. Regulatory focus may in the future also explain political and societal changes. To give an example, Inglehart (1977, 1990) advanced a model of societal value change that is based on Maslow's (1954) pyramid of human needs with a materialist orientation on the bottom and postmaterialist needs on the top level. Only if materialist needs are being fulfilled, people would strive to fulfill postmaterialist needs of self-actualization. If socioeconomic development occurs one may predict that societies prioritize goals of self-actualization and thereby a promotion focus may evolve. It is also possible that foci change by generations: If a younger generation takes materialist need fulfillment for granted, younger people may have a relatively stronger promotion focus (see Welzel, 2007) that may further explain generation conflicts evolving from a conflict between prioritization of different needs and goals.

Acknowledgments

Preparation of this chapter was supported by two grants from the Deutsche Forschungsgemeinschaft to Jens Förster (FO 244/6-1, FO244/8-1). We thank Sarah Horn for editing the manuscript and Tory Higgins for invaluable discussions and comments on this chapter.

Note

1. The relation between regulatory focus and interdependency or collectivism is more complicated. Lee, Aaker, and Gardner (2000) found that chronically interdependent people place more emphasis on prevention information than on promotion information, whereas chronically independent people place more emphasis on promotion information than on prevention information. Higgins, May, and Mendoza-Denton (2003) found vertical collectivism (self-sacrifice and duty) to be related to chronic prevention, but horizontal collectivism (nur-

turance and support) to be related to chronic promotion. Future research needs to determine the relations among regulatory focus and collectivism versus individualism.

References

Aaker, J. L., & Lee, A. Y. (2001). "I" seek pleasures and "we" avoid pains: The role of self-regulatory goals in information processing and persuasion. *Journal of Consumer Research, 28,* 33–49.

Anderson, M. C., & Neely, J. H. (1996). Interference and inhibition in memory retrieval. In E. L. Bjork & R. A. Bjork (Eds.), *Memory* (pp. 237–313). San Diego: Academic Press.

Atkinson, J. W. (1964). *An introduction to motivation.* Princeton, NJ: Van Nostrand.

Avnet, T., & Higgins, E. T. (2003). Locomotion, assessment, and regulatory fit: Value transfer from "how" to "what." *Journal of Experimental Social Psychology, 39,* 525–530.

Bandura, A. (1982). Self-efficacy mechanism in human agency. *American Psychologist, 37,* 122–147.

Bornstein, R. F. (1989). Exposure and affect: Overview and meta-analysis of research, 1968–1987. *Psychological Bulletin, 106,* 265–289.

Brendl, C. M., & Higgins, E. T. (1996). Principles of judging valence: What makes events positive or negative? In M. P. Zanna (Ed.), *Advances in experimental social psychology* (Vol. 28, pp. 95–160). San Diego: Academic Press.

Brown, J. S. (1948). Gradients of approach and avoidancce responses and their relation to level of motivation. *Journal of Comparative and Physiological Psychology, 41,* 450–465.

Cacioppo, J. T., Priester, J. R., & Berntson, G. G. (1993). Rudimentary determinants of attitudes: II. Arm flexion and extension have differential effects on attitudes. *Journal of Personality and Social Psychology, 65,* 5–17.

Cesario, J., Grant, H., & Higgins, E. T. (2004). Regulatory fit and persuasion: Transfer from "feeling right." *Journal of Personality and Social Psychology, 86,* 338–404.

Chernev, A. (2004). Goal-attribute compatibility in consumer choice. *Journal of Consumer Psychology, 14,* 141–150.

Coan, J. A., & Allen, J. J. B. (2003). Frontal EEG asymmetry and the behavioral activation and inhibition systems. *Psychophysiology, 40,* 106–114.

Crowe, E., & Higgins, E. T. (1997). Regulatory focus and strategic inclinations: Promotion and prevention in decision-making. *Organizational Behavior and Human Decision Processes, 69,* 117–132.

Derryberry, D., & Reed, M. A. (1998). Anxiety and attentional focusing: Trait, state and hemispheric influences. *Personality and Individual Differences, 25,* 745–761.

Derryberry, D., & Tucker, D. M. (1994). Motivating the focus of attention. In P. M. Niedenthal & S. Kitayama (Eds.), *The heart's eye: Emotional influences in perception and attention* (pp. 167–196). San Diego: Academic Press.

Easterbrook, J. A. (1959). The effect of emotion on cue utilization and the organization of behavior. *Psychological Review, 66,* 183–201.

Edwards, W. (1951). Probability preference among bets with differing expected values. *Psychological Bulletin, 51,* 380–417.

Fazio, R. H., Eiser, J. R., & Shook, N. J. (2004). Attitude formation through exploration: Valence asymmetries. *Journal of Personality and Social Psychology, 87,* 293–311.

Florack, A., Scarabis, M., & Gosejohann, S. (2005). Regulatory focus and consumer information processing. In F. R. Kardes, P. M. Herr, & J. Nantel (Eds.), *Applying social cognition to consumer-focused strategy* (pp. 235–263). Mahwah, NJ: Erlbaum.

Förster, J., & Friedman, R. (2008). Expression entails anticipation: Towards a self-regulatory model of bodily feedback effects. In G. R. Semin & E. R. Smith (Eds.), *Embodied grounding: Social, cognitive, affective, and neuroscientific approaches* (pp. 289–307). New York: Cambridge University Press.

Förster, J., Friedman, R. S., Özelsel, A., & Denzler, M. (2006). Enactment of approach and avoidance behavior influences the scope of perceptual and conceptual attention. *Journal of Experimental Social Psychology, 42,* 133–146.

Förster, J., Grant, H., Idson, L. C., & Higgins, E. T. (2001). Success/failure feedback, expectancies, and approach/avoidance motivation: How regulatory focus moderates classic relations. *Journal of Experimental Social Psychology, 37,* 253–260.

Förster, J., & Higgins, E. T. (2005). How global versus local perception fits regulatory focus. *Psychological Science, 16,* 631–636.

Förster, J., Higgins, E. T., & Idson, L.C. (1998). Approach and avoidance strength during goal attainment: Regulatory focus and the "goal looms larger" effect. *Journal of Personality and Social Psychology, 75,* 1115–1131.

Förster, J., Higgins, E. T., & Strack, F. (2000). When stereotype disconfirmation is a personal threat: How prejudice and prevention focus moderate incongruency effects. *Social Cognition, 18,* 178–197.

Förster, J., Higgins, E. T., & Taylor Bianco, A. (2003). Speed/accuracy in performance: tradeoff in decision making or separate strategic concerns? *Organizational Behavior and Human Decision Processes, 90,* 148–164.

Förster, J., Higgins, E. T., & Werth, L. (2004). How threat from stereotype disconfirmation triggers self-defense. *Social Cognition, 22,* 54–74.

Förster, J., & Liberman, N. (2007). Knowledge activation. In A. W. Kruglanski & E. T. Higgins (Eds.), *Social psychology: Handbook of basic principles* (2nd ed.). New York: Guilford Press.

Freitas, A. L., Liberman, N., & Higgins, E. T. (2002). Regulatory fit and resisting temptation during goal pursuit. *Journal of Experimental Social Psychology, 38,* 291–298.

Freitas, A. L., Liberman, N., Salovey, P., & Higgins, E. T. (2002). When to begin? Regulatory focus and initiating goal pursuit. *Personality and Social Psychology Bulletin, 28,* 121–130.

Freud, S. (1923). *Das Ich und das Es.* [The Ego and the Id]. GW XIII. Leipzig, Wien, Zurich: Internationaler Psychoanalytischer.

Friedman, R. S., & Förster, J. (2001). The effects of promotion and prevention cues on creativity. *Journal of Personality and Social Psychology, 81*, 1001–1013.

Friedman, R. S., & Förster, J. (2005). Effects of motivational cues on perceptual asymmetry: Implications for creativity and analytical problem solving. *Journal of Personality and Social Psychology, 88*, 263–275.

Friedman, R. S., & Förster, J. (2008). Activation and measurement of motivational states. In A. Elliott (Ed.), *Handbook of approach and avoidance motivation* (pp. 235–246). Mahwah, NJ: Erlbaum.

Galinsky, A. D., Leonardelli, G. L., Okhuysen, G. A., & Mussweiler, T. (2005). Regulatory focus at the bargaining table: Promoting distributive and integrative success. *Personality and Social Psychology Bulletin, 31*, 1–12.

Galinsky, A. D., & Mussweiler, T. (2001). First offers as anchors: The role of perspective-taking and negotiator focus. *Journal of Personality and Social Psychology, 81*, 657–669.

Gray, J. A. (1982). The neuropsychology of anxiety: An enquiry into the functions of the septo-hippocampal system. *Behavioural Brain Sciences, 5*, 469–484.

Heller, W., Koven, N. S., & Miller, G. A. (2003). Regional brain activity in anxiety and depression, cognition/emotion interaction, and emotion regulation. In K. Hugdahl & R. J. Davidson (Eds.), *The assymetrical brain* (pp. 533–564). Cambridge, MA: MIT Press.

Heller, W., & Nitschke, J. B. (1998). The puzzle of regional brain activity in depression and anxiety: The importance of subtypes and comorbidity. *Cognition and Emotion, 12*, 421–447.

Heller, W., Nitschke, J. B., Etienne, M. A., & Miller, G. A. (1997). Patterns of regional brain activity differentiate types of anxiety. *Journal of Abnormal Psychology, 106*, 376–385.

Higgins, E. T. (1996). The "self digest": Self-knowledge serving self-regulatory functions. *Journal of Personality and Social Psychology, 71*, 1062–1083.

Higgins, E. T. (1997). Beyond pleasure and pain. *American Psychologist, 52*, 1280–1300.

Higgins, E. T. (1998). From expectancies to worldviews: Regulatory focus in socialization and cognition. In J. M. Darley & J. Cooper (Eds.), *Attribution and social interaction: The legacy of Edward E. Jones* (pp. 243–309). Washington, DC: American Psychological Association.

Higgins, E. T. (2000) Making a good decision: Value from fit. *American Psychologist, 55*, 1217–1230.

Higgins, E. T. (2001). Promotion and prevention experiences: Relating emotions to non-emotional motivational states. In J. P. Forgas (Ed.), *Handbook of affect and social cognition* (pp. 186–211). Mahwah, NJ: Erlbaum.

Higgins, E. T. (2002). How self-regulation creates distinct values: The case of promotion and prevention decision making. *Journal of Consumer Psychology, 12*, 177–191.

Higgins, E. T., Bond, R. N., Klein, R., & Strauman, T. (1986). Self-discrepancies and emotional vulnerability: How magnitude, accessibility, and type of discrepancy influence affect. *Journal of Personality and Social Psychology, 51*, 5–15.

Higgins, E. T., Friedman, R. S., Harlow, R. E., Idson, L. C., Ayduk, O. N., & Taylor, A. (2001). Achievement orientations from subjective histories of success. Promotion pride versus prevention pride. *European Journal of Social Psychology, 31,* 3–23.

Higgins, E. T., Grant, H., & Shah, J. (1999). Self-regulation and quality of life: Emotional and non-emotional life experiences. In D. Kahnemann, E. Diener, & N. Schwarz (Eds.), *Well-being. The foundations of hedonic psychology* (pp. 244–266). New York: Russell Sage Foundation.

Higgins, E. T., Idson, L. C., Freitas, A. L., Spiegel, S., & Molden, D. C. (2003). Transfer of value from fit. *Journal of Personality and Social Psychology, 84,* 1140–1153.

Higgins, E. T., May, Mendoza-Denton (2003). Unpublished data set, Columbia University, New York.

Higgins, E. T., & Molden, D. C. (2003). How strategies for making judgments and decisions affect cognition: Motivated cognition revisited. In G. V. Bodenhausen & A. J. Lambert (Eds.), *Foundations of social cognition* (pp. 211–235). Mahwah, NJ: Erlbaum.

Higgins, E. T., Roney, C. J., Crowe, E., & Hymes, C. (1994). Ideal versus ought predilections for approach and avoidance distinct self-regulatory systems. *Journal of Personality and Social Psychology, 66,* 276–286.

Higgins, E. T., Shah, J., & Friedman, R. (1997). Emotional responses to goal attainment: Strength of regulatory focus as moderator. *Journal of Personality and Social Psychology, 72,* 515–525.

Higgins, E. T., & Silberman, I. (1998). Development of regulatory focus: Promotion and prevention as ways of living. In J. Heckhausen & C. S. Dweck (Eds.), *Motivation and self-regulation across the life span* (pp. 78–113). New York: Cambridge University Press.

Higgins, E. T., & Spiegel, S. (2004). Promotion and prevention strategies of self-regulation: A motivated cognition perspective. In K. Vohs & R. F. Baumeister (Eds.), *Handbook of self-regulation: Research, theory, and applications* (pp. 171–187). New York: Guilford Press.

Higgins, E. T., & Tykocinski, O. (1992). Self-discrepancies and biographical memory: Personality and cognition at the level of psychological situation. *Journal of Personality and Social Psychology Bulletin, 18,* 527–535.

Idson, L. C., & Higgins, E. T. (2000). How current feedback and chronic effectiveness influence motivation: Everything to gain versus everything to lose. *European Journal of Social Psychology, 30,* 583–592.

Idson, L. C., Liberman, N., & Higgins, E. T. (2000). Distinguishing gains from nonlosses and losses from nongains: A regulatory focus perspective on hedonic intensity. *Journal of Experiemental Social Pscyhology, 36,* 252–274.

Inglehart, R. (1977). *The silent revolution.* Princeton, NJ: Princeton University Press.

Inglehart, R. (1990). *Culture shift.* Princeton, NJ: Princeton University Press.

Kahneman, D., Knetsch, J. L., & Thaler, R. (1990). Experimental tests of the endowment effect and the Coase theorem. *Journal of Political Economy, 98,* 1325–1348.

Kahneman, D., Knetsch, J. L., & Thaler, R. H. (2005). Experimental tests of the endowment effect and the Coase theorem. In M. H. Bazerman (Ed.), *Negotiation, decision making and conflict management* (Vol. 1–3, pp. 92–115). Cambridge, MA: Edward Elgar Publishing.

Kahneman, D., & Tversky, A. (1979). On the interpretation of intuitive probability: A reply to Jonathan Cohen. *Cognition, 7,* 409–411.

Keltner, D., Gruenfeld, D. H., & Anderson, C. (2003). Power, approach, and inhibition. *Psychological Review, 110,* 265–284.

Lee, A. Y., & Aaker, J. L. (2004). Bringing the frame into focus: The influence of regulatory fit on processing fluency and persuasion. *Journal of Personality and Social Psychology, 86,* 205–218.

Lee, A. Y., Aaker, J. L., & Gardner, W. L. (2000). The pleasures and pains of distinct self-construals: The role of interdependence in regulatory focus. *Journal of Personality and Social Psychology, 78,* 1122–1134.

Leung, C. M., & Lam, S. F. (2003). The effects of regulatory focus on teachers' classroom management strategies and emotional consequences. *Contemporary Educational Psychology, 28,* 114–125.

Levine, J. M., Higgins, E. T., & Choi, H.-S. (2000). Development of strategic norms in groups. *Organizational Behavior and Human Decision Processes, 82,* 88–101.

Levine, J. M., & Moreland, R. L. (1998). Small groups. In D. Gilbert, S. Fiske, & G. Lindzey (Eds.), *The handbook of social psychology* (4th ed., Vol. 2, pp. 415–469). Boston: McGraw-Hill.

Lewin, K. (1951). *Field theory in social science; selected theoretical papers.* D. Cartwright (Ed.). New York: Harper & Row.

Liberman, N., & Förster, J. (in press). Expectancy, value and psychological distance: A new look at goal gradients. *Social Cognition.*

Liberman, N., Idson, L. C., Camacho, C. J., & Higgins, E. T. (1999). Promotion and prevention choices between stability and change. *Journal of Personality and Social Psychology, 77,* 1135–1145.

Liberman, N., Molden, D. M., Idson, L. C., & Higgins, E. T. (2001). Promotion and prevention focus on alternative hypotheses: A regulatory focus perspective on attributional functions. *Journal of Personality and Social Psychology, 77,* 1135–1145.

Lockwood, P., Chasteen, A. L., & Wong, C. (2005). Age and regulatory focus determine preferences for health-related role models. *Psychology and Ageing, 20,* 367–389.

Lockwood, P., Jordan, C. H., & Kunda, Z. (2002). Motivation by positive or negative role models: Regulatory focus determines who will best inspire us. *Journal of Personality and Social Psychology, 83,* 854–864.

Lockwood, P., Marshall, T. C., & Sadler, P. (2005). Promoting success or preventing failure: Cultural differences in motivation by positive or negative role models. *Personality and Social Psychology Bulletin, 31,* 379–392.

Lockwood, P., Sadler, P., Fyman, K., & Tuck, S. (2004). To do or not to do: Using positive or negative role models to harness motivation. *Social Cognition, 22,* 422–450.

Luu, P., Tucker, D. M., & Derryberry, D. (1998). Anxiety and motivational basis of working memory. *Cognitive Therapy and Research, 22,* 577–594.

Maslow, A. (1954). *Motivation and personality*. New York: Harper & Row.

McClelland, D. C. (1961). *The achieving society*. Princeton, NJ: van Nostrand.

McClelland, D. C. (1985). How motives, skills, and values determine what people do. *American Psychologist, 40,* 812–825.

Miller, N. E. (1944). Experimental studies of conflict. In J. McVicker Hunt (Ed.), *Personality and the behavioral disorders* (Vol. 1, pp. 431–465). New York: Ronald.

Miller, N. E. (1959). Liberation of basic S-R concepts: Extension to conflict behavior, motivation and social learning. In S. Koch (Ed.), *Psychology: A study of a science* (Vol. 2, pp. 196–292). New York: McGraw-Hill.

Milner, A. D., Brechmann, M., & Pagliarini, L. (1992). To halve and to halve not: An analysis of line bisection judgements in normal subjects. *Neuropsychologia, 30,* 515–526.

Molden, D. C., Lee, A., & Higgins, E. T. (2007). Motivation for promotion and prevention. In J. Shah & W. Gardner (Eds.), *Handbook of motivation science* (pp. 101–128). New York: Guilford Press.

Mowrer, O. H. (1960). *Learning theory and behavior*. New York: John Wiley.

Murray, H. A. (1938). *Explorations in personality*. New York: Oxford University Press.

Nitschke, J. B., Heller, W., Palmieri, P. A., & Miller, G. A. (1999). Contrasting patterns of brain activity in anxious apprehension and anxious arousal. *Psychophysiology, 36,* 628–637.

Pfaffmann, C. (1960). The pleasure of sensation. *Psychological Reviews, 4,* 253–268.

Pham, M., & Avnet, T. (2004). Ideals and oughts and the reliance on affect versus substance in persuasion. *Journal of Consumer Research, 30,* 503–518.

Pham, M., & Higgins, E. T. (2005). Promotion and prevention in consumer decision-making. In S. Ratneshwar & D. G. Mick (Eds.), *Inside consumption* (pp. 8–63). New York: Routledge.

Richards, J. E. (1997). Effects of attention on infants preference for briefly exposed visual stimuli in the paired comparison recognition memory paradigm. *Developmental Psychology, 33,* 22–31.

Roese, N. J., Hur, T., & Pennington, G. L. (1999). Counterfactual thinking and regulatory focus: Implications for action versus inaction and sufficiency versus necessity. *Journal of Personality and Social Psychology, 77,* 1109–1120.

Roney, C. J. R., Higgins, E. T., & Shah, J. (1995). Goals and framing: How outcome focus influences motivation and emotion. *Personality and Social Psychology Bulletin, 21,* 1151–1160.

Safer, D. A. (1998). *Preference for luxurious or reliable products. Promotion and prevention focus as moderators*. Unpublished doctoral dissertation, Columbia University, New York.

Sassenberg, K., Jonas, K. J., Shah, J. Y., & Brazy, P. C. (2007). Why some groups just feel better: The regulatory fit of group power. *Journal of Personality and Social Psychology, 92,* 249–267.

Sassenberg, K., Kessler, T., & Mummendey, A. (2003). Less negative = more positive? Social discrimination as avoidance or approach. *Journal of Experimental Social Psychology, 39,* 48–58.

Schooler, J. W., & Melcher, J. (1995). The ineffability of insight. In S. M. Smith, T. B. Ward, & R. A. Finke (Eds.), *The creative cognition approach* (pp. 97–134). Cambridge, MA: MIT Press.

Schwarz, N., & Clore, G. L. (2007). Feelings and phenomenal experiences. In E. T. Higgins & A. Kruglanski (Eds.), *Social psychology. Handbook of basic principles* (2nd ed., pp. 385–407). New York: Guilford Press.

Scholer, A. A., & Higgins, E. T. (2008). Distinguishing levels of approach and avoidance: An illustration using regulatory focus theory. In A. J. Elliot (Ed.), *Handbook of approach and avoidance motivation*. Mahwah, NJ: Erlbaum.

Scholer, A. A., Stroessner, S. J., & Higgins, E. T. (2008). Responding to negativity: How a risky tactic can serve a vigilant strategy. *Journal of Experimental Social Psychology, 44*(3), 767–774.

Seibt, B., & Förster, J. (2004). Stereotype threat and performance: How self-stereotypes influence processing by inducing regulatory foci. *Journal of Personality and Social Psychology, 87*, 38–56.

Semin, G. R., Higgins, E. T., DeMontes, L. G., Estourget, Y., & Valencia, J. F. (2005). Linguistic signatures of regulatory focus: How abstraction fits promotion more than prevention. *Journal of Personality and Social Psychology, 89*, 36–45.

Shah, J. Y., Brazy, P. C., & Higgins, E. T. (2004). Promoting us or preventing them: Regulatory focus and manifestations of intergroup bias. *Personality and Social Psychology Bulletin, 30*, 433–446.

Shah, J. Y., & Higgins, E. T. (1997). Expectancy x value effects: Regulatory focus as determinant of magnitude and direction. *Journal of Personality and Social Psychology, 73*, 447–458.

Shah, J. Y., & Higgins, E. T. (2001). Regulatory concerns and appraisal efficiency: The general impact of promotion and prevention. *Journal of Personality and Social Psychology, 80*, 693–705.

Spiegel, S., Grant-Pillow, H., & Higgins, E. T. (2004). How regulatory fit enhances motivational strength during goal pursuit. *European Journal of Social Psychology, 34*, 39–54.

Spiegel, S., & Higgins, E. T. (2001). *Regulatory focus and means substitution in strategic task performance.* Unpublished manuscript, Columbia University.

Steele, C. M. (1997). A threat in the air: How stereotypes shape the intellectual identities and performance of women and African Americans. *American Psychologist, 52*, 613–629.

Steidle, A., & Werth, L. (2008). *How motivational traits and skills interact in self-management.* Unpublished manuscript, University of Chemnitz, Chemnitz, Germany.

Strauman, T. J. (1988). Self-discrepancies and emotional syndromes: Evidence of distinctive vulnerabilities from particular self-structures. *Dissertation Abstracts International, 48*, 3427.

Strauman, T. J. (1992). Nothing ado about much: Overlooked opportunities for cognitive approaches to depression? *Psychological Inquiry, 3*, 266–269.

Strauman, T. J., & Higgins, E. T. (1987). Automatic activation of self-discrepancies and emotional syndromes: When cognitive structures influence affect. *Journal of Personality and Social Psychology, 53*, 1004–1014.

Strauman, T. J., & Higgins, E. T. (1988). Self-discrepancies as predictors of vulnerability to distinct syndromes of chronic emotional distress. *Journal of Personality, 56,* 685–707.

Tajfel, H. (1978). *Differentiation between social groups: Studies in the social psychology of intergroup relations.* London: Academic Press.

Tucker, D. M., & Williamson, P. A. (1984). Asymmetric neural control systems in human self-regulation. *Psychological Review, 91,* 185–215.

Van Dijk, D., & Kluger, A. N. (2004). Feedback sign effect on motivation: Is it moderated by regulatory focus? *Applied Psychology: An International Review, 53,* 113–135.

Welzel, C. (2007). Individual modernity. In R. J. Dalton & H.-D. Klingemann (Eds.), *Oxford handbook of political behavior* (pp. 185–275). New York: Oxford University Press.

Werth, L., & Förster, J. (2006). How regulatory focus influences consumer behavior. *European Journal of Social Psychology, 36,* 1–19.

Werth, L., & Förster, J. (2007). The effects of regulatory focus on braking speed. *Journal of Applied Social Psychology, 37,* 2764–2787.

Zhou, R., & Tuan Pham, M. (2004). Promotion and prevention across mental accounts: When financial products dictate consumers' investment goals. *Journal of Consumer Research, 31,* 125–135.

PART IV

CONSEQUENCES OF GOAL PURSUIT

CHAPTER 16

Self-Regulatory Resource Depletion
A MODEL FOR UNDERSTANDING THE LIMITED NATURE OF GOAL PURSUIT

KATHLEEN D. VOHS
ANDREW M. KAIKATI
PETER KERKHOF
BRANDON J. SCHMEICHEL

About 10 years ago, Baumeister and Heatherton reviewed the self-control literature and found an important ingredient missing. The content of goals had been studied at length (e.g., promotion vs. prevention goals: Higgins, 1987; autonomy vs. relatedness goals: Deci & Ryan, 1995). The process of goal setting had been examined too, such as the importance of setting suitable goals (e.g., Gollwitzer, 1990; Locke & Latham, 1990; Vaillant, 1977; for a more recent update see Oettingen, Pak, & Schnetter, 2001). Breakthroughs in the 1970s and 1980s underscored the vital role of self-awareness in starting and maintaining goal-pursuit efforts (Duval & Wicklund, 1972; Hull, 1981). Until the mid-1990s, however, theories depicting how people engage in self-control were sorely lacking. Hence a full understanding of why people so often fail at self-control remained somewhat elusive until a comprehensive model of how people move themselves from their current state to a more desirable state was developed. That model, variously called the "strength model," the "limited-resource model," the "ego-depletion model," or the "self-regulatory resource model," is the focus of this chapter.

Understanding Self-Regulation

We understand self-regulation as the process by which the self modifies an incipient response. Oftentimes overriding one response will be accompanied by a move to replace it with a less natural but more desired response, but this is not a necessary component of self-regulation. The term "modification" itself needs clarifying: Although a great deal of self-regulation is self-stopping (Polivy, 1998), modification of a response can also include prolonged maintenance or amplification of a response. (Think about how happy one can appear when opening a gift from Grandma while she looks on.)

Another important point is that self-regulation may best be conceptualized as a struggle between impulses and restraints (cf. Hoch & Loewenstein, 1991). To see a person with a neutral facial expression at a funeral, one does not know whether this person is a strong self-regulator or whether this person feels very little emotion. The strength of the urge and the restraints on the urge are theoretically orthogonal constructs, and presumably it requires more self-regulatory resources to wrestle with a strong urge than a weak urge, although to our knowledge this notion has not yet been tested empirically.

The Limited-Resource Model of Self-Regulation

The focus of this chapter is on the limits of self-regulatory capacity. Attempting to move from one's current state to a more desirable state requires a certain amount of energy. This psychic energy is called "self-regulatory strength" and is governed by a set of finite resources. When people engage in self-regulation, they expend some of their self-regulatory resources; and, consequently, fewer of these resources are able to be consumed during a subsequent regulatory task. The resulting state is termed "self-regulatory resource depletion" and is manifested in a temporary loss in self-control ability. This hangover effect of fewer regulatory resources to put toward a second self-regulation task explains why people typically cannot put forth equal amounts of motivational effort.

Self-regulatory resources are used for all controlled responses and actions, as well as other executive functions such as decision making and active (vs. passive) responding (Vohs et al., 2007). Because self-regulatory resources represent a general supply of resources that are used anytime a person attempts to modify responses or behaviors, the effects of resource depletion are not limited to difficulties in attaining goals in that specific domain (Baumeister, Bratslavsky, Muraven, & Tice, 1998; Vohs, Baumeister, & Ciarocco, 2005; Vohs & Heatherton, 2000). Indeed, one of the cornerstones of the model is that depletion of regulatory resources in one domain, such as managing one's feelings, directly affects attainment of goals in other domains, such as being polite or squashing unwanted habits.

Evidence of Self-Regulatory Depletion

The effects of self-regulatory depletion and the limited-resource pattern have been demonstrated in nearly 80 published studies (for full reviews see Baumeister, Schmeichel, & Vohs, 2007; Vohs, Baumeister, & Tice, 2008). What follows is a sampling of research demonstrating the effect of resource depletion on subsequent goal striving. First we review some of the experiments that test the basic tenets of the model. Next we discuss research findings in the domains of overeating, impulsive spending, and interpersonal processes.

Basic Premises and Tests Thereof

The limited-resource model of self-regulation comprises six main tenets. First, self-regulation consumes and therefore reduces or depletes a limited internal resource. Second, when the resource has been depleted, additional efforts at self-regulation are impaired. Third, the resource is domain general. That is, apparently disparate acts of self-regulation all rely on the same underlying resource. Fourth, efforts at self-regulation deplete the resource only temporarily. Rest or other interventions may help to restore the resource to its initial level. Fifth, the resource may be bolstered or strengthened over the long run, much like muscles are strengthened with exercise. And sixth, people may seek to conserve the self-regulatory resource well before it becomes fully depleted.

A series of experiments reported by Baumeister et al. (1998) provided broad, initial support for the limited-resource model by testing the effects of initial acts of self-regulation on subsequent acts of self-regulation. These experiments also distinguished the resource model from two alternative models of self-regulation, namely a skill model and a schema model. Briefly, a skill model of self-regulation would predict that engaging in one act of self-regulation may improve subsequent efforts at self-regulation, insofar as practicing a skill produces minor increments in performance. A schema model would make a similar prediction insofar as activating a self-regulatory schema during an initial task makes the schema more readily available for subsequent efforts at self-regulation. The limited resource model, by contrast, predicts that initial efforts at self-regulation would undermine subsequent efforts.

The first experiment in this series found that people who made themselves eat radishes instead of tempting chocolates and cookies gave up more quickly when they tried to solve difficult puzzles. Another experiment found that people who suppressed their responses to emotional film scenes went on to solve fewer anagrams than people who freely expressed their emotional responses. These experiments thus confirmed that initial efforts at self-regulation undermine subsequent efforts at self-regulation, as though both efforts rely on the same internal resource or strength. Moreover, the resource appeared to underlie diverse forms of self-regulation, ranging from resisting temptation and suppressing emotional expressions to persisting at difficult puzzles.

More recent experiments found that expending the limited resource affected not only subsequent efforts at self-regulation, but also the perception of time passage. More precisely, Vohs and Schmeichel (2003) found that people who suppressed their responses to an emotionally charged film scene estimated that the scene had lasted longer than it actually had. Suppressors also thought the scene lasted longer than did people who simply expressed their response to the scene. Hence effortful self-regulation produced a distorted sense of time passage.

Additional experiments in this series found that distorted (elongated) perceptions of time helped to explain the behavioral aftereffects of self-regulatory exertion. For example, in one experiment participants attempted to hold their breath for as long as they could. Some participants attempted the breath-holding task immediately after suppressing a forbidden thought, whereas other participants held their breath after freely expressing their thoughts. The breath-holding assessment revealed the typical resource-depletion effect: Participants who had just suppressed a thought showed a larger decrease in breath-holding ability than did participants who had just expressed their thoughts. Although participants who were depleted held their breath for less time, they estimated that they had held their breath for more time than participants who were not depleted did. Moreover, perceived duration of breath holding mediated the effect of resource depletion on breath-holding ability. When time perceptions were statistically controlled, the effect of depletion on subsequent performance disappeared. Thus, expending the self-regulatory resource not only impaired a subsequent attempt at self-regulation, but also disrupted the ability to monitor the duration of self-regulatory efforts, and this reduced monitoring ability explained the resource-depletion effect. Perceiving that self-regulatory efforts lasted overly long rendered people less likely to sustain subsequent self-regulation attempts.

Another tenet of the limited-resource model of self-regulation is that the resource may be bolstered or strengthened over time, much like a bicep muscle will be strengthened by daily dumbbell curls. A growing body of evidence provides some support for this element of the model. For example, one recent investigation had participants perform a resource-depletion task involving the suppression of stereotypic thoughts at two points in time: first during an initial experimental session and then again 2 weeks later (Gailliot, Plant, Butz, & Baumeister, 2007). In the 2-week interim period, participants assigned to the self-regulation practice condition were instructed to perform various forms of self-regulation such as using their nondominant hand to open doors, to brush their teeth, and while using a computer mouse. Other participants were given no particular instructions or tasks to perform during the 2-week interval. At the second experimental session, participants again attempted the stereotype suppression task. The results revealed strong support for the beneficial effect of regular practice at self-regulation. Participants who had used their nondominant hand regularly for 2 weeks showed a smaller resource-depletion effect relative to participants who had not practiced self-regulation. Thus, regular bouts of exertion appeared to make the limited self-regulatory resource more resistant to short-term depletion, even though the practice tasks were quite different from the experimental measures of self-regulation ability (see also Muraven, Baumeister, & Tice, 1999; Oaten & Cheng, 2006).

Everyday observation and a dose of common sense suggest that the limited self-regulatory resource is rarely depleted to a state of utter exhaustion. After all, people do not become helplessly impulsive after they have overridden responses or otherwise attempted self-regulation. Empirical evidence confirms that people conserve some of the resource, particularly when they anticipate needing it in the near future. For example, one experiment found that suppressing a forbidden thought led to reduced persistence on a test of pain tolerance (Muraven, Shmueli, & Burkley, 2006). This finding replicated the standard resource-depletion effect of poorer self-regulation due to prior, unrelated efforts at self-regulation. The magnitude of the depletion effect, however, was influenced by the type of task participants expected to perform following the pain test. Participants who were depleted who expected to perform another difficult task after the pain test showed lower pain tolerance compared to participants who were depleted who anticipated performing a simple (nonregulatory) task after the pain test. Thus, it appeared as though participants who were depleted who anticipated a future challenge conserved or withheld some of the resource during the pain test, presumably so that they would have some of it left to confront the next challenge.

In summary, research over the last 10 years has provided consistent and substantial support for the core tenets of the limited resource model of self-regulation. This self-regulatory resource becomes depleted with use, strengthened with practice, and occasionally conserved when other challenges loom on the horizon. The state of the resource helps to determine the efficacy of behaviors spanning the spectrum of self-regulation.

Domain-Specific Applications

Overeating among Dieters

Most of the research on the limited-resource model asks participants to follow through with a goal that has been assigned to them in the laboratory, such as stifling their amusement at a comedy film or keeping their attention glued to a boring video. Although these are important for understanding situational self-control demands, it is essential to test the contextual effects of self-control demands on self-imposed goals. This approach is not only quite naturalistic, but also provides a backdrop for asking whether chronic self-guides interact with situational demands to produce effects that are different than those externally placed on participants after their arrival to the laboratory. A series of studies by Vohs and Heatherton (2000) examined the effects of self-regulatory resource depletion in a context in which people have preestablished eating goals. The domain of eating was chosen because it represents a particularly pernicious self-control problem: Unlike other forms of self-regulation wherein one regulatory method would be to not interact with the stimulus whatsoever so as to avoid temptation (e.g., smokers could avoid cigarettes and alcoholics could avoid alcohol), everyone must to eat to stay alive and healthy. This means that controlling food intake is a special case of regulation in which one has to interact with—and hence engage in self-regulation—on the order of multiple times a day. The uniqueness of this situation renders dieting a particularly interesting case of chronic self-regulation.

The first experiment in this series exposed dieters and nondieters to tempting candies while they watched a video about Bighorn sheep (Vohs & Heatherton, 2000). The placement of the candies was manipulated so that participants were either next to or far away from the overflowing bowl of chocolates. Participants also received instructions that the candies were available to be eaten ("go ahead, help yourself") or that the candies were needed later in the day and should not be consumed ("please don't touch"). After watching the boring video for 10 minutes, participants were moved to a different room to for a task that involved judging three flavors of ice cream. To judge the ice creams, one needed only to consume a small amount; however, participants were left alone with large bowls of ice cream with their ad-lib eating being the measure of self-regulation.

It was expected that only dieters (and not nondieters) would expend regulatory resources in the presence of tempting snacks due to their long-term goal of limiting caloric intake. However, if the experimenter (an external force) prevented dieters from having to exert self-control to restrain themselves from eating the candies, their self-regulatory resources would not be expended. Thus, it was expected that dieters who sat close to the snacks and were allowed to eat them would consume the most ice cream.

In support of this prediction, dieters ate significantly more ice cream in the second setting after they had been tempted by sitting next to the candies and had to control themselves because they had been told the candies were available to be eaten. Dieters ate far less ice cream after they had been seated far from the chocolates and were told they could indulge in them (which they did not, because they were dieters). Given that nondieters are not regulating with respect to eating, they were not expected to become depleted by the presence of tempting chocolates in the initial task. In line with this assumption, nondieters' ice cream eating did not vary as a function of the situational factors.

Another study replicated the loss of self-control among dieters after having expended self-regulatory resources, this time because of emotion regulation (Vohs & Heatherton, 2000). Dieters watched a sad movie about a woman on her deathbed saying good-bye to her husband, mother, and two young sons. Participants were asked either to watch the movie naturally or to suppress their emotions, a task that was designed to leave intact or deplete participants' self-regulatory resources, respectively. As before, ice cream consumption during the taste-and-rate task was the measure of self-control. As expected, dieters who suppressed their emotions ate more ice cream later than those who were allowed to let their emotions flow freely. Notably, both groups reported similarly negative feelings after the movie, ruling out differences in mood as an explanation for eating differences.

For dieters, eating is a behavior that must be controlled, having to regulate emotions depleted the resource that later would have helped dieters control their ice cream consumption.

Impulsive Spending

A second context in which to assess the limits of self-regulation from a self-regulatory resources perspective is in terms of personal spending. Along not as essential as eating, regulating one's purchases is a strong motive for almost everyone, or should be. Even those who believe that they are not required to modify their spending can find themselves badly mistaken, as evidenced by celebrities such as MC Hammer who misspent $30 million and ended up in financial ruin in a few short years. The national savings rate in the United States in the negative, which means that people are spending more than they are saving. We thought it worthy indeed to test whether self-regulatory resources play a role in spontaneous, unnecessary purchases (Vohs & Faber, 2007).

"Impulsive buying" is defined as purchasing behavior that results from a spontaneous urge within the consumer to buy something (Rook, 1987): the to-be-purchased good is not specified in advance, but rather the urge is aimed at the act of purchasing and not the product per se. Vohs and Faber (2007) demonstrated the effect of self-regulation depletion on impulsive spending for a variety of products, such as pens, coffee mugs, decks of playing cards, cookies, pretzels, and potato chips. Overall, the findings of four studies indicate that self-regulatory resources are needed to control impulsive spending and that impulses to buy are acted upon more often when self-regulatory resources are reduced than when they are intact.

In two experiments, attentional control was used as a manipulation of self-regulatory ability. All participants watched a silent video of a woman being interviewed. The video simultaneously displayed irrelevant words at the bottom of the screen every 30 seconds. Some participants were not told anything about the irrelevant words, whereas participants in the depletion condition were instructed not to look at the words and to revert their eyes back to the interviewee if they did find themselves looking at the words. In one study, the dependent measure was an immediate buying impulses scale; in another study, the dependent measure was reported willingness-to-pay rates for high-end products such as watches and appliances. Both studies showed an effect of self-regulatory resource availability on impulsive spending tendencies. Participants who had earlier used their resources to ignore the distracting stimulus later reported stronger urges to spend impulsively (Experiment 1) and reported higher willingness-to-pay rates (Experiment 2), as compared to participants who did not engage in attention control.

Two additional studies tested behavioral indices of impulsive spending in a mock store environment. In these studies, participants in the self-regulatory resource-depletion condition were asked either to read a non-emotional text with exaggerated emotions or to suppress specific thoughts. In both studies, participants whose regulatory strength had been reduced bought more items and spent more money than participants whose regulatory resources were not reduced.

Section Summary

It is no secret that despite having firm, clear goals to manage food consumption or spending, people are oftentimes unable to achieve these goals. Ironically, many of these efforts can lead to an end-state that is worse than the point at which the goal was set (e.g., Mann et al., 2007). Having to exert self-control in an initial task was shown to increase subsequent rates of undesirable behaviors that would otherwise be controlled. Dieters, who have a chronic goal to curb caloric intake, ate more ice cream after they had engaged in self-control in an earlier task. People whose self-regulatory resources were depleted spent more money than people whose resources were not depleted.

The Limited-Resource Nature of Interpersonal Functioning

Social forms of self-regulation are emerging as an important domain in which people expend their self-regulatory resources. Work on impression management, stigma, and high-maintenance interactions indicate that active, regulatory processes deplete the self's resources in the context of managing the social self. As with many other goals, interpersonal goal pursuit takes self-control. It takes self-control not to give in to impulses such as shouting when angry with another person or become overly intimate with this wonderful colleague while at work. Being depleted because self-regulatory resources have been used while exercising self-control in other domains (e.g., being on a diet, working on difficult tasks) impairs the ability to pursue interpersonal goals and to resist impulses that may conflict with these goals. On the other hand, troublesome interpersonal interactions take up resources that may be needed while pursuing other goals. In the literature there is evidence for both processes.

Self-Presentation

Most people have a goal of social inclusion. People engage in self-presentation, which is the putting forth a specific public image to demonstrate to others that they would be or are a worthy member of a group. Self-presentation is effortful and may be strongly linked to self-control abilities. In a series of eight studies, Vohs, Baumeister, and Ciarocco (2005) found that reductions in self-regulatory resources led to impairments on self-presentation tasks, and that engaging in impression management resulted in reduced self-regulation ability.

In one of Vohs et al.'s (2005) eight studies demonstrating that the engaging in self-control can lead to inappropriate impression management behaviors, participants with one of three attachment styles (avoidant, anxious-ambivalent, or secure) were brought into the lab. All participants first performed the Stroop task and were asked either to read the ink color of a row of Xs or the ink color of color-name words. Vohs et al. predicted that people would generally attempt a moderate amount of self-disclosure, even among people who were anxious-ambivalent who would prefer to be more disclosing and among people who were avoidant who would prefer to be less disclosing. However, it was predicted that their predispositions toward being over- or underdisclosing were emerge if their self-regulatory resources were reduced.

The results supported these predictions. Under conditions in which people's resources were not depleted, individuals (regardless of attachment style) said they preferred to disclose moderately intimate details about themselves. However, after participants had engaged in the color-naming version of the Stroop and were therefore depleted of their self-regulatory resources, their disclosures were more extreme (according to their attachment style). Thus, in the absence of sufficient self-regulatory resources, people fail to portray themselves in the most desirable light.

Self-Control and Sexual Behavior

An important interpersonal goal is to prevent behaviors that are considered socially inappropriate. Many things people do are subject to strict social norms. It is typically not considered appropriate to shout at other people, to drink alcohol in the early morning, to play loud music in public transport, or to push other people when they are in the way. This is not to say that people do not sometimes feel the urge to do so. Controlling these urges takes self-control, and when the resources needed to self-control has been used for other goals, people have difficulties in controlling their social behavior.

The social ramifications of uncontrolled social behavior are particularly troublesome when this behavior is sex related. Even in the presence of abundant sexual cues in TV programs and advertising, people are supposed to restrain their sexual activities to certain times, certain places, and certain ways. Failing to do so would result in divorce, in unwanted pregnancies, getting fired, or getting arrested. Thus, a certain amount of self-restraint in sexual behavior is highly needed for proper social functioning. Gailliot and Baumeister (2007) reported several studies that show that ego depletion does indeed lead people to lose sexual restraint and to behave in a socially inappropriate way. For example, in one study couples were asked to come to the lab and to show their affection in a physical way. Half of the couples participated in a depleting task before, whereas the other half did a task that was not depleting. The showing of affection was done in a private room without any cameras. Afterwards, the couples were asked to report how passionate and sexual their behavior had been. The couples who were depleted reported that they behaved in a more passionate and sexual way, indicating impaired sexual self-regulation. In another study, participants were asked to look at different scenarios while imagining being involved in a committed long-term relationship. The scenarios provided the participants with an opportunity to engage in sexual behavior with somebody else than their (imagined) relationship partner.

Trait self-control and experimentally induced ego depletion turned out to be important predictors of the willingness to engage in infidelity, especially for male and participants who were sexually unrestricted.

Several other findings in the Gailliot and Baumeister (2007) studies show that self-control is essential in sexual self-restraint. For example, participants who were temporarily depleted and with chronically low self-control solved word stems and anagrams more often using sex-related words. Also, episodes in which sexual restraint was low were linked to circumstances in which self-control was low. These findings clearly show the vital role of self-control in social functioning. Lack of self-control leads to socially inappropriate behaviors and to behaviors that are destructive within an intimate relationship.

Racial Interactions and Stigmatizing Settings Impair Self-Control

Not only can interpersonal relationships and interpersonal behavior be affected by self-control, troubled interpersonal contacts can also be a source of impaired self-control. This becomes particularly clear in the literature on interracial interactions, which can be threatening for Whites and Blacks. For Whites, the main threat is to come across as prejudiced. For Blacks, there is the fear of social rejection. For Blacks and Whites, striving for the goals of appearing unprejudiced or preventing exclusion is effortful and requires self-restraint.

Several studies in which White participants meet Black confederates, Richeson and Shelton (2003) showed that performance on tasks that require response inhibition is impaired by previous interracial interactions. A task that typically requires participants to inhibit the first response is the Stroop task. In a Stroop task, people are asked to name the color of color words that are incompatible with the semantic meaning of the color word (e.g., saying "green" when reading the word "red" written in green letters). This uses self-regulatory resources because people need to suppress the natural tendency to just read aloud the word itself rather than its color. Richeson and Shelton showed that after meeting a Black confederate, White participants show more Stroop interference than after meeting a White confederate, but only when the participants' concerns about not appearing prejudiced had been made salient by feedback on an Implicit Association Test (IAT) score. When being told that the IAT score was an indication of performance on a category association test, there was no Stroop interference. However, when the experimenter told the participants that the IAT score indicated racial bias, Stroop performance was impaired after interracial contact.

A follow-up experiment made clear that the effect of interracial interactions on Stroop performance is indeed the effect of effortful self-regulation in order not to appear prejudiced. In this experiment, self-regulation during the interracial interaction was made less effortful by scripting the conversation with the confederate. Because carefully picking one's own words is no longer necessary in a fully scripted conversation, ego depletion would be less likely and the Stroop interference should not occur. This was exactly what happened: White participants who talked to a Black confederate about racial profiling only showed Stroop interference when the conversation was not scripted.

Self-regulation in interracial interactions is not only a matter of regulating behavior, but also involves dealing with emotions and with anxious arousal. Taking away the burden of emotion regulation should therefore also diminish the resources needed to self-regulate. This was done in a third experiment in which Richeson and Shelton (2003) manipulated attribution of arousal by telling half of the White participants that the room that they were in was known to make people feel uneasy. The other half was not given any reason why they would feel aroused and were more likely to attribute this to their conversation with a Black confederate. As predicted, the latter group showed stronger Stroop interference, indicating impaired self-control.

It is not only preventing to stigmatize that uses self-regulatory resources, running the danger of being stigmatized is depleting as well, as is shown in several studies by Inzlicht, McKay, and Aronson (2006). Inzlicht et al. proposed that the stress and uncertainty that come with feeling stigmatized drains self-regulatory resources. In a correlational study among Black students, they showed that race-based stigma sensitivity is related to self-efficacy in regulating one's learning strategies (e.g., to study even when it's attractive to spend time in a more appealing way). Black students who were sensitive to race-based stigma had more difficulties in self-regulating their learning behavior.

In an experimental study, Inzlicht et al. (2006) asked Black and White students to come to their lab. The participants were told that they would have to do a difficult verbal test that was randomly labeled as diagnostic (threat condition) or nondiagnostic (no-threat condition) for intelligence. Next, after having a look at the kind of questions they could expect in the test, the experimenter asked the participants to do a Stroop task. Indeed, in the stereotype threat condition, it took Black, but not White, students longer to correctly name the right color. In the no-threat condition there was no difference between the two groups of students, indicating that stereotype threat does indeed impair self-control.

This was confirmed in a third study among women, which started with the finding that women are prone to stereotype threat effects when being asked to do a math test. Inzlicht et al. (2006) told half of their participants in this study that they would take a math test, the other half were told to do a verbal test. As in the previous experiment, half of the participants were told that the test was indicative of their ability (threat condition), whereas the other half were not told so. Subsequent performance on a handgrip stamina task was taken as a measure of self-control (cf. Muraven, Tice, & Baumeister, 1998). As in the previous study, experiencing stereotype threat resulted in poorer performance on the self-control task: Women who were expecting a math test, and who had been told that this test was an indication of their ability, showed poorer performance on the handgrip task.

High-Maintenance Interactions Damage Self-Regulatory Ability

The previous examples were all based on stereotype threat: For the stigmatized and the stigmatizers it is depleting to interact with the other groups either directly or in an indirect way. One might conclude from these examples that it takes heavily burdened social relationships (e.g., Black–White relationships) for interpersonal interactions to become depleting. Recent work by Finkel et al. (2006) shows that interpersonal interactions that are not group based and that are not heavily taxed by hundreds of years of suppression can be depleting as well. Finkel et al. focused on the depleting effect of high-maintenance social interactions: everyday interactions that require extra energy because social coordination does not run as smoothly as usual. They let participants interact with a confederate who supposedly was to lead the participant through a computer maze only the confederate could see. Half of the participants received clear instructions from the confederate ("left," "right," "up," "down," for the other half 1 of 10 instructions was erroneous or confusing ("wait," "left, I mean right"). Experiencing difficulties in coordination was depleting as could be seen in subsequent preferences for easy tasks, and in poorer task performance on a task that required some concentration and persistence. A follow-up experiment including a control condition that did not involve any interaction showed that this effect was not due to low-maintenance interaction strengthening self-regulation. Also, the effects of high-maintenance interaction on self-regulation were not due to possibly bad moods that could result from troublesome coordination.

The depleting effect of high-maintenance interactions was replicated in a more naturalistic setting where participants talked with a confederate about a problem the confederate supposedly had. In the high-maintenance condition, the confederate was responding to any suggestion in a depressed way: Nothing the participant said would help to solve the problem. In the low-maintenance condition, the confederate responded in a more receptive way to the suggestions made by the participant. Again, high-maintenance interactions proved to be depleting: On a subsequent handgrip stamina test the high-maintenance group showed impaired performance. Interestingly, the effect of high-maintenance interactions holds even when the interaction is not consciously perceived as badly coordinated. Finkel et al. (2006) conducted an experiment where mimicry was varied. Again participants interacted with a confederate, who either did or did not mimic the participants' gestures. Because behavioral mimicry is known to facilitate social interactions without needing conscious awareness (e.g., Chartrand & Bargh, 1999), interactions without mimicry can be regarded as high-maintenance interactions. The results showed that indeed engaging in an interaction without being mimicked is depleting and impairs performance on a task that requires self-control, even when the high maintenance is not consciously perceived as such.

Section Summary

In this section, we reviewed findings that describe one level of interplay between interpersonal and intrapersonal processes: self-regulation. People attempt to regulate themselves privately, and there are interpersonal consequences. People must engage in good self-control interpersonally, and there are repercussions for their personal self-control endeavors. The breadth of findings connecting personal and social selves continues to expand (see Vohs & Finkel, 2006), and we are excited by the findings revealing the dynamic nature of self-regulation across these spheres.

What Is the Pool of Resources That Enable Goal Pursuit?

The precise nature of the resource for self-regulation has yet to be established, although a growing body of evidence is beginning to provide helpful clues. Here we consider the nature of the resource in two different lights: by reviewing evidence that compares and contrasts the limited resource for self-regulation with cognitive resources more generally (e.g., attention, effort, working memory), and then by reviewing evidence pertaining to a possible biological basis for the self-regulatory resource.

Resource models of cognitive processes have a notable and lengthy history in psychology, including also the controversy and disagreement that attends such a history. One main bone of contention with resource models has been their lack of specificity: Which processes are fueled by the resource, and perhaps more important, which processes are not fueled by it? This issue has motivated hundreds if not thousands of experiments in cognitive psychology. One prominent line of research, for example, has been devoted to distinguishing the processing resources devoted to spatial information from the processing resources devoted to verbal information (e.g., Baddeley & Hitch, 1974). Another more recent line of research has demonstrated that judgments about people and judgments about objects activate distinct areas of the brain (e.g., Mitchell, Heatherton, & Macrae, 2002) as though person knowledge and object knowledge rely on different underlying processing resources.

Regarding the limited resource for self-regulation, research has distinguished the regulatory resource from other cognitive resources such as attention and memory. For example, one experiment asked participants to suppress or to express their responses to an emotional film scene (Schmeichel, Vohs, & Baumeister, 2003). Then participants completed two cognitive tests. One was a test of general knowledge that required the test taker simply to consult long-term memory in search of the correct answer (e.g., "Who was the author of *Gone with the Wind?*"). The other test was a cognitive-estimation test that required the test taker to work from prior knowledge to generate plausible estimates for unknown quantities (e.g., "How many seeds are there in a watermelon?"). The results revealed that initial efforts at self-regulation caused participants to generate inaccurate (sometimes wildly inaccurate) estimates on the cognitive-estimation task but no reliable effect on performance on the general knowledge test. Hence expending the self-regulatory resource undermined one form of cognitive performance (when the person was required to play an active, decisive role) but left another form of cognitive performance (retrieving facts from long-term memory) unblemished.

Self-regulatory resource expenditure has also been distinguished from the expenditure of effort. One possibility is that expending effort undermines later self-regulation regardless of whether the initial effort is devoted to self-regulation. If that is true, then the resource would appear to be related to effort expenditure more generally rather than self-regulation specifically. To test this possibility, one experiment compared the aftereffects of three tasks that differed in terms of difficulty (Schmeichel, 2007). For the simplest task, participants read and then recalled two words at a time. For the moderately challenging task, participants read and then had to recall six words at a time. For the self-regulatory task, participants had to divide attention between recalling words and solving mathematical equations. Following their respective initial tasks, all participants watched an emotionally charged film scene under instructions to suppress all outward expressions of emotion. If prior effort expenditure or the difficulty of the initial task determines the magnitude of subsequent decrements in self-regulation, then performance on the emotion-suppression task should reveal a linear pattern such that suppression is poorest after the most difficult task and best after the easiest task, with suppression after the moderately difficult task falling somewhere in-between. If, however, only efforts at self-regulation reduce the regulatory resource, then emotion suppression should be poorest after the task that required people to recall words while solving math equations, but equally good after the other two recall-only tasks.

The results supported the idea that the expenditure of self-regulatory resources determines the magnitude of subsequent decrements in self-regulation. Emotion suppression was equally thorough after participants performed the easy or the moderately difficult recall-only tasks, but suppression was substantially impaired after participants performed the self-regulatory (recall plus math) task. Hence the self-regulatory requirements of the initial task, not task difficulty or effort expenditure, were the decisive determinant of subsequent self-regulatory ability.

One crucial distinction between cognitive resources and the self-regulatory resource concerns the manner in which they are studied. The limited nature of cognitive-processing resources is typically examined by having people perform two tasks at once. A vast body of research using this approach attests to the fact that cognitive load (e.g., having to perform two or more tasks simultaneously) undermines performances that require effort and attention. For example, people are less able to inhibit a response when they must actively maintain other information in working memory at the same time (e.g., Ward & Mann, 2000). Thus, cognitive load has a detrimental impact on goal pursuit by diverting processing resources away from the goal.

Research on the consequences of cognitive load has implicitly assumed that, once the load has been lifted, processing resources revert immediately to baseline capacity. The limited-resource model of self-regulation makes a different prediction, namely that juggling a cognitive load temporarily depletes a regulatory resource, and in the interim before the resource is replenished, further attempts at self-regulation are prone to failure.

Recent evidence has revealed that cognitive load has a detrimental aftereffect on self-regulation, consistent with the regulatory-resource model. One experiment, for example, found that a cognitive load manipulation early in the study made participants more likely later in the study to "seize and freeze" on salient, readily available information in lieu of elaborating less salient (although no less important) information (Dewitte, Pandelaere, Briers, & Warlop, 2005). Thus, cognitive load may not only undermine the performance of a concurrent task (e.g., Ward & Mann, 2000), but also may undermine the performance of a subsequent task insofar as it requires the expenditure of the self-regulatory resource.

Is the notion of a self-regulatory resource biologically plausible? Recent evidence suggests that it is. Glucose is one of the brain's major sources of energy, and it appears to be especially relevant for high-level cognitive processes such as self-regulation and cognitive load. For example, research has shown that an infusion of glucose into the bloodstream boosts memory performance, particularly when the encoding of to-be-remembered material occurs under conditions of cognitive load (Sünram-Lea, Foster, Durlach, & Perez, 2002).

Most relevant for current purposes is evidence that an infusion of glucose into the bloodstream eliminates the derogatory effect of self-regulatory exertion. For example, Gailliot and colleagues (Gailliot et al., 2007) found evidence for the typical resource-depletion effect by having participants exercise attention control (or not) while watching a boring videotape. More important, they found that the depletion effect was eliminated when participants consumed a glucose-rich drink immediately after the attention control manipulation. Thus, it appeared as though the glucose drink replenished whatever had been depleted by the attention control task. Additional experiments in this series replicated this finding and ruled out several alternative explanations.

Section Summary

Work on the precise nature of self-regulatory resources is mounting. Fuel for self-regulatory resources seems to come, in part, from glucose, which is a physiological chemical that gets used when people engage in high-level forms of executive functioning. Engaging in self-regulation and expending self-regulatory resources is not the same as engaging in any kind of mental operation: It is crucial that the executive aspect of the self be activated for self-regulatory resource depletion to occur. Last, we discuss the parent–sibling relationship between self-regulatory resource-depletion and cognitive load, noting that the latter is a subset of the former and itself produces hangover effects.

Developmental Aspects of Self-Regulatory Resource Use

The study of self-regulation from a limited-resource perspective has bloomed over the past 10 years and new pathways that appear quite fruitful continue to crop up. The notion of developmental changes in self-regulation resource usage is an area that is ripe for exploration, but one for which we know no direct evidence.

We consider the question of self-regulatory resources changing over the course of the life span as having two parts. One is that we assume that everyone has a supply of executive resources in their psyche when they are born, although we admit that there may be cases of disability or deformity in which impairments in self-regulation may stem from a complete lack of self-regulatory resources and therefore a lack of self-regulation ability. We think that would be a rare case, though. Hence we assume that people are born with a set of resources that enable them to modify their responses. For instance, it is clear that children can engage in self-regulation at young ages (Mischel & Ebbesen, 1970; Mischel, Ebbesen, & Zeiss, 1972), and so we presume they have self-regulatory resources.

The second part of the answer to this question is that there are likely myriad processes related to self-regulatory resources that develop over time. In this sense, one can think of another analogy, which is to intelligence. Intelligence is known to be highly heritable (Bouchard et al., 1990) but is also affected by nongenetic factors. As one instance, consider the Flynn effect, which describes the fact that intelligence scores have been increasing throughout the decades (Flynn, 1987) across a wealth of countries studied and across multiple forms of intelligence. In that same way, we think that there are environmental effects on the development (or, in the case of sweeping cultural changes in self-regulation, perhaps we should say "regression") of self-regulation and usage of self-regulatory resources.

Although children probably do have self-regulatory resources they most certainly do not have a repertoire of skills to recruit those resources. Those skills, we imagine, build up over time. Thus, although there is no direct evidence as to whether resource-capacity limits play a role in the self-regulation problems of children, we believe that the internal capacity for self-regulation exists in children and that cognitive, emotional, and other motivational strategies improve with age. These strategies, in turn, should aid in the use of self-regulatory resources.

In support of this notion, it seems that people's self-regulatory abilities can improve over time. Self-report studies of emotion regulation indicate better emotion regulation in older adults than in younger adults (i.e. Gross, Carstensen, Pasupathi, Hsu, & Tsai, 1997; Labouvie-Vief, Hakim-Larson, DeVoe, & Schoeberlein, 1989; Lawton, Kleban, & Dean, 1993). Additionally, Carstensen and her colleagues (e.g., Carstensen, Pasupathi, Mayr, & Nesselroade, 2000) have repeatedly demonstrated that people improve at regulating their emotions with age. In this work, older people, relative to younger people, consistently show better regulation of their emotional states in terms of frequency, intensity, and complexity. In the 2000 work, Carstensen et al. tracked participants aged 18 to 94 and found a steady improvement in emotional health over time. Negative emotions declined in frequency with age (from age 18 until 60, at which point they leveled off) and that positive emotions remained stable. Carstensen's data argue against the notion that older people experience incoming stimuli less intensely than young people; rather the evidence seems to suggest that their incipient emotions are just as strong and negative, but that the self-regulatory capacity of older adults is to credit for their improved emotional health.

This pattern indicates that the ability to recruit self-regulatory resources may well increase with age.

Some research suggests that cognitive strategies can modify depletion effects. Some self-regulatory resources are kept "in reserve," and consumers may learn if–then rules for when to decide whether to conserve or to expend their remaining self-regulatory resources. Recall that Muraven et al. (2006) demonstrated that people are able to conserve their resources in anticipation of an important upcoming task. This too would seem to be a skill that would develop with age, as the tendency to adopt a longer time horizon grows (Bettinger & Slonim, 2007). Other work has found that if people think positively about their ability to accomplish a goal, they may temporarily overcome depletion effects (Martijn, Tenbült, Dreezens, & de Vries, 2002). Children are often told childhood stories (about trains) that teach them to think, "I think I can, I think I can," which may well be another tactic to aid in recruiting self-regulatory resources once they have been diminished (cf. Martijn et al., 2002).

Section Summary

Although children are able to self-regulate while young and therefore are in clear possession of self-regulatory resources, there are strategies that children do not know that could help them better use their self-regulatory resources. We speculate that strategies are underdeveloped in children and may improve with age.

Brief Review and Concluding Remarks

This chapter reviewed and integrated some of the myriad findings on self-regulatory resource depletion that are being uncovered. We started by outlining work that was done to test basic parameters of the model, which have shown strong support for the six underlying components of the limited-resource model:

1. The resource is consumed by self-regulation attempts;
2. consequently, acts of self-regulation are impaired;
3. there is a broad range of activities that governed by self-regulatory resources, suggesting that they are global;
4. the deleterious effects of self-regulatory resource depletion are short lived;
5. people may engage in acts that promote the replenishment of the resource;
6. people may conserve the resource before it becomes fully depleted.

We parsed our discussion of the domain-specific findings into those related more closely to the intrapersonal or the interpersonal sphere. There seems to be ample evidence now that internal acts of self-control drain self-regulatory resources, such that engaging in one intrapsychic process relating to self-regulation has strong effects on other intrapsychic processes that require controlled responding. Evidence in the interpersonal sphere, on the other hand, is only beginning to emerge, but this effect seems to be just as strong—and with good reason. Self-regulation most likely did not emerge in human ancestral times for the initial purpose of regulating internal processes for internal needs. Rather, people engaged in self-regulation to be accepted by others and included into groups. Consider that one did not control one's emotional expressions unless it led to some interpersonal advantage, which apparently it did because humans have this capacity still today. Hence, the connection between interpersonal goals and internal self-control is likely quite robust because being a controlled person promoted social inclusion (see Vohs et al., 2005).

The discussion of the domains in which researchers have found linkages between self-control endeavors and other processes naturally leads to the question of what exactly is this resource that we have been discussing? We have answered that question by drawing upon two research streams, one distinguishing the self-regulatory resource model from other forms of basic cognitive processes. A crop of data indicates that engaging in self-regulation is not equivalent to engaging in just any kind of cognitive maneuvers. Vohs and Schmeichel (2003) showed evidence of this in their experiment contrasting emotion suppression to emotion reappraisal and found that only the former left traces of self-regulatory resource depletion. Schmeichel (2007) showed definitively that task difficulty and effort expended cannot account for self-regulatory resource-depletion effects, but that depletion only occurs after engaging the self-control system. A second research stream that we point to for answers to this question pertains to the active take-up of glucose during controlled responding (Gailliot et al., 2007), which seems to mediate the effects of self-regulation on later attempts at self-control.

Last, we discussed the implications of the limited-resource model for capacity to engage in self-regulation across the life span. This section of the chapter was admittedly less data driven, but we were encouraged by the linkages across developmental psychological findings regarding self-control and ideas from the limited-resource model. Children and older adults appear to use their self-regulatory resources differently, with the former not being aware of mental strategies to harness what self-regulatory resources they have and the latter group being quite adept at effective self-regulation. Much work could be done in this area to bridge the two perspectives, and we encourage interested readers to test some of these (or others) assertions and report back to us about their findings.

In closing, we hope this chapter has conveyed the power of the limited-resource model of self-regulation to predict and explain patterns of self-control. Work on self-regulation has multiplied over the decades, and unfortunately during this time losses of self-control have become widespread (perhaps this is an anti-Flynn effect). With better modeling of the processes that govern self-control, researchers and practitioners may be able to make strides in combating the temptations and impulses that surround people today.

References

Baddeley, A. D., & Hitch, G. (1974). Working memory. In G. H. Bower (Ed.), *The psychology of learning and motivation: Advances in research and theory* (Vol. 8, pp. 47–89). New York: Academic Press.

Baumeister, R. F., Bratslavsky, E., Muraven, M., & Tice, D. M. (1998). Ego depletion: Is the active self a limited resource? *Journal of Personality and Social Psychology, 74,* 1252–1265.

Baumeister, R. F., Schmeichel, B. J., & Vohs, K. D. (2007). Self-regulation and the executive function: The self as controlling agent. In A. W. Kruglanski & E. T. Higgins (Eds.), *Social psychology: Handbook of basic principles* (2nd ed., pp. 516–539). New York: Guilford Press.

Bettinger, E., & Slonim, R. (2007). Patience among children: Evidence from a field experiment. *Journal of Public Economics, 91,* 343–363.

Bouchard, T. J., Jr., Lykken, D. T., McGue, M., Segal, N. L., & Tellegen, A. (1990). Sources of human psychological differences: The Minnesota Study of Twins Reared Apart. *Science, 250,* 223–228.

Carstensen, L. L., Pasupathi, M., Mayr, U., & Nesselroade, J. (2000). Emotional experience in everyday life across the adult life span. *Journal of Personality and Social Psychology, 79,* 644–655.

Chartrand, T. L., & Bargh, J. A. (1999). The chameleon effect: The perception–behavior link and social interaction. *Journal of Personality and Social Psychology, 76,* 893–910.

Deci, E. L., & Ryan, R. M. (1995). Human autonomy: The basis for true self-esteem. In M. Kernis (Ed.), *Efficacy, agency, and self-esteem* (pp. 31–49). New York: Plenum.

Dewitte, S., Pandelaere, M., Briers, B., & Warlop, L. (2005). *Cognitive load has negative aftereffects on consumer decision making.* Available at *www.ssrn. com/abstract=813684.*

Duval, S., & Wicklund, R. A. (1972). *A theory of objective self-awareness.* San Diego: Academic Press.

Finkel, E. J., Dalton, A. M., Campbell, W. K., Brunell, A. B., Scarbeck, S. J., & Chartrand, T. L. (2006). High-maintenance interaction: Inefficient social coordination impairs self-regulation. *Journal of Personality and Social Psychology, 91,* 456–475.

Flynn, J. R. (1987). Massive IQ gains in 14 nations: What IQ tests really measure. *Psychological Bulletin, 101,* 171–191.

Gailliot, M. T., & Baumeister, R. F. (2007). Self-regulation and sexual restraint: Dispositionally and temporarily poor self-regulatory abilities contribute to failures at restraining sexual behavior. *Personality and Social Psychology Bulletin, 33,* 173–186.

Gailliot, M. T., Baumeister, R. F., DeWall, C. N., Maner, J. K., Plant, E. A., Tice, D. M., et al. (2007). Self-control relies on glucose as a limited energy source: Willpower is more than a metaphor. *Journal of Personality and Social Psychology, 92,* 325–336.

Gailliot, M. T., Plant, E. A., Butz, D. A., & Baumeister, R. F. (2007). Increasing self-regulatory strength can reduce the depleting effect of suppressing stereotypes. *Personality and Social Psychology Bulletin, 33,* 281–294.

Gollwitzer, P. M. (1990). Action phases and mind-sets. In E. T. Higgins & R. M. Sorrentino (Eds.), *Handbook of motivation and cognition* (Vol. 2, pp. 53–92). New York: Guilford Press.

Gross, J. J., Carstensen, L. L., Pasupathi, M., Hsu, A. Y. C., & Tsai, J. (1997). Emotion and aging: Experience, expression, and control. *Psychology and Aging, 12*(4), 590–599.

Higgins, E. T. (1987). Self-discrepancy: A theory relating self to affect. *Psychological Review, 94,* 319–340.

Hoch, S. J., & Loewenstein, G. F. (1991). Time-inconsistent preferences and consumer self-control. *Journal of Consumer Research, 17,* 492–507.

Hull, J. G. (1981). A self-awareness model of the causes and effects of alcohol consumption. *Journal of Abnormal Psychology, 90,* 586–600.

Inzlicht, M., McKay, L., & Aronson, J. (2006). Stigma as ego-depletion: How being the target of prejudice affects self-control. *Psychological Science, 17,* 262–269.

Labouvie-Vief, G., Hakim-Larson, J., DeVoe, M., & Schoeberlein, S. (1989). Emotions and self-regulation: A life span view. *Human Development, 32*(5), 279–299.

Lawton, M. P., Kleban, M. H., & Dean, J. (1993). Affect and age: Cross-sectional comparisons of structure and prevalence. *Psychology and Aging, 8*(2), 165–175.

Locke, E. A., & Latham, G. P. (1990). *A theory of goal-setting and task performance.* Englewood Cliffs, NJ: Prentice Hall.

Mann, T., Tomiyama, A. J., Westling, E., Lew, A., Samuels, B., & Chatman, J. (2007). Medicare's search for effective obesity treatments: Diets are not the answer. *American Psychologist, 62,* 220–233.

Martijn, C., Tenbült, P., Dreezens, E., & de Vries, N. K. (2002). Getting a grip on ourselves: Challenging expectancies about loss of energy after self-control. *Social Cognition, 20*(6), 441–460.

Mischel, W., & Ebbesen, E. B. (1970). Attention in delay of gratification. *Journal of Personality and Social Psychology, 16,* 329–337.

Mischel, W., Ebbesen, E. B., & Zeiss, A. R. (1972). Cognitive and attentional mechanisms in delay of gratification. *Journal of Personality and Social Psychology, 21*, 204–218.

Mitchell, J. P., Heatherton, T. F., & Macrae, C. N. (2002). Distinct neural systems subserve person and object knowledge. *Proceedings of the National Academy of Sciences, 99*, 15238–15243.

Muraven, M., Baumeister, R. F., & Tice, D. M. (1999). Longitudinal improvement of self-regulation through practice: Building self-control strength through repeated exercise. *Journal of Social Psychology, 139*, 446–457.

Muraven, M., Shmueli, D., & Burkley, E. (2006). Conserving self-control strength. *Journal of Personality and Social Psychology, 91*, 524–537.

Muraven, M., Tice, D. M., & Baumeister, R. F. (1998). Self-control as limited resource: Regulatory depletion patterns. *Journal of Personality and Social Psychology, 74*, 774–789.

Oaten, M., & Cheng, K. (2006). Longitudinal gains in self-regulation from regular physical exercise. *British Journal of Health Psychology, 11*, 717–733.

Oettingen, G., Pak, H., & Schnetter, K. (2001). Self-regulation of goal-setting: Turning free fantasies about the future into binding goals. *Journal of Personality and Social Psychology, 80*, 736–753.

Polivy, J. (1998). The effects of behavioral inhibition: Integrating internal cues, cognition, behavior, and affect. *Psychological Inquiry, 9*, 181–204.

Richeson, J. A., & Shelton, J. N. (2003). When prejudice does not pay: Effects of interracial contact on executive function. *Psychological Science, 14*, 287–290.

Rook, D. W. (1987). The buying impulse. *Journal of Consumer Research, 14*, 189–199.

Schmeichel, B. J. (2007). Attention control, memory updating, and emotion regulation temporarily reduce the capacity for executive control. *Journal of Experimental Psychology: General, 136*, 241–255.

Schmeichel, B. J., Vohs, K. D., & Baumeister, R. F. (2003). Ego depletion and intelligent performance: Role of the self in logical reasoning and other information processing. *Journal of Personality and Social Psychology, 85*, 33–46.

Sünram-Lea, S. I., Foster, J. K., Durlach, P., & Perez, C. (2002). Investigation into the significance of task difficulty and divided allocation of resources on the glucose memory facilitation effect. *Psychopharmacology, 160*, 387–397.

Vaillant, G. E. (1977). *Adaptation to life: How the best and the brightest came of age.* Boston: Little, Brown.

Vohs, K. D., Baumeister, R. F., & Ciarocco, N. J. (2005). Self-regulation and self-presentation: Regulatory resource depletion impairs impression management and effortful self-presentation depletes regulatory resources. *Journal of Personality and Social Psychology, 88*, 632–657.

Vohs, K. D., Baumeister, R. F., & Tice, D. M. (2008). Self-regulation: Goals, consumption, and choices. In C. P. Haugtvedt, P. Herr, & F. Kardes (Eds.), *Handbook of consumer psychology* (pp. 349–366). New York: LEA/Psychology Press.

Vohs, K. D., Baumeister, R. F., Schmeichel, B. J., Twenge, J. M., Nelson, N. M.,

& Tice, D. M. (2008). Making choices impairs subsequent self-control: A limited resource account of decision making, self-regulation, and active initiative. *Journal of Personality and Social Psychology, 94,* 883–898.

Vohs, K. D., & Faber, R. (2007). Spent resources: Self-regulatory resource availability affects impulse buying. *Journal of Consumer Research, 33,* 537–549.

Vohs, K. D., & Finkel, E. J. (2006). *Self and relationships: Connecting intrapersonal and interpersonal processes.* New York: Guilford Press.

Vohs, K. D., & Heatherton, T. F. (2000). Self-esteem and threats to self: Implications for self-construals and interpersonal perceptions. *Journal of Personality and Social Psychology, 81,* 1103–1118.

Vohs, K. D., & Schmeichel, B. J. (2003). Self-regulation and the extended now: Controlling the self alters the subjective experience of time. *Journal of Personality and Social Psychology, 85,* 217–230.

Ward, A., & Mann, T. (2000). Don't mind if I do: Disinhibited eating under cognitive load. *Journal of Personality and Social Psychology, 78,* 753–763.

CHAPTER 17

Goals and (Implicit) Attitudes
A SOCIAL-COGNITIVE PERSPECTIVE

MELISSA J. FERGUSON
SHANETTE C. PORTER

G oals and attitudes are two of the most central constructs within social psychology. They each have a long history of scholarship and remain key fixtures in contemporary research. However, the nature of the relationship between these two constructs has (understandably) received relatively less attention than each construct individually. Part of the problem may be that the definition of each (and especially of goals) lacks consistency in the literature (e.g., see Albarracín, Johnson, & Zanna, 2005; Elliot & Fryer, 2007), and each topic has become somewhat segregated from the other in terms of paradigms, research questions, and common operationalizations. We argue that the burgeoning work on automaticity over the last two decades, however, has helped to sharpen the social-cognitive definition of these two constructs, and this in turn encourages a potential theoretical integration of the two. In this chapter we explore this integration and review some recent empirical work relevant to it.

We describe two recent areas of research on the relationship between attitudes and goals. In the first empirical section (How Goals Influence Attitudes), we present evidence that the activation of a goal has implications for implicit attitudes toward goal-related stimuli (Ferguson, 2007c; Ferguson & Bargh, 2004; Seibt, Hafner, & Deutsch, 2007; Sherman, Presson, Chassin, Rose, & Koch, 2003). These effects on attitudes are unique to goal activation and cannot be reduced to mere semantic priming. We also consider the effects of conscious as well as nonconscious goal activation on attitudes, and the importance of regulatory success at obtaining a goal. In the second empirical section (How Attitudes Influence Goals), we review work that demonstrates the predictive validity and influence of implicit attitudes on motivation and successful goal pursuit. In this section we review the recent findings that implicit attitudes toward concrete goal-related stimuli can increase one's motivation to approach those stimuli (Aarts, Custers, & Holland, 2007; Custers & Aarts, 2005), and that implicit attitudes toward abstract goals can significantly predict goal success (Ferguson, 2007a). The findings that we summarize in the two empirical sections together suggest an iterative and dynamic relationship between goals and implicit attitudes. That is, our pursuit of goals has implications for how we evaluate the stimuli in our environment, and the way in which we evaluate the stimuli in our environment has implications for our goal pursuit.

Before reviewing the empirical work, we provide a social-cognitive account of goals and attitudes. Although there are, in our opinion, multiple and serious unanswered questions regarding the cognitive underpinnings of each construct, we try to identify some common elements in the literature today from a social-cognitive framework. We also describe the ways in which these two constructs are commonly measured in contemporary work. We begin with a social cognitive account of attitudes.

What Is an Attitude?

Attitudes represent one of the field's most central constructs. The definition of "attitudes" has fluctuated over the last 70 years but has always retained the notion of an evaluative component (e.g., Allport, 1935; Brown, 1998; Eagly & Chaiken, 1993; Higgins & Brendl, 1996; McGuire, 1969, 1985; Osgood, Suci, & Tannenbaum, 1957; Rosenberg, 1965; Tesser & Martin, 1996; Zajonc, 2000). In the mid-1990s, Fazio and colleagues argued that an attitude can be defined as the positivity or negativity associated with an object in memory, which is a process-oriented, social-cognitive elaboration of the evaluative element of traditional definitions of "attitudes" (see Fazio, 1990, 1995, 2001, 2007). In line with this definition, Fazio and colleagues (Fazio, Sanbonmatsu, Powell, & Kardes, 1986) developed a paradigm to measure the evaluative information that becomes spontaneously (vs. deliberately) activated in memory whenever the object is perceived (see section on Measures of Attitudes). In this way, this work heralded the beginning of research in social psychology on implicitly measured attitudes, and since then research on the topic has been accumulating rapidly (for reviews, see Petty, Fazio, & Brinol, in press; Wittenbrink & Schwarz, 2007).

Although we adopt this general definition of an attitude, we provide a more detailed social-cognitive account of an attitude, including what the attitude as well as the attitude *object* entails. We should note that there is considerable disagreement and uncertainty among researchers about what exactly an attitude reflects, how an explicitly measured attitude differs from an implicitly measured one, and so on. A discussion of these issues is beyond the purview of the current chapter, but we refer readers to recent chapters, articles, and books that cover such topics (e.g., Bassili & Brown, 2005; Ferguson, 2007b; Gawronski & Bodenhausen, 2006; Petty et al., 2007; Wittenbrink & Schwarz, 2007). We begin with some assumptions about the content as well as structure of memories involved in an attitude and attitude object.

Content of an Attitude and an Attitude Object

In terms of the content of memories related to an attitude, it seems necessary to address the content of memories underlying an attitude, as well as the content of memories that underlie the object with which an attitude is associated.

The Attitude

An "attitude" (or evaluation) has been defined simply as positivity or negativity. The question of whether affective processes are involved in evaluation is still a relatively open issue (i.e., "cold" vs. "hot" evaluative information). Although there seems to be a consensus that affective processes can influence how one's evaluation of an object develops, there is still some uncertainty about how often affective processing is involved each time the object is perceived (see Amodio & Devine, 2006; Fazio, 2007; LeDoux, 1996).

It should be noted that affective (or emotional) states share some similarities with evaluations. For example, both are generated in response to stimuli—and, in fact, both can be tied to a specific stimulus. Relative to evaluations, however, affective states tend to be longer lasting and more sustainable (e.g., Tesser & Martin, 1996). Moreover, whereas an evaluation is simply positive or negative, an affective state involves some degree of positive or negative (e.g., happy, surprised, angry, or sad). Perhaps most important is that affective states are, by definition, conscious experiences (see Davidson, Scherer, & Goldsmith, 2003), whereas the types of evaluations discussed here can be nonconscious.

Mood states also share some features with evaluations (e.g., they are often characterized as generally positive or negative). Like affective states, however, mood states can be distinguished from evaluations given classic assumptions that mood states occur consciously (see Davidson et al., 2003; though see Winkielman, Berridge, & Wilbarger, 2005). Mood states also tend to have lengthy durations (see Thayer, 1989) and tend not to be tied to a particular stimulus (see Thayer, 1989; Davidson et al., 2003), unlike attitudes.

The Attitude Object

The term "attitude object" has been traditionally used to refer to the stimulus that is being evaluated. An attitude object consists of anything that can be discriminated (Eagly & Chaiken, 1993) and merely needs to exist as a "psychological" entity (Thurstone, 1931). Thus, it can refer to people, images, values, goals, smells, letters, sounds, pictures, animals, physical objects, and so on. In this way, the content of memories involved in the perception and processing of any object can clearly vary widely. The term "attitude object" is therefore extremely broad and all encompassing and is essentially synonymous with "stimulus." We will use the terms "stimulus" and "object" interchangeably throughout the chapter.

Structure of an Attitude and an Attitude Object

We now outline some characteristics about the structure of the memories involved in an attitude (and attitude object). We should emphasize that these characteristics are not mutually exclusive but in many ways share considerable theoretical assumptions and overlap. We chose to highlight these three characteristics because they seem most relevant to the question of how goals and attitudes might influence one another from a social-cognitive perspective.

Multiple Memories

How is any given object represented? There is considerable controversy and ongoing research on this question that is beyond the scope of this chapter. However, we maintain and reiterate the basic assumption in the literature that the perception of any stimulus evokes a wide range of memories, rather than a single, static, and isolated category (e.g., Abelson, 1976, 1981; Barsalou, 1992; Bower, 1981; Carlston, 1994; Fishbein & Ajzen, 1975; Fiske & Pavelchak, 1986; Schank & Abelson, 1977; Smith, 1992; Smith & Zarate, 1992). For instance, reading the word "chocolate" should elicit a range of memories, the activation of some of which the perceiver undoubtedly remains consciously unaware (see also Ferguson & Bargh, 2004a). This means that an array of memories will be activated on the perception of any stimulus, and which memories are activated will depend on their baseline accessibility as well as the fit between them and the incoming stimulus (e.g., see Bruner, 1957; Higgins, 1996, for further discussion).

What does the above assumption imply for the attitude that is measured for a certain stimulus? We assume that many memories are stored in memory with valenced information. However, the critical question is whether the attitude that is observed (i.e., measured) reflects the evaluative information associated with a single memory (or category), or reflects an integration across pieces of evaluative information (see Bassili & Brown, 2005; Ferguson, 2007b). In the former case, the attitude could be understood as reflecting a unitary (evaluative) memory. However, in the latter case, the attitude would be understood as reflecting the integration of multiple evaluative memories. We return to this issue in the section on information processing.

Another relevant issue is whether a single attitude or multiple attitudes are associated with a given object in memory (e.g., Wilson, Lindsey, & Schooler, 2000). Given the complexity of information likely associated with any given object in memory, we assume that different types of evaluative information can be associated with the memories that relate to a given object.

Varying Accessibility

The accessibility of any (attitude) object varies in its accessibility in memory. Assuming that most objects are associated with evaluative information (however it may be represented), it also follows that the accessibility of the attitude toward any object will vary in accord with the object's accessibility. To what degree, however, is the accessibility of an attitude completely dependent on the accessibility of the corresponding object? Fazio and colleagues have shown that the association(s) between an object and its attitude can vary across situations and people (e.g., Fazio, 1990, 1995, 2001). For instance, the more that people express their attitude toward an object, the more quickly that attitude will be activated spontaneously when they encounter that object at a subsequent time point. However, making a nonevaluative judgment repeatedly about an object does not necessarily influence the ease with which its associated attitude will become activated subsequently. This suggests that the association between an attitude and an object is not fixed, or static, but rather changes depending on the nature of recent and frequent processing. We also note that if a measured attitude reflects the integration of multiple evaluative memories, then it naturally follows that the accessibility of that measured attitude may vary somewhat independently of the accessibility of some of the respective object memories.

There is an important implication of the fact that an object likely consists of multiple memories that fluctuate in their accessibility, and that those object memories in turn may be associated with various (and different) evaluative memories. Namely, the way in which any object is evaluated will depend on the way in which that object is perceived and constructed. That is, because the array of memories relevant to any given object can easily vary in their evaluative connotation, the attitude that is spontaneously activated in response to perceiving an object will depend on which object memories are most accessible at that time. There is considerable evidence for the contextual dependence of explicit and implicit attitudes (e.g., for reviews see Albarracin et al., 2005; Petty, Fazio, & Briñol, 2009; Schwarz & Bohner, 2001).

Principles of Information Processing

We assume that basic principles of information processing can describe the interconnections between object memories, the interconnections between evaluative memories, and the interconnections between the two (Anderson, 1983; Anderson & Reder, 1999; Collins & Loftus, 1975; Neely, 1977, 1991; Posner & Snyder, 1975; Shiffrin & Schneider, 1977). Although the overview of models of cognitive architecture and processing is beyond the scope of this chapter, we assume merely that memories can be interconnected via excitatory links, such that the activation of one memory leads to the activation of connected memories. Other memories can be connected via inhibitory links, where the activation of one memory leads to the inhibition of others.

In addition to the directional nature of associations between object and evaluative memories, associations also vary in their strength. Thus, some object memories may be strongly associated with each other, as well as with evaluative information, whereas others may not. Researchers have long claimed that the strength of the association between the evaluative information and the object influences the ease with which the attitude is activated spontaneously and unintentionally on perception of the object (e.g., for a review, see Fazio, 2001; in press; Petty et al., 2009).

As far as how the attitude itself (the evaluative information) is represented, researchers have tended to assume that memories are discrete and are associated with either a positive or negative summary tag of some sort (Bargh, Chaiken, Govender, & Pratt, 1992; Fazio et al., 1986; Fiske & Pavelchek, 1986; Wilson et al., 2000), or are distributed and instantiated within connectionist frameworks (e.g., Bassili & Brown, 2005; Eiser, Fazio, Stafford, & Prescott, 2003; Eiser, Stafford, & Fazio, 2008). We consider this to be an extremely important question for future research.

Measures of Attitudes

Throughout most of the history of social psychology, researchers have been measuring people's attitudes in an explicit manner, that is, by asking people to report their attitudes. For example, to assess how people feel about George Bush, researchers may ask respondents to indicate how positively they view him using a 10-point scale (with 1 = *not at all* and 10 = *very much*). Large segments of academic disciplines as well as private industries (e.g., psychology, advertising, political science, etc.) still rely on this kind of self-report methodology to assess people's attitudes toward any number of products, candidates, policies, and so on. It was commonly assumed until the last two decades that people's evaluations were primarily or solely based on a deliberate analysis about how they felt, taking into account various factors, issues, and dimensions (see Schwarz & Bohner, 2001). Many researchers assumed that evaluation is a process that is accessible to, and enabled by, conscious and intentional thought (see Albarracin et al., 2005).

Over the last two decades, however, the theory and methodology in the area of attitudes have changed dramatically. First, researchers have continued to document how easily and readily people edit their explicit attitudes for reasons that have little to do with their actual attitudes toward the stimuli. There is also some suggestion (more theoretical than empirical at this point; see Gawronski, LeBel, & Peters, 2007) that people may at times be unable to explicitly access the information relevant to their attitude (e.g., Wilson & Dunn, 2004). Thus, it is not always clear whether someone's explicitly reported attitude will match up with other indices that would reflect the person's attitude (i.e., their attitude-relevant behavior). This conclusion is in accord with the claim that explicit attitudes are better conceptualized as verbal expressions of the underlying attitudes, rather than as the attitudes themselves (see Thurstone, 1928, p. 531; Fazio, 2007).

Second, contemporary measures of attitudes have been adapted from the indirect methodologies of cognitive psychology and thus allow for implicit, or automatic, attitude measurement (e.g., Neely, 1977; Logan, 1980; Meyer & Shavaneveldt, 1971). Several implicit measures have been developed, such as the Go/No-go Association Task (Nosek & Banaji, 2001), the Affective Simon Task (De Houwer, 2003), and the Affect Misattribution Procedure (Payne, Cheng, Govorun, & Stewart, 2005). The most utilized of implicit attitude measures, however, continues to be the evaluative priming paradigm (Fazio et al., 1986) and the Implicit Association Test (IAT; Greenwald, McGhee, & Schwarz, 1998). Because most of the research described in this chapter utilized an evaluative priming paradigm, we briefly describe it below.

The evaluative priming paradigm measures the extent to which a stimulus activates particular evaluative information (positivity or negativity) using reaction times derived from a computer task. This paradigm can be thought of as a specialized case of sequential priming. Thus, first a "prime" stimulus (e.g., a picture of an elderly person, or the word "old") is presented on a computer screen either subliminally or supraliminally, but in either case, typically for fewer than 250 milliseconds (see Fazio et al., 1986; Neely, 1977). Next, a "target" stimulus is presented. This target stimulus is either positively (e.g., puppy) or negatively (e.g., spider) valenced. The participant then rapidly categorizes the target stimulus as positive or negative using labeled keys. Researchers have found that participants are quicker, on average, to make a correct decision about the target stimulus if it is evaluatively congruent with the prime stimulus (e.g., for a review, see Fazio, 2001; 2007; Fazio & Olsen, 2003; Musch & Klauer, 2003). Thus, it has been concluded that in addition to semantically related knowledge, evaluative information becomes activated without a person's awareness, intention, or control on perception of a stimulus.

What Is a Goal?

Goals have a long and interesting history in psychology. For a construct that figures so prominently in the literature, across areas of social psychology and the social sciences more broadly, the definition of a "goal" varies widely, and there seems to be little consensus (e.g., see Elliot & Fryer, 2007). For example, definitions vary in terms of the abstractness of the goal, the commitment involved, the consciousness involved, the future oriented aspect to goals, and so on. One common theme across definitions, however, is that goals reflect the end points toward which behavior is directed. Directed behavior can consist of trying to procure or maintain something (approach behaviors) or trying to avoid or get rid of something (avoidance behaviors).

Fishbach and Ferguson (2007) recently provided a definition of a "goal" as a cognitive representation of a desired end point that impacts evaluations, emotions and behaviors. Elements of this definition overlap to varying degrees with other definitions offered over the years (e.g., see Bargh, 1990; Carver & Scheier, 1981; Gollwitzer & Moskowitz, 1996; Higgins & Kruglanski, 2000; Locke & Latham, 1990; Moskowitz, Li, & Kirk, 2004; Sorrentino & Higgins, 1986). Fishbach and Ferguson also speculated on the content of a goal in memory, along with three structural aspects of a goal, which we review below. We have added some detail and additional explanation beyond what was provided by Fishbach and Ferguson. Several other conceptualizations of goals can be found throughout this volume.

Content of a Goal

End Point and Means

In terms of the content of memories included in a goal construct, Fishbach and Ferguson (2007) argued that goals will usually contain an end point along with various information about how to reach that end point (means, strategies), objects that are associated with the end point or associated goals, and related information about temptations to the goal, alternatives to the goal, and consequences of the goals (Hommel, Muesseler, Aschersleben, & Prinz, 2001; Jeannerod, 1997; Kornblum, Hasbroucq, & Osman, 1990; Kruglanski et al., 2002; Miller, Galanter, & Pribram, 1960; Powers, 1973). This information can presumably vary considerably in terms of referring to the short versus long term, concrete versus abstract, and simple versus complex. For example, an end point and its associated means might consist of making a cup of coffee within the next 10 minutes, or attempting to become more creative over the next year.

Affective Information

Second, to qualify as a goal, memories related to the end point (and perhaps means) have to be associated to some degree with positive or negative evaluative information. The affective information is what gives a goal its motivational force (Carver & Scheier, 1981; Custers & Aarts, 2005; Kruglanski et al., 2002; Peak, 1955; Pervin, 1989; Shah, Kruglanski, & Friedman, 2002; Young, 1961). This claim is in concert with previous work on goals and follows the assumption that people are motivated to approach those things they view as positive, and avoid those things that they regard as negative (Arnold, 1960; Bogardus, 1931; Corwin, 1921; Doob, 1947; Frijda, 1986; Lang, 1984; Lazarus, 1991; Lewin, 1935; Mowrer, 1960; Osgood, 1953; Thurstone, 1931; Young, 1959).

We also argue here that the evaluative information in a goal construct must be somewhat strong. Goals are usually considered as factors that guide our behavior and inform our decisions and therefore play a more or less central role in our daily lives. This means that goals must be sufficiently positive or negative to beat out all the other demands on our time and attention. It follows that an array of knowledge about some end point (building a tree house) and the associated means to reach it would not qualify as a goal if it were not associated with fairly strong evaluative information.

Commitment

Some researchers have argued that a person's commitment to a goal is a critical aspect of the definition (e.g., Elliot & Fryer, 2007). We agree that a person's commitment to a pursuit is an important aspect of what it means to possess a goal, but we argue that the degree of commitment that someone reports on an explicit measure may simply constitute an emergent phenomenon. That is, people may infer their level of commitment based on the kinds of memories that become activated when introspecting on the goal. We speculate here that one potentially important determinant of this inference is the degree of evaluative information that becomes activated in association with goal during introspection. The more strongly people experience affect when thinking about the goal (either positive or negative), the more commitment they may report to either attain or avoid it, respectively.

Expectancy Information

The extent to which a person expects to be able to meet a goal has been assumed to be part of what it means to possess a goal, in line with expectancy-value theories of motivation (e.g., Atkinson, 1974; Tolman, 1932). Expectancy has often been measured explicitly, and so we again argue that it may be an emergent characteristic that depends on the types of goal-related memories that become accessible while the person is speculating on the goal. In particular, it may depend on the degree to which people have available and accessible memories about their previous successes at the goal. The more that people can easily think about such successes, the more they should expect (and predict) success. Thus, it is unclear whether the notion of expectancy is an emergent belief (one that depends on the number of success or failure accessible memories) or as a stored belief in its own right. It is also possible that expectancy beliefs, however they are represented and generated, may interact with evaluative information to inform explicit assessments of commitment. For example, the more someone expects to be successful, and the more he/she feels positivity toward the goal, the more commitment he/she may report.

Structure of a Goal

The three structural aspects of goals outlined by Fishbach and Ferguson (2007) follow more or less seamlessly from the assumption that goals are represented in memory, an assumption that has been echoed by various theorists throughout the years (Bargh, 1990; Hull, 1931; Kruglanski, 1996; Moskowitz et al., 2004; Tolman, 1932) but has not always been explicitly emphasized. Additionally, these structural aspects also follow from assumptions about the content of goals listed above, as well as from basic social-cognitive principles of information processing.

Multiple Memories

One important structural aspect of a goal is that it likely does not consist of a static, uniform, singular memory but instead consists of many memories, all of which may vary in their format (e.g., visual, semantic, episodic) and content (e.g., end point, means, objects, affect). This suggests that perhaps we should refer to a goal as a "goal network" or "goal constellation" to explicitly highlight the fact that many memories are involved in any desired end point (e.g., see Kruglanski, 1996).

The claim that any given goal likely consists of many interconnected memories raises an important theoretical point. Namely, it is unclear when a cluster of memories should be classified as part of one goal versus another, or as unrelated to any goal. Where do the goal boundaries end? Future research could investigate this by perhaps testing, for instance, the memories that are relatively strongly (automatically) associated with some common theme of the goal. This kind of systematic analysis of the strength of the associations between goal-relevant memories could at least identify those goal-related memories that are most likely to exert an influence in goal-related situations.

Varying Accessibility

A second structural aspect of a goal is that it likely varies in its accessibility in memory, which means that a given goal will fluctuate in its influence on behavior. The more accessible a goal (over time, and also compared with other goal networks), the more influential it should be, a claim that is in line with assumptions about the relationship between the accessibility of knowledge and the influence of that knowledge in interpretation and behavior (Higgins, 1996). In fact, the influence of a goal on behavior should depend directly on it being relatively accessible in memory. In this way, when a person is in a goal state (e.g., thirsty), memories associated with that goal should by definition be more accessible in memory compared with when the goal is not active. Recent research as well as classical theory provides support for this notion (Aarts et al., 2007; Ach, 1935; Balcetis & Dunning, 2006; Bargh, 1997; Bruner, 1957; Bruner & Postman, 1948; Förster et al., 2005; Gollwitzer, 1996; Jones & Thibaut, 1958; Klinger, 1996; Kruglanski, 1996; Kuhl, 1987; McClelland & Atkinson, 1948; Moskowitz, 2002).

Given the previous structural characteristic that a goal consists of multiple memories, however, it should be clear that parts of the goal network may become more accessible than others at times. Thus, when sitting in the library studying, the memories associated with an academic achievement goal that are activated may be somewhat different from those memories associated with achievement that become activated while choosing classes for the semester. This means that the nature of a goal—in terms of its underlying representations and thus its impact on behavior—may be quite different across time and situations. This suggests that thinking about a goal as a singular, static construct is potentially misleading.

Because we view the evaluative information included in a goal network as the critical factor that provides the goal's motivational force, the accessibility of the evaluative information should also vary depending on whether the goal is "active" or not. In other words, the influence of a goal on behavior is due to not just the accessibility of the memories generally, but the accessibility of the evaluative information connected with those memories. Again, this implies that when the goal is active, there should be greater positivity or negativity toward at least some of the memories in the goal network, compared with when the goal is not active, and, importantly, compared with when the goal has been fulfilled.

Principles of Processing and Interconnections

The third structural characteristic of a goal provided by Fishbach and Ferguson (2007) is that the memories involved in a goal network become activated according to classical knowledge activation principles (Anderson, 1983; Anderson & Reder, 1999; Collins & Loftus, 1975; Neely, 1977, 1991; Posner & Snyder, 1975; Shiffrin & Schneider, 1977). Just as with the memories involved in any object, and perhaps any attitude, this means that some goal-related memories will be interconnected via excitatory connections whereas others will be connected via inhibitory links. For example, people who are highly skilled at a goal start thinking about that goal whenever they encounter temptations (Fishbach, Friedman, & Kruglanski, 2003), illustrating that temptations possess excitatory connections with the longer-term goal. On the other hand, when highly skilled regulators think about their goals, thoughts about alternative options or temptations may become inhibited (Fishbach, Friedman, & Kruglanski, 2003), which suggests that goals can be connected to temptations via inhibitory links. These examples illustrate the directedness of associations, in that even though X may activate Y in an excitatory manner, Y may activate X in an inhibitory way.

Just as with memories underlying any stimulus, the memories in a goal network are likely going to vary in terms of not only the nature of the connection, but also the strength of the association. That is, some of the associations will be sufficiently strong such that the activation of one memory will automatically lead to the activation of certain others. For instance, for some people, and not others, the memories reflecting "library" and "class" will be strongly (vs. weakly) interconnected within the goal network related to achievement. The degree to which the activation of memories in response to a given stimulus excites or inhibits other related memories may depend to some extent on the depth of processing of that first stimulus. Thus, whereas the mere inkling (i.e., shallow processing) of "summer" may activate certain memories about swimming in the ocean (refreshing water, fun waves), more extensive thought about the summer can activate different kinds of memories about swimming (salty water, potential sharks), or different summer-related memories altogether. This means that implicitly perceiving a goal-relevant stimulus may qualify as shallower processing compared with being consciously put into a goal state. Thus, there may be interesting differences in the "spread of activation" throughout a goal network after implicit versus explicit goal priming. It may be the case that a different set of memories is accessible in one versus the other case, with potential downstream consequences for behavior.

Although the processing that underlies goals is in accord with classical research on information processing, it does not seem to operate in the same way as with other, non-goal concepts (see Förster, Liberman, & Friedman, 2007). One distinctive characteristic of the operation of goals is that once the goal becomes accessible in memory, it will stay accessible or even increase in accessibility until the goal is met or abandoned (Atkinson & Birch, 1970; Gollwitzer & Moskowitz, 1996; Lewin, 1936; McClelland, Atkinson, Clark, & Lowell, 1953). This is quite unlike the accessibility of a non-goal concept, which tends to decay rapidly. Another distinctive characteristic of the memories underlying goals is that once a goal is fulfilled, the memories recede in accessibility (Goschke & Kuhl, 1993; Marsh, Hicks, & Bryan, 1999). This is also unlike what would happen with mere semantic concepts. For instance, when a concept such as "fruit" has been made accessible, any additional interaction with or reminder of that concept should further increase its accessibility.

What exactly is it about the memories involved in a goal that enable them to maintain or increase their activation potential depending on the goal status? There is still a lot of work to be done on this point, but we speculate that the critical aspect may be the (strong) affective information associated with the goal memories. It may be that once some strongly affective memories are activated, they tend to capture attention, and linger in accessibility, compared with less affective memories. Additionally, there may be something about (some) strongly valenced memories that once they are experienced, or met, they cease to become accessible. In other words, there may be a potential satiation for strong affect. Or, there may simply be a process whereby knowledge related to an intended and conscious action recedes in activation after that action is performed (see Sparrow & Wegner, 2006), which may again suggest some interesting differences in implicit versus explicit goal activation. Animal research on the neural substrates involved in goal pursuit provides some interesting correlates regarding this question. There are some so-called reward neurons in the orbitofrontal cortex in animals that cease firing when the animal has been allowed to eat its fill of a highly desirable food (see Berridge, 2003). Thus, there may be some neurons that are specifically tied to the satiation of a goal state, and that perhaps differ from other reward neurons that are tied to (perhaps milder) positive or negative experiences or events.

Last, although various theorists have proposed ways in which knowledge is represented (e.g., Carlston & Smith, 1996), we note again that the format of knowledge is still currently controversial. Therefore, although plenty of research strongly supports the notion that many different memories can be activated in response to a given stimulus, such as a goal concept (e.g., "fairness," "achievement"), and that the memories will be interconnected in certain ways (excitatory, inhibitory), we cannot yet specify the nature of those representations. This lack of clarity concerning the nature of representations more generally extends of course to the way in which evaluative information in particular may be represented, as we discussed earlier in our definition of an attitude.

Measurement of Goals

Throughout most of the last century of research in the social sciences on goal pursuit, researchers have assumed that goals operate consciously and intentionally. Thus, for example, when someone is pursuing a goal, she is assumed to be intentionally striving to achieve a certain end point and consciously monitoring her progress along the way (Bandura, 1986; Carver & Scheier, 1998; Deci & Ryan, 1985; Gollwitzer, 1990; Locke & Latham, 1990; see also Mischel, Cantor, & Feldman, 1996, for a review). This assumption about the operation of a goal naturally leads to the assumption that goals can be measured explicitly, that is, by asking people whether or how much they possess a given goal. Researchers typically assess this question by administering questions using Likert-type scales such as "How important is it to you to achieve X," or "How desirable would it be for you to attain X?"

However, given the social-cognitive perspective on goals outlined above, it should be possible to activate a goal implicitly. In support of this possibility, a considerable amount of work now shows that goals can be activated without the person's awareness, and then operate over time and in response to a changing environment (e.g., Aarts & Dijksterhuis, 2000; Aarts, Dijksterhuis, & De Vries, 2001; Bargh, 1990; Bargh, Gollwitzer, Lee-Chai, Barndollar, & Troetschel, 2001; Kruglanski, 1996; Fishbach et al., 2003; Shah, Kruglanski, & Friedman, 2002; Shah & Kruglanski, 2002, 2003; for reviews see Chapter 1, in this volume). This raises the possibility that asking people whether they have a goal or not may not be the most accurate, sensitive measure possible. Given people's well-documented tendencies to edit their explicit responses to probes, especially about issues about which they care very much, and people's potential inability to access the relevant memories for the question, it seems as though asking people to report their goals may be misleading. Thus, although there has been very little work on implicitly measuring people's goals, some recent work suggests that one possibility is to measure people's implicit positivity toward the abstract end state (see Ferguson, 2007a; Fishbach & Ferguson, 2007). Another possible method is to measure the accessibility of goal-relevant constructs (see Higgins, King, & Mavin, 1982).

How Goals Influence Attitudes

How do goals influence the ways in which we evaluate goal-related stimuli in our environment? The social-cognitive account of the two constructs we outlined above would predict that goals should be expected to influence the ways in which we evaluate the goal-related stimuli around us. Recall that from our perspective a goal, loosely speaking, consists of a network of many interconnected and related memories that are strongly valenced and that fluctuate in accessibility. This means that when a goal is active, versus not, objects, means, behaviors, and other kinds of memories related to the goal should be more accessible, and more positive. This suggests that the activation of a goal will lead to increased positivity of goal-related memories. Additionally, in our definition of a "goal" we reviewed research showing that when a goal has been met, the accessibility of goal-related memories decreases. In line with this reasoning, we argue that once a goal has been activated and then fulfilled, the positivity of related objects, means, and behaviors related to the goal should decrease relative to when the goal has not been met. We review empirical evidence for these predictions below.

Conscious Goals and Attitudes

Sherman and colleagues (Sherman et al., 2003) measured the implicit attitudes of smokers toward smoking-related paraphernalia. Participants were either allowed to smoke before the experiment, or were not allowed to

smoke. They then completed an implicit attitude measure of their attitudes toward stimuli such as cigarettes, an ashtray, and so on. The findings
showed that those participants who were not allowed to smoke—those
who were therefore in a nicotine need state—showed relatively greater
implicit positivity toward the smoking-related items compared with those
who had just smoked (and thus just fulfilled their need state). Interesting,
there were no effects of the manipulation on participants' explicit attitudes, which points toward the notion that goals may have a unique effect
on implicit versus explicit attitudes.

Recent work has also tested the effects of goals on implicit attitudes
(Ferguson & Bargh, 2004). Findings showed that participants who were
in an active goal state (vs. had already fulfilled the goal or never had the
goal) implicitly evaluated goal-relevant stimuli as significantly more positive. For example, in one experiment (Ferguson & Bargh, 2004, Experiment 1) participants played a Scrabble-type game where they had to create words out of letter tiles. We manipulated two variables. The first was
whether participants were motivated to do well in the game or not. The
second was whether they were still playing the game or not when we measured their implicit attitudes toward performance-relevant stimuli (e.g.,
points, achieve, win). Only those participants who had the goal to do well
and who were still playing the game—in other words, only those who
had an active (still unfulfilled) goal—implicitly evaluated the performance-
relevant stimuli as positive. Importantly, the findings also showed that
participants' active goal pursuit did not influence their explicit attitudes,
which implies again that implicit attitudes may be uniquely reflective of a
person's motivational priorities. Another experiment from Ferguson and
Bargh (2004) found that the goal of thirst only influenced participants'
implicit attitudes toward stimuli that were strongly related to the goal (e.g.,
the words "water," "drinking"), rather than weakly (e.g., "beer") or indirectly (e.g., "mug") related to the goal. These findings show that goals may
influence attitudes toward only those goal-related memories that are most
strongly associated with the goal.

There has also been recent work by Seibt et al. (2007). These researchers looked at the effect of hunger on implicit attitudes toward food-related
stimuli (e.g., sandwiches). They found that those participants who were
hungrier also exhibited more positive implicit attitudes toward food-
related stimuli, but not toward control stimuli. Again, this suggests that
the activation of a goal influences how we spontaneously and unintentionally evaluate goal-relevant stimuli in our environment.

Across all of this research, the findings demonstrate support for the
two predictions we outlined above. First, when a given goal becomes (consciously) activated in memory, some of the objects, behaviors, and means
associated with that goal become more implicitly positive. Second, goal-
related stimuli are more positive when the goal is active versus the goal has

been fulfilled. In some of the above research, the implicit positivity toward goal-related stimuli after a goal had been fulfilled was no different from when the goal had not been activated at all. This demonstrates a crucial difference between the effect of mere semantic priming on attitudes, versus the effect of a goal on attitudes. If the effect were just due to semantic priming, then we would expect the positivity to be the same or even greater when participants fulfilled the goal (and enjoyed doing so) versus had not yet fulfilled it.

How do these effects emerge? How exactly does the positivity of the word "water" change, for instance, when the person is thirsty versus has quenched her thirst or was never thirsty to begin with? One possibility is that the features and memories related to the object "water" fluctuate in accessibility depending on goal activation and fulfillment. When the goal of thirst becomes accessible in memory, then the features of water most interconnected with the goal (via excitatory links) will tend to become accessible, and these will also tend to be positive given that the goal is desirable and influential on behavior (see discussion in Ferguson & Bargh, 2004). These features might include for instance, "refreshing" and "cool," or, memories of how water tasted when the person last quenched her thirst by drinking it, and so on. These features and memories should be strongly associated with positivity. These more positive memories should be most accessible when the person then encounters the word "water," and thus the person will respond to the word with greater positivity than when the goal is not active or has already been met.

When the person finishes drinking, however, and has sated her thirst, then the goal-relevant knowledge and memories should recede in activation generally, and this means that the goal-relevant (and positive) features and memories of water should also recede (see Förster et al., 2005). In this way, when the person now encounters the word "water," those positive, goal-related memories are less accessible, and thus the word should not provoke as much positivity. From this perspective, the activation of a goal—almost by definition—constrains and shapes the construal of goal-related objects and behaviors and events. The fact that the activation and satiation of a goal change the accessibility of object-relevant features and memories implies that they will also change the evaluation of the object.

When a Goal Leads to More Positive Attitudes

Although it seems clear that the activation and satiation of a goal can change the way in which goal-related objects are construed and thus evaluated, one important issue is when the activation of a goal should make attitudes toward goal-relative stimuli more positive in particular. Should it happen for everyone and for all goals? For instance, once the academic achievement goal has been activated in students, when should the positivity of a goal-related object such as "grades" increase? What factors determine whether positivity becomes associated with grades in the achievement context? The positivity that becomes associated with a given object in a certain context (a goal in this case) reflects the tendency of the person to view the object, in that context, as positive and desirable, and to approach it. This means that only those who tend to view the object as desirable and who tend to approach it in that context should have positivity associated with it (in that context). Who are the people who should show this? Those who are the most likely to view the object as desirable in that context and approach the object in that context are probably also going to be the most skilled at the goal. This in turn suggests that the nature of the effect of a goal on attitudes toward goal-related objects should depend on people' general tendencies to positively view that object and approach it in that context—people who should on average be more successful at the goal.

This prediction was tested recently (Ferguson, in press). Participants were assigned to one of three conditions. They were consciously and overtly reminded of their goal to achieve academically, their goal to be social, or they were not reminded of any goal. The condition in which participants were reminded of a social goal was included so that some participants would be in a motivational state, but not one tied to academic achievement. Participants then completed an implicit attitude measure in which their attitudes toward objects related to academic achievement (e.g., grades) were assessed. At the end of the experiment, participants indicated their grade point average (GPA). Based only on the previous results described earlier (Ferguson & Bargh, 2004; Sherman et al., 2003), the prediction here would be that everyone should show more positive implicit attitudes toward the academic stimuli when the academic achievement goal has been activated versus the other two control conditions (social goal, control). On the other hand, if the positivity associated with objects and means related to the goal reflects people's tendency to view those objects as more positive when the goal is active, and possible to actually approach the objects when the goal is active, then those who are successful at the goal should be the ones who most strongly show the effect. This is what happened. Only those with a relatively high GPA showed more positive implicit attitudes toward the academic stimuli (and not control stimuli) when the academic goal was activated compared with the other two conditions (see Ferguson, in press, for more details).

Although a person's skill level (which is undoubtedly multiply determined) should determine whether they succeed at a given goal and develop goal-dependent implicit attitudes, those goal-dependent implicit attitudes should further enable and facilitate their success at the goal. Previous research has shown that the more that people can access their attitudes automatically (i.e., spontaneously, quickly), the better decisions they make (e.g., see Fazio & Powell, 1997). From this perspective, goal-dependent implicit attitudes can be thought of as a signature of successful goal pursuit, as well as a tool of successful goal pursuit.

If a person's skill is an important moderator for how a goal will influence implicit attitudes, how did the results (Ferguson & Bargh, 2004; Seibt et al., 2007; Sherman et al., 2003) described at the outset emerge? In almost every experiment in previous work, the goal was extremely easy to attain (e.g., thirst, nicotine satiation, hunger, performing well on an easy word game), and most if not all participants probably had plenty of successful experience meeting the goal. Thus, most of them probably had developed the associations between the goal and positive features and memories of goal-relevant objects. This suggests that when a goal is easy, the activation of that goal should lead to more positive implicit attitudes toward goal-relevant stimuli for most people. However, when a goal is more difficult, this kind of effect of the goal should emerge only for those who are relatively successful at the goal.

The Automaticity of the Effect of Goals on Attitudes

The recent findings outlined above illustrate how rapidly and effortlessly people transform (their interpretation of) the world around them in a way that facilitates their goals and needs. And yet, it should be noted that these findings together only indicate how quickly people can evaluate a stimulus in a goal-dependent way. They do not in fact reveal anything about how much conscious deliberation and intentional thinking may be required for such goal-dependent evaluations. This is because, in each experiment, participants were conscious of their goal state. In the experiment with the word game (Ferguson & Bargh, 2004, Experiment 1), for instance, participants were of course aware of the game and the importance of their performance. This raises the possibility that participants across the experiments were consciously and intentionally thinking about how to satisfy their goal (e.g., see Bandura, 1997; Oettingen & Gollwitzer, 2001) before they completed the implicit attitude measure. This means that participants in a goal state may have implicitly evaluated the goal-relevant stimuli as more positive only because they were explicitly thinking about the utility of those stimuli minutes earlier. For example, participants still playing the word game may have implicitly evaluated the word "achieve" as positive within 150 milliseconds after seeing the word only because they were consciously thinking about how to perform well beforehand.

Moreover, although the attitudes toward the goal-relevant stimuli were measured using an implicit paradigm (ensuring that they were generated spontaneously), the stimuli were still supraliminally presented, and thus consciously perceived. This allows the possibility that participants employed a strategic, evaluative process at some point (e.g., see Klauer, Roßnagel, & Musch, 1997). These issues together raise the broader question of whether people can implicitly evaluate stimuli in a goal-relevant manner even when the goal is activated nonconsciously and the stimuli are perceived subliminally.

The question of the automaticity of the effect of goals on attitudes was recently addressed (Ferguson, in press). To test how much conscious deliberation is involved, a double-barreled methodological approach was adopted across a series of experiments. First, the goal was activated in a covert or subliminal manner, ensuring that participants in the goal condition were not actively and consciously thinking about the goal (participants did not report any goal-related thoughts in the extensive debriefing). Second, the objects in the implicit attitude measure were presented subliminally rather than supraliminally. This helps to preclude any conscious rumination about the goal and related objects and means. Participants did not report any awareness of the subliminal attitude objects. Given the importance of a person's skill at the goal for the nature of any effects, in all experiments participants' skill was measured.

Across three experiments, participants who were nonconsciously primed with a goal state (e.g., academic achievement) implicitly evaluated goal-relevant, subliminally presented stimuli (e.g., books, library) in a more positive manner than those not primed. Moreover, this effect emerged only for participants who were relatively skilled. This pattern of results therefore suggests that (skilled) people do implicitly shift their interpretations of the stimuli around them in a way that is consistent with their goal, even while remaining largely unaware of the goal and the goal-relevant stimuli. It may be useful to reiterate the implications of these findings for the understanding of how goals influence people's (implicit) interpretations of the world around them. This work shows that a goal that people may not even realize is active can change the way in which they evaluate stimuli they do not even consciously notice. Such findings support the notion that the effect of goal activation on attitudes can remain largely below one's conscious radar, and implies that in some cases people may not realize whether or why their interpretations and reactions to the stimuli around them are fluctuating.

It is important to note that these recent findings (Ferguson, in press) provide critical evidence that the activation of a goal construct in particular was responsible for the effects on implicit attitudes. In line with classic and contemporary research on motivation reviewed earlier in our definition of a "goal," the effect of the nonconciously activated goal on implicit attitudes stayed the same or got stronger across a 6-minute delay (e.g., Aarts, Gollwitzer, & Hassin, 2004; Atkinson & Birch, 1970; Bargh et al., 2001; Lewin, 1936). If only nonmotivational knowledge was activated, the effect would be expected to decrease in strength over that same time period (Higgins, Bargh, & Lombardi, 1985; Srull & Wyer, 1979).

Conclusions of How Goals Influence Attitudes

These findings on how goals influence attitudes yield three central conclusions. First, it seems to be the case that goals influence implicit attitudes more than explicit attitudes. Although more work needs to be conducted on this issue, it may be the case that explicit attitude measures capture participants' (meta) theories about how they think they feel about the objects, rather than the online, currently accessible evaluative information about those objects. These theories may be relatively stable and impervious to fluctuations in the relevant evaluative information.

Second, these findings are in accord with previous work showing that the activation of a goal influences the types of memories that are most accessible concerning objects, events, and means related to the goal (e.g., for reviews, see Barsalou, 2005, 2008; Yeh & Barsalou, 2006). However, the current findings show that because the activation of a goal changes which features and memories will become accessible for a given related object, and because some of those memories will undoubtedly be evaluative, a goal can also change the evaluative nature of a related object. In this way, goals influence the way in which we implicitly evaluate the stimuli around us.

Third, these findings also tell us about how and when a goal will influence our attitudes. When we have had some success at a goal, this means that we tend to view certain goal-related means and actions as desirable whenever the goal is active, and also tend to approach them when the goal is active. This implies that those objects and actions will likely be associated with positivity in the context of the goal. That is, those features and memories for each object that are also linked up with the goal should be positive in nature. This implies that the effect of a goal on attitudes depends on a person's skill level at the goal. For those who tend to be successful, even a very subtle reminder of the goal can shift the evaluation of goal objects to be more positive and desirable. This is an effect that likely further enables and facilitates goal pursuit, suggesting that this effect may constitute a low-level, implicit mechanism of successful goal pursuit.

How Attitudes Influence Goals

The research we have reviewed so far indicates that the activation (and satiation) of a goal constrains and shapes the construal, and implicit evaluation, of goal-related objects. And, the direction of that effect indicates the person's likely success at the goal. Namely, the more positive a person's implicit attitudes toward goal-framed objects, the more successful that person likely is at that goal. This work suggests that people who are successful at a certain goal do not always view relevant objects in terms of that goal. However, once an object has been framed by a particular goal, once it has been contextualized, then the degree to which it spontaneously evokes positivity indicates the success of the person. In other words, the attitude that is evoked reflects the types of behavior the person will likely enact, and probably has enacted in the past, in relation to the object.

These findings are in line with the classic and contemporary research in the attitudes, emotions, and motivation literatures that suggests that the evaluative information associated with a stimulus should reflect the person's behavioral tendency to approach or avoid that stimulus (e.g., Petty et al., 2009). However, there are many remaining questions on this topic. We address two of them below and review recent work that addresses them. The first concerns the potential difference in the predictive validity of implicit attitudes toward concrete versus abstract goal memories for successful goal pursuit. The second concerns the potential causal influence of implicit attitudes on goal pursuit and motivation.

Implicit Attitudes toward Concrete versus Abstract Goal Memories

Are there certain goal-relevant memories that are particularly likely to become activated in goal relevant situations? If there are, then the attitude associated with them may possess predictive validity for the person's goal success. There may be an important difference between the predictive validity of attitudes toward concrete versus abstract goal knowledge on successful goal pursuit. Recent findings (Ferguson, in press) showed that people's implicit evaluations toward relatively concrete stimuli (e.g., tempting foods) related to a goal (e.g., be thin) did not significantly predict their success at meeting that goal. However, people's implicit evaluations of relatively more abstract goal knowledge (e.g., be thin) did significantly predict their success at the goal. For example, across several experiments, people's unintentional and rapid evaluations of abstract goal words (e.g., "equality," "thin") significantly predicted their success at pursuing those goals, and did so above and beyond participants' explicit (i.e., intentional, conscious) ratings of the desirability of the goals. For instance, people's implicit evaluation of the goal *equality* predicted their subtle prejudice toward the elderly, whereas people's explicit evaluation of the goal did not. The more people spontaneously and quickly responded to the word "equal" with positivity, the less likely they were to express subtle prejudice toward the elderly. As another example, people's implicit evaluation of the word "thin" significantly predicted how much they reported being able to successfully resist eating tempting foods over the previous week, and also how much of a tempting snack (i.e., cookies) they actually consumed while in the lab. The more people implicitly evaluated the goal to be thin as positive, the more they were able to resist eating tempting foods.

Why would implicit attitudes toward end-states prove so predictive of behavior? Some research even suggests that people preferentially rely on more abstract representations during the enactment of some behaviors (e.g., see Vallacher & Wegner, 1987). For example, when asked to describe familiar activities (e.g., brushing teeth, climbing a tree), people often choose the abstract versus concrete description. Brushing one's teeth is described as "cleaning" rather than "moving the brush bristles across one's teeth," and climbing a tree is described as "having fun" rather than "holding onto the branches." Assuming that an abstract versus concrete description of an action will conjure up different kinds or intensities of evaluative information, it follows that implicit attitudes toward abstract and concrete descriptions may not be redundant with one another. And, if abstract knowledge is at times more accessible in memory than concrete knowledge during some behaviors, then the implicit attitudes toward that abstract knowledge should best predict the corresponding behavior.

This research (Ferguson, in press) also tested whether implicit attitudes toward abstract end-states predicted relevant behavior better than explicit measures of attitudes and motivation. People may fail to accurately introspect on the strength of their motivation, or may be susceptible to various self-presentation norms and pressures, thus obscuring the predictive validity of explicit constructs. Indeed, across two experiments, participants' implicit attitudes toward abstract end-states predicted their behavior toward that end-state above and beyond their explicitly reported attitudes and motivation. This paper therefore introduces the possibility that implicit attitudes toward end-states can be conceptualized (and utilized) as an implicit measure of goal success. Moreover, this work suggests that the evaluation that people generate within 150 milliseconds after perceiving a stimulus is at times more predictive of their actual goal pursuit than their intentional, conscious reports of the importance of the goal.

The Causal Influence of Implicit Attitudes on Behavior

Almost all of the work on the predictive validity of implicit attitudes has been correlational. For example, in the work reviewed earlier, those who tend to be successful at a goal also tend to evaluate goal-framed objects as positive. But the data do not indicate whether these people's implicit attitudes played an active role in their success. Moreover, although people's implicit attitudes toward abstract goal memories predict their success at the goal, it is unknown whether those attitudes had any causal influence on their regulatory success.

Researchers have begun to examine the causal influence of implicit evaluative information associated with a concept on behavior related to that concept (see Aarts, Custers, & Holland, 2007; Custers & Aarts, 2005). Custers and Aarts (2005), for instance, examined whether the evaluative information associated with an activity can causally increase the motivation to pursue that activity. They argued that the more a person possesses positivity implicitly associated with an activity in memory, the more the person should show implicit approach behaviors toward that activity. In support of this claim, they found that participants who had received subliminal positive evaluative conditioning of words related to "puzzle" later showed more "implicit" motivation to start working on a puzzle. That is, these participants worked faster on the task that preceded the puzzle, presumably in an attempt to start the puzzle as soon as possible. This finding emerged even though participants did not consciously report any increased desire to begin working on the puzzle. These findings show that implicitly increasing the positivity associated with an activity does increase people's implicit motivation to pursue that activity.

One interesting aspect of this work is that there was no effect of the increased positivity on actual puzzle performance. Participants who had received positive evaluative conditioning of words related to "puzzle" did not perform any better, or work any longer, on the puzzle, compared with control participants. In future work, it may be interesting to compare the causal influence of implicit positivity (or negativity) toward concrete versus abstract goal knowledge on actual goal behavior. Given the difference in the predictive validity of implicit attitudes toward the two types of goal knowledge, it may be the case that implicitly increasing the positivity associated with abstract end-states has an impact on implicit motivation as well as on actual performance, whereas positivity associated with concrete goal knowledge may only have an effect on initiating the activity related to the concrete object or activity.

Conclusions

We presented a social-cognitive view of attitudes and goals, and how each influences the other. On the one hand, the findings we reviewed show that the activation of a goal has implications for people's implicit attitudes toward goal-relevant stimuli, and that the direction of the effect depends on the person's regulatory skill at the goal (Ferguson & Bargh, 2004; Seibt et al., 2007; Sherman et al., 2003). Specifically, people who are skilled at a goal automatically, without any deliberation or awareness of the goal or means, implicitly evaluate goal-framed objects as more positive, compared with when the same objects are not framed in terms of the goal, and compared with people who are unskilled. We also reviewed findings suggesting that people's implicit attitudes toward abstract goal knowledge, such as end-states, are significantly predictive of their success at the goal (Ferguson, in press). The more people implicitly evaluate end-states as positive, the more successful they are at pursuing the goal. Moreover, the more implicit positivity (negativity) associated with an activity, the more the person will be implicitly motivated to approach (avoid) that activity (Aarts et al., 2007; Custers & Aarts, 2005), which shows a causal influence of implicit evaluative knowledge on motivation. Together, these results suggest that the social-cognitive analysis of goals and attitudes can yield interesting information about each one separately as well as how they interact.

References

Aarts, H., Custers, R., & Holland, R. W. (2007). The nonconscious cessation of goal pursuit: When goals and negative affect are coactivated. *Journal of Personality and Social Psychology, 92,* 165–178.

Aarts, H., & Dijksterhuis, A. (2000). Habits as knowledge structures: Automaticity in goal-directed behavior. *Journal of Personality and Social Psychology, 78,* 53–63.

Aarts, H., Dijksterhuis, A., & De Vries, P. (2001). The psychology of drinking: Being thirsty and Perceptually Ready. *British Journal of Psychology, 92,* 631–642.

Aarts, H., Gollwitzer, P. M., & Hassin, R. (2004). Goal contagion: Perceiving is for pursuing. *Journal of Personality and Social Psychology, 87,* 23–37.

Abelson, R. P. (1976). Script processing in attitude formation and decision making. In J. S. Carroll & J. W. Payne (Eds.), *Cognition and social behavior* (pp. 33–45). Hillsdale, NJ: Erlbaum.

Abelson, R. P. (1981). Psychological status of the script concept. *American Psychologist, 36,* 715–729.

Ach, N. (1935). Analyse des willens [Analysis of the will]. In E. Abderhalden (Ed.), *Handbuch der biolagishen arbeitsmethoden* (Vol. 6, Part E). Berlin: Urban and Schwarzenberg.

Albarracin, D., Johnson, B. T., & Zanna, M. P. (2005). *The handbook of attitudes.* Mahwah, NJ: Erlbaum.

Allport, G. W. (1935). Attitudes. In C. Murchison (Ed.), *Handbook of social psychology* (pp. 798–844). Worcester, MA: Clark University Press.

Amodio, D. M., & Devine, P. G. (2006). Stereotyping and evaluation in implicit race bias: Evidence for independent constructs and unique effects on behavior. *Journal of Personality and Social Psychology, 91,* 652–661.

Anderson, J. (1983). *The architecture of cognition.* Cambridge, MA: Harvard University Press.

Anderson, J. R., & Reder, L. M. (1999). The fan effect: New results and new theories. *Journal of Experimental Psychology: General, 128*(2), 186–197.

Arnold, M. B. (1960). *Emotion and personality.* New York: Columbia University Press.

Atkinson, J. W. (1974). Strength and motivation and efficiency of performance. In J. W. Atkinson & J. O. Raynor (Eds.), *Motivation and achievement* (pp. 193–218). New York: Wiley.

Atkinson, J. W., & Birch, D. (1970). *The dynamics of action.* New York: Wiley.

Balcetis, E., & Dunning, D. (2006). See what you want to see: Motivational influences on visual perception. *Journal of Personality and Social Psychology, 91*(4), 612–625.

Bandura, A. (1986). *Social foundations of thought and action: A social cognitive theory.* Englewood Cliffs, NJ: Prentice Hall.

Bandura, A. (1997). *Self-efficacy: The exercise of control.* New York: Freeman.

Bargh, J. A. (1990). Auto-motives: Preconscious determinants of social interaction. In E. T. Higgins & R. M. Sorrentino (Eds.), *Handbook of motivation and cognition: Foundations of social behavior* (Vol. 2., pp. 93–130). New York: Guilford Press.

Bargh, J. A. (1997). The automaticity of everyday life. In R. S. Wyer, Jr. (Ed.), *The automaticity of everyday life: Advances in social cognition* (Vol. 10, pp. 1–61). Mahwah, NJ: Erlbaum.

Bargh, J. A., Chaiken, S., Govender, R., & Pratto, F. (1992). The generality of the automatic attitude activation effect. *Journal of Personality and Social Psychology, 62,* 893–912.

Bargh, J. A., Gollwitzer, P. M., Lee-Chai, A., Barndollar, K., & Troetschel, R. (2001). The automated will: Nonconscious activation and pursuit of behavioral goals. *Journal of Personality and Social Psychology, 81,* 1014–1027.

Barsalou, L. W. (1992). *Cognitive psychology: An overview for cognitive scientists.* Hillsdale, NJ: Erlbaum.

Barsalou, L. W. (2005). Situated conceptualization. In H. Cohen & C. Lefebvre (Eds.), *Handbook of categorization in cognitive science* (pp. 619–650). St. Louis: Elsevier.

Barsalou, L. W. (2008). Grounded cognition. *Annual Review of Psychology, 59,* 617–645.

Bassili, J. N., & Brown, R. D. (2005). Implicit and explicit attitudes: Research, challenges, and theory. In D. Albarracin, B. T. Johnson, & M. P. Zanna (Eds.), *The handbook of attitudes* (pp. 543–574). Mahwah, NJ: Erlbaum.

Berridge, K. C. (2003). Comparing the emotional brain of humans and other animals. In R. J. Davidson, H. H. Goldsmith, & K. Scherer (Eds.), *Handbook of affective sciences* (pp. 25–51). New York: Oxford University Press.

Bogardus, E. (1931). *Fundamentals of social psychology* (2nd ed.). New York: Appleton-Century-Crofts.

Bower, G. H. (1981). Mood and memory. *American Psychologist, 36,* 129–148.

Brown, J. D. (1998). *The self.* New York: McGraw-Hill.

Bruner, J. S. (1957). On perceptual readiness. *Psychological Review, 64*(2), 123–152.

Bruner, J. S., & Postman, L. (1948). Symbolic value as an organizing factor in perception. *Journal of Social Psychology, 27,* 203–208.

Carlston, D. E. (1994). Associated systems theory: A systematic approach to the cognitive representation of persons and events. In R. S. Wyer (Ed.), *Advances in social cognition: Associated systems theory* (Vol. 7, pp. 1–78). Hillsdale, NJ: Erlbaum.

Carlston, D. E., & Smith, E. R. (1996). Principles of mental representation. In E. T. Higgins & A. W. Kruglanski (Eds.), *Social psychology: Handbook of basic principles* (pp. 184–210). New York: Guilford Press.

Carver, C. S., & Scheier, M. F. (1981). *Attention and self-regulation: A control-theory approach to human behavior.* New York: Springer.

Carver, C. S., & Scheier, M. F. (1998). *On the self-regulation of behavior.* New York: Cambridge University Press.

Collins, A. M., & Loftus, E. E. (1975). A spreading activation theory of semantic processing. *Psychological Review, 82*(6), 407–428.

Corwin, G. (1921). Minor studies from the psychological laboratory of Cornell University. *American Journal of Psychology, 32,* 563–570.

Custers, R., & Aarts, H. (2005). Positive affect as implicit motivator: On the non-conscious operation of behavioral goals. *Journal of Personality and Social Psychology, 89*(2), 129–142.

Davidson, R., Scherer, K., & Goldsmith, H. (2003). *Handbook of affective sciences.* New York: Oxford University Press.

Deci, E. L., & Ryan, R. M. (1985). *Intrinsic motivation and self-determination in human behavior.* New York: Plenum.

De Houwer, J. (2003). The extrinsic affective Simon task. *Experimental Psychology, 50,* 77–85.

Doob, L. W. (1947). The behavior of attitudes. *Psychological Review, 54,* 135—156.

Eagly, A. H., & Chaiken, S. (1993). *The psychology of attitudes.* Fort Worth, TX: Harcourt Brace Jovanovich College.

Eiser, J. R., Fazio, R. H., Stafford, T., & Prescott, T. J. (2003). Connectionist simulation of attitude learning: Asymmetries in the acquisition of positive and negative evaluations. *Personality and Social Psychology Bulletin, 29*(10), 1221–1235.

Eiser, J. R., Stafford, T., & Fazio, R. H. (2008). Expectancy-confirmation in attitude learning: A connectionist account. *European Journal of Social Psychology, 38*(6), 1023–1032.

Elliot, A. J., & Fryer, J. W. (2007). The goal construct in psychology. In J. Shah & W. Gardner (Eds.), *Handbook of motivational science* (pp. 235–250). New York: Guilford Press.

Fazio, R. H. (1990). Multiple processes by which attitudes guide behavior: The MODE model as an integrative framework. In M. P. Zanna (Ed.), *Advances in experimental social psychology* (Vol. 23, pp. 75–109). New York: Academic Press.

Fazio, R. H. (1995). Attitudes as object-evaluation associations: Determinants, consequences, and correlates of attitude accessibility. In R. E. Petty & J. A. Krosnick (Eds.), *Attitude strength: Antecedents and consequences* (pp. 247–282). Hillsdale, NJ: Erlbaum.

Fazio, R. H. (2001). On the automatic activation of associated evaluations: An overview. *Cognition and Emotion, 14,* 1–27.

Fazio, R. H. (2007). Attitudes as object-evaluation associations of varying strength. *Social Cognition, 25,* 603–637.

Fazio, R. H., & Olson, M. A. (2003). Implicit measures in social cognition research: Their meaning and use. *Annual Review of Psychology, 54,* 297–327.

Fazio, R. H., & Powell, M. C. (1997). On the value of knowing one's likes and dislikes: Attitude accessibility, stress, and health in college. *Psychological Science, 8*(6), 430–436.

Fazio, R. H., Sanbonmatsu, D. M., Powell, M. C., & Kardes, F. R. (1986). On the automatic activation of attitudes. *Journal of Personality and Social Psychology, 50,* 229–238.

Ferguson, M. J. (2007a). On the automatic evaluation of end-states. *Journal of Personality and Social Psychology, 92,* 596–611.

Ferguson, M. J. (2007b). On the automaticity of evaluation. In J. A. Bargh (Ed.), *Social Psychology and the unconscious: The automaticity of higher mental processes* (pp. 219–264). New York: Psychology Press.

Ferguson, M. J. (2007c). *On evaluative readiness: The automatic attitudes of effective self-regulators.* Unpublished manuscript.

Ferguson, M. J., & Bargh, J. A. (2004a). Liking is for doing: The effects of goal pursuit on automatic evaluation. *Journal of Personality and Social Psychology, 87*(5), 557–572.

Ferguson, M. J., & Bargh, J. A. (2004b). How social perception automatically influences behavior. *Trends in Cognitive Sciences, 8,* 33–39.

Fishbach, A., & Ferguson, M. J. (2007). The goal construct in social psychology. In A. W. Kruglanski & E. T. Higgins (Eds.), *Social psychology: Handbook of basic principles* (pp. 490–515). New York: Guilford Press.

Fishbach, A., Friedman, R., & Kruglanski, A. W. (2003). Leading us not unto temptation: Momentary allurements elicit automatic goal activation. *Journal of Personality and Social Psychology, 84,* 296–309.

Fishbein, M., & Ajzen, I. (1975). *Belief, attitude, intention, and behavior: An introduction to theory and research.* Reading, MA: Addison-Wesley.

Fiske, S. T., & Pavelchak, M. A. (1986). Category-based versus piecemeal-based affective responses: Development in schema-triggered affect. In R. M. Sorrentino & E. T. Higgins (Eds.), *Handbook of motivation and cognition: Foundations of social behavior* (pp. 167–203). New York: Guilford Press.

Förster, J., Liberman, N., & Friedman, R. (2007). Seven principles of goal activation: A systematic approach to distinguishing goal priming from priming of non-goal constructs. *Personality and Social Psychology Review, 11,* 211–233.

Förster, J., Liberman, N., & Higgins, E. T. (2005). Accessibility from active and fulfilled goals. *Journal of Experimental Social Psychology, 41*(3), 220–239.

Frijda, N. (1986). *The emotions.* New York: Cambridge University Press.

Gawronski, B., & Bodenhausen, G. V. (2006). Associative and propositional processes in evaluation: An integrative review of implicit and explicit attitude change. *Psychology Bulletin, 132,* 692–731.

Gawronski, B., LeBel, E. P., & Peters, K. R. (2007). What do implicit measures tell us? Scrutinizing the validity of three common assumptions. *Perspectives on Psychological Science, 2,* 181–193.

Gollwitzer, P. M. (1990). Action phases and mind-sets. In E. T. Higgins & R. M. Sorrentino (Eds.), *Handbook of motivation and cognition: Foundations of social behavior* (Vol. 2, pp. 53–92). New York: Guilford Press.

Gollwitzer, P. M. (1996). The volitional benefits of planning. In P. M. Gollwitzer & J. A. Bargh (Eds.), *The psychology of action: Linking cognition and motivation to behavior* (pp. 287–312). New York: Guilford Press.

Gollwitzer, P. M., & Moskowitz, G. B. (1996). Goal effects on action and cognition. In E. T. Higgins & A. W. Kruglanski (Eds.), *Social psychology: Handbook of basic principles* (pp. 361–399). New York: Guilford Press.

Goschke, T., & Kuhl, J. (1993). Representation of intentions: Persisting activation in memory. *Journal of Experimental Psychology: Learning, Memory, and Cognition, 19*(5), 1211–1226.

Greenwald, A. G., McGhee, D. E., & Schwarz, J. L. K. (1998). Measuring individual differences in implicit cognition: The Implicit Association Test. *Journal of Personality and Social Psychology, 74,* 1464–1480.

Higgins, E. T. (1996). Ideals, oughts, and regulatory focus: Affect and motivation from distinct pains and pleasures. In P. M. Gollwitzer & J. A. Bargh (Eds.), *The psychology of action: Linking cognition and motivation to behavior* (pp. 91–114). New York: Guilford Press.

Higgins, E. T., Bargh, J. A., & Lombardi, W. (1985). The nature of priming effects on categorization. *Journal of Experimental Psychology: Learning, Memory, and Cognition, 11,* 59–69.

Higgins, E. T., & Brendl, C. M. (1996). Principles of judging valence: What makes events positive or negative? In M. P. Zanna (Ed.), *Advances in experimental social psychology* (Vol. 28, pp. 95–160). San Diego, CA: Academic Press.

Higgins, E. T., King, G. A., & Mavin, G. H. (1982). Individual construct accessibility and subjective impressions and recall. *Journal of Personality and Social Psychology, 43,* 35–47.

Higgins, E. T., & Kruglanski, A. W. (2000). *Motivational science: Social and personality perspectives.* Philadelphia: Psychology Press.

Hommel, B., Muesseler, J., Aschersleben, G., & Prinz, W. (2001). The theory of event coding (TEC): A framework for perception and action planning. *Behavioral and Brain Sciences, 24,* 849–937.

Hull, C. L. (1931). Goal attraction and directing ideas conceived as habit phenomena. *Psychological Review, 38,* 487–506.

Jeannerod, J. (1997). *The cognitive neuroscience of action.* Oxford, UK: Blackwell.

Jones, E. E., & Thibaut, J. W. (1958). Interaction goals as bases of inference in interpersonal perception. In L. Petrullo & R. Tagiuri (Eds.), *Person perception and interpersonal behavior* (pp. 151–178). Stanford, CA: Stanford University Press.

Klauer, K. C., Roßnagel, C., & Musch, J. (1997). List-context effects in evaluative priming. *Journal of Experimental Psychology: Learning, Memory, and Cognition, 23,* 246–255.

Klinger, E. (1996). Emotional influences on cognitive processing, with implications for theories of both. In P. M. Gollwitzer & J. A. Bargh (Eds.), *The psychology of action: Linking cognition and motivation to behavior* (pp. 197–218). New York: Guilford Press.

Kornblum, S., Hasbroucq, T., & Osman, A. (1990). Dimensional overlap: Cognitive basis of stimulus–response compatibility—A model and taxonomy. *Psychological Review, 97,* 253–270.

Kruglanski, A. W. (1996). Goals as knowledge structures. In P. M. Gollwitzer & J. A. Bargh (Eds.), *The psychology of action: Linking cognition and motivation to behavior* (pp. 599–619). New York: Guilford Press.

Kruglanski, A. W., Shah, J. Y., Fishbach, A., Friedman, R., Chun, W., & Sleeth-Keppler, D. (2002). A theory of goal-systems. In M. P. Zanna (Ed.), *Advances in experimental social psychology* (Vol. 34, pp. 331–378). New York: Academic Press.

Kuhl, J. (1987). Action control: The maintenance of motivational states. In F. Halisch & J. Kuhl (Eds.), *Motivation, intention, and volition* (pp. 279–291). Berlin: Springer-Verlag.

Lang, P. J. (1984). Cognition in emotion: Concept and action. In C. Izard, J. Kagan, & R. Zajonc (Eds.), *Emotion, cognition and behavior.* (pp. 196–226). New York: Cambridge University Press. .

Lazarus, R. E. (1991a). *Emotion and adaptation.* New York: Oxford University Press.

Lewin, K. (1935). *A dynamic theory of personality.* New York: McGraw-Hill.

Lewin,K. (1936). *Principles of toplogical psychology* (F. Heider & G. M. Heider, Trans.). New York: McGraw-Hill.

Locke, E. A., & Latham, G. P. (1990). *A theory of goal setting and task performance.* Englewood Cliffs, NJ: Prentice Hall.

Logan, G. D. (1980). Attention and automaticity in Stroop and priming tasks: Theory and data. *Cognitive Psychology, 12,* 523–553.

Marsh, R. L., Hicks, J. L., & Bryan, E. S. (1999). The activation of unrelated and canceled intentions. *Memory and Cognition, 27,* 320–327.

McClelland, D. C., & Atkinson, J. W. (1948). The projective expression of needs, I: The effect of different intensities of the hunger drive on perception. *Journal of Psychology, 25,* 205–232.

McGuire, W. J. (1969). The nature of attitudes and attitude change. In G. Lindzey & E. Aronson (Eds.), *Handbook of social psychology* (2nd ed., Vol. 3, pp. 136–314). Reading, MA: Addison-Wesley.

McGuire, W. J. (1985). Attitudes and attitude change. In G. Lindzey & E. Aronson (Eds.), *Handbook of social psychology, 3rd ed.* (Vol. 2, pp. 253–346). New York: Random House.

Meyer, D. E., & Schvaneveldt, R.W. (1971). Facilitation in recognizing pairs of words: Evidence of a dependence between retrieval operations. *Journal of Experimental Psychology, 90,* 227–234.

Miller, G. A., Galanter, E., & Pribram, K. H. (1960). *Plans and the structure of behavior.* New York: Henry Holt.

Mischel, W., Cantor, N., & Feldman, S. (1996). Principles of self-regulation: The nature of willpower and self-control. In E. T. Higgins & A. W. Kruglanski (Eds.), *Social psychology: Handbook of basic principles* (pp. 329–360). New York: Guilford Press.

Moskowitz, G. B. (2002). Preconscious effects of temporary goals on attention. *Journal of Experimental Social Psychology, 38,* 397–404.

Moskowitz, G. B., Li, P., & Kirk, E. R. (2004). The implicit volition model: On the preconscious regulation of temporarily adopted goals. In M. P. Zanna (Ed.), *Advances in experimental social psychology* (Vol. 36, pp. 317–404). New York: Academic Press.

Mowrer, O. H. (1960a). *Learning theory and behavior.* New York: Wiley.

Musch, J., & Klauer, K. C. (2003). *The psychology of evaluation: Affective processes in cognition and emotion.* Mahwah, NJ: Erlbaum.

Neely, J. H. (1977). Semantic priming and retrieval from lexical memory: Roles of inhibitionless spreading activation and limited-capacity attention. *Journal of Experimental Psychology: General, 106*(3), 226–254.

Neely, J. H. (1991). Semantic priming effects in visual word recognition: A selective review of current findings and theories. In D. Besner & G. W. Humphreys (Eds.), *Basic processes in reading: Visual word recognition* (pp. 264–336). Hillsdale, NJ: Erlbaum.

Nosek, B. A., & Banaji, M. R. (2001). The go/no-go association task. *Social Cognition, 19*(6), 625–666.

Oettingen, G., & Gollwitzer, P. M. (2001). Goal setting and goal striving. In A. Tesser & N. Schwarz (Eds.), *Intraindividual processes. Volume 1 of the Blackwell Handbook in Social Psychology* (pp. 329–347). Oxford: Blackwell.

Osgood, C. E. (1953). *Method and theory in experimental psychology.* New York: Oxford University Press.

Osgood, C. E., Suci, G. J., & Tannenbaum, P. H. (1957). *The measurement of meaning.* Chicago: University of Illinois Press.

Payne, B. K., Cheng, C. M., Govorun, O., & Stewart, B. D. (2005). An inkblot for attitudes: Affect misattribution as implicit measurement. *Journal of Personality and Social Psychology, 89,* 277–293.

Peak, H. (1955). Attitude and motivation. In M. R. Jones (Ed.), *Nebraska symposium on motivation* (Vol. 3, pp. 149–188). Lincoln: University of Nebraska Press.

Petty, R. E., Fazio, R. H., & Briñol, P. (Eds.). (2009). *Attitudes: Insights from the new implicit measures.* New York: Psychology Press.

Pervin, L. A. (1989). Goal concepts: Themes, issues, and questions. In L. A. Pervin (Ed.), *Goal concepts in personality and social psychology.* Hillsdale, NJ: Erlbaum.

Posner, M. I., & Snyder, C. R. R. (1975). Attention and cognitive control. In R. L. Solso (Ed.), *Information processing and cognition: The Loyola Symposium* (pp. 55–85). Hillsdale, NJ: Erlbaum.

Powers, W. T. (1973). *Behavior: The control of perception.* New York: Aldine de Gruyter.

Rosenberg, M. (1965). *Society and the adolescent self-image.* Princeton, NJ: Princeton University Press.

Schank, R. C., & Abelson, R. P. (1977). *Scripts, plans, goals, and understanding: An inquiry into human knowledge structures.* Hillsdale, NJ: Erlbaum.

Schwarz, N., & Bohner, G. (2001). The construction of attitudes. In A. Tesser & N. Schwarz (Eds.), *Blackwell handbook of social psychology: Intraindividual processes* (Vol. 1, pp. 436–457). Oxford, UK: Blackwell.

Seibt, B., Häfner, M., & Deutsch, R. (2007). Prepared to eat: How immediate affective and motivational responses to food cues are influenced by food deprivation. *European Journal of Social Psychology 37,* 359–379.

Shah, J. Y., & Kruglanski, A. W. (2002). Priming against your will: How goal pursuit is affected by accessible alternatives. *Journal of Experimental Social Psychology, 38,* 368–382.

Shah, J. Y., & Kruglanski, A. W. (2003). When opportunity knocks: Bottom-up priming of goals by means and its effects on self-regulation. *Journal of Personality and Social Psychology, 84,* 1109–1122.

Shah, J. Y., Kruglanski, A. W., & Friedman, R. (2002). A goal systems approach to self-regulation. In M. P. Zanna, J. M. Olson, & C. Seligman (Eds.), *The Ontario symposium on personality and social psychology* (pp. 247–276). Mahwah, NJ: Erlbaum.

Sherman, S. J., Presson, C. C., Chassin, L., Rose, J. S., & Koch, K. (2003). Implicit and explicit attitudes toward cigarette smoking: The effects of context and motivation. *Journal of Social and Clinical Psychology, 22,* 13–39.

Shiffrin, R. M., & Schneider, W. (1977). Controlled and automatic human information processing: II. Perceptual learning, automatic attending, and a general theory. *Psychological Review, 84,* 127–190.

Smith, E. R. (1992). The role of exemplars in social judgment. In L. L. Martin & A. Tesser (Eds.), *The construction of social judgment.* Hillsdale, NJ: Erlbaum.

Smith, E. R., & Zarate, M. A. (1992). Exemplar-based model of social judgment. *Psychological Review, 99,* 3–21.

Sorrentino, R. M., & Higgins, E. T. (Eds.). (1986). *Handbook of motivation and cognition: Foundations of social behavior.* New York: Guilford Press.

Sparrow, B., & Wegner, D. M. (2006). Unpriming: The deactivation of thoughts through expression. *Journal of Personality and Social Psychology, 91,* 1009–1019.

Srull, T. K., & Wyer, R. S. (1979). The role of category accessibility in the interpretation of information about persons: Some determinants and implications. *Journal of Personality and Social Psychology, 37*(10), 1600–1672.

Tesser, A., & Martin, L. (1996). The psychology of evaluation. In E. T. Higgins & A. W. Kruglanski (Eds.), *Social psychology: Handbook of basic principles* (pp. 400–432). New York: Guilford Press.

Thayer, R. E. (1989). *The biopsychology of mood and arousal.* New York: Oxford University Press.

Thurstone, L. L. (1928). Attitudes can be measured. *American Journal of Sociology, 33,* 529–554.

Thurstone, L. L. (1931). Measurement of social attitudes. *Journal of Abnormal and Social Psychology, 26,* 249–269.

Tolman, E. C. (1932). *Purposive behavior in animals and men.* New York: Appleton-Century-Crofts.

Vallacher, R. R., & Wegner, D. M. (1987). What do people think they're doing? Action identification and human behavior. *Psychological Review, 94,* 3–15.

Wilson, T. D., & Dunn, E. W. (2004). Self-knowledge: Its limits, value, and potential for improvement. *Annual Review of Psychology, 55,* 493–518.

Wilson, T. D., Lindsey, S., Schooler, T. Y. (2000). A model of dual attitudes. *Psychological Review, 107,* 101–126.

Winkielman, P., Berridge, K. C., & Wilbarger, J. L. (2005). Unconscious affective reactions to masked happy versus angry faces influence consumption behavior and judgments of value. *Personality and Social Psychology Bulletin, 31*(1), 121–135.

Wittenbrink, B., & Schwarz, N. (Eds.). (2007). *Implicit measures of attitudes.* New York: Guilford Press.

Yeh, W., & Barsalou, L. W. (2006). The situated nature of concepts. *American Journal of Psychology, 119,* 349–384.

Young, P. T. (1959). The role of affective processes in learning and motivation. *Psychological Review, 66,* 104–125.

Young, P. T. (1961). *Motivation and emotion.* New York: Wiley.

Zajonc, R. B. (2000). *Feeling and thinking: The role of affect in social cognition.* New York: Cambridge University Press.

CHAPTER 18

Mystery Moods
THEIR ORIGINS AND CONSEQUENCES

N. PONTUS LEANDER
SARAH G. MOORE
TANYA L. CHARTRAND

The affective consequences of positive or negative events often linger after these events have passed. We act differently when we are in good as opposed to bad moods: Our attitudes, goals, judgments, and behaviors are influenced by these transient feelings. Although it is well understood that moods affect our experiences, our reasons for being in particular moods are sometimes beyond our knowing. Although we can often point directly at the sources of our moods and identify what brought us into our current affective state, other times we cannot. Sometimes we might be in a particularly good or bad mood without any explanation for why we feel that way; other times we are so unaware of our feelings that it takes another person to remark on our behavior before we recognize our current mood. Indeed, we are often unaware of our own mental states and processes (Nisbett & Wilson, 1977; Wilson & Brekke, 1994), and moods are no exception. Moods that emerge without awareness, or for reasons beyond our knowledge, will be henceforth called "mystery moods."

This chapter examines the origins and consequences of mystery moods. The ways in which mystery moods emerge as a result of different nonconscious processes are described, and the consequences of mystery moods for cognition and subsequent goal pursuit are discussed. Before continuing, however, moods are defined and differentiated from emotions.

Differentiating Moods from Emotions

Moods, whether mysterious or not, differ from emotions on a variety of dimensions, but the two concepts are often defined in relation to one another. Russell and Feldman Barrett (1999) distinguished *prototypical emotional episodes,* which involve explicit cognitive processing and are specifically about something, from *core affect* or *mood,* which consists of general feelings of pleasure or displeasure. Similarly, emotions have been defined as "intense, short-lived, [with] a definite cause and clear cognitive content," while moods are "low-intensity, diffuse and relatively enduring affective states without a salient antecedent cause and therefore little cognitive content" (Forgas, 1992, p. 230).

More specifically, moods and emotions vary according to (1) duration: where emotions last for a shorter time than moods; (2) facial expressions: where emotions manifest through specific expressions and moods may not (Ekman, 1994); (3) specificity or discreteness: as emotions involve particular feelings such as anger, fear, and joy, whereas moods are a more diffuse mix, or rolling average, of feelings (Chartrand, van Baaren, & Bargh, 2006); (4) cause: where emotions (but not moods) are reactions to particular events such as goal success or failure, which trigger attributions, cognitions, and specific feelings (Higgins, Shah, & Friedman, 1997); and (5) action: as specific emotions prepare individuals to respond to situations in certain ways (Lerner & Keltner, 2000), but moods do not. Further, emotions are most often experienced consciously as a result of a specific incident and thus require deliberate processing or cognition to arise. In fact, some have argued that emotions can only be experienced consciously (Clore, 1994; however, see Zemack-Rugar, Bettman, & Fitzsimons, 2007). In contrast, moods may be triggered and experienced nonconsciously and need not be tied to a specific source (Berridge & Winkielman, 2003; Zajonc, 2000).

For the purposes of this examination, an "emotion" is characterized as a consciously experienced, discretely categorized hedonic feeling that stems from an identifiable source. A *mood,* on the other hand, is a diffuse experience that may or may not be experienced consciously, with origins that are either known or unknown. *Mystery moods,* the focus of this chapter, are nonconscious and/or stem from unknown sources. That is, *mystery moods* arise as a result of nonconscious processes such that we cannot identify their origins and may be experienced nonconsciously or without awareness. Thus, mystery moods can influence our attitudes, goals, and behavior when we do not even realize we are experiencing them.

The Origins of Mystery Moods

This chapter focuses on three major sources of mystery moods that have been identified and empirically tested. Each of these triggers of mystery moods is nonconscious, such that individuals are unaware of the origins of their mood. These three sources are not exhaustive but simply highlight the types of experiences that may produce mystery moods and provide some insight into their underlying mechanisms. First, success or failure at nonconscious goals has consequences for mood. Unlike the affect that results from conscious goal pursuit, however, mystery moods arising from nonconscious goal pursuit may not always be experienced consciously, and even when they are experienced consciously, their sources are typically unknown. Second, automatic evaluation systems may generate mood states that reflect the overall positive or negative valence of the environment and result in a corresponding mood. Given that automatic evaluations occur outside conscious awareness, moods stemming from them are not necessarily tied to a singular, specific source. Third, interpersonal motives might render individuals susceptible to social contagion effects, such that we might spontaneously and nonconsciously "catch" the moods of others. Social interaction may also lead us to be sensitive to nonconscious social acceptance or rejection cues, which can lead to mystery moods. Below, each of these sources of mystery moods is reviewed.

Nonconscious Goals

Goals are represented in memory such that they can be triggered spontaneously by situational cues, often outside of our awareness (Bargh, 1990; Kruglanski, 1996; Shah & Kruglanski, 2000). Nonconsciously triggered goals can guide behavior automatically and operate much in the same way as conscious goals, sharing many of their behavioral characteristics and outcomes (Bargh, Gollwitzer, Lee-Chai, Barndollar, & Trotschel, 2001; Chartrand & Bargh, 1996; Moskowitz, Li, & Kirk, 2004). Importantly, they also share affective consequences; just as success (or failure) at a conscious goal can produce a positive (or negative) mood (Bandura, 1997; Carver & Scheier, 1998), so too can success or failure at a nonconscious goal produce positive or negative moods. However, the moods resulting from nonconscious goals are of unknown origin: They are mystery moods.

Chartrand (2007a) demonstrated the existence of mystery moods stemming from nonconscious goal success or failure. In one study, participants who were supraliminally primed with an achievement goal and were then led to succeed or fail at this goal showed different effects on mood, despite being unaware of the goal. First, participants completed a scrambled sentence task, for which they were asked to unscramble lists of five words to create grammatically correct four-word sentences; for example, "He it hides box instantly" might become "he hides it instantly." In the achievement-goal condition, words related to "achievement" (e.g., success, achieve, attain) were embedded in the items, and in the control condition, these were replaced with neutral words. This procedure has been used in previous research to prime an achievement goal nonconsciously, or outside participants' awareness (see Bargh & Chartrand, 2000). Next, half the participants were assigned to an "easy" condition: They were given eight anagrams and were told that the task would take 8 minutes to finish (it actually required 2). The other half were assigned to a "difficult" condition: They were given 28 anagrams and were told that the task would take 2 minutes to finish (it actually required 8). All participants were given as much time as needed to complete the anagrams; however, given participants' different expectations about how long the task would take, those primed with a nonconscious achievement goal were set up to either succeed at that goal in the easy condition or fail at it in the difficult condition. Following this task, participants completed a self-reported mood scale and a funnel debriefing to assess whether any participants were aware of having an achievement goal active.

Results indicated that participants who were primed with a nonconscious achievement goal were in a better mood if they completed the "easy" task than if they had completed the "difficult" task. No such mood differences were observed in those who were not goal-primed. Thus, the nonconscious achievement goal was responsible for producing positive or negative changes in participant's explicit moods, depending on whether they felt they had succeeded or failed at the anagram task. These changes in mood were explicit, despite participants having no awareness that they had a goal to achieve and no awareness of the origin of their current mood: These participants were experiencing a mystery mood.

In a second study, moods generated as a result of nonconscious goal success or failure were found to mirror those resulting from conscious goal pursuit (Chartrand, 2007a). Participants first completed a computer task, wherein they were subliminally primed with words either related to forming an impression of another person (e.g., judgment, evaluate) or not (e.g., background, calendar). This way, participants were either primed with a nonconscious impression-formation goal or not (see Chartrand & Bargh, 1996, Study 2). Goal success or failure was then manipulated by having participants listen to one of two audio recordings describing the typical daily behaviors of a target person, Joe. To instantiate a conscious goal, half the participants in the control priming condition were then given explicit instructions to form an impression of Joe, and half were not. This resulted in three conditions: nonconscious goal, conscious goal, and no goal. Half the participants in each condition were then set up to succeed or fail at the impression-formation goal: Some heard consistent descriptions of Joe that made it easy to form an impression that he was clumsy, whereas others heard conflicting information that made it difficult to form an impression by describing Joe as sometimes clumsy and at other times graceful. Participants then completed a self-reported mood measure.

Results indicated that participants with conscious or nonconscious impression-formation goals were in a better mood when it was easy (as opposed to difficult) to form an impression of Joe, that is, those who easily formed impressions of Joe satisfied their goal and this improved their moods. Participants who had not been assigned an explicit or nonconscious goal indicated no significant changes in mood. These experiments demonstrate that nonconsciously pursued goals produce mood effects similar to consciously pursued goals, with the exception being that their sources are unknown. No participants in either study were suspicious of the nonconscious goal-priming procedure nor could any of them accurately report where their mood came from. In short, success or failure at nonconscious goals can create positive or negative mystery moods.

Nonconscious goals may also buffer us against potential changes in mood. For example, the prospect of having to perform an unpleasant task such as taking a test might typically shift our mood in a negative direction—but what if taking such a test serves some nonconscious goal? Might fulfilling that goal through completing an objectionable task protect us from the negative affect typically induced by that task?

Riketta and Dauenheimer (2003) conducted a study that investigated this question. First, participants were either given a nonconscious goal to seek knowledge or not; next, they were informed that they would be completing a test that would evaluate a personality trait of theirs. Mood was assessed either prior to being informed about the test or after being informed. Participants with a nonconscious goal to seek information reported no difference in mood, regardless of whether mood was measured before or after they were informed of the test. Participants without a knowledge-seeking goal, on the other hand, demonstrated a negative shift in mood when mood was measured after they had learned about the test. Thus, the prospect of completing the personality test negatively affected the moods of participants who could not use the test to attain a goal—as the opportunity to learn about their personalities was not motivationally relevant to them. However, those with a nonconscious goal to seek knowledge seemed to regard the test as a means to attain that goal, counteracting the negative mood it might otherwise have generated. These results help explain why our mood states can be difficult to predict: Sometimes even the most unpleasant of circumstances may incidentally provide goal-related opportunities that spare us from their negativity. In other words, nonconscious goals not only create mystery moods, but they may sometimes lead to mystery "unmoods," or a mysterious lack of mood change, by protecting us from the potentially mood-altering influence of certain tasks.

The studies described above highlight the nature and complexity of mood states and their relation to nonconscious goal success or failure. The pursuit of nonconscious goals significantly affects our mood states, actively by increasing or decreasing mood, and also more passively, by buffering us from potential changes in mood. These changes in mood states are of unknown origin, yet in the above studies participants could nevertheless report their mystery moods via explicit self-report measures. This suggests that although we are often not aware of our mental processes, we may sometimes be aware of the outcomes of these processes. In sum, mystery moods often signal the presence of one or more nonconscious goal pursuits, arising (or not) in response to their success or failure.

Automatic Evaluations

In addition to the influence of specific nonconscious goals on mood, the general valence of the environment may be sufficient to evoke a mystery mood. Indeed, we may find ourselves in a bad mood because we are embedded in a situation that we find gloomy, hostile, or tense. Just as emotions signal the status of our conscious goal pursuits, moods may signal the general valence of the environment. How do moods come to reflect the tenor of the overall environment? Two factors come into play: evaluation and repetition.

First, the environment is full of objects imbued with memory associations that trigger affect and allow us to classify objects as positive or negative. Thus, we may see a picture of a loved one on our desk and smile as we remember when and where it was taken. However, the evaluations we make of objects in the environment do not always occur consciously. Indeed, most situations contain so much stimulus information that we rely on automatic evaluations to manage this information and classify objects as either positive or negative in valence (Bargh, Chaiken, Govender, & Pratto, 1992; Fazio, Sanbonmatsu, Powell, & Kardes, 1986). Further, although a single stimulus is unlikely to generate a mood, repeated exposure to one stimulus or to several stimuli of a consistent valence may significantly alter mood. Our propensity to evaluate the environment automatically, combined with the fact that multiple, consistent evaluations may create positive or negative moods, leads to the potential for environmentally cued mystery moods. Thus, we may sometimes experience moods that are unexplained by a specific stimulus but are generated by the situation as a whole. These feelings stem from the aggregated valence of the global environment, from the sums of countless positive (or negative) evaluations assigned to various objects. Given the breadth of sources for such moods, it may be difficult to identify one particular source; thus, these environmentally cued moods are experienced as mystery moods.

In an empirical test of environmentally cued mystery moods (Chartrand et al., 2006), participants were subliminally primed with words of either a positive (e.g., music, friends), negative (e.g., war, cancer), or neutral valence (e.g., tree, carpet). Participants then completed self-report measures of mood. Results indicated that participants who were subliminally primed with positive words—despite having no awareness that any words had been flashed on the screen—reported more positive affect and those primed with negative words reported more negative affect, indicating that automatic evaluation can produce mood states as a result of repeated exposure to stimuli of a consistent valence. It is important to note again that no participants were aware of being subliminally primed because it suggests that the source of their altered mood was unknown as they completed the self-report measures.

Thus far, it has been suggested that mystery moods may arise from two sources: nonconscious goals and automatic evaluation of the environment. However, these two sources are not necessarily independent; the effects of automatic evaluations of the environment may be influenced by current goals. Nonconscious goals can bias automatic and conscious evaluations of stimuli, such that evaluation of and behavior toward the stimulus are, at least in part, determined by its relevance to active goals. The ability of specific stimuli to satisfy certain goals leads to changes in the valence we assign to these stimuli, such that goal-relevant stimuli are automatically evaluated as positive, whereas goal-irrelevant stimuli are automatically evaluated as negative (Ferguson & Bargh, 2004; Moors, De Houwer, & Eelen, 2004). For instance, the instrumentality of another person to our current goal pursuits might influence evaluations of the quality of our relationship with that individual, such that instrumental others are evaluated more favorably than noninstrumental others; this goal-driven automatic evaluation can occur even when a goal is nonconscious (Fitzsimons & Shah, 2008). Accordingly, Fishbach and Shah (2006) demonstrated a behavioral form of implicit self-control, where individuals automatically avoid tempting stimuli by pushing levers away from themselves faster than they push goal-related stimuli, and vice versa for pulling.

Thus, the way we automatically evaluate and behave toward stimuli in the environment is influenced by nonconscious goals. Such goal-driven automatic evaluations might lead to mystery moods that signal the ability of the current environment to help or hinder goal pursuit; negative mystery moods could be the result of perceiving either a lack of support for a goal in the environment (e.g., a lack of goal-relevant stimuli), or a direct threat against goal achievement (e.g., the presence of tempting stimuli). For example, phobic participants who are subliminally presented with images of feared stimuli such as snakes demonstrate heightened skin conductance responses (SCRs) and self-reported arousal, as well as low self-reported moods (Ohman & Soares, 1994). With the assumption that a phobia of snakes is likely associated with a strong goal to avoid them, the subliminal presentation of snake-filled images might suggest failure at that avoidance goal, leading not only to heightened states of arousal and specific fear responses, such as SCRs, but also to a negative mystery mood. Future research will likely shed further light on the relationship between our past or current goal pursuits and the automatic evaluations that lead to mystery moods.

Social Interactions

Finally, mystery moods may originate from our interpersonal interactions. Socially induced mystery moods can arise in two ways: through emotional contagion such that we nonconsciously "catch" the moods of others, or through the automatic activation of schemas and memories related to close others, wherein the valence of these memories influences our mood and behavior.

Emotional Contagion

Whether we are joining in the elation of an excited child or the tension of an anxious friend, we are sensitive to the moods of others (Hatfield, Cacioppo, & Rapson, 1994). That is, moods can be contagious, though we are not always aware of such social influences upon our moods. Further, human beings spontaneously mimic the behaviors of those around them, often without conscious awareness (Chartrand & Bargh, 1999). This affective and behavioral mimicry is part of an automatic link between perception and action or feeling. Thus, we can move automatically from perceiving a mood to feeling that mood, or from perceiving a behavior to engaging in that behavior (Dijksterhuis & Bargh, 2001).

Of particular interest in this chapter is the extent to which we mimic the moods of those around us. Indeed, a great deal of research indicates that we frequently and automatically "catch" other people's moods as a result of mimicking their facial expressions, postures, and voices (Hatfield et al., 1994). For example, we automatically mimic emotional facial expressions: The link between perceiving and doing is so strong that subliminally presented images of happy or angry faces can lead to facial electromyographic (EMG) responses in perceivers that are consistent with those emotions (Dimberg, Thunberg, & Elmehed, 2000). These contagion effects may be due to a two-step process of first (automatically) mimicking the emotional behavior of another person, which then triggers the corresponding mood through a self-perception process. Importantly, such self-perception can occur nonconsciously or without cognitive mediation.

Strack, Martin, and Stepper (1988) provided evidence for this process, showing that "self-perception" does induce corresponding moods in individuals. Study participants were asked to hold a pen in their mouth in such a way that the facial muscles used for smiling were either facilitated or inhibited. Participants whose smiling muscles were inhibited rated humorous material as less funny than those whose smiling muscles were facilitated. Note that this procedure precludes "cognitive" self-perception in which individuals actively think, "I'm smiling, therefore I must be happy," by instead using physiological cues that are merely associated with affective responses to influence participants.

Neumann and Strack (2000) also demonstrated that we can catch another person's affective state by perceiving and mimicking it and yet remain unable to explain why we are feeling that way. In a series of studies examining the contagion of moods, participants listened to a recorded speech given in either a happy or sad tone of voice. In the first study, after listening to the speech, participants completed a self-reported mood scale and a measure of discrete emotions (e.g., cheerfulness, anxiety). Consistent with our expectations for a mystery mood, participants who were exposed to the happy voice reported a more positive mood state than those who were exposed to the sad voice. Moreover, no results were observed for the discrete emotion measures, suggesting that the affect participants "caught" from the voice was of a positive or negative valence, and not specific to a particular emotion. A second study examined the behavioral consequences of mood contagion, in which participants were instructed to repeat the speech out loud as they heard it, purportedly for reasons unrelated to emotion. Independent raters who were blind to experimental conditions observed that participants who listened to and repeated the happy voice seemed more happy, whereas those who repeated the sad voice seemed more sad. Thus, we seem to pick up mystery moods from the moods of others in our environment, automatically and without awareness.

Much like automatic evaluations, emotional contagion is likely dependent on goals. Given the social nature of emotional contagion, this type of mystery mood is particularly related to affiliation goals. Indeed, the extent to which we adopt the emotions of others may be moderated by how much we mimic them, which may in turn be influenced by affiliation goals. For instance, Lakin and Chartrand (2003) gave participants either a nonconscious goal to affiliate (via subliminal priming), a conscious goal to affiliate via explicit instructions, or no goal at all. Next, participants watched a "live feed" of a participant in another room, which was actually a prerecorded confederate who deliberately touched her face while performing some unrelated task. Participants with an affiliation goal, whether conscious or nonconscious, touched their own faces more while watching the video than those who were not assigned an affiliation goal. These results suggest that simply having a nonconscious goal to affiliate increases mimicry.

Gump and Kulik (1997) provided additional evidence that goals to affiliate increase the degree to which we mimic others. Their research was based on the classic finding that individuals who are feeling threatened prefer the company of others facing a similar threat (Schachter, 1959). This desire to affiliate with similar others may be a result of perceiving those others to be instrumental in managing the threat, whether as allies or sources of guidance (see, for instance, Fitzsimons & Shah, 2008). Participants wishing to affiliate with these similar others should thus pay greater attention to their behavior, which might in turn increase mimicry. This hypothesis was tested by Gump and Kulik (1997), who demonstrated that participants did mimic the behaviors of those they believed were facing threats similar to their own. Moreover, these authors found that participants experienced emotional contagion from the individuals they mimicked. Interestingly, participants reported feeling anxiety, a specific emotion, around confederates who also appeared anxious (vs. calm) and were thought to be facing a similar threat. These results are intriguing given Neumann and Strack's (2000) evidence that contagion involves catching the general valence of the perceived emotion, but not the discrete emotion itself. However, in the Gump and Kulik study, there was no measurement of mood; participants only completed a measure specific to anxiety. Thus, it is difficult to conclude whether the mood caught through mimicry was anxiety per se or a general state of arousal that happened to be recorded with an anxiety measure, but would also have been observable with any measure of negative affect. Regardless, these studies provide some evidence that we mimic others with whom we want to affiliate, and this mimicry has consequences for our own moods.

In addition to the emotional contagion effects of mimicking others, being mimicked by others can also have affective consequences, again as a function of affiliation motivation. Human beings may be chronically motivated to be accepted by others socially and therefore are sensitive to cues suggesting success or failure at affiliation, including cues that are not consciously accessible (Baumeister & Leary, 1995). An example of such a nonconscious cue might be whether or not an individual is mimicking our behavior, wherein being mimicked by others is a positive cue (van Baaren, Fockenberg, Holland, Janssen, & Van Knippenberg, 2006). This feedback regarding success or failure at affiliation may in turn influence our moods.

A recent study provides initial evidence that there are indeed affective consequences of being mimicked by others (Ashton-James & Chartrand, 2007). Participants first engaged in an introductory social interaction with another "participant," actually a confederate who either mimicked the participant's nonverbal behavior or not. Participants then completed a word-recognition task on the computer, in which they responded to words of positive and neutral valence (see Koole, Dijksterhuis, & van Knippenberg, 2001). Those participants who were mimicked by the confederate responded faster to positive words than participants who were not mimicked, suggesting that their social interaction had produced a positive affective response. This positive mood increased the salience of mood-consistent information and allowed those who had been mimicked to respond more quickly to positive words, in accordance with an associative network model perspective of mood (Lerner & Keltner, 2000). Participants were unaware of having been mimicked, highlighting the nonconscious nature of the effects of mimicry on mood.

In sum, automatic, nonverbal social behaviors—both our own and those of others—may influence our current mood states for reasons beyond our conscious awareness, thereby creating mystery moods. However, mimicry is not the only way that mood can be influenced by other people; in the next section, an even more subtle mechanism for socially induced mystery moods is considered.

Relationship Schemas

Although mimicry certainly influences mood, a behavioral interaction with another person is not required to experience a socially induced mystery mood. Consider walking into an automotive repair shop with the intent of negotiating strongly to reduce the price of a botched repair job. The clerk at the front desk, however, resembles an old friend whom you have not seen in years. You always had a good time with this friend, and your memories of him/her are pleasant. The lucky clerk at the repair shop will benefit from these remembered feelings, as those pleasant memories may have made your mood slightly more positive and your behavior slightly less aggressive.

Indeed, social stimuli can lead us to recall past relationships, consciously or nonconsciously, and this may have consequences for affect (Andersen & Chen, 2002). As we perceive familiarity in features of new people we meet or learn about, previously formed *relational schemas* may activate as a function of associative memory (Baldwin, 1992). These relational schemas may be imbued with positive or negative affect, such that when they are recalled we are reminded of the joys or pains of their associated relationship. The mental activation of such emotionally laden relationships may have immediate effects on our current affective experiences, generating feelings that resemble mystery moods.

In a study examining the role of affective transference in social interactions (Andersen, Reznik, & Manzella, 1996), participants first provided the name of one significant other who was associated with positive feelings, and a second significant other who was associated with negative feelings. Participants then provided information regarding the traits of each of those persons before being dismissed with the belief that the experiment had been concluded. Before leaving, however, participants were recruited to participate in an "unrelated" study occurring approximately 2 weeks later. When participants returned for this "new" experiment, they were led to believe that they would be interacting with someone later in the experimental session. Participants were then instructed to read some information aloud that purportedly described the person with whom they were going to interact. The traits participants were given to describe the other person were experimentally manipulated as to either resemble the participant's own positive (or negative) significant other or not. Participants were unobtrusively videotaped while reading this trait list. Independent raters blind to experimental conditions were used to illustrate that participants expressed more positive affect when reading aloud traits resembling their own positive significant other, as opposed to the traits resembling their negative significant other or traits of a person they did not know. Thus, when reminded of a significant other associated with positive or negative feelings, participants nonverbally expressed emotions that reflected the tone of the relationship schemas that were triggered.

Although Andersen and colleagues demonstrated that the nonconscious activation of relationship schemas could change an on-line measure of affect, they found no evidence of corresponding change in self-reported mood (Andersen et al., 1996). An earlier version of the study produced some evidence that relationship schemas might influence mood (Andersen & Baum, 1994), though the results held only for the activation of positive significant others and not negative significant others. However, a recent study examining this issue provides further insight (Chartrand, 2007b). In this study, participants provided the name of one significant other who made them happy, and another who made them feel sad. Participants were then subliminally primed with one of those names during an unrelated computer task, after which mood was assessed. Those who were subliminally primed with the name of a positive significant other reported better moods than those who were primed with the name of a negative significant other. Thus, when something or someone in the environment triggers mental representations of significant others with whom we associate particular feeling states, this can evoke mystery moods.

Beyond activating general feelings about significant others, the nonconscious activation of relationship representations might provoke goal-specific automatic evaluations, which can have affective consequences. In other words, priming a significant other whom we believe provides useful feedback for our important goal pursuits can trigger affect in ourselves that corresponds to the feedback we receive from that person. In a study by Baldwin and colleagues (Baldwin, Carrell, & Lopez, 1990), practicing Catholics who read a sexually provocative passage reported more negative self-evaluations when subliminally primed with the scowling image of the Pope than when primed with the scowling image of someone they did not know. Interestingly, one of the subscales used in the study included a measure of self-reported anxiety, which was significantly affected by the relationship priming manipulation. Given that the Pope is likely perceived as an instrumental other for the goal of being a good Catholic, even nonconscious cues suggesting his disapproval were sufficient to produce negative affect in participants, specifically anxiety. Participants did not report their overall moods in this study, however, so it is unclear whether the affective results are specific to feelings of anxiety or whether they reflect a general negative mood state stemming from the nonconscious goal feedback. However, and further supporting a motivational perspective on mood, there were no affective consequences for practicing Catholics who were primed with someone they did not know, nor for nonpracticing Catholics who were primed with the scowling Pope's image—further supporting a motivational perspective on mystery moods. Results from this and prior studies suggest that the nonconscious activation of relationship representations has affective consequences that resemble those of mystery moods.

Summary

Thus far, three sources of mystery moods have been discussed: nonconscious goals, automatic evaluations, and significant others. That is, success or failure at nonconscious goals, automatic evaluations of the valence of our general environment, and the activation of relationship schemas have the ability to influence affective states. The studies reviewed have been used to demonstrate that these factors alter mood, and that individuals are often unaware of why they are experiencing a change in mood; that is, these changes in affect are mystery moods. Also highlighted is the role that goal pursuit plays in automatic evaluations of the environment and in social interactions with others, as well as how these factors combine to influence the creation of mystery moods.

The Consequences of Mystery Moods

Once an individual is in a mystery mood, how does it influence his/her subsequent behavior? The research reviewed below demonstrates that mystery moods, despite (or sometimes because of) their unknown origins, significantly affects cognition and behavior.

Cognition

Mystery moods influence the way we organize situational information in two ways. First, because individuals lack insight into the origins of their mystery moods, they may explain their current mood state using factors in the environment that are not related to their mood. This misattribution has consequences for downstream behavior and for experienced emotion. Second, mystery moods, as with other feeling states, influence the way in which we process information.

Misattribution

Mystery moods are "free-floating" affect in that they are not cognitively bound to their actual sources, which are often unknown to individuals. Thus, mystery moods can be reassigned or misattributed to whatever source is consciously available (see Berridge & Winkielman, 2003). In Schachter and Singer's (1962) two-factor theory of emotion, emotions consist of physiological arousal and cognitive attribution. As free-floating affect, mystery moods should consist solely of the physiological arousal component. They should not include the cognitive component; after all, they are mysterious in nature, and individuals are unable to correctly pinpoint the origins of these moods. As such, the arousal and valence associated with mystery moods may become linked to whatever cognitive source seems most appropriate at the time, including aspects of the situation that are in fact unrelated to the current feeling state (Schwarz & Clore, 1983). The nature and direction of such attributions can have significant consequences for discrete emotions, behavior, and cognitive processing.

In a well-known demonstration of misattribution (Dutton & Aron, 1974), an attractive female experimenter recruited male pedestrians to complete a survey at the edge of a very high bridge or in the middle of it. Following each survey, the experimenter gave participants her telephone number. She received more phone calls from men surveyed on the bridge, suggesting that these participants misattributed their arousal as attraction to the experimenter instead of as fear from standing on a bridge. Similarly, Schachter and Singer (1962) demonstrated that individuals may misattribute free-floating arousal to ready sources in the environment. In this classic study, individuals who were injected with epinephrine and misinformed about the drug's side effects were more likely to adopt the feelings and behavior of a confederate acting angrily or cheerfully, misattributing their unexplained physical symptoms to a specific emotion. These demonstrations suggest that, regardless of their true source, the ways in which we understand and explain mystery moods and arousal have significant effects on the discrete emotions we feel and on our social behavior.

In addition to the ability of misattribution to create discrete emotions from general arousal, the fact that mystery moods are "free floating" might lead us to generalize our current affective state onto unrelated targets. If our feelings generally provide information about our environment (Chartrand et al., 2006; Schwarz, 1990; Schwarz & Clore, 1983), then the misattribution of mystery moods may mean we sometimes receive faulty information from our feelings. In one study, participants who responded to a phone interview on a sunny day reported greater happiness, life satisfaction, and less desire to change than those who were called on a rainy day, so long as the interviewer did not mention the weather (Schwarz & Clore, 1983). If the interviewer did mention the weather, however, its effect on participant responses was attenuated. When the weather was not mentioned, the current weather was not cognitively accessible to participants; thus, the negative "free-floating" affect produced by the rain was generalized or misattributed to participants' assessments of life happiness and contentedness. Interestingly, the desire-to-change component of the dependent measure points toward the potential motivational consequences of mystery moods, even when they are misattributed. That is, the emotional barometers that manage goal pursuit could be misinformed by mystery moods, leading us to make incorrect inferences about goal success or failure. Indeed, we may automatically appraise rainy days as making some of our goals harder to attain—regardless of whether or not they actually do. This suggests that these unbound affective states have potentially negative consequences; the issue of mystery moods and subsequent goal pursuit is further examined below.

Information Processing

Just as the environment can generate moods without awareness, mystery moods can influence the ways in which we manage and process information in the environment. As discussed previously, feelings inform us of the general valence of our environment and of the current status of our goal pursuits. We feel good when goal progress is satisfactory and bad when it is not; these feelings are useful in that they signal a need for self-regulatory behavioral responses (Carver & Scheier, 1998). By nature, mystery moods are often not attached to a particular source. Although this may lead to problems of misattribution, mystery moods may be adaptive when they signal the general valence of the environment and trigger necessary changes in cognitive processing. Indeed, moods may be used to provide information about the current environment (Schwarz, 1990), pushing individuals toward one of two general types of information processing (Chaiken, 1980; Petty & Cacioppo, 1986). Heuristic processing is broad and superficial, often employing rules of thumb or stereotypes to reach a conclusion or attain a goal. When moods are positive, the environment is assumed to be safe, allowing for more risky or superficial processing (e.g., Bodenhausen, Kramer, & Susser, 1994). However, negative moods may signal that something is wrong, motivating us to identify the problem and use a systematic processing style that is vigilant, detail oriented, and analytical.

Supporting the idea of moods as information, Chartrand and colleagues (2006) found that participants who were subliminally primed with negatively valenced words demonstrated greater evidence of systematic processing than those primed with neutral words, including less reliance on heuristics for organizing social information. Moreover, these effects were mediated by the valence of participants' mystery moods. Such effects of mystery moods on processing style may be generally linked to differential reliance on automatic processing as a function of mood, where positive moods lead to more automatic and less effortful processing than negative moods (Hanze & Meyer, 1998).

Subsequent Goal Pursuit

In addition to influencing cognition through attribution or information processing, mystery moods can influence behavior through altering or initiating goal pursuit. First, the affect associated with mystery moods may be taken as an indicator of which goals to begin or continue pursuing, and which goals to stop or avoid pursuing. Second, we may adopt goals in response to mystery moods in an attempt to regulate these moods and change our current feelings.

Transferring Affect onto Goals

Mystery moods affect conscious and nonconscious goal pursuits in similar ways—through the transfer of the positive or negative mood to the goal itself. For instance, free-floating or "core" affect may sometimes be assimilated with or attributed to one's prospective and current goal pursuits. For example, one recent study found that participants expressed greater desire to pursue a prospective goal when they had been subliminally primed with positively valenced words moments before being presented with that goal (Custers & Aarts, 2005). Although participants were not consciously aware of the priming stimuli, the valence of the stimuli was readily transferred to the goal being evaluated, such that individuals who had some positive affect from being exposed to the positive words applied this positivity to the subsequently presented goal. Although the priming in this study does not map directly onto a mood manipulation, it mirrors previously discussed work where automatic evaluations of multiple similarly valenced words lead to changes in mood (Chartrand et al., 2006). Beyond demonstrating changes in mood from exposure to valenced stimuli, this work suggests that environmentally induced "free-floating" affect may be attributed to a consciously available target such as a goal, thereby influencing subsequent behavior as well as experienced mood.

In addition to influencing evaluations of prospective goals, nonconsciously triggered affect can be transferred to current goal pursuit. As discussed above, environmental stimuli are evaluated in terms of their relevance to our current goals; thus, mystery moods may provide signals about which goals to pursue in the current environment. For instance, study participants who were thirsty (e.g., have a current goal to satisfy their thirst) were found to drink more of a beverage when subliminally primed with happy as opposed to sad faces (Winkielman, Berridge, & Wilbarger, 2005). It may have been that participants sated their thirst more readily when their automatic evaluations were positive, suggesting that those evaluations facilitated goal pursuit. In a subsequent study, participants completed the same priming procedure but were given only a limited amount to drink afterwards, as to keep active their goal to quench their thirst. Participants were then given a series of questionnaires regarding the drink. Results indicated that when the environment signaled a generally positive valence, participants wanted to pursue their goal: They indicated a greater desire to drink more of the beverage than those receiving angry primes or those who were not thirsty. However, participants who were still thirsty who were subliminally primed with angry faces placed a lower dollar value on the drink, indicating a decreased desire to pursue the goal (Winkielman et al., 2005). These results demonstrate how affective responses to nonconscious stimuli influence conscious goal pursuits. Although participants in these studies did not demonstrate changes in self-reported mood, they behaved as if they were experiencing and responding to mystery moods. Moreover, the authors acknowledged the possibility that affective mechanisms might have been responsible for these motivated drinking behaviors; perhaps in this case, the mystery mood was created and experienced nonconsciously.

Further support for the transferring of affect demonstrates that positive moods induced by our environment may encourage the pursuit of existing affiliation goals. In a recent study, participants who were in a positive mood (from watching a funny video) mimicked an experimenter more than those in a negative mood (from watching a sad video; van Baaren et al., 2006). To the extent that we mimic to affiliate with others (Lakin & Chartrand, 2003), the positive valence of the environment might have been used by participants as a signal that the goal to affiliate could be attained in the experimental session.

In sum, mystery moods may be induced by the general valence of the environment and our propensity to evaluate environmental stimuli, as discussed above. Importantly, the affect resulting from environmentally induced mystery moods can transfer to current and future goal pursuit, significantly affecting behavior. Future research can examine whether the transfer of affect from sources other than automatic evaluation (i.e., from nonconscious goal pursuit or social interactions) occurs in the same way.

Mystery Mood Repair Strategies

When we are in a bad mood, we often take action to regulate or improve that mood; we might engage in behaviors designed to improve our mood directly (such as eating chocolate cake), or utilize a self-esteem enhancing strategy to improve our mood indirectly (Aspinwall & Taylor, 1993; Isen, 1984). These two mood repair strategies are discussed below.

Although negative emotions have been tied to self-regulation failure and engagement in behaviors that are unhealthy (binge eating) or dangerous (drug use), it has also been argued that we perform these behaviors strategically to help resolve negative mood states. To investigate this hypothesis, Tice and colleagues (Tice, Bratslavsky, & Baumeister, 2001) conducted a series of studies in which participants who were induced with a (conscious) negative mood were informed that scientific research had shown that a variety of negative behaviors (e.g., eating unhealthy food) either did or did not improve mood. They found that participants who were led to believe that negative behaviors would improve their mood were more likely to engage in those behaviors than those who were not led to such a belief; thus, individuals may sometimes adopt explicit affect-regulation goals in response to consciously experienced negative moods.

Similarly, we use repair strategies to improve negative mystery moods, and these repair-oriented behaviors may also be negative. Research on non-conscious goal pursuit has examined how individuals cope with the negative mystery moods that follow failure at automatically activated goals. One possibility is that we misattribute the cause of this free-floating affect to someone else, which may in turn lead to aggression toward them (e.g., Berkowitz, 1989). The role of nonconscious goal failure in interpersonal aggression was examined by Jefferis and Chartrand (2007). In one study, participants were supraliminally primed with an impression-formation goal via a scrambled sentence task. They were then led to succeed or fail at the impression-formation task by reading a consistent or inconsistent description of a target person. Next, participants were informed that another (fictitious) participant was in the next room and were asked to dole out a sample of hot sauce for that other participant to taste (McGregor et al., 1998). Despite being informed that the fictitious participant despised spicy foods, participants who were primed with an impression-formation goal and then led to fail at it subsequently poured more hot sauce for the fictitious participant to taste than did those who were led to succeed at the impression-formation task or those who did not have a impression-formation goal. Similar results were observed in another study wherein participants walked down a hallway toward another person (actually a confederate) who was also heading toward them: Those who had failed at a nonconscious goal got significantly closer to colliding with the confederate before stepping aside, suggesting greater aggression and thus the use of a mood repair strategy.

We might also utilize various self-esteem enhancement mechanisms to manage negative mystery moods. Self-esteem maintenance is argued to be a goal featuring the property of substitutability: that is, several different psychological mechanisms can be used to enhance self-esteem (Tesser, 2000). When the causes of moods are unknown, such as when we fail at a nonconscious goal, we may be motivated to repair that mood using one of our many available self-enhancement strategies (Tesser, Martin, & Cornell, 1996). Some recent research has begun to investigate this possibility (Chartrand, Cheng, Dalton, & Tesser, 2007). In one study, participants were given a nonconscious-achievement goal via a scrambled sentence task, a conscious-achievement goal via explicit task instructions, or no achievement goal, before completing an anagram task that was impossible to solve. After "failing" at a conscious, nonconscious, or nonexistent goal to achieve, participants completed a measure of self-enhancement in which they had the opportunity to create a "self-serving definition" of successful marriages (Dunning & Cohen, 1992). Results revealed that participants who had failed at their nonconscious-achievement goal reported the most self-serving bias, those with the conscious goal reported moderate bias, and those with no achievement goal demonstrated the least bias. Two subsequent studies demonstrated that when participants had attributed their mystery mood to a source, regardless of whether that source was the true cause of their mood or not, participants' tendency to self-enhance was attenuated. In other words, when participants had an explanation for their mystery moods and were able to attribute their moods to a particular source, they were no longer motivated to repair those moods through self-enhancement.

Summary

In this section, the consequences of mystery moods for our thoughts and behaviors were explored. Mystery moods influence cognition in two ways: First, we may misattribute mystery moods to irrelevant sources in the environment; second, mystery moods can be used as an indicator of whether we need to adopt a stringent or heuristic style of cognitive processing. Goal pursuit is also influenced by mystery moods; free-floating affect may be used as a barometer to indicate which goals we should pursue and which we should abandon. Finally, we might adopt mood-repair goals based on negative mystery moods, which significantly affect behavior.

Conclusions

Mystery moods are distinguished from moods by virtue of the role of non-conscious processes along one of two dimensions: either we are not aware of the source of our mood or we are unaware of the mood itself. These mysterious moods arise from different sources: nonconscious goal pursuit, environmental stimuli, and individuals in the social environment. Once created, mystery moods have important consequences for cognition and behavior; individuals use these moods as indicators of which goals to pursue, try to explain their mysterious feelings by attributing them to unrelated sources, and try to improve their moods by engaging in mood-repair strategies. Before concluding, two important themes from this chapter are highlighted: first, the recurring theme that goals are intimately related to the origins and consequences of mystery moods; and second, the idea that the environment may play a role in determining the consequences of mystery moods.

First, many, if not most, of our mystery moods (and their consequences) can be linked to some motivational source. Contemporary research on automatic motivation is exploring the ways in which nonconscious goals influence evaluations of environmental stimuli and social relationships. For example, the reviewed research demonstrated that automatic evaluations of the environment are dependent upon current goal pursuit, such that goal-relevant stimuli are evaluated more positively than irrelevant stimuli (Ferguson & Bargh, 2004). These findings lead to questions about whether environmentally and socially induced mystery moods are independent of goal pursuit or whether they are intimately linked to motivation. Although it is unclear whether mystery moods are entirely motivational, we hope future studies will help answer this question.

In returning to the idea that mystery moods are expressed in accordance with the current environment, the specific behaviors and emotions that are available to individuals in that environment must be considered. First, when they are consciously experienced, mystery moods are diffuse: They are not experienced as discrete emotions per se, but rather as general feelings of positive or negative valence. Although mystery mood states do not always manifest as discrete emotions, we are motivated to attribute these feelings to particular sources; this attribution (or misattribution) process may be one means through which mystery moods morph into specific subjective emotional experiences. Second, the specific behaviors that individuals engage in as a consequence of mystery moods may be determined by the environment. For example, individuals feeling diffuse negative affect may repair their moods in various ways, depending on the options available. These mood-regulating behaviors might involve behaving aggressively toward other individuals if they are present (such as refusing to move aside in the hallway), or might involve eating chocolate cake if one is near the refrigerator. The issue of how the environment influences the consequences of mystery moods in terms of specific emotions expressed and behaviors engaged in has great research potential.

The depth and complexity of the origins and consequences of mystery moods for cognition, emotion, and motivation is highlighted by existing research. The importance and ubiquity of mystery moods in our everyday experiences and goal pursuits is evident: Mystery moods may explain a great variety of our feelings and behaviors that are otherwise inexplicable.

References

Andersen, S. M., & Baum, A. (1994). Transference in interpersonal relations: Inferences and affect based on significant-other representations. *Journal of Personality, 62,* 460–497.

Andersen, S. M., & Chen, S. (2002). The relational self: An interpersonal social-cognitive theory. *Psychological Review, 109,* 619–645.

Andersen, S. M., Reznik, I., & Manzella, L. M. (1996). Eliciting facial affect, motivation, and expectancies in transference: Significant-other representations in social relations. *Journal of Personality and Social Psychology, 71*(6), 1108–1129.

Ashton-James, C., & Chartrand, T. L. (2007). *The creative chameleon: How non-conscious mimicry influences thinking styles.* Manuscript in preparation, University of British Columbia.

Aspinwall, L. G., & Taylor, S. E. (1993). Effects of social comparison direction, threat, and self-esteem on affect, self-evaluation, and expected success. *Journal of Personality and Social Psychology, 64*(5), 708–722.

Baldwin, M. W. (1992). Relational schemas and the processing of social information. *Psychological Bulletin, 112*(3), 461–484.

Baldwin, M. W., Carrell, S. E., & Lopez, D. F. (1990). Priming relationship schemas: My advisor and the pope are watching me from the back of my mind. *Journal of Experimental Social Psychology, 26*(5), 435–454.

Bandura, A. (1997). *Self-efficacy.* New York: Freeman.

Bargh, J. A. (1990). Auto-motives: Preconscious determinants of social interaction. In R. M. Sorrentino & E. T. Higgins (Eds.), *Handbook of motivation and cognition* (pp. 93–130). New York: Guilford Press.

Bargh, J. A., Chaiken, S., Govender, R., & Pratto, F. (1992). The generality of the automatic attitude activation effect. *Journal of Personality and Social Psychology, 62*(6), 893–912.

Bargh, J. A., & Chartrand, T. L. (2000). The mind in the middle: A practical guide to priming and automaticity research. In H. T. Reis & C. M. Judd (Eds.), *Handbook of research methods in social and personality psychology* (pp. 253–285). New York: Cambridge University Press.

Bargh, J. A., Gollwitzer, P. M., Lee-Chai, A., Barndollar, K., & Trotschel, R. (2001). The automated will: Nonconscious activation and pursuit of behavioral goals. *Journal of Personality and Social Psychology, 81*(6), 1014–1027.

Baumeister, R. F., & Leary, M. R. (1995). The need to belong: Desire for interpersonal attachments as a fundamental human motivation. *Psychological Bulletin, 117*(3), 497–529.

Berkowitz, L. (1989). Frustration-aggression hypothesis: Examination and reformulation. *Psychological Bulletin, 106*(1), 59–73.

Berridge, K. C., & Winkielman, P. (2003). What is an unconscious emotion? (The case for unconscious "liking"). *Cognition and Emotion, 17*(2), 181–211.

Bodenhausen, G. V., Kramer, G. P., & Susser, K. (1994). Happiness and stereotypic thinking in social judgment. *Journal of Personality and Social Psychology, 66*(4), 621–632.

Carver, C. S., & Scheier, M. F. (1998). *On the self-regulation of behavior.* Cambridge, UK: Cambridge University Press.

Chaiken, S. (1980). Heuristic versus systematic information processing and the use of source versus message cues in persuasion. *Journal of Personality and Social Psychology 39*(5), 752–766.

Chartrand, T. L. (2007a). *Mystery moods and perplexing performance: Consequences of succeeding and failing at a nonconscious goal.* Working paper, Duke University.

Chartrand, T. L. (2007b). Significant others can automatically induce mystery moods. Unpublished data, Duke University.

Chartrand, T. L., & Bargh, J. A. (1996). Automatic activation of impression formation and memorization goals: Nonconscious goal priming reproduces effects of explicit task instructions. *Journal of Personality and Social Psychology, 71*(3), 464–478.

Chartrand, T. L., & Bargh, J. A. (1999). The chameleon effect: The perception-behavior link and social interaction. *Journal of Personality and Social Psychology, 76*(6), 893–910.

Chartrand, T. L., Cheng, C. M., Dalton, A. N., & Tesser, A. (2007). *Consequences of failure at nonconscious goals for self-enhancement: A trip to the self zoo.* Manuscript submitted for publication, Duke University.

Chartrand, T. L., Huber, J., Shiv, B., & Tanner, R. (in press). Nonconscious goals and consumer choice. *Journal of Consumer Research, 35* 189–201.

Chartrand, T. L., van Baaren, R. B., & Bargh, J. A. (2006). Linking Automatic evaluation to mood and information processing style: Consequences for experienced affect, impression formation, and stereotyping. *Journal of Experimental Psychology: General, 135*(1), 70–77.

Clore, G. L. (1994). Why emotions are never unconscious. In P. Ekman & R. J. Davidson (Eds.), *The nature of emotion: Fundamental questions* (pp. 285–290). New York: Oxford University Press.

Custers, R., & Aarts, H. (2005). Positive affect as implicit motivator: on the non-conscious operation of behavioral goals. *Journal of Personality and Social Psychology, 89*(2), 129–142.

Dijksterhuis, A., & Bargh, J. A. (2001). The perception–behavior expressway: Automatic effects of social perception on social behavior. *Advances in Experimental Social Psychology, 33,* 1–40.

Dimberg, U., Thunberg, M., & Elmehed, K. (2000). Unconscious facial reactions to emotional facial expressions. *Psychological Science, 11*(1), 86–89.

Dunning, D., & Cohen, G. L. (1992). Egocentric definitions of traits and abilities in social judgment. *Journal of Personality and Social Psychology, 63*(3), 341–355.

Dutton, D. G., & Aron, A. P. (1974). Some evidence for heightened sexual attraction under conditions of high anxiety. *Journal of Personality and Social Psychology, 30*(4), 510–517.

Ekman, P. (1994). Moods, emotions, and traits. In P. Ekman & R. J. Davidson (Eds.), *The nature of emotion: Fundamental questions* (pp. 56–58). New York: Oxford University Press.

Fazio, R. H., Sanbonmatsu, D. M., Powell, M. C., & Kardes, F. R. (1986). On the automatic activation of attitudes. *Journal of Personality and Social Psychology, 50,* 229–238.

Ferguson, M. J., & Bargh, J. A. (2004). Liking is for doing: The effect of goal pursuit on automatically activated attitudes. *Journal of Personality and Social Psychology, 87*(5), 557–572.

Fishbach, A., & Shah, J. Y. (2006). Self-control in action: implicit dispositions toward goals and away from temptations. *Journal of Personality and Social Psychology, 90*(5), 820–832.

Fitzsimons, G. M., & Shah, J. Y. (2008). How goal instrumentality shapes relationship evaluations. *Journal of Personality and Social Psychology, 95*(2), 319–337.

Forgas, J. P. (1992). Affect in social judgments and decisions: A multi-process model. In M. Zanna (Ed.), *Advances in experimental social psychology* (Vol. 25, pp. 227–275). San Diego: Academic Press.

Gump, B. B., & Kulik, J. A. (1997). Stress, affiliation, and emotional contagion. *Journal of Personality and Social Psychology, 72*(2), 305–319.

Hanze, M., & Meyer, H. (1998). Mood influences on automatic and controlled semantic priming. *American Journal of Psychology, 111*(2), 265–278.

Hatfield, E., Cacioppo, J., & Rapson, R. (1994). *Emotional contagion.* New York: Cambridge University Press.

Higgins, E. T., Shah, J. Y., & Friedman, R. S. (1997). Emotional responses to goal attainment: Strength of regulatory focus as moderator. *Journal of Personality and Social Psychology, 72*(3), 515–525.

Isen, A. M. (1984). Toward understanding the role of affect in cognition. In R. S. Wyer, Jr. & T. Srull (Eds.), *Handbook of social cognition* (pp. 179–236). Hillsdale, NJ: Erlbaum.

Jefferis, V. E., & Chartrand, T. L. (2007). *Aggressive behavior and the role of nonconscious goal pursuit.* Manuscript in preparation, Duke University.

Koole, S. L., Dijksterhuis, A., & van Knippenberg, A. (2001). What's in a name:

Implicit self-esteem and the automatic self. *Journal of Personality and Social Psychology, 80*(4), 669–685.

Kruglanski, A. W. (1996). Goals as knowledge structures. In P. M. Gollwitzer & J. A. Bargh (Eds.), *The psychology of action: Linking cognition and motivation to behavior* (pp. 599–618). New York: Guilford Press.

Lakin, J., & Chartrand, T. L. (2003). Using nonconscious behavioral mimicry to create affiliation and rapport. *Psychological Science, 14*(4), 334–339.

Lerner, J. S., & Keltner, D. (2000). Beyond valence: Toward a model of emotion-specific influences on judgment and choice. *Cognition and Emotion, 14*(4), 473–493.

McGregor, H., Lieberman, J. D., Solomon, S., Greenberg, J., Arndt, J., Simon, L., et al. (1998). Terror management and aggression: Evidence that mortality salience motivates aggression against worldview threatening others. *Journal of Personality and Social Psychology, 74*, 590–605.

Moors, A., De Houwer, J., & Eelen, P. (2004). Automatic stimulus-goal comparisons: Support from motivational affective priming studies. *Cognition and Emotion, 18*(1), 29–54.

Moskowitz, G. B., Li, P., & Kirk, E. R. (2004). The implicit volition model: On the preconscious regulation of temporarily adopted goals. In M. Zanna (Ed.), *Advances in experimental social psychology* (Vol. 34, pp. 317–414). San Diego: Academic Press.

Neumann, R., & Strack, F. (2000). "Mood contagion": The automatic transfer of mood between persons. *Journal of Personality and Social Psychology, 79*, 211–223.

Nisbett, R. E., & Wilson, T. D. (1977). Telling more than we can know: verbal reports on mental processes. *Psychological Review, 84*, 231–259.

Ohman, A., & Soares, J. J. F. (1994). "Unconscious anxiety": Phobic responses to masked stimuli. *Journal of Abnormal Psychology, 103*, 231–240.

Petty, R. E., & Cacioppo, J. T. (1986). *Communication and persuasion: Central and peripheral routes to attitude change.* New York: Springer-Verlag.

Riketta, M., & Dauenheimer, D. (2003). Anticipated success at unconscious goal pursuit: Consequences for mood, self-esteem, and the evaluation of a goal-relevant task. *Motivation and Emotion, 27*(4), 327–338.

Russell, J. A., & Feldman Barrett, L. (1999). Core affect, prototypical emotional episodes, and other things called emotion: Dissecting the elephant. *Journal of Personality and Social Psychology, 76*(5), 805–819.

Schachter, S. (1959). *The psychology of affiliation: Experimental study of the source of gregariousness.* Stanford, CA: Stanford University Press.

Schachter, S., & Singer, J. E. (1962). Cognitive, social, and physiological determinants of emotional state. *Psychological Review, 69*(5), 76–93.

Schwarz, N. (1990). Feelings as information: Informational and motivational functions of affective states. In E. T. Higgins & R. Sorrentino (Eds.), *Handbook of motivation and cognition: Foundations of social behavior* (Vol. 2, pp. 527–561). New York: Guilford Press.

Schwarz, N., & Clore, G. L. (1983). Mood, misattribution, and judgments of well-being: Informative and directive functions of affective states. *Journal of Personality and Social Psychology, 45*(3), 513–523.

Shah, J. Y., & Kruglanski, A. W. (2000). Aspects of goal networks: Implications for self-regulation. In M. Boekaerts, P. R. Pintrich, & M. Zeidner (Eds.), *Handbook of self regulation* (pp. 85–110). San Diego: Academic Press.

Strack, F., Martin, L., & Stepper, S. (1988). Inhibiting and facilitating conditions of the human smile: A nonobtrusive test of the facial feedback hypothesis. *Journal of Personality and Social Psychology, 54*(5), 768–777.

Tesser, A. (2000). On the confluence of self-esteem maintenance mechanisms. *Personality and Social Psychology Review, 4,* 290–299.

Tesser, A., Martin, L., & Cornell, D. (1996). On the substitutability of self-protective mechanisms. In P. M. Gollwitzer & J. A. Bargh (Eds.), *The psychology of action: Linking motivation and cognition to behavior* (pp. 48–68). New York: Guilford Press.

Tice, D. M., Bratslavsky, E., & Baumeister, R. F. (2001). Emotional distress regulation takes precedence over impulse control: If you feel bad, do it! *Journal of Personality and Social Psychology, 80*(1), 53–67.

Van Baaren, R. B., Fockenberg, D. A., Holland, R. W., Janssen, L., & Van Knippenberg, A. (2006). The moody chameleon: The effect of mood on nonconscious mimicry. *Social Cognition, 24*(4), 426–437.

Wilson, T. D., & Brekke, N. (1994). Mental contamination and mental correction: Unwanted influences on judgments and emotions. *Psychological Bulletin, 116,* 117–142.

Winkielman, P., Berridge, K. C., & Wilbarger, J. L. (2005). Unconscious affective reactions to masked happy versus angry faces influence consumption behavior and judgments of value. *Personality and Social Psychology Bulletin, 31*(1), 121–135.

Zemack-Rugar, Y., Bettman, J. R., & Fitzsimons, G. (2007). The effects of nonconsciously priming emotion concepts on behavior. *Journal of Personality and Social Psychology, 93*(6), 927–939.

Zajonc, R. B. (2000). Feeling and thinking: Closing the debate over the independence of affect. In J. P. Forgas (Ed.), *Feeling and thinking: The role of affect in social cognition* (pp. 31–58). New York: Cambridge University Press.

CHAPTER 19

Regulatory Fit in the Goal-Pursuit Process

E. TORY HIGGINS

There are three major elements in goal pursuit: the goal itself, the motivational orientation toward the goal, and the manner or means of goal pursuit. Historically, psychologists and other scientists have paid most attention to the relation between the goal and motivational orientation, such as how the strength and the direction (approach vs. avoidance) of the motivation to pursue a goal is affected by anticipated goal-attainment outcomes (success vs. failure), and to the relation between the goal and the manner of goal pursuit, such as how different goal-pursuit strategies are more or less effective or efficient in goal attainment. In contrast to these two relations that concern goal attainment outcomes, relatively little attention has been paid historically to how the relation between motivation orientation and the manner of goal pursuit can affect performance, evaluative judgments, and life experiences independent of goal-attainment outcomes per se. Recently, however, the relation between motivation orientation and the manner of goal pursuit, and the effects of this relation, have begun to receive increasing attention in studies investigating regulatory fit. The purpose of this chapter is to review the different ways that regulatory fit can be created, the different kinds of effects that regulatory fit can have, and the different mechanisms that underlie these effects. It should be noted at the outset that this is just the beginning of the story on regulatory fit—much has yet to be learned about its antecedents, its consequences, and its very nature.

Regulatory Fit

As defined in the dictionary (*Webster's Ninth New Collegiate Dictionary*, 1989), when two things fit with one another, they suit or agree with each other; they are in harmony. This captures the sense of "fit" as an adaptive regulatory process. In addition, when something is experienced as fitting, it feels correct, proper, or even just. This captures the sense of "fit" as an experience of feeling right about what is happening. These two senses of "fit" are critical to the conceptualization of fit proposed in regulatory-fit theory (Higgins, 2000). According to regulatory-fit theory, people experience regulatory fit when the manner of their engagement in an activity sustains (vs. disrupts) their current regulatory orientation. Notably, the term "sustains" has two separate meanings in the dictionary (e.g., *Webster's Ninth New Collegiate Dictionary*, 1989, p. 1189). One definition of "sustain" is to hold up or prolong, to give support, sustenance, or nourishment. This first definition relates to the sense of fit as something that is adaptive by supplying what is needed to carry on. A second definition of "sustain" is to allow or admit as valid, to confirm, to support as true, legal or just. This second definition relates to the sense of fit as feeling right about something. Fit makes people engage more strongly in what they are doing and "feel right" about it.

Individuals, for example, can pursue (approach) the same goal with different orientations and in different ways. Consider, for instance, students in the same course who are working to attain an "A." Some students have a promotion focus orientation toward an "A," where a promotion focus represents goals as hopes and ideals. Others have a prevention-focus orientation toward an "A," where a prevention focus represents goals as responsibilities and oughts. With regard to how they pursue their goal, some students read material beyond the assigned readings as an eager way to attain an "A," whereas others are careful to fulfill all course requirements as a vigilant way to attain an "A." Previous studies have found that an eager manner fits a promotion focus better than a prevention focus, whereas the reverse is true for a vigilant manner (Higgins, 2000).

For all students, receiving an "A" in the course has certain outcome benefits regardless of the orientation or manner of their goal pursuit. Independent of this outcome value, however, there is an additional experience from regulatory fit. Specifically, when people engage in goal pursuit in a manner that fits their orientation (e.g., promotion/eager, prevention/vigilant), they engage in that pursuit more strongly and have more intense evaluative reactions (Higgins, 2000, 2006). Regulatory fit makes them "feel right" about their positive reactions to what they are doing or "feel right" about their negative reactions to what they are doing (see Cesario, Grant, & Higgins, 2004; Higgins, 2005).

It is the meaning of regulatory "fit" as described above—when the manner of goal pursuit sustains a person's orientation toward the goal—that is the concern of this chapter. I begin by briefly distinguishing regulatory fit from other "fit"-like concepts and from other kinds of self-regulatory value experiences. I then discuss the different ways in which regulatory fit can be created. Finally, I review evidence of the different kinds of effects that regulatory fit can have, while considering the different mechanisms that underlie these effects.

Regulatory Fit as a Distinct Variable

Regulatory fit is distinct as a goal-pursuit concept and as a type of self-regulatory value experience. This section briefly considers each of these distinctive qualities of regulatory fit (see also Higgins, 2002).

Regulatory Fit as a Distinct Goal-Pursuit Concept

"Compatibility" refers to an action's instrumentality toward attaining a goal outcome. There is substantial evidence that specific actions are valued to the extent that they support attaining more abstract goals (e.g., Carver & Scheier, 1981; Shah & Kruglanski, 2000; for a review, see Brendl & Higgins, 1996). People more highly value those process goals (e.g., "making conversation") that are compatible with the attainment of their broader-purpose goals (e.g., "achieving interpersonal closeness"; Harackiewicz & Sansone, 1991; Sansone & Harackiewicz, 1996; Tauer & Harackiewicz, 1999). Work on "self-concordance" also demonstrates that an action's value to a person increases as its relevance to that person's broader aims increases (e.g., Sheldon & Elliot, 1999).

   In the persuasion literature, there is also considerable evidence that matching the content of a persuasive message to some characteristic of the message recipient's cognitive, motivational, or affective system can increase the attitude-behavior correlation and persuasion (e.g., Millar & Tesser, 1986; Petty & Wegener, 1998). The characteristics of the message recipient include the psychological functions served by the recipient's attitudes (e.g., Clary, Snyder, Ridge, Miene, & Haugen, 1994) and the recipient's chronic self-guides (e.g., Evans & Petty, 2003). A mediator of message-matching effects is the degree to which participants expect that the actions the messages describe will be instrumental in affecting the outcomes toward which the messages are focused (DeSteno, Petty, Rucker, Wegener, & Braverman, 2004).

   What research on action-goal compatibility, self-concordance, and message matching have in common is that they all emphasize the instrumental value of the manner of goal pursuit for outcomes: They identify relations between actions and outcomes as important sources of action value. Regulatory fit differs from these other goal-pursuit concepts in its concern with the relation between the manner of goal pursuit and the actor's current orientation— independent of the efficiency (low costs) or effectiveness (high benefits) of the manner of goal pursuit (i.e., independent of outcomes). Indeed, there is evidence that regulatory fit is not related to the actual or perceived efficiency or effectiveness of the goal pursuit (e.g., Higgins, Idson, Freitas, Spiegel, & Molden, 2003) and that it can affect evaluative judgments of an object or message even when it is induced prior to presentation of the object or message (e.g., Cesario et al., 2004; Higgins et al., 2003).

Regulatory Fit as a Distinct Self-Regulatory Experience

The self-regulatory experiences that have received the most attention historically are value experiences, particularly the hedonic-value experiences of feeling pleasure or pain. This attention to hedonic experiences again reflects the importance given to outcomes when considering self-regulation in general and goal pursuit in particular. People are motivated to pursue goals that produce positive outcomes. When making choices, for example, they want the alternative whose mix of pleasant or painful outcomes is the most positive. Goal pursuit, such as making a decision, has outcome benefits and outcome costs. The means used to pursue goals can contribute to outcome benefits by, for instance, being enjoyable in themselves ("getting there is half the fun"). The means used can also contribute to outcome costs, such as having high emotional costs (e.g., Janis & Mann, 1977) or high costs in cognitive effort or time (e.g., Payne, Bettman, & Johnson, 1993).

The benefits or costs of the manner of goal pursuit are outcomes of the goal-pursuit process itself and are weighed along with the positive and negative consequences of goal attainment in some kind of costs–benefits analysis. Emphasizing people's experiences of outcome benefits and costs is natural because they concern whether a decision is experienced as "worthwhile" or "worth it." It is reasonable to relate a decision's value to its worth because value relates to utility, and one sense of "utility" is "worth to some end" (*Webster's Ninth New Collegiate Dictionary*, 1989, p. 1300). However, "utility" has another sense: "fitness for some purpose" (*Webster's Ninth New Collegiate Dictionary*, 1989, p. 1300). This is what distinguishes the regulatory-fit experience from other value experiences. The regulatory-fit experience concerns this additional sense of utility having to do with experiencing the fitness of how the goal is pursued . Rather than being a diffuse, global hedonic feeling of pleasure, the regulatory-fit experience involves a more specific sense of "feeling right" about what one is doing. Empirically supporting this distinction is evidence that goal pursuit with regulatory fit produces a regulatory-fit experience (i.e., "feels right"; "feels like a good fit") that is distinct from hedonic feelings of pleasure (e.g., Cesario & Higgins, 2007; Appelt, Zou, Arora, & Higgins, in press), and has effects that are independent of hedonic feelings (Cesario et al., 2004; Higgins et al., 2003).

This is not to say that regulatory fit is the only value experience from how a goal is pursued that is independent of instrumental outcomes. There is another such value experience from which regulatory fit must be distinguished—*value from the use of proper means*. It has been recognized for centuries that there is value from *how* a goal is pursued that is independent of the outcomes of goal attainment, as captured in such cultural maxims, "It is not enough to do good, one must do it the right way" and "The ends do not justify the means." These maxims distinguish between value from the outcomes of goal pursuit and value from pursuing goals with proper means (see Merton, 1957). The proper means value experience derives from the goal pursuit process being the right or proper way to attain outcomes according to established normative rules. In contrast, the regulatory-fit value experience derives from the relation between the manner of goal pursuit and the current self-regulatory orientation of the person pursuing the goal. What matters for the regulatory-fit experience is not whether the process of goal pursuit agrees with established rules (value from the use of proper means), but whether the manner of goal pursuit sustains the actor's current orientation while pursuing the goal (see Higgins, 2000, 2002, 2006). Thus, the use of proper means experience and the regulatory-fit experience are distinct value experiences, even though people can sometimes confuse them (see Camacho, Higgins, & Luger, 2003).

In sum, regulatory fit is a distinctive motivational principle. It can be distinguished conceptually from other "fit"-like concepts having to do with compatibility, concordance, and matching. In addition, the regulatory-fit value experience itself can be distinguished from other kinds of value experiences, including hedonic outcome experiences (pleasure or pain) and moral process experiences. The next section considers the different ways in which regulatory fit can be created (see also Cesario, Higgins, & Scholer, 2008; Lee & Higgins, in press).

Different Ways to Create Regulatory Fit

As discussed earlier, people experience regulatory fit when the manner of their engagement in an activity sustains (vs. disrupts) their current regulatory orientation. A study by Freitas and Higgins (2002) provides an early example of how regulatory fit (and nonfit) can be created. The fit involved the relation between participants' regulatory focus orientation and the strategic way that they pursued their task goal. It should be emphasized that regulatory-fit effects are not restricted to the case of regulatory focus orientations and the strategies that do or do not fit these orientations (see, e. g., Avnet & Higgins, 2003; Bianco, Higgins, & Klem, 2003). However, most regulatory-fit studies have used regulatory focus variables to create fit or nonfit. Thus, I need first to describe the regulatory focus variables and then return to the Freitas and Higgins study.

Regulatory focus theory (Higgins, 1997, 1998) distinguishes between two basic self-regulatory orientations: a promotion-focus orientation and a prevention-focus orientation. When people have a promotion-focus orientation they represent goals as hopes or aspirations (ideals) and are concerned with nurturance, accomplishment, and advancement. They are concerned with gains and nongains and are more sensitive to the difference between the status quo or neutral state and a positive deviation from that state (the difference between "0" and "+1") than to the difference between the status quo or neutral state and a negative deviation from that state (the difference between "0" and "–1"). In contrast, when people have a prevention-focus orientation they represent goals as duties or obligations (oughts) and are concerned with safety and security. They are concerned with losses and nonlosses and are more sensitive to the difference between "0" and "–1" than to the difference between "0" and "+1" (cf. Brendl & Higgins, 1996). Because nurturance and security are each necessary for survival, each regulatory focus orientation is available to all people (with varying accessibility), and all people will pursue goals in each focus at least some of the time. However, there are chronic individual differences in the strength of each orientation, and, moreover, there are situational features that can momentarily make one orientation or the other predominate.

Regulatory focus theory also proposes that there are different pre-ferred goal-pursuit strategies for each orientation. In other words, different strategic means fit a promotion focus versus a prevention focus (Cesario et al., 2004; Crowe & Higgins, 1997; Higgins et al., 2003; Liberman, Molden, Idson, & Higgins, 2001; Shah, Higgins, & Friedman, 1998). The nature of this preference stems from the ability of one or the other strategic means to sustain (vs. disrupt) a given regulatory focus orientation. When an actor in a promotion focus pursues goals, he/she will prefer to use *eager strategic means* of goal attainment. "Eager means" are means that ensure gains (look for means of advancement) and ensure against nongains (do not close off possible advancements) and are sensitive to the difference between "0" and "+1." In contrast, when an actor in a prevention focus pursues goals, he/she will prefer to use *vigilant strategic means* of goal attainment. "Vigilant means" are means that ensure nonlosses (be careful) and ensure against losses (avoid mistakes) and are sensitive to the difference between "0" and "–1."

Let us now return to the Freitas and Higgins (2002) study. Participants began the experimental session by first describing either their hopes and aspirations in life or their beliefs about their duties and obligations in life to induce experimentally either a promotion state or a prevention state, respectively. The participants then began the "next study" in which they acted as scientists working with organic material whose goal was to find as many four-sided objects as possible among dozens of multiply shaped objects drawn on a sheet of paper. Half of the participants were instructed that "the way to do well on the task was to be eager and to try to maximize the helpful four-sided objects." The other half were instructed that "the way to do well on the task was to be vigilant and to try to eliminate the harmful four-sided objects." Thus, all participants pursued the same goal of searching for and noting as many four-sided objects as possible, but they were induced to pursue this goal in either an eager manner or a vigilant manner. The study found that, independent of their actual success on the task, the participants with an experimentally induced promotion orientation evaluated the task more positively when they pursued it an eager than a vigilant manner, whereas the reverse was true for the participants with a prevention orientation. (For an illustration of creating fit for regulatory mode orientations, rather than regulatory focus, see Avnet & Higgins, 2003.)

In the Freitas and Higgins (2002) study the participants' goal-pursuit orientation (promotion or prevention) and the manner in which they pursued the goal (eager or vigilant) were experimentally manipulated. Thus, the regulatory-fit conditions (promotion/eager, prevention/vigilant) and nonfit conditions (promotion/vigilant, prevention/eager) were created by situationally inducing participants' goal-pursuit orientation. It is also possible, however, to create regulatory fit and nonfit by having different participants who vary chronically in their regulatory focus orientations and then having them pursue a goal in an eager or vigilant manner. A study by Higgins et al. (2003, Study 2) illustrates this way of creating regulatory fit and nonfit. The participants first completed the Self-Guide Strength measure as part of a larger battery of measures. The Self-Guide Strength measure is an idiographic measure that asks participants to list attributes of their ideal self, defined as the type of person they ideally would like to be, the type of person they hope, wish, or aspire to be; and to list attributes of their ought self, defined as the type of person they believe they ought to be, the type of person they believe it is their duty, obligation, or responsibility to be. The computer recorded the time each participant took to produce each attribute. The reaction times were transformed using a natural logarithmic transformation. Then one total ideal-strength assessment and one total ought-strength assessment were calculated by summing attribute reaction times across the three ideal attributes and, separately, across the three ought attributes.

After the Self-Guide Strength measure, the participants were told that, over and above their usual payment for doing this task, they could choose between a coffee mug and a pen as a gift. (Pretesting indicated that the mug was clearly preferred.) The means of making the decision was manipulated through framing. Half of the participants were told to think about what they would gain by choosing the mug or the pen (an eager manner of making the decision), and the other half were told to think about what they would lose by not choosing the mug or the pen (a vigilant manner of making the decision). Note that both the eager and the vigilant participants were directed to consider the positive qualities of the mug and the pen. As expected, almost all participants chose the coffee mug. These participants were then given the opportunity to actually buy the mug— the amount of their own money that they offered to buy the mug was the dependent measure. The study found a positive interaction between ideal strength and strategic framing indicating that the stronger was participants' promotion focus the higher was the price offered in the eager "gain" condition than in the vigilant "loss" condition. Independent of this effect, the study also found a negative interaction between ought strength and strategic framing indicating that the stronger was participants' prevention focus the higher was the price offered in the vigilant "loss" condition than in the eager "gain" condition. It is notable that there were no main effects. This indicates that neither chronic promotion strength nor chronic prevention strength nor the strategy used to make the decision (i.e., eager "gain" vs. vigilant "loss") affected the price offered. Only the interactions reflecting fit had significant effects on the price offered.

There is another combination of orientation and manner of goal pursuit that can create regulatory fit. Rather than it involving a personality difference in orientation, it involves a commonly held difference in concerns about different kinds of activities. For example, the goal can be to eat more fruits and vegetables for the sake of protection from harmful daily elements (safety concerns), which would commonly induce a prevention orientation, or for the sake of increased energy and general fulfillment (accomplishment concerns), which would commonly induce a promotion orientation. Persuasive messages advocating eating more fruits and vegetables for the sake of these two different concerns can then be framed such that the goal of eating more fruits and vegetables would be pursued in an eager manner (gain framing) or would be pursued in a vigilant manner (nonloss framing). Using this way to create regulatory fit and nonfit, Cesario et al. (2004, Study 1) found that the message was more persuasive in the fit conditions (accomplishment/gain, safety/nonloss) than in the nonfit conditions (accomplishment/nonloss, safety/gain) (see also Lee & Aaker, 2004, discussed later below).

A somewhat different version of this way of creating regulatory fit from different concerns about different activities was used in a study by Bianco et al. (2003, Study 1). In a separate pretest, participants rated different activities on the extent to which they agreed each was "fun" and the extent to which each was "important." An activity was considered to have a consensual orientation when a clear and significant majority of respondents in a pretest rated it either as more "fun" than "important" (a consensual "fun" activity) or as more "important" than "fun" (a consensual "important" activity). In this way, "Financial Duties" was selected for Study 1 as a consensual "important" activity and "Dating Games" was selected as a consensual "fun" activity. Study 1 gave participants the same computer activity disguised as either a Financial Duties task or a Dating Game task. The goal of the activity was to determine how to use given cues to best predict the correct answer. In the Dating Game condition, participants were asked to predict the bachelor eligibility ratings of fictitious bachelors on the basis of sense of humor, good looks, and intelligence, with the cues interpreted as "points" for a bachelor. In the Financial Duties condition, participants predicted students' financial status on the basis of checking accounts, savings accounts, and credit card payments, with the cues interpreted as dollars.

Given the chronic consensual orientations to these two different activities, participants were expected to have either a "fun" orientation toward the goal of correct prediction for Dating Game or an "important" orientation for Financial Duties. For each of these goal-pursuit orientations, the task instructions suggested engaging in the activity either in a fun manner (experience doing the task as an enjoyable diversion from your "real" academic work) or in an important manner (experience doing the task as an important part of your life). As predicted, performance on the task was better when there was a fit between consensual orientation and manner of engagement ("dating game"/fun, "financial duties"/important) than when there was a nonfit ("dating game"/important, "financial duties"/fun).

In the above method of creating regulatory fit, the goal-pursuit orientation and the manner of goal pursuit are manipulated within the current situation (i.e., within the task activity itself; within the persuasive message itself). In direct contrast to such integral regulatory-fit manipulations (see Koenig et al., 2007), regulatory fit can be ambient or incidental to a focal task by being created before or after the focal task (e.g., Higgins et al., 2003, Study 4; Cesario et al., 2004, Study 3; Hong & Lee, 2008, Study 4; see also Cesario et al., 2008; Lee & Higgins, in press). For example, in a study by Cesario et al. (2004, Study 3), participants were asked first to think about their hopes and aspirations (promotion-orientation goals) or their duties and obligations (prevention-orientation goals), and then write down either five eager strategies or five vigilant strategies to attain the goals. Later, all participants were given the identical persuasive message. Participants who experienced fit prior to receiving the message (i.e., eager strategies for attaining their hopes & aspirations, vigilant strategies for attaining their duties & obligations) were more persuaded by the message than participants who experienced prior nonfit (i.e., vigilant strategies for attaining their hopes & aspirations; eager strategies for attaining their duties & obligations).

All of the above methods for creating regulatory fit involve participants pursuing (or imagining pursuing) a goal in a particular manner that fits or does not fit their orientation toward the goal, which then affects their response in the fit-inducing task or carries over to affect their response in a separate task. Studies have also found that it is possible to create regulatory fit (and nonfit) by manipulating the manner of goal pursuit displayed by another person for recipients who vary in their orientation to the goal. A study by Cesario and Higgins (2008, Study 2) provides an especially powerful demonstration of this effect.

All participants were exposed to a video message that advocated implementing a new after-school program for grade schools, with the speaker in the video ostensibly being a teacher who had worked on developing the program. The text of the persuasive messages was identical across all video conditions. The only difference between the videos concerned whether the speaker's nonverbal gestures, speech rate, and body position and movement while delivering the message conveyed a sense of eager versus vigilant goal pursuit. The participants' chronic regulatory focus orientation was determined using the Regulatory Focus Questionnaire (see Grant & Higgins, 2003; Higgins et al., 2001, for reliability and validity), operationalized as a person's subjective history of success with promotion-related versus prevention-related strategies. Participants' predominant focus is computed by subtracting the mean of prevention items from the mean of promotion items, yielding a single continuous measure with positive numbers corresponding to predominant promotion focus and negative numbers corresponding to predominant prevention focus.

Cesario and Higgins (2008, Study 2) found that participants in the regulatory-fit conditions (predominant promotion/eager speaker, predominant prevention/vigilant speaker) expressed that they "felt right" during the message to a greater degree and were more persuaded by the message than participants in the nonfit conditions (predominant promotion/vigilant speaker, predominant prevention/eager speaker). Moreover, "feeling right" functioned as the mediator between regulatory fit and persuasion. Another study by Cesario and Higgins (2008, Study 1) using the same nonverbal eager versus vigilant videos found that participants' ratings of *processing fluency* (ease of attention) were higher in the regulatory-fit conditions than in the nonfit conditions. These findings suggest that when people are pursuing a goal, or imagining pursuing a goal, their orientation toward the goal can be sustained or disrupted by observing the manner in which another person pursues the goal. This has intriguing implications for social influence because it means that sharing another person's goals is not sufficient to make that person "feel right" about their reaction to what is going on. It is also necessary to display a manner of goal pursuit that fits that person's orientation to the goal.

In sum, regulatory fit can be created, and have its effects, in many different ways. The participants' goal-pursuit orientation and the manner in which they pursued the goal can be experimentally manipulated. It is also possible to create fit and nonfit by having participants who differ chronically in their regulatory orientations and then having them pursue a goal in one or another manner. Rather than involving a chronic personality difference in orientation, the chronic difference can also be a commonly held difference in concerns about different kinds of activities. In addition, rather being integral to the focal task activity itself, regulatory fit can be ambient or incidental to a focal task by being created before or after the focal task. Finally, rather than manipulating individuals' own manner of goal pursuit, it is possible to create regulatory fit (and nonfit) by manipulating the manner of goal pursuit displayed by another person for recipients who vary in their regulatory orientation. Not only can regulatory fit be created in many different ways, it can also have many different effects. This has already been suggested by the studies reviewed above, which demonstrate effects of regulatory fit on how much they enjoy their pursuit of a goal, how much they value an object they have chosen, how well they perform on a task, and how persuaded they are by a message they receive. The next section reviews regulatory-fit effects in more detail while also considering the different mechanisms that can underlie regulatory fit effects.

Regulatory-Fit Effects and the Mechanisms Underlying Them

Regulatory fit makes people "feel right" about, and engage more strongly in, what they are doing (Higgins, 2000). Feeling right about and engaging more strongly in what one is doing can also increase the fluency of the process. Thus, one can consider these elements of the regulatory-fit experience as a unified syndrome. It is also possible, however, that each of these elements can have its own independent effects. In addition, not all three elements need to be present for there to be effects. As is discussed below, there is evidence supporting the role of each of these elements in regulatory-fit effects, although given their natural co-occurrence, evidence for any one element does not preclude the possibility that one of the other elements was also involved in the obtained effect. This section is organized in terms of different regulatory effects, with evidence for the role of the underlying mechanisms being discussed in relation to these effects.

Regulatory Fit and Value

The Freitas and Higgins (2002) study and the Higgins et al. (2003, Study 2) study described above illustrate how regulatory fit can influence the value of activities and objects. In Freitas and Higgins, the positive value, that is, enjoyment, of the goal activity of finding as many four-sided objects as possible was higher for those participants who experienced regulatory fit while engaging in the task, and in Higgins et al. (Study 2) the positive value of the chosen mug, as reflected in the money offered to buy it, was higher for those participants who made their decision with regulatory fit. In more recent studies on fit and value creation by Brodscholl, Kober, and Higgins (2007), participants varied chronically or situationally in their promotion and prevention orientations and the manipulation of the manner of goal pursuit concerned goal attainment versus goal maintenance rather than eagerness versus vigilance.

All participants earned tokens by solving anagrams and were motivated to end up with enough tokens to win a coffee mug as a prize. However, half of the participants began with no tokens and needed to solve anagrams to add enough tokens to reach criterion (the token attainment condition), whereas the other half began with tokens and needed to solve the anagrams to stop enough tokens from being subtracted to reach criterion (the token maintenance condition). The strategic "addition" in the attainment condition fits promotion whereas the strategic "stop subtraction" in the maintenance condition fits prevention. All participants successfully reached the criterion and won the prize mug. They were then asked to assign a monetary price to it. Partipants in the fit conditions (promotion/attainment, prevention/maintenance) assigned a higher monetary price than participants in the nonfit conditions (promotion/maintenance, prevention/attainment).

A study by Avnet and Higgins (2003) provide another example of how fit can affect value with an orientation other than the regulatory focus orientations of promotion and prevention; specifically, with the regulatory mode orientations of locomotion and assessment (see Higgins, Kruglanski, & Pierro, 2003). A locomotion orientation is concerned with movement from state to state, whereas an assessment orientation is concerned with making comparisons. In the Avnet and Higgins study, either a locomotion orientation or an assessment orientation was experimentally induced at the beginning of the experiment. The participants then chose one book-light from a set of book-lights using either a progressive elimination strategy (i.e., eliminate the worst alternative at each phase until only one alternative remains) or a full evaluation strategy (i.e., make comparisons among all of the alternatives for all of the attributes and then choose the one with the best attributes overall). The progressive elimination strategy allows for steady movement toward the goal (a locomotion fit), but it steadily restricts the number of comparisons possible as the process continues (an assessment nonfit). In contrast, the full evaluation strategy allows for all possible comparisons to be made (an assessment fit), but movement toward narrowing down the options is restricted until the end of the process (a locomotion nonfit). Avnet and Higgins found that the participants offered more of their own money to buy the same chosen book-light in the fit conditions (assessment/"full evaluation," locomotion/"progressive elimination") than in the nonfit conditions. In addition, this fit effect was independent of the participants' pleasant or painful mood at the time that they offered to buy the book-light.

Regulatory-fit effects on increasing the value of activities and objects like those illustrated above could result from several mechanisms. Novemsky, Dhar, Schwarz, and Simonson (2007) found that the ease or difficulty of making preferential choices, that is, preference fluency, can influence decision making because people use these experiences as information (see Schwarz, 1990; Schwarz & Clore, 1983, 1988) to make inferences about what their evaluations of the choices must be. One possibility, then, is that when regulatory fit increases processing fluency, people experience the decision-making process, such as choosing between the mug and the pen in the Higgins et al. (2003, Study 2) above, as being relatively easy. They then use this information to infer that the chosen object, for example, the mug, must have been of high value because it was easy to choose it. And if it is of high value then it is worth offering a higher price to buy it.

Although this "feelings-as-information" mechanism could contribute to past regulatory-fit effects on increasing the value of objects and activities, it cannot account for all of the findings. Indeed, another study by Higgins et al. (2003, Study 4) explicitly addressed this possibility by creating regulatory fit using the ambient rather than integral technique discussed above. In this study, participants were asked first to think about their hopes and aspirations (promotion-orientation goals) or their duties and obligations (prevention-orientation goals), and then write down either five eager strategies or five vigilant strategies to attain the goals. Later, all participants were asked to rate the good-naturedness of some depicted dogs in an allegedly unrelated study. Participants who had earlier experienced fit (i.e., eager action plans for hopes and aspirations, vigilant action for duties and obligations) rated the dogs as more good-natured than did those who had earlier experienced nonfit (i.e., vigilant action plans for hopes and aspirations, eager action plans for duties and obligations). Thus, regulatory fit increased the value of the target object without any manipulation of fit during the evaluation task itself that could have produced greater fluency when evaluating the dogs' good-naturedness. Another study by Higgins et al. (2003, Study 5) on evaluating middle school as an object measured the perceived efficiency, that is, the fluency, of proposing strategies for improving middle school (How easy was it for you to list things to improve students' experiences?; How quickly were you able to list things to improve students' experiences?). The study found that regulatory fit increased the evaluated importance of middle school even when fluency was statistically controlled.

There is another kind of feeling mechanism that might also contribute to regulatory-fit effects on increasing the value of objects and activities: mood transfer. There is evidence that processing fluency can elicit positive affect (e.g., Winkielman & Cacioppo, 2001). It is possible, then, that when regulatory fit increases processing fluency, positive affect is generated, and this positive affect transfers to objects and activities, thereby increasing their value. Such transfer of positivity could itself be an ambient factor and transfer positivity when later evaluating something, such as depicted dogs, despite the object evaluation being independent of the process that created regulatory fit to begin with.

Another "mug versus pen" study by Higgins et al. (2003, Study 3) investigated whether regulatory-fit effects on increasing value was independent of people's positive mood. The procedure for this study was basically the same as described earlier for Study 2 of Higgins et al. except that the participants completed the Self-Guide Strength measure of chronic promotion and prevention focus in a separate session a week before the choice study. After participants had made their choice between the mug and the pen, the experimenter gave them a questionnaire with mood items (e.g., how good, positive, happy, relaxed, content they felt) and price items. (The order of price items and mood items was counterbalanced and there were no order effects.) The study found that the chosen mug was assigned a higher price in the fit conditions, and this effect was independent of participants' positive mood. In another study involving a different kind of evaluation—evaluating the "rightness" of a conflict resolution—Camacho et al. (2003) found not only that participants' evaluations of rightness were stronger when the manner of the conflict resolution (i.e., eager manner of resolution, vigilant manner of resolution) fit participants regulatory focus than when it didn't, but also that this regulatory-fit effect was independent of the positivity of participants' mood. Thus, once again, although a "transfer-of-positive-mood" mechanism might in some cases contribute to regulatory-fit effects on value, fit effects can occur independent of this mood mechanism.

In sum, regulatory-fit effects on increasing the value of objects and activities cannot be explained just in terms of increased fluency from fit making what one is doing feel easier or more positive, although these factors could contribute to regulatory-fit effects in some cases. Generally speaking, the underlying mechanism that was proposed in early studies of regulatory-fit effects was that fit made people "feel right" about what they were doing (e.g., Camacho et al., 2003; Higgins et al., 2003). As discussed above, this "feel-right" experience is not the same as just experiencing what one is doing as more positive or efficient. There is an additional "correctness" property to this experience from the manner of goal pursuit "sustaining" one's current orientation—the second definition of "sustain," as mentioned earlier, being "to allow or admit as valid, to confirm, to support as true, legal or just." How might the "feel-right" experience increase the value of objects and activities? Two different possibilities have been proposed. The first proposal (Higgins et al., 2003) was that feeling right about what one is doing is a value experience, and this value experience, like any other experience or feeling, can last for awhile. Later, at the time that the value judgment is made (e.g., deciding the monetary value of the mug), this value experience could transfer to other value experiences regarding the target object or activity, such as those deriving from the target's remembered or perceived hedonic properties, and thus increase the overall value of the target. That is, the "feel right" value experience from fit transfers to the overall experience of the target's value, analogous to arousal or excitation from one source later transferring to the emotional experience of something (Schachter & Singer, 1962; Zillman, 1978).

The notion that the "feel-right" experience transfers to the value experience of some target has an important implication: It would always make the target object or activity more valuable than it would otherwise be. This is not a problem with respect to the studies reviewed above because the targets did, indeed, increase in value when there was regulatory fit. However, in these studies the initial reaction to the target was always positive. What if the initial reaction to the target was negative instead? According to the value-transfer notion, the positive "feel-right" experience would transfer some positive value to the experience of the target, thereby making the value experience of the target less negative than it would otherwise be. The second possibility for how the "feel-right" experience might affect the value of objects and activities makes a different prediction.

Rather than the "feel-right" experience from fit transfering value to the target object or activity, it is possible that fit makes people "feel right" about their reaction to the target. My statement in the original presentation of regulatory-fit theory (Higgins, 2000, pp. 1218–1219) was as follows: "I propose that, independent of outcomes, people experience a *regulatory fit* when they use goal pursuit means that fit their regulatory orientation, and this regulatory fit increases the value of what they are doing." The question, then, is what is meant by "what they are doing"? It could be, for example, their engagement in the target activity itself, such that it becomes more enjoyable as in the Freitas and Higgins (2002) study. However, "what they are doing" could instead be conceptualized as their reacting to or evaluating the target activity or object, in which case it would be their reaction or evaluation that increases in value and importance. That is, whatever their reaction to the target happens to be—positive or negative—would increase in value and importance. With respect to the "feel-right" experience in particular, regulatory fit would make people feel that their reactions to the target were valid and true, that is, "correct." This would intensify whatever the reaction happens to be, making positive reactions more positive and making negative reactions more negative. As is seen in the next section on persuasion, this is precisely what was found in a study by Cesario et al. (2004, Study 4). A recent study by Levine, Alexander, and Higgins (2007) on group reactions to a deviate also directly tested this possibility.

Group members' reactions to opinion deviance is typically quite negative. Levine et al.'s (2007) question was whether this negative reaction would be intensified when there was a fit between a group's regulatory focus state (promotion vs. prevention) and the way a deviate delivered his or her deviant message (eager vs. vigilant). They addressed this question by experimentally inducing a promotion state in all the members of some groups and a prevention state in all the members of other groups. Each group then engaged in a discussion in which they came to a unanimous group decision against implementing a senior comprehensive examination. They then watched a videotape of another student, who like them was a psychology student at the university, deliver a message that supported the senior comprehensive exam requirement. The delivery style of the deviate's message presentation was either eager or vigilant. The study found that the group members' subsequent evaluation of the deviate was more negative in the regulatory-fit conditions (promotion group/eager deviate, prevention group/vigilant deviate) than in the nonfit conditions (promotion group/vigilant deviate, prevention group/eager deviate).

Additional support for the idea that regulatory fit affects the value of objects and activities by intensifying a person's value reaction to something is provided in studies by Idson, Liberman, and Higgins (2004). Their studies involved participants making prospective evaluations of how good or bad they would feel if they were to make a choice that produced a positive or negative outcome, respectively. They modified a Thaler (1980) scenario in which participants imagined buying a book and choosing between paying with cash or paying with a credit card, with the book's price being higher for the latter choice. In one study, for example, the scenario was written to induce either a promotion focus ("discount" language) or a prevention focus ("penalty" language) and the outcomes were framed either in gain-related terms or loss-related terms such that promotion gain and prevention loss involved regulatory fit. The prediction was that both feeling good and feeling bad would be intensified in the regulatory-fit conditions, such that feeling good when imagining a positive outcome would be greater for promotion/gain than prevention/nonloss, and feeling bad when imagining a negative outcome would be greater for prevention/loss than promotion/nongain. This prediction was confirmed.

The specific intensification mechanism examined in the Idson et al. (2004) studies was not that fit makes people "feel right" about their evaluative reactions to something but, rather, that fit increases motivational intensity: how strongly motivated people are to make a positive outcome happen or a negative outcome not happen. This is basically the same as the strength of engagement mechanism described earlier (see Higgins, 2006). Once again, this mechanism emphasizes that regulatory fit affects value by intensifying whatever a person's reaction to something happens to be. But it does so not because people "feel right" about their reaction, but because stronger engagment increases the experience of the motivational force toward the target—either an increase in the experience of the force of attraction or an increase in the experience of the force of repulsion. This motivational force experience can affect value independent of the effect of hedonic experience on value (see Higgins, 2006).

Studies by Idson et al. (2004) provided evidence for such independent effects of increased motivational force (i.e., engagement strength) from fit and pleasure/pain hedonic experience from outcome. In addition to measuring how good or bad participants felt about the imagined decision outcome, separate measures of pleasure/pain intensity and strength of motivational force were taken. Different studies used slightly different measures to provide convergent validity. For example, in a study that manipulated regulatory focus through priming rather than scenario framing, pleasure-pain intensity was measured by asking the participants how pleasant the positive outcome would be or how painful the negative outcome would be; and strength of motivational force was measured by asking them how motivated they would be to make the positive outcome happen (in the positive outcome condition) or how motivated they would be to make the negative outcome not happen (in the negative-outcome condition). The framing and the priming studies found that pleasure/pain intensity and strength of motivational force each made significant *independent* contributions to the perceived value of the imagined outcome (i.e., its goodness/badness). The results of these studies, as well as the Levine et al. (2007) study, support the idea that regulatory fit affects the value of objects and activities by intensifying a person's value reaction to something, whether that reaction is positive or negative. Either the "feeling-right" or the engagement-strength mechanism could produce such fit effects on value. Further support for the intensification idea is considered in the next section on regulatory fit and persuasion.

Regulatory Fit and Persuasion

To change people's attitudes and behavior, one needs to convince them of the value of the advocated change. A standard method is to provide information about the positive outcomes or benefits of such a change. Regulatory fit permits another method for change. To the extent that people have a basically positive response to what is being advocated, then creating a regulatory fit should make that positive response "feel right" and/or intensify it from stronger engagement, thereby increasing persuasion. The results of several studies support this idea (for fuller discussions of fit and persuasion, see Lee & Higgins, in press; Cesario et al., 2008). For example, in an early study by Spiegel, Grant-Pillow, and Higgins (2004, Study 2) that was similar to the Cesario et al. (2004, Study 1) study described earlier, where the same goal (eating more fruits and vegetables) was associated with different concerns (promotion vs. prevention) and would be pursued in different ways (eager vs. vigilant), the participants recorded over 7 days how many servings of fruits and vegetables they ate in a daily nutrition log. As discussed above, "feeling right" and engagement strength from fit should be higher for promotion than prevention when eager pursuit is emphasized and should be higher for prevention than promotion when vigilant pursuit is emphasized. The results supported these predictions, with participants in the regulatory-fit conditions eating about 20% more fruits and vegetables over the following week than those in the nonfit conditions.

Pham and Avnet (2004) examined regulatory focus differences in the preferred manner of decision making and found that individuals with a promotion orientation preferred to rely more on their affect whereas those with a prevention orientation preferred to rely more on reasons. Using these findings, Avnet and Higgins (2006) had participants choose between two brands of correction fluids in either an affect-based manner or a reason-based manner. They found that participants who were promotion oriented who chose in an affect-based manner were willing to pay much more for their chosen product than those who chose in a reason-based manner, and the reverse was true for participants who were prevention oriented.

Cesario et al. (2004) examined fit effects on persuasion in more detail. How an ambient or incidental effect of creating fit in one phase can make the same persuasive message more effective in a second phase was discussed earlier (Cesario et al., 2004, Study 3). In another study by Cesario et al. (2004, Study 2), participants who varied chronically in the strength of their promotion or prevention focus read an article eliciting support for a new city tax to create an after-school program that would help elementary- and high-school students in their personal and academic lives. The structure, content, and primary goal of the article was identical for both versions. The only difference was the strategic framing used to advocate the policy. For example, the eager-framed article said that "the primary reason for supporting this program is because it will advance children's education and support more children to succeed," whereas the vigilant-framed article said that "the primary reason for supporting this program is because it will secure children's education and prevent more children from failing." The study found that the message was perceived as more persuasive and was more effective in changing attitudes when there was a fit between its manner of presentation and participants' chronic focus orientation (eager/promotion, vigilant/prevention) than when there was a nonfit (eager/prevention, vigilant/promotion). Importantly, this fit effect was independent of participants' positive or negative mood.

Cesario et al. (2004, Study 3) also investigated the role of the "feel-right" experience for the effect of fit on persuasion. To test for the importance of this experience, participants' attention either was or was not drawn to the true source of their "feeling-right" experience prior to their receiving the message (e.g., Schwarz & Clore, 1983). In addition, because of the importance of attitude confidence and certainty for persuasion (e.g., Tormala & Petty, 2002), participants were asked how confident they were in their attitude toward the after-school proposal. In the standard condition where participants' attention was not drawn to their "feel-right" experience, participants in the fit conditions were more confident in their attitudes than participants in the nonfit conditions. However, when participants' attention was drawn to their "feeling-right" experience, participants in the fit conditions actually reported being less confident in their attitudes than participants in the nonfit conditions (see also Spiegel & Higgins, 2002, described in Higgins et al., 2003).

The results of this study suggest that the regulatory-fit "feel-right" experience does contribute to people's confidence in their subsequent evaluations, and if the appropriateness of using this experience is brought into question, as by drawing attention to its source, then its effect is suppressed and reversed, perhaps through overcorrection (cf. Petty & Wegener, 1998). Moreover, as discussed above, the recent study by Cesario and Higgins (2008, Study 2) that created fit by having messages delivered with eager versus vigilant nonverbal styles to recipients with chronic promotion versus prevention orientations found that the "feel-right" experience mediated the relation between fit and persuasion.

Cesario and Higgins (2008, Study 1) also found, as mentioned earlier, that processing fluency (subjective ease of attention) was higher in the regulatory-fit conditions than in the nonfit conditions. In earlier studies, Lee and

Aaker (2004, Study 4A) directly tested for the role of processing fluency in fit effects on persuasion. Participants were presented with an advertisement for Welch's grape juice that emphasized either promotion concerns (e.g., energy creation, enjoy life) or prevention concerns (e.g., cancer and heart disease prevention) and eager or vigilant means to pursue these concerns. The advertising appeal was found to be more persuasive in the fit conditions (promotion/eager, prevention/vigilant) than in the nonfit conditions (promotion/vigilant, prevention/eager). Processsing fluency (self-reported ease of processing and comprehensibility) was also higher in the fit than the nonfit conditions. Moreover, the study found that processing fluency mediated the relation between fit and persuasion. In another study by Lee and Aaker (Study 4B), participants first reviewed an appeal message framed in one of the above four fit/nonfit conditions and then were presented very briefly target words from the message which they had to identify—an accessibility measure of processing fluency. The study found that more target words from the message were identified in the fit conditions.

Processing fluencing as indexed by ease of processing and comprehensibility and by accessibility is like a mild kind of "flow" experience (see Csikszentmihalyi, 1975). It has properties that are like "feeling right" on the one hand (i.e., subjective ease of processing and comprehensibility) and like engagement strength on the other hand (i.e., accessibility). Thus, these studies provide support for all three hypothesized elements of the regulatory-fit experience. What about the proposed "intensification" mechanism? Another study by Cesario et al. (2004, Study 4) directly tested for the role of this mechanism in fit effects on persuasion. It is well known in persuasion studies that individuals can vary in their positive or negative thought reactions to a message (e.g., Greenwald, 1968). If participants are generating positive thoughts, their experience of "feeling right" about and strongly engaging in those positive thoughts would make the message more positive and thus more persuasive. In contrast, if participants are generating negative thoughts, their experience of "feeling right" about and strongly engaging in those negative thoughts would make the message more negative and thus less persuasive (cf. Petty, Briñol, & Tormala, 2002). Cesario et al. (2004, Study 4) used the standard thought-listing technique to obtain participants' positive and negative thoughts about the message. They found that the fit effect on increasing attitude change occurred only for participants who had positive thoughts about the message. For participants who had negative thoughts about the message, fit had the opposite effect: It decreased attitude change.

This study provides strong evidence for the intensification mechanism of regulatory fit operating in the persuasion domain as well. Additional evidence is provided in an early study by Aaker and Lee (2001, Study 3). They manipulated argument strength and regulatory fit in an advertising message about tennis racquets. Regulatory fit was created by priming participants' independent or interdependent self-construals that have been shown to be associated with distinct regulatory orientation (Lee, Aaker, & Gardner, 2000) and by making the manner of goal pursuit either eager (to win the tennis tournament) or vigilant (to not lose the tennis tournament). Aaker and Lee found that the tennis racquet was evaluated more positively with the fit than the nonfit message—but only when the arguments were strong, which is when they were likely to respond positively to the mesage. When the arguments were weak, which is when they were likely to respond negatively to the message, the tennis racquet was evaluated less positively in the fit conditions.

Regulatory Fit and Performance

The mechanism that provides the best explanation for regulatory-fit effects on performance is increased strength of engagement (see Higgins, 2005, 2006). The fit effects on performance that I now review provide indirect evidence of fit increasing engagement strength, but there is also more direct evidence. One set of studies by Förster, Higgins, and Idson (1998), for example, examined chronic and situational instantiations of regulatory focus orientation. The participants performed an anagram task in either an eager or vigilant manner. Performing the task in an eager versus vigilant manner was manipulated by using an arm pressure technique (Cacioppo, Priester, & Berntson, 1993). While performing the anagram task, the participants either pressed downward on the plate of a supposed skin conductance machine that was attached to the top of the table (a vigilance/avoidance-related movement of pushing away from oneself) or pressed upward on the plate attached to the bottom of the table (an eagerness/approach-related movement of pulling toward oneself). Participants' arm pressure while pressing downward or upward on the plate was recorded and served as the measure of engagement strength. On a measure of overall on-line arm pressure during task performance, strength of engagement was stronger when there was regulatory fit (i.e., promotion/eager, prevention/vigilant) than nonfit (i.e., promotion/vigilant, prevention/eager). Another study by Förster et al. used persistence as the measure of strength of engagement and found that persistence was greater when there was fit than nonfit.

Using a similar paradigm as the Förster et al. (1998) arm pressure studies, while also experimentally controlling for participants' outcome expectancies during task performance, Förster, Grant, Idson, and Higgins (2001) replicated another Förster et al. finding: On a measure of the steepness of the arm pressure gradients (calculated over the recorded arm pressure values from the beginning to the end of the set of anagrams), the approach gradient (the recorded upward pressure values when the plate was attached to the bottom of the table) was steeper for participants in a promotion than a prevention focus. In contrast, the avoidance gradient (the recorded downward pressure values when the plate was attached to the top of the table) was steeper for participants in a prevention than a promotion focus. Förster et al. (2001) also replicated the fit effect on persistence found by Förster et al. (1998). Importantly, the fit effects found by Förster et al. (2001) and by Förster et al. (1998) were independent of participants' positive or negative feelings during the task performance. Additional evidence that regulatory fit increases strength of engagement is provided by the Idson et al. (2004) finding described earlier that participants in the regulatory-fit conditions reported higher motivational intensity than participants in the nonfit conditions.

Task performance can be enhanced in different ways through regulatory fit. In studies on anagram performance by Shah, Higgins, and Friedman (1998), for example, participants' regulatory focus varied either chronically or through experimental induction, and either an eager or vigilant manner was manipulated by designating particular anagrams in vigilance terms (avoid losing payment by solving) or eagerness terms (gain payment by solving). As predicted, anagram performance was better when there was regulatory fit (i.e., promotion focus/eager strategy, prevention focus/vigilant strategy) than nonfit. Förster et al. (1998) also found that anagram performance was better when there was regulatory fit (i.e., promotion focus/eager strategy, prevention focus/vigilant strategy) than nonfit. Finally, Freitas, Liberman, and Higgins (2002) found that participants with a prevention focus did better than participants with a promotion focus on a task that required vigilance against a tempting distractor.

The Bianco et al. (2003) study on "fun" and "importance" described earlier illustrates another way in which regulatory fit can enhance performance: how performance is affected by the fit between people's consensual theories of a given task being either fun or important and task instructions to engage that task in either a fun or important way. On tasks of predictive learning (discussed above), paired-associate learning, and free recall of movie scenes, they found that performance was enhanced when there was a fit (vs. a nonfit) between participants' implicit theories and task instructions regarding the fun and importance of the task. Interestingly, in one study where participants' implicit theory of an "academic activity" was that it was "important but not fun," instructing participants that doing the task would be high in importance and fun (a nonfit) actually undermined performance compared to high importance/low fun instructions (a fit).

There is yet another way that regulatory fit can influence performance. Previous researchers have suggested that the mental simulation of steps needed to implement goal completion facilitates goal achievement (e.g., Gollwitzer, 1996). Given the tactical preference of people with a promotion focus for eagerly approaching matches to desired end-states, rather than vigilantly avoiding mismatches to desired end-states, Spiegel et al. (2004) predicted that people who were promotion focused would perform better at a task if they prepared by eagerly simulating and developing approach-oriented plans rather than avoidance-oriented plans, and the reverse would be true for people who were prevention focused. In one study, participants were asked to write a report on how they would spend their upcoming Saturday, and to turn it in by a certain deadline, to receive a cash payment. Before they left the lab, all participants were asked to imagine certain implementation steps that they might take in writing the report (i.e., simulations related to when, where, and how to do the report), and the steps were framed to represent either eager-approach means or vigilant-avoidance means. Spiegel et al. (2004) found that participants in the fit conditions were almost 50% more likely to turn in their reports than participants in the nonfit conditions.

Yet another kind of performance is effectiveness as a leader. Regulatory-fit effects on leader effectiveness have recently been examined in regard to regulatory mode orientations. Kruglanski, Pierro, and Higgins (2007), for example, examined leadership effectiveness in diverse organizational contexts. They compared the effectiveness of two leadership styles: (1) a "forceful" leadership style, represented by coercive, legitimate, and directive kinds of strategic influence; and (2) an "advisory" leadership style, represented by expert, referent, and participative kinds of strategic influence. A forceful leadership style fits individuals high in locomotion more than an advisory leadership style because the former pushes for moving a task along, whereas the latter waits to allow reflection before moving ahead. In contrast, an advisory leadership style fits individuals high in assessment more than a forceful leadership style because the former allows for critical comparison of alternatives, whereas the latter dictates one course of action (the leader's). Consistent with regulatory-fit predictions, Kruglanski et al. (2007) found that subordinates who were high in locomotion preferred and reported greater job satisfaction for forceful than advisory leadership, whereas the reverse was true for subordinates who where high in assessment. Benjamin and Flynn (2006) have also recently found, using experimental data and data collected from a survey of executives, that the effectiveness of transformational leadership depends on followers' regulatory mode. They hypothesized that transformational leadership would be more effective (e.g., increasing motivation, eliciting positive evaluations) when followers had a locomotion orientation than an assessment orientation because transformational leaders emphasize movement and change through their strong sense of purpose, perseverance, and direction. The results supported their prediction.

Future Directions

In this chapter, I distinguished regulatory fit from other "fit"-like concepts and from other kinds of self-regulatory value experiences. I also discussed the various ways in which regulatory fit can be created. Finally, I reviewed evidence of the different kinds of effects that regulatory fit can have and considered the different mechanisms that underlie these effects. In closing, I want to consider more the regulatory-fit mechanisms that have been identified and discussed.

I reviewed evidence supporting the role of the regulatory-fit experience of "feeling right" about what one is doing, engaging more strongly in what one is doing, and feeling more fluent about what one is doing. Different studies provide evidence for the role of each of these elements of the regulatory-fit experience, including evidence for the mediating role of each element and/or the independence of its effect on value, persuasion, or performance from just hedonic experience. It makes sense to conceptualize the regulatory-fit experience as a unified syndrome of these three elements, especially given that each element could contribute psychologically to the others: "feeling right" about what one is doing could contribute to engaging more strongly and more fluently in what one is doing; engaging more strongly in what one is doing could make what one is doing "feel right" and be more fluent; engaging more fluently in what one is doing could make the engagement stronger and "feel right." The possibility should also be considered, however, that each element can make its own unique, or at least major, contribution to some regulatory-fit phenomena (see also Lee & Higgins, in press; Cesario et al., 2008).

With regard to this latter possibility, there do seem to be phenomena for which one or another of the regulatory-fit elements is most critical. One example would be some of the regulatory-fit effects on performance described above. For instance, the regulatory-fit mechanism of increased engagement strength is likely to underlie the increase in arm pressure found by Förster et al. (1998, 2001) when people are in regulatory-fit conditions. There are other regulatory-fit effects where increased engagement strength is likely to be the underlying mechanism. For instance, recent research by Hong and Lee (2008) examined the effects of regulatory fit and nonfit using a variety of self-regulation tasks. They found that participants who experienced regulatory fit could squeeze a handgrip longer and control their food intake better (i.e., choose a healthy apple over a chocolate bar for a snack) compared to those who experienced regulatory nonfit.

Another example would be regulatory-fit effects where "feeling right" from fit, and "feeling wrong" from nonfit, is likely to be the mechanism underlying the phenomena. A study by Grant, Higgins, Baer, and Bolger (2007) provides an instance of this case. They conducted a daily diary study of college students who recorded each day the extent to which they used eager coping strategies and vigilant coping strategies to deal with a problem or life hassle they had that day. The students varied in the strength of their promotion focus and prevention focus. The study found that the students felt less distressed at the end of the day when they used coping strategies during the day that fit their predominant regulatory focus and felt more distress when they used coping strategies that did not fit. The results from this study suggest that people "feel right" when they pursue life goals in a manner that fits their goal orientation and "feel wrong" when they pursue life goals in a manner that does not fit.

What the above examples illustrate is the possibility that the different elements of the regulatory-fit experience can contribute differentially to particular regulatory fit effects. What is clear now is that the "feel right," engagement strength, and fluency elements of the regulatory-fit experience have significant effects on value creation, persuasion, and performance. We need to turn now to the second- and third-generation questions of when and how these elements of the regulatory-fit experience influence one another, when and how they work together, and when and how they work independently. These are the critical questions for future research.

Acknowledgments

The research by the author and his collaborators that is reported in this chapter, as well as the writing of this chapter, was supported by Grant 39429 from the National Institute of Mental Health to E. Tory Higgins.

References

Aaker, J. L., & Lee, A. Y. (2001). I seek pleasures and we avoid pains: The role of self regulatory goals in information processing and persuasion. *Journal of Consumer Research, 28* (June), 33–49.

Appelt, K. C., Zou, X., Arora, P., & Higgins, E. T. (in press). Regulatory fit and negotiation: Effects of "promotion-seller" and "prevention-buyer" fit. *Social Cognition.*

Avnet, T., & Higgins, E. T. (2003). Locomotion, assessment, and regulatory fit: Value transfer from "how" to "what." *Journal of Experimental Social Psychology, 39,* 525–530.

Avnet, T., & Higgins, E. T. (2006). How regulatory fit affects value in consumer choices and opinions. *Journal of Marketing Research, 43,* 1–10.

Benjamin, L., & Flynn, F. J. (2006). Leadership style and regulatory mode: Value from fit? *Organizational Behavior and Human Decision Processes, 100,* 216–230.

Bianco, A. T., Higgins, E. T., & Klem, A. (2003). How "fun/importance" fit affects performance: Relating implicittheories to instructions. *Personality and Social Psychology Bulletin, 29*, 1091–1103.

Brendl, C. M., & Higgins, E. T. (1996). Principles of judging valence: What makes events positive or negative? In M. P. Zanna (Ed.), *Advances in experimental social psychology* (Vol. 28, pp. 95–160). New York: Academic Press.

Brodscholl, J. C., Kober, H., & Higgins, E. T. (2007). Strategies of self-regulation in goal attainment versus goal maintenance. *European Journal of Social Psychology, 37*, 628–648.

Cacioppo, J. T., Priester, J. R., & Berntson, G. G. (1993). Rudimentary determinants of attitudes II: Arm flexion and extension have differential effects on attitudes. *Journal of Personality and Social Psychology, 65*, 5–17.

Camacho, C. J., Higgins, E. T., & Luger, L. (2003). Moral value transfer from regulatory fit: "What feels right is right" and "what feels wrong is wrong." *Journal of Personality and Social Psychology, 84*, 498–510.

Carver, C. S., & Scheier, M. F. (1981). *Attention and self-regulation: A control-theory approach to human behavior.* New York: Springer-Verlag.

Cesario, J., Grant, H., & Higgins, E. T. (2004). Regulatory fit and persuasion: Transfer from "feeling right." *Journal of Personality and Social Psychology, 86*, 388–404.

Cesario, J., & Higgins, E. T. (2008). Making message recipients "feel right": How nonverbal cues can increase persuasion. *Psychological Science, 19*, 415–420.

Cesario, J., Higgins, E. T., & Scholer, A. A. (2008). Regulatory fit and persuasion: Basic principles and remaining questions. *Social and Personality Psychology Compass, 2*, 444–463.

Clary, E. G., Snyder, M., Ridge, R. D., Miene, P. K., & Haugen, J. A. (1994). Matching messages to motives in persuasion: A functional approach to promoting volunteerism. *Journal of Applied Social Psychology, 24*, 1129–1149.

Crowe, E., & Higgins, E. T. (1997). Regulatory focus and strategic inclinations: Promotion and prevention in decision-making. *Organizational Behavior and Human Decision Processes, 69*, 117–132.

Csikszentmihalyi, M. (1975). *Beyond boredom and anxiety.* San Francisco: Jossey-Bass.

DeSteno, D., Petty, R. E., Rucker, D., Wegener, D. T., & Braverman, J. (2004). Discrete emotions and persuasion: The role of emotion-induced expectancies. *Journal of Personality and Social Psychology, 86*, 43–56.

Evans, L. M., & Petty, R. E. (2003). Self-guide framing and persuasion: Responsibly increasing message processing to ideal levels. *Personality and Social Psychology Bulletin, 29*, 313–324.

Förster, J., Grant, H., Idson, L. C., & Higgins, E. T. (2001). Success/failure feedback, expectancies, and approach/avoidance motivation: How regulatory focus moderates classic relations. *Journal of Experimental Social Psychology, 37*, 253–260.

Förster, J., & Higgins, E. T. (2006). How global vs. local perception fits regulatory focus. *Psychological Science, 16*,(8), 631–636.

Förster, J., & Higgins, E. T., & Idson, C. L. (1998). Approach and avoidance strength as a function of regulatory focus: Revisiting the "goal looms larger" effect. *Journal of Personality and Social Psychology, 75,* 1115–1131.

Freitas, A. L., & Higgins, E. T. (2002). Enjoying goal-directed actions: The role of regulatory fit. *Psychological Science, 13* (January), 1–6.

Freitas, A. L., Liberman, N., & Higgins, E. T. (2002). Regulatory fit and resisting temptation during goal pursuit. *Journal of Experimental Social Psychology, 38,* 291–298.

Gollwitzer, P. M. (1996). The volitional benefits of planning. In P. M. Gollwitzer & J. A. Bargh (Eds.), *The psychology of action: Linking cognition and motivation to behavior* (pp. 287–312). New York: Guilford Press.

Grant, H., & Higgins, E. T. (2003). Optimism, promotion pride, and prevention pride as predictors of quality of life. *Personality and Social Psychology Bulletin, 29,* 1521–1532.

Grant, H., Higgins, E. T., Baer, & Bolger, N. (2007). *Coping style and regulatory fit: Emotional ups and downs in daily life.* Unpublished manuscript, Columbia University.

Greenwald, A. G. (1968). Cognitive learning, cognitive response to persuasion, and attitude change. In A. G. Greenwald, T. C. Brock, & T. M. Ostrom (Eds.), *Psychological foundations of attitudes* (pp. 147–170). San Diego, CA: Academic Press.

Harackiewicz, J. M., & Sansone, C. (1991). Goals and intrinsic motivation: You can get there from here. In M. L. Maehr & P. R. Pintrich (Eds.), *Advances in motivation and achievement* (Vol. 7, pp. 21–49). Greenwich, CT: JAI Press.

Higgins, E. T. (1997). Beyond pleasure and pain. *American Psychologist, 52,* 1280–1300.

Higgins, E. T. (1998). Promotion and prevention: Regulatory focus as a motivational principle. In M. P. Zanna (Ed.), *Advances in experimental social psychology* (Vol. 30, pp. 1–46). New York: Academic Press.

Higgins, E. T. (2000). Making a good decision: Value from fit. *American Psychologist, 5,* 1217–1230.

Higgins, E. T. (2002). How self-regulation creates distinct values: The case of promotion and prevention decision making. *Journal of Consumer Psychology, 12,* 177–191.

Higgins, E. T. (2005). Value from regulatory fit. *Current Directions in Psychological Science, 14,* 209–213.

Higgins, E. T. (2006). Value from hedonic experience and engagement. *Psychological Review, 113,* 439–460.

Higgins, E. T., Friedman, R. S., Harlow, R. E., Idson, L. C., Ayduk, O. N., & Taylor, A. (2001). Achievement orientations from subjective histories of success: Promotion pride versus prevention pride. *European Journal of Social Psychology, 31,* 3–23.

Higgins, E. T., Idson, L. C., Freitas, A. L., Spiegel, S. & Molden, D. C. (2003). Transfer of value from fit. *Journal of Personality and Social Psychology, 84,* 1140–1153.

Higgins, E. T., Kruglanski, A. W., & Pierro, A. (2003). Regulatory mode: Locomotion and assessment as distinct orientations. In M. P. Zanna (Ed.), *Advances in experimental social psychology* (Vol. 35, pp. 293–344). New York: Academic Press.

Hong, J., & Lee, A. Y. (2008). Be fit and be strong: Mastering self-regulation through regulatory fit. *Journal of Consumer Research, 34,* 682–695.

Idson, L. C., Liberman, N., & Higgins, E. T. (2004). Imagining how you'd feel: The role of motivational experiences from regulatory fit. *Personality and Social Psychology Bulletin, 30,* 926–937.

Janis, I. L., & Mann, L. (1977). *Decision making: A psychological analysis of conflict, choice, and commitment.* New York: Free Press.

Kruglanski, A. W., Pierro, A., & Higgins, E. T. (2007). Regulatory mode and preferred leadership styles: How fit increases job satisfaction. *Basic and Applied Social Psychology, 29,* 137–149.

Labroo, A., & Lee, A. Y. (2006). Between two brands: A goal fluency account of brand evaluation. *Journal of Marketing Research, 43,* 374–385.

Lee, A. Y., & Aaker, J. L. (2004). Bringing the frame into focus: The influence of regulatory fit on processing fluency and persuasion. *Journal of Personality and Social Psychology, 86*(2), 205–218.

Lee, A. Y., Aaker, J. L., & Gardner, W. L. (2000). The pleasures and pains of distinct self-construals: The role of interdependence in regulatory focus. *Journal of Personality and Social Psychology, 78*(6), 1122–1134.

Lee, A. Y., & Higgins, E. T. (in press). The persuasive power of regulatory fit. In M. Wänke (Ed.) *The social psychology of consumer behavior.* New York: Psychology Press.

Levine, J. M., Alexander, K. M., & Higgins, E. T. (2007). *Regulatory fit and reaction to deviance in small groups.* Unpublished manuscript, University of Pittsburgh.

Liberman, N., Molden, D. C., Idson, L. C., & Higgins, E. T. (2001). Promotion and prevention focus on alternative hypotheses: Implications for attributional functions. *Journal of Personality and Social Psychology, 80,* 5–18.

Merton, R. K. (1957). *Social theory and social structure.* Glencoe, IL: Free Press.

Millar, M. G., & Tesser, A. (1986). Effects of affective and cognitive focus on the attitude–behavior relation. *Journal of Personality and Social Psychology, 51,* 270–276.

Novemsky, N., Dhar, R., Schwarz, N., & Simonson, I. (2007). Preference fluency in consumer choice. *Journal of Marketing Research, 44,* 347–356.

Payne, J. W., Bettman, J. R., & Johnson, E. J. (1993). *The adaptive decision maker.* Cambridge, UK: Cambridge University Press.

Petty, R. E., Briñol, P., & Tormala, Z. L. (2002). Thought confidence as a determinant of persuasion: The self-validation hypothesis. *Journal of Personality and Social Psychology, 82,* 722–741.

Petty, R. E., & Wegener, D. T. (1998). Attitude change: Multiple roles for persuasion variables. In D. T. Gilbert, S. T. Fiske, & G. Lindzey (Eds.), *The handbook of social psychology* (4th ed., pp. 323–390). New York: McGraw-Hill.

Pham, M. T., & Avnet, T. (2004). Ideals and oughts and the reliance on affect versus substance in persuasion. *Journal of Consumer Research, 30,* 503–518.

Sansone, C., & Harackiewicz, J. (1996). "I don't feel like it": The function of interest in self-regulation. In L. L. Martin & A. Tesser (Eds.), *Striving and feeling: Interactions among goals, affect, and self-regulation* (pp. 203–228). Mahwah, NJ: Erlbaum.

Schachter, S., & Singer, J. E. (1962). Cognitive, social and physiological determinants of emotional state. *Psychological Review, 69,* 379–399.

Schwarz, N. (1990). Feelings as information: Informational and motivational functions of affective states. In E. T. Higgins & R. M. Sorrentino (Eds.), *Handbook of motivation and cognition: Foundations of social behavior* (Vol. 2, pp. 527–561). New York: Guilford Press.

Schwarz, N., & Clore, G. L. (1983). Mood, misattribution, and judgments of well-being: Informative and directive functions of affective states. *Journal of Personality and Social Psychology, 45,* 513–523.

Schwarz, N., & Clore, G. L. (1988). How do I feel about it? The informative function of affective states. In K. Fiedler & J. Forgas (Eds.), *Affect, cognition and social behavior* (pp. 44–62). Toronto, Canada: C. J. Hogrefe.

Shah, J., Higgins, E. T., & Friedman, R. (1998). Performance incentives and means: How regulatory focus influences goal attainment. *Journal of Personality and Social Psychology, 74,* 285–293.

Shah, J. Y., & Kruglanski, A.W. (2000). Aspects of goal networks: Implications for self-regulation. In M. Boekaerts & P. R. Pintrich (Eds.), *Handbook of self-regulation* (pp. 85–110). San Diego: Academic Press.

Sheldon, K. M., & Elliot, A. J. (1999). Goal striving, need satisfaction, and longitudinal well-being: The self-concordance model. *Journal of Personality and Social Psychology, 76,* 482–497.

Spiegel, S., Grant-Pillow, H., & Higgins, E. T. (2004). How regulatory fit enhances motivational strength during goal pursuit. *European Journal of Social Psychology, 39,* 39–54.

Tauer, J., & Harackiewicz, J. (1999). Winning isn't everything: Competition, achievement orientation, and intrinsic motivation. *Journal of Experimental Social Psychology, 35,* 209–238.

Thaler, R. H. (1980). Toward a positive theory of consumer choice. *Journal of Economic Behavior and Organization, 1,* 39–60.

Tormala, Z. L., & Petty, R. E. (2002). What doesn't kill me makes me stronger: The effects of resisting persuasion on attitude certainty. *Journal of Personality and Social Psychology, 83,* 1298–1313.

Webster's Ninth New Collegiate Dictionary. (1989). Springfield, MA: Merriam-Webster.

Winkielman, P. & Cacioppo, J. T. (2001). Mind at ease puts a smile on the face: Psychophysiological evidence that processing facilitation elicits positive affect. *Journal of Personality and Social Psychology, 81,* 989–1000.

Zillmann, D. (1978). Attribution and misattribution of excitatory reactions. In J. H. Harvey, W. J. Ickes, & R. F. Kidd (Eds.), *New directions in attribution research* (Vol. 2, pp. 333–368). Hillsdale, N.J.: Erlbaum.

Index